GLOSSARY OF LIBRARY AND INFORMATION SCIENCE
(Vol. I)

Dr. Amjad Ali
Deputy Librarian
Aligarh Muslim University, Aligarh

Ess Ess Publications

4837/24, Ansari Road, Darya Ganj,
New Delhi-110002
✆ : 23260807
Fax : 23274173
E-mail: info@essessreference.com
url:http://www.essessreference.com

First Published 2004

ISBN: 81-7000-410-1 (Set of 2 Volumes)

Rs.1700/- (Set of 2 Volumes)

Published by:
Ess Ess Publications
4837/24, Ansari Road, Darya Ganj,
New Delhi-110 002.
Phone: 23260807
Fax: 23274173
E-mail: info@essessreference.com
url: http://www.essessreference.com

Printed in India at:
Printline, New Delhi

Dedicated to

My Parents

Preface

Libraries are affected by changes taking place in the society. The change is reflected in their services, practices and techniques of information management. The last two decades witnessed adoption of a record number of new terms for library and information related activities as influenced by the application of computers and advent of Internet.

This Glossary of about 4,500 terms includes traditional as well as the latest items which will be useful for the students of library and information science, working librarians and information professionals at every stage of their career from students life to management positions.

My thanks are due to the individuals and organizations which have put the relevant resources on the Net as I referred some of them to compile this Glossary. My thanks are also due to M/s Ess Ess Publications, New Delhi for bringing out this multi-volume book in a very short time.

Dr. Amjad Ali

E-Mail: amjad_alig@yahoo.co.in

GLOSSARY

AACR Anglo American Cataloging Rules, A detailed set of standardized rules for cataloging various types of library materials which had its origin in Catalog Rules: Author and Title Entries published in 1908 under the auspices of the American Library Association and the Library Association (UK), and the A.L.A. Cataloging Rules for Author and Title Entries (1949), with its companion volume Rules for Descriptive Cataloging in the Library of Congress. Cooperation between the ALA, the Library Association, and the Canadian Library Association resumed with the joint publication in 1967 of Anglo-American Cataloging Rules, which is divided into two parts: rules for creating the bibliographic description of an item of any type, and rules governing the choice and form of entry of headings (access points) in the catalog.

AACR2 Anglo-American Cataloguing Rules (2nd ed.); established in 1978 and revised in 1988. "These rules are designed for use in the construction of catalogues and other lists in general libraries. The rules cover the description of, and provision of, access points for all library materials commonly collected." A second edition (AACR2) was published in 1978 and revised in 1988 (AACR2R) to reflect changes in information formats. The 1998 revision includes changes and corrections authorized by the Joint Steering Committee (JSC) for revision of AACR since 1988, including amendments authorized through 1997. Additional amendments were issued in 1999 and 2001. AACR2-e is a hypertext version published by ALA Editions that includes all amendments through 2001.

AB Bookman's Weekly A trade publication used mainly by antiquarian booksellers to locate rare, out of print, and difficult to find titles, AB Bookman's Weekly began as a section of Publisher's Weekly under the title Antiquarian Bookman. In 1948 it became an independent weekly of the same title published by R. R. Bowker. Publication under the current title began in 1967.

Abbreviation A shortened form of a word or phrase used for brevity in place of the whole, consisting of the first letter, or the first few letters, followed by a period (full stop), for example, assoc. For association or P.O. for post office. Some terms have more than one abbreviation (v. Or vol. For volume). Abbreviated abbr.

Abecedarium A book containing the letters of the alphabet and basic rules of spelling and grammar, used in Europe as a primer before the invention of the printing press. Early printed examples (sometimes in the form of a broadsheet) displayed the alphabet in uppercase and lowercase letters in both roman and gothic type, with separate lists of vowels, dipthongs, and consonants. By 1700, some ABC books included children's rhymes. Synonymous with abecedary.

Aberrant copy A copy of a book containing obvious printing and/or binding errors which are more serious than minor defects.

ABI/Inform A database of articles in more than 800 business-related periodicals and specialty publications since 1986.

Aboutness The totality of subjects explicitly or implicitly addressed in the text of a document, including but not limited to the meaning(s) of the title, the stated and unstated intentions of the author, and the ways in which the information may be used by readers. Levels of specificity must be considered in ascertaining the subject(s) of a work. In the case of the hypothetical title The Japanese Teamwork Approach to Improving High School Effectiveness, is the work about:

Above the fold The half of a broadsheet newspaper that appears above the horizontal fold. Articles printed near the top have greater prominence because most languages are read from top to bottom of page.

Abridged A shortened version of a book, audio cassette, etc.

Abridged Decimal Classification (ADC) A shortened version of Dewey Decimal Classification developed for use in small libraries.

Abridgment A shortened version or edition of a written work, which preserves the overall meaning and manner of presentation of the original but omits the less important passages of text, and usually the illustrations, notes, and appendices. Often prepared by a person other than the original author or editor, an abridged edition is generally intended for readers unlikely to purchase the unabridged version because of its length, complexity, or price (example: The New Shorter Oxford English Dictionary). Also spelled abridgement. Abbreviated abr. Synonymous with condensation. Compare with simplified edition.

Absenteeism The failure of an employee to report for work, usually due to illness, accident, family responsibilities, or personal business. A persistently high rate of absenteeism may be a sign of low morale among the staff of a library or library system.

Absorbency The capacity of paper to absorb and retain moisture, which varies with type of paper, and is of particular importance in printing processes that use liquid ink.

Absorption The assimilation of one serial by another. The note Absorbed: followed by the title of the assimilated serial is added to the bibliographic record representing the assimilating publication, and the corresponding note Absorbed by: giving the title of the assimilating serial is added to the record for the assimilated publication.

Abstract A brief, objective summary of the essential content of a book, article, speech, report, dissertation, or other work, which presents the main points in the same order as the original, but has no independent literary value. An abstract can be indicative, informative, critical, or written from a particular point of view (slanted). In a scholarly journal article, the abstract follows the title and the name(s) of the author(s), and precedes the text. In an entry in a printed indexing and abstracting service or bibliographic database, thc abstract accompanies the citation.

Abstracting journal A periodical devoted to publishing abstracts, usually in a specific field of research. For example, Chemical Abstracts or Psychological Abstracts. Abstract journals enable researchers to peruse recent work in their area of interest, and serve as an archive of bibliographic information. Many important abstracting journals are now available in electronic format. (See the Marriott Databases & Indexes page.) Many indexes which formerly provided only citation information are now providing abstracts as they convert to electronic formats.

Abstracting service A commercial indexing service that provides both a citation and a brief summary or abstract of the content of each document indexed (example: Information Science Abstracts). Numbered consecutively in order of addition, entries are issued serially in print, usually in monthly or quarterly supplements, or in a regularly updated bibliographic database available by subscription. Abstracting services can be comprehensive or selective within a specific academic discipline or subdiscipline.

Abstracting The preparation of a brief, objective statement (abstract) of the content of a written work, to enable the researcher to quickly determine whether reading the entire text might satisfy the specific information need. Abstracting is usually limited to the literature of a specific discipline or group of related disciplines, and is performed by an individual or commercial entity, such as an indexing and abstracting service, that provides abstracts regularly to a list of subscribers.

Academic freedom The principle that faculty members employed at institutions of higher education (including librarians with faculty status) should remain free to express their views and teach in the manner of their own choosing, without interference from administration, government, or outside organizations which may have an axe to grind.

Academic library A library that is an integral part of a college, university, or other institution of post-secondary education, administered to meet the information and research needs of its students, faculty, and staff. In the United States, the professional association for academic libraries and librarians is the Association of College and Research Libraries (ACRL).

Academic status Recognition given by an institution of higher education that the librarians in its employ are considered members of the teaching or research staff, but are not entitled to ranks, titles, rights, and benefits equivalent to those of faculty. Compare with faculty status.

Acanthus A representation of the elegant leaf-form of Acanthus spinosus, a species of herbaceous plant native to the Mediterranean region, used by the ancient Greeks to ornament Corinthian capitals, and as a decorative motif in the illuminated initial letters and borders of medieval manuscripts, where it is often found painted in a unrealistic colors (red, yellow, purple, blue).

Acceptable use policy Guidelines established by a library or library system concerning the manner in which its computer systems and equipment may be used, for example, most public libraries forbid the use of public workstations for commercial or unlawful activities. In most libraries, a printed copy of acceptable use policy is posted near the workstations to which the restrictions apply. Some libraries also make the statement available on their Web site.

Access code An identification code, such as a username, password, or PIN which a user must enter correctly to gain access to a computer system or network. In most proprietary systems, access codes are tightly controlled to exclude unauthorized users. Synonymous with authorization code.

Access point A unit of information in a bibliographic record under which a person may search for and identify items listed in a library catalog or bibliographic database. Access points have traditionally included the main entry, added entries, subject headings, classification or call number, and codes such as the standard number, but with machine-readable cataloging almost any portion of the catalog record (name of publisher, type of material, etc.) Can be used as an access point. In the MARC record, most access points are found the following fields, with XX in the range of 00-99:

Access policy A formal written statement issued by the person(s) or body responsible for managing archives or special collections, specifying which materials are available for access and by whom, including any conditions or restrictions on use, usually posted or distributed in some manner to users.

Access Provider The company that provides you with Internet access and, in some cases, an online account on their computer system.

Access services The provision of access to a library's resources and collections, which includes the circulation of materials (general circulation, reserves, interlibrary loan, document delivery), reshelving, stack maintenance, and security. Large libraries employ an access services librarian to manage these activities.

Access The right of entry to a library or its collections. All public libraries and most academic libraries in the United States are open to the general public, but access to certain areas such as closed stacks, rare books, and special collections may be restricted. In a more general sense, the right or opportunity to use a resource which may not be openly and freely available to everyone.

Access time The amount of time it takes a computer system to provide stored data to a person who logs on and follows correct procedures for retrieval. Access time may be slower during periods of peak use.

Access tool A tool which identifies or directs you to a source of information. The Online Catalog is an access tool in the Mary Couts Burnett Library. It will give you call numbers and location information for most of the items kept in the library. An index like the Readers' Guide to Periodical Literature (Ref. Room - AI3 .R48) is also an access tool. It will give you the title of the article, the title of the periodical it appeared in, the date and issue numbers for the periodical, and the pages on which the article appears.

Accessibility As specified in Section 508 of the 1998 Rehabilitation Act, the process of designing and developing Web sites and other technology that can be navigated and understood by all people, including those with visual, hearing, motor, or cognitive impairments. This type of design also can benefit people with older/slower software and hardware.

Accession number A unique number assigned to a bibliographic item in the order in which it is added to a library collection, recorded in an accession record maintained by the technical services department. Most libraries assign accession numbers in continuous numerical sequence, but some use a code system to indicate type of material and/or year of accession, in addition to order of accession.

Accession record A list of the bibliographic items added to a library collection in the order of their addition. Normally such a list includes the accession number, brief bibliographic identification, source, and price paid for each item. Synonymous with accession catalog, accession register, and accession list.

Accession To record in an accession list that a bibliographic item has been added to a library collection.

Also refers to the document added. The process of making additions is known as accessions. The opposite of deaccession.

Accompanying material Related material issued with an item, for example, a floppy disk, CD-ROM, slide set, answer book, teacher's manual, atlas, or portfolio of prints or plates intended by the publisher to be used and stored with it, often in a pocket inside the cover or loose inside the container. When such an item is cataloged by a library, the presence of accompanying material is indicated in the physical description area of the bibliographic record.

Accountability The extent to which persons in government and the workplace are held answerable for their conduct in office, and for the quality of their performance of assigned duties, particularly when incompetence, dereliction, or malfeasance is at issue.

Accreditation The regular evaluation process by which an educational or service organization establishes that its program of study or services, or the institution as a whole, meets certain pre-existing standards of quality. In the United States, institutions of higher learning are evaluated by regional accrediting bodies, and academic libraries are evaluated as part of the institutional accreditation process. The formal evaluation of individual competence is called certification.

Accredited library school In the United States, a library school offering a degree program regularly evaluated by the American Library Association and found to meet established standards of quality, as opposed to an approved library school offering a program recognized or certified by a state board or educational agency as meeting its standards. Some approved library schools are also ALA-accredited.

Accuracy The quality of correctness as to fact and precision as to detail in information resources and in the delivery of information services. In libraries, it is essential that the resources used by librarians to provide reference service be free of error. Accuracy is also an important criterion in judging the reliability of information provided on the Internet. The accuracy of a statement can be verified by checking other sources that provide the same information. The opposite of inaccuracy (the quality of being incorrect or mistaken).

Acid migration The movement of acid from a material containing acid to one that is less acidic, ph neutral, or alkaline. The process can occur through direct contact or vapor transfer. One of the most common problems in document preservation is the migration of acid from the boards, endpapers, or paper covers of a book to the less acidic paper of the text block (or vice versa). Acid can also migrate from bookplates, inserts, tissues used in interleaving, and labels that are not acid-free. The result may be discoloration and eventual embrittlement. The process can be arrested by removing the contaminating material and subjecting the sheet(s) or volume to deacidification. Synonymous with **acid transfer**.

Acid paper Paper that has a ph value less than 7.0 (neutral). The primary source of acid in paper is **lignin**, an organic substance contained in untreated wood pulp, but acid can also develop from the addition of certain types of sizing or from residual chlorine used in bleaching. It can also be introduced by acid migration or atmospheric pollution (sulphur dioxide). Because acidity weakens the cellulose in plant fiber, it can cause paper, board, and cloth to yellow and become brittle over time, making it an important factor in the preservation of printed materials. To ensure durability, publishers are encouraged to use acid-free permanent paper in printing trade books. Buffering helps neutralize acids that develop after manufacture. Acid can be removed from fiber-based materials by means of an expensive process called deacidification.

Acid-free Materials with a ph value of 7.0 (neutral) or higher (alkaline), preferred in printing and binding to prevent deterioration caused by acid over time. Acid-free papers are often buffered to counteract acids that may develop with age as a result of bleaching and sizing, or be introduced through acid migration or atmospheric pollution.

Acidic Substances which have a ph value less than 7.0 (neutral). The main source of acid in paper products is lignin contained in wood used for pulp. Because acid causes the paper and board used in printing and binding to deteriorate over time, lignin is removed in all but the lowest-grade papers. A buffer such as calcium carbonate or magnesium carbonate may be added in papermaking to neutralize acids that develop or are introduced in paper after it is manufactured. The opposite of alkaline.

ACIS Academic Computing and Information Services.

Acknowledgments The section of the front matter of a book in which the author gives formal recognition to the contributions others have made to the work. The acknowledgments usually follow the preface or foreword and precede the introduction. Some authors include their acknowledgments in the preface. Also spelled acknowledgements.

ACLIS Academic Computing and Library Information Services; the department of Marriott Library responsible for: library information systems; campus computing services such as e-mail, test scanning, and student access computing labs; the Faculty Assistance Center; the Help Desk (581-6494), etc.

ACM Association for Computing Machines; a professional society for computer scientists, and a major publisher in the field. Marriott subscribes to virtually all of the ACM journals and special interest group (SIG) conference proceedings in full-text electronic format.

ACORN Vanderbilt's automated library system, including an online catalog and circulation, acquisitions, and cataloging functions.

Acoustic Coupler A type of modem which converts digital signals into sound for transmission through telephone lines, and performs the reverse operation when receiving such signals. Acoustic couplers generally have cups for the telephone handset.

Acquisition number A unique number used by the acquisitions department of a library to identify a specific bibliographic item on a purchase order. Some libraries use a standard number such as the ISBN (International Standard Book Number) or ISSN (International Standard Serial Number) as the acquisition number.

Acquisitions The process of selecting, ordering, and receiving materials for library or archival collections by purchase, exchange, or gift, which may include budgeting and negotiating with outside agencies, such as publishers, dealers, and vendors, to obtain resources to meet the needs of the institution's clientele, in the most economical and expeditious manner.

ACRL Association of College and Research Libraries (a division of ALA).

Acrobat A set of programs from Adobe: 1) Acrobat Exchange is used for converting documents into PDF (portable document format) files that retain the original "look and feel" with special formatting, graphics, and color intact; and 2) Acrobat Reader is used for viewing and printing PDF formatted files such as the OIT user documentation; a program distributed via the OIT Software To Go web site. More information can be found at http://www.adobe.com.

Acronym A new name or word (neologism) that is pronounceable and hence memorable, coined from the first or first few letters or parts of a phrase or compound term (example: ERIC for Educational Resources Information Center). Compare with abbreviation and initialism.

Acrostic A verse or list of words composed in such a way that certain letters of each line (usually the first and/or last), when read in order of appearance, spell a word, phrase, or sentence. An abecedarius is an acrostic in which the pattern consists of the letters of the alphabet in traditional order. An acrostic can be single, double, or triple, depending on how many words in each line are composed in this way. As a matter of policy, newspaper and magazine editors routinely check verses for acrostics prior to publication to avoid embarrassment. The following well-known example is an all around acrostic in Latin:

ACS American Chemical Society; a professional society and major publisher in all areas of chemistry. Marriott subscribes to most ACS journals in both print and full-text electronic format; the electronic access is being provided through UALC.

Act One of the major divisions in the action of a play, usually marked by the dropping of the curtain, followed by an intermission. In modern drama, most plays are divided into three acts which may be further subdivided into scenes.

Acta Diurna A daily gazette published in ancient Rome from the period of the late Republic onward, devoted primarily to matters of state (official events, public speeches, legal proceedings, public building projects, major military actions) and announcements of births, marriages, and deaths. It also contained news of unusual occurrences (earthquakes, strange accidents, portents) and information about the private lives of prominent persons (scandals, divorces, lawsuits).

Acting edition An edition of a play intended for the use of actors and others directly involved in theater production, which includes fuller stage directions (entrances, exits, stage properties, etc.) Than one intended for reading, usually published in limp paper covers and priced lower than other editions of the same work.

Active records Records required by an agency or individual to function effectively on a daily basis, usually kept close at hand, organized in a manner that renders them readily accessible. Synonymous with current records. The opposite of inactive records.

Active Window The top or front window in a multiple window environment.

Activex A technology from Microsoft that links desktop applications to the worldwide Web. Using activex tools, interactive web content can be created. Example: In addition to viewing Word and Excel documents from within a browser, additional functionality such as animation, credit card transactions, or spreadsheet calculations.

Ad hoc Latin for "to this," used to indicate that something was created or exists for the particular purpose in view at the moment. Also refers to something organized for a specific purpose, for example, an ad hoc committee elected or appointed to address a specific issue or handle an unanticipated contingency, usually dissolved once the need has been met.

Ad loc. An abbreviation of the Latin phrase ad locum meaning "at the place [cited]".

ADA: The Americans with Disabilities Act; wide-ranging legislation intended to make society more accessible to people with disabilities. As web-based information continues to diversify, it is increasingly important that web pages be designed with consideration for different types of access. Recommendations for universally accessible design can be found at the Center for Applied Special Technology (CAST) web site at http://www.cast.org.

Adaptation A work that has been edited or rewritten, in part or in its entirety, for a new use, audience, or purpose. Also, a work converted to another literary form or artistic medium to serve a different or related purpose, while retaining as much of the action, characters, language, and tone of the original as possible, for example, a novel adapted for performance on the stage, a play adapted for the motion picture screen, or an engraving based on a painting. Under AACR2, adaptations of texts are cataloged under the name of the adapter, or under the title if the adapter is unknown, with a name-title added entry for the original work.

Adaptive workstation Computer designed to accommodate users with disabilities.

Add note A brief note in the Dewey Decimal Classification schedules instructing the cataloger to append to a given base number one or more numerals found elsewhere in the classification in order to build a class number. For example, the instruction to "add to base number 027.1 (private and family libraries) notation from 1-9 from Table 2, e.g., family libraries in the United Kingdom 027.141."

Added copy A copy of an item already owned by a library, added to the collection usually when demand warrants. Compare with duplicate.

Added entry An entry additional to the main entry, by which an item is represented in a catalog. This is an access point, such as editor, subject, etc., which can be used in a search. For example, a book edited by John Smith would have "Smith, John" as an added entry.

Added title page A title page preceding or following the one that the cataloger uses as the chief source of information in creating the bibliographic description of an item. It can be more general (a series title page) or of equivalent generality (a title page in a different language).

Added volume Pieces of a book set that are received after the initial piece is cataloged. For example, volume 2 of a set that is received after volume 1 is cataloged.

Addendum Brief printed matter, less extensive than a supplement or appendix, included in a book or other publication after the work has been typeset because it is considered essential to the meaning or completeness of the text, usually printed separately on a slip of paper tipped in at the beginning or end of the text. Plural: addenda. Compare with errata.

Additive Primaries Red, green, and blue are the primary colors of light from which all other colors can be made.

Add-ons Programs that provide extra facilities for a WWW browser (e.g. Sound, video) (see helper application, plug-in, viewer)

Address Identifies the location of an Internet resource. Examples: an e-mail address (doe.999@osu.edu); a web address (http://www.osu.edu); or an internet address (128.146.999.9).

In computing, a character or set of characters used to identify a specific location in main memory or peripheral storage, usually for the purpose of accessing stored data.

Address Resolution Conversion of an IP Address to the corresponding low-level physical address.

Adds Items which are a part of a monograph or serial series and are added to the library collection automatically.

Adhesive A substance applied to a material to make it stick to another surface by chemical or mechanical action. Gummed adhesives require moisture to be effective. Solid at room temperatures, hot-melt adhesives liquify when heated and set up quickly as they cool. Some types of adhesive are pressure-sensitive. Adhesives of various kinds are used extensively in binding and technical processing in libraries. In document conservation, adhesives are often selected for their reversibility.

Adhesive binding A generic term for binding methods in which the leaves are held together by a strong adhesive applied directly to the back of the text block, usually done after the binding edge is milled, but sometimes after the sections are sewn. The most commonly used adhesives are animal glues, hot-melts, and polyvinyl acetate (PVA). Synonymous with threadless binding and unsewn binding.

Adjunct A librarian employed part-time in an academic library at an institution that grants librarians faculty status. Synonymous with part-time faculty.

Administration The range of activities normally

associated with the management of a government agency, organization, or institution, such as a library or library system. Also refers collectively to the persons responsible for such activity, from director to secretary.

Administrative history In archives, the part of a finding aid that provides pertinent information concerning the records it lists and describes, such as the history and organizational structure of the agency (or group of related agencies) that generated them, or significant details in the life and career of the individual or family with which they are associated, usually in the form of a biographical note.

Adobe Acrobat A document exchange program created by Adobe Systems which allows data files created on one software platform (DOS, Windows, Macintosh, etc.) To be displayed and printed on another without loss of text formatting. This capability is particularly important in communication over the Internet which interconnects computers of all types and sizes. Adobe Systems sells the software required to create or convert documents to its Portable Document Format, but does not charge users for the software needed to read PDF documents. The Acrobat Reader program can be downloaded directly from the company Web site at: www.adobe.com.

Adobe Acrobat Reader Stand-alone program or Web browser plug-in from Adobe that lets you view a PDF (Portable Document Format) file in its original format and appearance. Adobe Acrobat Reader is free and can be downloaded from Adobe at http://www.adobe.com.

Adult A fully grown, mentally competent person of sufficient age to be considered capable of making mature decisions and held legally accountable for the consequences of his (or her) actions. Libraries operate on the assumption that adult patrons are capable of deciding independently what they wish to read and borrow. Although it is the responsibility of the parent to supervise the actions of a child, it is appropriate for librarians to provide guidance to children in the selection of materials suitable to their age level and interests, if asked to do so.

Adult education Courses designed specifically for adults who have spent their lives outside the system of formal higher education. Because nontraditional students often lack the library skills of students who follow a traditional course of study, they may require more assistance at the reference desk and a more basic level of bibliographic instruction.

Adult learner A person older than traditional college age, who pursues an independent, organized course of study, usually without the benefit of formal instruction at an established educational institution. When enrolled as a nontraditional student at a college or university, such a person may require reference services and bibliographic instruction at a more basic level than traditional students.

Adult services Materials, services, and programs intended to meet the needs of the adult users of a public library, as opposed to those designed for children and young adults.

Advance copy A copy of a book or other publication bound in advance of the normal press run to enable the publisher to check that all is in order before binding of the edition proceeds. Advance copies are also sent to booksellers, book club selection committees, and reviewers before the announced publication date, sometimes unbound or in a binding other than the publisher's binding, often with a review slip laid in. Copies sent unbound are known as advance sheets. Synonymous with early copy. Compare with reading copy and review copy.

Advance on royalty An amount paid to the author(s) of a new book prior to its publication against the royalties it is expected to earn, usually offered as an inducement to sign a book contract with the publisher. Synonymous with author's advance.

Advance order An order placed for a new book prior to its date of publication, usually in response to prepublication promotion. The number of copies ordered in advance may assist the publisher in determining the size of the first printing, the price, and how much to spend on advertising.

Advanced search One of the search modes available in the library catalog. This search mode uses a series of dropdown menus and textboxes to construct a search.

Advertorial Advertising text written in editorial style and format. To avoid confusion, most magazine publishers add the word "Advertisement" to the running head.

Adverts Advertisements bound into a book, usually at the end of the back matter. Abbreviated ads or advrts.

Aerial map A map of the earth, or of another planetary body, composed of one or more photographs taken from a position above its surface, usually from a passing aircraft, satellite, or space vehicle.

Affiliate A separately administered organization closely connected with another by formal agreement, for example, the various organizations affiliated with the American Library Association (ALA.

Affiliated library A library which is, by formal agreement, part of a larger library system but administered independently by its own board or management structure. Medical and law libraries at large universities often fall into this category. Compare with branch library.

Affirmative action An active effort, begun in the late 1960's, to enhance opportunities in the United States for minority groups and women, through federal regulations and programs intended to counteract bias and discrimination in government employment and contracting, and in admissions to state-supported educational institutions. Most publicly supported libraries in the U.S. are affirmative action employers. The legality of affirmative action has been called into question by individuals and political groups who believe that legislating equality discourages initiative and results in reverse discrimination. Against the Grain (ATG) A bimonthly journal providing news about libraries, publishers, book jobbers, and subscription agents, with reports on the issues, literature, and people affecting books and journals.

Agency For archival purposes, any commercial enterprise, organization, institution, or other corporate body that creates and manages records of its business, activities, or affairs. In very large organizations, subordinate units (sections, departments, offices) may function as separate agencies. In a more general sense, any person (agent) or organization that has the authority to perform a specific function, for example, the National Endowment for the Humanities (NEH).

Agenda A list of topics or issues to be discussed at a meeting, sometimes solicited from prospective attendees in advance by the person who calls or chairs the meeting. It is customary to distribute the agenda before the meeting begins, to allow attendees time to prepare. A hidden agenda is a goal or intention consciously or unconsciously concealed, usually to gain the advantage of surprise, a tactic that often backfires when unsuspecting persons discover that they have been manipulated.

Agent An individual or company that acts as middleman between a library or library system and a publisher in the purchase of materials, for example, a subscription service such as EBSCO or FAXON that manages periodical subscriptions for client libraries.

Aggregator A bibliographic service that provides online access to the digital full-text of periodicals published by different publishers. Because aggregator databases can be very large, tracking their coverage is not an easy task for serials librarians. A task group of the Program for Cooperative Cataloging (PCC) is working on standards for analytic catalog records for serials titles available electronically from aggregator services. Currently, the top three journal aggregators in the United States are EBSCO, Gale Group, and proquest. Recently, EBSCO has been building market share by offering higher up-front payments to secure exclusivity from the publishers of certain journals. The effects of this competitive practice on libraries and the end-user are as yet unclear.

Agrarian A group of twelve writers who discussed the benefits of an agricultural economy published as "i'll Take My Stand" in 1930. The original manuscript and papers of the members are part of Special Collections.

Agricultural Research Information System (ARIS) The project "Agricultural Research Information System (ARIS)" is being implemented to bring information management culture to National Agricultural Research System (NARS) so that agricultural scientist can carry out research more effectively by having systematic access to research information available in India as well as in other countries, better project management of agricultural research, and modernization of the office tools. The basic infrastructure required required for linking all ICAR institutes has already been created. The E-mail connectivity has been established to 72 out of 86 ICAR institutes by linking through dial-up including six institutes with VSAT connectivity using NICNET and ERNET services. ARIS has four information modules namely Agricultural Research Personnel Information System (ARPIS); Agricultural Research Financial Information System (ARFIS); Agricultural Research Library Information System (ARLIS) and Agricultural Research Management Information System (ARMIS). The ICAR is also running an Agricultural Research Information Centre (ARIC) as the Central source of information on all research projects and schemes financed by the ICAR. Databases on A.P. Cess Fund Schemes, Deputation reports and research projects of institutions were computerized and updating of the databases is taken up. The ARIC is the national input centre for the AGRIS and CARIS agricultural databases of the FAO, which is the largest information system of its kind in the world. The ARIC is also the national focal point for the SAARC Agricultural Information Centre (SAIC). It has published several directories in addition to a half-yearly Directory of conferences, seminars, symposia and workshops in agriculture. It is being upgraded to provide on line uplinking and downlinking facilities to the ICAR system, and to the agricultural information system of the entire world.

Agriculture Online Access (Agricola) It is an index to all aspects of agricultural sciences

AGRIS International Information system for Agricultural Scinces and Technology AGRIS provides worldwide bibliographic coverage of agricultural science and technology literature. Developed by the AGRIS Co-ordinating Centre, the Food and Agriculture Organization (FAO) of the United Nations, AGRIS offers an international perspective on crucial agricultural research. The database coverage is from 1975 till present.

Aiche American Institute of Chemical Engineers; a professional society and major publisher in chemical engineering.

AIP American Institute of Physics; a professional society and major publisher in the field of physics; Marriott subscribes to most AIP journals in both print and full-text electronic format.

Aisle The space left unoccupied between two parallel bookcases or shelf ranges, or at right angles to a bank of ranges, to allow library patrons and staff to access the stacks. Minimum aisle width is 36 inches in libraries open to the public in the United States. Some types of compact shelving allow staff or users to shift movable ranges, usually along tracks in the floor, opening aisles as needed.

AIX Advanced Interactive Executive - IBM's version of Unix.

ALA Allied Professional Organization (APA) A separate adjunct organization operating under bylaws approved by the governing Council of the American Library Association at the 2002 Midwinter Meeting, which allows the ALA to conduct activities prohibited under its current 501(c)(3) tax status. In the planning stages since 1996, the APA will be able to offer postgraduate specialty certification, advocate for pay equity, and address other issues related to the professional status of librarians, as a 501(c)(6) entity.

ALA American Library Association.

ALA character set The set of characters defined by the American Library Association for use in the MARC record, including the characters of the Latin alphabet, special characters, diacritics, 14 superscript characters, 14 subscript characters, and 3 Greek letters.

ALA Editions Established in 1886, the Publishing Section of the American Library Association first evolved into ALA Books and Pamphlets, and then into ALA Editions in 1993. Its roster of first editions includes Reference Books for Libraries (1902), Books for College Libraries (1967), Anglo-American Cataloging Rules (1967), and the Intellectual Freedom Manual (1974). Income from annual sales of over 100,000 copies of titles published by ALA Editions supports ALA's other programs. Publications currently available from ALA Editions are listed in its trade catalog.

ALA Filing Rules A set of guidelines for determining the order in which entries are to be filed in a library catalog, originally published by the American Library Association in 1942 under the title A.L.A. Rules for Filing Catalog Cards. Revised in 1967 to correspond with Anglo-American Cataloging Rules, the filing rules were expanded and published under the current title in 1980 to cover any form of bibliographic display (print, microform, digital, etc.) And any catalog code.

ALA Graphics A marketing section of the American Library Association that sells posters, bookplates, bookmarks, T-shirts, and other graphic materials designed to promote libraries, literacy, and reading. ALA graphics can be ordered from a printed catalog or electronically from the ALA Online Store.

Album A bound or loose-leaf book containing blank

pages for mounting stamps, photographs, poems, quotations, newspaper clippings, or other memorabilia, or for collecting autographs. Also, a book containing a collection of pictures, with or without accompanying text. Also refers to a book of sleeves designed to hold phonograph records, usually enclosed in an illustrated pasteboard cover with a list of the contents and descriptive notes printed on the inside.

Alcove A semi-private recessed area within a library, formed when two free-standing shelving units are placed at right angles to one or more units of wall shelving, usually large enough to provide access to materials on the shelves and to accommodate a small number of readers, seated at desks or around a study table. The architect Sir Christopher Wren is credited with originating this style of seating in his design of the library at Trinity College, Cambridge in 1676. Synonymous with cell.

ALCTS Association for Library Collections and Technical Services.

Alexandrian Library Founded by Ptolemy I in about 300 BC, the great library at Alexandria in Egypt became the most important center of Hellenistic culture in antiquity. At its peak, it contained over 500,000 manuscripts, mostly papyrus scrolls, some of which were translated into Greek from other languages. The collection was cataloged in the "Pinakes" of Callimachus which included the author's name and a summary of the content of each item. The main library was part of a museum that functioned as an academy, attracting scholars from all parts of the Mediterranean world. A smaller library was established in the Temple of Serapis by Ptolemy III in about 235 BC.

Algorithm A finite sequence of unambiguous steps or instructions, designed to solve a complex problem or accomplish a specific task in a way that produces at least one output, for example, a formula used to encrypt data. Algorithms can be expressed in natural language (example:

a culinary recipe or the instructions for assembling an item shipped in pieces), in a symbolic language such as that used in mathematical logic, or in a computer programming language. One measure of proficiency in programming is the ability to create elegant algorithms that achieve the desired result in a minimum number of ingenious steps.

Alias A short, easy to remember name created for use in place of a longer, more complicated name; commonly used in e-mail applications.

Aliasing Visibly jagged steps along angled or object edges, due to sharp tonal contrasts between pixels.

Alibris A commercial company that specializes in supplying rare, out of print, and hard-to-find books to bookstores, libraries, and retail customers through a worldwide network of booksellers and distribution capabilities.

Alignment In typography, the arrangement of characters in a line of type in such a way that the tops and bottoms form a straight line across the page, parallel with other lines. Also, the setting of type in lines that are even at both right and left margins. Compare in this sense with justification.

ALISE Association for Library and Information Science Education.

Alkaline Substances with a ph exceeding 7.0 (neutral), for example, calcium carbonate or magnesium carbonate added to paper in manufacture as a reserve or buffer to neutralize any acids that might develop with age. Alkaline substances are also used in the deacidification of materials made from acid paper or board.

All along A sewing method used in hand-binding in which each section of the text-block is sewn separately to cords or tapes, from kettle stitch to kettle stitch inside the fold. For the sake of economy or to reduce swell, sections may be hand sewn two on. Synonymous with all across and all on.

All firsts An expression used in the antiquarian book trade and in library cataloging to indicate that all the items in a group of publications are known to be first editions.

All over A style of binding in which the whole of both sides (front and back covers) are decorated, in contrast to design on the front cover only, on the centers and/or corners, or on the borders.

All published A note in the bibliographic record describing a publication originally proposed in more than one part or volume but never completed, usually because it was discontinued by the publisher. Similarly, a note describing all the issues of a periodical for which publication ceased.

All rights reserved A phrase printed in or on a published work, usually on the verso of the title page of a book, giving formal notice that all rights granted under existing copyright law are retained by the copyright holder and that legal action may be taken against infringement.

Allegory A narrative that can be interpreted literally, but which also has at least one symbolic meaning, usually expressing or elucidating an abstract idea or moral principle. Also, a form of extended metaphor used primarily in works of fiction and poetry in which an event, idea, thing, or person stands for itself and simultaneously for something else. A dream allegory is a medieval poem or story about a dream that has allegorical significance, for example, King Rene's Book of Love (Le Cueur d'Amours Espris).

Allocation A quantity of time, money, materials, or other resources reserved by an organization for a specific purpose, usually to meet a need essential to realizing its goals and objectives. In most libraries and library systems, funds are allocated in accordance with an annual or biennial budget determined by the availability of funds.

Allonym The name of a person known to have existed, assumed as a pen name by another writer, as opposed to a fictional pseudonym. For example, the name "Publius" for the Roman tribune Publius Clodius Pulcher, used by Alexander Hamilton, John Jay, and James Madison in writing The Federalist.

Allusion A brief figurative or symbolic reference in a literary text, usually made indirectly to a familiar person, place, thing, or event outside the text, or to another literary work or passage in it. Allusions are sometimes indexed and published in collections.

Almanac Originally, a book introduced by the Moors to Spain, listing the days, weeks, and months of the year and providing information about festivals, holidays, astronomical phenomena, etc. In modern usage, an annual compendium of practical dates, facts, and statistics, current and/or retrospective, often arranged in tables to facilitate comparison. Almanacs can be general (example: World Almanac and Book of Facts) or related to a specific subject or academic discipline (Almanac of American Politics

Alpha test The first full-scale test of a newly designed computer software system or hardware device, or of substantially revised software or hardware that has undergone a major upgrade, usually conducted in a laboratory environment. Compare with beta test.

Alphabet book A picture book for preschool children with illustrations designed to teach the letters and sequence of the alphabet by showing on each page or double spread, one or more objects, animals, etc., belonging to a class whose name begins with the letter displayed (a for apple, etc.). Compare with counting book.

Alphabet The complete set of characters used to write or indicate the speech sounds of a language, usually arranged in traditional order. The roman alphabet used in writing the English language contains 26 letters (5 vowels and 21 consonants), each with an uppercase and lowercase form. The roman alphabets used to write other languages may contain fewer or additional letters, with diacritical marks used to indicate specific sounds.

Alphabetical In the customary order of the letters of the alphabet of a language. Alphabetizing can be letter-by-letter, ignoring punctuation and divisions between words, or word-by-word, with entries beginning with the same word alphabetized by the next word, and so on. The terms in this dictionary are listed alphabetically letter-by-letter.

Alphabetization Arranging items or entries in the conventional order of the letters of the alphabet of a language, usually by author, title, subject, or other heading.

Alphanumeric A contraction of alphabetic-numeric, referring to a character set containing letters of the alphabet, numerals, and/or special characters. The access codes used in computer systems are often alphanumeric (example: the username smith003). Synonymous with alphameric.

Alpha-Numeric System for Classification of Recordings (ANSCR) A scheme for classifying sound recordings of all types, based on a set of 23 major subject categories represented by letters of the Latin alphabet (example: M for popular music), with some categories subdivided and represented by double letters (MJ for jazz). To the alphabetic category is added a three- or four-letter code representing type of subarrangement (by title of work; name of composer, performer, or author; name of skill, language, or sound; etc.). The third part of the classification number is composed of the first letter of each of the first three keywords in the title of the work or album, or a number if the work is known by form and numbered. The fourth part is composed of a letter representing the name of an individual closely associated with the performance on the recording, followed by the last two digits of the commercial recording number:

Alternative press A small, politically progressive publisher not controlled by the handful of giant multinational corporations that dominate the publishing industry worldwide. Alternative press publications often address important social issues and publish innovative and experimental works largely ignored or covered superficially in the mainstream press. For the past thirty years, the Alternative Press Center (APC), an affiliate of the Social Responsibilities Round Table (SRRT) of the American Library Association, has provided access to such publications through Alternative Press Index, available in the reference section of large academic and public libraries.

Alternative title The second part of a title consisting of two parts, each of which is a title in itself, connected by the word "or" or its equivalent in another language (example: The Female Quixote, or, the Adventures of Arabella). Compare with subtitle.

Ambient conditions The prevailing characteristics of the environment within the room or building in which library or archival materials are stored or used, including temperature, humidity, natural and artificial light, dust, etc., important considerations for long-term preservation.

Ambient light The level of illumination in an enclosed space, from natural or artificial sources, an important consideration in the preservation of materials that deteriorate when exposed to light (especially the ultraviolet in direct sunlight).

Amelia Frances Howard-Gibbon Illustrator's Award A literary award established in 1971, presented annually for the best illustrated children's book published in Canada during the preceding year. The illustrator must be a citizen or permanent resident of Canada and the text must be worthy of the illustrations. The award is sponsored by the National Book Service and administered by the Canadian Association of Children's Librarians.

America Online (AOL) The largest Internet service provider in the world, America Online was founded as Quantum Computer Services in 1985, reached one million subscribers in 1994, purchased its closest rival compuserve in 1997, and merged with Time Warner in 2001. Known by the initialism AOL, the company offers e-mail, a chat directory, a Web browser and subject directory of Web sites, online shopping, and information and entertainment services, in addition to providing Internet access to businesses and individuals, usually for a monthly fee.

American Antiquarian Society (AAS) An independent national research library founded in 1812 in Worcester, Massachusetts to document the history of the American people from the colonial period through the Civil War and Reconstruction. The collections of the AAS include books, pamphlets, newspapers, periodicals, manuscripts, broadsides, juvenile literature, music, graphic arts, genealogy, and local history.

American Association of Law Libraries (AALL) Founded in 1906, AALL has a membership of librarians and related information professionals who serve the legal profession in bar associations, courts, law schools, law societies, private law firms, businesses, and government. AALL seeks to promote and enhance the value of law libraries to the legal community and general public, fosters the profession of law librarianship, and provides leadership in the field of legal information. An affiliate of the American Library Association, AALL has published the quarterly Law Library Journal since 1908

American Association of School Librarians (AASL) Founded in 1951, AASL is a division of the American Library Association with a membership of elementary and secondary school library media specialists and others interested in the improvement and extension of services for children and young adults. AASL publishes the quarterly journal School Library Media Research and its bimonthly companion Knowledge Quest.

American Association of University Professors (AAUP) A professional association founded in 1915 to represent college and university faculty, the AAUP is also open to administrators, graduate students, and the general public. The organization is dedicated to defending academic freedom and tenure, advocating collegial governance, developing policies to ensure due process in the workplace, and providing statistics and analysis of trends in academic employment. Library faculty members at colleges and universities in the United States who are members of the AAUP may be covered by a collective bargaining agreement negotiated by their chapter.

American Book Trade Directory (ABTD) Published annually by R. R. Bowker, the ABTD provides basic directory information on booksellers, jobbers, dealers, and antiquarians in the United States and Canada, listed geographically by state/province and indexed by name and type of store, as well as information about auctioneers of literary property, appraisers of library collections, book exporters and importers, and national and regional associations involved in the book trade.

American Booksellers Association (ABA) Founded in 1900, the ABA is the oldest trade association of independent bookstores with store front locations in the United States. Its mission is to meet the needs of its members through advocacy, education, research, and the dissemination of information. The ABA actively supports fee speech, literacy, and programs that encourage children to read. The organization also publishes an annual handbook for book buyers and maintains the bookweb.org site on the World Wide Web.

American Chemical Society Free Search Database Gives access to ACS journals' full text, images, illustrations, halftones, structures, figures and supporting information.

American Folklife Center Created by Congress in 1976, the American Folklife Center is an agency within the Library of Congress, dedicated to preserving and presenting the American folk tradition. It incorporates the Archive of Folk Culture, established in 1928 as a repository of American folk music

American Indian Library Association (AILA) Founded

in 1979, AILA is an affiliate of the American Library Association with a membership of individuals and institutions committed to promoting the development, maintenance, and improvement of library services and collections for Native Americans, particularly cultural and information resources needed on reservations and in communities of Native Americans and Native Alaskans. AILA publishes the quarterly AILA Newsletter.

American Institute of Graphic Arts (AIGA) Founded in 1914 in New York, AIGA is a nonprofit organization that fosters excellence in graphic design as an academic discipline, communication medium, business tool, and cultural force by providing a forum for design professionals to exchange ideas and information, participate in research and critical analysis, and enhance education and ethical practice. AIGA publishes Trace: AIGA Journal of Design in three issues per year.

American Libraries (AL) A professional magazine for librarians, published since 1907 by the American Library Association, AL provides news and announcements, analysis of trends, feature articles, job postings, and advertising by library-related businesses in eleven issues per year.

American Library Association (ALA) The leading professional association of public and academic libraries and librarians in the United States, the ALA was founded in Philadelphia in October, 1876 by a group of library leaders (90 men and 13 women) that included Melvil Dewey. An "association of associations," the ALA is organized in divisions, each with its own officers, budget, and programs, and is closely tied to over 50 state and regional chapters. The Association also sponsors round tables on specific issues and topics, and is affiliated with other independent library-related organizations. Its imprint is ALA Editions. The most widely read periodicals published by the ALA are the trade journal American Libraries and the review publication Booklist.

American Library Directory (ALD) A serial published annually by R. R. Bowker, available in the reference sections of most libraries, providing directory information (name, location, phone and FAX number(s), department heads, budget, collection size, special collections, electronic resources, network participation, etc.) For over 30,000 academic, public, research, county, provincial, regional, medical, law, and other special libraries in the United States, Canada, and Mexico. ALD also includes separate sections listing library networks and consortia, library systems, libraries for persons with special needs, and state and federal library agencies. It also contains an alphabetically arranged Personnel Index of all the individuals named in the entries for libraries, library systems, and library consortia, with contact information.

American National Standards Institute (ANSI) A nonprofit national clearinghouse founded in 1918 to facilitate standardization by voluntary consensus in the United States in both the public and private sectors, and to coordinate and administer standards of all types. ANSI membership includes over 1,400 companies, organizations, government agencies, and other institutions. The U.S. is represented by ANSI in the International Organization for Standardization (ISO). Standards for library and information science are developed by the National Information Standards Organization (NISO), a nonprofit association accredited by ANSI.

American Printing History Association (APHA) Founded in 1974, APHA encourages study and research in printing history and related arts and skills, including calligraphy, type founding, papermaking, bookbinding, illustration, and publishing. From its headquarters in New York City, APHA publishes the APHA Newsletter and the biannual journal Printing History.

American Reference Books Annual (ARBA) A reference serial published annually by Libraries Unlimited, ARBA provides comprehensive coverage of English-language reference books and CD-roms published in the United States and Canada during the previous year, presenting reviews in a classified arrangement, indexed by author/title and subject. Reviews are usually 100-300 words long, written by scholars, librarians, and library educators who are asked to examine new works and provide well-documented critical comments (positive and negative). All reviews are signed. ARBA is shelved in the reference section of large academic and public libraries.

American Society for Civil Engineers CE Database ASCE CEDB Provides Access to over 90,000 bibliographic and abstracted records of its publications. The current coverage is form January 1973-June 2001.

American Society for Information Science and Technology (ASIST) An affiliate of the American Library Association, ASIST is a non profit association established in 1937 to provide opportunities for professionals in the information science field to communicate across the disciplines of library science, computer science, linguistics, mathematics, and the physical sciences.

American Theological Library Association (ATLA) Founded in 1947, ATLA is an affiliate of the American Library Association with an ecumenical membership that includes theological librarians, persons interested in theological librarianship, and theolog ASI is an affiliate of the American Library Association that seeks to promote indexing, abstracting, and database construction. Its members are professional indexers, librarians, editors, publishers, and organizations that employ indexers. ASI publishes the semiannual journal The Indexer and the bimonthly bulletin Key Words.

Americana A term used in the book trade and by collectors to refer to books and other materials written about the Americas (North, South, and Central America), not necessarily published in the Americas or written by authors from the Americas. Libraries that own extensive or valuable collections of Americana often store them in special collections.

Americanize To convert to American English the style and spelling of a work written in (or translated into) British English. Compare with briticize.

Americans with Disabilities Act (ADA) Legislation passed by Congress in 1990 guaranteeing right of access to public facilities and resources to persons with physical disabilities and prohibiting discrimination against them in employment. The ADA has had a profound effect on the delivery of library services in the United States, from architectural planning (ramps, elevators, automatic door-openers, signage in Braille, etc.) To the design and placement of furniture, equipment, and shelving, and even the design of computer interfaces. To learn more, click here or see the print publication How Libraries Must Comply with the Americans with Disabilities Act (ADA) by Donald Foos and Nancy Pack (Oryx: 1992).

Ampersand The symbol & derived from a fusion of the letters of the Latin word et, meaning "and." Under AACR2, when the title proper contains an ampersand (example: **Notes & Queries**), it is transcribed in the title and statement of responsibility area of the bibliographic description exactly as it appears on the chief source of information, and an added entry is made under the title with "and" spelled out.

AMS: American Mathematical Society; a professional society and major publisher in mathematics.

Ana, -iana A suffix added to the name of a person, place, or institution to signify the body of related literature, information, memorabilia, etc., that has accumulated over time (examples: Conradiana, Americana, librariana). In libraries such materials are usually housed in special collections.

Analects From the Greek analekta meaning "things gathered up." A collection or "gleaning" of miscellaneous literary excerpts or fragments (example: the teachings of Confucius).

Analog A representation of an object, physical condition, or process, that closely replicates the original, reflecting any variations in its state. In technology, analog devices are designed to monitor conditions such as sound, movement, or temperature, and convert the resulting measurements into electrical signals or mechanical patterns representing the fluctuations of the actual phenomenon (example: sounds recorded on a phonograph record). Analog data is encoded in signals that are continuous over a range or interval of values, for example, data transmitted over a telephone line which must be converted by a device called a modem into the discrete values of digital code in order to be processed by a digital computer.

Analytical bibliography The comparative and historical study of books as physical objects, including the methods and techniques of book production and their influence on texts. Synonymous with critical bibliography. Analytical bibliography has three main branches:

Analytical entry An entry in a library catalog for a part of a work (chapter in a book) or for an entire work (story, play, essay, or poem) contained in an item, such as an anthology or collection, for which a comprehensive entry is made. Analytical entries are made under the author, title, and subject of the part, and include a reference to the title of the work containing the part. Because preparation of analytical entries is time-consuming, the level of bibliographic description provided in a catalog depends on the administrative policy of the library and its assessment of local needs. Synonymous with analytics.

Analytical note The statement in an analytical entry indicating the relationship of the work, or part of a work, to the more comprehensive work of which it is a part, for example, the title of an anthology containing a short story, play, essay, or poem.

Anchor: Either the starting point or the destination of a hyperlink (or link) within a document. Example: a highlighted word within an online help file may display additional information related to the word. This information is "anchored" to the highlighted word.

Anet Advanced Research Projects Agency network, the first computer network to use packet switching. Funded by the U.S. Advanced Research Projects Agency in 1969, arpanet linked research computers on two University of California campuses with the Stanford Research Institute and the University of Utah. In 1983, with more than 300 computers connected, its protocols were changed to TCP/IP and it became known as the Internet. In 1987, when the National Science Foundation (NSF) began to develop a high-speed fiber-optic backbone to connect supercomputer centers, intermediate networks of regional arpanet sites began connecting to the backbone. In 1995, commercial Internet service providers assumed control of the major backbones in the United States. Traffic over the "Net" continues to expand.

Animated graphics A graphic design technique in which a sequence of related still images, such as cartoon drawings or diagrams, is displayed in such rapid succession that the illusion of continuous motion is created on a computer screen. Animated graphics require less bandwidth than full-motion video when transmitted over the Internet (and also less memory), so they can be downloaded more quickly when a Web site containing them is selected by the viewer.

Animation The illusion of continuous motion created on film by photographing a sequence of drawings, still pictures, or cartoon cels, each representing a slight change from the preceding one, and viewing them in rapid succession. Developed into an art form by animators in the studios of Walt Disney, the technique continues to provide pleasure to audiences worldwide.

Annals A periodical in which the transactions of a society or organization, or events and developments in a specific discipline or field of study are recorded (example: Annals of the American Academy of Political and Social Science published since 1890). In a more general sense, a list of events recorded in chronological order.

Annex An addition to an existing library or archive, or a nearby facility used as an addition to the main building, usually of smaller size. A library annex is sometimes used to store low-use materials in closed stacks.

Annotate To add notes to a written document to explain, comment on, or evaluate its content, as in an annotated edition. Also, to add brief notes, called annotations, to the entries in a bibliography or catalog to describe, explain, or evaluate the sources listed.

Annotated Bibliography A list of books, articles, or other documents on a topic or by a particular author containing a citation of each item, as well as a brief description and/or a critical evaluation of it.

Annotated edition An edition that includes comments written by the author or another annotator, which are explanatory or supplemental rather than evaluative. Compare with critical edition.

Annotation is an explanatory or critical note or commentary. Annotation is also the process of adding an explanatory or critical note or commentary to a text. Reference lists are often annotated with comments about what each resource covered and how useful it was.

Annual Comprehensive Index Bibliographic Database The database has approximately 38,818 bibliographic entries. The entries for the period 1976 to 1987 come from INFORMS journals, while for the period 1988 to 2001 they come from a total of approximately 663 different INFORMS as well as non-INFORMS journals. The subjects include operations research, management, computing etc.

Annual Issued once a year, every year, as in an annual report or annual review. Also refers to a form of literary anthology popular during the 19th century, usually illustrated with engravings. According to Geoffrey Glaister (Encyclopedia of the Book, Oak Knoll: 1996), this type of book was intended mainly for female readers.

Annual report A printed publication, usually less than one hundred pages in length, submitted each year by the officers of a publicly held company to its board of directors (or other governing body) and issued in softcover for distribution to current and prospective shareholders, describing the firm's activities during the preceding fiscal year and its current financial position. Some corporations make their annual reports available online. In business libraries, annual reports are usually retained in a company file for a fixed number of years and subsequently discarded.

Annual Report Collection Collection of annual reports for a wide selection of public companies. Held on microfiche and housed near the Microfilm/fiche readers on level 3. Arrangement is alphabetical by company name. More recent reports are available ON-Line vai the Library database page.

Annual review A serial publication that surveys the most important works of original research and creative thought published in a specific discipline or subdiscipline during a given calendar year (example: Annual Review of Information Science and Technology). In most academic libraries, annual reviews are placed on continuation order. In the workplace, an inspection or personnel evaluation conducted once a year.

Annual Review of Information Science and Technology (ARIST) Issued once a year by the American Society for Information Science and Technology (ASIST) and Information Today, **ARIST** provides scholarly reviews of current topics in information science and technology, as substantiated by the published literature of the field. Publication of ARIST began in 1966 with the financial support of the National Science Foundation. Because the field is broad and dynamic, no single topic is treated on an annual basis. The reviews are critical in the sense of presenting the contributor's opinion concerning activities, developments, and trends within the subject area reviewed. Each volume includes a cumulative keyword and author index to the entire series. Indexing and abstracting of **ARIST** is provided in Library and Information Science Abstracts, Library Literature & Information Science, and ERIC.

Anonym An anonymous publication or a person or author whose name is not known; 3. A pseudonym.

Anonymous A work in which the author's name does not appear and cannot be traced with certainty in catalogs, bibliographies, or any other reliable source. Of unknown authorship. For an entertaining introduction to the methods used to detect the identities of writers of anonymous works, please see.

Anonymous FTP Archive sites where Internet users can, log in and download files and programs without a special username or password. Typically, you enter anonymous as a username and your e-mail address as a password.

Anonymous Login Convention (FTP) Standard username (anonymous) and password (guest) which allows login within FTP for the purpose of retrieving an unprotected file.

ANSCR It is used mainly by libraries holding large numbers of sound recordings. Libraries with smaller collections generally use accession number or some other "home-grown" classification system to organize sound recordings. Pronounced "answer."

ANSI American National Standards Institute. This organization is responsible for approving U.S. standards in many areas, including computers and communications. Standards approved by this organization are often called ANSI standards (e.g., ANSI C is the version of the C language approved by ANSI).

Anthology A collection of extracts or complete works by various authors, selected by an editor for publication in a single volume or multi-volume set. Anthologies are often limited to a specific literary form or genre (short stories, poetry, plays) or to a national literature, theme, time period, or category of author. The works anthologized are listed in the table of contents by title in the order of their appearance in the text. In the card catalog, analytical entries are prepared for works published in anthologies. In the online catalog, the individual works contained in an anthology are listed in the bibliographic record in a contents note searchable by keyword(s) in most catalog software. Compare with compilation.

Anthropological Index Online It is an Anthropological Index to Current Periodicals in the Anthropology Library at the British Museum.

Antiphonary A liturgical work containing hymns, psalms, or verses chanted or sung responsively by the choir in a worship service. Also, a book containing the choral parts of the Divine Office (canonical hours) of the Catholic Church.

Antiquarian book An old out-of-print used book, more valuable than most second-hand books because of its rarity and/or condition, usually sold by an antiquarian bookseller. Very rare and valuable old books are sold at auction. Price guides are available for appraising old books.

Antiquarian bookseller A bookseller who deals in old, rare, fine, out of print, and secondhand books.

Antiquarian Booksellers Association of America (ABAA) Founded in 1949, the ABAA encourages interest in fine and antiquarian books and manuscripts (and other rare or valuable printed materials), promotes ethical standards and professionalism in the antiquarian book trade, encourages collecting and preservation, advances technical and general knowledge useful to the trade, sponsors book fairs, and facilitates collegial relations among booksellers, librarians, scholars, and collectors

Antique binding A modern binding done in the style of an earlier period, with no intent to mislead prospective buyers as to its actual age.

Antique In papermaking, the unpolished matte finish produced when uncoated paper is not processed through a calendering machine. Eggshell is a smooth, slightly pitted antique finish. Also refers to a contemporary calf binding designed to imitate an older binding.

Anti-virus software A computer program designed to periodically check the hard drive of a computer (or all the computers attached to a network) for the presence of man-made computer viruses and eliminate them if found. The anti-virus software used on computer networks usually includes an update feature that automatically downloads profiles of newly-created viruses soon after they are detected.

Antonym A word or phrase which is the opposite in meaning of another term. Dictionaries of antonyms are available in the reference section of larger libraries. In some indexing languages, one of the terms in a pair of opposites may be selected to represent both, with a cross-reference made from the other. The opposite of synonym.

APA style A guide for typing research papers in the social sciences, developed by the American Psychological Association, which includes the proper format for typing notes and bibliographic citations. APA style is described fully in the most recent edition of the Publication Manual of the American Psychological Association, available in the reference section of most academic libraries.

Aperture card A card containing one or more small windows in which individual frames cut from a strip of microfilm are mounted. This format allows microfilm images to be used independently and provides a convenient surface for recording pertinent information about each frame. Synonymous with image card.

Aphorism A very concise sentence or statement ("nugget") that expresses, in a pointedly memorable way, a universally recognized truth or principle. A maxim (example: "Well begun is half done."). Aphorisms published in collections are usually shelved in the reference section of a library (example: Oxford Book of Aphorisms).

Apocryphal Writings which scholars consider to be of dubious authorship or authenticity (not genuine), for example, the 14-15 books of the Greek translations of the Old Testament (Septuagint), known as the Apocrypha, accepted as authoritative by the Roman Catholic and Greek Orthodox churches, but rejected in Judaism and not considered canonical in Protestantism. Compare with anonymous.

Apostil A marginal note or annotation in a book or manuscript. Also spelled apostille.

Appendix A part of a written work, not essential to the completeness of the text, containing complementary information such as statistical tables or explanatory material too long to be included in the text, or in footnotes or endnotes. An appendix differs from an addendum in having been planned in advance as an integral part of the publication, rather than conceived after typesetting occurs. Appendices usually appear in the back matter, following the text and preceding the notes, glossary, bibliography, and index. Abbreviated app.

Applet :A small Java program that can be embedded in an HTML page. Applets differ from full-fledged Java applications in that they are not allowed to access certain resources on the local computer, such as files and serial devices (modems, printers, etc.), and are prohibited from communicating with most other computers across a network. The common rule is that an applet can only make an Internet connection to the computer from which the applet was sent.

Applicant A person who has made a formal request to be considered for employment, usually by filling out an application form or by sending a resume or curriculum vitae with cover letter to a prospective employer in response to a job posting. Compare with candidate.

Application Computer software that allows the user to process data or perform calculations necessary to achieve a desired result, as opposed to the operating system designed to control the computer's hardware and run all other programs. Common microcomputer applications include word processing, spreadsheet, e-mail, presentation graphics, desktop publishing, database management systems, and Web browsers..

APPM Archives, Personal Papers, and Manuscripts, a standard for the description of archival materials based on AACR2, accepted by most archives in the United States.

Appraisal The monetary valuation of gifts, usually done at the request of an archives, library, or museum, by a professional appraiser familiar with the market for the type of item(s) donated. Also refers to the process of evaluating records to determine whether they are to be archived indefinitely, retained for a shorter period, or disposed of in some other way (sold, donated, destroyed, etc.).

Approval plan A formal arrangement in which a publisher or wholesaler agrees to select and supply, subject to return privileges specified in advance, publications exactly as issued which fit a library's pre-established collection development profile. Approval profiles usually specify subject areas, levels of specialization or reading difficulty, series, formats, price ranges, languages, etc. Some plans provide advance notification slips instead of sending the actual physical item. Compare with blanket order and book lease plan.

Approval shelf A shelf or shelves, usually located in or near the acquisitions department of a library, where new books ordered on approval are stored pending examination by the selectors responsible for deciding whether they are to be added to the collection or returned to the publisher or wholesaler.

Approvals New books sent automatically by a publisher or wholesaler in accordance with a pre-established profile of the library's needs, rather than ordered title-by-title by the selectors responsible for collection development. Approvals not returned within an agreed upon time are understood to have been accepted by the library.

Approved library school In the United States, a library school that offers a program recognized or certified by a state board or educational agency as meeting its standards of quality and professionalism. Some approved library schools are also ALA-accredited.

Approximate the whole Said of a work which is nearly coextensive with the subject(s) represented by a in Dewey Decimal Classification, or which covers more than half the content of the heading, or which covers representative examples from three or more subdivisions of the class. The cataloger is permitted to add standard subdivisions to a work that approximates the whole of a subject (adapted from DDC). Compare with standing room.

ARA Appletalk Remote Access. A protocol (and product) that provides system-level support for dial-in (modem) connections to an appletalk network. With ARA, you can call your desktop Mac from a powerbook and remotely access all the available services - files, printers, servers, e-mail, etc.

Arabic numeral One of the ten digits (0 1 2 3 4 5 6 7 8 9) developed in India in the 6th century to indicate number in a system of place value based on ten. Arabic numerals were adopted by the Arabs around 900 AD, who introduced them in Europe via Spain about 100 years later, where they replaced roman numerals. Colonization introduced them to the rest of the world.

Archetypal novel Early fictional tales and romances considered to be precursors of the novel in its modern form (example: The Tale of Genji by Lady Shikibu Murasaki).

Archie A tool (software) for finding files stored on anonymous FTP sites. You need to know the exact file name or a substring of it. By 1999 Archie had been almost completely replaced by web-based search engines. Back when FTP was the main way people moved files over the Internet archie was quite popular.

Architectural binding A form of ornamental bookbinding popular during the 16th century in which the front cover was decorated with architectural columns on either side, supporting an arch or lintel across the top, beneath which the title is displayed on a panel, the style of the cover bearing no relation to the content of the work.

Architectural drawing A drawing or sketch of a proposed construction project, done by an architect or architectural firm. A full set of drawings, showing all phases of the construction process, includes the specifications used by contractors for bidding, purchase of materials and equipment, etc. Synonymous with blueprint, a term derived from the process used to duplicate them which produces a white image on a blue ground. Compare with architectural rendering.

Architectural rendering A pictorial representation of a building or other structure, usually from an angle showing the front or main entrance, created by the architect or an architectural firm to give an accurate, if somewhat idealized, impression of how the structure will appear after it is constructed. Sometimes used in fund-raising to promote capital projects, such as the construction of a new library facility or the renovation and/or expansion of an existing one. Compare with architectural drawing.

Architecture library A specialized library associated with a graduate school of architecture or a large architectural firm, containing books and periodicals on architecture and architectural engineering, building codes and standards, architectural drawings and renderings, indexes and abstracting services, databases, and other reference materials for research in architecture and related fields.

Archival copy A copy of a document specifically created or designated for archival storage by the company, government, organization, or institution that wishes to preserve it, usually for legal, evidential, or historical purposes.

Archival database An organized collection of records in digital format, containing information to be retained for an indefinite period of time, usually for future reference, for example, the messages received and distributed by an e-mail discussion list, or the reference questions received by an electronic reference service, including the answers provided.

Archival journal A journal published mainly for archival purposes, as opposed to one intended for distribution to retailers and individual subscribers, usually priced for the library market with little or no attempt to market it to a wider audience.

Archival paper A grade of paper that is permanent and highly durable, particularly with respect to fading and physical deterioration caused by acidity, used for printing materials of archival quality.

Archival quality The physical properties of records in all (paper, microform, magnetic tape or disk, optical disk, etc.) Which make them suitable for permanent storage in archives. Items printed on paper must have a ph of 7 or higher and be free of other contaminates (chemicals, mildew, etc.). Synonymous with archival standard.

Archival value The decision, following appraisal by a knowledgeable expert (or experts), that a document, record, or group of records is worth preserving, permanently or for an indefinite period. Records are retained for their:

Archive It is a place in which historical documents and other records are preserved. Usually operated by large organizations, they may or may not be open to the public. The University of Toronto, for example has an archive that requires a five story building and contains several climate controlled vaults. A virtual archive is similar except the documents have no physical presence and seldom have historical value.

Archives An organized collection of the noncurrent records of the activities of a business, government, organization, institution, or other corporate body, or the personal papers of one or more individuals, families, or groups, retained permanently (or for a designated or indeterminate period of time) by their originator or a successor for their permanent historical, informational, evidential, legal, administrative, or monetary value, usually in a repository managed and maintained by a trained archivist. Also refers to the office or organization responsible for appraising, selecting, preserving, and providing access to archival materials.

Archives box A container of standard size with a hinged or lift-off lid, used to store and facilitate the handling of archival materials, usually constructed of acid- and lignin-free cardboard held together without glue or metal staples. Boxes made of inert polypropylene plastic are also used for this purpose. See also: archival copy, archival database, archival paper, archival quality, archival value, digital archives, and Society of American Archivists.

Archives Information Center Integrated Web site designed to guide users to materials related to the history of the IPFW campus.

Archives policy A formal written statement defining the authority under which an archives operates, the scope of its activities (mission, objectives, conditions/restrictions, etc.), and the range of services it provides. Compare with access policy.

Archivist The person responsible for managing and maintaining an archival collection, usually a librarian with special training in archival practices and methods, including the identification and appraisal of records of archival value, authentication, accessioning, description/documentation, facilitation of access and use, preservation and conservation, and exhibition and publication to benefit scholarship and satisfy public interest. Archivists are organized in the Society of American Archivists.

Archivists and Librarians in the History of the Health Sciences (ALHHS) An association of librarians, archivists, and other specialists actively engaged in the librarianship of the history of the health sciences, dedicated to the exchange of information and to improving standards of service.

Area One of the major portions of description comprising the bibliographic record created to represent a specific item in a library catalog or bibliographic database. Each area ia reserved for data elements of a specific category (or categories). In AACR2, the standard areas of a bibliographic description are:

Area study A publication that provides factual information about a specific region of the world (Africa, Asia, Europe, Latin America, the Middle East, etc.), including a description of its physical and social geography, economy, history, governments, and cultures, and which may also contain pertinent statistical and directory information. Area studies are often published serially (example: The Far East and Australia in the series Regional Surveys of the World, published annually by Europa). Compare with country study.

Argot The idiomatic vocabulary of a group or class of people, or of the members of a specific occupation or profession, particularly those who are on the margins of conventional society. Dictionaries of argot are available in the reference section of larger libraries. Compare with slang.

Ariadne An electronic journal for academic information science professionals, reporting on issues and developments in information service and information networking worldwide. Published quarterly by UKOLN, Ariadne is aimed at keeping the practitioner informed of current digital library initiatives.

Ariel A document transmission system developed by the Research Libraries Group (RLG) which provides rapid, inexpensive, high-quality document delivery over the Internet by integrating scanning, sending, receiving, and printing functions. The user can send text and gray-scale images (illustrations, photographs, etc.) In letter, legal, and other sizes to another Ariel workstation, to an e-mail account used by an Ariel machine, or to anyone who uses MIME-compliant e-mail software and a multipage TIFF viewer. The system is used in libraries to facilitate interlibrary loan and document delivery service.

Armarian The person charged with keeping the manuscripts and books owned by a medieval monastery in good order and repair, also responsible for maintaining an accurate catalog of the library's contents. It was also the armarian's duty to keep the scribes and illuminators in the scriptorium well-supplied with parchment, vellum, pens, ink, pigments, gold and silver leaf, and other materials needed to copy, illustrate, and bind books by hand. Synonymous with armarius. Compare with armarium.

Armarium A wooden cupboard or free-standing piece of furniture with shelves and doors, first used to store scrolls, and eventually manuscripts and books. Known to have existed during the Roman Empire, armaria were used in medieval monasteries until the end of the Renaissance. Compare with armarian.

Armorial binding A binding, usually in leather, decorated with a coat-of-arms or other heraldic device to indicate the royal or noble lineage of its original owner.

ARP Address Resolution Protocol. Used to dynamically discover the low-level physical network hardware address that corresponds to the high level IP Address for a given host, for instance. ARP is limited to physical network systems that support broadcast packets that can be heard by all hosts on the network.

Arrangement A portion of a musical work, or an entire work, rewritten for a medium of performance or market other than the one for which the original was intended (synonymous in this sense with transcription); or a simplified or amplified version of a musical composition, written for the same medium. In AACR2, an arrangement is, as a general rule, cataloged under the name of the composer, with an added entry under the name of the arranger. In archives, the process of putting records into order, following accepted archival principles; with special attention given to their provenance and original order. If, upon careful scrutiny, the original order is found to be completely random, the archivist may, after carefully documenting the original sequence, substitute an impartial arrangement that is more convenient to use. In indexing, the process of putting in systematic and consistent order the headings under which entries are listed. The sequence can be alphabetical, numerical, or classified in some manner.

Arranger A person who transforms an entire musical work, or a major portion of a such a work, to a medium of performance other than the one intended by the original composer, or who extends or simplifies a work in the same medium, retaining a substantial amount of the original musical structure. Under AACR2, an arrangement is, as a general rule, cataloged under the name of the composer, with an added entry under the name of the arranger.

Array From the Latin arredare meaning "to arrange in order." In an index or thesaurus of indexing terms, a display of entries, headings, descriptors, etc., in an orderly sequence. In classification, a set of mutually exclusive and exhaustive coordinate subclasses dividing a class by a single characteristic, for example, the array "newspaper," "newsletter," "magazine," and "journal" dividing the class "periodical" by form.

Arrears Library materials in need of cataloging, which have accumulated to the point of requiring a special effort to process, usually the result of heavy ordering, receipt of a large gift, or insufficient personnel to maintain normal workflow. Synonymous in this sense with backlog. Also refers to the state of being behind in the payment of salaries, wages, invoices, etc.

Art book A volume, usually of relatively large size,

containing high-quality reproductions of works of visual art (paintings, drawings, prints, etc.) Or photographs of sculpture, architecture, or other three-dimensional works of art, usually with accompanying text. In an exhibit catalog, the text may be minimal. Because art books are expensive to produce, they are sometimes co-published to achieve economies of scale. Compare with coffee table book.

Art Libraries Society/North America (ARLIS/NA) Founded in 1972, ARLIS is an organization of librarians, institutions, and individuals with an interest in art librarianship and the curatorship of visual art resources in public and academic libraries, museums, galleries, art institutes, and publishing houses. An affiliate of the American Library Association, ARLIS publishes the.

Art library A library newsletter ARLIS/NA Update five times a year. See also: art librarycharged with acquiring, organizing, preserving, and providing access to information and resources in the diverse fields constituting the visual arts (architecture, drawing, graphic design, painting, photography, sculpture, etc.). An art library usually functions as a unit within a larger academic or public library, or as a special library maintained by a host organization such as a gallery, museum, art institute, or publishing house. The first modern art library in the United States was founded in 1871 by the San Francisco Art Association (now the San Francisco Art Institute).

Art original An original work of art created by an artist in two or three dimensions, as distinct from a reproduction of such a work. The term is not applied to photographs and art prints which can be produced in multiple copies by a person other than the artist.

Article A self-contained nonfiction prose composition on a fairly narrow topic or subject, written by one or more authors and published under a separate title in a collection or periodical containing other works of the same form. The length of a periodical article is often an indication of the type of publication—magazine articles are usually less than five pages long, articles published in scholarly journals longer than five pages. Periodical articles are indexed, usually by author and subject, in periodical indexes and abstracting services, called bibliographic databases when available on computer. Compare with editorial and essay. Also refers to the words a, an, or the, or their equivalent in another language, used as adjectives preceding a noun, the being the definite article, and a and an indefinite articles. In library filing, an initial article is ignored at the beginning of a heading. An initial article is also ignored at the beginning of a title in a search of an online catalog or bibliographic database by title.

Artifact An object made or modified by the work of one or more persons (replicas excluded), as distinct from a natural object called a specimen when collected. Objects created for their aesthetic value are considered works of art. The value of an item to collectors as a physical object is usually reduced by any modification. Also spelled artefact.

Artifactual value The worth of a thing as a physical object, for example, a copy of a book that has little value in the antiquarian market, but is important to textual scholars because of its typographic characteristics, or to 'book historians because of its unusual binding. Normally, any modification of such an object reduces its value. Compare with archival value.

Artificial digit In Dewey Decimal Classification, a letter or symbol used optionally as a substitute for the numerals 0-9 to give various languages, literatures, religions, cultures, and ethnic groups a more prominent location or shorter notation (adapted from DDC). For example, under classes 810-890 (Literature of specific languages), Option B to "give preferred treatment by placing before 810 through use of a letter or other symbol, e.g., literature of Arabic language 8A0, for which the base number is 8A."

Artificial intelligence (AI) Mechanical and electronic

devices and applications designed to closely mimic the human ability to learn, reason, and make decisions. AI is used in voice recognition technology, expert systems, natural language and foreign language processing, and robotics.

Artificial language A language constructed from a pre-established set of rules. Its vocabulary can be a subset of a natural language, as in a classification system, or composed of symbols, as in a language used in programming computers. Synonymous with synthetic language.

Arts and humanities Archaeology, classical studies, communication, folklore, history, language and literature, performing arts (dance, film, music, theater), philosophy, religion and theology, visual arts

Artwork A general term used in publishing and printing to refer to illustration originals in any medium, as opposed to reproductions of art originals. Such works may have artistic and monetary value independent of the publication for which they were created.

As issued A term used in the antiquarian book trade to indicate the condition of an item that exists in the same unaltered form in which it was first published, as opposed to one that has been rebound, processed by a library, damaged, etc. Compare with doctored.

As New/Mint In the same flawless condition as when published (no defects, missing pages, or ownership marks); dust jacket in perfect condition (no chips, marks, or tears).

As well.

ASCE American Society of Civil Engineers; a professional society and major publisher in all areas of civil engineering.

Ascender In typography and calligraphy, the stroke of a lowercase letter that extends above the highest point of an x-height letter (a, c, e, m, etc.). The letters of the Latin alphabet with ascenders are: b, d, f, h, k, l, and t. The ascender line is an imaginary horizontal line connecting the tops of ascender letters, often, but not necessarily, the same as the cap line. Compare with descender.

ASCII An acronym for American Standard Code for Information Interchange (pronounced "askee"), the binary code built into most minicomputers and all personal computers to represent uppercase and lowercase letters, numerals, and special characters in digital format. Each ASCII character consists of seven information bits and one parity bit for error checking. Designed to facilitate information exchange between nonstandard data processing and communications equipment, ASCII is recognized by the American National Standards Institute (ANSI). Also refers to text that has been converted to ASCII code. Unlike text containing special formatting, ASCII can be imported and exported by most application programs without conversion, and requires no special software for display and printing. ASCII text is also called vanilla text.

ASERL Association of Southeastern Research Libraries.

Asian Development Bank ADB gives access to social and economic data of its developing member countries. The type of data includes national accounts, financial accounts, trade, population, labour and employment etc.

Asian/Pacific American Librarians Association (APALA) Founded in 1980, APALA is an affiliate of the American Library Association with a membership consisting of of librarians and information specialists of Asian Pacific (APA) descent employed in the Unites States, and other interested persons. APALA provides a forum for the discussion of issues and ideas of interest to APA librarians, supports and encourages library services to APA communities, establishes scholarships for APA library school students, recruits and mentors APA library and information science professionals, and fosters cooperation with other organizations with similar interests. APALA publishes the quarterly APALA Newsletter

Asiatic Society Journals Index Provides access to

bibliographic details of articles published in Asiatic Society journals published between 1700 to 1960

Askeric Initiated in 1996 as a project of the ERIC Clearinghouse on Information & Technology, askeric is an e-mail-based reference and referral system that provides answers to questions, assistance, and referral services to K-12 educators via the Internet. Askeric also provides news of interest to educators and a growing virtual libary collection of full-text resources at its Web site, including lesson plans, ERIC Digests in full-text, completed ERIC searches on current topics in education, resource guides, answers to faqs, and the archives of education-related electronic mailing lists.

Askjake A search engine designed to identify the bibliographic databases (aggregators) that contain full-text articles or provide indexing and abstracting for a given periodical title. The askjake development site is currently hosted by Simon Fraser University Library.

Askwisconsin Virtual Reference This is a collaborative virtual reference service of academic, private and public member libraries in Wisconsin. Chat reference is run on a consortial basis, which means that answers may come from a librarian at any of the member libraries. E-mail questions submitted from this site are answered by UW-W librarians. To use this service, go to the askwisconsin Virtual Reference home page.

ASME American Society of Mechanical Engineers; a professional society and major publisher in mechanical engineering. ASME is a major publisher of standards; Marriott does not have a standing subscription to ASME standards, but will purchase them on demand by UU faculty.

Aspect In Dewey Decimal Classification, an approach to a subject from a discipline other than the one in which the subject is classified, for example, the economic or sociological aspects of health care delivery.

Assessment Quantitative and qualitative measurement of the degree to which a library's collections, services, and programs meet the needs of its users, usually undertaken with the aim of improving performance. Assessment is accomplished by various methods, including direct observation, analysis of feedback obtained through interviews, user surveys, testing, etc. When conducted by the library, rather than an outside agency, the process is known as self-assessment.

Assignment indexing A method of indexing in which a human indexer selects one or more subject headings or descriptors from a list of controlled vocabulary to represent the subject(s) of a work. The indexing terms need not appear in the title or text of the document indexed. Synonymous with assigned indexing. Compare with derivative indexing.

Associate Linking a document with the program that created it so that both can be opened with a single command.

Association copy A copy of a book, which has a special association with the author, with a person closely connected to the author or its content, with a well-known individual other than the author, or with a particular library or collection, as indicated by an autograph, bookplate, dedication, inscription, marginalia, special binding, or other physical characteristic.

Association des bibliothecaires francais (ABF) Founded in 1906, L'ABF is the oldest and largest association of librarians in France, with approximately 3,500 members. L'ABF publishes the quarterly Bulletin d'informations.

Association for Information Management (Aslib) Founded in 1924, Aslib is a nonprofit organization with an international membership consisting of over 2,000 private and public companies and organizations in 70 countries, which have an interest in the efficient management of information resources. Divided into 14 special interest groups covering approximately 60 SIC areas, Aslib specializes in advising organizations, from small companies to large corporations and government agencies, on issues and problems related to information management.

Association for Information Management Professionals (ARMA) A nonprofit international association serving over 10,000 information management professionals in the U.S., Canada, and over 30 other countries, including records managers, MIS and ADP professionals, imaging specialists, archivists, hospital and legal administrators, librarians, and educators, ARMA provides education, research, and networking opportunities enabling its members to maximize the value of records, information, and knowledge as corporate assets. Formerly known as the Association of Records Managers and Administrators, ARMA publishes the bimonthly Information Management Journal and the monthly newsletter infopro Online.

Association for Library and Information Science Education (ALISE) Founded in 1915, ALISE is an affiliate of the American Library Association, dedicated to promoting excellence in research, teaching, and service in library and information science education. Its members are graduate schools offering degree programs in library and information science, and their faculties. ALISE publishes the quarterly Journal of Education for Library and Information Science (JELIS).

Association for Library Collections and Technical Services (ALCTS) A division of the American Library Association since in 1957, ALCTS has a membership consisting of librarians and other persons interested in the acquisition, identification, cataloging, classification, reproduction, and preservation of library materials.

Association for Library Service to Children (ALSC) A division of the American Library Association since in 1900, ALSC has a membership consisting of librarians and persons interested in improving the quality of services for children in all types of libraries. ALSC publishes the journal Children and Libraries.

Association for Library Trustees and Advocates (ALTA) A recently formed division of the American Library

Association, ALTA has a membership consisting of library trustees and persons interested in promoting outstanding library service through educational programs that develop excellence in trusteeship and actions that advocate access to information for all.

Association for Recorded Sound Collections (ARSC) Founded in 1966, with headquarters in Annapolis, Maryland, ARSC has a membership consisting of persons in the broadcasting and recording industry, librarians, archivists, curators, private collectors, and institutions such as museums, national libraries, and foundations. ARSC publishes the semiannual ARSC Journal and the quarterly ARSC Newsletter.

Association of Academic Health Sciences Libraries (AAHSL) Founded in 1977, AAHSL is an organization of the directors of medical libraries at over 140 accredited medical schools in the U.S. and Canada belonging to the Association of American Medical Colleges. Its goal is to promote excellence in academic health science libraries and assure that health practitioners acquire the information skills necessary for quality health care delivery, education, and research..

Association of American Publishers (AAP) The principal trade association of the book publishing industry in the United States, AAP was created in 1970 by the merger of the American Book Publishers Council (ABPC) and the American Educational Publishers Institute (AEPI). Directed by standing committees, AAP is currently focused on a variety of core issues, such as intellectual property; new technology and telecommunications; First Amendment rights, censorship, and libel; international freedom to publish; funding for education and libraries; postal rates and regulations; and tax and trade policy.

Association of American University Presses (AAUP) Established in 1937, AAUP is a trade association representing over 120 scholarly presses, large and small, associated for the most part with colleges and universities in the United States and Canada. Its members publish in a wide range of disciplines, including the arts and humanities, social sciences, and science and technology. Some also publish books of regional interest, others include fiction and poetry in their lists. Through its programs, AAUP seeks to further the interests of scholarly publishing by monitoring legislation affecting university presses, fund-raising for projects beneficial to scholarly publishers, and helping its members market their publications and train personnel effectively.

Association of College and Research Libraries (ACRL) A division of the American Library Association since 1889, ACRL has a membership of academic and research librarians committed to improving quality of service in academic libraries, promoting the career and professional development of academic and research librarians, and supporting the programs of academic and research libraries.

Association of Independent Information Professionals (AIIP) Founded in 1987, AIIP is an organization of entrepreneurs owning professional firms that provide information-related services, including online and manual information retrieval and research, document delivery, database design, library support, consulting, writing, and publishing.

Association of Jewish Libraries (AJL) Founded in 1965 with headquarters in New York City, AJL seeks to advance the interests of Jewish libraries and promote publications of Jewish bibliographical interest. AJL publishes the semiannual journal Judaica Librarianship and the quarterly AJL Newsletter.

Association of Moving Image Archivists (AMIA) A nonprofit professional association devoted to advancing the field of moving image archiving by encouraging cooperation among the individuals and organizations concerned with the collection, preservation, exhibition, and use of moving image materials, AMIA publishes the quarterly AMIA Newsletter

Association of Research Libraries (ARL) Founded in 1932, ARL is an organization of large research libraries dedicated to influencing major decisions affecting the future of research libraries and their ability to serve effectively the needs of students, faculty, and the research community, by articulating concerns, forming coalitions, suggesting policy, and supporting innovations and improvements in operations. An affiliate of the American Library Association, ARL provides access to proprietary databases, training and consultation in management and program development, directories, and statistics on its membership.

Association of Specialized and Cooperative Library Agencies (ASCLA) A division of the American Library Association representing state library agencies, specialized library agencies, independent libraries, and multi-type library cooperatives. ASCLA publishes the quarterly newsletter Interface.

Association of Vision Science Librarians (AVSL) An international association of information professionals employed at educational institutions, eye clinics and hospitals, and private companies whose library collections and services include the literature of vision, AVSL is a special interest group of both the Association of Schools and Colleges of Optometry and the Medical Library Association. The organization publishes standards and guideliness for vision science libraries, a union list of vision-related serials, and a core list audiovisual collection.

Association The group of persons who have joined a formal organization devoted to pursuing a common interest or purpose, usually by paying an annual membership fee. Professional associations, such as the American Library Association, are dedicated to promoting the interests of a specific profession and its practitioners. The most comprehensive directory of such organizations is the Encyclopedia of Associations published by Gale Group, available in the reference section of most libraries in the United States.

Associative relation A semantic relation in which two words or phrases are conceptually connected, sometimes within a specific context, but are not related hierarchically (example: "Library extension" and "Library outreach.

Asterisk A special character in the shape of a star (*) produced on a standard keyboard by pressing the Shift+8 keys. The asterisk is used as a reference mark in printing to indicate a footnote or other reference on the same page. A series of asterisks is sometimes used in text to indicate ellipsis, for example, to suggest an unprintable word (D***). In most bibliographic databases, the asterisk is used as the end truncation symbol in keywords searches.

ASTM American Society for Testing and Materials; a major publisher of standards in the area of materials and engineering. Marriott purchases a full set of ASTM standards every 3 years which is kept at the Science & Engineering Desk.

Asynchronous Communication Electronic communication involving messages that are sent and received at different times. E-mail is an example of asynchronous communication. Asynchronous Occurring at different times. In communications, a response that is delayed due to the nature of the transmission medium. The opposite of synchronous.

Asynchronous communication Communication in which sending, reading, and responding to messages is not simultaneous. E-mail is a form of asynchronous communication; chat is synchronous.

Asyndetic Lacking cross-references. Compare with syndetic structure.

At command set An industry standard set of commands beginning with the letters "AT" that are used to control a modem. Example: ATDT tells the modem to dial (D) using touch-tone dialing (T). ATDP specifies pulse dialing (P). Also referred to as the "Hayes Command Set".

Athenaeum The temple of Athena, goddess of knowledge and learning, where scholars and writers met in the city of Athens in ancient Greece to exchange ideas. In early 19th century New England, the name was applied to certain proprietary libraries, reading rooms, and buildings containing libraries. The Redwood Library & Athenaeum in Newport, Rhode Island is the oldest surviving library of this kind in the United States.

Atlas A bound or boxed collection of maps, usually related in subject or theme, with an index of place names (gazetteer) usually printed at the end. The first bound collection of maps is known to have been issued in Europe in the mid-16th century. In most atlases, the maps are printed in uniform style and format, on a fairly consistent scale. An atlas may be issued as an independent publication or as accompanying material, with or without descriptive text, plates, charts, etc. Some have a special focus (example: The Times Atlas of World Exploration), others are intended for a specific use (road atlases). In a library, large atlases may be stored in a specially designed atlas case.

Atlas case A free-standing piece of display furniture used mainly in libraries, usually about waist-high with a sloping top and a book stop along the front edge for displaying an open atlas. Most atlas cases are made of wood, with several deep, wide, closely-spaced shelves for storing oversize reference works. Some designs have sliding shelves to facilitate use. Compare with dictionary stand.

Atlas folio The largest widely used folio, usually about 16 x 25 inches in size, used mainly for large atlases. Compare with elephant folio.

Attachment A computer file of any type linked to an e-mail message in such a way that the two are transmitted together to the designated address. Nontext attachments, such as graphics and database files, may require special encoding and decoding software. Particular care should be taken when opening attachments as they are sometimes used to transmit computer viruses.

Attribute In classification, one of the distinguishing

characteristics of a class, identified as a means of differentiating it from other classes. As defined in FRBR (Functional Requirements for Bibliographic Records), one of a set of characteristics enabling users of information to formulate queries and evaluate responses when searching for information about a specific entity. Attributes can be inherent in the entity (physical characteristics, labeling information, etc.) Or imputed by an external agent (assigned identifiers, contextual information, etc.). For example, the logical attributes of a creative work include its title, form, date of creation, intended audience, etc. As a general rule, a given instance of an entity exhibits a single value for each attribute, but multiple values are possible (example: a work published under more than one title) or a value may change over time (date of publication for a serial). Nor is it necessary for every instance of an entity to exhibit all its attributes—some may be appropriate to a specific subtype of the entity, for example, the attribute "coordinates" applicable only to cartographic materials.

Attributed A creative work ascribed to a known person or corporate body, usually on the basis of reliable supporting evidence. Degree of certainty concerning authorship depends on the strength of the existing evidence, for example, some scholars believe the plays and sonnets of William Shakespeare to be the work of another Elizabethan writer, but the available evidence is insufficient to resolve this dispute. When evidence of authorship is inconclusive, a work is said to be of unknown authorship.

Attributed author A person believed to have written or created a work published anonymously or which is of doubtful authorship (example: The Second Maiden's Tragedy attributed to the 17th century writer Thomas Middleton). Attribution is usually based on supporting evidence, but uncertainty may arise when the evidence is meager or conflicting (The Two Noble Kinsmen ascribed to John Fletcher but sometimes erroneously attributed to William Shakespeare). In the library cataloging, attributed authorship is indicated in the note area of the bibliographic description. Synonymous with supposed author. Compare with suppositious author.

AU sounds A type of audio format used in the World Wide Web.

Audience The people who actually read a literary work or attend an artistic performance or exhibition, not necessarily the same as the target audience for whom the work is intended by the author or creator, or by the publisher or producer.

Audiocassette An audiotape permanently enclosed in a hard plastic case containing two take-up reels to which the ends of the tape are attached for playback and rewinding. Libraries that allow audiocassettes to circulate usually place them in a section reserved for sound recordings, arranged by composer, performer, genre, or some other means of classification. In AACR2, the term "sound cassette" is used in the physical description area of the bibliographic record representing an audiocassette, with "analog" given as type of recording.

Audiorecording A generic term for any medium on which sounds are recorded for mechanical or electronic playback, including phonograph records (vinyl), audiotape, and compact disc. Synonymous with sound recording.

Audiotape A continuous strip of thin magnetic tape on which sounds can be recorded as electrical signals, and converted back into sound with the proper playback equipment. The most common size in libraries is 1/4-inch wide, stored on audiocassette. Synonymous with tape recording.

Audiovisual A work in a medium that combines sound and visual images, for example, a motion picture or videorecording with a sound track, or a slide presentation synchronized with audiotape. Directory information for products and services provided by the audiovisual industry is available in AV Market Place (AVMP), published annually by R. R. Bowker. Also spelled audio-visual. Abbreviated a-v

Audiovisual materials Library materials in non-print form, such as audio cassettes, video cassettes, compact discs, and DVD's.

Audio-Visual Non-book materials such as various formats of audio and video recordings, which require equipment to be usable. Marriott's collection of audio-visual materials is housed in the Multimedia Center.

Audit An official examination of the accounts or records of an individual, company, organization, or institution to determine if they are correct. Also, to conduct such an examination, usually on a regular basis.

AUL Associate University Librarian; occasionally referred to as Assistant University Librarian.

AUSTROM A CD-ROM database of Australian material. This is made up of a number of well known indexes such as Australian Education Index and APAIS.

Authentication In online systems, the procedure for verifying the integrity of a transmitted message. Also, a security procedure designed to verify that the authorization code entered by a user to gain access to a network or system is valid.

Authenticity The quality in a thing of being what it is claimed to be (valid, real, genuine, etc.), verified in archives and special collections through an investigative process known as authentication, essential in appraising the value of an item.

Author abstract A brief summary, called an abstract, written by the person responsible for creating the work summarized, as opposed to one written by someone other than the author, usually a professional abstractor or indexer.

Author affiliation The name of the organization with which the author of a publication is formally connected, usually given in books on the back flap of the dust jacket or on the title page, and in journal articles in a note at the foot of the first page, sometimes with the writer's position title and contact information.

Author bibliography A bibliography of works written by or about a specific author, which can vary in detail and extent from an unannotated list of selected titles to a comprehensive, in-depth descriptive bibliography.

Author entry The entry in a catalog, index, or bibliography under the authorized heading for the first-named author of a work, whether it be a person or corporate body. In most library catalogs, the author entry is the main entry.

Author index An alphabetically arranged index in which the headings are the names of the individuals and corporate bodies responsible for creating the works indexed. Author entries may be combined with the subject index or title index, rather than listed separately. Compare with name index.

Author interview A conversation in which a writer is questioned about his/her life and work by an interviewer who intends to publish the results verbatim in a book or periodical, or incorporate them into a radio or television broadcast, in their entirety or excerpted. Also refers to the article or program based on such an interview.

Author mark Letters, numerals, or other symbols representing the last name of an author, added by the cataloger to the call number to distinguish an item from others of the same classification (example: the Cutter-Sanborn number D548 to identify works by Charles Dickens). When a work mark is added to the author mark, the result is known as the book number (D548d for David Copperfield). Synonymous with author number.

Author portrait A plate in a book, bearing a full-page image of the author, usually a photograph or a reproduction of a painting, drawing, or engraving, printed on the verso of the leaf preceding the title page. Common in books published in the 19th and early 20th centuries, most show just the head and shoulders, with the author's name and source of portrait given in a caption. In medieval manuscripts, the authors of the gospels were sometimes depicted in a drawing or miniature accompanying the text of their work. In modern book production, a small portrait photograph of the author is usually printed on the back flap of the dust jacket in hardcover editions.

Author search In an electronic catalog or index, to search for an article or book by a particular author. "Author" may include persons responsible for the work, such as composers, artists, actors, directors, etc., and organizations may also be authors ("corporate author" in library parlance).

Author The person responsible for producing a written work (essay, monograph, novel, play, poem, screenplay, short story, etc.), whose name is printed on the title page of a book, or given elsewhere in or on a manuscript or other item, and in whose name the work is copyrighted. A work may have two or more joint authors. In library cataloging, the term is used in its broadest sense to include editor, compiler, composer, creator, etc. Compare with personal author and corporate author.

Author tour A tightly-scheduled trip, usually arranged by the publisher of a new trade book, in which the author (or a well-known illustrator) agrees to help promote sales by participating in book signings, author interviews, book talks, etc., usually at trade bookstores and through the mass media. Travel expenses are paid by the publisher, but the writer is usually not compensated for his or her time. Author tours are announced in the trade journal Publishers Weekly.

Authoritative A source that is official. Also, a work known to be reliable because its authority or authenticity has been widely recognized by experts in the field.

Authority control The procedures by which consistency of form is maintained in the headings (names, uniform titles, series titles, and subjects) used in a library catalog or file of bibliographic records, through the application of an authoritative list called an authority file to new items as they are added to the collection. Authority control is available from commercial service providers.

Authority file A list of the authoritative forms of the headings used in a library catalog or file of bibliographic records, maintained to ensure that the headings are applied consistently as new items are added to the collection. Separate authority files are usually maintained for names, uniform titles, series titles, and subjects. All the references made to and from a given heading are also included in the authority file.

Authority record A printed or machine-readable record of the decision made concerning the authoritative form of a name (personal or corporate), uniform title, series title, or subject used as a heading in a library catalog or file of bibliographic records, listed in an authority file governing the application of headings to new items as they are added to the library collection. An authority record may also contain See from and See also from records, as well as notes concerning the application of the authorized form.

Authority The knowledge and experience qualifying a person to write or speak as an expert on a given subject. In the academic community, authority is based on credentials, previously published works on the subject, institutional affiliation, awards, imprint, reviews, patterns of citation, etc.

Authority work The process of deciding which form of a name, title, series title, or subject will be used as the authorized heading in a library catalog or file of bibliographic records, including the establishment of appropriate references to the heading, and its relationship to other headings in the authority file.

Authorization In computing, a username, password, PIN, or other access code issued to a person who is allowed access to a specific electronic resource, application program, network, or other computer system, which the user must enter correctly in order to log on. Authorization codes are usually subject to periodic renewal. A single authentication may have multiple authorizations.

Authorized biography A biography written with the explicit consent and sometimes the cooperation of its subject, or the subject's family if the biographee is deceased. Authorized biographies are more likely to be scrutinized by reviewers for bias because the biographer may have been expected to overlook or downplay embarrassing events or unflattering qualities in exchange for access to first-hand information and confidential sources. Compare with unauthorized biography.

Authorized edition An edition issued with the explicit sanction of the author or holder of rights in the work or, in the case of a biography, by the person who is its subject or the subject's family if the biographee is deceased. The opposite of unauthorized edition. Compare with definitive edition.

Author's advance An amount paid by the publisher to the author of a work before the completed manuscript is submitted for publication, established by contractual agreement between the two parties, usually refundable if the work is not completed. Synonymous with advance on royalty.

Author's copy One of six or more complimentary copies of a published work normally provided to the author free-of-charge by the publisher at the time of first publication. Faculty members sometimes donate complimentary copies of their works to the academic library at the college or university with which they are affiliated.

Author's edition An edition of all the unpublished and previously published works of an author, issued in one or more uniform volumes, usually bearing a collective title or some other indication on the title page that all known works are included. Synonymous with complete works and uniform edition. Compare with collected edition.

Author's editor An editor familiar with the publishing industry, employed by a university or research institution to assist faculty and researchers in preparing their work for publication, and to help them negotiate the intricacies of the publishing process, as distinct from an editor employed by a publishing company to help prepare a manuscript for printing once it has been accepted for publication.

Authorship The origin of a manuscript, book, or other written work, with reference to its author(s). In a more general sense, the source of an idea or creative work in any form, with reference to its creator or originator, for example, the composer of a musical work. When authorship of an anonymous work cannot be determined with reasonable certainty, it is said to be of unknown authorship.

Autobiography An account of a person's life written by its subject, usually in the form of a continuous narrative of events considered by the author to be the most important or interesting, selected from those he or she is willing to reveal. The first fully-developed autobiography, the Confessions of St. Augustine, was written in the 4th century A.D. Some autobiographies are largely fictional (example: Confessions of Jean-Jacques Rousseau). Contemporary autobiographies of famous people are often written with the assistance of a ghost writer. An autobiography differs from a diary or journal in being written for others, rather than for purely private reasons. Compare with biography.

Autograph A manuscript written entirely in the author's own handwriting. Also refers to a person's own signature. Compare with holograph.

Autographed copy A copy of a book or other published work signed by the author. Autographed copies may be of considerable value to collectors if the author is very well-known and signed copies rare. Compare with inscribed copy.

Autographed edition An edition of a work in which all the copies are personally signed by the author, possible only in relatively small editions.

Autolib autolib - Integrated Library Automation

Management Software has been designed, developed and promoted by M/s autolib Software System.

Automated checkout Some computerized circulation systems allow patrons to check out materials on their own, without the assistance of library staff, usually by means of barcodes on the item and on the patron's library card. Automated checkout is part of a trend toward self-service in library operations.

Automatic indexing A method of computerized indexing in which an algorithm is used to extract words or phrases representing subjects from the title and/or text of a work, for use as headings under which entries are made in an index. Compare with machine-aided indexing.

Autonym A person's own name. Also refers to a work published under the real name of its author, rather than under a pseudonym or allonym.

Autotron A device which keeps track of the number of copies made on a photocopying machine. No longer used in Marriott's copy centers.

Auxiliary schedule In library classification, a separate list of classes (with their notations) which serve only to subdivide the classes listed in the main schedules, for example, the standard subdivisions listed in Table 1 of Dewey Decimal Classification.

AV Audio-Visual. AV Macintosh models have video-capture hardware and have sophisticated sound (and video) recording capabilities.

Available An indication in an online catalog of the circulation status of an item that can be found on the shelf ready to be checked out. In a more general sense, any item that can be seen, used, or obtained by a library patron, including reference materials and items in special collections for which access may be subject to certain restrictions. Compare with out of circulation.

Average price The sum of the prices of individual items

within a specific category (or a representative sample), divided by the number of items selected for the purpose of calculation. In library acquisitions, average price per title is used to compute the annual rate of inflation in the cost of various types of materials, an important consideration in budgeting and the allocation of funds. The average price of books and serials sold in the United States is broken down by subject in the Bowker Annual Library and Book Trade Almanac, available in the reference section of larger libraries.

B Byte. One character of information, usually eight bits wide.

Back file All the issues of a periodical which precede the current issue, usually bound in annual volumes or converted to microfilm or microfiche to conserve space. In the catalog record, the extent of the back file is indicated in the holdings note

Back fold The fold along which a signature is gathered to form the binding edge of a book, left uncut in sewn bindings but trimmed in perfect binding to allow the adhesive to bond more securely.

Back issue Any issue of a periodical that precedes the current issue. Back issues are usually retained in a back file which may be stored in a different location in the periodicals section of a library, sometimes converted to a more compact format, such as microfilm or microfiche. In the catalog record, the extent of the back file is indicated in the holdings note. Synonymous with back number.

Back matter The pages following the text at the end of a book, on which the appendices, notes, bibliographies, list of contributors, indices, imprint, and any advertising normally appear. In scholarly works, the back matter may be considerable. Back matter is paginated in arabic numerals continuously with the text. Blank leaves may be included at the end to make up a full section. Synonymous with end matter, postliminary matter, and subsidiaries. Compare with front matter.

Back number A synonymous with back issue; any issue of a periodical older than the most recent issue.

Back order (BO) An order for library materials that could not be filled when originally placed because at least one of the items requested was not in stock or as yet unpublished. Back orders are held open for future delivery, usually for a designated period of time, after which they are canceled. Synonymous in the U.K. with dues.

Back The sewn or binding edge of the gathered sections of a book, to which the lining is applied. The back may be flat, but more often it is given a convex curve in a binding procedure called rounding. A flexible or hollow back is preferable because it allows a volume to open flat. Compare with backstrip and spine.

Backbone In telecommunication, the portion of a physical network that covers the longest distance and handles the heaviest traffic. To operate at the highest possible transmission speed, it must be constructed of cable that provides maximum bandwidth. On the Internet, regional networks are connected to the fiber-optic backbone, smaller networks are connected to regional networks, and so on down the line.

Backdate To make a document or transaction effective from a date earlier than its actual date, for example, a book order given a prior date with the publisher's permission, to allow the purchaser to qualify for an expired discount.

Backing In bookbinding, the process of shaping a shoulder on each side of the binding edge of the text block after rounding, before lining is applied to the back. In hand-binding, a backing hammer is used to bend the backs of the sewn sections from the center of the text block toward the front and back, forming two ridges against which the boards of the cover will fit. By folding the leaves over each other close to the binding edge, backing also helps maintain the rounded shape of the spine, preventing the leaves from working their way forward as the volume is used. The process also enhances the openability of a volume by creating a slight crease in each leaf near the spine. In edition binding and library binding, backing is done by machine. Also, a conservation treatment in which an additional layer is applied to an item to provide support, usually on the reverse side of a weakened paper sheet. Also refers to the material added in this type of reinforcement.

Backlist Items still available for sale from a given publisher, though they are not on the publisher's "new" or "current" list. Since most books go out of print within a year or two of publication, backlists generally consist of works of long-standing value or demand.

Backlog An accumulation of work that remains to be done, often the cause of delays and bottlenecks in workflow. A cataloging backlog may result when staffing is insufficient to meet the demands of acquisitions, for example, when a substantial gift is received within a short period of time. Synonymous in this sense with arrears.

Backslanted A typeface or handwriting that inclines to the left of center.

Backslash A character consisting of a straight line slanting diagonally from upper left to lower right, used mainly in computer programming notation and to separate directory and file names in DOS and Windows (example: c:\bib\bib.txt referring to the bib.txt file in the bib folder stored on the c:\ disk drive). Also spelled back slash. Synonymous with reverse solidus. Compare with slash.

Backstrip In bookbinding, the central portion of the covering material, extending from the front joint to the back joint over the inlay separating the boards, stamped with the title and author's name in most editions. Sometimes used synonymously with spine. Compare with back.

Backup file In Windows 95, a compressed version of the original file and its locations created by Backup.

Backup In data processing, to make a second copy of an important data file in case the original is lost, damaged, or destroyed. Also refers to computer files, equipment, and procedures created and maintained specifically for use in the event of loss or failure of normal systems. In a more general sense, any strategy designed to be implemented if a preferred method or system fails. Also, to print the reverse side of a sheet that has already been printed on one side. Also spelled back up.

Baker & Taylor A jobber in the business of supplying books, videocassettes, and music materials to retailers and libraries, usually at a discount, and of providing value-added and customized services to meet the needs of libraries of all types. B&T products and services are listed and described in its trade catalogs

Balance In budgeting, to keep expenditures in line with income, usually for the duration of a fixed accounting period. In printing and Web page design, to arrange text and graphics on a page in a configuration that is aesthetically pleasing.

Balanced A library collection containing materials that present the full range of opinion on controversial issues and sensitive topics, for example, the "for" and "against" positions on legalized abortion, or religious books representing various faiths. Although it is an elusive goal, balance is particularly important in developing public library collections which must meet the information needs and reflect the reading tastes of a wide range of patrons.

Ballad Originally, an orally transmitted narrative song composed in an impersonal style for public performance, often sung to a traditional tune that served as a musical accompaniment to a dance. Most ballads tell a popular story of tragic romance or personal catastrophe in short stanzas with a refrain, usually in the form of a dialogue with action. Repetition over an extended period of time tends to produce variants. Synonymous in this sense with folk ballad. Beginning in 16th century Britain, broadside ballads about contemporary issues and events were printed on a single sheet of paper and sold in the streets to be sung to well-known popular tunes. In the late 18th century, a new literary form developed in which long narrative poems were written in deliberate imitation of earlier popular ballads (example: Coleridge's Rime of the Ancient Mariner).

Balloon In cartoons, comic books, and graphic novels, a space encircled by a line drawn from the mouth of one of the characters, containing dialogue or the character's unspoken thoughts.

Bands In older hand-bound books, the sections were sewn to cords of flax or hemp, spaced at regular intervals across the binding edge, producing a series of parallel ridges in the material covering the spine, unless sunk by the binder into grooves sawn across the back (the term refers to both the cords and the ridges). Bands replaced the leather thongs originally used to bind books in codex form. In modern bookbinding, bands have been replaced by tapes in quality bindings, or omitted entirely in most hardcover trade editions.

Bandwidth The maximum carrying capacity of a line in an electronic communications network. For digital devices, bandwidth is measured measured in bits or bytes per second; for analog devices, in Hertz (cycles per second). Bandwidth determines the amount of data that can be transmitted in a fixed amount of time. During periods of peak use, it may also determine speed of transmission, particularly for large data files (graphics, audio, video, etc.). On the Internet, the fiber-optic backbone has greatest bandwidth.

Banned book A book, the publication and/or sale of which has been prohibited or suppressed by ecclesiastical or secular authority because its content is considered objectionable or dangerous, usually for political reasons (example: The Grapes of Wrath) or social reasons (Leaves of Grass). Banned Books Week has been celebrated annually in the United States since 1981. Lists of banned books are available in the reference section of most large libraries. Compare with expurgated edition.

Banned Books Week An annual event observed in the United States since 1981 during the last week of September, Banned Books Week is sponsored by the American Booksellers Association, American Booksellers Foundation for Free Expression, American Library Association, Association of American Publishers, American Society of Journalists and Authors, and National Association of College Stores, and endorsed by the Center for the Book at the Library of Congress. Libraries and bookstores throughout the country celebrate the freedom to read by displaying recently banned books and books that have been banned throughout history

Barcode A printed label containing machine-readable data encoded in vertical lines of equal length but variable thickness, which can be read into an attached computer by an optical scanner. In libraries barcodes are used to identify books and other materials for circulation and inventory, and to link the borrower's library card to the appropriate patron record in automated circulation systems. Also spelled bar code.

Base line In typography, the imaginary horizontal line connecting the bottoms of lowercase letters lacking descenders, used to measure the intervals between lines of type. The line connecting the tops of letters lacking ascenders is called the mean line. Also spelled baseline.

Base map A topographic map, usually on a scale of 1:10,000 to 1:50,000, used as the basis for other maps. In the United States, the base map is the 1:24,000 7.5-minute topographic quadrangle published in series by the U.S. Geological Survey, popularly known as the quad. Synonymous with mother map.

Base number A class number in the Dewey Decimal Classification schedules to which other numerals are appended (example: 020 representing the library and information sciences) to which a decimal fraction can be added to indicate a subclass (.5 for an item that is a periodical). Compare with base of notation.

Base of notation The set of characters or symbols used in the notation of a given classification system. In Dewey Decimal Classification, the arabic numerals 0-9 are used (decimal notation). In Library of Congress Classification, the letters of the English alphabet are used (alphabetic notation), minus the letters O and I which are easily mistaken for the numerals zero and one. As a general rule, the shorter the base, the longer the notation representing a given class is likely to be. Compare with base number.

Baseband System A baseband system transmits signals without converting them to another frequency and is characterized by its support of one frequency of signals. Ethernet-based networks inside campus buildings are transmitted via baseband coaxial cable, with ethernet being the only service supported by the coaxial cable.

BAT Filename extension for a batch file.

Batch processing A group of records accumulated so that they can be processed together, rather than one-by-one, used mainly in automated cataloging and interlibrary loan to increase efficiency and reduce costs. Synonymous with batchload processing.

Batch Scanning Sequential scanning of multiple originals using previously defined, unique settings for each.

Bathymetric map A topographic map showing the depth and features of the sea floor, including coastal zones (bays and estuaries), usually by means of contour lines called isobaths.

Battledore A type of school primer used in the late 18th century, made of folded paper varnished on the inside, resembling a horn book when opened, but sometimes lacking a handle.

Baud Originally, a unit of telegraph signaling speed (one Morse code dot per second) proposed in 1927 at the International Telegraph Conference and named after the French engineer Jean-Maurice-Emile Baudot (1845-1903) who designed the first teleprinter. In telecommunications, a unit of measurement indicating the number of signaling elements (changes of voltage or frequency) transmitted per second over a communication channel, at slower speeds synonymous with bits per second (bps). At higher speeds, more than one bit may be encoded per second, for example, a speed of 4,800 baud may transmit 9,600 bits per second. For this reason, bps has replaced the term baud as a measure of data transmission speed. The baud rate of a modem is one of the factors determining the speed of an Internet connection in dial-up access. Pronounced bawd. Plural: baud.

Baud rate The actual rate of signal changes per second between two modems. At one signal per second, 300 baud translates to 300 bits per second (bps). However, depending on the signal's code, a baud rate may have more than one bps rate.

Bbanner A narrow band of graphic promotional material displayed on a Web site that has leased or sold space on its page(s) to a commercial advertiser. Also, a narrow strip logo across the top or bottom of a Web page, identifying the host organization or suggesting the content of the site. Also refers to a newspaper headline of one or two lines, large enough to extend across an entire page or most of a page. Compare with skyline.

BBS Bulletin Board System : A computerized meeting and announcement system that allows people to carry on discussions, upload and download files, and make announcements without the people being connected to the computer at the same time. In the early 1990's there were many thousands (millions?) Of BBS?S around the world, most arc very small, running on a single IBM clone PC with 1 or 2 phone lines. Some are very large and the line between a BBS and a system like AOL gets crossed at some point, but it is not clearly drawn.

Beast epic A series of stories popular during the Middle Ages in which the characters are animals with human qualities, usually written in the form of an allegory satirizing the Catholic Church, the royal court, or some other powerful person, group, or institution (example: Pierre de Saint-Cloud's 12th century Roman de Renart). A more recent example is George Orwell's Animal Farm (1945), written in the same tradition. Compare with bestiary.

Beginning reader A heavily illustrated work of fiction or nonfiction designed specifically for young children learning to read, in which the text is brief, the vocabulary and grammar simplified, and the type size large, shelved in the juvenile collection in public libraries (example: Harry and the Lady Next Door by Gene Zion).

Beilstein A massive compendium of data on organic chemical compounds. The actual title is Handbuch der Organischen Chemie, and its call number is QD251 .B4.

Beilstein Netfire A bibliograhic database covers 140 Chemistry journals.

Belles lettres A French phrase meaning "beautiful letters," referring to polite, refined literature (poetry, essays, drama, orations, letters, literary criticism, etc.) And to the aesthetics of literary studies.

Benchmark A term borrowed from surveying to indicate the superior quality of a product or service recognized as a standard or point of reference in comparisons made by other producers or providers intent on improving their performance. In computing, a measure of the performance of a hardware or software component. Also spelled bench mark.

Benefits Compensation to which an employee is entitled in addition to salary or wages, such as health and dental insurance, pension or retirement contributions, free tuition, etc., usually specified in the contract or collective bargaining agreement governing terms of employment. Persons employed part-time are usually not entitled to full benefits. Synonymous with fringes. Compare with perk.

Berne Convention An international copyright agreement creating an International Union for the Protection of Literary and Artistic Works signed in Berne, Switzerland in 1886, ratified in 1887 by several European countries and their colonies, and revised periodically. By 1974, there were 64 signatories. The United States joined in 1988. To receive copyright protection under the Berne Convention, first publication of a work must occur in a member country. Works published in nonsignatory nations receive protection if published simultaneously in a signatory nation. Protection is for the author's lifetime plus fifty years..

Berners-Lee, Tim The inventor of the World Wide Web, Tim Berners-Lee graduated from Oxford University in physics and worked in the telecommunications industry in England beforc he was granted a fellowship in 1984 at CERN, a high-energy physics lab in Geneva. In 1989, he proposed that CERN fund the development of a hypertext data system and spent the next five years facilitating the design of what quickly became a global electronic communications system. In 1994, Berners-Lee moved to the Laboratory for Computer Science at MIT where he continued to develop Web tools and standards. Although Berners-Lee has received awards for his work, he elected not to copyright or profit from his invention because he wanted the Web to remain widely accessible. He has been quoted as saying, "....you can have an idea...and it can happen. It means that dreamers all over the world should take note and not stop."

Best books A selection of recently published books considered by reviewers to be superior in the field or the type of publication they represent. Most library review publications publish annual lists of highly recommended titles in the various categories reviewed (reference, fiction, nonfiction, young adult, children's books, etc.). Recommended lists are also published in book form (example: Best Books for Beginning Readers by Thomas G. Gunning) for use in collection development. Compare with bestseller.

Best practice In the application of theory to real-life situations, any procedure which, when properly applied, consistently yields superior results, and is therefore used as a reference point in evaluating the effectiveness of alternative methods of accomplishing the same task.

Bestiary A type of literature popular during the Middle Ages, containing myths and folklore about exotic animals, real or imaginary, in which text and illustrations were employed to teach both natural history and Christian morals through the use of allegory. Compare with beast epic.

Bestseller A highly publicized trade book currently in such high demand in bookstores and libraries that large numbers of copies are sold and circulated. Major newspapers and review publications often publish ranked lists of bestsellers in adult fiction and nonfiction (and sometimes in children's literature) based on sales volume over a given period of time (example: The New York Times Best-Seller Lists). The Bowker Annual Library and Book Trade Almanac usually includes an essay analyzing the previous year's bestsellers

Beta test A full-scale test of a new software or hardware system involving actual users under normal operating conditions in the field, usually preceded by alpha testing in a laboratory environment.

Better Telnet A program for Macintosh distributed via the OIT Software To Go web site; enables you to open a telnet connection to a remote computer.

Beveled boards A technique used in hand-binding in which the upper surface of the edges of heavy boards are cut at a sloping angle, instead of the usual 90-degrees, to give the cover a more elegant appearance or in conscious imitation of an earlier style. Also spelled bevelled boards.

Beveled edge Any edge tapered at less than a 90-degree angle to make the transition from upper to lower surface more gradual than in a right-angle cut. Beveled boards are sometimes used in hand bookbinding. The edges of mats used in framing are normally beveled at a 60-degree angle.

BGI Binary Gateway Interface. Provides a method of running a program from a Web server. Similar to a Common Gateway Interface (CGI). The BGI uses a binary DLL which is loaded into memory when the server starts. While more efficient han a CGI, the BGI must be compiled and is not easily portable to other environments.

Bi-annual A publication (e.g. A magazine) which is issued twice a year. Because of confusion with the term biennial (a publication issued every two years), the terms "half-yearly," "twice yearly" or "semi-annual" are more commonly used.

Bias Judgment unfairly influenced by subjective opinion when the situation calls for reliance on objective fact. Bias exists even in reference books (compare the entries for "Holocaust" and "Inquisition" in the Encyclopedia Judaica, Encyclopedia of Religion, and New Catholic Encyclopedia). In publicly supported libraries in the United States, bias in employment practices is prohibited by law..

Bibelot A French term for a small decorative object of exceptional beauty, rarity, or curiosity. In literature, a book of unusually small size, elegantly designed, and crafted from the finest materials. Also known as a thumb book.

Bible paper A strong, thin, opaque printing paper made from new cotton or linen rags, or from flax fiber, used to reduce the bulk of large volumes such as dictionaries, encyclopedias, bibles, and prayer books that would otherwise be too thick to be easily handled. Sometimes used synonymously with India paper.

Bible style A general term for any flexible leather binding that has rounded corners, especially one of dark color.

Biblia Pauperum Latin for "Bible of the Poor," a block book issued in large numbers beginning in about 1450, consisting mainly of pictures with explanatory text in Latin or German providing lessons from the Scriptures. According to Jean Peters (The Bookman's Glossary, Bowker: 1975), this form of book was not superseded by the invention of movable type, but continued to be produced into the early part of the 16th century. Extremely rare, fewer than two dozen examples are known to survive.

Biblio From the Greek word biblion meaning "book," used in combination to form a host of terms pertaining to books and libraries (bibliography, bibliomania, bibliophile, bibliophobia, bibliotherapy, etc.). In interactions with patrons, most public services librarians avoid the "B-words" because the general public is not familiar with the technical terminology of librarianship.

Bibliocaper A term coined by George Eberhart (The Whole Library Handbook, ALA: 2000) to refer to an odd or wacky event, harebrained prank, or bizarre petty crime involving libraries, librarians, library patrons, or books.

Biblioclast A person who destroys or mutilates books, for one reason or another. Fortunately for bibliophiles, this form of aberrant behavior occurs infrequently.

Bibliofile A CD-ROM database of millions of Library of Congress catalogue records used mainly for acquiring and cataloguing books.

Bibliogony Of or relating to the production of books in all their forms. Synonymous with bibliogenesis.

Bibliographee A person concerning whom a bibliography is compiled, as in a list of references at the end of a biographical essay or book-length biography.

Bibliographer A person who describes and lists books and other publications, with particular attention to such characteristics as authorship, publication date, edition, typography, etc. The result of this endeavor is a bibliography. A person who limits such efforts to a specific field or discipline is a subject bibliographer.

Bibliographic citation Synonym for bibliographic reference, identifying information about a publication, used in catalogs and indexes as well as in lists of "literature cited" or "references" in scholarly publications. Formats vary, but a book citation generally includes at least information on the author, title, publisher, and date of publication; an article citation includes author, title, date, and information on the periodical in which it was published.

Bibliographic control A broad term encompassing all the activities involved in creating, organizing, managing, and maintaining the file of bibliographic records representing the items held in a library or archival collection, or the sources listed in an or database, to facilitate access to the information contained in them. Bibliographic control includes the standardization of bibliographic description and subject access by means of uniform catalog code, classification systems, and preferred headings; the creation and maintenance of catalogs, union lists, and finding aids; and the provision of physical access to the items in the collection.

Bibliographic database A computer file consisting of electronic entries called records, each containing a uniform description of a specific document or bibliographic item, usually retrievable by author, title, subject heading (descriptor), or keyword(s). Some bibliographic databases are general in scope and coverage, others provide access to the literature of a specific discipline or group of disciplines. An increasing number provide the full-text of at least a portion of the sources indexed. Most bibliographic databases are proprietary, available by licensing agreement from vendors, or directly from the indexing and abstracting services that create them.

Bibliographic description In a general sense, all the elements of data necessary to conclusively identify a specific document, presented in some form of record. In library cataloging, the detailed description of a copy of a specific edition of a work, intended to identify and distinguish it from other works by the same author, of the same title, or on the same subject. In AACR2, the bibliographic record representing an item in the catalog includes the following standard areas of description: title and statement of responsibility (author, editor, composer, etc.), edition, material specific details, details of publication and distribution, physical description, series, notes, and standard number and terms of availability (ISBN, ISSN, price).

Bibliographic essay A critical essay in which the bibliographer identifies and evaluates the core literature of a subdiscipline or field of study, providing guidance to students, researchers, and collection development librarians (example: the bibliographic essay published at the beginning of each issue of the review journal CHOICE). Compare with literature review.

Bibliographic format The standardized sequence and manner of presentation of the data elements constituting the full description of an item in a specific cataloging or indexing system. The machine-readable MARC record format has become the standard for library catalogs in many countries of the world.

Bibliographic instruction (BI) Instructional programs designed to teach library users how to locate the information they need quickly and effectively. BI usually covers the library's system of organizing materials, the structure of the literature of the field, research methodologies appropriate to the discipline, and specific resources and finding tools (catalogs, indexing and abstracting services, bibliographic databases, etc.). In academic libraries, bibliographic instruction is usually course-related or course-integrated. Libraries which have a computer-equipped instruction lab are in a position to include hands-on practice in the use of online catalogs, electronic databases, and Internet resources. Instruction sessions are usually taught by an instructional services librarian with specialized training and experience in pedagogical methods. Synonymous with library instruction and library orientation. Compare with user education.

Bibliographic item In AACR2, a document or set of documents in any physical format (print or nonprint), given a single bibliographic description in library cataloging based on the fact of having been published, issued, released, or otherwise treated as a single entity. As defined in FRBR (Functional Requirements for Bibliographic Records), a single concrete exemplar of a manifestation of an expression of an intellectual or artistic work, in most cases a single physical object, such as a copy of an edition of a single-volume . All the items constituting a manifestation normally contain the same intellectual/artistic content and are identical in physical form, but variations can occur subsequent to production, as in the case of a monograph rebound by a library. In some cases an item consists of more than one physical object, for example, a videorecording released on more than one cassette or a multivolume set of reference books.

Bibliographic record An entry representing a specific item in a library catalog or bibliographic database, containing all the data elements necessary for a full description, presented in a specific bibliographic format. In modern cataloging, the standard format is machine-readable (example: the MARC record), but prior to the use of computers, the traditional format was the catalog card. Compare with catalog record, check-in record, item record, and order record.

Bibliographic retrieval The process in which a user queries a library catalog or bibliographic database, usually by author, title, subject heading (descriptor), or keyword(s), and receives a list of records representing items that satisfy the parameters of the search. Most commercial databases allow the searcher to use techniques such as Boolean logic, truncation, and proximity to refine search statements.

Bibliographic service center A regional broker in the business of handling access, communication, training, billing, and other services for libraries located within a given geographic area which are connected to an online bibliographic network, for example, Nelinet which provides access to and support for OCLC and a variety of bibliographic databases to libraries in the northeastern U.S. Compare with bibliographic utility.

Bibliographic utility An organization that provides access to and support for machine-readable bibliographic databases directly to member libraries or through a network of regional bibliographic service centers, usually via a proprietary interface. The largest bibliographic utility in the United States is OCLC.

Bibliographical Society of America (BSA) Organized in 1904, the BSA promotes bibliographical research and issues publications on bibliographical topics. Membership is open to all who have an interest in bibliographical problems and projects, including libraries and librarians. The BSA publishes the quarterly journal Papers of the Bibliographical Society of America.

Bibliography A list of sources, usually appearing at the end of a research paper, an article, a book, or a chapter in a book that documents evidence used in the work and points out sources that might be useful for further research. Each entry provides enough information about each source so that a reader can track it down. (2) A list of recommended readings on a given topic, usually sorted into subcategories. A systematic list or enumeration of written works by a specific author or on a given subject, or which share one or more common characteristics (language, form, period, place of publication, etc.). When a bibliography is about a person, the subject is called the bibliographee. A bibliography may be comprehensive or selective. Long bibliographies may be published serially or in book form. The person responsible for compiling a bibliography is the bibliographer. Bibliographies are indexed by subject in Bibliographic Index: A Cumulative Bibliography of Bibliographies published by H. W. Wilson. Compare with catalog.

Biblioholism An addiction to books and book collecting, a lesser affliction than bibliomania, but more intense than bibliophily. A term coined by Tom Raabe which appears in the title of his book

Biblioklept A thief who steals books. A bibliokleptomaniac is a person suffering from a compulsion to steal books. When library collections are targeted, biblioklepts are considered problem patrons.

Bibliolatry Excessive reverence for books, carried to the point of emotional dependence on them. A person who is an habitual bookworm may be at risk of becoming a bibliolater. Compare with bibliophile and biblioholism.

Bibliology The historical and scientific study and description of books as physical objects, from their origins in human society to the present, including knowledge of the processes and materials (booklore) involved in making them. Compare with codicology.

Bibliomancy The art of divination through the use of books or verses of the Bible or some other sacred text. Also, the practice of opening the Bible, or a book of verses or aphorisms such as the I Ching, without previously marking the page, to discover meaning or significance in the passage found.

Bibliomania An obsession or mania for collecting and possessing books, especially rare books and editions. In the International Encyclopedia of Information and Library Science (Routledge: 1997), the origin of the term is attributed to Thomas Frognall Dibdin (1776-1845), a writer and bibliographer who helped establish book collecting as a popular pursuit among English aristocracy of the 19th century. Some bibliomaniacs are driven by apparent obsession to become biblioklepts. In a recent case, Stephen C. Blumberg was convicted on four felony counts, sentenced to five years and eleven months in prison, and fined $200,000 after a collection of 21,000 rare books was found in his home in Iowa, stolen over a period of years from approximately 140 libraries in the United States and Canada. The fact that Mr. Blumberg had a very comfortable independent income from family trusts suggests that his larceny was motivated by the desire to possess rather than profit from his illegal activities. Compare with bibliophile and biblioholism.

Bibliometrics The use of mathematical and statistical methods to study and identify patterns in the usage of materials and services within a library, or to analyze the historical development of a specific body of literature, especially its authorship, publication, and use. Prior to the mid-20th century, the quantitative study of bibliographic data and usage was known as statistical bibliography.

Bibliopegy The fine art of binding books by hand, performed by a bibliopegist (bookbinder).

Bibliophilately The collection and study of library-related postage stamps, usually as a hobby (see "Bibliophilately Revisited" by Larry Nix in the February 2000 issue of American Libraries).

Bibliophile A person who loves and treasures books (especially their physical form), and is sufficiently knowledgeable to be able to distinguish editions by their characteristics and qualities. Most bibliophiles are book collectors. The opposite of bibliophobe. Synonymous with booklover and bibliophilist. Compare with biblioholism and bibliomania.

Bibliophobia An irrational fear or dread of books, so intense that the afflicted person, known as a bibliophobe, avoids them whenever possible. The opposite of bibliophily.

Bibliopole A bookseller, especially one who deals in rare books and editions.

Bibliotaph A person who hoards books and hides them from others, even to the extent of keeping them under lock and key.

Bibliotheca From the Greek biblion ("book") and theke ("to place"). A library or collection of books. Also refers to a list or catalog of books, especially one prepared by a bibliographer.

Bibliotheque nationale de France (bnf) The national library of France, located in Paris. The history of the bnf spans five centuries. King Charles V ("The Wise") made the initial gift of his private library in 1368, but continuity in collection development did not begin until the reign of Louis XI (1461-1483). Francis I established the legal depository in 1537, and the collection was first classified in 1670 by Nicolas Clement. During the French Revolution, the royal library was proclaimed a national library. After the rise of Napoleon Bonparte in 1799, it became an imperial library until the Republic was re-established in 1870. The creation of a Master Catalog of Printed Books was initiated in 1874 by Leopold Delisle, a medievalist who served as administrator general of the library from 1874 until 1905. In 1994, the Bibliotheque Nationale (BN) and the newly built Bibliotheque de France (BDF) merged to form a single entity, the Bibliotheque nationale de France, one of the leading libraries in the world. The collections have been brought together in two locations, the "Site Richelieu" and the "Site Francois Mitterand." The latter welcomes both scholars (2,000 seats) and the general public (1,700 seats). Thc Library of Congress currently hosts the online exhibit Creating French Culture: Treasures from the Bibliotheque Nationale de France.

Bibliotherapy The use of books selected on the basis of content in a planned reading program designed to facilitate the recovery of patients suffering from mental illness or emotional disturbance. Ideally, the process occurs in three phases: personal identification of the reader with a particular character in the recommended work, resulting in psychological catharsis, which leads to rational insight concerning the relevance of the solution suggested in the text to the reader's own experience. Assistance of a trained psychotherapist is advised..

Biennial A serial publication issued every two years.

Bifolium In bookbinding, a pair of conjoint leaves (as opposed to a single leaf), forming four pages when folded. Plural: bifolia.

Bildungsroman From the German word Bildung (meaning education, culture) and the French word roman (novel). A novel in which the author traces the maturation of the hero or heroine, from the subjectivity of childhood and early adolescence through the development of objective self-awareness (examples: The Magic Mountain by Thomas Mann and The Tin Drum by Gunter Grass). Compare with Kuntslerroman.

Bilevel A type of image containing only black and white pixels.

Bilingual edition A book or periodical published in two languages, usually because both languages are spoken in the country in which the work was published (example: English and French in Canada) or because the work was co-published in countries with different national languages.

Billed A code used in library catalogs and circulation systems to indicate the circulation status of an item unavailable due to loss or damage, for which a previous borrower has been charged an amount usually based on the cost of replacement. Most libraries make an effort to replace lost and damaged items, even if the patron fails to pay the bill, provided demand exists and a reasonably priced edition is still in print.

Bi-monthly A serial publication issued every two months.

Binary **A numbering system with only two values: 0 (zero) and 1 (one).**

Binary file A file that cannot be read by standard text editor programs like Notepad or Simple Text. Examples: documents created by applications such as Microsoft Word or wordperfect or DOS files with the extension ".com" or ".exe".

Binary Information consisting entirely of ones and zeros. Also, commonly used to refer to files that are not simply text files, e.g. Images.

Bind To fasten the leaves of a book together and enclose them in a protective cover, a process known as binding, originally done by hand, but in modern book production, almost entirely by machine.

Binder A removable cover used for filing and storing loose sheets, pamphlets, and issues of periodicals. Commercially-made binders used in libraries to protect current issues of magazines usually have a transparent front cover to facilitate browsing.

Binder's board A stiff, sturdy board made from pulped fiber derived from rope, wood, or recycled paper, used since the early 18th century to give rigidity to the covers of books published in hardcover, and preferred in hand-binding. Modern high-quality binder's board is single-ply, made by pressing pulp between heavy rollers to achieve the desired thickness and smoothness. Synonymous in the U.K. with millboard. Compare with pasteboard.

Binder's title The title stamped or lettered on the spine of a volume by the binder, as distinct from the cover title on the publisher's edition or the title printed on the title page. Compare with side title.

Bindery An establishment that performs one or more of the various types of binding. Some large libraries and library systems have an in-house bindery usually associated with centralized technical processing. In smaller libraries, materials in need of binding or rebinding (back issues of periodica

Bindery Department responsible for binding periodicals between hard covers and repair of items with damaged bindings. At Marriott, periodicals are sent to an off-campus commercial bindery. Items are generally inaccessible for approximately 2 weeks while being bound.

Binhex Binary hexadecimal: A method for converting non-text files (non-ASCII) into ASCII. This is needed because Internet e-mail can only handle ASCII.

Biography/Biographical An account of a person's life.

BIOS Basic Input-Output System. Part of the computer's operating system that is built into the machine, rather than read from a disk drive at startup.

BIP Books in Print; a publication or database from R.R. Bowker Company.

Bit A unit of measurement that represents one figure or character of data. A bit is the smallest unit of storage in a computer. Since computers actually read 0s and 1s, each is measured as a bit. The letter A consists of 8 bits which amounts to one byte. Bits are often used to measure the capability of a microprocessor to process data, such as 16-bit or 32-bit.

Bit Depth The number of bits used to represent each pixel in an image, determining its color or tonal range.

Bit-map Generally used to describe an illustration or font file as being created by a predefined number of pixels.

BITNET An academic computer network that provides interactive electronic mail and file transfer services, using a store-and-forward protocol, based on IBM Network Job Entry protocols. BITNET-II encapsulates the BITNET protocol within IP packets and depends on the Internet to route them. There are three main constituents of the network: BITNET in the United States and Mexico, NETNORTH in Canada, and EARN in Europe. There are also asianet, in Japan, and connections in South America. See CREN.

Bi-weekly Serial publication issued every two weeks (similar to a semi-monthly).

Black Point A movable reference point that defines the darkest area in an image, causing all other areas to be adjusted accordingly.

Blackboard and webct. Synonymous with authorware.

Blended learning Instruction that combines aspects of both face-to-face (F2F) and online learning experiences. An increasing number of courses at OSU now offer this type of mix.

Blogs They are typically updated daily using software that allows people with little or no technical background to update and maintain the blog. Postings on a blog are almost always arranged in chronological order with the most recent additions featured most prominently.

Blurb A brief summary or description of a work printed on the book jacket, publisher's catalog or advertisement to entice potential purchasers.

BMP Bitmap file; a common image format on Windows computers. Files of this type usually have the suffix ".bmp" as part of their name.

Book jobber A book supplier.

Book number The part of a call number which distinguishes an item from all others in that subject class. Book numbers may be author numbers and/or work numbers, and are assigned to place materials in the desired order on the shelves. (See Cutter number .) Example in the call number HM206 .D48 1997, D48 is the book number, and is an author number, for author Jared Diamond.

Book return A place to bring books borrowed from the library back to the library. Large metal book return boxes are located outside the library and at other campus sites. There is a book return slot on your right as you are entering the library.

Book rpair lab The library's in-house facility for the assessment and repair of damaged library materials. See Preservation Team for additional information.

Book Sale Items weeded from the collection and donated materials not needed for the collection, which are offered for sale to the public. In general, hardback books are $1 and paperbacks are 50 cents. Funds raised are used for purchase of needed materials. The Book Sale is managed by the Gifts department, and the sale shelves are located on Level 3 in the Duplication Center.

Bookmark A function in a Web browser that allows users to mark frequently visited Web sites for easy accessibility. When a site is bookmarked, the site's URL is added to a list that the user can return to later. (2) A tag used in a Web page that links directly to a part of the Web page.

Boolean logic or key searching Phrases used to describe the connecting of terms that enable the user to do a more specific search in a database. Boolean terms like "and", "or", and "not" are used in Boolean Logic. "And" narrows, "or" broadens, and "not" eliminates items from a search.

Boolean operator Conjunctions AND, OR, and NOT in logical expressions; named for mathematician George Boole (1815-1864). In library usage, refers to these conjunctions in electronic search criteria.AND retrieves items in which both terms are found wolves and Yellowstone OR retrieves items in which either term is found woman or women NOT retrieves items in which the first term is present but the second term is not AIDS not United States

Boolean Operator or Boolean Logic Boolean operators, otherwise known as logical operators, are used to construct more complex searches in a database. They help make a search more accurate. There are 3 logical operators: AND, OR and NOT.

Boolean Searching Uses three basic Boolean operators (AND, OR, NOT) to link concepts in database searching. For more information, see the Search Strategy guide.

Boom dummy A wooden or plastic marker, like a block, with a call number or message on it. The block is placed on the shelf in place of an item with information explaining where the item is, or why it is not on the shelf.

Booting Starting up a computer via the power switch, which loads the system software into memory. Restarting the computer via a keystroke combination is called rebooting or a warm boot.

Borrowers Card A card issued by the Library, in conjunction with the Student Association, to each student, identifying a person as an authorised borrower and providing information for the loan record.

Borrowing Being able to take books from the library. It is the same as check out.

Bounce A term applied to an e-mail message when it is returned to you as undeliverable.

Bound Journals Several issues of a journal that have been sewn together between hard covers like a book.

BPS Bits per second; the standard measure of data transfer speed. Example: a 9600 bps (9600 bits per second) modem. Often improperly referred to as the "baud rate".

Bridge A dedicated computer used to connect two different networks. It uses data link layer address (i.e., ethernet physical addresses) to determine if packets should be passed between the networks.

Broadband A high-speed Internet connection; at present, cable modems and DSL (Digital Subscriber Lines) are the two technologies that are most commonly available to provide such access.

Broadband System A broadband system is capable of transmitting many different signals at the same time without interfering with one another. For local area networks, a broadband system is one that handles multiple channels of local area network signals distributed over Cable Television (CATV) hardware.

Broadcast A packet whose special address results in its being heard by all hosts on a computer network.

Browse To inspect something casually, particularly to use an internet browser to casually inspect Web pages. This involves following links from page to page (also called surfing) rather than searching directly. The main difference between browsing and searching is that with browsing you have very little advance knowledge of what will be on thc next page.

Browser A World Wide Web tool (software program) for navigating the Internet. Most browsers display graphics and formatted pages. They let a user click on hyperlinks to jump from one Web page to another. The most popular Web browsers right now are Netscape Navigator and Internet Explorer. The very first Web browsers, such as Lynx, only allowed users to see text.

BSD Berkeley Software Distribution. Implementation of the UNIX operating system and its utilities developed and distributed by the University of California at Berkeley. BSD is usually preceded by the version number of the distribution, e.g., 4.3 BSD is version 4.3 of the Berkeley UNIX distribution. Many Internet hosts run BSD software, and it is the ancestor of many commercial UNIX implementations.

BTW Commonly used in electronic communications, an acronym meaning "by the-way". Can be written in either upper- or lower case.

Buckeye Bundle A collection of software available to OSU faculty, staff, and students under the terms of an agreement between OSU and Microsoft. Buckeye Bundle includes products such as Office, frontpage, Visual Studio Professional, and operating system upgrades for Windows. For more information, go to http://www.osu.edu/units/uts/site_license/mslicense or to http://www.osu.edu/bookstores/buckeyebundle.

Buffer On a multitasking system, a certain amount of RAM that is allocated as a temporary holding area so that the CPU can manipulate data before transferring it to a particular device.

Buffered Data that is collected but not made immediately available. Compare to a language translator who listens to a whole statement before repeating what the speaker has said rather than providing a word-by-word tranlsation. Example: Streaming media data viewable using a tool like realmedia Player is buffered.

Bug A mistake, or unexpected occurrence, in a piece of software or in a piece of hardware.

Bulletin board system (BBS) The electronic equivalent of a notice board, generally subject-specific. A BBS is a form of electronic mail in which users post messages to a common receiver (the bulletin board) and have access to all messages posted.

Bus the electronic pathway along which signals travel from one part of the computer to another: address bus allocates memory addresses data bus moves data between the processor and memory control bus carries signals from the control unit

By subject (or in classified arrangement) and sometimes under the author's last name. Periodical indexes may be general (Reader's Guide to Periodical Literature), devoted to a specific academic discipline (Education Index) or group of disciplines (Humanities Index), or limited to a particular type of publication (Alternative Press Index). In libraries, periodical indexes are available in print, as online electronic databases, or on CD-ROM. Some electronic indexes will provide full-text articles. Print indexes and some electronic indexes only provide citations to articles. The actual periodicals would have to be located for the full articles.

Byte A set of Bits that represent a single character. Usually there are 8 Bits in a Byte, sometimes more, depending on how the measurement is being made.

Cable modem A special type of modem that connects to a local cable TV line to provide a continuous connection to the Internet. Like an analog modem, a cable modem is used to send and receive data, but the difference is that transfer speeds are much faster. A 56 Kbps modem can receive data at about 53 Kbps, while a cable modem can achieve about 1.5 Mbps (about 30 times faster). Cable modems attach to a 10Base-T Ethernet card inside your computer.

Cache Refers to: 1) a region of computer memory where frequently accessed data can be stored for rapid access; or 2) a optional file on your hard drive where such data also can be stored. Examples: Inernet Explorer and

Netscape have options for defining both memory and disk cache. OIT provides caching of web pages via an HTTP proxy server at wwwcache.service.ohio-state.edu. The act of storing data for fast retrieval is called "caching".

Caching A process in which frequently accessed data is kept on hand, rather than constantly being from the place where it is stored.

Cadastral map From the Latin word capitastrum meaning "register of the poll tax." A map showing boundaries and subdivisions, made to record ownership and rights in land, and to describe and establish the value of property, usually for the purpose of tax assessment.

CAG Circulation Advisory Group.

CALA Chinese American Librarians Association.

Calcutta Library Network (CALIBNET) It is the first library network visualized and started by NISSAT. At a meeting in 1986 in Calcutta, DSIR initiated action for preparation of a feasibility study for networking about 40 libraries in Calcutta. CALIBNET now is a society under West Bengal Societies Registration Act 1961 and responsible for Calcutta Library Network, a project sponsored and supported by NISSAT. NISSAT also contributed to the development of MAITRAYEE software package based on INGRESS 5.2 for CALIBNET. This package was developed through CMC Ltd. And given to CALIBNET. So far, no data has been created in machine readable from using MAITRAYEE. At present, CALIBNET has become a centre for CD-ROM databases.

Caldecott Medal A literary award given annually since 1938 under the auspices of the American Library Association to the illustrator of the most distinguished children's picture book published in the United States during the preceding year. The medal is donated by the family of Frederic G. Melcher.

Calendar A list of the days in a year, usually arranged by month and within each month by week, sometimes indicating the dates of important events such as national and religious holidays. Also, an almanac listing days of the year which are of special significance to a particular culture or political entity. Compare with chronology. Also refers to a list of the documents included in an archival collection (rolls, charters, state papers, etc.), usually annotated to indicate the date, contents, and other characteristics of each item.

Calendar year The one-year period beginning on January 1 and ending on December 31. Most journal subscriptions run for a single calendar year, although an incentive may be offered to subscribe or renew for two or more years. Compare with publication year. Calender The part of a papermaking machine consisting of a series of rollers designed to smooth paper after drying, reducing its permeability to moisture by closing the pores in its surface. In calendering, the degree of smoothness depends on the amount of pressure applied by the rollers.

Calf A leather binding made from the skin of a calf usually no more than a few weeks old. The smooth, unblemished surface of calf made it the preferred material in England for hand-binding trade editions, but not on the Continent where printed books were usually sold in paper covers to be bound at the discretion of the purchaser. Calf bindings can be dyed any color and decorated in various ways (marbled, mottled, speckled, stained, tooled, etc.).

Call Number A unique identifying number given to each book acquired by a library. The call number serves to group books together according to subject in an organizational scheme. The uconn Libraries use primarily the Library of Congress Classification system, with some older items in the Dewey Decimal Classification. In the Homer Babbidge Library, Federal

Call slip A brief form that must be filled out by a registered borrower to request an item from the closed stacks of a library, usually retrieved by hand by a staff member called a page, although automated and semi-automated systems are used in some large libraries.

Calligraphy The art of elegant handwriting. A highly skilled penman is a calligrapher. The term also refers to handwritten characters, words, pages, and even entire documents which meet the aesthetic requirements of highly skilled penmanship. In Far Eastern cultures, calligraphy is done with a pointed brush held in a vertical position. In Western and Islamic cultures, it is done with a reed, quill, or nib pen held at an angle to the writing surface.

Cameo A typeface used for special effect in which the normal method of printing is reversed, the characters appearing in white against a solid or shaded background, instead of in black against a light background. Compare with outline letter.

Cameo binding A style of bookbinding popular in Italy from about 1500-1560 in which the centers of the boards forming the cover are stamped in relief in imitation of a coin or medallion. The decoration may be left blind, or embellished with ink, silver, or gold leaf. Synonymous with plaquette binding. Compare with centerpiece.

Cameo stamp In binding, a metal tool of oval shape, engraved with a design, usually in the form of a picture, used from the 11th to 16th century in blind tooling to make an impression resembling cameo jewelry on the side of a leather-bound book.

Camera microfilm In reprography, an image of an original source document, made with a camera on high-quality film, usually retained by the producer for the purpose of making archival or distribution copies. Synonymous with first generation and master negative.

Camera-ready copy (CRC) In printing, copy typed using word processing software, or produced by some other means, which has been fully edited and is ready to be photographed for platemaking without having to be typeset. Synonymous with camera copy.

Campus mail Internal mail delivery and routing

system. This system is independent from the U.S. Postal Service.

Canadian Booksellers Association (CBA) A nonprofit national trade association devoted to promoting the current and future interests of the bookselling industry in Canada and to meeting the needs of Canadian booksellers. Its members include over 1200 bookstores and over 350 publishers across Canada. CBA publishes the trade journal Canadian Bookseller in nine issues per year.

Canadian Library Association(CLA) Founded in 1946, CLA has a membership of librarians and other persons involved or interested in libraries, librarianship, and information science in Canada. An affiliate of the American Library Association, CLA sponsors a national conference held at a different location in Canada each year. CLA is also co-publisher with the ALA and the Library Association (UK) of Anglo-American Cataloging Rules.

Canadian Publishers' Council (CPC) Founded in 1910, CPC is a trade association representing the interests of Canadian publishers of English-language books and media for schools, colleges and universities, professional and reference markets, and the retail and library sectors. Located in Toronto, CPC also represents the Canadian publishing industry internationally and maintains a liaison with the Association of American Publishers.

Cancel A new leaf or leaves printed to replace part of a book or other publication when changes are required in the text or illustrations, usually before binding but after the work has gone to press, more common in the 17th and 18th centuries than today because as printing developed, the frequency of printing errors declined.

Canceled Said of a regular order, continuation order, or periodical subscription terminated for some reason by the library or the seller. A nonserial item may be reordered if it is still available. Library holdings of a canceled serial title are noted in the catalog record in a closed entry. Serial cancellations have increased in recent years, particularly in academic libraries, due to the rising cost of print subscriptions and the availability of full-text in periodical databases. Compare with discontinued.

Cancellation period The period of time a library allows a publisher, jobber, or other vendor for shipment of a book or item before the order is automatically canceled, usually 90-180 days. The item may subsequently be reordered from the same vendor, or a different source.

Cancerlit It is a bibliographic database that contains more than 1.8 million citations and abstracts from over 4,000 different sources including biomedical journals, proceedings, books, reports, and doctoral theses. The database contains references to cancer literature published from the 1960s.

Candidate A person whose application for employment has been accepted and who is being seriously considered for a position. Also refers to a person taking an examination, running for an elected office, considered for an award or degree, or destined for a particular purpose or fate.

Canon In literature, the accepted list of works by a given author, considered by scholars to be authentic, for example, the thirty-seven plays of William Shakespeare. Also refers to the approved list of works included in the Christian Bible. In the most general sense, a criterion or standard of judgment applied for the purpose of evaluation. Compare with apocryphal.

Canonical order The arrangement of headings, parts, divisions, or items in an order established by law or tradition, the classic example being the sequence of the books of the Christian Bible.

Canto A major subdivision of a long narrative or epic poem, serving the same function as a chapter in a novel. Cantos are traditionally numbered in roman numerals. Examples of works divided in this way are Dante's Divina

Commedia, Spenser's Faerie Queene, and Byron's Don Juan.

Cap line In typography, the imaginary horizontal line connecting the tops of the uppercase letters of a type font, often, but not necessarily, the same as the ascender line. Compare with mean line.

Capital expenditure In budgeting, an allocation made on a one-time basis, usually for the construction of new facilities, the renovation or expansion existing facilities, or a major upgrade of automation equipment or systems, as opposed to the operating budget allocated annually or biennially to meet ongoing expenses incurred in running a library or library system.

Capital improvement The acquisition of a long-term asset, such as a new or renovated facility, initial book stock, or new equipment, furnishings, or vehicle(s), funded on a one-time basis from a budget for capital expenditures, as distinct from the ongoing purchase of library materials, payment of salaries and wages, routine repair and replacement of existing equipment and furnishings, and regular maintenance of facilities, funded from the operating budget.

Capital letter A large letter of the roman alphabet (A, B, C, etc.) Which prior to the 4th century A.D. consisted of capitals only. The name is derived from the lapidary Roman letterforms incised with a chisel at the top (capital) of architectural columns and on other stone monuments. Also, any letter written or printed in a form larger and usually different from that of the corresponding small letter. Abbreviated cap. Synonymous with uppercase. Compare with majuscule.

Capitalization The writing or printing of a letter, word, or words in uppercase, rather than lowercase. Also refers to the conventions in a language with respect to words written or printed with certain letters in uppercase. For example, in English the first letter of the first word of a paragraph, and of each of the parts of a proper name, is normally capitalized (unless you are a cockroach and not heavy enough to depress the "Caps" key). The general rules governing capitalization in library catalog entries can be found in Appendix A of AACR2.

Capsa A box of cylindrical shape used in ancient libraries to store scrolls in an upright position..

Caption From the Latin word for "capture" or "seizure." A brief title, explanation, or description appearing immediately above, beneath, or adjacent to an illustration or photograph on a page, sometimes indicating the source of the image. Synonymous in this sense with cut line or legend.

Caption title A title printed at the beginning of a chapter, section, or other major division of a book, or at the beginning of the first page of the text, which, in the absence of a title page, is sometimes used as the title of the whole in creating the bibliographic description. The cataloger usually adds "caption title" as a note in the bibliographic record to indicate its source. In a musical score, the title that appears immediately above the opening bars may be used as the caption title. Synonymous with head title. Compare with drop-down title.

Card catalog A list of the holdings of a library, printed, typed, or handwritten on catalog cards, each representing a single bibliographic item in the collection. Catalog cards are normally filed in a single alphabetical sequence (dictionary catalog), or in separate sections by author, title, and subject (divided catalog), in the long narrow drawers of a specially designed filing cabinet, usually constructed of wood. Most large and medium-sized libraries in the United States have converted their card catalogs to machine-readable format. Also spelled card catalogue. Compare with online catalog.

Caricature A deliberately distorted picture of a person, or imitation of a performance or literary style, achieved by grossly exaggerating certain features or mannerisms peculiar to the object of satire.

Carnegie library A library facility constructed wholly or in part with grant funds provided by the American steel magnate and philanthropist Andrew Carnegie (1835-1919) who, in his later years, devoted his considerable wealth to the promotion of libraries and world peace. Between 1881 and 1917, over 2,500 Carnegie libraries were built around the world, the majority in the United States, United Kingdom, and Canada. The libraries of many small towns in the United States still occupy facilities built with Carnegie funds.

Carnegie Medal A literary award presented annually since 1936 by the Library Association of the United Kingdom to the author of the most outstanding English-language children's book published in the U.K. during the preceding year. The prize is named after the American steel magnate and philanthropist Andrew Carnegie (1835-1919) who devoted the last years of his life to the advancement of libraries and world peace.

Carolingian minuscule The first script to introduce small letters, Carolingian minuscule was developed in the late 8th century by Alcuin of York, Abbot of St. Martin's at Tours, in response to Charlemagne's desire for a standard alphabet in which books of the Catholic Church could be copied throughout his realm. It quickly became the dominant book hand in Europe where it was used through the 11th century and adopted in England following the Norman Conquest. Its letterforms are wide and curved, with ligatures sparingly used, each letter written separately. Carolingian style standardized the practice of beginning each sentence with a single majuscule and completing it in minuscules, and formed the basis for the lowercase letterforms developed after the invention of movable type. Synonymous with Caroline minuscule.

Carousel A detachable, circular slotted container, usually made of plastic, in which dozens of slides can be queued for sequential viewing on a specially-designed slide projector. Although carousels are bulky, they can also be used to store slides when not in use. Compare with magazine.

Carrel Originally a small stall or pew in a medieval cloister containing a desk for reading, writing, and semi-private study. In modern libraries, a small room or alcove in the stacks designed for individual study. Also refers to a free-standing desk (or two desks face-to-face) with low partitions at back and sides to provide some degree of privacy, with a shelf across the back facing the reader. Newer study carrels have built-in illumination and may be wired to provide network access for patrons using laptops.

Cartobibliography A list of references to maps and/or works about maps, arranged in some kind of order, with or without annotations. Also, the branch of bibliography pertaining to maps and mapping.

Cartogram A simplified map in which the size, outline, or location of geographic features is altered or exaggerated to illustrate diagrammatically a principal concept or set of statistical data.

Cartographic A term that refers to maps, atlases and globes which represent the whole or part of the earth or a celestial body.

Cartographic material Any representation of part or all of the surface of the earth or any other celestial body (real or imaginary) on any scale, including two- and three-dimensional maps, atlases, globes, aeronautical and navigational charts, aerial photographs, sections, cartograms, bird's-eye views, etc. In the bibliographic record representing a cartographic item, the nature of the material is described in the material specific details area (MSD).

Cartography The art and craft of making maps and other cartographic materials. A person who makes or produces maps is a cartographer. Synonymous with mapmaking..

Cartoon A symbolic or representational drawing in one or more panels, intended to caricature a person or institution, or satirize in a witty and imaginative way an action or situation of current popular interest. Usually published in a newspaper or magazine, cartoons may be captioned or use balloons to convey monologue or dialogue. Political cartoons usually appear on or near the editorial page of a newspaper. Successful cartoonists are often syndicated.

Cartouche An ornamental frame in the form of a scroll, drawn or printed in the corner of a map around an inscription giving the map's title or subject, name of cartographer, scale, and other descriptive information. In older maps, the cartouche often includes decorative elements. Sometimes seen on older book bindings.

CAS Registry Number A unique identifying number assigned to a chemical by the Chemical Abstracts Service. Useful for searching for a particular chemical in some databases, including Chemical Abstracts and the spectra databases, and in many physical property reference works.

Case binding A form of bookbinding in which a hard cover, called a case, consisting of two boards and an inlay covered in cloth, leather, or paper, is manufactured separately from the book and subsequently attached to it. The process of attaching the case to the sewn and glued sections by pasting the endpapers to the boards is called casing-in.

Case In machine binding, a cover made completely before it is attached to the body of a book, consisting of two boards and a paper inlay covered in book cloth or some other protective material. The edition binder submits a specimen case to the publisher for approval showing the size, boards, covering, lettering, and squares. The process of attaching the case to the text block by pasting down the endpapers is called casing-in..

Case Sensitive Capital letters (upper case) retrieve only upper case. Most search tools are not case sensitive or only respond to initial capitals, as in proper names. It is always safe to key all lower case (no capitals) in search engines because lower case will always retrieve both upper and lower case.

Case study In the social and medical sciences, analysis of the behavior of one individual in a population, or a single event in a series, based on close observation over a period of time. A case study may be published as an article in a journal, as an essay in a collection, or in book form. In bibliographic databases that permit the user to limit retrieval by type of publication, case studies may be one of the options (example: psycinfo). Compare with casebook.

Casebook A book containing records or descriptions of actual cases that have occurred in a professional discipline (law, medicine, psychology, sociology, social work, counseling, etc.), selected to illustrate important principles and concepts, for the use of students as a textbook and practitioners for reference. Compare with case study

Case-dependent Software differentiation between upper and lower case characters. Also referred to as case sensitive.

Case-sensitive A computer system or software program in which uppercase letters (A, B, C...) And lowercase letters (a, b, c...) Are not interchangeable as input (JAVA versus java). On the Internet, Web addresses (urls) are case-sensitive, but e-mail addresses and filenames usually are not. Generally applies to a data input field; a case-sensitive restriction means lower-case letters are not equivalent to the same letters in upper-case. Example: "cat" is not recognized as being the same word as "Cat" or "CAT".

Casetable Alphabetical list of court opinions by name of plaintiff; sometimes by name of defendant also (Law Library).

Cash discount Usually 1-2%, offered by publishers to booksellers in exchange for payment within 10 days of the end of the billing month

CASSI Chemical Abstracts Service Source Index. A 3-volume reference listing all titles cited in Chemical Abstracts, arranged alphabetically by abbreviation; very useful for identifying sources cited, and housed at the Science & Engineering desk.

Casstte Small case, as an encased video or audio tape.

CAT SEP Abbreviation for a publication that is part of a series, but is cataloged separately as a monograph with an individual (different) call number.

Catalog A comprehensive list of the books, periodicals, maps, and other materials in a given collection, arranged in systematic order to facilitate retrieval (usually alphabetically by author, title, and/or subject). In most modern libraries, the card catalog has been converted to machine-readable bibliographic records and is available online. The purpose of a library catalog, as stated by Charles C. Cutter in Rules for a Dictionary catalog notification. Printout of the record made available to serials to establish the check-in information on SAGE.

Catalog record In the manual card catalog, all the information given on a library catalog card, including a description of the item, the main entry, any added entries and subject headings, notes, and the call number. In the online catalog, the screen display that represents most fully a specific edition of a work, including elements of description and access points taken from the complete machine-readable bibliographic record, as well as information about the holdings of the local library or library system (copies, location, call number, status, etc.) Taken from the item records attached to the bibliographic record. British spelling is catalogue record. Compare with entry.

Cataloger A librarian primarily responsible for preparing bibliographic records to represent the items acquired by a library, including bibliographic description, subject analysis, and classification. Also refers to the librarian responsible for supervising a cataloging department. British spelling is cataloguer. Synonymous with catalog librarian..

Cataloger's Desktop Published on a single CD-ROM, Cataloger's Desktop is a product of the Library of Congress that provides basic cataloging documentation (including MARC formats), the Library of Congress Subject Headings list, Cutter table, and much more, based on the 1998 revision of AACR2, including all Amendments.

Cataloging agency A library or other institution that provides authoritative cataloging data in the form of new bibliographic records and modifications of existing records, for the use of other libraries. In the United States, the leading source of cataloging data is the Library of Congress. In the MARC record, the identity of the cataloging agency is indicated by its three-letter OCLC symbol in the cataloging source field (example: DLC for Library of Congress).

Cataloging Distribution Service (CDS) An agency within the Library of Congress that develops and markets, on a cost-recovery basis, bibliographic products and services that provide access to its resources for libraries in the United States, the American public, and the international information community. To accomplish its goals, the CDS employs librarians, product developers, systems analysts, programmers, operators, marketers, shippers, customer service representatives, accountants, and production staff.

Cataloging source Field (040) of the MARC record, reserved for the three-letter OCLC symbol representing the cataloging agency that created, transcribed, or modified the bibliographic record (example: DLC for Library of Congress). If English is not the language of the cataloging agency, the 040 field may also contain information about the language in which the item is cataloged.

Cataloging The process of creating entries for a catalog. In libraries, this usually includes bibliographic description, subject analysis, assignment of classification notation, and all the activities involved in physically preparing the item for the shelf, tasks usually performed under the supervision of a librarian trained as a cataloger. British spelling is cataloguing.

Cataloging-in-publication (CIP) A prepublication

cataloging program in which participating publishers complete a standardized data sheet and submit it with the front matter or entire text of new book (usually still in galleys) to the Library of Congress for use in assigning an LCCN and preparing a bibliographic record which is sent back to the publisher within ten days to be printed on the verso of the title page. The Library of Congress distributes CIP records to large libraries, bibliographic utilities, and book vendors on a weekly basis to facilitate book processing. If incomplete, the initial record may be amended by the Library of Congress after the U.S. Copyright Office receives the deposit copy of the published work. The CIP Program began at the Library of Congress in 1971 and is used throughout the world. British spelling is cataloguing-in-publication.

Cataloguing in progress (CIP) Preliminary cataloging based on pre-publication information supplied by publishers. The CIP is generally created by national cataloging agencies such as the Library of Congress, the British Library Bibliographic Services, or the National Library Of Canada, and usually appears on the verso of the Title Page. Occasionally publishers also will create their own CIP-like information.

Catch letters A sequence of letters (usually three) printed at the top of a page in a dictionary, gazetteer, or similar work, which duplicate the first few letters of the first or last word on the page. Those printed on the verso indicate the first letters of the first word on the page; those on the recto, the first letters of the last word on the page. In some works, the letters appear in two groups separated by a hyphen, representing the first and last words on the page. Compare with catchword.

Catchword A word or part of a word printed in boldface or uppercase at the top of a column or page in a dictionary or encyclopedia, which repeats the first and/or last heading appearing in the column or on the page. Synonymous with guideword. Compare in this sense with catch letters.

Catchword title A partial title composed of an easily remembered word or phrase likely to be used as a heading or keyword in a search of the library catalog, sometimes the same as a subtitle or the alternative title. Synonymous with catch title.

Cathedral binding A cloth or leather binding decorated with architectural motifs of the Gothic period, sometimes even including a rose window, popular in France and England from about 1815 to 1840 when interest in Gothic art underwent a revival.

Catholic Library Association (CLA) Established in 1921, CLA has a membership of librarians, teachers, and booksellers involved with Catholic libraries and the writing, publication, and distribution of Catholic literature. CLA publishes the quarterly Catholic Library World.

Catme OCLC's **Cataloging Micro Enhancer**, software that enables catalogers to search the worldcat database and OCLC Authority File interactively online, edit bibliographic and authority records offline, and send updates to OCLC in batches to increase cataloging efficiency and reduce costs.

CATP (Caffeine Access Transport Protocol): Common method of moving caffeine across Wide Area Networks such as the Internet, CATP was first used at the Binary Cafe in Cybertown and quickly spread world-wide. There are reported problems with short-circuits and rust and decaffinated beverages were not supprted until version 1.5.3

Caucus An interest group within a political faction or party, legislative body, or organization, formed (sometimes spontaneously) to address an immediate need for action on a given issue or series of related issues, usually by formulating policy, supporting candidates for political office, drafting campaign strategy, lobbying, etc. (example: Black Caucus of the ALA). Compare with task force.

Caxton, William, C. 1422?-1491 England's first printer, Caxton learned the trade relatively late in life while living in Cologne and Bruges. He brought the first printing press to

England and installed it in the Chapter House at Westminster Abbey, issuing the first dated book known to have been printed in England (probably his The Dictes and Sayings of the Philosophers) in 1477. By the time he died in 1491, his press had issued approximately one hundred works, including folio editions of Chaucer's Canterbury Tales (1478) and Mallory's Morte D'Arthur (1485) which he sold to English readers in bound copies. He was an expert editor and translated into English many of the works he printed. For a succinct, informative essay on the life and work of William Caxton, see the entry under his name in Geoffrey Glaister's Encyclopedia of the Book (Oak Knoll: 1996).

CBT Computer-Based Training; a type of training in which a student learns a particular application by using special programs on a computer. Sometimes referred to as "CAI" (Computer-Assisted Instruction) or "CBI" (Computer-Based Instruction), although these two terms may also be used to describe a computer program used to assist a teacher or trainer in classroom instruction.

CCD Charge-coupled device. An integrated, micro-electrical light sensing device built into some image capturing devices.

CCH Commerce Clearing House.

CD Short for CD-ROM.

CDAG Collection Development Advisory Group.

CDATA The Australian Bureau of Statistics census data on CD-ROM. Data can be manipulated to produce tables, graphs, charts and maps.

CD-BURNER Another name for a CD-R DRIVE.

CD-R drive A type of disk drive that can create CD-roms and audio cds. CD-R drives that feature multisession recording allow you to continue adding data to a compact disk which is very important if you plan on using the drive for backup.

CD-R Short for CD-RECORDABLE, write once compact

disc storage. This type of compact disc can be recorded on only once. CD-R allows multiple write sessions to different areas of the disc, but you cannot write to areas that are already burned..

CD-Recordable Write once compact disc storage. This type of compact disc can be recorded on only once. CD-R allows multiple write sessions to different areas of the disc, but you cannot write to areas that are already burned.

CD-Rewritable A type of compact disk that enables you to write onto it in multiple sessions. With CD-RW drives and disks, you can treat the optical disk just like a floppy or hard disk, writing and erasing data onto it multiple times.

CD-ROM (Compact Disc - Read Only Memory) - A technology for putting a large amount of information on a small disk that can be accessed by a computer; CD-roms in the Libraries contain periodical indexes, abstracts, statistics, directories, and other complete texts.

CD-ROM Database A computer technology which allows information to be stored on a compact disk and accessed through a microcomputer. NOTE: CD-ROM databases at NSU include those which provide access to periodical article citations, full text, and statistical data. The library has many CD-ROM databases such as Moodys, National Trade Data Bank, etc.

CD-RW Short for CD-REWRITABLE disk, a type of compact disk that enables you tu write onto it in multiple sessions. With CD-RW drives and disks, you can treat the optical disk just like a floppy or hard disk, writing and erasing data onto it multiple times.

CD-RW, CD-R disk: A CD-RW disk allows you to write data onto it multiple times instead of just once (a CD-R disk). With a CD-R drive you can use a CD-RW disk just like a floppy or zip disk for backing up files, as well as for creating CD-roms and audio cds.

CDS/ISIS CDS/ISIS was developed by UNESCO in the year 1985 for information management in the libraries, information centers and archives at the national and international level. The software was originally written for a super computer, which was later on customized to be used on the other types of computers also. CDS/ISIS is operational on MS dosand Windows. It is suitable for creating larger databases and the changes can be made in view of the local needs of libraries.

Ceased publication Said of a periodical no longer published. Publication may start up again under the same title or an altered title. Also said of a work published in more than one volume, which was never completed. Library holdings are indicated in a closed entry. Compare with canceled and discontinued.

Ceased title Serial title which is no longer being published.

Cel A thin sheet of transparent material of standard size (usually acetate), having the same proportions as a frame of motion picture film, on which is drawn or painted a single image in a sequence of animation. Original cels from early animated films may have independent value as works of art. Also refers to a transparent sheet used as an overlay against an opaque background, as in textbooks on anatomy to show in layers the various systems of the human body (circulatory, nervous, skeletal, etc.).

Cellulose The fibrous vegetable material used in papermaking, derived primarily from wood pulp, but formerly from cotton or linen rags. The cellulose in paper and board made from wood pulp is weakened over time by the presence of acid unless lignin is removed in manufacture and an alkaline buffer added.

Censorship Prohibition of the production, distribution, circulation, or display of a work by a governing authority on grounds that it contains objectionable or dangerous material. The person who decides what is to be prohibited is called a censor. Commonly used methods include decree and confiscation, legislation, repressive taxation, and licensing to grant or restrict the right to publish.

Census An official count and statistical analysis of the population of a given geographic entity (city, county, state, province, country, etc.) Taken at a particular point in time. The earliest known census of taxpaying households was recorded in China in the 3rd century B.C. More complete enumerations were conducted for military and tax purposes in ancient Rome by special magistrates called censors. The development of the modern census began in Europe in the 17th century and today includes questions concerning age, gender, ethnicity, income, housing, etc., formulated to generate data used in social planning, political redistricting, business marketing, etc. In most countries, participation in the census is compulsory and the information collected on individual households and businesses is confidential.

Census Information Provides statistics of All India population totals as per the Census 1991 and Census 2001, India and State maps, etc.

Census tract One of many small geographic areas into which a state or country is divided for the purpose of gathering and reporting census data. In the United States, the average tract contains 4,000 residents or approximately 1,200 households. Census tract outline maps are available from the U.S. Census Bureau.

Center for Book Arts (CBA) Founded in 1974, CBA is a non-profit organization with headquarters in New York City, dedicated to preserving the traditional craft of bookmaking and encouraging contemporary interpretations of the book as an art object, through exhibitions, lectures, publications, and services to artists, including courses, workshops, and seminars on all aspects of the book arts.

Center for Research Libraries (CRL) Founded in 1949, CRL's members are large research libraries that seek to improve access to scholarly collections. CRL publishes a bimonthly newsletter and serves as a depository for infrequently used research materials which its members may use cooperatively.

Center for the Book An educational outreach program established in 1977 by the Library of Congress to stimulate public interest in and awareness of books, reading, and libraries, and to encourage the study of books and the printed word. The Center is a public-private partnership between the Library of Congress, 35 affiliated state centers, and over 50 national and civic groups.

Centerpiece In bookbinding of the late 16th and early 17th centuries, an ornamental design such as an arabesque, stamped on the center of the front and/or back cover, usually accompanied by matching cornerpieces. Also refers to a piece of embossed or engraved metal attached to the center of the front cover of a book. Also spelled centrepiece

Central library The administrative center of a library system, where system-wide management decisions are made, centralized technical processing is conducted, and principal collections are located. Synonymous with main library.

Central processing unit (CPU) The hardware component of a computer that houses the circuitry for storing and processing data according to instructions contained in the programs installed on it, including the operating system, utilities to run peripheral devices, and application software. Generally speaking, the more memory and disk storage a CPU has, the more processing it can handle within a given amount of time, and the faster it can accomplish a task.

Centralized cataloging The preparation of bibliographic records for books and other library materials by a central cataloging agency which distributes them in printed and/or machine-readable form to participating libraries, usually for a modest fee. Also refers to the cataloging of materials for an entire library system at one of its facilities, usually the central library, to achieve uniformity and economies of scale. Also spelled centralized cataloguing.

Centralized processing The practice of concentrating in a single location all the functions involved in preparing materials for library use, as opposed to technical processing carried out at multiple locations within a library or library system. Centralization allows processing methods to be standardized, but increased efficiency may be offset by the cost of distributing materials to the units where they will be used.

Centre for Airospace Information Technical Report Server The CASI TRS database contains bibliographic citations and abstracts for publicly available aerospace documents, journal articles, and conference proceedings.

Certificate Authority An issuer of Security Certificates used in SSL connections.

Certificate of issue In a limited edition, the statement in each copy giving the total number of copies printed and the copy number. In an autographed edition, the certificate may also bear the signature of the author, editor, or illustrator.

Certification In archives, the formal act of attesting to the official identity and nature of an original document or its reproduction. Compare with authentication.

Cessation A serial or annual that has ceased publication. Cessations are listed alphabetically by title in a separate section of Ulrich's International Periodicals Directory published annually by R. R. Bowker, and in The Serials Directory published by EBSCO. In library cataloging, the holdings of a serial that has ceased publication are indicated in a closed entry (example: v. 1-26, 1950-76).

CEU Continuing Education Unit One CEU is equal to one hour of instruction or contact time. Ceus are required for public school educators, including Library Media Specialists. (LINK)

CGI (Common Gateway Interface): A set of rules that describe how a Web Server communicates with another piece of software on the same machine, and how the other piece of software (the ?CGI program?) Talks to the web server. Any piece of software can be a CGI program if it handles input and output according to the CGI standard.

Challenge A complaint lodged by a library user acting as an individual or representing a group, concerning the inclusion of a specific item (or items) in a library collection, usually followed by a demand that the material be removed. Library programs may also be targeted. Public libraries are challenged far more frequently than other types of libraries because they are supported by public funds and must provide resources and services for a highly diverse clientele ("this library has something to offend everyone"). An unambiguously worded collection development policy is a library's best defense against such objections.

Changed title The title proper of a publication that has undergone a change of title from the one under which it was previously published. Title changes occur most frequently in periodicals, compounding the work of serials librarians and complicating access for users. In library cataloging, a note (Continues:) is included in the bibliographic record representing the new title, and a similar note (Continued by:) is added to the record for the previously published title. Synonymous with title change.

Channel A pathway along which data is transmitted electronically from one computer, terminal, or device to another. The term also refers to the physical medium carrying the signal (optical fiber, coaxial cable, etc.) And to the properties that distinguish a specific channel from others. In data storage, a track on a specific storage medium (magnetic tape, magnetic disk, CD-ROM, DVD, etc.) On which electrical signals are recorded.

Chapbook From the Anglo-Saxon root ceap. A small inexpensive paperbound book or pamphlet containing a popular legend, tale, poem, or ballad, or a collection of prose or verse, hawked in the streets of London from the 16th to the 18th century by traveling peddlers called chapmen. The content was usually sensational (abduction, murder, witchcraft etc.), educational (travel), or moral. Chapbooks were typically of small size (6 x 4 inches), containing up to 24 pages illustrated with woodcuts, usually with a decorated cover title. Also refers to a modern pamphlet of the same type. Also spelled chap-book.

Chapter drop The position below the chapter heading at which the text of a chapter begins—lower than on succeeding pages of the text and, in most books, the same for all chapters.

Chapter heading A display heading in a book or manuscript, usually consisting of a roman numeral indicating the chapter number, followed by the chapter title, written or printed on the first page of the chapter in uniform style and position above the first paragraph of the text. Set in a type size larger than the text and running heads, chapter headings are sometimes embellished with an illustration or head-piece in older editions.

Chapter One of two ore more major divisions of a book or other work, each complete in itself, but related in theme or plot to the division preceding and/or following it. In works of nonfiction, chapters are usually given a chapter title, but in works of fiction they may simply be numbered, usually in roman numerals. Chapters are listed in order of appearance by title and/or number in the table of contents in the front matter of a book. Compare with canto.

Chapter title The title that appears at the beginning of a chapter in a book, usually bearing some relation to the content of the division of the work. Chapters may simply be numbered (usually in roman numerals), or given a number and a title. They are listed in order of appearance by number and/or title in the table of contents in the front matter.

Character Any mark, sign, or symbol conventionally used in writing or printing, including letters of the alphabet, numerals, punctuation marks, and reference marks. In indexing, the smallest unit used in the arrangement of headings

Character set A group of symbols in a specific font, used for printing and/or electronic display. Character sets for languages written in the roman alphabet usually contain 256 symbols of which the first 128 are the same.

Characteristic An attribute, property, or quality that forms the basis for dividing a class into clearly differentiated subclasses, for example, the characteristic "period" dividing the class "European literature" into the subclasses "classical," "medieval," "renaissance," "modern," and "contemporary," as opposed to the characteristic "form" dividing the same class into "drama," "essay," "novel," "poetry," "short story," etc.

Charge To record the loan of a book or other item from the circulating collection of a library to a borrower. In modern libraries, this task involves the use of a computer. Also refers to the library's record of such a transaction, including the identity of the borrower, the title and call number of the item, and its due date. Compare with discharge.

Charged If a library item is checked-out, the online catalog will indicate that the status of the item is Charged, or not available. In such cases, users may request a hold or recall on the item. Another option, if the item is a book, is Borrow Direct.

Charging The process of recording the loan of library material to an individual, another library, etc.

Chart A map designed to meet the requirements of navigation, or one showing meteorological phenomena or heavenly bodies. A nautical chart indicates soundings, currents, coastlines, and other important maritime features. An aeronautical chart shows features of interest to aircraft pilots. Also refers to an opaque sheet on which data are displayed in the form of graphs or tables, or by other graphic techniques.

Charter A legal document recording the franchise or granting of specific rights to an individual or corporate body by a governmental authority such as a legislature or sovereign (example: the Charter of the United Nations). The texts of important charters are usually available in the government documents or reference section of large libraries. The originals are preserved by the institutions that own them, usually in archives or special collections.

Chartered Institute of Library and Information Professionals (CILIP) A new professional association formed in April 2002 by the unification of the Institute of Information Scientists (IIS) and the Library Association (UK.

Charts A collection of posters and large pictures in the map cabinet near the level 3 Information Desk.

Chase In letterpress, the portable rectangular metal frame in which assembled type and display matter, composed into pages, is firmly locked into position. The resulting forme is then ready to be transferred to the bed of the press for printing. The expression in chase means "ready for printing."

Chased edges A small wavy or crimped repeating pattern impressed as decoration on the gilt edges of a book, using heated finishing tools called gauffering irons, popular in 16th and 17th century ornamental bindings. Synonymous with gauffering and goffered edges.

Chat Real-time communication between two or more users via networked-connected computers. After you enter a chat (or chat room), any user can type a message that will appear on the monitors of all the other participants. While most isps offer chat, it is not supported by OIT. However, the webct software supported by TELR does provide the capability for live chat among students participating in online courses.

Check digit A digit added to a sequence of digits, related arithmetically to the sequence in such a way that input errors can be automatically detected whenever the sequence is entered as data into a computer (example: last digit of the ISBN).

Checked out The circulation status of an item that has been charged to a borrower account and is not due back in the library until the end of the loan period. In the online catalog, the due date is usually displayed as a status code in the catalog record to indicate that the item is currently not available for circulation. Synonymous with on loan.

Checked-in card On SAGE, a display with receipt/ claiming information for serials. Also called Check-in Grid.

Check-in record A separate record attached to the full bibliographic record for a serial publication, in which the receipt by the library of individual issues or parts is entered, usually by an assistant working in the serials department. Most online catalogs allow users to view the check-in record to determine if a specific issue has arrived. The check-in record may also indicate whether an issue is missing, claimed, or at the bindery. Compare with item record.

Checklist A comprehensive list of books, periodicals, or other documents, which provides the minimum amount of description or annotation necessary to identify each work—briefer than a bibliography. Also, the log kept by a library to record the receipt of each number of a serial publication, or part of a work in progress. Also refers to a list of items required, or procedures to be followed, such as the steps in a library's opening or closing routine. Also spelled check-list.

Checkout period loan period.

Chef-d'oeuvre See: magnum opus and masterpiece.

Chemise A loose leather or cloth cover designed with pockets to fit over the wooden boards of a hand-bound book, sometimes secured to the boards with bosses, used in Europe from the 12th to 15th century as a substitute for full binding.

Chemweb.com Provides access to abstracts of articles published in over 350 journals and 15 databases from a variety of publishers. A number of databases offer structure-based searching and manipulation of molecular structures.

Chief Information Officer (CIO) The title of the person in a commercial company or nonprofit organization who is responsible for managing the flow of official information, including computing and any library services—a relatively new position in companies and organizations that recognize the need for such a management function.

Chief source of information The source of bibliographic data preferred by catalogers in preparing the bibliographic description of an item, usually the title page or a substitute, for example, the title frame at the beginning of a filmstrip or motion picture, or the title screen of a Web page.

Chiffon silk Extra-thin but strong silk tissue used to mend or strengthen a leaf in a book or other document printed on paper.

Child Abuse and Neglect Database Its document database contains over 32,000 records on child abuse and neglect and child welfare issues. Childnet Bibliographical Database (Global) This database contains an ever growing number of screened bibliographical citations on child-related issues.

Child Serial titles received on membership or as part of a group/package.

Children's book A book written and illustrated specifically for children up to the age of 12-13. Included in this category are juvenile fiction and nonfiction, board books, nursery rhymes, alphabet books, counting books, picture books, easy books, beginning readers, picture storybooks, and storybooks. Children's books are shelved in the juvenile collection of most public libraries and in the curriculum room in most academic libraries. Currently available children's titles are indexed in Children's Books in Print published by R. R. Bowker

Children's book award A literary award or prize given to the author or illustrator of a book published specifically for children. In the United States, the two best-known awards are the Caldecott Medal and the Newbery Medal.

Children's Book Council (CBC) Established in 1945, the CBC is a nonprofit trade association dedicated to encouraging literacy and the use and enjoyment of children's books. Its membership includes publishers and packagers of children's trade books, and producers of book-related multimedia for children. The CBC sponsors Children's Book Week, celebrated in schools, libraries, and bookstores throughout the United States each November, and Young People's Poetry Week celebrated in April in conjunction with National Poetry Month.

Children's Book Week Sponsored since 1919 by the Children's Book Council, Children's Book Week is a local and national celebration held each November in which librarians, booksellers, publishers, and educators schedule book exhibits, read-a-thons, story hours, swap sessions, contests, book raffles, an other activities to stimulate interest in books and reading among young people. Synonymous with Book Week.

Children's Books in Print An author, title, and illustrator index to currently available books for children and young adults, published annually by R. R. Bowker. The separately published Subject Guide to Children's Books in Print includes indexes by publisher, wholesaler, and distributor..

Children's Internet Protection Act of 1999 (CIPA) Legislation passed by Congress in 1999 that makes discounted Internet access and internal connection services for schools and libraries under the E-rate provisions of the 1996 Telecommunications Reform Act contingent on certification that certain "Internet safety policies" have been put in place, most notably technology that filters and blocks access to visual depictions considered obscene or harmful to minors. Implemented by the Federal Communications Commission (FCC), CIPA was strongly opposed by the education/library lobby and civil liberties groups, and remains controversial.

Children's librarian A librarian who specializes in services and collections for children up to the age of 12-13. Most children's librarians have extensive knowledge of children's literature and are trained in the art of storytelling.

Children's literature Literary works created specifically for children, as distinct from works written for adults and young adults, including poetry and prose, fiction and nonfiction. Children's literature began with the oral transmission of nursery rhymes, songs, poems, fairy tales, and stories. During the early 17th century, the horn book came into widespread use in Britain and the American colonies, but it was not until the late 17th century with the publication of the popular Tales of Mother Goose by Charles Perrault (1628-1703) that written literature for children emerged as a separate genre.

Children's Literature Review (CLR) An annual reference serial published since 1976 by the Gale Group, providing excerpts from reviews, criticism, and commentary on books for children and young adults, arranged alphabetically by name of author, with cumulative author and title indexes at the end of each volume.

Children's room The area in a public library or one of its branches, reserved for collections and services intended specifically for children up to the age of 12-13, usually staffed by at least one children's librarian and furnished to accommodate persons of small stature. Some children's rooms include a comfortable corner or alcove designed for group storytelling, puppetry, etc.

Children's services Library services intended for children up to the age of 12-13, including juvenile collection development, lapsit services, storytelling, assistance with homework assignments, and summer reading programs, usually provided by a children's librarian in the children's room of a public library. Compare with adult services and young adult services.

Chinese American Librarians Association (CALA) Established in 1983, CALA seeks to promote better communication between Chinese American librarians employed in the United States, and serves as a forum for discussion of the problems of its members. An affiliate of the American Library Association, CALA publishes the semiannual Journal of Library and Information Science in English and Chinese, the CALA Newsletter in three issues per year, and the semiannual CALA E-Journal.

Chinese style In China and Japan, the evolution of the book proceeded as in the West, from scroll to leaves enclosed in a cover, but by a different route. Instead of binding separately cut leaves in codex form, a continuous roll of writing material was accordion-pleated, creating a series of folded leaves left uncut at the fore-edge with writing (and later printing) on one side only. Also known as Japanese style.

Chip A shortened form of microchip, a high-speed miniaturized integrated circuit, etched in a semiconducting material (usually silicon) on the surface of a tiny, wafer-thin piece of metal, for use as microprocessor and memory in computers and other electronic equipment. The design of increasingly powerful microchips has been the driving force behind the information technology revolution that began in the second half of the 20th century.

Chip board A thin, cheap, low-density board manufactured from recycled paper and other cellulose fibers. Although chip board is sometimes used in case binding, binder's board is preferred in hardcover trade editions. Also spelled chipboard.

Chipped The condition of a book that has small pieces missing from the edges of its cover, dust jacket, or pages, not as prized in the market for antiquarian books as a copy in mint condition.

Choice Current Reviews for Academic Libraries A review publication founded in 1964 by the Association of College and Research Libraries (ACRL) and published in eleven issues/year, choice provides reviews of 6,000-7,000 English-language books, Web sites, and other resources per year, focusing on titles of interest to the librarians and teaching faculty responsible for collection development in college and university libraries. Arranged by discipline, CHOICE reviews are prepared by academic reviewers from completed books, not galley proofs. Each issue also includes an editorial, a bibliographic essay, and at least one feature article, with separate author, title, and topic indexes at the end. Reviews on Cards (ROC) contains the same set of reviews as the printed magazine, each printed on heavy-duty 4.25" x 5.5" paper stock to facilitate routing to individual selectors. Choice is also available online by subscription under the title Choice Reviews.online.

Choropleth map A map on which color, shading, or some other graphic technique is used to show the density or frequency of a variable (e.g., mortality, population, precipitation) in each of several areas, based on the average number of occurrences per unit of area..

Chorus score The score of a musical work originally written for solo voice and chorus, which shows only the choral parts and any accompaniment arranged for keyboard instrument.

Chrestomathy A collection of choice passages from the literary works of an author (or authors), especially one compiled as a sample of literary specimens as an aid in the study of a language.

Christian fiction Novels and stories in which Christian religious belief is a major (sometimes predominant) element in the development of plot, theme, and character. The market for Christian fiction has expanded considerably in the United States in recent years. New titles are regularly reviewed in Booklist and Library Journal.

Chronicle Originally, a detailed chronological record of contemporary events, usually written over an extended period of time, with no pretense of literary style and little or no interpretation or analysis. The first extant example is the Anglo-Saxon Chronicle which begun in the 9th century during the reign of King Alfred, which covered the history of England from 60 BC to the 12th century. In modern usage, a list of events described and recorded in the order in which they occurred. The treatment is fuller and more connected than in annals.

Chronicle play A drama based on material from the chronicle histories of England, for example, those written by Hall and Holinshead. Popular during the Elizabethan period, chronicle plays were at first loosely structured, but evolved into sophisticated character studies, exemplified by the history plays of William Shakespeare. A more recent example of a history play is A Man for All Seasons by Robert Bolt (1960).

Chronological The arrangement of data, records, items, headings, entries, etc., according to their relation in time, from earliest to latest. In library classification systems, the period subdivisions added to subject headings are listed in chronological order (example: Antiquity—Medieval—Renaissance—then by century from the 15th to 20th). The opposite of reverse chronological.

Chronology A book or section of a book that lists events and their dates in the order of their occurrence. Most chronologies are limited to a specific period (example: Roman Empire), event (World War II), or theme (women's history). Book-length chronologies are usually shelved in the reference section of a library (example: Day by Day: The Sixties published in 1983 by Facts on File). Compare with calendar.

Chrysography From the Greek words chrys ("gold") and graphia ("writing"). The art and craft of writing letters in gold, as practiced by the skilled copyists who produced medieval illuminated manuscripts. Also refers to writing done in gold letters.

CIDC The Cornell Institute for Digital Collections (CIDC) is a cross-disciplinary team established to explore the use of emerging technologies for providing greater access to cultural and scientific collections. Digital imaging has enabled CIDC to make many of Cornell University's rare and fragile collections available on the World Wide Web. Partnerships with academic institutions, museums, corporations, and libraries, national and international, have permitted CIDC to create digital collections from around the world. For more information see the CIDC web site in the CU Library Web Sites section of the Library Gateway.

CIE The "Commission Internationale de l'Eclairage". An organization that has established a number of widely-used color definitions.

Cinema A broad term encompassing the motion picture industry and distribution system, the films produced, and the art form they represent. It is also used in Europe and the UK to refer to the theater in which motion pictures are publicly shown.

CIP Cataloging in Publication: Cataloging information located on the verso of the title page of a book (or other type of material). Provides call number, main entry, subject headings, etc.

Cipher The initials of a personal name, written or arranged in ornamental form of such complexity and/or artistry as to form a private mark or symbol. Compare with cryptonym.

Circa A Latin word meaning "about," used to indicate lack of certainty but reasonable probability concerning a date, for example, the approximate birth and/or death date(s) of a person for whom official records are lacking. Abbreviated c. Or ca.

Circuit-switched A type of network connection which establishes a continuous electrical connection between calling and called users for their exclusive use until the connection is released. Ericsson PBX is a circuit-switched network.

Circular An advertisement, announcement, or directive, usually in the form of a printed letter or leaflet, distributed to a large circle of people at the same time and intended to be passed on to others to whom its content might be of interest.

Circulating book A book that can be charged to a borrower account for use inside or outside the library facility, as opposed to one restricted to library use only. Compare with noncirculating.

Circulating collection Books and other materials which may be checked out by registered borrowers for use inside or outside the library. In most academic and public libraries in the United States, circulating materials are shelved in open stacks to facilitate browsing. Compare with noncirculating.

Circulating library A library containing materials that can be borrowed by persons authorized to do so, usually for a fixed period of time, after which prompt return is expected. The idea of a subscription library to circulate fiction and other books of general interest was first conceived and implemented by London booksellers in the 17th century. By the Victorian period, this type of library was sufficiently widespread to provide a market for the publication of quality fiction in Britain.

Circulating Material that can be checked out of the library. Some materials, such as those in Reference, and Archives/ Special Collections, are non-circulating.

Circulation The library department responsible for activities connected with the lending and return of library materials, including re-shelving, searching, rush requests for material in process, etc.

Circulation analysis Close examination of statistics compiled on the circulation of library materials, usually broken down by classification, material type, category of borrower, time of year, etc., to determine patterns of usage, an important tool in budgeting, collection development, staffing, etc.

Circulation desk The service point at which books and other materials are checked in and out of a library, usually a long counter located near the entrance or exit, which may include a built-in book drop for returning borrowed materials. In small and medium-sized libraries, items on hold or reserve are usually available at the circulation desk, which is normally staffed by one or more persons trained to operate the circulation system and handle patron accounts. Synonymous with loan desk. Compare with reference desk.

Circulation on the fly Creating a new "MINI" BIB item record when checking out a book that has a barcode not found in the system. This enables the patron to check out the book. Also called on the fly.

Circulation Services Steps involved in lending library materials, including check out and renewal, recalls for overdue items, holds for items needed by another user, and fines for lost materials.

Circulation statistics A count maintained of the number of items checked out from a library during a given period (usually a year), or the number of times a specific item is checked out during a given period, usually broken down by type of material and/or classification. Circulation statistics can be kept by hand, but most automated circulation systems provide detailed statistical reports by day, week, month, and year, which can be analyzed to determine usage patterns, an important aid in budgeting, collection development, staffing, etc.

Circulation status The conditions under which a specific item in a library collection is available for use. An item may be on order, in process, at the bindery, for library use only, available to be checked out, on loan until a certain due date, recently returned, missing, lost, or billed. Compare with loan status.

Circulation system The methods used to record the loan of items from a library collection by linking data in the patron record to the item record for each item loaned. An effective circulation system provides the means of identifying items on loan to a specific patron (including those which are overdue) and enables circulation staff to place holds, recall items needed before the due date, and notify borrowers when items are overdue. An automated circulation system is capable of generating circulation statistics for planning and reporting purposes. Abbreviated circ system. Synonymous with charging system..

CIRRI Database of International Rehabilitation Research It contains citations relating to rehabilitation research conducted outside of the United States. The database is updated monthly. It presently includes citations from 1996 to the present and will eventually include citations from 1990 to the present.

CISER The Cornell Institute for Social and Economic Research (CISER) is a cross-disciplinary organization founded in 1981 to enhance the environment for social science research at Cornell University. Its membership includes more than 400 social science faculty who are dispersed administratively, organizationally, and geographically in nine colleges. CISER provides research services to faculty members and encourages collaborative research among Cornell's social scientists. CISER's research support services include assistance in preparing proposals, a data archive, computing consulting support, and computing systems support. In addition, CISER helps investigators identify colleagues with similar research interests, issues publications supporting social science research, and organizes seminars and workshops. For more information see the CISER web site in the CU Library Web Sites section of the Library Gateway.

Citation analysis A bibliometric technique in which works cited in publications are examined to determine patterns of scholarly communication, for example, the comparative importance of books versus journals, or of current versus retrospective sources, in one or more academic disciplines.

Citation chasing A legitimate research technique in which the bibliographies of works already located in a literature search are examined ("mined") for additional sources containing further information on the topic. The process can be facilitated by using a citation index.

Citation In the literary sense, any written or spoken reference to an authority or precedent, or to the verbatim words of another speaker or writer. In library usage, a written reference to a specific work or portion of a work (book, article, dissertation, report, musical composition, etc.) By a particular author, editor, composer, etc., which clearly identifies the document in which the work is to be found. The frequency with which a work is cited is sometimes considered a measure of its importance in the literature of the field. Citation format varies from one field of study to another but includes at a minimum author, title, and publication date. An incomplete citation can make a source difficult if not impossible to locate. Abbreviated cite..

Citation index A three-part index in which works cited during a specific year are listed ly by name of author cited, followed by the names of the citing authors (sources) in a "Citation Index." Full bibliographic information for the citing author is given in a "Source Index." Also provided is a "Subject Index," usually listing articles by significant words in the title. Researchers can use this tool to trace interconnections among authors citing papers on the same topic, and to determine the frequency with which a specific work is cited by others, an indication of its importance in the literature of the field.

Citation order In Dewey Decimal Classification, the

order in which the facets or characteristics of a class are to be combined in number building. For example, juvenile court procedure in the United States is expressed in a notation built or synthesized from four facets: 345/.73/081/0269. The citation order for the discipline of law (34) is branch of the law (criminal 5), jurisdiction (United States 73), topic in the branch of law (juvenile court 081), and standard subdivision (0269 for procedure). Instructions for citation order are provided in the Schedules. When number building is not permitted or possible, an order of precedence with respect to the choice of facets or characteristics is provided (DDC).

Citation search A search, by name, of all references to an individual. Some databases have a specific citation search option, otherwise you use a full-text search. For an example of a database that has a specific citation search option go to the University of Michigan Library Database.

Citation trail A process used by researchers to track down additional sources on a topic. The tracing of citations to reference works is sometimes referred to as following the path of a "citation trail" or "citation network."

Cited article An article referenced in another scholarly publication. In a citation search, the known relevant article - the user is looking for later papers that have cited that item.

Cited author An author whose publication has been referenced in a scholarly work. In a citation search, users are often trying to determine the frequency with which a particular author (perhaps themselves) has been cited in later publications.

Citrix A program that allows our DOS and Windows programs and databases to be run in a World Wide Web environment; this enables users to access such programs from outside the library.

City directory A three-way directory that lists the residents and businesses located in a specific town or city alphabetically by name, with street address and telephone number included in each entry. In a second section, name(s) and addresses are listed by phone number, and in a third section, names and phone numbers are listed by street address. Published annually and sold by subscription, current city directories often include zip code and census tract locators for use in marketing. In libraries, they are usually shelved in ready reference or in the reference stacks. Synonymous with cross reference directory.

City map A map, larger in scale than a road map, showing in considerable detail the streets, public transportation lines, hospitals, schools, libraries, museums, parks, and other major institutions and landmarks within the boundaries of a city.

CJK An abbreviation that refers to materials published in the Chinese, Japanese, and Korean languages.

CLA Book of the Year for Children A literary award established in 1947 and presented annually under the auspices of the Canadian Library Association to the author of the most outstanding children's book of creative writing (fiction, poetry, retelling of traditional literature, etc.) Published in Canada during the preceding year. The author must be a citizen or permanent resident of Canada. Click here to see a list of past award winners. Compare with Amelia Frances Howard-Gibbon Illustrator's Award.

Claim A notice from a library informing the publisher or subscription agency that a specific issue of a periodical on subscription, or item on continuation order, has not been received within a reasonable time, with a request that a replacement copy be sent. Claimed items are noted in the check-in record attached to the bibliographic record created to represent the publication in the library catalog.

Clasp A hinged catch made of ornamented metal, ivory, or bone, attached to the fore-edge of the boards of a book, used from the 14th to the early 17th century to keep the leaves pressed firmly together and to prevent the cover from warping. Today, clasps are used mainly on personal diaries and albums, and may include a lock to prevent the volume from being opened by someone other than the person who holds the key.

Class A grouping of objects or concepts based on one or more characteristics, attributes, properties, qualities, etc., which they have in common, for the purpose of classifying them according to an established system. In hierarchical classification systems, the members of a class (example: books) are divided into more specific subclasses (children's books), sub-subclasses (picture books), and so on.

Class number The first part of a call number, which corresponds to the item's primary subject, and indicates its place in the classification system and its physical location on the shelves. All books with the same class number will be about the same subject. Example: TK 2842 (TK=electrical engineering; 2842=circuit breakers)

Class Web Site Registry A local TELR web site that enables you to find web sites for Ohio State courses by entering one or more keywords (course title, course number, instructor's last name, or another keyword). You also can refine your search by selecting a specific department in a particular quarter/year. Access this search tool at http://telr.ohio-state.edu/apps/classwebsites.

Classic A widely read work recognized as outstanding in its field. Such a work remains in print long after initial publication; is translated, adapted, and issued in multiple editions; and continues to be the subject of criticism, commentary, study, and analysis (example: The Adventures of Huckleberry Finn by Mark Twain). Also refers to a feature film (Chaplin's The Gold Rush) or documentary (Robert Flaherty's Nanook of the North) that has withstood the test of time. Compare with classics.

Classics All the non-Christian works written in the Greek and Latin languages prior to 600 AD (example: The Republic of Plato). In a broader sense, outstanding books on any subject, fiction or nonfiction, written for adults or children. Compare with classic.

Classification the arrangement of knowledge into specific groups or systems. The main classification systems used at Marriott are: Library of Congress (LC) QH45.5 .G68 1991 used for most of the collection Dewey Decimal (DCC) 813.4 A355 M512s for juvenile and older works Superintendent of Documents (sudocs) A 57.38/26: G13 for U.S. Government publications

Classification (DDC) library classification system which divides knowledge into ten main classes (000-999); named for its inventor, Melvil Dewey, and its use of decimals as necessary for subdivisions. DDC is used in most school and public libraries; at Marriott, DDC is used for juvenile and older (pre-1960's) materials.

Classification number Number assigned to a book or other library material to show the subject area. The Libraries use Library of Congress classification for books and periodicals in the regular collection, and SUDOC (Superintendent of Document) Classification for Government Documents. See also Call Number.

Classification schedule The names assigned to the classes in a classification system, listed in the order of their symbolic notation. In a hierarchical classification system, the arrangement of the schedule(s) indicates levels of specificity.

Classification Society of North American (CSNA) A nonprofit interdisciplinary organization devoted to promoting the scientific study of classification and clustering, and to the dissemination of scientific and educational information related to its fields of interest. The CSNA publishes the biannual Journal of Classification and the CSNA Newsletter.

Classification system A list of classes arranged according to a set of pre-established principles, for the purpose of organizing items in a collection, or entries in an index, bibliography, or catalog, into groups based on their similarities and differences, to facilitate access and retrieval. In the United States, most library collections are classified by subject. Classification systems can be enumerative or hierarchical, broad or close. In the United States, most public libraries use Dewey Decimal Classification, but academic and research libraries prefer Library of Congress Classification.

Classified catalog A type of subject catalog in which the entries are filed according to a pre-established classification system, with bibliographic records entered under as many subject headings as apply to the content of each item. An alphabetical subject index facilitates the use of a classified catalog, which is usually maintained alongside an author and/or title catalog. Compare with dictionary catalog and divided catalog.

Classified index An index in which entries are arranged under headings and subheadings indicating hierarchical divisions and subdivisions within classes based on the subject matter indexed, rather than in alphabetical or numerical sequence. To use such an index effectively, a subject index is required.

Classified Personal Council (CPC) Campus-wide elected group of employees who represent state classified personnel employed by the University.

Classified staff All permanent University employees not included in the academic faculty or administrative professional staff are in the state classified personnel system.

Classified The status of a document to which access is restricted to a few authorized individuals within a military or government agency, research institution, private corporation, or other organization, usually because it contains highly sensitive information which might be misused by unauthorized persons. When secrecy is no longer required, the document may be declassified..

Classroom collection A small semi-permanent collection of library materials selected by a school library or academic library for the general classroom use use of an instructor and the students enrolled in a course (or courses). Compare with classroom library and classroom loan.

Classroom library A small collection of library materials located permanently in a school classroom for the use of instructor and students in support of the general curriculum. Such a collection may include reference materials such as a dictionary, thesaurus, atlas, general encyclopedia, etc. Compare with classroom collection and classroom loan.

Classroom loan A small collection of library materials on temporary loan from a school library or academic library to a classroom, for the use of instructor and students, usually in support of a specific project or curriculum unit. Compare with classroom collection and classroom loan.

Clay tablet The earliest known books were inscribed on small, thin, wet slabs of clay, using a thin, sharp instrument called a stylus to incise the wedge-shaped cuneiform characters of the written languages of ancient Mesopotamia. The finished tablets were sun-dried or kiln-fired, then enclosed in a protective outer shell of dried or fired clay inscribed with a title or abstract of the contents. Although clay tablets were too heavy to be portable in large numbers and too small to record long texts effectively, they were much more durable than the papyrus scrolls that superseded them.

Clearinghouse An organization or unit within an organization that functions as a central agency for collecting, organizing, storing, and disseminating documents, usually within a specific academic discipline or field. A clearinghouse may also assist the research process by maintaining records of information resources for referral (examples: ERIC and LOEX). Also spelled clearing house.

Cliche From the French word clicher meaning "to stereotype." A word, phrase, or expression so overused that it has lost its impact and, to some degree, its original meaning. Considered unimaginative, cliches are avoided by serious writers and speakers, except in dialogue when the author wishes to make a point about the mentality of the speaker. Dictionaries of cliches are available in the reference section of larger libraries.

Clickable Image Any image that has instructions embedded in it so that clicking on it initiates some kind of action or result. On a web page, a clickable image is any image that has a URL embedded in it.

Click-and-drag To change the position of an icon, filename, window, or other movable element on a computer screen by clicking on it with a pointing device, such as a mouse, and then holding down on the button to shift the element to another location on the screen. The technique can be used to reposition windows on a microcomputer desktop, move computer files from one directory or subdirectory to another in storage, and organize bookmarked Web sites in folders in most Web browsers.

Client A software program that is used to contact and obtain data from a Server software program on another computer, often across a great distance. Eachclient program is designed to work with one or more specific kinds of Server programs, and each Server requires a specific kind of Client. A Web Browser is a specific kind of Client.

Client/server relationship A client application is one that resides on a user's computer, but sends requests to a remote system to execute a designated procedure using arguments supplied by the user. The computer that initiates the request is the client and the computer responding to the request is the server. Many network services follow a client and server protocol.

Client-server technology Refers to a connection between networked computers in which the services of one computer (the server) are requested by the other (the client). Information obtained is then processed locally on the client computer.

Client-server Wide-area (WAN) or local-area network (LAN) architecture that makes it possible for a client computer (usually a PC workstation) to download information or processing from a server machine, as opposed to a system that uses dedicated terminals connected to a minicomputer or mainframe. The size and speed of computer required as a server (microcomputer, minicomputer, or mainframe) depends on the nature of the applications to be installed and the amount of anticipated use. Also refers to the software used to establish the connection between a client and server.

Clipboard A small amount of computer memory reserved as a temporary storage place in the exchange of data between software applications. In word processing, this is normally accomplished by selecting the option to "cut" or "copy" from one document and "paste" into another. Data transferred to the clipboard is lost when another cut/copy operation commences, unless saved as a separate file.

Clipping A page, piece of a page, or pages cut or torn from a printed publication, usually from a newspaper or magazine, by a person who wishes to save an article, editorial, letter to the editor, photograph, cartoon, etc. Large collections of clippings are usually stored in a clipping file, arranged by subject or some other method of classification. Synonymous with cutting. Compare with tear sheet.

Clipping service A service, usually performed in a special library, in which news announcements, articles, photographs, and other items of interest to the host organization are clipped from current periodicals and news services on a daily or weekly basis, to be forwarded to appropriate personnel within the organization, based on pre-established interest profiles. Directory information for clipping services is available in the reference serial Literary Market Place. Synonymous with clipping bureau.

Cloisonne An elegant style of book cover produced by Italian and Greek craftsmen of the 11th century in which an ornamental design in narrow metal strips was soldered onto a metal plate, and the open spaces between the strips filled with enamel in various colors, to form the outer surface of the cover. Books bound in this style are usually very valuable, especially if they are in good condition..

Close classification A classification system in which the main classes and divisions are minutely subdivided, allowing very specific characteristics of each subject to be differentiated. The opposite of broad classification.

Close out A book title offered for retail sale at a significantly reduced price because the publisher is allowing it to go out of print. A rebate may be offered by the publisher to the bookseller for copies that do not sell.

Close score A vocal music score in which all the parts are given on a minimum number of staves, usually two, as in a hymn.

Closed caption (CC) A continuous moving line of text (called a crawl) along the bottom of the screen in a television broadcast, giving the narration or dialogue, and noting any non-speech vocalizations (laughter, screams, dogs barking, etc.) Or sound effects (music, applause, doorbells, etc.). Used mainly for the hearing-impaired and in bilingual programming, closed captioning is visible only with the aid of a special decoder. In library cataloging, the phrase closed captioned is entered in the note area of the bibliographic description to identify an item that includes the feature.

Closed catalog A library catalog to which new bibliographic records are no longer added, or in which additions are restricted to certain categories, although existing records continue to be removed as they are revised, corrected, and/or converted to machine-readable format. After retrospective conversion is completed, a closed catalog is usually removed from public access and eventually discarded. Compare with frozen catalog and open catalog.

Closed circuit television (CCTV) A video system used

internally in some large libraries, for conferencing and to monitor traffic for security purposes.

Closed collection A library collection, such as university archives or rare books, not open to the public but accessible by appointment only. Ask at the Service Desk for assistance. Course Reserves Supplementary reading materials assigned by faculty, available in physical and/or electronic format.

Closed entry A note in the bibliographic record for a serial or continuation, giving the complete information for all the parts or volumes published, or in the holdings note in the catalog record for such a title, indicating all the parts or volumes held by a the library (example: v. 1-10, 1936-46), as distinct from the open entry for an ongoing serial subscription or continuation order (example: v.1- ,1936-). For periodicals, a closed entry usually indicates that the subscription was canceled or the publication ceased.

Closed file In archives, a collection of documents in which additions or changes are unlikely to occur, or a file of records to which access is restricted or denied, except under special circumstances.

Closed reserve An item on reserve which may be checked out by a registered borrower, but may not be removed from library premises. Also, a reserve collection shelved in a closed stack from which requested items must be retrieved by a member of the library staff. Compare with open reserve.

Closed stacks collections in which library staff retrieve requested items for users rather than allowing users to browse the shelves and retrieve items on their own. Closed stacks are generally for materials that require special protection or handling, such as archival and rare materials. A shelving area in a library to which only to members of the library staff have access, established to protect the collection or conserve space by using aisles narrower than the standard-width in open stacks. Materials are retrieved from closed stacks by staff members upon request.

Closed-end index An index covering one or more documents or publications, compiled all at one time (example: **Canadian Feature Film Index, 1913-1985**). Compare with open-end index..

Closet drama A play written to be read rather than performed on the stage, for example, the dramatic works of the French poet Alfred de Musset. Also refers to a drama originally intended for performance, which survives as a work of literature but is rarely if ever performed (Byron's Manfred).

Closing All the procedures followed by the staff of a library when the facility closes at the end of a day, such as informing patrons that it is time to leave, checking the premises to be certain all users have vacated, logging off computer systems, turning off lights and equipment, locking doors, switching on pre-recorded phone messages, activating security alarms, etc. Size and design of facility determine the length of time and number of staff required to close. In very large facilities, a checklist may be followed for each floor, and one or more security guards may assist in clearing the building. Compare with opening.

Cloth A generic term for any woven material used since the early 19th century to cover the boards of a book, as opposed to the leather, parchment, or vellum used in earlier bookbinding, or the paper covers used today. Dyed book cloth used in edition binding is woven from cotton or linen, filled with starch sizing, or coated or impregnated with some other compound, then pressed under heat. Because the covers of cloth-bound trade editions are not designed to withstand heavy use, publishers add an attractively designed paper dust jacket for protection (and marketing purposes). Volumes that must withstand heavy use are often given a library binding in a heavier, more durable material such as buckram. The term is also used in publishers' catalogs to distinguish the hardcover from the softcover edition of a work. Synonymous with clothbound.

Cloth book A small, illustrated children's book printed entirely on sturdy woven fabric and given a flexible binding for toddlers who have not yet developed sufficient manual dexterity to turn paper pages without tearing them. To withstand drooling, the cloth pages may be treated with a moisture-resistant substance. In the 19th century, this type of toy book was called a rag book.

Cloth joint A strip of cloth used to reinforce the inside of the front and back joints in some library bindings, and in very large, thick, or heavy books. In volumes of normal size and thickness, the unreinforced joints are usually formed on the inside by the fold in each endpaper.

CLR Council on Library Resources.

Club line A single indented line at the beginning of a paragraph when it appears at the foot of a printed column or page of text, considered awkward by skilled typesetters and avoided whenever possible. Compare with orphan.

CMS Color management system. This ensures color uniformity across input and output devices so that final printed results match originals. The characteristics or profiles of devices are normally established by reference to standard color targets.

CMYK Cyan, magenta, yellow, and black are the base colors used in printing processes. CMY are the primary colorants of the subtractive color model. .

Coalition for Networked Information (CNI) Founded in 1990. Sponsored by the Association of Research Libraries (ARL) and EDUCAUSE, CNI's membership include, CNI is a nonprofit organization with headquarters in Washington D.C., dedicated to supporting the future of networked information technology for the advancement of scholarly communication and the enhancement of intellectual productivity s 200 institutions representing higher education, publishing, telecommunication, information technology, libraries, and library-related activities.

Coaster Slang term for a CD-R disk that has been written to improperly and therefore serves no other purpose but to set drinks on.

Coated The smooth surface of papers to which a thin layer of mineral, wax, resin, plastic, or emulsion has been applied, either in the papermaking machine prior to drying and finishing, or by a separate coating machine after manufacture (some papers are double-coated using both methods). Coated papers are used to print posters, wall calendars, dust jackets, magazine and catalog covers, and other materials in which detailed visual elements predominate (art books, exhibit catalogs, coffee table books, etc.). The finish can be glossy or dull. Also known as art papers.

Coaxial cable A high-capacity metal cable consisting of four layers: a solid or stranded wire encased in insulation, shielded by braided wire covered in plastic insulation. Various types of coaxial cable are used extensively in cable television transmission and computer networks because "coax" can carry more data and is less susceptible to interference than the twisted pair wire used in older telephone systems. Compare with optical fiber.

Cocked A serious binding defect in which the spine of a book is angled or twisted in a way that prevents the boards from lining up evenly with each other.

Cockle A slightly puckered finish produced naturally or artificially when paper shrinks unevenly as it is dried under little or no tension, as in the production of onionskin. The boards and paper in a finished book may cockle if heat is applied following exposure to excessive moisture. The condition can be prevented by controlling temperature and relative humidity in storage.

Cockled The condition of a book in which the leaves or boards appear puckered, wavy, wrinkled, or curled, usually due to excessive heat and/or humidity in drying. In a book cover, the condition can result from the incorrect use of adhesive (too much or the wrong kind).

Coda From the Latin word cauda meaning "tail." An independent passage added at the end of a musical work or literary composition to bring the piece to a graceful conclusion by drawing preceding motifs and themes together in a satisfying resolution. The last chapter of a biography, the last essay in a collection of essays, or the last story in a book of short stories is sometimes written as a coda to tie the other parts together.

Code of ethics A set of standards governing the conduct and judgment of librarians, library staff, and other information professionals in their work. The ALA Code of Ethics sets standards for equitable access, intellectual freedom, confidentiality, respect for intellectual property rights, excellence, accuracy, integrity, impartiality, courtesy, and respect for colleagues and library patrons.

Coden A system of alphanumeric codes developed by the American Society for Testing and Materials (ASTM) to uniquely and permanently identify sci-tech serial and monographic publications. Responsibility for administering the system was transferred to Chemical Abstracts Service (CAS) in 1975. The CODEN is used in electronic information systems to process bibliographic data because it is more concise than the full title and less ambiguous than an abbreviated title.

Codes Laws of a state or nation arranged by subject (Law Library).

Codex Originally, an ancient manuscript written with a stylus on hinged wax-covered tablets made of metal, wood, or ivory, called codices. Later, a manuscript written on sheets of parchment, vellum, or papyrus, fastened at one side to allow the leaves to open like a book. This format was used for law books in ancient Rome, and for devotional works and the classics during the Middle Ages. According to Harrod's

Librarians' Glossary, the oldest Greek vellum codex known to exist (the Codex Sinaiticus) has been in the possession of the British Library since 1933. Also refers to the form of the modern book, consisting of individual leaves of writing material bound together along one edge and enclosed in a protective cover.

Codicology The study of the physical characteristics of manuscript books. By identifying the scribes and workshops that produced them, codicologists are able to establish interrelationships among manuscripts, which assist scholars in detecting alterations (accidental and intentional) in classical and medieval texts. Compare with bibliology.

Codification The process of creating systematic rules to govern a specific activity, such as the cataloging of bibliographic materials. In the United States, Britain, and Canada, the joint efforts of the American Library Association, the Library Association (UK), and the Canadian Library Association have produced Anglo-American Cataloging Rules which apply to library materials in various formats (books, manuscripts, cartographic materials, music, sound recordings, motion pictures and videorecordings, graphic materials, computer files, three-dimensional artifacts and realia, microforms, and serials).

Co-edition An edition for which two or more publishers share responsibility, for example, The Great Libraries: From Antiquity to the Renaissance, published in 2000 by Oak Knoll Press and The British Library. In most cases, the original publisher grants the exclusive right to market and distribute the publication within a specific sales territory to one or more other publishers (see co-publishing). The title page of a co-edition may bear the imprint of the originator, of one of the companies granted distribution rights, or of all the co-publishers. Compare with export edition and joint publication.

Coextensive entry The principle in indexing that the subject heading or descriptor assigned to a work should encompass all the significant concepts covered in the item (and no more). Thus a book about painters and poets would require the heading "Painters and poets," rather than separate headings for "Painters" and "Poets." Coextensive indexing is attempted in the PRECIS system. Also spelled co-extensive entry. Compare with specific entry.

Coextensive heading A subject heading that indicates all or most of the subjects of a bibliographic item, for example, the Library of Congress subject heading United States—History—Civil War, 1861-1865—Participation, African American—Juvenile literature assigned to the juvenile book Black, Blue & Gray: African Americans in the Civil War (Simon & Schuster: 1998). Also spelled co-extensive heading. Compare with post-coordinate indexing. COF OCLC location code for CSU Libraries.

Coffee table book An expensive book on a popular subject, usually oversize and lavishly illustrated, with the text clearly subordinate to the illustrations. Designed primarily for display and casual browsing rather than cover-to-cover reading, coffee table books are often marketed on the decorative appeal of their colorful dust jackets. In trade bookstores, they may be sold at a deep discount, especially at Christmas to attract gift buyers. Public libraries may add them to the collection when received as gifts, provided demand exists for the subject and their condition is good. Academic library approval plans generally exclude them. Compare with table book.

Cognitive style The manner in which an individual habitually organizes a problem-solving or learning experience, especially whether the person prefers content that is already structured (lecture-style) or is more likely to impose his/her own structure on the material (hands-on approach). Differences in learning style have important implications for the delivery of reference services and bibliographic instruction, and for the design of online tutorials and library Web pages.

Cold boot To restart a computer by turning the power off and turning it back on again, causing the files in its operating system to be re-executed. This procedure is sometimes helpful in getting a computer "unstuck" when it locks up unexpectedly during processing and rebooting fails to get it going again, but the user should be aware that powering down will result in loss of unsaved data.

Cold-crack The tendency of the adhesive on the spine of a perfect-bound book to split at very low temperatures, reducing the text block to a pile of loose leaves. The inability of hot-melt adhesives to withstand cold temperatures makes them unsuitable for use in bindings marketed in countries like Finland and Russia where winter temperatures can be severe. The problem is eliminated in Otabind adhesive binding which uses slower drying, cold-resistant polyvinyl acetate (PVA) adhesive.

Coleection policy statements Narrative statements used to describe the Libraries collections by subject, the programs they support, and the level at which they are collected.

Collaborator A person who works closely with one or more associates in producing a work to which all who participate make the same kind of contribution (shared responsibility) or different contributions (mixed responsibility), for example, essays written by different authors for publication in a collection, or illustrations for a children's book in which the text is written by a person other than the illustrator.

Collate To determine, usually by close examination of signatures, leaves, illustrations, and other characteristics, if a copy of a book is complete and perfect, or to compare it with descriptions of ideal copies found in bibliographies for the same purpose. Also, to compare two printed works page-by-page and line-by-line, to establish whether they are identical copies or variants of the same text.

Collation In library cataloging, a synonym for the

physical description area of a bibliographic record, which has fallen into disuse.

Collected edition An edition of the previously published works of an author, issued in a single volume or uniform set of volumes, usually under a collective title. Compare with author's edition.

Collecting archives An independent organization, or unit within a larger organization or institution, responsible for building a collection of records and documents from a variety of sources, in keeping with the mission of the parent institution, for example, a manuscript repository in the library of a major university. Archives of this type may provide online access to a portion of their resources (example: Declaring Independence: Drafting the Documents exhibit at the Library of Congress) or be completely electronic (usgenweb Archives hosted by rootsweb).

Collection agency A commercial enterprise that specializes in collecting past-due bills from people who owe them, usually by informing the person that their credit record will suffer unless prompt payment is received. Most public libraries enter into a contractual agreement with such an agency to handle the collection of unpaid bills for items lost, damaged, or long overdue. Academic institutions have the option of withholding grades or diploma from a student until library fines are paid.

Collection assessment The systematic evaluation of the quality of a library collection to determine the extent to which it meets the library's service goals and objectives and the information needs of its clientele. Deficiencies are addressed through collection development. Synonymous with collection evaluation.

Collection Books not meant to be read cover-to-cover, such as dictionaries, handbooks, and encyclopedias, shelved together in a special section of the library called the reference area. Reference books may not be checked out because they are needed by librarians to answer questions at the reference desk. Their location and circulation status is usually indicated by the symbol "R" or "Ref" preceding the call number in the catalog record and on the spine label.

Collection development policy A formal written statement of the principles guiding a library's selection of materials, including the criteria used in making selection and deselection decisions (fields covered, degrees of specialization, levels of difficulty, languages, formats, balance, etc.) And policies concerning gifts and exchanges. An unambiguously worded collection development policy can be very helpful in responding to challenges from pressure groups.

Collection development The process of planning and building a useful and balanced collection of library materials over a period of years, based on an ongoing assessment of the information needs of the library's clientele, analysis of usage statistics, and demographic projections, normally constrained by budgetary limitations. Collection development includes the formulation of selection criteria, planning for resource sharing, and replacement of lost and damaged items, as well as routine selection and deselection decisions.

Collection evaluation See: collection assessment.

Collection In library cataloging, three or more independent works or long excerpts from works by the same author, or two or more independent works or excerpts from works by different authors, not written for the same publication or occasion, published in a single volume or uniform set of volumes, for example, a book of essays written by one or more essayists. Selected for publication by an editor, the works are listed in order of appearance in the table of contents in the front matter. Synonymous with collected work. Compare with anthology and compilation.

Collection level cataloging The encoding level used to control separately published documents (maps, pamphlets, ephemera, etc.) Which are unrelated bibliographically and do not warrant the expense of full level or even minimal level cataloging, but have research value and can be cataloged as a single item under a collective title because they share at least one unifying characteristic (author, issuing body, language, subject, genre, etc.). Synonymous with collective cataloging.

Collection maintenance Measures taken on a routine basis or as needed to preserve the materials in a library collection in usable condition, including mending, repairing, binding, rebinding, and reformatting, usually the responsibility of the technical processing and serials departments.

Collection management The application of quantitative techniques, such as statistical and cost-benefit analysis, to the process of collection development, usually limited to large libraries and library systems. In a more general sense, the activity of planning and supervising the growth and preservation of a library's collections, based on an assessment of existing strengths and weaknesses, and an estimate of future needs.

Collective bargaining agreement A legally binding contract signed on behalf of library staff organized in a collective bargaining unit, by elected representatives authorized to negotiate terms of employment with management, including salaries and wages, benefits, job responsibilities, evaluation for promotion and tenure, grievance procedures, etc. Librarians employed at colleges and universities which grant librarians faculty status may be members of the same bargaining unit as the teaching faculty.

Collective bargaining unit See: collective bargaining agreement.

Collective biography A work in one or more volumes containing separate accounts of the lives of two or more individuals who lived within a specific time period, distinguished themselves in the same field or activity, or have some other characteristic in common (example: Ordinary

Women, Extraordinary Lives: Women in American History edited by Kriste Lindenmeyer). Written by one or more biographers, the essays in a collective biography are usually longer than the entries in a biographical dictionary, and may include a biobibliography or list of references for further reading.

Collective title In library cataloging, the title proper of a bibliographic item containing several works by one or more authors, issued in a single volume or uniform set of volumes, each with its own title distinct from that of the whole. Also refers to the title assigned by a cataloger to a group of separately published materials cataloged collectively.

College and career collection Collection of books on colleges, financial aid, vocations, educational testing, resume writing and interviewing housed in the Young Adult Department of the Main Library. In the library catalog, this collection is designated with YA CC.

College bookstore A retail outlet operated in association with a college or university, selling new and second-hand textbooks and trade editions used by professors as assigned reading in their courses. College bookstores also sell popular reference books, school supplies, greeting cards, college memorabilia, general interest magazines, bestsellers, and nonfiction trade titles of interest to the student market. They can be owned and managed by the institution served, operated by an independent contractor, or run as a cooperative. Compare with trade bookstore.

College library A type of academic library maintained by an independent four-year college, or by one of several colleges within a larger university, for the use of students and faculty. Compare with undergraduate library.

Collocation In library cataloging, the process of bringing together all the bibliographic records representing works by the same author, of variant titles, of different editions, of the same series, or on closely related subjects, by assigning the same access point to facilitate retrieval. For exampie, the preparation of entries under a heading for the predominant name of an author who wrote under one or more pseudonyms. Collocation often requires the use of cross-references to direct the user to the authorized form of the name, title, subject heading, etc

Colloquy A literary work written in the form of a conversation or dialogue (example: Aelfric's Colloquy). Plural: colloquies.

Co-location Most often used to refer to having a server that belongs to one person or group physically located on an Internet-connected network that belongs to another person or group. Usually this is done because the server owner wants their machine to be on a high-speed Internet connection and/or they do not want the security risks of having the server on thier own network.

Colon Classification A classification system in which subjects are analyzed into facets based on their uses and relations, and then represented by synthetically constructed classes with the parts separated by the colon (:). Developed by S. R. Ranganathan in the 1930s, Colon Classification is used in libraries in India and in research libraries throughout the world.

Colophon A Greek word meaning "finishing touch." A statement given at the end of the text of an early manuscript, indicating the title of the work, name of scribe, and place of copying. The colophon may also include an expression of gratitude to the patron or client who commissioned the copy, and a warning against unauthorized copying. Early printed colophons followed the manuscript tradition, giving the name and emblem (imprint) of the printer, date of printing, number of copies printed, and sometimes an apology to the reader for any errors in the text. Synonymous with explicit.

Color Cast An overall color imbalance in an image, as if viewed through a colored filter.

Color plate An illustration in color, usually printed separately from the text on a different grade of paper and bound with others in one or more sections of a book. Also spelled colorplate. Compare with duotone and monochrome plate.

Color supplement A magazine printed in color to be issued with a Sunday newspaper (example: The New York Times Magazine). Also refers to a section of illustrations printed in color for insertion in the center of a magazine or book, whether removable or not.

Colorimeter A light-sensitive device for measuring colors by filtering their red, green, and blue components, as in the human eye. See also spectrophoto-meter.

Column inch In newspaper and magazine publishing, the unit of measurement in which the length of an article or size of a paid advertisement is expressed, equivalent to the width of a column of type multiplied by one inch of depth.

Column One of two or more vertical sections of written or printed text separated from each other by a ruled line or blank space, as in ancient scrolls, newspapers, and language dictionaries. The length of a newspaper article is expressed in column inches. Abbreviated col.

Columnist A journalist who writes regular commentary on current issues for publication in a magazine or newspaper, or in more than one newspaper, usually from a political position left or right of center, or expressing an original point of view on a matter of interest to readers. National political columnists are often syndicated. Also refers to a specialist in a particular field or on a given subject who writes regular commentary for a magazine or trade journal (example: Roy Tennant who writes the Digital Libraries column in Library Journal).

COM port On an IBM PC or compatible computer, a serial port often used to connect a mouse or a modem.

COM1, COM2, etc. Most serial ports and internal modems on DOS/WIN pcs can be configured to either COM1 or COM2 in order to accommodate the situation where both may exist. The DOS MODE command is used to change the output direction to such serial devices as modems.

Comb binding A form of mechanical binding in which a row of interconnected curved plastic teeth is inserted into slots punched along the binding edge of the leaves of a publication to hold them together, used for binding calendars, lab manuals, instruction manuals, and workbooks which must open flat to be used conveniently. If the plastic spine is wide enough, the title may be printed on it. Compare with spiral binding and loose-leaf.

Comedy A dramatic work in which an amusing event, or series of events with a happy ending, is presented for the enjoyment of the audience or reader. Comic effect is usually achieved by emphasizing incongruity of character in dialogue and/or action. When such an effect is achieved with subtle insight, the result is "high" comedy, as distinct from "low" comedy which appeals to cruder perceptions. The earliest surviving examples of classical comedy are the eleven plays of Aristophanes, thought to have been written and performed in Athens in the 5th century B.C. Compare with farce.

Comic book A booklet, usually printed in color on paper made from wood pulp, containing one or more stories told pictorially in a continuous strip of cartoon panels, with any dialogue or monologue enclosed in balloons or given in captions. An extended form of the comic strip seen in daily newspapers, comic books are often published in series classified by genre (adventure, fantasy, romance, science fiction, etc.). They are acquired by libraries for special collections on popular culture, and are of considerable interest to private collectors.

Command search In GIL, a special kind of keyword searching using Boolean operators (and, or, not).

Command-driven A computer interface in which the user must type a command statement or query to achieve the desired result, usually faster than a menu-driven interface, but not as user-friendly for novices who must invest time and effort in learning the system's command language.

Commands symbols and/or terms used to retrieve computer stored information.

Comment Faculty/staff newspaper at Colorado State University, available in both electronic and print versions.

Commentary A critical or explanatory note or collection of notes on a sacred or literary work, accompanying the text or issued separately, usually written by a person (or persons) other than the author. Commentaries are usually devoted to major works that have been the subject of considerable interpretation (Bhagavad-Gita, Bible, Koran, etc.). Also refers to an historical narrative written largely from personal experience (Seven Commentaries on the Gallic War by Julius Caesar). Synonymous in this sense with memoirs. In a more general sense, a series of remarks or observations, made by someone with authority to speak and be heard on the subject, for example, a journalist writing a column on a political or social issue.

Commercial journal A scholarly journal or trade journal published by a for-profit company (example: Elsevier), as opposed to a journal published by a university press or nonprofit organization, such as a scholarly society or professional association. Relentless price increases have become an important issue for libraries that subscribe to commercially published journals.

Commercial publisher A publisher in the business of producing and selling books and/or other publications for profit, as opposed to a university press or the publishing arm of a scholarly society, professional association, or other nonprofit organization that operates on a cost-recovery basis. The term includes trade publishers and popular presses. In commercial publishing, the decision to publish is influenced by sales potential, sometimes at the expense of originality and quality.

Common carrier (CC) A telecommunication service, such as a telephone or cable company, that provides wire and/or microwave services to businesses and the general public, usually at rates regulated by federal, state, or local government.

Common Gateway Interface (CGI) A program interface installed on a Web server, that allows Web pages to be linked to databases and other programs in such a way that input can be entered via the Web page and sent to a database management system for searching. Results are sent back by the DBMS and presented to the user in HTML format.

Commonplace book A book with blank pages in which passages in prose or verse are recorded irregularly by its owner as ideas for future exploration or contemplation, sometimes arranged by subject. The writer may note only his own thoughts and ideas, or excerpt those of other writers or speakers. Commonplace books kept by persons of stature, such as Ralph Waldo Emerson and Thomas Jefferson, have been deemed worthy of publication. Although interest in this form of literary expression has waned, it is still used by poets (example: A Certain World by W. H. Auden). See also: diary and journal.

Communications The transfer of information from one physical location to another by electronic means. The term telecommunication refers to both analog and digital communications, including the transmission of voice and video. Data communications refers to digital communications only, occurring via modem over a telephone line, by direct cable to another PC equipped with file transfer software, from a remote terminal connected to a minicomputer or mainframe, from one node to another on a local area network (LAN), or between client and server in a network environment. A communications device is a piece of hardware, such as a modem, cable, or port, designed to facilitate data transmission.

Compact disc (CD) A digital audiorecording medium

introduced in 1982, capable of storing up to 74 minutes of high-fidelity stereophonic sound in a single spiral track on one side of a 4.75-inch disc, similar to the track on a phonograph record. Designed to be read by a laser beam and decoded inside a device called a CD player, compact discs not only provide clearer sound than phonograph records and audiotape, but are capable of recording a much wider range of volume. In libraries, cds are usually shelved separately, often in specially designed display cases. Some libraries provide listening equipment on the premises. In AACR2, the term "sound disc" is used in the physical description area of the bibliographic record representing a compact disc, with "digital" given as type of recording.

Compact edition An edition in which the physical size of a long work is reduced, usually by altering the format without changing the content, for example, The Compact Oxford English Dictionary (second edition) reproduced micrographically and issued in a slipcase with a microprint reader. Compare with concise edition.

Compact Pro A file compression utility for Macintosh computers; files compressed using Compact Pro end with a ".cpt" extension.

Compact shelving Library shelving designed to maximize the storage capacity of a given space by incorporating movable elements such as shelf ranges on tracks. Because it is considerably heavier than normal shelving when filled, compact shelving requires more structural support, an important design consideration in the construction of a new library facility.

Compact storage A library shelving area, often reserved for low-use materials, in which narrow aisles, higher than normal shelves, and/or compact shelving is employed to maximize storage capacity. The building must be structurally capable of supporting the additional weight. Compact shelving with movable parts may be subject to electrical or mechanical failure.

Company file A collection of information about one or more commercial enterprises, usually maintained by a corporation or business library for the use of employees, business students, investors, career counselors, job seekers, etc. Annual reports, SEC filings, trade catalogs, issues of house organs, news clippings, photographs, etc., are usually organized alphabetically by name of firm. Synonymous with corporation file.

Comparative librarianship The study and analysis of similarities and differences in librarianship as practiced in different countries, to identify or clarify underlying principles, expand awareness of successful practices, facilitate cooperation, etc.

Comparative table An alphabetical list of selected topics in a complete or extensive revision of Dewey Decimal Classification, giving the class number in the current edition and the corresponding number used in the preceding edition. In most cases, only numbers for comprehensive works are given...

Compatibility The ability of computer software to run on hardware other than that for which it was originally designed. Compatibility can be upward (or forward) in programs capable of running on newer, more powerful machines, or downward (backward) in programs that will run on older, less powerful machines.

Compendium A work that presents in condensed form the main points of a longer work, prepared by a person other than the original author. Also, a work that treats a broad subject or entire field of knowledge briefly and concisely, sometimes in the form of an outline. Used synonymously with digest and epitome.

Competencies The capabilities expected of a person hired to perform a specific job, or upon successful completion of a course of study or training. In librarianship, the knowledge, skills, and experience necessary to effectively handle professional responsibilities, usually within a specialization, expressed inclusively rather than as a set of minimum standards. For an example, please see the

Compile To gather and put together pieces of information or materials from various sources in an orderly structured whole, as in the creation of a bibliography or index. The person who assembles such a work is the compiler and the resulting work is called a compilation.

Compiler A person who selects and assembles written or printed material from the works of various persons or bodies, or the various works of a single person or body, into a ordered whole, without editorial alteration of the original text. The resulting document is called a compilation. When the compiler's name is indicated in or on the chief source of information, it is entered in the statement of responsibility area of the bibliographic record that represents the item in the library catalog. Compare with editor.

Completeness An indication of how much of the published run of a serial title is held by a library, usually given in the holdings note as: complete (95-100% held), incomplete (50-94% held), or scattered (less than 50% held).

Complex Search Engine A type of search engine that allows you to type in multiple search terms and combine them with and, or, or not. Some complex search engines allow limiting by additional criteria such as date or Web page domain (.com, .edu, etc.)

Complimentary copy In publishing, a copy of a book sent without charge to an instructor for consideration as a textbook for students enrolled in courses on the subject. Faculty members sometimes donate complimentary copies to the library at the institution with which they are affiliated. Synonymous in this sense with inspection copy. In a more general sense, any copy of a book or periodical given away by the publisher to promote sales, including author's copies, desk copies, and review copies.

Composer The original creator of a musical work in any form, entered as author in the bibliographic record created to represent the work in the library catalog. Compare with arranger and performer.

Composite volume A bound volume containing two or more separately published works, for example, a collection of brochures or music scores.

Composite work An original work produced as the result of a collaboration between two or more authors or composers in which the contribution of each is a separate and distinct part of a planned whole (example: Festschrift). Compare with joint author.

Composition The putting together of words to express an idea, sentiment, thesis, analysis, or conclusion, as in a work of poetry or prose, or in the form of a writing exercise assigned as school work. In a musical composition, the message is expressed in musical notation. Also refers to the piece of writing or music that is the result of such activity.

Compositor The worker responsible for setting (composing) the type used to print a book or other publication. In letterpress, the compositor holds the composing stick in his left hand and removes the individual elements of type, called sorts, each bearing an individual letter or other character, from the case with his right hand, assembling each line in sequence until the stick is full and ready to be transferred to a tray called a galley. The compositor is also responsible for making up the galleys into pages, a process that includes inserting display matter, dividing the matter into page lengths, adding running heads, page numbers, footnotes, etc., and imposing the pages in a frame called a chase which, when locked up, constitutes a forme ready to be placed on the bed of the press for printing.

Compound name A name formed by joining two or more proper names with a hyphen (example: Marie-Louise), conjunction (Simon & Schuster), or preposition (Alcuin of York)..

Compound subject heading A subject heading consisting of two or more words that together represent a single concept (examples: "Bibliotherapy for children," "Book reviewing," "Library catalogs") or two closely related concepts ("Libraries and adult education"). In some cases semantic factoring yields false drops (School + Library —> Library school / School library).

Compound surname A surname composed of two or more proper names, usually joined by a hyphen, conjunction, or preposition. Under AACR2, compound surnames are entered under the element preferred by the person, with cross-references from the other elements (example: Lloyd George, David, 1863-1945 with a reference from George, David Lloyd, his correct paternal surname). Hyphenated surnames are entered under the first element (Bourke-White, Margaret, 1904-1971).

Comprehensive All-inclusive or all-encompassing. An index, bibliographic database, or other work of reference, compiled with the stated goal of covering all possible aspects of a subject, or all the published literature on a subject or in a field or discipline. In bibliography, an attempt to list of all the works that meet the criteria for inclusion established by the bibliographer as to author, subject, publication type, currency, etc. The opposite of selective.

Compress The process of making a file smaller so that it will save disk space and transfer faster over a network. The most common compression utilities are PKZIP for IBM PC or compatible computers (.zip files) and Compact Pro (.cpt files) or Stuffit (.sit files) for Macintosh computers.

Compression A method (e.g. Zipping) for reducing the size of files to save space or transmission time; compressed files must be uncompressed before use.

Compulsory arbitration The process in which representatives organized labor and management, having reached an impasse in contract negotiations, submit their differences to a legally designated arbitrator or arbitration board authorized to hear arguments from both sides on unresolved issues and reach a final binding decision. Both sides are required to accept the outcome..

Compulsory retirement Mandatory retirement at a fixed age, usually established by the employer and stipulated in its personnel policy. Compulsory retirement is a controversial legal issue in the United States. Organizations that have no mandatory retirement age may offer periodic retirement incentives to long-time employees, aimed at reducing payroll costs.

Computer A programmable machine. The two principal characteristics of a computer are: 1. It responds to a specific set of instructions in a well-defined manner; 2. It can execute a prerecorded list of instructions (a program). Modern computers are electronic and digital. The actual machinery — wires, transistors, and circuits — is called hardware; the instructions and data are called software.

Computer file Data or programs encoded in machine-readable format for processing by a computer. Data files stored on a computer are usually organized by topic or other characteristic in directories and subdirectories. Synonymous with machine-readable data file.

Computer literacy The skills required to retrieve information efficiently and communicate effectively using computer hardware and software, based on a conceptual understanding of computer technology and how it can be used to accomplish specific tasks, including an awareness of its inherent limitations, as well as its advantages. Because most hardware and software is progressively upgraded, an ongoing effort is required of the user to remain computer literate. Compare with information literacy.

Computer output microform (COM) Computer output produced directly on microfiche or microfilm without ever having been printed on paper. A device called a COM recorder converts digital data into a form that can be read by the human eye before recording it on film.

Computer output microform catalog A library catalog produced directly on microfiche or microfilm from a file of machine-readable bibliographic records, using a special recording device called a COM recorder. Comcatalogs are more compact than card catalogs, but a microform reader-printer machine is required to display and print individual catalog records. Prior to the development of online catalogs, this format was preferred for state, regional, and consortial union catalogs.

Computer program A set of instructions written in a programming language to enable a computer to process data, perform operations, and solve logical problems. Synonymous with software.

Computer Search Service Computer Search Service (CSS), a fee-based service, offers access to more than 500 databases, primarily in the sciences and social sciences, from which the Library can create customized bibliographies.

Computer terminal Electronic device through which a user can communicate with a central server over a computer network.

Computerized Archives An indexing tool that helps in finding gopher files.

Comstock, Anthony, 1844-1915 An American reformer with a high school education who in 1873, after serving in the Union army during the Civil War, founded the New York Society for the Suppression of Vice and devoted the rest of his life to waging an aggressive crusade against pornography, abortion, gambling, swindling, medical quackery, and other activities he considered morally offensive. Comstock used his influence to persuade Congress to pass what became known as the "Comstock laws" empowering the U.S. Postal Service to exclude from the mail books and other publications which he considered indecent or obscene, including information about contraception. After Comstock publicly attacked the first American production of George Bernard Shaw's play Mrs. Warren's Profession, the British playwright dubbed his rigid views and repressive methods "comstockery," turning his name into a public symbol of censorship based on prudery.

Concatenate From the Latin con ("together") and catenare ("to chain"). To join two or more data fields within a record to create a single field. In a more general sense, to link items together in a series, for example, several related essays or long excerpts for publication in a collection.

Concertina A form of bookbinding in which the spine is continuous with the front and back covers, but folded in narrow accordion-style pleats to which the leaves or folios are attached along the peaks or valleys of the folds. Compare with zig-zag book.

Concise edition An edition in which the content of a longer work is stated in the fewest possible words, sometimes aimed at beginners in the field (example: The Concise AACR2 published by ALA Editions). In the concise edition of a dictionary, infrequently used words and phrases in the full edition are omitted, and long definitions may be shortened. In a concise encyclopedia, the text is shortened and less important entries may be dropped entirely. The adjective "concise" is sometimes used in the titles of works not based on a longer work, to indicate that the content is expressed succinctly. Compare with compact edition..

Concordance An alphabetically arranged index of the principal words or selected words in a text, or in the works of an author, giving the precise location of each word in the text, with a brief indication of its context. A glossarial concordance includes a brief definition of each term. Concordances are usually devoted to very well-known works, such as the Bible, or to the works of a major writer (Chaucer, Shakespeare, etc.). Compare with dictionary.

Condensed A typeface narrower in proportion to its height than the normal version of the same style, used in printing to fit more text than normal in a column or on a page. The opposite of expanded.

Condensed book A single volume, usually published

in inexpensive hardcover edition, containing abridgments or long extracts from several separately published works, usually of fiction. In the United States, the Reader's Digest Condensed Book Club is a prolific distributor of condensed books. Most libraries specify in their collection development policy that works are to be purchased in unabridged form.

Condensed score The score of a musical work composed for orchestra or band in which the principal parts, usually given by type of instrument (woodwind, brass, strings, percussion), are reduced to a minimum number of staves.

Condition The physical state of existence of a book or other document at a particular point in time, designated in the antiquarian and used book trade by a two-part code (example: VG/G) in which the first part (VG) indicates the condition of the book itself and the second part (G) the condition of its dust jacket. A hyphen or dash following the slash indicates that the dust jacket is missing. Antiquarian book dealers grade condition as follows:

Conference In library terms, a gathering in which scholars report their recent research findings to peers in the same field. Papers presented at a conference are often published in volumes known as "conference proceedings," which are therefore important sources for current information. The work presented may or may not later be revised and published in a refereed journal. Also defined as a formal meeting of a group of individuals, or representatives of several bodies, to provide the opportunity for discussion or consultation on topics of mutual interest. When published colelctively, the papers presented at such a meeting are called proceedings. Abbreviated conf. Compare with workshop.

Conference name The official name of a meeting, conference, workshop, symposium, exhibition, exposition, festival, athletic contest, scientific expedition, etc., used as the corporate name heading in cataloging any publications issued in its name. Form of heading is subject to authority control.

Confidentiality In the delivery of library services, the right of patrons to have the nature of their research and library transactions remain private. Under the guidance of the ALA Code of Ethics, librarians and library staff members are encouraged to "protect each library user's right to privacy and confidentiality with respect to information sought or received and resources consulted, borrowed, acquired or transmitted." For this reason, automated circulation systems are designed to delete from the patron record all indication that a specific item has been borrowed once it has been returned to the library, and to limit access to borrower accounts to authorized personnel. Confidentiality when it is transmitted over a publicly accessible network.

Configuration The physical arrangement and functional relationships of the various components of a computer system, usually established to meet the needs and preferences of its users. The term configurability has been coined to refer to the ease with which a computer system can be modified or customized to meet changing needs and requirements.

Conjoint leaves Two leaves formed by one piece of parchment, vellum, or paper, usually folded lengthwise down the center. In a book, they may be bound into a section in such a way that they are not adjacent in the resulting sequence of leaves, but when traced through the back of the volume are found to be of a single piece, for example, in a 16-page signature, pages 3-4 (leaf 2) would be the conjugate of pages 13-14 (leaf 7) and vice versa.

Connect A term that commonly refers to accessing a remote computer; also a message that appears at the point when two modems recognize each other.

Connect time The length of time a user is logged on to a remote computer network or system. Some Internet service cproviders began by charging subscribers on the basis of connect time, but most isps now provide unlimited access for a fixed monthly fee. Connect time is still used by some database vendors as the basis for billing (example: DIALOG).

Connexion Connexion is an OCLC service that integrates all cataloging functions into a single interface that can be accessed from either a browser or a client interface. It provides one-stop access to cataloging tools and to worldcat.

Conser An acronym for Cooperative online serials, a cooperative online serials cataloging program that began in the early 1970s as a project to convert manual serials cataloging to machine-readable format. Since then it has evolved into a program for creating and maintaining high quality bibliographic records for serial publications.

Conservation binding Binding or rebinding intended to ensure the long-term survival of a manuscript or book while maintaining the integrity of its original form, as opposed to binding or rebinding for appearance or durability regardless of the implications for conservation.

Conservation center An organization that specializes in the protection and rehabilitation of printed and photographic materials, especially damaged or deteriorating items. Conservation centers support the enhancement of preservation programs in libraries, archives, museums, and other historical and cultural organizations. Some conservation centers also provide disaster assistance (example: Northeast Document Conservation Center).

Conservation The use of physical or chemical methods to ensure the survival of manuscripts, books, and other documents, for example, the storage of materials under controlled environmental conditions or the treatment of mildew-infected paper with a chemical inhibitor. Non-invasive techniques are preferred as a means of preserving items in their original condition. In a more general sense, any measures taken to protect archival or library collections from damage or deterioration, including initial examination, documentation, treatment, and preventive care supported by research. A person educated, trained, and experienced in such procedures is a conservator: Resources for Conservation Professionals, a project of the Preservation Department of the Stanford University Libraries.

Consistency In indexing, the degree of similarity between the subject headings or descriptors assigned to the same item or document by different indexers, or at different times by the same indexer.

Consolidated shipment In the book trade, a batch of materials sent by a publisher, jobber, or other vendor to a library or bookseller which includes both recently ordered titles and items on back order, combined to reduce shipping costs.

Consolidation The merger of two or more separately administered libraries, or organizational units within a library, into one unit under a single administration, usually for reasons of efficiency and/or economy, or to improve quality of service.

Consortium An association of independent libraries and/or library systems established by formal agreement, usually for the purpose of resource sharing. Membership may be restricted to a specific geographic region, type of library (public, academic, special), or subject specialization. One of the leading examples in the United States is ohiolink which includes Ohio's college and university libraries and the Ohio State Library. Plural: consortia. Compare with network.

Conspectus A survey of a topic or body of literature that takes a general or comprehensive view of the subject. Also, a summary or digest that retains the basic pattern or structure of a larger work, but condenses the content considerably. In libraries, a method of uniform collection assessment developed in North America in 1979 to facilitate resource sharing. The system uses codes to survey strengths, levels of difficulty, linguistic and geographical coverage, etc., recorded on worksheets in subject areas based on Library of Congress Classification. In 1982, the Research Libraries Group initiated the RLG Conspectus Online to provide electronic access to data on the collections of research libraries in the United States. The system was subsequently adopted by the Association of Research Libraries for its North American Collection Inventory Project (NCIP). It has also been adapted by the National Library of Canada and is used in the UK, Australia, and some European countries. In the 1990s, after the Western Library Network (WLN) developed PC software that enables libraries to develop and maintain local collection assessment databases, use of RLG Conspectus Online dwindled and the files were removed from RLIN in 1997.

Constituency The persons represented by a library or library system when it seeks funding for daily operations, new programs, and capital improvements, and when it lobbies for legislation favorable to its interests. Successful library administration depends on winning the approval of the library's external constituency (voters, users, supporters, etc.) Through quality of service, public relations, and community outreach programs. A library also has an internal constituency consisting of its employees and management.

Consultant A person with knowledge and experience in a specialized field, hired by a library or other institution to analyze a problem and provide professional or technical advice concerning possible solutions, especially when the required level of expertise is not available within the organization or the opinion of an outsider is desirable. A consultant may also participate in the planning and implementation phase of a recommended change.

Consultation Service In-depth reference assistance from a librarian, available by appointment.

Consumer guide A publication containing practical information and advice for prospective purchasers concerning the quality of products and services available in the market place. Some consumer guides are published serially (example: Consumer Reports Buying Guide). High-demand consumer guides may be shelved in the reference section of a library, sometimes in ready reference. Used synonymously with buying guide.

Container A box or holder used for storing a bibliographic item, group of items, or part of an item (example: pull-case, slipcase, or solander). Physically separable from its contents, a container can be open or lidded. Compare with physical carrier.

Conte The French term for a narrative tale or short story of the medieval period, originally dealing with events of an imaginative nature (example: Guigemar by Marie de France, as distinct from her lais). In modern usage, the term is associated with any brief story of a few printed pages, regardless of genre.

Contemporary Africa Database Contains information on African people, organizations and history. At present a Who's Who of prominent Africans now living or who have died since 1950, in all fields of expertise is available online.

Contemporary In the antiquarian and used book trade, a work published within the most recent decade. Also refers to a book in which all the parts (particularly the binding) were created at the time the edition was printed.

Content analysis Close analysis of the explicit and implicit message of a work or body of communicated information through classification and evaluation of the important concepts, symbols, and themes it addresses, to determine its meaning and account for the effect it has on its audience.

Content designation Codes and conventions that explicitly identify and characterize the data elements within a record to facilitate the manipulation of data

Content designator Characters used as tags, indicators, and subfield codes in a machine readable bibliographic record to identify or provide additional information about the data elements of which it is composed.

Content The essential matter or substance of a written

work or discourse, as opposed to its form or style. In a more general sense, all the ideas, topics, facts, or statements contained in a book or other written work. Synonymous in this sense with subject matter. Also refers to the matter which is the subject of a course of study. Compare with contents.

Contents All the divisions, chapters, articles, or individual works contained in a book, periodical, or other publication, usually listed with locators (page numbers) in order of appearance in the table of contents in the front matter of a book, or on a page near the front of an issue of a periodical. Compare with content.

Contents note A note in the bibliographic record for a book, listing its major divisions (books, chapters, etc.) Or the works contained in it (essays, interviews, short stories, poems, plays, etc.), usually by title.

Context In the most general sense, the entire situation, background, or environment relevant to an event, action, statement, work, etc. In a literary sense, the parts of a sentence, paragraph, or text that occur just before and after a specific word, phrase, or passage and determine its precise meaning. Quoting out of context may give a misleading impression of the intentions of the original speaker or author. Context is included in certain types of keyword indexing (see: KWAC, KWIC, and KWOC).

Context-sensitive In computing, an interface designed to provide assistance to the user at the point when help is needed, as opposed to a program that provides a general help screen which the user must first locate and then navigate to find instructions or advice concerning a specific problem.

Contingency fund A special fund set aside in a library budget to cover unanticipated expenditures and emergencies. Contingency funds are commonly included in budgets for major capital improvements to allow for possible cost overruns.

Contingency plan An alternative plan of action prepared in advance to be put into effect should it become impossible to implement normal arrangements, or when certain predetermined conditions arise. An example might be the decision of a library to cut spending on monographs rather than cancel serials subscriptions in the event of an unexpected budget cut. Compare with disaster plan and emergency plan.

Continuation A book or other uncompleted work continued by another writer, usually after the death of the original author. Compare with sequel.

Continuation order An order placed by a library with an agent or publisher to automatically supply until further notice each succeeding issue, volume, or part of a serial or series as published. If a continuation order does not specify a maximum price, it is assumed that the item may be shipped regardless of price. Some publishers offer a discount on continuation orders (usually 5-10%). Annuals (example: Literary Market Place), reference sets (Dictionary of Literary Biography), and monographs revised and reissued in frequent editions (travel guides) are often purchased in this way. A special order record is created and maintained to track the receipt of such items. Synonymous with standing order. Compare with approval plan.

Continuing education Formal instruction for persons who have completed an academic degree, moved into the workplace, and wish to keep up with changes and innovations in their field. For librarians, continuing education opportunities include courses offered online or traditionally through a library school, training provided by commercial vendors, and workshops sponsored by bibliographic service centers and library associations, as well as independent study.

Continuous pagination Numbering the pages of two or more volumes or parts of a set, or the issues of a periodical comprising a volume, in a single unbroken sequence, beginning with number one. Compare with separately paginated..

Continuous paging Page numbers which continue from one issue or volume to the next instead of starting each issue or volume with page one.

Continuous revision The process of updating a textbook or reference work by revising a portion of the text and/or illustrations with each printing, as opposed to updating the entire content of the work all at once and publishing the result as a revised edition.

Contone (CT) An abbreviation for continuous tone. A color or greyscale image format capable of illustrating continuously varying tonal ranges, as opposed to line art.

Contour map A topographic map that indicates relief by continuous lines, traditionally shown in brown ink, connecting points of equal elevation, with or without shading. The number of feet represented by the intervals between contour lines varies with the scale of the map. A topographic map of the sea floor is called a bathymetric map. Compare with relief map.

Contract A legally binding written agreement between an employer and 1) an individual librarian or other member of the library staff, or 2) librarians and/or staff organized in a collective bargaining unit for the purpose of negotiating terms of employment (salaries and wages, duties and responsibilities, promotion and tenure, vacation and sick leave, benefits, etc.) Usually for a specified period of time..

Contraction A shortened form of a word or phrase used for brevity in place of the whole, formed by the omission of one or more letters or sounds, usually replaced by a hyphen (e-mail for electronic mail) or an apostrophe (isn't for is not). Compare with abbreviation and elision.

Contraries Impurities in the rag, waste paper, or other fibrous material from which paper is made, usually bits of wool, feathers, or twine, or hard materials such as metal staples, bone, or plastic which must be removed in the papermaking process to maintain quality of product.

Contraries occasionally show as blemishes in a sheet of finished paper.

Contrast The degree of difference between the high and low tonal values in a print, photograph, or image on motion picture film, video, or television, maximum contrast being black and white with no intermediate gray tones.

Contributor One of several persons, each of whom writes one or more signed or unsigned portions of a book, periodical, or other edited work. A contribution may consist of an article or column in a magazine or journal, an essay in a collection, a poem or story in an anthology, an entry in an encyclopedia, or one or more terms and definitions in a dictionary or glossary. Contributors are usually listed by name in the front matter or back matter of a book, on one page of a periodical, or in the last volume of a reference set, alphabetically by name or in the order in which their work appears. Compare with joint author.

Control file File maintained in the accounting office, in numerical order, of all purchase orders for material purchased on the material budget, filed by purchase order number.

Control ID Unique identifier, replacing the accession number, derived from the barcode. Items in inventory are shelved in control number order.

Control key A key located in the lower left-hand corner of a standard computer keyboard, usually labeled Ctrl or **Ctl**, which can be used simultaneously with one or more other keys to give a specific command, for example, Ctrl+Alt+Del to reboot the operating system.

Controlled access Entry into a library, or use of a library collection, which is limited to registered members of the library's user group or some other category of user specifically granted access. The libraries of large private universities may extend access to all or part of their collections only to registered students, faculty, and staff. Use of special collections may be limited to authorized library staff, except by appointment. Compare with restricted access.

Controlled vocabulary Descriptive words added to the items in a database that make it easier for researchers to find works on a particular topic. When compilers of a database decide on which words to use in these descriptions (called descriptors or subject headings), they control the vocabulary users of the database will use. Researchers will retrieve more items searching with controlled vocabulary than they will using synonyms. See also descriptors and subject heading.

Convention discount A discount given on orders placed at a publisher's exhibit booth during a conference or convention, usually 10-20%, with 15% the norm. Librarians sometimes compile lists of selected new books prior to attending a major library conference, to be prepared to take advantage of the anticipated discount. At the end of the conference, display copies may be sold at an even deeper discount, especially if the dust jackets are no longer in perfect condition. Synonymous with show discount.

Convention issue An issue of a trade journal devoted to a forthcoming conference or convention, providing a brief description of the program, information about exhibits, registration procedures, advice about travel and accommodations, and whom to contact for more details. Follow-up articles usually appear in the issue immediately following the event.

Conventional name A name, distinct from the real or official name by which a thing, place, or corporate body has become known, for example, "Wall Street" for the New York Stock Exchange. Compare with nickname.

Cookbook A type of how-to book that gives instructions for preparing food, including recipes for specific dishes, notes about tools and ingredients, weights and measures, and sometimes directory information for culinary suppliers. Most cookbooks are specialized, focusing on a particular cuisine, type of dish, or category of food. Cookbooks for beginners often include color illustrations, but those intended by the author to be comprehensive are usually sparsely illustrated. Most public libraries include a diverse selection of cookbooks in the nonfiction section. Synonymous with recipe book.

Cookie The most common meaning of "Cookie" on the Internet refers to a piece of information sent by a Web Server to a Web Browser that the Browser software is expected to save and to send back to the Server whenever the browser makes additional requests from the Server. Depending on the type of Cookie used, and the Browsers' settings, the Browser may accept or not accept the Cookie, and may save the Cookie for either a short time or a long time. Cookies might contain information such as login or registration information, online "shopping cart" information, user preferences, etc. When a Server receives a request from a Browser that includes a Cookie, the Server is able to use the information stored in the Cookie. For example, the Server might customize what is sent back to the user, or keep a log of particular users' requests. Cookies are usually set to expire after a predetermined amount of time and are usually saved in memory until the Browser software is closed down, at which time they may be saved to disk if their "expire time" has not been reached. Cookies do not read your hard drive and send your life story to the CIA, but they can be used to gather more information about a user than would be possible without them.

Cooperative cataloging An arrangement in which a library or library system agrees to follow established cataloging practices and work in automated systems or utilities that facilitate the creation of bibliographic and authority records in a form that can be shared with other libraries. In North America, cooperative cataloging is facilitated by the uniform cataloging practices established under AACR2R. OCLC is the bibliographic utility used for cooperative cataloging in the United States.

Cooperative collection development Cooperative activity between institutions for purposes of reducing competition, assessing strengths and weaknesses of individual collections, setting guidelines, assigning primary collecting responsibilities, operating within network associations, and encouraging direct interaction in order to save staff time and MATERIALS BUDGET dollars.

Cooperative Online Resource Catalog (CORC) A Web-based metadata system designed to facilitate access to electronic resources, CORC provides a catalog of bibliographic records for electronic resources, an authority file, a pathfinder database, and an enhanced version of Dewey Decimal Classification called webdewey. Based on technology developed at OCLC, the CORC toolkit supports flexible automated bibliographic record creation, authority control, URL maintenance, subject heading assignment, and pathfinder creation.

Coprocessor A chip designed specifically to handle a particular task, such as math calculations or displaying graphics on-screen. A coprocessor is faster at its specialized function than the main processor is, and it relieves the processor of some work. A coprocessor can reside on the motherboard or be part of an expansion card, as with an accelerator.

Co-publishing The simultaneous publication of an edition by two or more publishers, usually in different countries, to achieve economies of scale when the home market is not sufficient to guarantee a reasonable profit. Typically, a work is printed in the country of the originating publisher and then supplied to a publisher in another country with a title page bearing the imprint of the second publisher (or both). Subsequent printings may occur independently or cooperatively. In journal publishing, the result may be separate editions for each country or a bilingual edition marketed in both countries. Compare with export edition.

Copy card A small plastic debit card available for purchase from a vending machine or at the circulation desk of a library, which can be used in photocopiers and microform reader-printer machines instead of cash to pay for paper copies of documents.

Copy cataloging Adaptation of a pre-existing bibliographic record (usually found in OCLC, RLIN, NUC, or another bibliographic database) to fit the characteristics of the item on hand, with modifications to correct obvious errors and minor adjustments to reflect locally accepted cataloging practice, as opposed to creating a completely new record from scratch. Synonymous with derived cataloging. Compare with original cataloging.

Copy editor A person employed by a publisher to meticulously edit and mark up an author's typescript in preparation for printing, usually in accordance with house style as to spelling, abbreviation, punctuation, grammar, syntax, usage, citation style, etc. A good copy editor also checks the accuracy of facts, quotations, and citations, and is alert to possibilities of libel, plagiarism, etc.

Copy number When multiple copies of the same edition are added to a library collection, the cataloger numbers each copy sequentially, beginning with the second. In the catalog record for the edition, each copy is listed separately in the holdings, with the copy number given at the end of the call number following the abbreviation cop. It is also printed at the end of the call number on the spine label attached to the outside of the physical item.

Copy rite II Copy Rite II manages and maintains the photocopiers in CSUL. Copy Rite II is a company that governed by the Lory Student Center. Copy Rite II is located on the 2nd floor in the JOURNAL ROOM.

Copy service A unit of the Office of the University Librarian that manages the copiers and reader printers in all library divisions except Law and Biomedical.

Copy To make a duplicate of a document or other work, by hand or any other process. Many early books were produced in only one copy. In medieval Europe, devotional works and the classics were laboriously hand-copied by monks and copyists known as scribes. Modern methods rely on printing and reprography. In data processing, to reproduce data from one file, location, or storage medium to another without alteration.

Copyright Clearance Center, Inc. (CCC) The largest licenser of photocopy reproduction rights in the world, CCC was established in 1978 by a group of authors, publishers, and users of copyrighted material in an effort to facilitate compliance with U.S. copyright law. CCC manages the rights to over 1.75 million works and represents approximately 9,600 publishers and hundreds of thousands of individual authors and creators.

Copyright compliance The responsibility of a library to ensure that its interlibrary loan requests, reserve materials, instruction guides, Web pages, etc., conform to existing copyright law. In the OCLC interlibrary loan system, the codes ccg ("conforms to copyright guidelines") and ccl ("conforms to copyright law") are used by the borrowing library to inform the lending library that a request is compliant.

Copyright date The year in which a specific work was granted copyright protection, usually printed on the verso of the title page, sometimes following the letter "c" with a circle around it. If more than one copyright date is given, the earliest is the date of the first edition, which is the same as the date of first publication. Subsequent dates indicate revisions in the text of an extent requiring renewal of copyright.

Copyright depository A library designated by law or custom to receive and preserve a specified number of free copies of works published under national copyright law. In the United States, the copyright depository is the U.S. Copyright Office at the Library of Congress. In Great Britain it is the Bodleian. In Canada, copyright law is administered by the Canadian Intellectual Property Office (CIPO). Synonymous with copyright library.

Copyright fee The payment required by a national copyright depository to register copyright of a creative work, which must be submitted with the completed application form and a deposit copy of the work. Also refers to the fee that must be paid to the holder of copyright, in exchange for the right to use all or part of a work in a manner not defined under U.S. copyright law as fair use, for example, the right to include a poem or short story in an anthology, or an excerpt or quotation in a published work.

Copyright piracy The systematic unauthorized reproduction or use without permission of a work protected under copyright law, usually for the purpose of profiting from such activity. This type of egregious infringement is subject to legal action by the copyright owner(s) in countries that have accepted international copyright agreements, but in countries which have not, the holder of intellectual property rights may have little recourse.

Copyright The exclusive legal rights granted by a government to an author, editor, compiler, composer, playwright, publisher, or distributor to publish, produce, sell, or distribute copies of a literary, musical, dramatic, artistic, or other work, within certain limitations (fair use). Copyright law also governs the right to prepare derivative works, reproduce a work or portions of it, and display or perform a work in public.

CORC Cooperative Online Resource Catalog.

Core collection A collection representative of the basic information needs of a library's primary user group. In public libraries, core collections are selected in anticipation of popular demand and maintained on the basis of usage. In academic libraries, selection is based on curriculum need and collections are maintained to meet the research interests of students and faculty. Also refers to an initial collection developed for a new library, usually with the aid of standard lists and other selection aids (example: Books for College Libraries: A Core Collection... Published by the American Library Association).

Core journal A scholarly journal that reports original research of such significance to the academic community that the publication is considered indispensable to students, teachers, and researchers in the discipline or subdiscipline. For this reason, it is included in the serials collections of academic libraries supporting curriculum and research in the field (example: American Historical Review in American history). Compare with primary journal.

Core level cataloging An encoding level developed for use in the Program for Cooperative Cataloging (PCC), which allows the cataloger to create bibliographic records containing fewer data elements than in full level cataloging, but more than in minimal level cataloging. Fields of fixed length are fully coded, but a list of exceptions applies to certain fields of variable length.

Core list A list of the best books, periodicals, etc., on a subject or in a discipline, usually compiled as a selection aid for librarians whose responsibilities include collection development (example: Core List of Best Books and Journals in Education by Nancy O'Brien and Emily Fabiano). Although useful when first published, such lists become outdated within a few years..

Corner The juncture of two edges of the cover of a book. Corners can be rounded, square, or mitered, and are sometimes covered in contrasting material, such as leather or heavier cloth, for protection and decorative effect. To make library corners, the turn-in is folded; on Dutch corners, it is cut.

Cornerpiece In bookbinding of the late 16th and early 17th centuries, an ornamental design such as an arabesque, stamped on the corners of a book cover, usually with a matching centerpiece. Also refers to decorative metal corners attached to the binding of a book. In modern usage, a temporary guard made of metal or some other hard material, attached to the corners of a book to protect against damage in shipping. Compare with boss and shoe.

Corpora Initial capital letters inserted by a rubricator in blank spaces left for that purpose by the copyist in a manuscript or by the printer in an early printed book.

Corporate author A corporate body such as an association, company, government agency, institution, or nonprofit organization in whose name a publication is issued. In libraries, the official name or title of such a body is used as the corporate name in cataloging publications issued in its name (example: American Library Association). Compare with personal author.

Corporate body A commercial enterprise, government agency, association, nonprofit organization, institution, or group of individuals identified by a collective name, which has the capacity to act as a single entity, including territorial authorities and groups constituted as meetings, conferences, congresses, expeditions, exhibitions, etc., whether operating or defunct. In libraries, the official name or title of such a body is used as the corporate name in cataloging publications issued in its name..

Corporation library A type of special library established and maintained as a unit within an incorporated company or organization, to meet the information needs of its employees and facilitate the achievement of its mission and goals. Some corporation libraries also serve as the repository for the official records of the organization. For internal security reasons, most corporation libraries are closed to the public except by special appointment. Synonymous with company library. Compare with business library.

Correctional library A type of special library maintained inside the walls of a prison or other correctional institution for the use of inmates and staff, usually managed by a prison librarian (example: Federal Bureau of Prisons Library). The collection usually includes general interest titles for recreational reading, educational and vocational materials, and legal resources. Synonymous with prison library.

Correspondence Letters or recorded messages exchanged between two or more people, usually archived with the personal papers of the correspondents. Often used in preparing biographical and historical works, correspondence may be published separately or with other papers. In AACR2, collected correspondence is cataloged under the name that appears first on the title page, with an added entry for each of the other correspondents and for the editor or compiler.

Corrupted text A text in which words or passages have been added, deleted, or altered to suggest a meaning other than the one intended by the original author. In medieval manuscripts, this was sometimes the result of accidental copying errors, but in modern texts tampering may be done by an individual or organization for other purposes, such as propaganda or public relations..

COSG RLIN library identifier for CSU Libraries.

Cost-effective A decision or practice that reduces expenditure in relation to the amount of resources invested (time, money, materials, etc.). Monetary savings can be difficult to determine when costs are intangible, intermittent, or incurred over an extended period of time.

Cost-recovery A product or service offered at a price that allows the vendor or provider to cover the costs incurred without generating a profit, for example, document delivery service in most academic libraries.

Cottage binding A style of decorative leather binding popular in England during the 17th century in which the center panel is surrounded by designs tooled to resemble the gables of a building, with the style of binding bearing no relation to the content of the work. Synonymous with cottage style.

Council on Library and Information Resources (CLIR) Originally named the Council on Library Resources, CLIR is an independent foundation that supports initiatives in preservation awareness, digital libraries, information economics, resources for scholarship, and international developments in library and information science. CLIR publishes the bimonthly newsletter CLIR Issues.

Counter A long cabinet top, shelf top, or other horizontal work surface of sufficient height to accommodate a person standing in front of it who wishes to transact business with the person standing or sitting behind it. In most libraries, the circulation desk is a long counter near the entrance to the building. In the children's room of a library, countertops (and furniture) are usually lower than normal to accommodate persons of small stature.

Countermark A smaller, secondary watermark on antique papers, usually located in the center or lower center of the half-sheet opposite the watermark, indicating the name of the papermaker and sometimes the date and place of hand manufacture.

Countersunk Said of a depression stamped or impressed on the surface of a book cover to display a label, inlay, or decoration.

Counting book A picture book designed to teach preschool children to count (usually from one to ten or twelve) by providing illustrations in which the number of objects displayed on each page or double spread corresponds to the numeral printed with them. Compare with alphabet book.

Country code The last portion of an e-mail or Internet address outside the United States, consisting of two alphabetic characters indicating the country in which the host computer is located (examples: .ca for Canada and .uk for Great Britain). Some Web search engines allow the user to specify country code in a query.

Country study A publication that provides factual information about a specific nation, including its history, geography, demography, society and culture(s), economy, government and politics, etc., with statistical information sometimes given in an appendix. Country studies often include at least one map and may be published in series, for example, the Country Studies/Area Handbook Program sponsored by the U.S. Department of the Army and issued by the Federal Research Division of the Library of Congress. Compare with area study.

Courier A person or service hired by a library to retrieve materials on request from an off-site storage facility, or to transport materials from one library to another within a library system or consortium, as opposed to relying on the postal service or a commercial delivery service.

Course catalog A comprehensive list, usually published annually, of all the courses taught at a school, college, or university during a given academic year, usually arranged by department and course number, with brief descriptions of course content and a list of instructors and their credentials at the end. Institutions offering both undergraduate and graduate programs may publish separate catalogs. Course catalogs for educational institutions in the United States and around the world are available online in collegesource, a searchable database provided by the Career Guidance Foundation.

Course reserves Supplementary reading materials assigned by faculty, available in physical and/or electronic format.

Course-integrated Bibliographic instruction designed to complement the content of a specific course of study, integral to completing the library research component embedded in the course. Compare with course-related.

Courseware A computer application designed to assist teachers and librarians in creating Web-based courses and online tutorials. Courseware requires little knowledge of HTML and may include presentation management software, the ability to include graphics and audio/video files, online chat and threaded discussions, auto-marked quizzes, course calendaring, and grading (examples: Blackboard and webct). Synonymous with authorware.

Court hand The cursive style of writing used by scribes from about 1100 AD until the end of the 16th century in copying charters, legal records, and other official documents, in contrast to the book hand used for copying literary and devotional works in manuscript form.

Court library A large private library housed in a monumental building, similar to the libraries known to have existed in ancient Rome, financed by a wealthy nobleman, aristocratic family, or high-ranking church dignitary of the Italian Renaissance, whose love of books manifested itself in collecting. An expression of the humanist revival of interest in classical culture, court libraries were open for use by outsiders at the discretion of the owner and, according to Konstantinos Staikos (The Great Libraries: From Antiquity to the Renaissance, Oak Knoll/British Library, 2000), some even functioned as lending libraries for educated readers.

Courtesy book A literary genre popular during the Renaissance, devoted to the detailed description of the code of personal conduct, training, and view of life expected of a gentleman, soldier, and courtier by the society in which he lived (example: Castiglioni's The Courtier).

Cover letter A letter of introduction, usually no longer than one page, sent with a resume or curriculum vitae when applying for employment. A good cover letter usually indicates that the applicant meets all the qualifications listed in the job posting, and expresses an interest in being considered for the position. In a more general sense, a brief letter of explanation sent with a document.

Cover paper The heavier grades of paper used for the outer cover of pamphlets, trade catalogs, and paperback books, manufactured in a range of colors and finishes.

Cover story The article in a magazine or trade journal that corresponds to the headline and illustration on the cover, usually longer and more extensively illustrated than other feature articles in the same issue. Some periodical indexes and bibliographic databases are designed to indicate whether an article is a cover story.

Cover The outer protective material attached to the bound leaves of a manuscript or printed publication, consisting in books of two panels (front and back), each attached to the inlay over the spine along a flexible joint. Books bound in paper, cloth, or leather over boards are said to be published in hardcover. The cover of a machine-bound book is called a case. Books bound in flexible paper covers are called paperbacks. Periodicals are almost always issued in softcover..

Cover title The title printed or impressed on the cover of a publication as issued by the publisher (in books usually on the spine), which may be a shortened form of the title proper. Compare with binder's title.

Coverage The extent of a library collection (or section of a collection), or of a catalog, index, abstracting service, database, bibliography, or other finding tool, usually indicated by the number and types of publications indexed, and a publication date range. The range of subjects or fields indexed determines the scope of such a resource.

Covered Process of placing a cover on items such as monographs and indexes. Usually done in-house.

Covers bound in A term used in the book trade to describe a volume in which the original covers are enclosed in a later binding. This usually occurs in rebinding when the bindery decides to retain the original covers as endpapers or flyleaves.

Covers bound in A term used in the book trade to describe a volume in which the original covers are enclosed in a later binding. This usually occurs in rebinding when the bindery decides to retain the original covers as endpapers or flyleaves.

CPU Central processing unit; the part of a computer that oversees all operations and calculations.

Cracked The condition of a book that has developed one or more long, narrow breaks in the cover or down the length of the spine. The usual method of rehabilitation is rebinding.

Cracker A slang term for a person who tries to gain access to a supposedly secure computer system without proper authorization, usually with malicious or criminal intent. Compare with hacker.

Crash In bookbinding, a narrow strip of thin, loosely woven, starched muslin attached with adhesive to the back of a book after the sections have been sewn to help hold them together. In some editions, a strip of kraft paper is applied to the layer of fabric as a second lining for added strength. Synonymous with gauze, mull, and super (in United States).

Crawler A robot software program that searches "intelligently" for information on the World Wide Web, for example, one that looks for new documents and Web sites by following hypertext links from one server to another, indexing the files it finds according to pre-established criteria. Crawlers used to fetch urls listed as entries by Web search engines are designed to adhere to standard rules of politeness by asking each server which files may not be indexed, observing firewalls, and allowing an interval of time to pass between requests to avoid tying up the server. Synonymous with spider and webcrawler.

Creasing In binding, the process of impressing a dull rule or disk on a sheet or leaf of paper to create an indentation along the line where a fold is to be made. By compressing the fibers, creasing produces a cleaner fold and increases the number of times the sheet can flex before it detaches at the fold. Compare with scoring.

Creator In archives, the individual or agency responsible for creating, receiving, accumulating, or otherwise producing records or documents for which some form of disposition must be made once their archival value has been appraised. Also refers to the person responsible for producing an original work of visual art.

Credential A letter, certificate, degree, or other document certifying that a person, organization, or institution is qualified to fill a specific position, offer a service, or exercise authority in a given field. For librarians in the United States, the most desirable credential is the M.L.S. or M.L.I.S. degree from an ALA-accredited library school.

Credenza Originally, a sideboard from which a lord's food was tested for poison ("credence"). In libraries, a furnishing that doubles as a bookshelf and study table, having two or three tiers of shelves under a flat surface low enough to accommodate a person standing or seated on a high stool or chair.

Credit Any textual statement at the beginning or end of a motion picture, videorecording, or television program, identifying by name the director, producer, screenwriter, performers, narrator, and other persons responsible for creating the work, usually with musical accompaniment. In filmmaking, considerable artistic attention is devoted to the style in which credits are presented, to set the tone for what is to follow (or add a final touch).

Credit line A brief statement giving the name of the author, artist, agency, or publication that is the source of a picture, photograph, or quotation used in an article or book, usually printed immediately below the illustration or quotation, or at the end of the caption. Credit lines are sometimes printed together in a separate section in the front matter or back matter of a book, or in a paragraph on a separate page in a periodical.

Credit memo A refund provided by a VENDOR/ supplier for a book or other item returned to them because of damage or error in filling the error. It is applied to a future INVOICE from the same vendor.

CREN Corporation for Research and Educational

Networking. This organization was formed in October 1989, when BITNET and CSNET (Computer + Science network) were combined under one administrative authority. CSNET is no longer operational, but CREN still runs BITNET. See BITNET.

Crime in the library Because many libraries in the United States and other countries are open to the public, they are not immune to the disruption caused by unlawful behavior, including theft of materials and equipment, verbal abuse and assault on patrons and staff, indecent exposure, drug use and sale by patrons and staff, mutiliation of materials, vandalism of equipment and facilities, arson, and more recently, computer crimes. Statistics indicate that crime is increasing in libraries, placing an additional burden on library budgets to provide adequate security.

Critical abstract An abstract that includes a brief evaluation of the content and/or style of presentation of the work abstracted, usually written by a subject specialist. Compare with indicative abstract and informative abstract.

Critical annotation In a bibliography or list of references, an annotation that includes a brief evaluation of the source cited, as opposed to one in which the content of the work is described, explained, or summarized.

Critical edition An edition of a work based on scholarly research and close examination of earlier manuscripts, texts, documents, letters, etc., which sometimes includes analysis and commentary by one or more qualified scholars who have studied and interpreted its meaning and significance.

Critical thinking In research and scholarship, the skill required to develop effective and efficient search strategies, assess the relevance and accuracy of information retrieved, evaluate the authority of the person(s) or organization producing information content, and analyze the assumptions, evidence, and logical arguments presented in relevant sources. Critical thinking is essential in evaluating information available online because the process of peer-review that exists in print publishing has yet to be stablished in electronic publishing. For this reason, instruction librarians have focused an increasing amount of attention on teaching critical thinking skills in recent years.

Criticism From the Greek word kritikos meaning "judge." The thoughtful analysis, interpretation, and evaluation of an artistic or literary work, in which the primary considerations are its essential nature ("message"), the intentions of the artist or author, the effect of the work on its audience, its relationship to works of similar style or content, its influence on subsequent works, and its implications for critical theory. Literary criticism is considered to have originated with the ancient Greeks (Aristotle's Poetics). Modern criticism is classified by school or type, depending on the approach taken by the critic.

Critique A critical examination of a topic, idea, thing, or situation by a person intent on determining its essential nature, its strengths and/or limitations, and the degree to which it conforms to accepted standards or prevailing beliefs or assumptions. Sometimes used synonymously with review.

CRL The Center for Research Libraries (CRL) is an international not-for-profit consortium of colleges, universities, and libraries that provides access to a variety of scholarly research resources, including newspapers, serials, archival materials in microform, microform sets, and foreign government publications in many subject areas. The CRL catalog is available in the Library Gateway. CRL resources are available to Cornell researchers through interlibrary loan.

Cropped A photograph or illustration from which a portion of the top, bottom, or sides has been eliminated in the process of reproduction to omit unnecessary detail or make its proportions fit the space available in thc layout of a printed page. Also refers to a book trimmed to such an extent that the text is cut into, causing it to bleed. Compare with shaved.

Cross aisle A corridor or passageway that intersects at

a 90-degree angle the ranges and range aisles in the stack area of a library, allowing staff and patrons to move from one range to another without walking to the end of the range.

Cross reference database: a collection of records that have one or more fields that reference other related records. These connections (for example between "marketing" and "promotion") make browsing very productive and allow related-items searches.

Cross-check To verify the results of an investigation by using an alternative source or method. In library research, facts are usually confirmed or disconfirmed by consulting a second (independent) source. When conflicting evidence or opinion is found, a third or fourth source may be required to resolve the discrepancy.

Cross-classification The inclusion of a subclass under more than one class in a hierarchical classification system, for example, the subject heading "Library bonds" under the broader terms "Library finance" and "Municipal bonds" in the list of Library of Congress Subject Headings.

Cross-grain A book or other bound publication in which the grain of the paper runs perpendicular to the spine, instead of parallel to it, reducing its openability and making the leaves more difficult to turn.

Cross-index A book index that covers the contents of more than one bibliographic item, such as a group of related reference works. The author and title indexes to the various parts of the Gale Literary Criticism Series are a good example.

Cross-platform Refers to software (or anything else) that will work on more that one platform (type of computer).

Cross-reference A reference from one heading to another in the same catalog, index, or reference work. The most common are see references instructing the user to look elsewhere for the preferred form of the heading, and see also references directing the user to related headings under which additional information may be found. A work containing cross-references is said to have syndetic structure. Abbreviated x-ref.

Crosswalk A table that enables search engines to operate across databases with dissimilar record formats, by mapping the relationships between metadata elements..

Cryptography Writing in cipher, usually for the purpose of concealment. Also refers to the study and decoding of such writing. In computing, the conversion of data into a code that can be deciphered only by those who have the key, usually to ensure confidentiality when it is transmitted over a publicly accessible network.

Cryptonym A secret name, for example, a name written in code or cipher, or in the form of an anagram.

CSS (Cascading Style Sheet). A standard for specifying the appearance of text and other elements. CSS was developed for use with HTML in Web pages but is also used in other situations, notably in applications built using XPFE. CSS is typically used to provide a single "library" of styles that are used over and over throughout a large number of related documents, as in a web site. A CSS file might specify that all numbered lists are to appear in italics. By changing that single specification the look of a large number of documents can be easily changed.

CSUNET California State University Network. A packet-switched network that connects the 22 campuses of the CSU system.

Cubic feet Measurement of the size of archival and manuscript holdings, e.g.1ft. X 1ft. X 1ft.

Cubook A unit of volume used to measure library stack capacity, equal to 1/100 of a standard section of shelving (3 feet wide by 7 1/2 feet high), the amount of space needed to shelve a book of average height and depth (thickness), assuming 10% of the length of each shelf remains unoccupied.

Cuir bouilli A French term meaning "boiled skin." An early form of bookbinding in which the leather used in the cover was soaked in scalding water, then hammered or molded on a die to create a design in relief, usually incorporating motifs popular in the medieval book arts (vines, leaves, flowers, birds, mythical beasts, etc.). When the skin dried, it became so hard that boards were unnecessary.

Cum privilegio A Latin phrase meaning "with permission," printed in old books to notify readers that the work was published with the approval of existing secular or ecclesiastical authorities. The Roman Catholic Church still requires imprimatur and nihil obstat in books representing its official teachings. Synonymous with cum licentia.

Cumdach An Irish word for a rectangular box made of bronze, brass, or wood, usually ornamented in elaborate style with gold, silver, and precious stones, used to store and protect medieval manuscript books. Synonymous with book shrine.

Cumulation An index, which is formed as a result of the combination of various parts of a resource. Often refers to an index, which combines indexing for a year or several years into one alphabetical arrangement.

Cumulative index An index designed to save the user's time by combining in a single sequence the entries listed in two or more previously published indexes, for example, the ten-year indexes to Current Biography Yearbook. Most printed periodical indexes are issued in monthly or quarterly paperback supplements, cumulated at the end of the publication year in one or more annual volumes. In a more general sense, any index that combines in a single sequence entries for previously published volumes of a book or periodical.

Cuneiform From the Latin cuneus (wedge) and forma (shape or form), referring to the pictographic characters used in ancient Akkadian, Assyrian, Babylonian, Persian, and Sumerian inscriptions from about 4,000 to 100 BC, each of which consisted of an arrangement of wedge-shaped marks incised in a wet clay tablet using a sharp, pointed implement called a stylus. If a text was long enough to be continued on more than one tablet, each tablet was numbered and incised with a catchword at its foot to link it to the next. The last tablet usually ended with a colophon.

Cunningham Classification system used to classify books published before 1970 (Biomedical Library).

Curator person responsible for the development, care, organization, and supervision of a museum, gallery, or other exhibit space and all the objects stored or displayed in it. Also, a person in charge of a special collection, trained to assist users in locating and interpreting its holdings.

Curiosa Books or pamphlets that are highly unusual in subject or treatment, usually somewhat indecent by conventional standards.

Currency The quality of being in progress, recent, or up-to-date. In information retrieval, the extent to which the content of a document or source reflects the existing state of knowledge about the subject. In the research process , the importance of currency varies, depending on the discipline. In medicine and the sciences, information can become outdated in less than five years, but in the arts and humanities, materials decades old may be just as useful as more recent information.

Current awareness service A service or publication designed to alert scholars, researchers, readers, customers, or employees to recently published literature in their field(s) of specialization, usually available in special libraries serving companies, organizations, and institutions in which access to current information is essential. Such services can be tailored to fit the interest profile of a specific individual or group. Some onlinc catalogs and bibliographic databases include a "preferred searches" option that allows the library user to archive search statements and re-execute them as needed. Synonymous with selective dissemination of information (SDI).

Current bibliography A bibliography that includes

only references to recently published sources on a subject, or in a specific field or discipline (example: Annual Bulletin of Historical Literature published by the Historical Association, London). The opposite of retrospective bibliography.

Current contents A periodical that reproduces the tables of contents of the leading scholarly journals in an academic field or discipline, to assist researchers in keeping abreast of the most recently published literature in their areas of interest or specialization, usually published weekly or monthly. Because currency is the raison d'etre of this type of publication, libraries may limit back files to the most recent 3-5 years.

Current Index to Statistics Current Index to Statistics is a bibliographic index to publications in statistics and related fields. The CIS Extended Database (CIS-ED) includes coverage, in most cases from 1974. The free access is available only to the records up to 1994.

Current issue The latest number of a serial publication, bearing the most recent issue date. In some libraries, current issues are displayed with the front cover facing forward on sloping shelves or on a periodical stand to facilitate browsing. Back files are typically stored in a different location, sometimes on microfilm or microfiche to conserve space. Synonymous with current number. Compare with back issue.

Current Journal Recent, unbound issues. For titles which are collected in microform, paper issues are retained until the microform is received.

Current periodical The most recent issues of journals and magazines, not yet bound between hard covers; since current periodicals are in high demand, they are non-circulating.

Curresnt awareness collection Books and documents shelved in the Current Awareness area. Materials cover topics of current interest to patrons.

Curriculum All the required and elective subjects/ courses taught at a school or institution of higher learning, usually listed by department and course number in an annual course catalog. Courses required of all students for graduation constitute the core curriculum.

Curriculum guide A written plan covering one or more facets of curriculum and instruction (goals and objectives, teaching strategies, learning activities, specific resources, evaluation and assessment techniques) for use within an instructional unit as small as a classroom or as large as a school district or state. Curriculum guides are indexed and abstracted as documents in ERIC.

Curriculum material collection CURRIC or CMC) Collection of secondary and elementary school texts, and other educational materials at the secondary and elementary levels. **Curriculum room** A room or designated area within an academic library containing curriculum-related materials such as kits, textbooks, workbooks, educational software, and juvenile fiction and nonfiction, for the use of students enrolled in teacher education courses. Synonymous with curriculum lab.

Curriculum vitae (c.v.) A brief summary of a person's professional career, including basic biographical information, degrees and post-graduate education, honors and awards, employment history, publications and presentations, memberships, service, etc., for use in employment (hiring, tenure, promotion, etc.). Compare with resume.

Cursive A right-sloping style of handwriting also known as running script, in which the letters within words are connected, having been written continuously without lifting pen or pencil from paper or other writing surface. Used in humanist manuscripts and papal documents of the Renaissance, and for writing letters. In printing and word processing, any typeface that has the appearance of handwriting.

Cursor A small illuminated point, vertical bar, underline, or other symbol on a computer screen which can be positioned by the user via a keyboard, mouse, or other control device to indicate where a new character will appear when typed as input, or a new operation is to occur when initiated by the user. In Windows and other graphical user interfaces, the cursor may change shape when moved from one window or dialog box to another, turning into an I-beam for text-editing, an arrow or finger for selecting an option from a menu or toolbar, an hour-glass while an operation is in progress, or a small pen in graphics programs. In many applications, the symbol blinks steadily to make it easier to locate on the screen. Synonymous with pointer.

Custodian The person responsible for the care and protection of something of value. Over the past one hundred years, the model of librarianship has evolved from custodianship of materials in physical form, to one in which the librarian is seen as a mediator of access to information in a wide range of formats, including electronic resources. However, custodianship remains a high priority in archival and special collections.

Custody In archives, the official guardianship of books, manuscripts, papers, records, and other documents, based on physical possession, with or without legal title or the right to control access or disposition. The person responsible for such care is their custodian.

Custom binding A book bound to the specifications of its owner or a dealer, or in accordance with special instructions from the publisher, rather than the general instructions for the edition.

Cut An illustration printed (captioned or uncaptioned) with the text page, as opposed to a plate printed on a separate leaf, usually of different quality paper, to be added to the publication in binding.

Cut and paste A type of editing in which data is copied or moved from one location to another. Example: rearranging paragraphs within a document.

Cut flush Said of a book cover that has edges perfectly even with the edges of the leaves, the result of having been cut after it was attached to the sections. Most paperback books are cut flush in binding. Synonymous with flush boards and trimmed flush. Compare with squares.

Cut-and-paste A feature built into most graphical user interfaces that allows the user to move an element displayed on the computer screen, such as a portion of text or graphic, from one location to another within the same document, from one document to another, or even from one application to another, usually by highlighting the element to be moved, selecting "cut" or "copy" under the "edit" option in a toolbar, and then using the option to "paste" after positioning the cursor at the point to which the element is to be moved. The element cut or copied is transferred to a temporary storage area called a clipboard until the next cut-and-paste operation is initiated. Most software includes an "undo" option that allows the user to reverse the operation if a mistake is made.

Cut-in note A side note printed wholly or partially inside the edge of a paragraph of text, instead of in the margin, usually in a typeface heavier and smaller in size than the text type. Synonymous with cut-in side note, in-cut note, and let-in note.

Cutter number A system of alphanumeric author marks developed by Charles A. Cutter to enable bibliographic items of the same classification to be subarranged alphabetically by author's last name. A Cutter number consists of one to three letters from the name, followed by one or more arabic numerals from the Cutter-Sanborn Table added to the end of the call number by a cataloger. Synonymous with Cutter author mark..

Cutter-Sanborn Table In 1880, Charles A. Cutter first circulated a two-figure table designed to assist catalogers in adding author marks to call numbers, as a means of differentiating items of the same classification by author. The Cutter Table was subsequently extended by Kate A. Sanborn to allow three arabic numerals to be assigned, following the initial letters of the author's last name.

Cuweblogin cuweblogin allows you to access restricted library resources in the Library Catalog and Find Articles/ Find Databases/Find e-Journas without needing sidecar. It does this by allowing you to log in to a web form, and then passing your authentication information back to the web server in a cookie. For more information about how cuweblogin works, see the help page for cuweblogin.

Cybercafe A high-tech coffee house equipped with microcomputers for the use of its customers.. Cybercafes originated in New York City in the 1990's and have since spread throughout the world. Some large academic libraries have installed them on their premises to give students a place to relax and read their e-mail. Synonymous with Internet cafe and netcafe.

Cybernetics From the Greek word kybernetes meaning "helmsman." A branch of science developed by Norbert Wiener in the 1940's that utilizes the concept of feedback in comparing human and machine processes, particularly mental processes, to understand their similarities and differences, with the ultimate goal of creating machines capable of imitating human behavior and intelligence.

Cyberporn A nelorgism coined from the terms "cyberspace" and "pornography" to refer to sexually explicit materials available electronically over the Internet. Cyberporn is of particular concern to parents who would like to see their children become computer literate, but hesitate to expose them to adult influences prematurely. Filtering software designed to block access to adult material remains controversial.

Cyberspace A neologism coined by the writer William Gibson in his science fiction novel Neuromancer (1984) to refer to the cyberspace A neologism coined by the writer William Gibson in his science fiction novel Neuromancer (1984) to refer to the virtual world of digital communication, in which human beings interact with one another electronically via computer networks, instead of face-to-face.

Cybrarian A shortened form of cyberlibrarian, coined from the terms "cyberspace" and "librarian" to refer to a librarian whose work routinely involves information retrieval and dissemination via the Internet, and the use of other online resources. Despite its catchy sound, the appellation has not been widely adopted within the library profession.

Cycle A group of literary works (poems, plays, stories, novels) that share a unifying theme, for example, the Yoknapatawpha stories of William Faulkner. An epic cycle is a group of individual epics or ballads joined, usually by a process of accretion, to form a whole, as in the Iliad of Homer or the narratives comprising the Arthurian legend.

Cyrillic An alphabet used in Russia and countries formerly part of the Soviet Union, Cyrillic evolved from the Greek uncial alphabet. Formalized during the 9th or 10th century, it contains characters not included in the Latin alphabet, which represent sounds peculiar to the Slavic languages. Cyrillic typefaces of 43 letters were introduced in the 18th century, based on the civil script established by Peter the Great in 1710. In 1918, the alphabet was reduced to its present 32 letters as a result of reforms introduced after the Russian Revolution.

Daemon The Greek word for "guardian spirit." In computing, an auxiliary systems program initiated at startup and executed in the background that performs a specific task when needed, for example, running a scheduler to start another process automatically at a pre-established time, checking incoming e-mail messages for addresses that cannot be found, or notifying the sender that a message could not be delivered. Pronounced "demon."

Dagger In printing, a character in the shape of a vertical stroke crossed above its mid-point, used in text as a second-order reference mark following use of the asterisk. When it appears before a personal name in the English language, the dagger indicates that the individual is deceased. Also called an obelisk or long cross.

Daguerrotype Historically, the first photographic process that actually worked, producing a positive image directly on a highly polished, silvered copper plate sensitized with iodide vapor. By exposing the plate to light in a camera obscura, an image was captured in the photosensitive layer of silver iodide which could be developed through the application of mercury vapor. Made public in 1839, the process was named after its French inventor, the painter of dioramas Louis Jacques Mande Daguerre, who relied heavily on earlier experiments by Joseph Nicephore Niepce. Easily scratched and tarnished, daguerrotypes were normally protected by a metal mat and a sheet of glass. Early examples are valued by collectors because each one is unique, not having been made from a negative. Also spelled daguerreotype.

Daily Issued on a daily basis, with the possible exception of Sundays. Also refers to a serial issued daily, especially a newspaper.

Damaged An item returned to the library in such poor condition that it cannot be placed back on the shelf for circulation, for example, a water-soaked or pet-chewed book. The borrower is normally charged the cost of repair or replacement. New items received from the shipper in damaged condition are returned by the library to the seller for credit or replacement.

Dana, John Cotton, 1856-1929 A public librarian for over forty years, John Cotton Dana began his career in 1889 as head of the Denver Public Library, moved to the City Library of Springfield in 1898, and ended his career at the Free Public Library in Newark, New Jersey. A leader in the library profession, he served as president of the American Library Association from 1895-96, as a member of its council from 1896-1902, and as president of the Special Libraries Association from 1909-10, an organization he helped establish. His philosophical approach to librarianship is best expressed in his book Suggestions, published in 1921 by F. W. Faxon.

Dandy roll The cylinder that exerts pressure in mechanized papermaking, smoothing the surface and creating designs such as the watermark, countermark, and the lines characteristic of laid and wove paper.

Dartmouth Medal A literary award presented annually since 1974 by the Reference and User Services Association (RUSA), a division of the American Library Association, to the most outstanding reference work published during the preceding calender year.

Dash A short length of horizontal rule used for punctuation, to separate text, and for decorative effect. In printing, dashes vary in length from the two-em (longest) to the hyphen (shortest). In typing, a dash is made by striking the hyphen key twice in succession (—). In descriptive cataloging, the dash is given a space on either side, but when used in subject headings to indicate subdivision, no spaces are included.

DAT Digital Audio Tape. The most common type of tape backup.

Data bank Sometimes used synonymously with database, the term applies more specifically to a collection of nonbibliographic data, usually numeric (example: the Global Soil Moisture Data Bank available online from the Department of Environmental Studies at Rutgers University). Large data banks containing information about individuals (social security numbers, credit history, health records, etc.) Have become the subject of controversy as the rapid development of high-speed information technology poses new threats to personal privacy.

Data compression A method of reducing the amount of memory required to store data on a computer by encoding it and minimizing redundancy. Compressed data requires less transmission time, but more computation time to restore it to its original form for processing.

Data Content Defined by external standards such as AACR2, Library of Congress Subject Headings (LCSH), etc.

Data conversion The process of translating data from one form to another, usually from human-readable to machine-readable format or vice versa, from one file type to another, or from one recording medium to another (example: film to videotape or videodisc).

Data jacks Wall plates throughout the library typically have both phone and data jacks. Just as phone cables plug into the phone jacks, data cables connect staff and public computers to data jacks and provide access to the local area network. Live data jacks are available west of the EIC area and third floor, northwest.

Data processing The systematic performance of a single operation or sequence of operations by one or more central processing units on data converted to machine-readable format, to achieve the result for which the computer program that controls the processing was written, for example, the compilation of circulation statistics from records of circulation transactions occurring in a library over a given period of time.

Data recovery The methodology of restoring lost data due to physical damage or software corruption to any storage medium.

Data The plural of the Latin word datum meaning "what is given," often used as a singular collective noun. Facts, figures, or instructions presented in a form that can be comprehended, interpreted, and communicated by a human being, or processed by a computer. Compare with information and knowledge.

Database A large, regularly updated file of digitized information (bibliographic references, abstracts, full-text documents, directory entries, images, statistics, etc.) Related to a specific subject or field, consisting of records of uniform format organized for ease and speed of search and retrieval, and managed with the aid of database management system (DBMS) software. Content is created by the database producer (example: American Psychological Association) which usually publishes a print version (Psychological Abstracts) and leases the content to a database vendor (example: EBSCO or OCLC) that provides electronic access to the data after it has been converted to machine-readable form (psycinfo), usually on CD-ROM or online via the Internet using proprietary search software.

Database field In a library database, a field is one piece of information (such as author name, for example) in a database record.

Database management system (DBMS) A computer application designed to control the storage, retrieval, security, integrity, and reporting of data in the form of uniform records organized in a large searchable file called a database. The range of available DBMS software extends from simple systems intended for personal computers to highly complex systems designed to run on mainframes.

Database record in a library database, a record contains one reference and also includes fields such as subject heading fields.

Database vendors Database vendors are businesses and companies that specialize in creating, developing and maintaining databases of articles, some being citations, or full text. Libraries subscribe to the vendors to obtain the services. Patrons, faculty, and staff can then search through the different database products depending on the subject area. Some common database vendors include OCLC, EBSCO, JSTOR, OVID, silverplatter, NISC and Lexis Nexis.

Date due slip A card or slip of paper inserted in an item charged from a library collection, or a small printed form attached to the inside of the front or back cover (or to one of the endpapers), on which is stamped the date the item is due back in the library. Date due slips are sometimes removed by borrowers in an attempt to avoid overdue fines, but automated circulation systems have put an end to this strategy.

Date line The line printed at the beginning of a story in a newspaper or article published in a magazine, indicating the date and place of origin of news that is not local.

Date range An interval of time marked by a beginning and ending date. Some online catalogs and bibliographic databases allow the user to limit a search to a specific range of publication dates. A year followed by a hyphen (1946-) limits retrieval to information published in the year specified or any succeeding year, a year preceded by a hyphen (-1945) limits retrieval to sources published up to and including the year specified, and a year followed by a hyphen and a subsequent year (1939-1945) limits retrieval to sources published in those or any intervening years.

Dater Adjustable stamping device used to stamp date on material. Used in access services to stamp the date due on charged out material.

Daughterboard A board that attaches to (rides piggyback on) another board, such as the motherboard or an expansion card. For example, you can often add a daughtercard containing additional memory to an accelerator card.

Day use card Card that can be purchased to gain access to libraries four times; valid for a period of a year.

DBMS database management system.

DCS Desktop color separation. An image format consisting of four separate CMYK postscript files at full resolution, together with a fifth EPS master for placement in documents.

DDN Defense Data Network. A global communications network serving the US Department of Defense composed of MILNET, other portions of the Internet, and classified networks which are not part of the Internet. The DDN is used to connect military installations and is managed by the Defense Information Systems Agency (DISA).

Deaccession The process of deleting from an accession record documents and other materials which are to be removed from a library collection. Also refers to any item so removed. The opposite of accession.

Deacidification A general term for a variety of costly preservation processes that chemically reduce the acid content of paper documents to a ph of 7.0 (neutral) or higher, usually undertaken at a professional conservation center to prevent further deterioration. An alkaline buffer may be deposited in deacidification to neutralize any acids that develop in the future. Brittleness is not reversed by deacidification. Mass deacidification is the shipment of a quantity of documents to a center for processing in small batches, rather than individually.

Deacidification Process used in preservation of library materials involving the removal of acid from paper. Conservation treatment that acts chemically to stabilize paper against further acid deterioration. Involves neutralizing acids present in the paper and buffering to leave an alkaline reserve to guard against future acid attack. Does not reverse any damage to the paper already done.

Dead file Term used for a serial title that is no longer received because it is a ceased publication or a canceled subscription.

Dealer An individual or commercial company in the business of buying and selling new books, used books, and/or rare books for resale to libraries, collectors, and other booksellers. Compare with antiquarian bookseller and jobber.

DEC Digital Equipment Corporation.

Decennial Issued every ten years (example: U.S. Census). Also refers to a serial publication issued every ten years.

Decimal point The period used in the numeric portion of Library of Congress Classification notation (example: DK 265.9) and following the third numeral of a class number in Dewey Decimal Classification (947.084) to indicate that succeeding numerals are to be treated as a decimal fraction.

Deckle edge The uneven or feathered edge of a sheet of handmade paper, created by the flow of liquified fibrous stock between the frame (deckle) and sieve of the mould used in manufacture. The same effect is achieved in machine-made paper by exposing the edge to a jet of air or water. In quality bookbinding, deckle edges are considered tasteful, but since books tend to collect dust when stored on an open shelf, and rough edges are difficult to clean, this feature is not practical.

Declassified A document no longer protected against unauthorized disclosure because the security classification assigned to maintain confidentiality has been officially changed or canceled. The opposite of classified.

Decompress Opposite of compressing a fiie; the process of restoring the file to its original size and format. The most common programs for decompressing files are PKUNZIP for IBM PC and compatible computers (.zip files) and Compact Pro (.cpt files) or Stuffit Expander (.sit files) for Macintosh computers. Certain DOS files with the extension ".exe" are self-extracting and do not require a program for decompressing. All Macintosh files with the extension ".sea" are self-extracting.

Decompression The expansion of compressed image files. See also lossy and non-lossy.

Dedicated In computing and communications, a device or channel reserved for a specific use. In libraries, dedicated servers are used to run the online catalog and provide access to the library's Web site.

Dedicated line A direct pathway to the Internet or some other computer network via a separate telecommunications channel not shared with multiple users as in dial-up access, but available around the clock to a specific user or group of users, for a designated purpose. When accessed through a common carrier, the channel is called a leased line.

Dedication A brief note in which the creator of a work addresses it to one or more persons, usually a colleague, mentor, or family member, as a sign of honor, appreciation, or affection. In books, the author's dedication appears in the front matter, usually printed on the recto of the leaf following the title page. Compare with acknowledgments.

Dedication copy A copy of a book or other work inscribed by the author, editor, or illustrator to the person or persons to whom the work is dedicated. In the antiquarian book trade, a dedication copy may be of considerably greater value than a copy with no inscription.

Deduping Removal of all but one occurrence of a bibliographic record from a file of machine-readable records, one of the initial steps in processing a MARC database. Deduping is a batch process that prevents confusion in the minds of users, conserves computer storage, and allows reliable usage statistics to be collected. Duplicate records are not uncommon because the "cancel holdings" command in OCLC software does not delete a record from the library's OCLC tapes. Synonymous with duplicate removal and duplicate resolution.

Deed of gift A signed document stating the terms of agreement under which legal title to real or personal property, such as a gift to a library or archives, is transferred, voluntarily and without recompense, by the donor to the recipient institution, with or without conditions specifying access, use, preservation, etc.

Default A value, option, or setting automatically selected in a hardware or software system in the absence of specific instructions from the user. The default setting may be displayed on the data entry screen to allow the user to see what action will be taken if no input is provided.

Default route A routing table entry which is used to

direct packets addressed to networks not explicitly listed in the routing table.

Definition One meaning of a word, expressed clearly and concisely. Because some words have more than one meaning, a word may have more than one definition. In lexicography, a word or phrase is defined by first specifying the class (genus) to which its referent belongs, then indicating the characteristics that distinguish the referent from others of the same class. Definitions are listed in dictionaries and glossaries, and are also provided in some concordances and thesauri. In most dictionaries, the modern definition of a word is given first and the oldest last, but there are notable exceptions to this rule. Abbreviated def.

Definitive edition An edition of the complete text of an author's work or works, usually edited and published after the person's death in a form considered final and authoritative. Also refers to the text of an anonymous work considered by scholars or other experts to be closest to the original version. Compare with authorized edition.

Delete To remove, erase, or omit a character, word, or passage from a text or document. In computing, to erase a character, word, passage, or entire file from memory, usually by pressing the "Backspace" key on a keyboard, or by highlighting text and pressing the "Delete" key or selecting the "Delete" option from a menu or toolbar. Some software systems allow the user to "Undo" a deletion while the application remains open.

Delhi Public Library Delhi Public Library is Owned by the Delhi Government, the Delhi Public Library Network is probably the oldest in town. It was inaugurated on 27th of October, 1951, by Pt. Jawahar Lal Nehru. Today the library has a total of 25 branches, and sends its Mobile Van Library services to every nook and corner of the city, including the Central Jail. Most of them have a section on children's books. Some branches also have the facility of Braille Services for the benefit of visually challenged people.

Delimiter A symbol used in a MARC record as the first character of a two-character subfield code to indicate the beginning of a subfield, separating one data element from another within a field. OCLC uses the double dagger as a delimiter; the Library of Congress uses the $ (dollar) sign. In a more general sense, any character or sequence of characters used in an electronic database to separate discrete elements of data within a field (or fields) contained in a record.

Deluxe edition An edition printed on better quality paper than the standard trade edition, sometimes from specially cast type, usually bound in leather or some other material of fine quality. Deluxe editions may also be larger in size, more lavishly illustrated, and published in limited edition. Also spelled de luxe edition. Synonymous with fine edition.

Demand publishing A commercial service that supplies single copies of rare or out of print books in response to individual demand, usually by photocopying prints made from a microform master, for example, Dissertation Express from Bell & Howell.

Demand The number of people who need or request a product or service. In libraries, high-demand items may be ordered in multiple copies or placed on reserve to ensure access. In public libraries, low-demand items in the circulating collection may be candidates for weeding. Demand for library services usually peaks at different times during the day, week, month, and year. Transaction logs can be helpful in tracking and anticipating patterns of usage.

DEMCO A commercial company that provides furniture, equipment, and supplies for the library, school, office, and home. DEMCO also provides periodical subscription services.

Demographic and Health Surveys Demographic and Health Surveys (DHS) datasets are available for most countries. The datasets include individual women's data, household data, men and husband's data, couple's data, children data and service availability/facility, etc.

Densitometer A measuring instrument that registers the density of transparent or reflective materials. Colors are read as tonal information. See also colorimeter and spectrophotometer.

Density Density is a brightness control to lighten or darken a printout to more closely reflect its screen appearance and to compensate for deficiencies in toner or paper quality.

Department of Statistics, Government of India Broad statistical information like national accounts statistics, energy statistics, consumer expenditure, annual survey of industries, live stock statistics, etc. Can be found here. Most of these statistics is brought out by its agencies Central Statistical Organisation and National Sample Organisation.

Department purchase order (DPO) A special order form to use when purchasing items paid for by the Libraries. Can only be issued through accounting service.

Departmental library A type of academic library that serves the information and research needs of the faculty members of a department within an institution of higher learning, usually a large university. Departmental libraries are also used by students enrolled in courses in the discipline(s) taught by the department, especially graduate students. If acquisitions are funded through the department, selection is usually the responsibility of the teaching faculty in collaboration with the departmental librarian.

Dependent work In library cataloging, a work that is contingent in some way on a previously published work by another author. Included in this category are: abridgments, arrangements, commentaries, continuations, dramatizations, sequels, revised editions, and supplements. Synonymous with related work. Compare with derivative work.

Deposit account Specified amount of money deposited with a vendor to pay for future services, not to exceed the amount deposited. The Library normally discourages the use of Deposit Accounts unless it is the only way to purchase a service.

Deposit Any addition to archival holdings, usually a transfer of materials from some other location or agency, but the term also applies to materials on loan for a period of fixed or indefinite duration. The depositor usually retains legal ownership and responsibility, except in the case of gifts.

Deposit copy A copy of a new publication sent without charge to a copyright depository or other designated library by the author or publisher in compliance with national copyright law. In the United States, the deposit copy is sent with the completed copyright application form and copyright fee to the U.S. Copyright Office of the Library of Congress in Washington, D.C. Synonymous with statutory copy.

Depository A library which receives the publications of a government or official body. GSW is a depository for United States government documents.

Depository library A library legally designated to receive without charge all or a portion of the government documents provided by the U.S. Government Printing Office (GPO) and other federal agencies to the Superintendent of Documents for distribution under the Federal Depository Library Program (FDLP). Some federal depositories also collect publications issued by state government agencies. Federal documents are usually classified and shelved by sudocs number. Compare with repository.

Depth indexing An indexing system that attempts to extract all the concepts covered in a work, including any subtopics, as opposed to summarization, in which a work is indexed only under its dominant subject. Library catalogers have traditionally looked for the single concept that best describes the entire content of an item, leaving depth indexing to commercial services that index parts of items (articles in periodicals, book chapters, essays in collections, etc.).

Depth The thickness of a bound volume at its thickest point included (usually at the spine) with the covers included. Average depth determines how many volumes will fit on a shelf of given length. Also refers to the width of a book shelf from front to back. Most library shelving is 10 or 12 inches deep.

Derivative indexing A method of indexing in which a human indexer or computer extracts from the title and/or text of a document one or more words or phrases to represent subject(s) of the work, for use as headings under which entries are made. Synonymous with derived indexing and extractive indexing. Compare with assignment indexing.

Derivative work A work based on another work, which transforms the content of the original in a significant way (abridgment, adaptation, arrangement, revision, translation, etc.). Under U.S. copyright law, the rights to produce derivative works are retained by the copyright holder. Compare with dependent work.

Descender In typography and calligraphy, the stroke of a lowercase letter that extends below the lowest point of an x-height letter (a, c, e, m, etc.). The letters of the roman alphabet which have descenders are: g, j, p, q, and y. The descender line is an imaginary horizontal line connecting the bottoms of descender letters, not to be confused with the baseline. Compare with ascender.

Descreening Removal of halftone dot patterns during or after scanning printed matter by defocusing the image. This avoids moire patterning and color shifts during subsequent halftone reprinting.

Descriptive bibliography The close study and description of the physical and bibliographic characteristics of books and other materials, including detailed information about author, title, date and place of publication, format, pagination, illustration, printing, binding, etc., as opposed to an examination of their content. Also, a work that is the result of such study.

Descriptive cataloging The part of the library cataloging process concerned with identifying and describing the physical and bibliographic characteristics of the item, and with determining the name(s) and title(s) to be used as access points in the catalog, but not with the assignment of subject and form headings. In the United States, Great Britain, and Canada, descriptive cataloging is governed by Anglo-American Cataloging Rules (AACR2).

Descriptor In indexing, a preferred term, notation, or sequence of symbols assigned as an access point in the bibliographic record representing a document, to indicate one of the subjects of its text (synonymous in library cataloging with the term subject heading). In bibliographic databases, descriptors appear in the DE or subject field of the record. Major descriptors are distinguished from minor descriptors by a special character, usually the asterisk. Some indexing and abstracting services, such as ERIC and Psychological Abstracts, provide a list of authorized indexing terms in the form of a printed or online thesaurus. Compare with identifier.

Deselection In serials, the process of identifying subscriptions for cancellation, usually in response to subscription price increases and budgetary constraints. In book and nonprint collections, the process of identifying titles for weeding, usually on the basis of currency, usage, and condition. The opposite of selection.

Desensitization The process of deactivating the magnetic strip affixed to a book or other printed item to prevent the security alarm from sounding when the borrower exits the library, a step performed by circulation staff when the item is checked out, using a device called a desensitizer. A different machine is required to desensitize magnetic media (audiocassettes, videocassettes, etc.).

Desiccant A drying agent such as silica gel used in museums and libraries to remove water vapor from an enclosed space when control of relative humidity is an important factor in the preservation of specimens, documents, and other materials in storage or on exhibit. Because desiccants release moisture when heated, they can usually be reused.

Desiderata A list of books and other materials needed and wanted by a library, to be purchased when budget permits or a cash donation is received. Synonymous in this sense with waiting list and want list. Also refers to a list of subjects or topics on which a writer or researcher requires information.

Desk copy A copy of a new book or recently revised edition, provided without charge by the publisher as an instructor's copy when additional copies are ordered by a college or university bookstore for students enrolled in a course of study. A complimentary copy may become a desk copy once an instructor decides to assign the work as required reading.

Desk dictionary A single-volume dictionary of approximately 150,000 words, intended for use by an individual sitting at a desk or in a workspace (example: Webster's New World Dictionary of the American Language). Entries usually indicate orthography, syllabication, pronunciation, etymology, and definition. Synonyms, antonyms, and brief biographical and gazetteer information are included in some editions. Synonymous with college dictionary. Click here to connect to the online version of Merriam-Webster's Collegiate Dictionary and Thesaurus. Compare with pocket dictionary and unabridged dictionary.

Desk schedule A list of the hours during which librarians and other public services staff are regularly assigned to assist users at the circulation desk, reference desk, information desk, or other public service point in a library, usually prepared by the staff member responsible for supervising the operations performed at the location.

Desktop On computers like IBM PC or compatibles and Macintoshes, the backdrop where windows and icons for disks and applications reside.

Desktop publishing (DTP) The use of microcomputer hardware and software for page layout, graphic design, and printing to produce professional quality camera-ready copy for commercial printing at a fraction of the cost of using the services of a commercial publisher. Used extensively to produce in-house brochures, fliers, newsletters, posters, etc., **DTP** requires desktop publishing software and a high-speed PC equipped with a large monitor and high-resolution laser printer to produce text and graphics in WYSIWYG format.

Destruction In archives, the process of physically doing away with records that are no longer of value, but remain too sensitive to be simply discarded as trash. For paper records, the most common methods are shredding and pulping. Incineration is used for records in all other formats.

Detachable materials Accompanying material issued with, and intended to be used with, the item being cataloged. Examples are folded maps or charts, computer disks or CD-ROMS. Usually housed in a pocket inside the back cover of the book.

Detective fiction A novel or short story in which the details of a crime (or suspected crime) are uncovered by an amateur or professional sleuth who looks for clues and interprets them, sometimes using ingenious methods, to solve the mystery of who-done-it. The modern detective story began with Edgar Allan Poe's Murders in the Rue Morgue and has since become a popular subgenre of mystery fiction. Some detective stories qualify as historical fiction (example: chronicles of Brother Cadfael by Ellis Peters).

Deterioration Damage that occurs to an item by physical, chemical, or biological means after it has been produced, usually over a period of time. Examples include bindings weakened by adhesives that dry out and crack, printing papers embrittled by acid, and paper documents discolored by the growth of mildew under damp conditions.

Developing Library Network (DELNET) Delnet started as a network of libraries in Delhi in 1988 and was named as Delhi Library Network. It is the first operational library network in India. It was initiated as a project of the India International Centre with the financial and technical assistance by National Information System for Science and Technology (NISSAT), Department of Scientific and Industrial Research, Govt. Of India. It was registered as a society in June 1992 under the Societies Registration Act of 1860 and is currently being promoted by the National Informatics Centre (NIC), Planning Commission, Govt. Of India and India International Centre, New Delhi.

Development services Department overseen by the director of development; responsible for exploring methods of funding beyond the traditional Libraries budget

Device An ornament or symbol used in printing, such as the north pointer used on maps to indicate compass orientation. Also refers to an insignia used as a publisher's identifying mark, for example, the small design of a house stamped on the spine and printed on the title page of books published by Random House. Synonymous in this sense with colophon.

Dewey Decimal Classification (DDC) A hierarchical system for classifying books and other library materials by subject, first published in 1876 by the librarian and educator Melvil Dewey who divided human knowledge into ten main classes, each of which is divided into ten divisions, and so on. In Dewey Decimal call numbers, arabic numerals and decimal fractions are used in the class notation (example: 996.9). An alphanumeric book number is added to subarrange works of the same classification by author, and by title and edition (996.9 b3262h).

Dewey, Melvil, 1851-1931 One of the founders of the American Library Association, Melvil Dewey served as editor of Library Journal from 1876 to 1881, published the Dewey Decimal Classification system in 1876, and served as librarian at Columbia University from 1883 to 1888 where he founded the first professional library school in 1887. He became the director of the New York State Library in Albany in 1888, taking the library school with him. Dewey was also a spokesman for professionalism in librarianship, for library education, and for equality of opportunity for women in the profession. A dynamic man, he also advocated standardization of library education, methods, tools, equipment, and supplies.

DHTML (Dynamic hypertext Markup Language) DHTML refers to web pages that use a combination of HTML, javascript, and CSS to create features such as letting the user drag items around on the web page, some simple kinds of animation, and many more.

Diacritical mark A mark written or printed above or below an alphabetic character, to indicate a change in its pronunciation, for example, the cedilla used in French under the letter c when it is pronounced like ts or s, instead of k.

Diagnostics Software designed to automatically test hardware components (disks, keyboard, memory, etc.) Whenever a computer session begins, to determine if they are functioning properly. If a component fails on startup, a warning message appears on the screen.

Diagram A figure, chart, or graphic design intended to explain or illustrate a principle, concept, or set of statistical data. Also, a drawing, sketch, or plan that shows the steps in a process, or the relationship of the parts of an object or structure to the whole, usually simplified for the sake of clarity. A diagram is usually accompanied by a line or two of explanation, or by explanatory text in the document in which it appears.

Dial up connection A connection from your computer that goes through a regular telephone line. You use special communications software to instruct your modem to dial a number to access another computer system or a network. May also be referred to as "dial up networking".

DIALOG A vendor that provides per-search access to a wide selection of online databases via a proprietary interface. Established in 1972, DIALOG led the market for many years in online information retrieval, and remains strong in business, science, and technology. The company also provides technical support for Internet users and e-commerce. In most libraries,

Dialog box A small square or rectangular area that opens in a graphical user interface in response to a selection made by the user, usually providing additional information or listing other options and/or settings available at that point in the program. A dialog box differs from a window in being neither movable nor resizable. Some applications are designed to open a dialog box automatically when certain operations are selected, but this feature can usually be set "off" when not desired.

Dialogue Conversation, real or imagined, between two or more persons, especially the exchange of ideas and opinions between individuals who do not share the same point of view. Also refers to a written work in the form of a conversation between two or more people, or to the portions of a work of fiction (novel, short story, play, etc.) Consisting of words spoken by the characters, as opposed to passages of narrative or description. In the text of a narrative work, dialogue is set apart by the use of quotation marks. Compare with monologue.

Dial-up access Connection to a network, online service, or computer system from a terminal or workstation via a telephone line, usually in exchange for payment of a monthly fee to a service provider, as opposed to access via a dedicated line. Dial-up access requires a modem to convert the digital signals produced by a computer into the analog signals used in voice transmission, and vice versa.

Diary A private written record of day-to-day thoughts,

feelings, and experiences, kept by a person who does not expect them to be published. Also refers to the blankbook or notebook in which such experiences are recorded. Diaries are sometimes published posthumously and some have become famous literary and historical works, for example, the Diary of Samuel Pepys and more recently that of Anne Frank. Compare with journal and memoirs.

Dictionary A single-volume or multi-volume reference work containing brief explanatory entries for terms and topics related to a specific subject or field of inquiry, usually arranged alphabetically (example: Dictionary of Neuropsychology). The entries in a dictionary are usually shorter than those contained in an encyclopedia on the same subject, but it is not uncommon for the word "dictionary" to be used in the title of works that should more appropriately be called encyclopedias (example: Dictionary of the Middle Ages in 13 volumes).

Dictionary catalog A type of catalog, widely used in the United States before the conversion of the card catalog to machine-readable form, in which all the entries (main, added, subject) and cross-references are interfiled in a single alphabetic sequence, as opposed to one divided into separate sections by type of entry (author, title, subject). Compare with classified catalog.

Dictionary stand A free-standing piece of display furniture usually made of wood, at least waist-high with a sloping top and a book stop, used in libraries to display an open dictionary or other large reference work. A dictionary stand is narrower than an atlas case and may contain shelves for storing other s. Small revolving table-top models are also available from library suppliers.

Different edition When the author and title match an earlier record, but the publisher, imprint date, edition statement or series differ or there is a major difference in pagination.

Differential pricing The controversial practice of

charging libraries a substantially higher price for periodical subscriptions than the amount an individual subscriber is required to pay, which some journal publishers claim is justified because a library subscription makes the publication available to more readers, an effect known in the publishing trade as pass-along. Also refers to the practice in Europe of charging North American subscribers a rate substantially higher than normal, presumably because they can afford to pay more.

Diffuse authorship A work created by four or more persons or corporate bodies in which no single individual or body can be identified as the primary author. In libraries, such works are cataloged under the title, with an added entry for the first-named person or body. Under AACR2, if three or fewer persons or bodies are primarily responsible for a work, the main entry is under the heading for first-named author, with added entries for the other principal authors. Compare with unknown authorship.

Digerati The digital version of literati, it is a reference to a vague cloud of people seen to be knowledgeable, hip, or otherwise in-the-know in regardsto the digital revolution.

Digest An orderly, comprehensive abridgment or condensation of a written work (legal, scientific, historical, or literary), broader in scope than a synopsis, usually prepared by a person other than the author of the original. Headings and subheadings may be added to facilitate reference. Also refers to a periodical or index containing excerpts or condensations of works from various sources, usually arranged in some kind of order .

Digital archives Archival materials that have been converted to machine-readable format, usually for the sake of preservation or to make them more accessible to users. A prime example is American Memory, a project undertaken by the Library of Congress to make digital collections of primary sources on the history and culture of the United States available over the Internet.

Digital asset Intellectual content which has been digitized and can be referenced or retrieved online; for example, powerpoint slides, audio or video files, or files created in a word processing application, etc.

Digital collection A collection of library or archival materials converted to machine-readable format for preservation, or to provide access electronically (example: Thomas Jefferson Digital Archive, a project of the Electronic Text Center, University of Virginia Library). In the United States, the Digital Library Federation is developing standards and best practices for digital collections and network access.

Digital Data recorded or transmitted as discrete, discontinuous voltage pulses represented by the binary digits 0 and 1, called bits. In digitized text, each alphanumeric character is represented by a specific eight-bit sequence called a byte. The computers used in libraries transmit data in digital format. Compare with analog.

Digital divide A term coined by former Assistant Secretary of Commerce for Telecommunication and Communication, Larry Irving, Jr., to focus public awareness on the gap in access to information resources and services between those with the means to purchase the computer hardware and software necessary to connect to the Internet, and low-income families and communities that cannot afford network access. Public libraries are helping to bridge the gap between information "haves" and "have-nots" with the assistance of substantial grants from industry leaders such as Microsoft's Bill Gates. The E-rate established by the Telecommunications Act of 1996 (TCA) has helped schools, public libraries, and rural health care institutions bridge the gap. Digital Divide Network is a Web site devoted to the issue. Synonymous with information gap.

Digital imaging The field within computer science covering all aspects of the capture, storage, manipulation, transmission, and display of images in digital format, including digital photography, scanning, and bitmapped graphics. In libraries, images of text documents are created for electronic reserve collections and digital archives. They are also available in full-text bibliographic databases and reference resources.

Digital Library A digital Library is an assemblage of digital computing, storage, and communications machinery together with the content and software needed to reproduce, emulate, and extend the services provided by conventional libraries based on paper and other material means of collecting, cataloging, finding, and disseminating information. A full service digital library must accomplish all essential services of traditional libraries and also exploit the well-known advantages of digital storage, searching, and communication.

A library in which a significant proportion of the resources are available in machine-readable format, rather than in print or on microform. In libraries, the process of digitization began with the catalog, moved to periodical indexes and abstracting services, then to periodicals and large reference works, and finally book publishing. Abbreviated d-lib. Compare with virtual library.

Digital Library Federation (DLF) A consortium of major libraries and library-related agencies dedicated to promoting the use of electronic technologies to extend collections and services, DLF is committed to identifying standards and best practices for digital collections and network access, coordinating research-and-development in the use of information technology by libraries, and assisting in the initiation of projects/services that individual libraries lack the means to develop on their own.

Digital Millennium Copyright Act of 1998 (DMCA) Legislation passed by Congress and signed into law in October, 1998 to prepare the United States for the ratification of international treaties protecting rights to intellectual property in digital form, drafted in 1996 at a conference of the World Intellectual Property Organization (WIPO). The bill was supported by the software and entertainment industries, and opposed by the library, research, and education communities.

Digital object identifier (DOI) The Digital Object Identifier (DOI) is a system for identifying and exchanging intellectual property in the digital environment. It provides a framework for managing intellectual content, for linking customers with content suppliers, for facilitating electronic commerce, and enabling automated copyright management for all types of media.

Digital preservation The process of maintaining, in a condition suitable for use, materials produced in digital formats. Problems of physical preservation are compounded by the obsolescence of computer equipment, software, and storage media. Also refers to the practice of digitizing materials originally produced in nondigital formats (print, film, etc.) To prevent permanent loss due to deterioration of the physical medium. Synonymous with e-preservation and electronic preservation.

Digital Rights Management (DRM) Short for digital rights management, a system for protecting the copyrights of data circulated via the Internet or other digital media by enabling secure distribution and/or disabling illegal distribution of the data. Typically, a DRM system protects intellectual property by either encrypting the data so that it can only be accessed by authorized users or marking the content with a digital watermark or similar method so that the content can not be freely distributed

Digital thesis A master's thesis or Ph.D. Dissertation created in electronic form ("born digital"). Most universities require a paper or microform copy for archival purposes, but for some hypermedia theses, a print version may not be an accurate representation of the original (or even possible). Preservation dilemmas posed by the rapid obsolescence of digital equipment and formats underscore the need for standards.

Digitial Libraries Initiative (DLI) A multi-agency interdisciplinary research program of the National Science Foundation (NSF), that provides grants to facilitate the creation of large knowledge bases, develop the information technology to access them effectively, and improve their usability in a wide range of contexts.

Digitization The process of converting data to digital format for processing by a computer. In information systems, digitization usually refers to the conversion of printed text or images (photographs, illustrations, maps, etc.) Into digital signals using some kind of scanning device that enables the result to be displayed on a computer screen. In telecommunication, digitization refers to the conversion of continuous analog signals into pulsating digital signals.

Digitize Sometimes referred to as digital imaging; the act of translating an image, a sound, or a video clip into digital format for use on a computer. Also used to describe the process of converting coordinates on a map to x,y coordinates for input to a computer. All data a computer processes must be digitally encoded as a series of zeroes and ones.

Dime novel A melodramatic fictional narrative of adventure, romance, and action, published in inexpensive paperback edition in the United States during the second half of the 19th century, sold mainly at news stands for 10-25 cents a copy. The term originated with the Dime Novel Library introduced in 1860 by Beadle and Adams of New York. Hundreds of thousands of titles, written according to formula, were issued before this form of pulp fiction waned in the early 20th century. Among of the most popular was Buffalo Bill, King of the Border Men (1869) by E. Z. C. Judson, writing under the pseudonym Ned Buntline. His other works included Bigfoot Wallace, the Giant Hero of the Border (1891) and The Red Warrior, or, Stella delorme's Comanche Lover: A Romance of Savage Chivalry (1869). The influence of this genre on popular culture is studied by literary historians. Compare with penny dreadful and yellowback.

Dimensions The actual physical size of a bibliographic item, given in centimeters the physical description area of the bibliographic description unless some other unit of measurement is more appropriate.

DIMM Dual In-line Memory Module; a small circuit board that can hold a group of memory chips. A DIMM is capable of transferring 64 bits instead of the 32 bits each SIMM can handle. Pentium processors require a 64-bit path to memory so simms must be installed two at a time as opposed to one DIMM at a time.

DIO Documents in Information Science dois is a searchable database of articles and conference proceedings published in electronic format in the area of Library and Information Science. At the moment it holds about 9455 articles and 2884 papers, 6345 of them are downloadable from the site.

Diorama A museum exhibit or display on any scale in which inanimate objects and life-like figures representing animate beings are carefully placed in front of a background scene drawn or painted in perspective on a flat or curved surface to create the illusion of greater depth of field than actually exists. Special lighting and recorded sound effects are sometimes added to make the impression more realistic. Small portable examples are made for traveling exhibits.

Diptych A portable hinged tablet consisting of two pieces of wood, ivory, or metal covered with wax on the inside surface, on which the ancient Greeks and Romans wrote with a stylus. Also, a picture or design painted or carved on the inside surfaces of two hinged tablets. In medieval Europe, three tablets called a triptych were also used for the same purpose, hinged in such a way that the outer tablets folded over the center panel. Compare with pugillaria.

Direct connection A connection from your computer directly to a network; much faster than a dial up connection. Examples: Most office computers in OSU buildings and many computers in dorms wired for resnet have direct connections.

Direct delivery Putting library materials directly into the hands of the patron who requests them, without requiring a trip to the library to pick them up, for example, through a books-by-mail program. Direct delivery is practical for special libraries located on the premises of the host organization. It is also used by public libraries on a limited scale to serve homebound users.

Direct edition An edition of a work for which the author provides the publisher with camera-ready copy produced on a computer with the aid of word processing software. Used mainly for works that cannot be produced economically from type.

Direct entry in indexing that a concept describing the content of an bibliographic item should be entered under the subject heading or descriptor that names it, rather than as a subdivision of a broader term, thus a book about "academic libraries" would be assigned the heading Academic libraries, not Libraries—Academic.

Direct order An order for materials placed by an acquisitions librarian directly with the publisher, rather than through a jobber or subscription agency. The percentage of orders placed in this manner has declined as wholesalers and subscription agents have positioned themselves to offer economies of scale to their customers and provide services that add value. Some publishers no longer accept direct orders and sell only to wholesalers (example: Random House).

Directional question One relating to location of sources, floor plan of library, hours, etc. EXAMPLE: "Where are the periodical indexes located?" (Compare with reference question.)

Directional Said of a question that can be answered at the information desk or reference desk by directing the patron to the location of specific resources, services, or facilities within the library, as opposed to a question requiring substantive information, instruction in the use of library resources, or referral to an outside agency or authority.

Director of Development The title for the individual who coordinates the Libraries development activities and directs development services.

Director of Fiscal Services The title for the individual who is responsible for accounting services.

Director The person who has overall responsibility for directing the performance of a work written for stage or screen. The director's name appears in the credits at the beginning or end of a motion picture, videorecording, or television program, and is indicated in the note area of the bibliographic record created to represent the work in the library catalog. Compare with producer, and screenwriter.

Directory A list of people, companies, institutions, organizations, etc., in alphabetical or classified order, providing contact information (names, addresses, phone/ FAX numbers, etc.) And other pertinent details (affiliations, conferences, publications, membership, etc.) In brief format, often published serially (example: American Library Directory). In most libraries, current directories are shelved in ready reference or in the reference stacks.

Direct-To-Press Elimination of intermediate film and printing plates by the direct transfer of image data to printing cylinders in the press.

Dirty proof In printing, a proof of typeset copy containing many errors, or one returned to the printer heavily corrected. A clean proof contains no errors or corrections.

Disaster manual Written plan for the Libraries for disaster preparedness and disaster response and recovery including procedures and directions for staff members involved in disaster response.

Disaster plan A set of written procedures prepared in advance by the staff of a library to deal with an unexpected occurrence that has the potential to cause injury to personnel or damage to equipment, collections, and/or facilities sufficient to warrant temporary suspension of services (flood, fire, earthquake, etc.). In archival records management, securing vital records in the event of disaster is one of the highest priorities. An effective disaster plan begins with a thorough risk assessment to identify the areas most susceptible to various kinds of damage and evaluate measures that can be taken in advance to ensure preparedness. Both an initial action plan and a recovery plan should be included. Compare with contingency plan and emergency plan.

Disaster plan quick manual guide An abbreviated form of the CSU Disaster Manual designed for quick referral in case of an emergency.

Disaster preparedness Steps taken by a library or archives to prepare for serious damage to facilities, collections, and/or personnel in the event of a major occurrence such as a fire, flood, or earthquake, including preventive measures, formulation of an effective disaster plan, maintenance of adequate insurance, etc.

Disavowal form A form that is completed by a donor donating a gift in kind to the Libraries. The form asks what type of funds (state, federal, personal) were used to purchase the items. There is also a place for the donor to indicate the estimated value of the donation. Forms are available from gifts and exchange.

Disbound A book or other printed publication from which a previous binding has been removed, usually in preparation for rebinding, part of the process called pulling. Compare with unbound.

Disc A generic term for a direct-access magnetic storage medium that is read-only, as distinct from rewritable, including audio compact discs, CD-roms, videodiscs, etc. Compare with disk.

Discard To officially withdraw an item from a library collection for disposal, a process that includes removing from the catalog all references to it. Also refers to any item withdrawn for disposal, usually stamped "discard" to avoid confusion. Materials are usually withdrawn when they become outdated, cease to circulate, wear out, or are damaged beyond repair. When shelf space is limited, duplicates may be discarded to make room for new acquisitions. Withdrawn items may be exchanged or given as gifts to other libraries, but the most common method of disposal is in a book sale. Unsold items may be given to a thrift store or thrown away as trash, depending on the policy of the library.

Discharge In circulation, to cancel the record of a loan upon return of the borrowed item and payment of any overdue fine. Compare with charge.

Discipline a academic field of study such as history, psychology, or biology. Often books and articles published by members of a discipline intended for other scholars are called the literature of the discipline—referring not to literary expression but to research publications in the field.

Disclaimer A legal notice posted on a Web page, appended to an e-mail message, given on a product, or provided with a service, informing the reader or consumer that the host or producer does not guarantee and cannot be held responsible for all aspects of its content or performance.

Discography A list or catalog of audiorecordings, usually of works by a specific composer or performer, of a certain style or genre, or of a specific time period. Each entry in a discography provides some or all of the following descriptive elements: title of work, name of composer and performer(s), date of recording, name of manufacturer, manufacturer's catalog number, and release date. Also refers to the systematic cataloging of audiorecordings, and to the study of sound recording as a medium of expression. The person who compiles such a catalog is called a discographer. Compare with filmography.

Discontinued A serial publication for which a library subscription or continuation order has ended. In the catalog record for the title, the library's holdings are indicated in a closed entry.

Discontinued number A class number from an earlier edition of the Dewey Decimal Classification, which is no longer used, indicated at the appropriate location in the schedule by a note to "class in" a more general number.

Discount A percentage deducted from the price of any product or service, for example, the reduction in the rate paid for telecommunication services by schools and public libraries under the federal E-rate program. In publishing, a percentage deducted from the publisher's list price for an item, as an inducement to purchase. In book sales, the discount system includes:

Discountinued title Publication of serial has ceased; may be resumed at a later date. Library no longer receives the title.

Discourse analysis Linguistic analysis of segments of spoken or written language which are longer than one sentence and form a unit having recognizable structure, for the purpose of identifying regularities in the occurrence of phonological, grammatical, and semantic elements. In computer science, the results of discourse analysis have been applied to the study of human/computer interaction, for example, in the development of voice recognition systems.

Discussion group Another term for an online newsgroup or forum. Also, the webct software supported by TELR provides the capability for online discussion groups relating to course sections.

Discussion list e-mail-based asynchronous conversation among members of a group with a shared interest. E-mail messages are posted to all members of a group using software protocols such as Listserv or Majordomo. Participants have the opportunity to hold a wide-ranging discussion on a common topic with hundreds of others. See also asynchronous communication.

Disintermediation Elimination of the mediator or

"middle man." In the delivery of information services, the need for professional assistance is minimized in user-friendly systems designed to facilitate end-user searching.

Disintermediation Elimination of the mediator or "middle man." In the delivery of information services, the need for professional assistance is minimized in user-friendly systems designed to facilitate end-user searching.

Disk A generic term for a direct-access magnetic storage medium which is rewritable, as opposed to read-only, including floppy disks, hard disks, and Zip disks. Synonymous with magnetic disk. Compare with disc.

Disk Defragmenter Arranges the blocks of information for a file into adjacent blocks on your hard drive, which may significantly improve the file access times.

Disk drive In computing, a generic term for the hardware component that physically manipulates a specific type of magnetic disk (hard, floppy, WORM, Zip), allowing the user to read data from and write data to it. Disk drives can be internal or external. Also spelled disc drive.

Diskette A portable magnetic disk most often used for secondary file storage. Diskettes come in 3 1/2 inch and 5 1/4 inch sizes and in both high-density (DSHD) and double-density (DSDD) formats. Also referred to as a "floppy disk".

Display case A box or set of shelves enclosed in glass or plexiglass to allow books and other items to remain protected while on exhibit. A display case can be free-standing, wall-mounted, or built-in. Modern designs are usually lockable. Cases used for perishable museum specimens may be climate-controlled to prevent deterioration. Synonymous with exhibit case. Compare with display rack.

Display copy A copy of a new book or other publication put on view, usually in a bookstore or as part of publisher's exhibit at a conference or convention. At the end of the event, display copies are sometimes sold to conference participants at a discount, especially if their dust jackets are no longer in new condition.

Display matter Any printed matter that is not part of the text of a work, including illustrations, headings, captions, printer's ornaments, etc. To distinguish it from body matter, textual display matter is set in type of a different size and/or font.

Display rack A library furnishing in metal, wood, or plastic, designed to display printed material, such as brochures, announcements, instructional handouts, reading lists, etc., face-forward to encourage users to browse and select what they need. Sold by library suppliers, display racks are available in wall-mounted and free-standing designs, from small counter-top models to large floor units. Compare with display case.

Display type Type sizes larger than 14-point, used mainly for headings, titles, banners, and other display purposes, in contrast to the smaller text type used to print the body of the text, and even smaller extract type used for quotations, notes, etc.

Disposal In U.S. government archives, the destruction of noncurrent records that are no longer needed. Also used synonymously with disposition.

Disposition schedule A systematic list of documents used by an archivist to determine: 1) which of the recurring records of an agency or individual will be retained, 2) the period of time for which they will be held, 3) where they will be housed during the retention period (archives or intermediate storage), and 4) any other decisions concerning their disposition, based on their utility and value to the organization. Synonymous with retention schedule.

Disposition The manner in which the noncurrent records of an agency or individual are handled once their utility has been appraised, whether stored (temporarily or permanently) in a repository in their original format, reproduced and stored on microform, sold, donated, or destroyed. Compare with disposal.

Dissertation A lengthy, formal written treatise or thesis, especially an account of scholarly investigation or original research on a specialized topic, submitted to a university in partial fulfillment of the requirements for a Ph.D. Degree. Dissertations submitted at universities in the United States, Canada, Great Britain, and other European countries are indexed and abstracted in Dissertation Abstracts International (DAI) available in print, on CD-ROM, and online from Bell & Howell. In most academic libraries, copies of dissertations may be requested on interlibrary loan or ordered via document delivery. Abbreviated diss. Compare with thesis.

Dissertation Abstracts International (DAI) A service of Bell & Howell that provides indexing and abstracting of Ph.D. Dissertations and master's theses in all academic disciplines, submitted at universities in the United States, Canada, Great Britain, and other European countries since 1861 (dissertations abstracted since 1980, theses since 1988). **DAI** is available in print, on CD-ROM, and as an online bibliographic database directly from Bell & Howell or via OCLC firstsearch (updated monthly). Print copies of dissertations can be obtained from Dissertation Express (Bell& Howell) upon payment of a fixed fee.

Distance education: May also be referred to as "online learning" or "elearning." A means of instruction that implies a course instructor and students are separated in space and perhaps, in time. Interaction may be synchronous (facilitated) or asynchronous (self-paced). Students can work with various course materials, or they may use tools like chat or discussion groups to collaborate on projects.

Distance learning A method of instruction and learning designed to overcome barriers of time and space by allowing students to study in their own homes or at local facilities, often at their own convenience, using materials available electronically or by mail. Communication with the instructor is normally by telephone or e-mail. Telecommunication networks and teleconferencing have facilitated distance learning. Libraries are working to support distance learning by providing online catalogs and databases, electronic reserves, electronic reference service, online tutorials, and electronic document delivery service.

Distance Library Services One can request books, journals, theses, etc. There are no charges for this service except for the return postage for books. NOTE: The service specifically designed for distance students at NSU is called Distance Library Services. The Electronic Library (http://www.nova.edu/library) has electronic request forms that you can use.

Distinctive title A title that is unique to a specific work. Distinctiveness of title is important in registering copyright, and makes the entry for a document easier to retrieve from a library catalog or other finding tool in a search by title.

Distribution copy In reprography, a microform copy from which additional copies of equal legibility can be reproduced.

Distribution imprint The statement printed on the verso of the title page of a book giving the official name(s) of the distributor(s) from which copies can be obtained, as distinct from the imprint of the publisher that issued the edition, or the printer responsible for printing the edition.

Distribution list In e-mail software, a feature that allows the user to establish a list of e-mail addresses under a common name, enabling messages to be sent simultaneously to everyone on the list when addressed to the list name. Although the term is sometimes used synonymously with mailing list, the latter generally supports a much larger group, requiring special software for automatic maintenance (example: listsserv).

Distribution rights Legal arrangements made by a publisher to transfer to another company or person the exclusive right to market a publication, usually within a designated geographic area. In books, distribution rights are usually indicated in the distribution imprint on the verso of the title page.

Distributor An agent or agency that owns the exclusive or shared rights to market a published work, usually within a designated geographic area. In domestic publishing, the distributor is usually, but not always, the publisher. Foreign publications are often distributed by a domestic publishing company under an agreement with the original publisher. Abbreviated distr.

Diversity Inclusiveness with regard to variation in age, gender, sexual orientation, religious belief, and ethnic, racial, and cultural background within a given population. In the United States, libraries strive to achieve diversity in library school admissions, hiring, collection development, services, and programs.

Divided catalog In the 1930s, when it became apparent that dictionary catalogs were becoming cumbersome, large libraries in the United States began dividing their catalogs into two sections, one for subject entries and the other for main and added entries other than subject (authors, titles, series, etc.). Eventually, some libraries divided their catalogs into three sections (author, title, and subject). Divided catalogs have the disadvantage of requiring that the user know in advance which type of entry is required (entries for works written by a specific author are filed separately from works written about the same person), but once the initial determination is made, the user is spared the time and effort of looking through entries which are not of the type desired. Synonymous with split catalog. Divide-like note A note added to a heading in a classification schedule to inform the user that the heading is subdivided in the same way as another heading in the same schedule.

Division In Dewey Decimal Classification, the first level of subdivision of the ten main classes, usually representing a discipline or subdiscipline, indicated by the first two digits in the notation (example: 94 in 940 for European history). There are one hundred divisions in DDC (10 x 10). The next level of subdivision, indicated by a third digit other than zero, is called a section (944 for works on the history of France).

Divisional title The title printed on the recto of the leaf preceding the first page of the text of a major division of a book, sometimes with the number of the division (if they are numbered). The verso is normally left blank. Synonymous with part title and section title.

DLC The OCLC symbol for the LIBRARY OF CONGRESS.

Dmin The point of minimum density in an image or an original.

DNA: Departmental network administrator; the person within an OSU department, college, or building responsible for networking services. Also referred to as a "SONNET administrator".

DNS Domain Name System. A general purpose distributed, replicated, data query service. Its principal use is the lookup of host IP addresses based on host names. The host names are also known as domain names. Some important domains are: .COM (commercial), .EDU (educational), .NET (network operations), .GOV (U.S. government), and .MIL (U.S. military). Most countries also have a domain. For example, .US (United States), .UK (United Kingdom), .AU (Australia).

DOC Location notation on SAGE for government documents collection.

DOC Oversize Oversized documents; located within the governement document collection.

Docking station A piece of computer hardware that enables a laptop to function as a desktop computer by providing a single large plug and socket that duplicates the individual cable connections to monitor, keyboard, mouse, and printer. Some docking stations include built-in peripherals such as audio speakers and CD-ROM drive, and a network interface card to allow the user to connect to a local area network. Because no standard exists for docking stations, compatibility with the specific type of laptop is an important consideration in making a purchase decision.

Doctored A book that has been altered from its original condition, usually as a consequence of mending, repairs, restoration, or the addition or removal of parts. Compare with as issued.

Docudrama A shortened form of the term documentary drama, a dramatization of events that actually happened, usually produced for film or television. Although some elements may be fictionalized, a serious attempt is made to be historically accurate (example: Edward Hopper, the Silent Witness, a film by Wolfgang Hastert). Compare with documentary and feature film.

Document A physical entity consisting of any substance on which is recorded all or a portion of one or more works, in the words of Marshall mcluhan, the "medium" in which a "message" (information) is communicated. Document formats range from print (books, manuscripts, pamphlets, periodicals, reports, maps, charts, prints, etc.) To microform and nonprint media. Abbreviated doc.

Document camera A table-top device used in bibliographic instruction and other visual presentations to project text and/or images from an opaque surface or transparency onto a large screen using an LCD projector. Document cameras have superseded overhead projectors in well-equipped libraries.

Document delivery It refers to the transfer of a database record, or other information resource, to the end user. It can involve direct internet or email transfers, CD delivery via mail, paper delivery via mail, or delivery via interlibrary loan.

Document delivery service (DDS) The provision of published or unpublished documents in hard copy, microform, or digital format, usually for a fixed fee upon request. In most libraries, document delivery service is provided by the interlibrary loan office on a cost-recovery basis. The patron is usually required to pick-up printed material at the library, but electronic full-text may be forwarded via e-mail. Also refers to the physical or electronic delivery of documents from a library collection to the residence or place of business of a library user, upon request.

Document trail All the authenticated sources of information about a topic, recorded in any medium, traced backward in time to determine conclusively the origins of an existing state of affairs, a technique used in archives to establish provenance and in news reporting to uncover the details of a story.

Documentary A motion picture that records actual events or depicts social conditions without fictionalization, often through the use of historical footage and still photographs, usually accompanied by a narration dramatically structured to highlight important individuals who participated in the action. The term was coined by the Scottish film-maker John Grierson in the late 1920's to describe the cinematic works of Robert Flaherty, the first person to produce films of social commentary depicting actual people in real-life situations (example: Louisiana Story). Compare with docudrama and feature film.

Documentation center An organization or agency that specializes in receiving, processing, preserving, abstracting, and indexing publications, usually within a scholarly discipline or field of research and study (example: ERIC). Documentation centers also issue bulletins on the progress of such work for distribution to interested parties and may also prepare bibliographies on special topics, make copies or translations, and engage in bibliographic research.

Documentation The acquisition, organization, storage, retrieval, and distribution of specialized documents, especially of a legal, technical, or scientific nature. Also refers to a collection of documents pertaining to a specific subject, especially when used to substantiate a point of fact.

Documents processing Part of acquisition service that handles material received from theu S Government Printing Office. Documents are cataloged in their own classification system called the superintendent of collection classification or "SUDOC." State of Colorado documents are also processed by the Documents Processing Unit.

Dog-eared The condition of a book that shows definite signs of wear, especially pages that have been folded down at a corner to mark a place.

Doggerel Versification that is loose, irregular, crude, and/or superficial due to the writer's ineptitude, or by intention, usually for comic effect, as in John Skelton's Colin Clout.

Domain All the hardware and software resources controlled by a single computer system. In a local area network (LAN), all the clients, servers, and devices under the control of a single security database, administered under a common set of rules and procedures. On the Internet, all the clients, servers, and devices sharing a common portion of the IP address, the highest level domain being the category of host, indicated in the United States by the three-letter suffix at the end of the domain name. In database management, all the possible values of the data contained in a specific field present in every record in a file.

Domain Name The unique name that identifies an Internet site. Domain Names always have 2 or more parts, separated by dots. The part on the left is the most specific, and the part on the right is the most general. A given machine may have more than one Domain Name but a given Domain Name points to only one machine. For example, the domain names: matisse.net, mail.matisse.net, workshop.matisse.net. Usually, all of the machines on a given Network will have the same thing as the right-hand portion of their Domain Names (matisse.net in the examples above). It is also possible for a Domain Name to exist but not be connected to an actual machine. This is often done so that a group or business can have an Internet e-mail address without having to establish a real Internet site. In these cases, some real Internet machine must handle the mail on behalf of the listed Domain Name.

Domain Name Server A computer that converts host names, such as rohan.sdsu.edu to its corresponding IP Address, such as 191.130.1.10. An SDSU computer provides this service any time mail is sent or received and permits users to use TELNET and FTP between SDSU and other sites.

Domain Name System (DNS) A table used to translate numerical IP addresses (example: 123.456.78.9) into the alphanumeric domain name addresses (www.thisuniversity.edu) familiar to Internet users, and vice versa.

Donation In archives, a voluntary deposit of records by a person or organization, in which both legal title and physical custody are formally transferred by the donor. Compare with gift.

Donor file A systematic record of the names of persons and/or organizations that have donated materials to a library or archives. A well-maintained donor file should document any restrictions on the preservation, use, or disposition of donated items or files, and provide current contact information. In a weeding project, it is wise to check discards against such a file to ascertain if a prior agreement was made with the donor concerning final disposition.

Door stop Library slang for a piece of equipment so obsolete that it cannot be given away. Such items are usually consigned to a storage room in the basement until renovation or a move into a new facility makes disposal unavoidable.

DOS An acronym for Disk Operating System (pronounced "dahss"), the first operating system for IBM-compatible personal computers, developed for IBM in a version called PC-DOS by Bill Gates' fledgling company Microsoft. Gates subsequently marketed the Microsoft version (MS-DOS) which became the underlying control program for early versions of Windows. Windows NT and later versions of Windows are not dependent on DOS, although they are capable of supporting DOS applications. Because it is nongraphical, line-oriented, and command-driven, the DOS interface is not as user-friendly as Windows.

Dos-a-dos An English term for a type of binding in which two books are bound back-to-back, sharing the back cover, with the fore-edges of one aligned with the spine of the other, so that they open in opposite directions. Popular during the 17th century, this style was used to bind in a single volume the New Testament with the Prayer Book and Psalms. Compare with tete-beche.

Dot A full stop used to divide the elements of an Internet address.

Dot.com A commercial enterprise that does all or a substantial portion of its business over the Internet (example: Amazon.com).

Dotted Decimal Notation The convention for writing 32-bit IP Addresses as a set of four 8-bit numbers written in base 10 with periods separating them.

Double column A book or other publication in which the text is set to half the width of a page, usually with a blank space or rule dividing the two columns, a format commonly used in dictionaries, encyclopedias, and other large-format reference works.

Double dagger In printing, a character in the shape of a vertical stroke crossed twice, above and below the mid-point, used as the third-order reference mark, following the use of the asterisk and the dagger. The double dagger is also known as a double obelisk or diesis.

Double fold See: double leaf.

Double leaf A leaf twice the page size in a book, folded in half at the fore-edge or top edge, with the fold uncut and no printing inside the fold. When such a leaf is unnumbered, it is counted as two pages. In the bibliographic description of the item, the total number of pages is recorded as in the following example: [32] pp. (on double leaves). Synonymous with double fold.

Double numeration A system of enumeration, used

mainly in textbooks, law books, and technical publications, in which two numbers are assigned, usually separated by a period, hyphen, or other symbol, the first being the number of the chapter or other major division of the work, and the second indicating a section of the text or one of several illustrations, maps, graphs, charts, etc., numbered in the sequence in which they appear within the division.

Double plate A single illustration that extends across facing pages in an open book or other publication, usually printed on a double-size leaf folded down the center and bound at the fold. A caption may be printed on the preceding or following page. Compare with double spread and face up.

Double shelving Storing books two rows to a shelf, one behind the other, a shelving method used in libraries only when space is severely limited. Shelves must be at least ten inches deep for this alternative to work. The method can potentially double shelf capacity, but it reduces browsability and makes materials more difficult to locate and reshelve. These drawbacks can be minimized by installing graphic signage or limiting its use to series, such as legal case law, or to the back files of bound periodicals and reports.

Double spread Text and/or illustration printed across facing pages in a book or other publication, as if on a single page, usually for visual effect. Compare with double plate.

Double-fan adhesive binding A type of adhesive binding in which the binding edge of the text block is milled and splayed, first in one direction while a slow-drying adhesive is applied, and then in the opposite direction as a second application is made, allowing the adhesive to penetrate no more than 1/32 inch between the leaves, so that each leaf is tipped to the next. The method is not practical for books with a text block more than two inches thick. The strength of fan adhesive binding can be enhanced by notching the binding edge, but this technique has the disadvantage of restricting openability. Compare with perfect binding.

Doublure An ornamental lining of silk, satin, vellum, leather, or some other material of fine quality, affixed to the inside cover of a book, especially in leather-bound deluxe editions. In older books, the doublure was often elegantly decorated. Synonymous with ornamental endpaper.

Doubtful authorship A work for which authorship has not been conclusively established, which is ascribed to one or more persons on the basis of incomplete or unconvincing evidence. Some scholars believe the works of William Shakespeare to have been written by another author, but the evidence in support of this contention is inconclusive.

Down time Any period during which a computer or system is out of operation, usually due to hardware or software failure or regular maintenance. In libraries, the amount of time a public access workstation or system is "down" is a measure of its reliability and can directly affect quality of service, particularly during periods of peak use. Also spelled downtime.

Download Transfer of data from a server to your computer's hard disk. You can use your browser or an FTP program to download files to your computer. When you're retrieving your mail, you're downloading your mail to your computer.

Down-Sampling The reduction in resolution of an image, necessitating a loss in detail.

Dpi Dots per inch; a measure of a printer's resolution. The higher the number, the better the print quality. A minimum of 300 dpi usually is required for professional-looking results.

Draft A handwritten, typed, or printed version of a document, not intended to be final, which is subject to future modification, correction, revision, etc., sometimes by a person or persons other than the original author. A rough draft usually provides only a preliminary or sketchy version of the work or plan. The last version of a work that has seen multiple revisions is the final draft. To avoid misunderstanding, a document not yet completed should be clearly marked "Draft."

Dramatization An adaptation of a nondramatic work of fiction or nonfiction for performance on stage or screen, usually by a person other than the original author. In library cataloging, a dramatization is entered under the name of the playwright, with added entries under the author and title of the work on which it is based..

Dreamweaver Software from Macromedia used to build and manage websites and Internet applications.

Driver A program routine specifically designed to link a peripheral device to the operating system of a computer, allowing it to perform the functions requested by application software. Some drivers, such as the keyboard driver, are included in the operating system, but when a new piece of hardware is added to a computer (printer, scanner, disk drive, etc.), the appropriate driver must usually be installed on the CPU so that the operating system can call upon it to run the device. Also called a device driver.

Drop A telecommunication outlet in a library or other facility, usually consisting of a voice jack and at least one data jack to

Drop initial A large decorated or undecorated initial letter in a manuscript or printed work, aligned horizontally with the tops of succeeding letters in the same line, but extending below the line into a space left by indenting the next line (or lines). Drop initials are used mainly at the beginning of a chapter or other major division of a work. Synonymous with drop cap. Compare with raised capital.

Drop shipment Publications ordered from a jobber by the acquisitions department of a library, sent by the publisher directly to the library at the request of the jobber, usually to reduce shipping costs when the jobber does not have the items in stock.

Drop-down title The shortened version of the title of a

book, printed on the first page of the text, usually the same as the running title. Compare with caption title.

Drum Scanner Early drum scanners separated scans into CMYK data, recording these directly onto film held on a second rotating drum.

DSL (Digital Subscriber Line), A method for moving data over regular phone lines. A DSL circuit is much faster than a regular phone connection, and the wires coming into the subscriber's premises are the same (copper) wires used for regular phone service. A DSL circuit must be configured to connect two specific locations, similar to a leased line (howeverr a DSL circuit is not a leased line. A common configuration of DSL allows downloads at speeds of up to 1.544 megabits (not megabytes) per second, and uploads at speeds of 128 kilobits per second. This arrangement is called ADSL: Asymmetric Digital Subscriber Line. Another common configuration is symmetrical: 384 Kilobits per second in both directions. In theory ADSL allows download speeds of up to 9 megabits per second and upload speeds of up to 640 kilobits per second. DSL is now a popular alternative to Leased Lines and ISDN, being faster than ISDN and less costly than traditional Leased Lines.

Dublin Core (DC) A set of metadata elements designed to facilitate the description of document-like resources in a networked environment. Dublin Core is the result of an international cross-disciplinary consensus achieved through the ongoing efforts of the Dublin Core Metadata Initiative (DCMI). It has the potential to provide a foundation for standardizing bibliographic description of information resources available via the Internet.

Dublin Core Metadata Initiative (DCMI) The Dublin Core Metadata Initiative is an open forum engaged in the development of interoperable online metadata standards that support a broad range of purposes and business models. DCMI's activities include consensus-driven working groups, global workshops, conferences, standards liaison, and educational efforts to promote widespread acceptance of metadata standards and practices.

Due Date A date stamped in the front or back of a book (or other library item) that indicates when the item must be returned to the library. Fines are charged for items not returned by the due date. Patrons can extend a due date by requesting a renewal.

Dues Titles ordered from a publisher that cannot be supplied until additional stock arrives from the printer, usually new books for which stock has not been received or backlisted titles in the process of being reprinted. Such items are usually back ordered.

Dummy A single prototype of a book, made up of the same number of leaves (usually blank) of the same grade of paper as the final product, trimmed and sewn but usually unbound, to give the binder an idea of bulk and page size, and to assist the graphic designer in planning the layout of the dust jacket.

Dump A computer operation that copies raw data from one location to another in a system, usually with little or no formatting, for example, the transfer of the contents of memory to a printer or computer screen to display the status of a program at the moment it crashed, useful in diagnosing the nature of a problem.

Duodecimo (12mo) A book, approximately 8 inches in height, made by folding a full sheet of book paper to form signatures of twelve leaves (twenty-four pages).

DUP Common abbreviation for a duplicate book, order, card, etc.

Duplex In communications, a channel capable of transmitting signals in both directions (sending and receiving) at the same time. In computer networks, this is usually achieved by using paired wires or by dividing bandwidth into two frequencies. A half-duplex connection is capable of transmitting signals alternately but not simultaneously in either direction (example: two-way radio).

Synonymous with full-duplex. Compare with simplex.

Duplicate An additional copy of an item already in a library collection, which is not needed. Public libraries often order high-demand items in multiple copies, then weed duplicates as they cease to circulate. Compare with added copy.

Duplicate exchange union (DEU) Operating under the auspices of the Association for Library Collections & Technical Services, a division of the American Library Association, the DEU is an association of libraries who cooperate in the exchange of usable library material. Although composed primarily of small college and public libraries, the DEU aims to serve all libraries in finding a place for their duplicate or unwanted materials. The exchange lists distributed by DEU members have also proven to be a valuable source for locating needed items.

Duplicate paging The numbering of pages in duplicate, usually on facing pages, used mainly in books containing parallel texts, for example, a text in translation and the same text in the original language.

Duplicate record A bibliographic record that occurs more than once on a library's catalog. In MARC files, this usually occurs when a record is used more than once in OCLC cataloging procedures. When a bibliographic database is created or updated, duplicate records are removed in a batch process known as deduping.

Duplication Center The library's photocopy service center. Marriott's main

Durability The degree to which a material retains its physical integrity when subjected to stress, for example, heavy use in the

Durability The degree to which a material retains its physical integrity when subjected to stress, for example, heavy use in the case of some library materials. A durable material, such as the buckram used as a covering in some library bindings, will generally last a relatively long time under conditions of normal use. The opposite of fragile.

Dust jacket The removable paper wrapper on the outside of a hardcover book, usually printed in color and given a glossy finish to market the work to retail customers and protect it from wear and tear. The front of the dust jacket bears the title, the author's full name, and a graphic design. The title also appears on the spine of the jacket, with the author's last name and the publisher's name or symbol. In most trade titles, a promotional blurb written by the publisher appears on the inside flap. The back flap usually provides brief biographical information about the author, which may include a small portrait photograph. The ISBN is printed on the back of the dust jacket, usually in the lower right-hand corner, following brief quotes from positive reviews of the work. Textbooks, reference books, and sci-tech books are usually published without a dust jacket.

DVD An initialism that stands for digital videodisc, a type of optical disk of the same size as a compact disc, but with significantly greater recording capacity, partly because it is double-sided. DVD is expected to supersede video cds, laserdiscs, and videotape as the preferred medium for motion pictures for home use. DVD players can also read most CD media.

Dwell In tooling, the length of time the heated finishing tool is in contact with the leather or cloth surface being decorated.

Dye Sublimation A printing process using small heating elements to evaporate pigments from a carrier film, depositing these smoothly onto a substrate.

Dynamic map A map on which flow lines and/or arrows of varying width are used to indicate the direction and amount of movement (migration), action (military maneuvers), or change in conditions (weather). Synonymous with flow map.

EARN European Academic Research Network.

Earthquake Engineering Abstracts Provides access to

world literature in earthquake engineering since 1971. The database contains 96,000 abstracts. A maximum of 200 records will be returned on any individual search.

EBCDIC Extended Binary-Coded Decimal Interchange Code. A standard character-to-number encoding used primarily by IBM computer systems..

Ebook An electronic version of a book.

EBSCO Database vendor offering access to full text articles; also a vendor for serial subscriptions.

Eccles Library The University of Utah Health Sciences Library, located near the University Hospital.

Echo (Local, Remote) Local echo ON causes all transmitted data to be sent to the screen of the sending computer. Remote echo ON causes everything that the remote computer (the one you are communicating with) transmits to be duplicated on your computer's screen. See Duplex.

Ecommunis Personalized Economic Research Community Economics is the most featureful free economics research platform and network online, with many useful features for economists. It includes paper database from repec and other institutions, free blogger.com compatible weblog, per-paper discussion and rating, free email notification of new papers on specific topics and many community features and discussion possibilities. Registration is required to avail this FREE service.

Economywatch.com Economywatch.com is a commercial site provides information and data on Indian economy. The data type available on this site include statistics related to national income, foreign investment, agriculture, industry, money and banking, balance of payments, population etc.

Editing 1. Process of proofreading a bibliographic record and verifying it against the piece being cataloged, ensuring that the record is accurate and conforms to accepted cataloging standards and local practices. 2. To prepare (written material) for publication presentation, as by correcting, revising, or adapting.

Edition All copies of a bibliographic item produced from the same master copy. A citation will not usually indicate a "first edition," but will note later editions: "revised edition," "fifth edition," etc. 2) one of the various editions of a newspaper or magazine printed at different times of the day, etc.; for example: " daily edition," "evening edition" or "special edition."

Editor One who prepares for publication or supervises the publication of a work or collection of works or articles that are not his/her own. Responsibility may extend to revising and providing commentaries, introductory matter, etc.

Education library A division of the library system including materials in education, special education, child study, curriculum materials, psychology related to education, and applied art; located on the Peabody campus.

Educational Resources Information Centre (ERIC) U.S. Dept. Of Education sponsored national clearinghouse for information on education. ERIC consists of Resources in Education ED reports and Current Index to Journals in Education EJ articles. ED reports are available on microfiche in the Journal Room. They can also be ordered for a fee through the ERIC Document Reproduction Service, EDRS. EJ articles are available from education journals owned by CSU. Many full text articles are available through SFX Citation Linker in Sage, via ERIC in OCLC firstsearch and via ERIC through CSUL databases.

Eectronic Information Centre (EIC) The EIC provides access to SAGE, the online public access catalog, CD-ROM databases, and online electronic databases in the areas of science and technology, social sciences, humanities and business. It also provides access to the World Wide web, Microsoft Office Suite, multi media stations, GIS, and CD-Burner

E-Journal An electronic version of a journal. Ejournals can be searched using citation linker.

Elearning Electroning learning; applies to a wide scope of processes including Web-based learning, computer-based instruction, virtual classrooms, and digital collaboration. Content may be delivered in a variety of ways including via the Internet, satellite broadcast, interactive TV, and DVD- or CD-roms.

Elec Media Collection of books, maps, documents in digitized format on compact disks available for checkout. Located in Morgan Library Lower Level.

Elec Ref Collection of databases and other reference materials in digitized format on compact disks. Like all reference materials, these are non-circulating. Some Elec Ref materials are installed on Public Computer Stations in the EIC, others are installed as needed.

Electronic book An electronic version of a book..

Electronic index A database of citations which may include full-text digitized articles, generally searchable by author, title, or keyword.

Electronic Journal A publication, often scholarly, that is made accessible in a computerized format and distributed over the Internet. An electronic journal or e-journal may have a traditional paper counterpart or historical antecedent. For example, the journal American Literature can be found in both paper and electronic versions at Cornell. The electronic versions are available through the Library Gateway, and the holdings for the paper copies can be found in the CU Library Catalog.

Electronic mail Electronic communication through institutional, community or commercial networks.

Electronic ordering The INNOPAC ordering module which allows orders to be sent electronically to vendors who are equipped to receive them.

Electronic reserve service Managed by the loan/

reserve desk materials selected by faculty for required class reading, are digitized and placed on Electronic Reserve for displaying to screen, downloading or printing.

Electronic resource and service fund This development fund was created to support special library technological initiatives.

EM Abbreviation for East Mesa Regional Library, the former name for our Red Mountain Branch Library. You may see EM on the spine labels of books belonging to the Red Mountain Branch.

Email (Electronic Mail), Messages, usually text, sent from one person to another via computer. E-mail can also be sent automatically to a large number of addresses.

Employee Association Program The Employee Assistance Program is a free and confidential counseling service with an office on campus that is open to all Colorado State University employees. It is a partnership between Colorado State University and EAP International which has offices in all 50 states and worldwide.

Employee Enhancement Committee (EEC) To provide the staff of the CSU Libraries with opportunities for personal and professional development, and to foster communication and interest among CSU Libraries staff about what they would consider beneficial training and development activities.

ENB Health Care Databases Health Care Database is a bibliographical database with abstracts for each entry. As at July 2001, the Database contains nearly 55,000 records from UK health care journals since 1986.

Encoded retrieval description (EAD) The Encoded Archival Description (EAD) standard is used by digital libraries to create machine-readable finding aids. Archival finding aids are descriptive bibliography or metadata tools which take the form of inventories, registers, indexes, guides, and similar resources created by museums, libraries, repositories, and other kinds of archives. Archival finding aids are descriptive bibliography or metadate tools which take the form of inventories, registers, indexes, guides, and similar resources created by museums, libraries, repositories, and other kinds of archives.

Encoding File transfer formatting that enables encrypted, compressed or binary files to be transferred without corruption or loss of data.

Encryption A way of coding information in a file or e-mail message so that if it is intercepted by a third party as it travels over a network it cannot be read.

Encumbrabce Money set aside for a puechase order which has been placed with a vendor, but not yet paid for because the product or service has not yet been received.

Encyclopedia A reference source containing information on a variety of topics. This information may be supplied in short paragraphs or in lengthy articles that include citations to other works on the same topic. Encyclopedias can be general - covering all topics, or specialized - focusing on a particular discipline such as art or philosophy.

Endnote Colorado State University researchers can use bibliographic reference software such as endnote to manage book and journal citations that are pertinent to work in their field. Endnote can also automatically format citation styles within a word processor. As an added software feature, the Z39.50 protocol in endnote enables the researcher to directly search and automatically import citations from the SAGE library catalog and selected online databases.

Endowmwnt Any bequest or GIFT that provides an income for an institution or person.

Energy Citations Database Contains bibliographic records for energy and energy-related scientific and technical information from the Department of Energy and its predecessor agencies, the Energy Research and Development Administration (ERDA) and the Atomic Energy Commission

(AEC)of USA. The Database provides access to DOE publicly available citations from 1948 through the present.

Engenius Engenius is a bibliographic database covering abstracts of articles published in the last 2 years in key engineering journals. It is a product of elsevierengineering.com. Search is completely FREE for registered members.

Enliven A multimedia player from Narrative that provides interactive streaming video, sound and animation (see Quicktime and Shockwave).

Entry Is any record, or a field in a record, that has been included, or entered, into a database. An entry word is the headword in a dictionary, encyclopedia, or glossary.

Entry word Word by which the entry is arranged in a catalog, usually the first word (other than an article) of a heading.

ERIC database ERIC is the world's largest source of education information, with more than 1 million abstracts of documents and journal articles on education research and practice. The data is available from 1966 onwards.

ERNET ERNET India, an autonomous scientific society under Ministry of Communications and Information Technology, is providing Internet access to Education and Research community in the country for over 10 years. ERNET is a nation-wide terrestrial and satellite network with points of presence located at leading education and research institutions in major cities. ERNET infrastructure is a judicious mix of satellite and terrestrial networks ideally suited for the Education and Research community in the country.

Errata Sheet of corrections printed after a publication has already been published and sent to those who purchased the publication so errors can be corrected.

Error correction A feature available with MNP-standard modems; this helps to assure integrity of data transmissions over phone lines when connected to another error-correcting modem. The V.32 and V.42 standards also offer error recovery capabilities.

ETC The Electronic Text Center (ETC), located on the first floor of Olin Library, provides access to scholarly electronic text and multimedia documents from a set of dedicated workstations in the library and from the Center's Web site. For more information about the ETC and the resources available there, see the ETC web site.

Ethernet A very common method of networking computers in a LAN. There is more than one type of Ethernet. By 2001 the standard type was "100-baset" which can handle up to about 100,000,000 bits-per-second and can be used with almost any kind of computer.

Ethernet card An adapter card that fits into a computer and connects to Ethernet cabling; different types of adaptor cards fit specific computers. Microcomputers connected to SONNET have some type of Ethernet card installed. Example: computers in campus offices or in dorms rooms wired for resnet. Also referred to as "Ethernet adapter".

Eudora Light The freeware version of the Eudora Pro client; the professional version distributed by OIT contains many extra features not available in the light version.

Eudora Pro A client program for Macintosh and Windows distributed via the OIT Software To Go web site; enables you to compose, send, receive and store e-mail messages on your own computer.

Eurostat Provides latest and the most complete statistical information on the EU and the zero-zone. The topics include general statistics, economy and finance, population and social conditions, industry, trade and services, agriculture and fisheries, etc. But only the key indicators are available for free of cost.

Exchange Arrangement with another Library or agency to receive materials automatically in return for materials our library or university sends them. A record of exchanges is kept in the gift and exchange section of acquisition.

Exchange Department The library division which handles exchanges of publications among cooperating institutions. Marriott no longer has an Exchange department; our only exchanges are for periodicals, which are handled by the Serials division.

Executable File Refers to a file that is a program. Executables in DOS and Windows usually have an .exe or a .com extension. In UNIX and Macintosh environments, executable files can have any name.

Exempt (Personnel) A status of employment as defined by the U.S. Department of Labor indicating exemption from payment of overtime. Positions are usually salaried (monthly) and meet criteria set by the federal government.

Exhibits Displays of books and/or visual material addressing particular topics of interest to the campus community.

Exit permit The printed form used to issue otherwise non-circulating material to authorized faculty and graduate students, generally for a few hours or overnight, and sometimes only with the consent of the librarian responsible for the subject area.

Expansion card Also referred to as an expansion board; a circuit board you can insert into a slot inside your computer to give it added functionality. A card can replace an existing one or may be added in an empty slot. Some examples include sound, graphics, USB, Firewire, and internal modem cards.

Extension A suffix preceded by a period at the end of a filename; used to describe the file type. Example: On a Windows computer, the extension ".exe" represents an executable file.

Extensive revision Subdivisions reworked, but the basic outline of the schedule is left untouched

External viewer Program used for presenting graphics, audio and movies while browsing World Wide Web pages via a Web client program. Helper applications is another term for these external programs.

Extranet An intranet that is accesible to computers that are not hysically part of a companys' own private network, but that is not accessible to the general public, for example to allow vendors and business partners to access a company web site. Often an intranet will make use of a Virtual Private Network. (VPN.)

Face-to-face Sometimes abbreviated as F2F; a term that is commonly used to desibe the traditional classroom learning environment where both the course instructor and students are in the same room.

Facilities management Department on campus responsible for buildings' condition and maintenance throughout the University.

Faculty Assistance Center A service division of ACLIS which assists faculty in classroom uses of technology, such as putting course materials on the web; using the internet for course-related communication; general training in technological literacy, etc.

Faculty council Representative body for Colorado State University faculty.

Faculty library representative A faculty member who serves as the department's contact for library matters; faculty representatives often funnel requests from their colleagues to the appropriate selector librarian, transmit library announcements to the department, and consult on major purchases and cancellations.

Fair An imited set of exemptions to copyright law. Copyright law protects authors and other owners of intellectual property so their expression of ideas cannot be copied by others without payment. Some exemptions to these protections are allowed under law for limited reproduction of texts for educational purposes.

Faostat Faostat is an on-line and multilingual databases currently containing over one million time-series records covering international statistics in the areas of production, trade, food balance sheets, fertilizer and pesticides, land use and irrigation, forest products, fishery products etc. At a time, maximum 1000 records on any topic of different combinations can be downloaded from their site free of cost.

FAQ (Frequently Asked Questions) faqs are documents that list and answer the most common questions on a particular subject. There are hundreds of faqs on subjects as diverse as Pet Grooming and Cryptography. Faqs are usually written by people who have tired of answering the same question over and over. Faqs are documents that list and answerthe most common questions on a particular subject. There are hundreds of faqs on subjects as diverse as Pet Grooming and Cryptography. Faqs are usually written by people who have tired of answering the same question over and over.

Fascicle 1. Portion of a work which, for convenience of publishing or printing, is issued in small installments. It is distinguished from a PART by being a temporary portion of a unit rather than a complete unit. 2. One of the parts of a book published in separate sections. Also called fascicule

Fascimile edition Exact replica of an edition of a book usually made either by a photochemical process or a type-facsimile.

FDDI Fiber Distributed Data Interface. An emerging standard for network technology based on fiber optics that has been established by the American National Standards Institute (ANSI). FDDI specifies a 100-million bit per second data rate.

Fetch : A program for Macintosh distributed via the OIT Software To Go web site; enables you to transfer files across the Internet to or from your desktop computer.

Ffacsimile an exact replica of a bibliographic item, both in text and physical appearance. Some of the items in Special Collections are facsimiles of rare editions.

Fiche Short for microfiche. A small sheet (4" x 6") containing microfilmed images of pages, read with a microfilm reader. Many pages of text fit onto a single fiche, and their major advantage is in saving shelf space.

Fiche Another name for microfiche.

Fiction A literary work based on imagination and not necessarily on fact. Fiction items are shelved in alphabetical order by the author's last name.

Field A particular area, as in a record in a database, in which the same type of information is regularly recorded. A field in an article database may contain the titles of articles, for example, while another field may contain the names of journals the articles are in. Some search engines allow a user to limit a search to one or more specific fields.

Field Limiter In the library catalog, and many online indexes and databases, a means of limiting a search to a particular field or fields. Imposing a field limiter on a search term(s) results in the retrieval only of those records containing the term(s) as searched within the specified field(s). Frequently called limits or limiters.

Field Searching Ability to limit a search by requiring a word or phrase to appear in a specific field of a document (e.g. Title, url, link).

File A collection of information on a disk, usually a document or a program, that's lumped together and called by one name.

File compression A method of transmitting more data bits using a modem; compression is a feature available at several different levels of MNP and with the V.42 and V.42 bis standards.

File Permissions When you place files on a UNIX system you can assign the files various levels of permission, specifying who can access them, and what type of access they can have.

File Server A computer that shares its resources, such

as printers and files, with other computers on the network. An example of this is a Novell netware Server which shares its disk space with a workstation that does not have a disk drive of its own.

File Transfer Protocol (FTP) File Transfer Protocol, the protocol used on the Internet for exchanging files. It is a very common method of moving files between two Internet sites. FTP is a way to login to another Internet site for the purposes of retrieving and/or sending files. There are many Internet sites that have established publicly accessible repositories of material that can be obtained using FTP, by logging in using the account name "anonymous", thus these sites are called "anonymous ftp servers". FTP was invented and in wide use long before the advent of the World Wide Web and originally was always used from a text-only interface. See also: Login, WWW. A method of transfering files from one computer to another. Usually, it is used to copy files from a personal computer to a server, so that they can be accessed by others. There are several common software programs that are used to transfer files (depending on which operating system your computer is running): WS_FTP, Internet Neighborhood, or Fetch. FTP is often used to download files from Internet sites, many of which allow users to log in anonymously and download public repositories of material (programs, images, text, etc.). These sites are called "anonymous ftp sites."

Fill-in form a document of a WWW page in which you can enter information

Film Recorder Used in reference to color transparency recording devices, and sometimes also to imagesetters.

Filter A piece of software that an application uses for file-format conversion or special effects. Pagemaker, for example, has a filter that lets it import Microsoft Word files, while Photoshop has dozens of filters for special effects (such as image blurring). Filters can be part of the main application or external programs called plug-ins.

Finding aid Guide,catalog, or index to non-current records. Finding aids, many computerized, are available to most of the non-classified archives held by the university archives.

Finger An Internet software tool for locating people on other Internet sites. Finger is also sometimes used to give access to non-personal information, but the most common use is to see if a person has an account at a particular Internet site. Many sites do not allow incoming Finger requests, but many do.

Firewall A mechanism that isolates a network from the rest of the Internet, permitting only specific traffic to pass in and out.

Firewire A way to connect different pieces of equipment so they can quickly and easily share information. Firewire (also referred to as IEEE1394 High Performance Serial Bus) is very similar to USB. It preceded the development of USB when it was originally created in 1995 by Apple. Firewire devices are hot pluggable, which means they can be connected and disconnected any time, even with the power on. When a new firewire device is connected to a computer, the operating system automatically detects it and prompts for the driver disk (thus the reference "plug-and play").

Firm order books Books ordered directly by a selector librarian, rather than arriving by default on an approval plan. At Marriott, funds available to selectors to purchase materials for their subjects are split into "approval" and "firm order" accounts. Any amount left over from the approval plan at the end of the fiscal year may be used for firm orders.

Firm order Order which placed for a title new to the libraries or an additional copy. "Firm" implies that the library has made a commitment to the supplier to purchase the item.

Firstsearch (OCLC) Comprehensive online remote databse offering over 70 different databases including worldcat, which has some 49 million records in over 400 languages from over 15,000 libraries worldwide.

Firstsearch A subscription service that provides access to a number of databases through a common interface. Many academic libraries subscribe to the service, though each chooses which databases it will allow users to search. Access is usually provided through the library's Web page.

Fiscal services Also known as accounting Office in administratice service which is responsible for monitoring budgets and expenditures and maintaining financial records and overseeing the Libraries shipping and receiving.

Fiscal value Utility in the conduct of financial business or fiscal accounting

Fiscal year Budget year running from July 1 to June 30. The Libraries is allotted state-appropriated funds which must be totally spent within the current fiscal year.

Fixed fields Areas within the bibliographic order, item, check-in, and patron record which contain coded information, with contents always validated by the system, are not repeatable, and with placement or order within the record; cannot be changed.

Flagging Goldenrod and pink colored flags used to identify an item with destination within main library andbranch. Also used to note an errata, detachable materials, need of repair or binding, and format.

Flame Originally, "flame" meant to carry forth in a passionate manner in the spirit of honorable debate. Flames most often involved the use of flowery language and flaming well was an art form. More recently flame has come to refer to any kind of derogatory comment no matter how witless or crude.

Flame War When an online discussion degenerates into a series of personal attacks against the debators, rather than discussion of their positions. A heated exchange.

Flaming/Flame War Reacting to someone's newsgroup

posting or e-mail in a hostile manner by publicly chastising the person or bombarding the person with nasty e-mail.

Flatbed Scanner Any scanning device that incorporates a flat transparent plate, on which original images are placed for scanning. The scanning process is linear rather than rotational.

Flexible binding temporary cardboard binding; often used for binding incomplete runs of a periodical - in hopes that the missing item(s) will be obtained, at which time the volume will be re-bound. Also called tie-bound.

Floating-point Processor A special chip that handles sophisticated calculations, such as those used in spreadsheets, CAD, and scientific programs.

Floppy disk A flexible plastic disk coated with magnetic material and covered by a protective jacket, used primarily by computers to store data magnetically. Also called diskette. Diskettes are received with some serials issues; retained at the loan desk;

Folder An area on a hard disk that contains a related set of files or alternatively, the icon that represents a directory or subdirectory.

Folio Folio are the larger of our oversized books shelved in special locations throughout the library. These items will show a location of "folio" or will have a "f" in the call number.

Font A complete assortment of letters, numbers, and symbols of a specific size and design. There are hundreds of different fonts ranging from businesslike type styles to fonts composed only of special characters such as math symbols or miniature graphics.

Format The physical form in which information appears. (bound, microfilm, microfiche, audio, video, etc.)

FPO For Position Only. A low resolution image placed in a document to indicate where the final version is to be positioned.

Fragmentation A condition where parts of a file are

stored in different locations on a disk. When a file is fragmented, the drive's read/write head has to jump from place to place to read the data; if many files are fragmented, it can slow the drive's performance.

Frame Technology introduced in Netscape 2.0 that allows Web designers to break the browser window into several smaller windows, each of which can load different HTML pages. Note: NSU's home page uses frames to create navigation bars that stay on the screen as you click through NSU pages.

Frame-grabbing System A combination of hardware and software, designed to capture individual frames from video clips for further digital manipulation, or consecutive replay on computer platforms.

Frames A feature of some web browsers that enables a page to be displayed in separate scrollable windows. Frames can be difficult to translate for text-only viewing via ADA guidelines, so their use is increasingly being discouraged.

Free Agent A client program for Windows distributed via the OIT Software To Go web site; enables you to read network newsgroups and to submit postings.

Freebies Items offered to CSUL patrons free of charge. This includes items received as gifts which are not added to the collection or items that have been withdrawn.

Freedom of Information Act (FOIA) Law enacted by Congress in 1976 that provides for public access to the records of federal executive agencies, with certain exceptions.

Free-text search(1) is a simple word or character search, usually with very few Boolean, proximity, or scope limiting options. It is simple and fast. A free-text search(2) is a search in which all the entries are freed from their original format of presentation. Text that originated in a journal article looks much the same as text that originated in a glossary or chat room. A free-text search(3) refers to the deliberate limiting of the scope of the search parameters to include only records that are available free of charge or a simple word or character search, usually with very few Boolean, proximity, or scope limiting options. It is simple and fast. A free-text search(2) is a search in which all the entries are freed from their original format of presentation. Text that originated in a journal article looks much the same as text that originated in a glossary or chat room. A free-text search(3) refers to the deliberate limiting of the scope of the search parameters to include only records that are available free of charge.

Freeware Copyrighted software available for downloading without charge; unlimited personal usage is permitted, but you cannot do anything else without express permission of the author. Contrast to shareware; copyrighted software which requires you to register and pay a small fee to the author if you decide to continue using a program you download.

French collections A collection of materials in French including the W.T. Bandy Center for Baudelaire Studies on French Poet Charles Baudelaire, the Pia Collection on French literary critic Pascal Pia, and the Sigaux Collection on Gilbert

Front office Common designation for the Administrative Office, which includes the administrative assistants to the dean.

Frontpage Microsoft's web authoring program for Macintosh and Windows. Frontpage Editor is used for page design, and frontpage Explorer is the management tool for constructing and maintaining the entire site.

FTE Full Time Equivalent. A term used for budgeting purposes to designate the number of staff allocated to each state department. One FTE is a full time professional or classified staff member working for one month. In the computation of hourly employees, one FTE is 173.4 hours worked.

FTP (File Transfer Protocol), A very common method of moving files between two Internet sites. FTP is a way to login to another Internet site for the purposes of retrieving and/or sending files. There are many Internet sites that have established publicly accessible repositories of material that can be obtained using FTP, by logging in using the account name "anonymous", thus these sites are called "anonymous ftp servers". FTP was invented and in wide use long before the advent of the World Wide Web and originally was always used from a text-only interface.

Fuel Property Database [Advanced Petroleum based Fuels] Provides key data on advanced compression ignition fuels. The database includes data on various physical; chemical; operational; and environmental, safety, and health properties. The data result from tests conducted according to standard test methods i.e. ASTM.

Fugitives A group of sixteen poets and critics who met in Nashville in the early 1920's and published "The Fugitive" from 1922 - 1925. Most members were faculty or students at Vanderbilt, including America's first Poet Laureate, Robert Penn Warren.

Full Image orfull Content Full image or full content is an exact replica of the printed page. This means that the text and any graphics or supplemental material such as tables and charts are available.

Full text database It is a collection of records containing complete versions of the original source, rather than just bibliographies, abstracts, or abridgements. An example is wilsonselectplus. A related concept is that of a full text search which searches only sources that are complete, and ignores those records that are mere abstracts or descriptors.

Full texts Complete documents from databases and Web sites. (Note: Illustrations or diagrams may be omitted from a full-text document.) Some databases run searches through full-text documents; others search only the citation or abstract. In some cases researchers can set their own preferences.

Full-time position For benefits purposes, any position in the university that is 30 or more hours per week.

Fund codes Collection managementacquisition and acoounting staff use five-character codes to identify conveniently the large number of fund accounts within the material budget. The INNOPAC Acquisitions System recognizes these codes in the Fund Field and will not accept invalid codes. Each subject area has a fund code. Subject funds are further subdivided by type.

Fuzzy And In a search, it is a method of ranking results in which documents with any terms (Boolean OR) are retrieved, but those with all terms (Boolean AND) are ranked first.

FWIW Commonly used in electronic communications, an acronym meaning "for what it's worth". Can be written in either upper- or lower case.

FWSP Federal Work Study Program; a program through which the federal government pays a portion of the student employees' salaries.

FYI an acronym meaning "for your information". Can be written in either upper- or lower case.

Gale Group A publisher of major reference serials (Contemporary Authors, Encyclopedia of Associations, Market Share Reporter, etc.), in print and online, for libraries, educational institutions, and businesses worldwide. Gale is also one of the three leading aggregators of journals in electronic format, providing online access to a range of bibliographic and full-text databases.

Galilio is (1) the name of the virtual library of Georgia. It allows library users to access dozens of periodical indexes and fulltext databases. Librarians have also created lists of World Wide Web sites that are potentially useful for academic (and other) research. You can find information on getting the password at the Circulation desk if you want to use the indexes from your home computer. (2) While Galileo is the entire statewide consortium, the term is also applied to the collection of online indexes and fulltext databases.

Galley In printing, a long narrow tray open at one end, into which assembled lines of type are transferred by the compositor from a manual composing stick, or from a typesetting machine, to await make-up into pages. Galleys were originally about 10 x 6 inches in size and made of wood, but in the early 19th century, metal trays came into use and their length was extended to about 22 inches to accommodate several pages of type. Also used as a shortened form of galley proof.

Galley proof An impression taken from type composed in long columns, arranged in trays called galleys, before it has been made up into pages, to allow the author and proofreader to inspect the text and make any corrections before the work goes to press. Although galley proofs usually do not include illustrations and indexes, reviews may be written from them. Synonymous with galleys and slip proof.

Game A set of materials designed for play according to an established set of rules, usually housed in a container to keep the pieces together. Educational games are usually stored in the curriculum room or children's room of a library. Compare with kit.

Gamma Correction The correction of tonal ranges in an image, normally by the adjustment of tone curves.

Gamut The limited range of colors provided by a specific input device, output device or pigment set.

Gang Scanning Sequential scanning of multiple originals using the same previously defined exposure setting for each.

Gap In the record representing a serial in a library catalog or union catalog, an indication that items issued are missing from the sequence held by the library. This happens when a subscription is canceled and later resumed, or when issues or volumes are lost due to damage or theft. Most libraries make an effort to fill gaps in periodical subscriptions with microfilm or microfiche if online full-text is not available. Compare with nongap break.

Garland A type of anthology containing a collection of prose extracts or short literary compositions, usually ballads or poems (example: A Little Garland of Celtic Verse published in 1905 by T. B. Mosher).

Gate count The number of times a counting device, attached to or located near the security gate at the entrance to or exit from a library, is activated during a designated period of time (day, week, or month). Gate counts provide statistical information on traffic patterns which can be helpful in establishing library hours and anticipating staffing needs.

Gatefold An illustration, map, or other insert, larger than the volume in which it is bound, which must be unfolded horizontally to the left or right to be fully viewed. Also, a method of folding a sheet of paper into three sections in which the two ends are folded toward each other over the center, like a triptych, used in advertising, performance programs, restaurant menus, etc.

Gateway A special-purpose dedicated computer that attaches to two or more disparate networks and converts data packets from one form to another.

Gathering In binding, the process of assembling and arranging in correct sequence the folded sections of a book prior to sewing them through the back fold, or before milling the clamped back folds and gluing the sections to the cover in adhesive binding. Sometimes used synonymously with signature and quire.

Gay, Lesbian, Bisexual, and Transgendered Round Table (GLBTRT) Founded in 1970 as the Task Force on Gay Liberation of the American Library Association, GLBTRT is a permanent round table that serves as an advocate for gays, lesbians, and bisexuals employed in libraries, and for the inclusion of materials on gay, lesbian, and bisexual issues in library collections. GLBTRT hosts the electronic mailing list

GLBTRT-L, sponsors annual literary awards in fiction and nonfiction, and publishes the quarterly GLBTRT Newsletter

Gaylord A library supplier that provides office and library supplies, furniture, security systems, and automation software to libraries, schools, and other educational institutions largely through its trade catalog.

Gazette A news sheet in which current events, legal notices, public appointments, etc., are recorded on a regular basis. Formerly, a journal devoted to current news. Also, a journal officially issued by a government, particularly in Great Britain. The word is derived from the name of an Italian coin that was equivalent at one point in time to the price of a news sheet.

Gazetteer A separately published dictionary of geographic names that gives the location of each entry (example: The Columbia Gazetteer of the World). Also, an of the names of the places and geographic features shown in an atlas, usually printed in a separate section following the maps, with locations indicated by page number or map number and grid coordinates. Some book-length gazetteers include basic information about major geographic features such as rivers, lakes, mountains, cities, etc. Abbreviated gaz.

GB Gigabyte. A unit of data storage size which represents 10^9 (one billion) characters of information.

GCG (Grey Component Replacement) A technique for replacing all the neutral tones of an image with an appropriate amount of black.

Genealogical table A diagram, usually in the form of an inverted tree, with branches showing the lineage of a person or group of persons who share a common ancestor, sometimes printed on the endpapers of biographical or historical works, particularly those concerning the reigns of sovereigns or the lives of titled nobility.

Genealogy The study of the descent from a common ancestor (or ancestors) of a specific individual, family, or group of persons. Genealogical research often requires the use of archival materials. Genealogical resources are increasingly available in digital form (example: US genweb Archives).

General encyclopedia An encyclopedia that provides basic information on a broad range of subjects, but treats no single subject in depth (example: Encyclopedia Americana), as distinct from a subject encyclopedia that provides greater depth of coverage within a limited scope (example: Encyclopedia of 20th Century American Humor).

General interest magazine A magazine of interest to a wide audience (example: Reader's Digest). Most public libraries make an effort to subscribe to the most popular general interest magazines, but are more selective in subscribing to special interest magazines. Compare with news magazine.

General library building Library building at 419 21st Avenue, South, housing Central Library, Special Collections, Divinity Library, and the Office of the University Librarian (Often abbreviated as GLB).

General material designation (GMD) An optional term added in square brackets to the bibliographic description of a nonbook item following the title proper to indicate type of material, for example, [videorecording]. Separate lists of general material designations are provided in AACR2 for British and North American libraries. In some categories, the British list is more general (object includes diorama, game, microscope slide, model, and realia). The Library of Congress does not to include the GMD in catalog records for manuscripts, maps, music, and text. Compare with material type.

General Technical Services Former name of the division of the library system which performed centralized technical

Generalia Works that cannot be assigned to a particular class on the basis of subject, theme, or treatment because their nonspecialized or diverse nature defies specific classification, for example, general encyclopedias and world almanacs. In library classification and bibliography, a separate category is reserved for general works, usually appearing at the beginning of the schedule or list. Synonymous with generalities.

Generation In reprography, the degree to which a copy is removed from the original document. In microfilm, the master negative developed from film taken of the original image is first-generation, print masters made from the master negative are second-generation, and service copies made from a print master for use in libraries are third-generation. Sharpness of image usually declines with each succeeding generation.

Generic searching In searching computerized catalogs or indexes, to search under broader subject headings than the most specific ones relating to one's topic, in order to retrieve more material.

Genre A type, class, or style of literature, music, film, or art. Genre criticism originated with Aristotle who divided literature into three basic categories: dramatic, epic, and lyric. In fiction, genre are based on form (novel, short story, etc.), theme (Christian, fantasy, horror, mystery, romance, science fiction, western, etc.), or format (graphic novel).

Geographic index An index in which the entries are listed by their geographic location (city, state, country, etc.). Also refers to an index that lists the geographic locations mentioned in the text of a document. Synonymous with place index.

Geographic information system (GIS) A computer-based system (hardware and software) designed to facilitate the mathematical manipulation and analysis of spatially distributed data (geographic phenomena, geologic resources, etc.), which provides an automated link between the data and its location in space, usually in relation to a system of coordinates. The data can be on any scale, from microscopic to global. A GIS differs from a map in being a digital, rather than an analog, representation. Each spatial feature is stored as a separate layer of data which can be easily altered using techniques of quantitative analysis. A map can be input or output in a **GIS**, but the output may also be one or more data sets. In the plural, the term refers to the field within the earth sciences, which is devoted to the study of computer-based systems for analyzing spatial data.

Geographic name The name most commonly used to identify a specific geographic location, feature, or area, preferred by catalogers in establishing the correct form of entry, not necessarily the same as the political name (example: France instead of Republique francaise).

Geographic subdivision In library classification, the subdivision of a class by geographic location (region, country, state, city, etc.). For example, in Library of Congress Classification the subdivision of the class P (literature) into PR (English literature), PS (American literature), etc. Also, the extension of an existing subject heading by the addition of a subheading indicating the place or geographic unit to which it applies (example: School violence—United States). In the Library of Congress subject headings list, the option to subdivide geographically is indicated by the note (May Subd Geog) or (Not Subd Geog)). Synonymous with local subdivision and place subdivision.

Geologic map A map showing the geological structure of an area. These very often have "geologic map" in the title, and the subject heading will always include "geology" and "maps" (for example, Geology—Utah—Rich County—Maps); to find them in UNIS, try a keyword search including geology and maps.

Geological survey An organization that prepares and publishes maps, charts, and other cartographic material concerning the geography of a specific nation and its territories, usually with government approval or sponsorship (example: U.S. Geological Survey). In libraries without a separate map section, publications of the USGS may be shelved in the government documents collection.

German Library Association (DBV) Founded in 1949 with headquarters in Berlin, the Deutscher Bibliotheksverband e. V. Promotes library services and professional librarianship in Germany, and publishes the journal Bibliotheksdienst.

Getcited.org getcited is an online, member-controlled academic database, directory and discussion forum. Its contents are entered and edited by members of the academic community.

Getty Thesaurus of Geographic Names (TGN) A searchable database of controlled vocabulary, containing over one million names and other details concerning places, maintained on the Internet by the Getty Research Institute in Los Angeles, California. Although the terms are not linked to maps, longitude and latitude are given in each entry, with the place name's position in a hierarchy of geographic names.

Ghost A work or edition of a work recorded in bibliographies, catalogs, or other sources, of whose actual existence there is no conclusive evidence. Synonymous with bibliographical ghost.

Ghost writer A person who writes or prepares a work for, and in the name of, another person who may be famous but is usually not a writer by profession. Autobiographies and memoirs are often written in this way. A ghost writer is normally paid for his or her services, and may or may not be listed on the title page as joint author.

GIF An acronym for Graphics Interchange Format, one of the two most commonly used file formats for storing graphic images displayed on the World Wide Web (the other being JPEG). An algorithm developed by Unisys, GIF is protected by patent, but in practice the company has not required users to obtain a license. The most recent version of GIF supports color, animation, and data compression. Pronounced jiff or giff (with a hard g).

Gift book An elaborately printed, expensively illustrated, ornately bound book of poetry or prose, usually published annually, popular as a gift item during the early part of the 19th century. Also known as a keepsake. In modern usage, a book purchased as a gift for another person (or persons). Coffee table books are often purchased for this purpose. Also spelled giftbook.

Gift One or more books or other items donated to a library, usually by an individual, but sometimes by a group, organization, estate, or other library. In academic libraries, desk copies and review copies are sometimes received as gifts from members of the teaching faculty. Donated items are usually evaluated in accordance with the library's collection development policy, and either added to the collection or disposed of, usually in a book sale or exchange with another library. Compare with donation.

Gigabyte (Gig or GB) 1024 x 1024 x 1024 (2 to the 30th power) bytes; it's usually sufficient to think of a gigabyte as approximately one billion bytes.

GIGO In computing, an initialism that stands for "garbage in, garbage out," a slang expression for the axiom that the quality of output a user receives from a computer is directly proportional to the quality of the input submitted.

GIL Is the GALILEO Interconnected Libraries system. It is our online catalog of library holdings. Since most University System of Georgia institutes have the same system, their catalogs are also called GIL.

Gilt edges In deluxe editions, gold leaf is sometimes applied to the head, tail, and/or fore-edge of each copy, then burnished to create an especially luxurious appearance. In the book trade, the abbreviation "ge" means gilt edges, "aeg" means all edges gilt, "gt" means gilt top, and "teg" means top edge gilt. Left unburnished, a gilt edge is called antique.

GISTNIC The information available on database includes banking statistics, industrial statistics, public finance, social sector statistics, census data etc.

Given name One or more names chosen for a person, usually by the parents at birth or christening (example:

Emily), sometimes the same as that of a living relative or ancestor, but distinct from the surname identifying members of the same family (example: Dickinson). Given names can be compound (example: Marie-Louise). Compare with first name.

Glair An adhesive preparation made from egg whites, used in edge gilding and tooling to permanently fix silver and gold leaf. Glair is usually purchased dry as albumen and mixed with water or vinegar prior to use. It melts with the application of heat and sets up quickly as soon as the hot finishing tool is removed, securing the leaf firmly to the surface. Also spelled glaire.

Glassine A type of thin, dense, translucent glazed paper sometimes used to protect the covers of new books. Also used for panels in window-envelopes and as wrapping material because it is resistant to the passage of air, water, grease, etc.

Glitch A malfunction in the hardware of a computer system, usually temporary or random, sometimes difficult to distinguish from a bug in the software. In a more general sense, any unanticipated problem that brings a process to a halt. Also spelled glytch.

Global Statistics Globall Statistics deals with statistics on the human population. The main kind of data you can find here is on the population of regions, countries, provinces and cities. Next to that there are some statistics on economic factors like wealth, infrastructure, etc.

Globe A representation of the surface of the earth, or of another celestial body, on a relatively permanent spherical object. A globe is usually more accurate than a map because it is free of the distortion inherent in a two-dimensional representation of a three-dimensional object. Globes are made of heavy paper, papier-mache, cardboard, plastic, metal, or glass, mounted on a full- or half-meridian axel, in a free cradle, or with gyroscopic support. Expensive models may be illuminated and/or animated for special effect. In the United States, the most common sizes are 12 inches and 16 inches in diameter.

Gloss In old manuscripts, an explanation, definition, or interpretation of a word or phrase, sometimes in a more familiar language, written on a margin, above the line of text to which it refers, or in a special appendix called a glossary, compiled by a person known as a glossator, glossographer, or glossarist. In modern printing, a note on the left- or right-hand margin is called a side note and is usually set in a type size smaller than that of the text to which it refers. Compare with interlinear matter.

Gloss ink Printing ink that appears shiny even when dry because it contains a higher than normal proportion of varnish, used mainly in display work.

Glossarial index An index at the end of a book (or set of books) that includes in each entry a definition or description of the term indexed, as well as the page number(s) referenced.

Glossary - An alphabetical list of words, limited to a special area of knowledge, with their definitions. What you are viewing now is a glossary of library terms.

Glossy A finish in which the surface of paper or board is given a smooth, shiny coat of varnish to enhance the appearance of visual material (illustrations, posters, etc.). Most magazines are printed on glossy paper to attract readership, as are dust jackets to heighten the sales appeal of new books. In publishing, the term also refers to a photograph printed on smooth, shiny paper, the format preferred by printers in reproduction work.

Glue A type of adhesive made from protein derived from the collagen in animal by-products (bone, hooves, hides, etc.) Boiled to form a brownish gelatin that can be thinned with water. Most glues are not suitable for use in binding because they become brittle with age. Compare with paste.

Gluing off In bookbinding, the application of adhesive to the binding edge of a book, after the sections have been sewn and before the steps called rounding and backing. The adhesive is forced between the sections to help hold them together. Compare with pasting down.

Glyphic In printing, a typeface derived from a carved or chiseled form, rather than from a calligraphic hand.

Gmelin A massive compendium of data on inorganic compounds; the full title is Gmelins Handbuch der Anorganischen Chemie, call number QD151.G521.

Gnawed A book that shows signs of having been chewed by an animal on at least one edge or corner, a condition that reduces its value considerably in the used book market, and makes it a candidate for weeding in libraries.

Goal In strategic planning, a general direction or aim that an organization commits iself to attaining, in order to further its mission. Goals are usually expressed in abstract terms, with no time-limit for realization. The specific means by which they are to be attained is also left open. Compare with objective.

Goatskin Leather made from the skin of a goat, used extensively in hand bookbinding. Older books bound in fine-quality goatskin, known in the antiquarian book trade as morocco, can be very valuable. The names of the various types of goatskin reflect their place of origin (Levant, Niger, etc.).

Gold foil An inexpensive substitute for gold leaf, made by spraying a thin deposit of gold or a look-alike substitute onto an adhesive backing, used extensively to decorate edition bindings and library bindings, and also in hand-binding when economy is desired. Syonymous with blocking foil.

Gold leaf Gold beaten by hand or mechanical means into very thin sheets, used in bookbinding to embellish lettering, tooling, and the edges of the sections. The gold leaf used in bookbinding is sold in sheets 3 1/2 inch square, made from an alloy of 23 carat gold, and 1 carat silver and copper, beaten to a thinness of 1/200,000-1/250,000 of an inch. Silver is used less often for the same purpose. Compare with gold foil.

Gone to press A term used in printing to indicate that the process of preparing the final plates for a work has commenced. Subsequent changes or corrections must be added as errata after printing is completed. In newspaper publishing, the corresponding term is gone to bed.

Good (G) - an obviously worn book in which all the pages or leaves are present; defects must be noted.

Gopher Before the World Wide Web was developed, files and resources available on the Internet were accessed by means of a hierarchical menu system installed on a Gopher server (named after the mascot of the University of Minnesota where the software was developed). Although they have fallen into disuse since the introduction of graphical Web browsers, Gopher servers have two advantages over Web search engines: they list Internet resources of all types (FTP files, Usenet newsgroups, etc.), not just Web sites, and they present resources in a logical hierarchy of directories created by a human being, rather than relying on an automated Web crawler ("spider") to locate information. The tools developed for searching Gopher file directories are named Veronica and Jughead. Gopher addresses begin with the prefix gopher://..

Gopher server Information on a gopher server is organized into a hierarchy of menus that become more specific as the levels descend. Usage has declined recently due to the superiority of the hypertext-based interface used for World Wide Web sites. Also refers to the Internet protocol that enables users to search for files via menus or directory structures.

Gopherspace A term that describes the collection of files accessible through gopher servers.

Gothic A style of dark, angular script executed with a broad-nib pen, widely used as a book hand in northern Europe during the late medieval period and adapted as a typeface in early printed books, particularly Bibles and other devotional works. Also refers to any modern typeface resembling gothic script, characterized by compressed letterforms, broad main strokes, fine hair strokes, regular verticals, uniform counters, diagonal couplings, and a lack of curves. The first book printed in Europe from movable type (the Gutenberg Bible) was set in gothic type. Synonymous with black letter and lettre de forme. Compare with roman and white letter.

Gothic novel Originally, a type of novel in which a medieval castle formed the setting for a plot with chillingly sinister overtones, intended to evoke irrational fear in the heart of the reader. Horace Walpole's Castle of Otranto, A Gothic Story (1764) established this genre. In modern usage, a subgenre of romance fiction, popular during the 18th and early 19th centuries, in which the setting is dark and gloomy, the action grotesque or violent, the characters strange or malevolent, the plot mysterious, and the mood often one of decadence or degeneration (example: Wuthering Heights by Emily Bronte). Synonymous with roman noir.

Gouge A nick or hole made accidentally in the cover or spine of a book. Also refers to a finishing tool used in bookbinding to make curved lines on a book cover.

Governance The arrangements by which the faculty and administration of an academic institution control and direct institutional affairs (bylaws, elective offices, committees, etc.). In some academic libraries, participation in governance may be a factor in tenure and promotion decisions affecting librarians who have faculty status.

Government agency A unit of government authorized by law or regulation to perform a specific function, for example, the U.S. Government Printing Office (GPO) authorized to collect, publish, and distribute government documents to the American public. Each agency of the U.S. federal government normally maintains its own records, which may or may not be publicly accessible depending on whether its activities are exempted from public disclosure under the Freedom of Information Act (FOIA).

Government archives A government agency authorized by legislation to provide centralized archival services for all, or a portion of, the agencies or units that administer a country's government (legislative, executive, and judicial). For the federal government of the United States, that agency is the National Archives and Records Administration (NARA). Each of the 50 U.S. state governments maintains its own state archives, sometimes as a unit of the state library.

Government Document A publication produced by a government agency. These items are often shelved separately and are arranged by an identification number assigned by the issuing agency. Go to the Government Documents home page.

Government Document or Publication Any document issued by, under the authority of, or at the expense of a recognized government. Government documents include publications from states, the federal government, and transnational or international organizations such as the United Nations.

Government documents or resources Are resources produced by the U.S. government. They may be books, periodicals, CD-roms, videos, maps or posters. Books and pamphlets are shelved by Superintendent of Documents classification number on the first floor. Periodicals are shelved in title order behind the regular government documents stacks. Other resources are shelved in special cabinets in the Government Documents area of the library. Videos are shelved in the Audiovisual room on the second floor of the library.

Government library A library maintained by a unit of government at the local, state, or federal level, containing collections for the use of its staff. Some government libraries have a wider mandate that includes accessibility to the general public (example: Smithsonian Libraries & Archives). Government librarians are organized in the Government

Documents Round Table (GODORT) of the American Library Association.

Government Publications Provide all types of information ranging from broad, general information to focused, contemporary information. Materials may be published by governmental agencies including local, state, and national governments.

GPO Access A service of the U.S. Government Printing Office that provides free electronic access to over 1,500 databases of government information, including the Federal Register, Code of Federal Regulations, and Congressional Record. GPO Access is funded by the Federal Depository Library Program under the Government Printing Electronic Information Enhancement Act of 1993 (Public Law 103-40).

Grace period A designated period of time following the due date during which a borrower may renew an overdue item or return it to the library without incurring a fine. To encourage the return of long overdue materials, some libraries also set aside one day (or several days) each year during which overdue items may be returned without penalty. Not all libraries provide a grace period. Synonymous with amnesty period and fine-free period.

Graduate library The academic library at a university that maintains separate collections (and usually facilities) for undergraduates and graduate students, containing the major research collections, staffed and equipped to meet the information needs of graduate students and faculty.

Grain In a sheet of machine-made paper or board, the direction in which most of the fibers lie, determined by forward movement of the papermaking machine in manufacture. Books are printed with the grain parallel to the spine because paper bends more readily with the grain than against it. One way to determine the grain in a sheet of paper is to do a tear test—paper tears more cleanly with the grain than across it. There is little or no grain in a sheet of handmade paper. Woven material used as covering material in bookbinding also has grain—as a general rule, the warp threads run parallel to the spine. Grain in leather depends on the direction in which the hairs lay before removal, indicated by tiny puncture marks on the surface.

Grangerized An edition into which illustrations, letters, and/or other matter is inserted after publication. The practice began in 1769, when James Granger (1723-1776) published A Biographical History of England containing blank leaves for the insertion of portrait engravings after printing. Synonymous with privately illustrated.

Grant Funds received from a private foundation (example: Council on Library and Information Resources) or government sponsored organization (example: National Endowment for the Humanities) by an individual, group, or institution, in support of a worthy project or cause. In most cases, the recipient must compete for such funds by submitting a proposal. The art of obtaining grants is called grantsmanship. Guides for proposal writing are available in academic libraries and large public libraries. Information on funding sources can be found in the Annual Register of Grant Support published by R. R. Bowker and The Foundation Directory published annually by The Foundation Center.

Granthalaya Granthalaya is an Indian software package for libraries developed by INSDOC in India. It is based on MS DOS but is now available in UNIX and LAN versions also.

Grant-in-aid Funds received by a library or library system from a state or federal government agency in support of regular operations, or a special project or program, as opposed to funds derived from the community or district served. In most cases, the library must apply in a competitive process by submitting a proposal (example: certain LSTA funds).

Grantsmanship The art of successfully obtaining and administering grants and grants-in-aid, including the ability to recognize when an idea is fundable, locate funding sources, research the information necessary to fill out the application, establish a realistic timetable, write the proposal, and manage the grant process once funding is approved. When grant funding is a high priority, a college or university usually employs a trained and experienced grants administrator to help teaching faculty and librarians negotiate the process.

Granularity The level of descriptive detail in a record created to represent a document or information resource for the purpose of retrieval, for example, whether the record structure in a bibliographic database allows the author's name to be parsed into given name and surname.

Graph A diagram that shows 1) quantity in relation to a whole (pie graph), 2) the distribution of separate values of a variable in relation to another (scatter graph), or 3) change in the value of a variable in relation to another, for example, the change in the average price of a journal subscription over time (coordinate graph, histogram, etc.).

Graphic Any two-dimensional nontextual, still representation. Graphics can be opaque (illustrations, photographs, diagrams, maps, charts, graphs, etc.) Or designed to be viewed or projected with the aid of optical equipment (slides, filmstrips, etc.). Magazines and art books usually contain a high proportion of graphic material. The graphic design of the dust jacket is important in marketing new books. Computer graphics are created with the aid of graphic design software.

Graphic novel A term coined by Will Eisner to describe his semi-autobiographical novel A Contract with God (1978), written and illustrated in comic book style, the first work in a new genre that presents an extended narrative as a continuous sequence of pictorial images printed in color and arranged in panel-to-panel format, with dialogue enclosed in balloons. A precursor can be found in the picture story albums of the 19th century Swiss writer Rodolphe Topffer, who also wrote novels in conventional form. This new literary form is viewed with suspicion by traditionalists who regard it as a marketing ploy aimed at attracting adult readers to comic books by removing the stigma attached to them.

Graphical user interface (GUI) A computer interface that allows the user to provide input and receive output interactively by manipulating menu bars, icons, and movable, resizable windows by means of a keyboard or pointing device such as a mouse. Guis are used in Web browsers and in most word processing, spreadsheet, and graphics applications. The quality of a GUI depends on its functionality and usability. Pronounced "gooey." Synonymous with graphic user interface and WIMPS.

Graticule A grid composed of horizontal and vertical lines printed over an image, such as a map, to assist the viewer in locating specific features. In an atlas, the grids are usually keyed to a gazetteer of place names giving page number and grid coordinates for each entry.

Gray literature Printed works such as reports, internal documents, phd dissertations, master's theses, and conference proceedings, not usually available through regular market channels because they were never commercially published, listed, or priced. Alternative methods of supply and bibliographic control have evolved in response to the need of libraries to preserve and provide access to such material. In the United States, the gray literature of science and technology is indexed in the NTIS database. Theses and dissertations are indexed and abstracted in Dissertation Abstracts International and are available in hard copy via Dissertation Express. Also spelled grey literature. Compare with ephemera.

Gray scale Variations in the density of black, arranged in sequence (usually from 10% to 90%) for use in printing and film developing.

Greatest Hits List A listing of hypertext links that represents the most frequently used resources in the Library Gateway. The Greatest Hits list can be accessed from the Find Databases page.

Green paper A printed document issued in green paper covers by a ministry or department of the British government to elicit public comment and debate on a proposed new policy (or change in an existing one). The practice began in 1967. Compare with white paper.

Greenaway Medal A literary award presented annually since 1956 by the Library Association (UK) to the artist judged to have produced the most distinguished work in the illustration of children's books published in the United Kingdom during the preceding calendar year. Compare with Carnegie Medal.

Greenaway Plan A form of blanket order plan in which a large library or library system agrees to receive from a publisher for a nominal price one advance copy of all the trade books it publishes, to encourage acquisitions librarians to order selected titles in advance of publication. The publisher relies on the probability that enough titles will be ordered in multiple copies to cover its costs. The plan is named after Emerson Greenaway, the librarian at the Philadelphia Free Library who conceived the idea in 1958.

Grey Balance The balance between CMY colorants required to produce neutral greys without a color cast.

Grey Levels Discrete tonal steps in a continuous tone image, inherent to digital data. Most CT images will contain 256 grey levels per color.

Grey literature See: gray literature.

Greyscale A continuous tone image comprising black, white, and grey data only.

Grid Two sets of parallel lines intersecting at right angles, usually at regular intervals, which when superimposed on a map or other two-dimensional surface, can be used to locate specific points by means of coordinates, usually a sequence of numbers or letters printed across the top and/or bottom margin, with a second sequence along one or both sides. A pattern of squares used to locate specific points or items on a sheet; in libraries, used in reference to microfiche and maps.

Grievance In the workplace, a formal complaint concerning a specific action or policy, set of circumstances, or persistent condition, addressed by an employee or group of employees to management, to a special committee established to hear grievances, or to some other appropriate authority, to protest its unfairness and request a remedy. Most organizations have an established procedure for filing grievances and negotiating their settlement. In library employment governed by collective bargaining agreement, the grievance procedure and conditions under which it applies may be explicitly stated in the contract.

Groupware Computer software designed to support more than one user connected to a LAN, usually colleagues working together on related tasks whose offices are not in the same location. Although groupware is an evolving concept, most products include a messaging system, document sharing and management software, a calendaring and scheduling system for coordinating meetings and tracking the progress of group projects, electronic conferencing, and an electronic newsletter (example: Lotus Notes).

Guard A flexible strip of cloth or strong paper inserted along the inner margin between two leaves prior to sewing the sections of a book, used to mount a plate or insert too stiff to turn like a normal page. Synonymous in this sense with hinge. Also, a strip of paper or other material added to reinforce a signature in a book.

GUI (pronounced "gooey") graphical user interface; a program in which the user executes commands, selects files, etc. By using a mouse or other pointer device to select items (such as program icons, commands in a drop-down menu or options in a dialog box) rather than by typing in text commands.

Guide Information provided by a library, usually in the

form of a printed handout or leaflet, that 1) explains how to use a library service (online catalog, interlibrary loan, etc.); 2) describes important resources on a subject (World War II), in a discipline (history), or of a specific form (periodical articles, government documents, biography, etc.); or 3) explains how to accomplish something (compile an annotated bibliography, cite sources in a particular bibliographical style, etc.).

Guidebook A handbook that provides useful current information for travellers to a city, state, region, country, or other geographic area, or for visitors to a museum, park, historical site, etc.

Guillemets French quotation marks printed << like this >>, also seen in some German texts. Synonymous with duck-foot quotes.

Guillotine A power-driven or hand-operated machine with a long, sharp-edged blade, used in binding to cut and trim large numbers of flat or folded sheets to the desired dimensions.

Gutenberg Bible The earliest known book to have been produced from movable type, probably printed between 1450 and 1455 at Mainz, Germany by Johann Gutenberg and his associate Peter Schoffer, with the financial assistance of a merchant named Johann Fust. Also known as the Mazarin Bible because a copy was found by a French bookseller in the private library of the bibliophile Cardinal Mazarin (1602-1661) one hundred years after his death. It is a Latin bible printed in black ink in gothic type set in two 42-line columns per page. Of approximately 180 copies printed, only forty-eight copies are known to have survived, which makes them very rare and valuable. Twelve are printed on vellum and thirty-six on paper. The British Library owns two copies, and the Bibliotheque nationale de France one. In the United States, there are thirteen copies, one each at the Library of Congress, the New York Public Library, the Huntington Library in California, and libraries at Harvard, Princeton, and

Yale. The Pierpont Morgan Library in New York City owns three copies.

Gutenberg,Johann, C. 1399-1468 A goldsmith by trade, Johann Gensfleisch zum Gutenberg is credited with the invention printing from movable type, probably at Mainz in Germany. His first printed work was a 42-line Bible set in gothic type probably printed no later than 1456. Uncertainty regarding Gutenberg's accomplishment arises from the lack of recorded information about his life and the fact that no extant work bears his name, nor have any of his presses survived. The printing press spread rapidly to the Netherlands, Italy, France, and England, becoming well-established in Europe by the 1480's. The Gutenberg Museum was established in Mainz in 1900 as a center for the study of Gutenberg's life and work, and early history of typography.

Gutter press Tabloid newspapers and magazines that publish salacious gossip, usually of a personal nature concerning the lives of prominent people. Synonymous with yellow press.

Gutter The blank space formed by the inner margins of facing pages in an open book, from the binding edge to the area that bears printed matter. The width of the gutter is an important factor in determining whether a book can be rebound.

Gutting The practice, abhorred by publishers, of reviewing a book, not by critically evaluating its strengths and/or weaknesses, but by revealing the main lines of its plot, ruining the experience of first-time readers. Also refers to the practice in publishing of carefully quoting out of context, in the blurb on the dust jacket and in advertising, only the most complimentary passages from reviews which, in their entirety, expressed mixed or even negative opinions of the work.

H. W. Wilson A commercial company that began publishing reference serials for libraries and researchers (especially periodical indexes) long before library finding tools were automated. Most of its publications are now available on CD-ROM and online. Some of its bibliographic databases include full-text

Hachure A series of short lines drawn or printed on a land map to indicate gradient: long thin, widely-spaced lines indicating a moderate grade and short, thick, closely-spaced lines a steep grade, with direction of slope indicated by direction of line. Hachuring is common on maps produced by the National Geographic Society and the U.S. Forest Service.

Hacker Slang term for a technically sophisticated computer user who enjoys exploring computer systems and programs, sometimes to the point of obsession.

Hagiography A form of biography, widespread during the Middle Ages and Renaissance, in which the life described is that of a saint. Also refers to a book containing such writing, often a collective biography covering the lives of two or more saints. An author who writes about the lives (and legends) of saints is a hagiographer.

Half cloth A book bound in a cloth spine and paper-covered boards. Synonymous with half linen.

Half leather A book with spine and corners covered in leather and the rest of the binding in paper or cloth. Compare with quarter leather.

Half uncial The stage in the development of Latin calligraphic letterforms at which cursive characteristics and ligatures were added to the uncial style, and ascenders and descenders introduced. A transitional phase on the path to Roman minuscules, half-uncial script was used as a book hand in Europe from the 7th to the 9th century. Synonymous with semi-uncial.

Half-binding A style of bookbinding in which the spine and corners are covered in a different material than the sides, usually selected for greater durability. Compare with full binding, quarter binding, and three-quarter binding.

Half-title The title of a book as printed, in full or in brief, on the recto of a leaf preceding the title page, usually in a smaller size of the font used to print the title on the title page. In books published in series, the series title page often appears on the verso of the leaf bearing the half-title.

Halftone Art made ready for printing by photographing the image through the fine, diagonally crossed lines of a screen made of glass or film, converting it into a field of tiny graded dots that reproduce by optical illusion the tonal values of the original. Halftone screens range from 50-200 rulings per inch. The finer the screen, the greater the range of tonal values. Printing papers with a smooth finish require a finer screen than coarse papers. Also refers to a print made by this process. Also spelled half-tone. Compare with **line art.**

Halo A light line around object edges in an image, produced by the USM (sharpening) technique.

Handbill A small notice or advertisement printed on a single unfolded sheet, intended for distribution by hand, but also used as a poster.

Hand-binding The art and craft of binding books by hand without the aid of mechanization. Medieval manuscripts and early printed books were hand-bound in wooden boards covered in leather. Today, trade editions are case bound and hand-binding is limited to fine books.

Handbook Intended for ready consultation or reference, a handbook (or manual) either compiles facts about a subject or provides instructions of methods or procedures for how to perform a specific set of functions.

Handle Unique character string identifier assigned to each entry in the NIC WHOIS database.

Handout A printed sheet, or group of sheets, usually stapled together at one corner, intended for distribution during an oral presentation or instruction session to give the attendees a record of content covered (summary, outline, hard copy of powerpoint slides, etc.) Or provide supplementary or complementary information (supporting data, examples, suggestions for further reading, contact information, etc.).

Handshaking The process computers and modems go through in order to establish a connection and agree on the speed and protocols for data transmission.

Hands-on A library instruction session or one-on-one reference transaction in which the student or patron has the opportunity to practice, usually at a computer workstation, research techniques demonstrated by the instructor or reference librarian.

Hang Having a computer freeze during a session so that it does not respond to user input, usually with no indication of the probable cause. Downloading a very large data file can create the appearance of a hang-up. Closing the application or rebooting will usually get the system unstuck, but unsaved data will be lost in the process.

Hanging indention A form of indention in which the opening line is flush with the left-hand margin and subsequent lines are indented one or more spaces. Used in typed and printed catalog cards and in some styles of bibliographic entry. Hanging indention is used for the terms and definitions in this online dictionary.

Hard copy Data printed on paper, in human-readable form, usually by a computer. Compare with soft copy, which is an image on a computer screen.

Hard disk A magnetic medium capable of storing a large quantity of data, which resides permanently within a computer, as opposed to a portable disk (floppy, Zip, etc.) That can be inserted in a disk drive by the user whenever a data file needs to be opened or saved, and removed once the operation is completed. In microcomputers, the hard disk is usually the **c:/** drive. In networked systems, users may also have access to a portion of the hard drive on a shared server.

Hardcover A book bound in an inflexible board case or cover, usually covered in cloth, paper, plastic, leather, or some other durable material, as distinct from a book bound in a cover made of flexible material. In modern publishing, a new trade title is usually issued first in hardcover, then in a paperback edition after sales in hardcover decline. Synonymous with cloth bound, hardback, and hard bound. Compare with softcover.

Hardware Mechanical, electrical, electronic, or other physical equipment and machinery associated with a computer system, or necessary for the playback or projection of nonprint media. Basic microcomputer hardware includes a central processing unit (CPU), keyboard, and monitor. The techencyclopedia describes the distinction between hardware and software as the difference between "storage and transmission" and "logic and language."

Hardwired A term that originally referred to a computer device containing unalterable circuitry designed to perform a specific task, as opposed to circuits that are programmable or controlled by a switch. However, the meaning has broadened to include constants built into computer software. Synonymous in this sense with hard-coded. In a more general sense, hardware or software that cannot be modified.

Hashmark The symbol # used to represent the word "number" in lists and street addresses, in touch-tone telephone systems that allow the caller to key input, in Web addresses (urls) to create a link to another location in the same document, etc. Abbreviated hash.

Hayes Compatible A modem is considered Hayes Compatible if it supports the Hayes command set (a language used to communicate with and control a modem).

Hazordous Chemical Database This database will allow the user to retrieve information for any of 3995 hazardous chemicals or 'generic' entries based on a keyword search. Potential keywords include names, formula and registry numbers (CAS, DOT, RTECS and EPA).

Head The top edge of a book. Also refers to the margin

at the top of a page, as opposed to the margin at the tail or foot of the page. Also, a word or phrase used as a brief headline in a book or periodical.

Headband In bookbinding, a band of woven cotton or silk, sometimes colored or multi-colored, glued or sewn to the back of a book at the head, to protect the end of the bound sections and take the strain off the covering material at the top of the spine when the volume is pulled from the shelf. The corresponding band at the lower end of the spine is called the tailband. Collectively, the headband and tailband are known as endbands.

Headcap The thickened edge at the upper end of the spine of a leather-bound book, created by inserting a piece of cord inside the turned-in end of the covering material after the text block has been attached to the cover. The same edge at the lower end of the spine is called the tailcap. Compare with headband.

Header The portion of a packet, preceding the actual data, containing source and destination addresses, error checking and other fields. A header is also the part of an electronic mail message that precedes the body of a message and contains, among other things, the message originator, date and time.

Heading The name of a person, corporate body, or geographic location; the title proper of a work; or an authorized content descriptor (subject heading), used as an access point in a catalog or index. In library cataloging, form headings are also used. In AACR2, form of entry is subject to authority control.

Headings List A button in the library catalog that, when clicked, returns the user to the list of headings (author or subject) that were retrieved by a search.

Headline A few words printed in large display type across the top of the front page of a newspaper to give prominence to the most important news story of the day, or above the text of one of the other articles in the newspaper to give the reader a sense of its content. Headlines are carefully worded to capture the reader's interest.

Headnote A brief explanatory note printed at the beginning of a chapter, short story, poem, or other work, to serve as a preface.

Headpiece A decoration printed in the blank space at the beginning of a chapter or other division of a book, usually a printer's ornament or a small illustration done by a professional illustrator. Also spelled head-piece. Synonymous with headband and head ornament. Compare with tailpiece.

Headword A word or phrase used as a main entry in a dictionary or encyclopedia, usually printed in boldface or some other distinctive type at the beginning of a definition or other entry. In most dictionaries, headwords are arranged in a single alphabetical sequence. In classified reference works, headwords may be listed alphabetically within each section, usually with a subject or keyword index to the entire work at the end of the last volume.

Hearings Publications of the U.S. federal government containing the transcripts of testimony given before Congressional committees and subcommittees, usually available in the government documents section of a library. Congressional hearings are also available online via GPO Access. Not all hearings are published by the U.S. Government Printing Office. In a more general sense, the printed transcript of testimony given before any government committee or executive body authorized to hold investigative or fact-finding proceedings.

Height The dimension of a book or other bound item from head to tail, usually greater than its width, the exception being volumes square or oblong in shape. In the library cataloging, the height of a book is given in centimeters in the physical description area of the bibliographic description. In many libraries, books over a certain height are labeled oversize and shelved in a separate section. Also refers to the vertical dimension of a unit of single- or double-faced shelving. Most commercially-made library shelving is sold in units 42, 60, 72, or 84 inches high.

Helmke Library Homepage Find us on the Web at http://www.lib.ipfw.edu/.

Help Desk an ACLIS service desk providing assistance to users of the campus modems, e-mail, web and other ACLIS services. The Help Desk is located at 464

Help line A telephone number that a person may call to receive assistance of a certain kind, for example, instructions or advice on how to use a specific type of computer hardware or software. Some help lines are more helpful than others.

Help screen The screen or sequence of screens in an online catalog, bibliographic database, or other application program, providing instructions to users who need assistance in learning how to use the system. In well-designed software, the help screens are context-sensitive. Compare with wizard.

Helper application: A program used for viewing multimedia files that your web browser cannot handle internally; files using a helper application must be moved to your computer before being shown or played. Contrast to a plug-in which enables you to view the file over the Internet without first downloading it.

Her Majesty's Stationery Office (HMSO) The government agency in the United Kingdom responsible for printing official government publications, and for regulating and licensing the use of all information produced by the government, the British equivalent of the U.S. Government Printing Office. Click here to connect to the homepage of the HMSO.

Hermeneutics The study of the art and science of interpretation and understanding, as opposed to the practice of exposition. The term originally applied to Biblical exegesis, but was subsequently extended to secular texts. In the 19th century, literary theorists recognized the paradox that understanding a work as a whole requires knowledge of its parts, but understanding the parts presupposes at least some knowledge of the whole. In the 20th century, as objectivity gave way to subjectivity in literary theory, interpretation was found to be rooted in culture and history, turning the meaning of a text into the history of its interpretations.

Heuristic From the Greek word heuriskein meaning "to discover." A course of action or method of problem-solving in which progress toward the best possible outcome or solution is continuously evaluated through trial and error. Both positive and negative results are incorporated as feedback into the discovery process, allowing procedure to be adjusted as the best next step is determined. Library research is usually a heuristic process.

Hickie Printer's slang for an unintended spot or defect on a printed page, usually caused by a speck of dust, lint, or dried ink on the printing plate or negative. Also spelled hickey.

Hierarchic relation A semantic relation between two terms in which the concept represented by one is a subclass of the concept represented by the other (example: Library books / Books).

Hierarchical classification A classification system in which the classes are subdivided on the principle of logical subordination, from the most general subjects to the most specific. Hierarchical classification can be broad or close.. Synonymous with analytic classification. Compare with enumerative classification and synthetic classification.

Hierarchical force In classification systems based on logical subordination, such as Dewey Decimal Classification, the basic principle that the attributes of a class (example: periodical) identified in the heading assigned to represent it and in certain explanatory notes, apply to all its subdivisions (examples: newspaper, magazine, journal) and to all other classes to which reference is made in the notes.

Hierarchical/Topical Search Engines These organize

indexed Web pages by topics, subtopics, etc. You can use this type of search engine to follow hyperlinks (or "mouse walk") through subject menus until you reach the level of specificity needed. Yahoo is an example of this type of search engine.

Hierarchy The arrangement of classes in a classification system, from the most general to the most specific. In a classification schedule, hierarchy is usually indicated by indention, as in the following example from Dewey Decimal Classification:

Hieroglyphics From the Greek hieros ("sacred" or "powerful") and glyphikos ("carving"). A writing system in which pictures or symbols, rather than letters of a phonetic alphabet, are used to represent words, syllables, and sounds. The ancient Egyptians wrote in hieroglyphs that were not deciphered until the discovery of the Rosetta Stone in 1799. Also refers to a form of written expression that is difficult to read or understand.

Hieronym A surname based on a sacred name (example: Perse Saint John).

High fidelity Any method of sound recording that minimizes distortion by reproducing such a wide range of audible frequencies that the result is very faithful to the original.

High Key A light image that is intentionally lacking in shadow detail.

Highlight To use a broad-tipped pen to mark in light-colored ink a section of text in a book or document, usually for future reference. College textbooks donated to libraries are often heavily highlighted. In a similar fashion, the "edit" option in some computer applications allows the user to mark in a shaded or contrasting background portions of electronic text to be cut or copied. In a more general sense, to give prominence to the part of a whole that is the most outstanding, interesting, pertinent, useful, etc.

Highlighting Words, phrases, or passages of text marked in a book with a broad-tipped, brightly colored pen for future study. The presence of highlighting diminishes the value of a book for resale, particularly for collectors. As a general rule, donated materials containing highlighting are added to a library collection only in exceptional cases. Compare with underlining.

High-risk collection An archival or library collection for which the likelihood of vandalism or theft is higher than normal due to its exceptional value (rare books) or unusual content (special collections). Tighter security precautions are taken, especially when such items are placed on exhibit.

Highsmith Inc. Company in the business of providing equipment, supplies, and furnishings to libraries and schools, marketed through its trade catalog.

High-speed In computing, equipment that functions at a higher than normal speed, usually purchased at a premium. Also refers to a fast Internet connection (compare T3 with T1).

Hinge A narrow strip of muslin or paper, attached with adhesive along the line dividing the two halves of an endpaper to reinforce the flexible joint along which the body of a book is attached to the cover. In volumes lacking this reinforcement, the hinge is formed by adhering the covering material (leather, cloth, paper, etc.) Directly to the fold in the endpaper.

Histogram A graph representing quantitative data in a series of vertical or horizontal bars or lines drawn from a base line. The position of each bar (or line) along the base indicates the class or value of one variable, with the length of the bar (or line) indicating the corresponding value of a second variable. A third variable can be added if the bars are displayed in groups and distinguished graphically, by color, shading, etc. Synonymous with bar graph.

Historiated border An ornamental band around a miniature or portion of text on the page of an illuminated manuscript, decorated with figures of animals and/or human beings, sometimes in a scene illustrating the accompanying text.

Historiated initial An initial letter in an illuminated manuscript, decorated with animal and/or human figures. Sometimes in a scene that illustrates the accompanying text. Compare with figure initial and inhabited initial.

Historical atlas A book of maps showing the progressive changes that have occurred over a given period of time in a geographic area or in the development of a spatial phenomenon (example: Historical Atlas of United States Congressional Districts, 1789-1983).

Historical bibliography The branch of bibliography devoted to the study of the history and methods of book production, including hand-copying, illustration, publishing, printing, papermaking, binding, and preservation. Historical bibliography has merged with the field of book history.

Historical fiction A narrative in the form of a novel, set in a specific period of history or based on an event or sequence of events that actually happened. The characters may be completely fictional, but if they are known to have existed, their feelings, words, and actions are reconstructed and to some degree imagined by the author. The presence of dialogue in an historical work is usually a clue that the account is fictionalized. Sir Walter Scott established the genre in 1814 with the publication of Waverly, a novel of life in the Scottish borderlands, followed by several more historical romances, including Ivanhoe (1819). Compare with nonfiction.

Historical society A nonprofit organization devoted to preserving the historical record of a state or municipality (example: Oregon), place (Martha's Vineyard), institution (U.S. Supreme Court), people (Huguenots), activity (Seafaring), or thing (Pipe organs). Well-established historical societies often support a public museum, maintain an archive or library for the use of members, and may publish books and other materials related to their sphere of interest.

Historical value Capacity to document past events,

providing information about the lives and activities of persons involved in them

History note A brief note in an entry in a thesaurus of indexing terms, giving the date the descriptor was added to the list of preferred terms, and indicating any changes that have occurred in its meaning, scope, relationships to other terms, etc.

Hit In information retrieval, a record retrieved from a database that matches the information need expressed in the query. The term is sometimes used loosely to refer to a record that satisfies the syntactic requirements of the query without necessarily meeting its semantic requirements (a false drop), but this is an imprecise use of the term. Hit rate is the percentage of all the records retrieved in a search that are relevant to the query.

HMSO See: Her Majesty's Stationery Office.

Hold When a book or other item is currently on loan, the library permits another borrower to place a "hold" on it by contacting the circulation desk. The patron who has the item checked out will not be permitted to renew it, and the person placing the "hold" will be entitled to check it out after it has been returned. The CU Library online catalog includes a feature that allows the user to place an item on hold without staff assistance. This service is available through the requests link at the top of any online catalog record.

Holdings display In a union catalog, a list of all the libraries and other participating institutions that own a specific item. In the OCLC worldcat database, the three-letter OCLC symbols attached to the bibliographic record for an item, representing the institutions that own at least one copy, used in interlibrary loan to generate lender strings.

Holdings note A note added to the catalog record for an item in a library collection, indicating the copies, volumes, issues, or parts held by the library or library system in an open or closed entry, usually with information concerning the location of the item. For serials, separate notes may be provided for print and microform holdings. Compare with numeric and/or alphabetic, chronological, or other designation area.

Holdings rate The percentage of items requested by the users of a library that are in its collections. In most libraries, items not held locally may be borrowed on interlibrary loan (ILL) or obtained via document delivery service (DDS).

Holdings the exact items a library owns. The term is most typically used to refer to the specific issues of a magazine or journal in a library. This information is often listed in a library's catalog as a holdings statement.

Hollow back A type of binding in which the cover is not glued to the back of a book, leaving an open space that allows the binding to flex easily when the volume is opened, without cracking the spine. Most hardcover trade editions are bound with a hollow back. Synonymous with loose-back and open back. Compare with tight back.

Hollow The open space between the cover and the back of a book in which the sections are not glued directly to the cover. A hollow back allows a book to open flat and stay open without damaging the spine.

Holograph A document written entirely in the handwriting of the person (or persons) to whom it is attributed. A holographic reprint is a reproduction of such a document, made by mechanical means. Also refers to a three-dimensional image of an object recorded on photosensitive film by the pattern of interference made by a split laser beam, in a process called holography.

Homepage The first or main page of a site on the World Wide Web, displayed whenever a user logs on to a Web browser and opens the site address (URL). The filename at the end of a homepage address is often home.html, index.html, main.html, or something similar. A well-designed homepage gives the title of the site, name of author, host, date of last update, notice of copyright, table of contents, and links to subpages providing more detailed information about the site, usually the best starting point when navigating the site for the first time. Also spelled home page.

Homework center A space set aside in a public library, usually with established hours and assigned staff trained to provide clearly defined services to students in need of assistance with their homework assignments.

Homily A sermon that explains a point in the Christian Bible, usually accompanied by instructions for the congregation hearing it. In a more general sense, any tendentious, moralizing speech or lecture.

Homograph A word spelled the same as one or more other words, but different in meaning and sometimes in origin, for example, current (ocean) and current (up-to-date), but not currant (the fruit). Every effort is made to avoid homographs in indexing, but when necessary, a parenthetical qualifier is added to the heading, as in the Library of Congress Subject Heading Mice (Computers). Compare with homonym and homophone.

Homonym A word pronounced the same as one or more other words, but different in meaning and origin (and usually in spelling), for example, plate (illustration) and plait (braid or pleat). The word "plate" is also a homograph: plate (food dish). Synonymous with homophone. Compare with synonym.

Homophone A word pronounced the same as one or more others, which has a different spelling, meaning, and derivation (toad, toed, and towed). Synonymous with homonym.

Honorific title A formal title conferred on a person by a recognized authority as a mark of honor, rank, nobility, or royalty (example: Cardinal Richelieu). In AACR2, an honorific title is included in a personal name heading only when commonly used in referring to the person. In such cases, the title follows the personal name and precedes the birth and death dates (Newton, Isaac, Sir, 1642-1727).

Horizon a Web-based, graphical-interface library catalog system which will be used by all academic institutions in Utah except BYU; Marriott's catalog will move to a Horizon system in March 1999.

Horn book A type of child's primer used in England and America from the 15th to the 18th century, consisting of a sheet of parchment or paper bearing the letters of the alphabet, usually the first ten numerals, basic spelling rules, the Lord's Prayer, and sometimes a hand-colored illustration, protected by a thin, transparent sheet of cattle horn, mounted on an oblong bat of wood or leather with a projecting handle by which it could be fastened to a child's girdle. Its paddle shape suggests that it may have been used in playing the game shuttlecock. The term is used in the title of Horn Book Magazine, a review publication devoted to children's literature. Also spelled hornbook.

Horn Book Magazine Published since 1924, Horn Book Magazine provides articles, author interviews, editorials, columns, and lengthy reviews of children's books in each bimonthly issue. The title is derived from the name of an educational toy, called a horn book, used by young children from about the 15th to the 18th century.

Horror A subgenre of gothic fiction in which supernatural events, macabre effects, and obsessive introspection are combined with chilling suspense to produce in the reader a sensation of fear and revulsion. Early literary examples are Mary Shelley's novel Frankenstein (1818), the short story "The Fall of the House of Usher" (1839) by Edgar Allan Poe, and Dracula (1897) by Bram Stoker. In motion pictures, the earliest examples are The Cabinet of Dr. Caligari (1919) directed by Robert Wiene and Nosferatu (1922) by F. W. Murnau, two classics of German expressionism. More recent examples include Alfred Hitchcock's Psycho (1960) and episodes of Rod Serling's television series The Twilight Zone. Compare with thriller.

Hors texte A French phrase meaning "outside the text,"

referring to illustrations not printed with the text, such as plates. They are usually numbered in roman numerals to distinguish them from illustrations printed with the text, which are numbered in arabic numerals or referenced by page number.

Hospital library A medical library maintained within the walls of a hospital, containing a collection of print and online resources on medicine and allied health, to serve the information and research needs of doctors, nurses, patients, and staff, usually managed by a medical librarian.

Hospitality In classification, the property that allows new classes to be added to a system of notation as needed, without requiring the alteration of previously established schedules.

Host A computer that serves as a source of data for other terminals or computers, for example, a central computer providing files to terminals connected directly to it, or a network server accessed by client machines. Also refers to the organization or institution that provides the server on which a Web site is installed, usually indicated in its Internet address.

Host organization The organization in which a special library functions as an administrative unit, for example, a museum that maintains a library on its premises for the use of curators, researchers, and members, or a corporation that maintains a library for the use of employees in their work.

Hostname Name which officially identifies each computer attached to the Internet.

Hot spot An icon of any size, or portion of a larger image displayed on a computer screen, that functions as a live link to another file or document available on the same or a different server. When it is clicked with a pointing device such as a mouse, a coded instruction is executed to retrieve and display the linked material. Also refers to the precise pixels within a clickable icon or image which are sensitive to selection by the user.

Hotlist A file containing lists of Internet Web pages, enabling you to easily access your favorite Web pages.

Hot-melt A tough, flexible chemical adhesive used in commercial bookbinding. Solid at room temperatures, hot-melt adhesive liquifies under high heat. In perfect binding, it is applied to the binding edge of a book in a single shot at temperatures of 135-175 degrees C. Unlike the adhesives used in sewn bindings which take time to dry, hot-melt adhesive sets up in seconds as it cools, significantly reducing production costs. Unfortunately, it has a clamping effect which reduces openability, and it is not resistant to cold-crack which makes it unsuitable for bindings marketed in countries where winter temperatures are severe. Also spelled hotmelt.

Hours The times during a day, week, and year that a library is open to its users, usually posted near the front entrance and available by phone or via the library's Web site, including any days the library is not open, usually holidays. A library's hours are determined by the needs of its users and by budgetary constraints. Also refers to the times during which a specific service is available from a library, which may be shorter (or longer) than the hours the facility is open.

House organ A periodical issued by a commercial or industrial organization for distribution internally to its employees and/or externally to its customers, not intended for wider publication. Synonymous with house journal. Compare with trade journal.

House style The uniform standards of a publisher, printer, company, or organization with reference to writing style (grammar, syntax, usage, punctuation, etc.) And presentation (spelling, abbreviation, uppercase/lowercase, citation format, etc.) To be followed, in the absence of contrary instructions, in publications issued in its name, usually explained in a style sheet.

Housekeeping Routine chores that must be performed methodically in a library to maintain manual or automated systems in good order, usually delegated to a trained assistant, for example, the task of checking in serial parts in a timely manner to make them available to users and identify missing issues that need to to be claimed.

How-to publication A book, pamphlet, or videocassette that provides practical information and advice about how to accomplish a task, acquire a skill, or achieve a desired result, usually in the form of step-by-step instructions accompanied by diagrams (example: home improvement and auto repair manuals). How-to titles are available in public libraries, shelved by call number in the nonfiction section. Compare with self-help publication.

HP Hewlett Packard.

HTML A collection of platform-independent styles (indicated by markup tags) that define the various components of World Wide Web document. The tags of electronic text indicate how the text should be displayed on screen by Web browsers.

HTTP (Hypertext Transfer Protocol) - The communication standards or protocol used by browsers and servers to move HTML documents across the Web.

Human resources A collective term for all the people employed by a company, agency, organization, or institution. Also, the administrative department responsible for matters pertaining to employment (hiring, evaluation, promotion, termination, etc.). Large independent libraries and library systems usually have their own human resources office. Libraries that function as a unit within a larger organization may rely on the parent organization for such services. Synonymous with personnel.

Humanistic script In 15th century Europe, the renaissance of interest in classical art and culture had a profound effect on calligraphy, producing a script that abandoned many characteristics of gothic letterforms and embraced some of features of the earlier Carolingian script, but in a more compressed form. Appearing concurrently with the invention of movable type, scrittura umanistica was quickly adapted by type founders, particularly the lowercase letters which are very close to the forms used in modern printing. According to Warren Chappell in A Short History of the Printed Word (1970), chancery script, from which italic developed, was a direct descendant of scrittura umanistica.

Humidity The amount of water vapor held in air. Absolute humidity is the weight (mass) of water vapor in a given volume of air, usually expressed as grams of water per cubic meter of air. Relative humidity is the ratio of the amount of water vapor present in a given volume of air to the amount required to reach saturation (condensation into droplets) at the same temperature, expressed as a percentage. Relative humidity varies with temperature and air pressure—warm air can hold more water vapor than cooler air. Forty percent relative humidity is considered ideal for permanent storage of library and archival materials made from paper. Mold can become a serious problem when relative humidity exceeds 70%.

Huntington Library Located in San Marino, California, the Huntington Library is one of the world's leading libraries of Americana and English literature, surpassed only by the British Library and the Bodleian. Its collections include over five million manuscripts, rare books, reference works, and other materials on Anglo-American history, literature and the arts, the history of science, and maritime history. The library includes a conservation center, exhibition hall, art collection, and botanical gardens.

Hybrid journal A periodical that functions as both a magazine and a journal by including features typical of both. A prime example is Analytical Chemistry published by the American Chemical Society, which includes a magazine section in the front of each issue, followed by a longer section of research articles with its own table of contents and separate pagination.

Hybrid learning: A course environment that combines

elements of both online and face-to-face instruction; also may be referred to a "blended learning."

Hydrologic map A map showing the drainage of surface waters (streams, rivers, etc.) And other features related to hydrology in a geographic area (lakes, reservoirs, glaciers, ground water, springs, wetlands, water quality, etc.).

Hygrometer Any one of several meteorological instruments designed to measure atmospheric humidity. Hygrometers are used to monitor conditions in facilities such as libraries and museums that house materials easily damaged by water vapor (rare books, manuscripts, specimens, film, etc.).

Hype An abbreviation of hyperbole. Publisher's slang for advertising copy written in an exaggerated style to attract attention to a new publication, not intended to be taken literally by prospective customers. Objective reviews are the best antidote. Compare with puff.

Hyperlink Highlighted term or image within the hypertext of a WWW page. When you click on it, it connects or "links" to other information about that term.

Hypermedia A hypertext document in which text is combined with graphics, audio, animation, and/or full-motion video (example: National Geographic Channel).

Hypertext The basic concept behind the WWW, whereby one resource can be linked to other relevant information elsewhere on the WWW. The user can view information non-sequentially; the idea is that the information is available in much the way that humans think - by association rather than linear sequence.

Hyphen In printing, the shortest rule used as punctuation. Also used to join the parts of a compound name (Jean-Pierre) or compound word (dog-eared), and to divide a long word at the end of a line of written or printed text. Compare with dash.

Hyphenation Use of the hyphen to divide a word (co-opt), to compound two or more words (son-in-law), to give the impression of stuttering or faltering speech (n-n-no), or to indicate that a word is to be spelled out (h-y-p-h-e-n-a-t-e).

Hyponym A word or phrase that can be replaced without exception by another, without changing the meaning of a sentence, but not vice versa, for example, azure by blue or sparrow by bird.

I.e. An abbreviation of the Latin phrase id est meaning "that is."

I-beam The blinking vertical line that shows the point at which text or graphics will be inserted.

Ibid.: abbreviation for Latin ibidem, "in the same place." Used in references and citations to refer to the last work cited, saving re-typing the author and title. EXAMPLE: 1. Wessel, Janet A. Fitness for the Modern Teenager. New York. The Ronald Press, 1963. P.70. 2. Ibid., p.87.

IBM International Business Machines Corporation.

Icon A small graphic element or symbol displayed on a computer screen, which the user can select with a pointing device such as a mouse to summon a menu of options, access a data file, or initiate a process or operation in an application program that uses a graphical user interface, for example, a small image of a trash can or recycle bin to which unwanted documents can be moved for disposal.

Iconic document A publication or other document in which the content is presented in predominantly graphic or pictorial form. Examples include atlases, children's picture books, exhibit catalogs, visual dictionaries, posters, postcards, etc.

Iconography The art of illustration or representation by means of pictures, figures, or images, developed to a high degree in the artistic tradition of the Eastern Orthodox faith. Also refers to the study of the pictorial representation of objects or people, in portraits, paintings, photographs, sculpture, coins, etc., and to the result of such study, especially when it takes the form of detailed lists of representations.

ID card Plastic card issued to all University faculty, staff, and students used for various University activities including charge-out of Library materials. Information on the card is utilized by the Libraries' computerized circulation system.

Ideal copy In analytical bibliography, a detailed description of the most perfect copy of the first impression of an edition, based on close inspection of as many copies as possible, to which all other copies of the same impression, and any subsequent impressions, are compared in determining issue and state (adapted from The ALA Glossary of Library and Information Science).

Identifier A keyword or indexable concept assigned to a document to add depth to subject indexing, not listed in the thesaurus of indexing terms because it either represents a proper name (geographic name, personal name, test or program name, piece of legislation, etc.) Or a concept not yet approved as an authorized descriptor. Identifiers are usually listed in a separate field of the index entry or bibliographic record, immediately following the descriptors. Major identifiers may be marked with an asterisk or distinguished in some other manner. Form of entry may be subject to authority control. In some indexing systems, identifiers are periodically reviewed for suitability as new descriptors. Not all indexing systems use identifiers. Compare with provisional term.

Ideogram A picture or symbol that represents an object or idea without expressing phonetically the sounds of its name, for example, the characters used in Chinese and Japanese writing systems. Also refers to a symbol that represents an idea, for example, the equal sign = or the plus sign +. Synonymous with ideograph. Compare with phonogram.

Idiom A well-known expression that has a different

meaning than the literal interpretation of its words (example: **holy terror**). Idioms are sometimes coined from the lexicon of a particular occupation or pastime (example: Monday morning quarterback). Because idioms are specific to a given language, they can be difficult to translate. Dictionaries of idioms are usually shelved in the reference section of a library.

Idyll A narrative poem based on a romantic, epic, or tragic theme, for example, Idylls of the King (1859) by Alfred, Lord Tennyson, an episodic retelling of the fables of the Holy Grail, Camelot, Round Table, and Morte d'Arthur. Compare with idyl.

IEE Often called "I double E." The Institution of Electrical Engineers, the major British professional society for electrical engineers. IEE produces the INSPEC database as well as a number of journals.

IEEE Often called "I triple E." The Institute of Electrical and Electronics Engineers, the major American professional society for electrical engineers as well as computer engineers. IEEE publishes a large number of journals, magazines and conference proceedings; Marriott Library subscribes to essentially all of them. Their conferences change names constantly and are best found in UNIS with a keyword search.

Iformation and Reference (INFOREF) Group within reference services responsible for 1) providing maximum access to information 2) location assistance in the book stacks, 3) service at the branch libraries, 4) help with assisteive technology, 5) the evaluation of effective function and improvement of public service desks: reference desk,electronic information centre, Journal/Microtext Assistance Desk and 6) development of aids to research including electronic and print guides.

III PAC WEB/PAC A subcommittee of Sage coordinstion group responsible for recommendations concerning all aspects of public displays on the ASCII and WEB version of the online catalog, SAGE.

ILA Indian Library Association. It is the largest body of librarians and information professionals of India with its headquarters in New Delhi.

ILL COURIER A contracted agent not employed by CSU is responsible for delivering materials to/from CSUL and other libraries in the state of Colorado. CSU is part of the High Plains Courier system; High Plains works with other courier systems to ensure a statewide delivery network.

Illiad This is the name of the University Library's Interlibrary Loan (ILL) software.

Illuminate To decorate an initial letter or word in a manuscript with designs or tracings in bright colors and gold or silver, or to decorate a border or an entire page with initial letters, hand-painted miniatures, and/or colorful designs highlighted in gold or silver, techniques commonly used in medieval manuscripts and incunabula. An artist who decorates books by hand is an illuminator..

Illuminated From the Latin luminaire meaning "to give light." A manuscript or incunabulum richly decorated by hand with ornamental polychrome letters, designs, and/or illustrations highlighted in gold or silver. Illumination flourished during the medieval period when books were hand-copied on parchment and vellum, mainly by Catholic monks who produced books for devotional use and for exchange with other monasteries (example: Book of Kells).

Illuminated initial An initial letter in a illuminated manuscript decorated in bright colors and highlighted in gold or silver. Compare with rubric.

Illustrator An artist who creates drawings, paintings, or designs to elucidate or embellish the text of a book or other printed publication. The illustrator of a children's picture book may receive higher honors than the author of the text. In AACR2, when illustration is added to the text of a work, main entry is made under the heading appropriate to the text, with an added entry for the illustrator if appropriate. However, if the work is the result of a collaboration between author and illustrator, main entry is under the person named first on the chief source of information unless greater prominence is given to the other by typography or some other means.

Imagemap an image in a Web browser in which different areas act as hyperlinks. Images can be found in UNIS under "Landsat." Marriott's collection is of Utah only, taken in the 1970's and 1980's. Most are in room 457B (ask at Science Reference desk); a few are computer tapes for mainframes and stored separately (ask at General Reference desk). Letter-by-letter alphabetization: alphabetization sequence which ignores the spaces between words. Compare with word-by-word alphabetization. Letter-by-letter word-by-word thermal copying thermal copying thermally processed thermal plastic film thermal plastic film thermally processed

Imagesetter A device used to record digital data (images and text) onto monochrome film or offset litho printing plates by means of a single or multiple intermittent light beams. Color separated data is recorded as a series of slightly overlapping spots to produce either solid areas of line-art or halftone dots for printing continuous tones.

IMAP (Internet Message Access Protocol), IMAP is gradually replacing POP as the main protocol used by email clients in communicating with email servers. Using IMAP an email client program can not only retrieve email but can also manipulate message stored on the server, without having to actually retrieve the messages. So messages can be deleted, have their status changed, multiple mail boxes can be managed, etc.IMAP is defined in RFC 2060

Imbrication In the book arts, a decorative pattern designed to give the impression of overlapping scales, tiles, shingles, leaves, etc.

IMHO (In My Humble Opinion) A shorthand appended to a comment written in an online forum, IMHO indicates that the writer is aware that they areexpressing a debatable view, probably on a subject already under discussion. One of many such shorthands in common use online, especially in discussion forums.

Imitation binding A contemporary binding executed in a style intended to closely resemble that of an earlier period.

Impensis Latin for "at the expense of," a word appearing in an imprint or colophon at the end of a work printed prior to the end of the 17th century, followed by the name of the person or entity responsible for financing the publication, usually the publisher, or a bookseller or patron.

Imperfect Said of a book discovered upon examination to have pages or sections missing, duplicated, or bound out of order or upside-down. The publisher will usually exchange or perfect copies containing binding errors, and reimburse the purchaser for shipping costs. Compare with imperfections.

Imperfections Printed sheets rejected in the binding process because they contain defects or errors that require replacement sheets.

Import A publication produced and issued in one country and brought into another for sale in the same unaltered form. The name of the importer may be printed on the title page in addition to, or in place of, the original publisher, or indicated on a label added to the title page after printing. Compare with co-publishing.

Impression All the copies of a book or other publication printed in the same press run from the same setting of type or plates. An edition may comprise several impressions in which the typesetting remains unchanged. Compare with reprint.

Imprimatur A Latin phrase meaning "let it be printed." The license for publication granted by an ecclesiastical or secular authority, usually printed on the verso of the title page of a book, indicating the name of the licenser and the date on which it was granted. Found most often in books printed during the 16th and 17th centuries, imprimatur is still used in the doctrinal publications of the Roman Catholic Church to indicate official approval (example: New Catholic Encyclopedia). See also: cum privilegio and nihil obstat.

Imprint The statement in a book that identifies the publisher and/or printer. The publisher's imprint consists of the official name of the publishing company and the date and place of publication. It usually appears at the foot of the title page, and more completely on the verso of the title page. The printer's imprint, indicating the name of the printing company and the place of printing, usually appears on the verso of the title page, at the foot of the last page of text, or on the page following the text. Synonymous with biblio.

In sheets A book in flat or folded unbound sheets, before the sections have been gathered. Synonymous with in quires.

In stock An item for which a publisher, dealer, jobber, distributor, or bookseller has a sufficient number of copies in inventory to fill an order at the time it is placed. Compare with out of stock and temporarily out of stock.

Inactive records Records no longer required by an agency or individual in the daily conduct of business or affairs, which may be placed in intermediate storage, transferred to archival custody, destroyed, or disposed of in some other way without affecting normal operations. The opposite of active records. Synonymous with nonactive records.

Inactive serial Serial title that has either ceased publication, suspended publication until further notice, been canceled, or cannot be activated through claims or correspondence.

Inactive Window A window that is open but is not the top window.

INC Incomplete. Used on certain library records such as for items bound together incompletely; to indicate missing issues.

Incipit Latin for "here begins," a word used to indicate the point at which the text commences in a medieval manuscript or incunabulum that lacks a title page, usually written or printed in majuscules or in a distinguishing color, often including the name of the author and the title of the work. Compare with explicit and colophon.

Incunabula A Works printed in Europe from movable type between 1454-1501. Located in university archives.

Incunabula From the Latin word cunae meaning "cradle." Books, pamphlets, calendars, and indulgences printed in Europe from movable type prior to 1500 during the earliest years (infancy) of printing. A prime example is the Gutenberg Bible believed to have been printed in Mainz before 1456 , Germany by Johann Gutenberg who is credited with the invention of printing from movable metal type. Singular: incunabulum. Synonymous with cradle books and incunables.

Indent To set back a line of type or column of figures by one or more spaces from a margin, to mark or distinguish it from preceding and succeeding lines or columns, as at the beginning of a new paragraph. Indention is heavily used in outlines and subject thesauri to indicate logical arrangement and semantic hierarchy. It is also used in typed and printed catalog cards to designate specific areas of bibliographic description.

Indention A space between the margin on a page and the beginning of a line of type, as at the beginning of a paragraph of text. The points listed in an outline are usually indented to indicate the logical structure of the content covered. Indention is also used in subject thesauri to indicate semantic relations, and in typed and printed catalog cards to designate specific areas of bibliographic description. Compare with full measure.

Independent Publisher A trade publication, formerly titled Small Press, that provides articles, announcements of new books, excerpts, and over 100 reviews of small press publications in each bimonthly issue. Independent Publisher is known for reviewing works not reviewed elsewhere.

Index A list of citations to journal articles and/or books arranged by subject, author, or title; indexes may be in print format, electronic format, or both. Also, a list of subjects covered in a book, usually published at the end of the book.

Index Librorum Prohibitorum An "Index of Forbidden Books" prepared in 1558 at the request of Pope Paul IV by a special "Congregation of the Inquisition." Published in 1559, the list included works which Catholic laypersons were prohibited from owning or reading because ecclesiastical authorities considered them to be detrimental to faith and morals, usually because they contained teachings condemned as heretical. Also known as the Index Expurgatorius, the list was not abolished by the Vatican until 1966.

Index map A map showing the complete extent of the geographic coverage of a set or series of more detailed maps, with or without segmentation. Compare with map index.

Indexable matter The parts of a book or other publication included when the document is analyzed for indexing, not necessarily limited to the text. Notes, appendices, and other complementary or supplementary material may or may not be indexed, depending on its usefulness to potential readers, and the policy of the publisher. Bibliographies and glossaries are rarely indexed.

Indexes that require them.

Indexing language An artificial language consisting of subject headings or content descriptors selected to facilitate information retrieval by serving as access points in a catalog or index, including any lead-in vocabulary and rules governing form of entry, syntax, etc.

Indexing The process of compiling one or more indexes for a single publication, such as a monograph or multi-volume reference work, or adding entries for new documents to an open-end index covering a particular publication format (example: newspapers), works of a specific literary form (biography, book reviews, etc.), or the literature of an academic field, discipline, or group of disciplines.

Indian District Database Indian district database provides district-level data from census and agricultural sources between 1961 and 1991.

Indicative abstract An abstract that describes the type and form of the work abstracted, indicating the main topics covered and providing a brief description of the treatment, but which does not summarize the content or evaluate quality. Compare with critical abstract and informative abstract.

Indicator One of two single-character positions following the tag at the beginning of a field in a MARC record (except fields 001 to 009) which can be used to specify certain conditions for the field. The positions nearly always contain a digit from 0-9, although alphabetic characters are permitted. The first indicator may be field dependent, for example, in the physical description (field 300), it can be set to supply the text label Descript in the catalog display. The second indicator may specify the number of characters to be ignored in filing or sorting the field, for example, 2 for "a," 3 for "an," or 4 for "the" at the beginning of a title. In some fields, the first or second position is used; in others, both or neither. When one of the positions is not used, the indicator is undefined and the position is left blank. In some fields, the absence of a character in one of the indicator positions has a specific meaning.

INDMED Index to Indian biomedical lournals ICMR-NIC Centre for Biomedical Information (Indian MEDLARS Centre) has designed and developed a bibliographic database from Indian biomedical literature. To start with 75 prominent Indian journals, have been selected to build up the database entitled indmed. The coverage of database is from 1985.

Inedita The plural of the Latin word ineditum meaning

"not made known," literary works not published, for example, the personal papers of a writer or well-known person. Works of this kind are usually available in the special collections of the library that purchased them or received them as a gift.

Infolibrarian.com is a group of professionals working in the area of library and computer fields. Its objective is to give maximum information to working library and information science professionals, teachers and students at one place by collecting information from different sources and giving brief description, wherever possible.

Infonation infonation is an easy-to-use, two-step database that allows you to view and compare the most up-to-date statistical data for the Member States of the United Nations.

Infopath Internet gopher for the University of California at San Diego.

Informatics The formal study of information, including its structure, properties, uses, and functions in society, in particular the technology used to record, organize, store, retrieve, and disseminate it. For a discussion of the history and current state of informatics, please see the entry by A. E. Cawkell in the International Encyclopedia of Information and Library Science (1997).

Information and Library Network (INFLIBNET) Information and Library Network (INFLIBNET) is regarded as a landmark in the information scenario of higher education. It is the brainchild of Prof. Yashpal, an eminent scientist and the former Chairman of the University Grants Commission. Incepted in the year 1988, INFLIBNET became operational in 1991 and got the status of an autonomous body in 1996. INFLIBNET is now an Inter-University Centre of the University Grants Commission (UGC) of India. It is a major National Programme initiated by the UGC with its Head Quarters at Gujarat University Campus, Ahmedabad. Initially started as a project under the IUCAA, INFLIBNET is involved in modernizing university libraries in India and connecting them as well as information centres in the country through a nation-wide high speed data network using the state-of-art technologies for the optimum utilisation of information. INFLIBNET is set out to be a major player in promoting scholarly communication among academicians and researchers in India.

Information and referral (I&R) A service available at no charge, usually from a public library or other public service agency, providing contact information about other organizations, agencies, and individuals qualified to offer specific information and services, both free and fee-based, usually within a local community.

Information broker A self-employed professional, skilled in information retrieval and delivery, who markets his or her research services commercially, usually on a freelance basis. Information brokers are organized in the Association of Independent Information Professionals (AIIP).

Information commons An area in the Lied library which provides access to information electronically through microcomputer workstations. The Info Commons is located on the first floor of the Lied library adjacent to R & I 1. Patrons are able to access numerous databases, both indices and fulltext, navigate the Internet, and use selected software for their research papers.

Information Data presented in readily comprehensible form, to which meaning has been attributed within a context for its use. In a more dynamic sense, the message conveyed by the use of a medium of communication or expression. Whether a specific message is informative or not depends in part on the subjective perception of the person receiving it.

Information desk A desk in a large public or academic library, usually located near the main entrance, staffed by a nonprofessional trained to screen questions, provide basic information about library services and collections, and direct users to the reference desk or some other public service point, when further assistance is needed. The presence of an information desk reduces the number of directional questions received by reference librarians, freeing them to focus on the needs of patrons who require professional services.

Information ethics The branch of ethics that focuses on the relationship between the creation, organization, dissemination, and use of information, and the ethical standards and moral codes governing human conduct in society. In the United States, the ALA Code of Ethics is the leading statement of ethical standards for the library profession. Compare with information law.

Information industry A broad term covering all the companies and individuals in the business of providing information and access to information for a profit, including the mass media, commercial publishers, software and database producers and vendors, indexing and abstracting services, and freelance information brokers. Public libraries, academic libraries, and many types of special libraries function outside the information industry because they operate on a nonprofit basis. Because the industry encompasses such a wide range of commercial enterprises, it has no single trade journal.

Information law The regulation and control of information by the state, including laws concerning censorship, copyright and intellectual property, forgery, freedom of information, intellectual freedom, privacy, computer crime, and public funding of information providers, such as libraries and museums. Also refers to a specialized branch of legal studies dealing with the regulation of information..

Information literacy Skill in finding the information one needs, including an understanding of how libraries are organized, familiarity with the resources they provide (including information formats and automated search tools), and knowledge of commonly used research techniques. The concept also includes the skills required to critcally evaluate information content, and an understanding of the technological infrastructure on which information transmission is based, including its social, political, and cultural context and impact. Compare with computer literacy.

Information management The skillful exercise of control over the acquisition, organization, storage, security, retrieval, and dissemination of the information resources essential to the successful operation of a business, agency, organization, or institution, including documentation, records management, and technical infrastructure. For a detailed discussion of information management as a field, please see the entry by T. D. Wilson in the International Encyclopedia of Information and Library Science (1997).

Information need A gap in a person's knowledge which, when experienced at the conscious level as a question, gives rise to a search for an answer. If the need is urgent, the search may be pursued with diligence until the desire is fulfilled. Persons with information needs often end up at the reference desk of a library where it is the responsibility of the reference librarian to determine the precise nature of the need, usually by conducting an informal reference interview, as a basis for recommending relevant sources. In order to to search the online catalog or bibliographic databases, the need must be expressed in the form of a query.

Information overload A condition in which too much information is available on a topic, a common occurrence in online searching, particularly when the query is expressed in terms that are too broad. Systems that facilitate the retrieval of high-quality resources, sifting out the chaff, are badly needed. In the meantime, consumers of information must develop their own analytical and critical skills.

Information policy A governing prrnciple, plan, or course of action concerning information resources and technology, adopted by a company, organization, institution, or government, for example, the political decision to use public funds to subsidize Internet access for schools and public libraries. In the United States, Congress and the President are advised by the National Commission on Library and Information Science (NCLIS) on decisions concerning national library and information policy. For a detailed discussion of information policy, please see the entry by Charles Oppenheim and Noreen macmorrow in the International Encyclopedia of Information and Library Science (1997).

Information retrieval (IR) The process, methods, and procedures used to selectively recall recorded information from a file of data. In libraries and archives, searches are typically for a known item or for information on a specific subject, and the file is usually a human-readable catalog or index, or a computer-based information storage and retrieval system, such as an online catalog or bibliographic database. In the design of such systems, a balance must be attained between speed, accuracy, cost, and effectiveness.

Information Science Abstracts (ISA) An indexing and abstracting service established in 1966 that provides abstracts of books, conference proceedings, and articles from over 450 journals and trade publications in information science, ISA covers abstracting and indexing, bibliometrics, cataloging, classification, electronic publishing, information management, the information industry, Internet search engines, and online information retrieval. Published nine times per year in print by Information Today Inc., ISA provides author and subject indexes in the last issue of each annual volume. The service is also available online from DIALOG.

Information science The systematic study and analysis of the sources, development, collection, organization, dissemination, evaluation, use, and management of information in all its forms, including the channels (formal and informal) and technology used in its communication. Compare with informatics and library science.

Information storage and retrieval (ISAR) Operations performed by the hardware and software used in indexing and storing a file of records, whenever a user queries the system for information relevant to a specific topic. For records to be retrieved, the search statement must be expressed in syntax that is executable by the computer.

Information technology (IT) A very broad term encompassing all aspects of the management and processing of information by computer, including the hardware and software required to access it.

Information theory The systematic statement of principles concerning the phenomenon of information and its transmission, based on the collection and analysis of quantitative and qualitative data as a means of testing hypotheses about its nature and properties. Compare with informatics.

Informational value Usefulness for reference and research

Informative abstract An abstract that summarizes as much of the essential content of a work as possible, within the limitations of a single paragraph. Compare with critical abstract and indicative abstract.

Infornet It is a networking project of the University Grants Commission of India. Indian Universities constitute one of the largest higher education systems in the world. With 325 universities/institutions, 15000 affiliated colleges, 100.00 lakh students and 4.27 lakh teachers; it is a great challenge to ensure effective coordination and communication. Fast changing curricula and frequent introducing of new subjects impose a great demand on the system in general. Indian Universities need to be given the required thrust to entire the third millennium with a leading edge. Technology is a driving force in the contemporary education systems. University Grant Commission has launched an ambitious programme to bring about a qualitative change in the academic infrastructure, especially for higher education.

Under this initiative UGC is modernizing the University Campuses with State-of-the-art campus wide networks and setting up its own nationwide communication network named UGC-Infonet.

Infotrieve Online Article Finder Gives access to bibliographic details with abstract on Science and technology. The data coverage is from 1966 to present from over 30000 journals.

Infrastructure A collective term borrowed from military parlance, encompassing all the components that support a particular activity, especially the permanent systems and structures that constitute its foundation. In modern information technology, all the hardware and software developed and maintained to keep a communication system (large or small) operating smoothly. The state of a society's infrastructure represents its commitment to investing in the future.

Infringement The use without permission of material protected by copyright or patent, in a manner reserved under law to the holder of rights in the work. Such use may be subject to legal action at the discretion of the copyright owner.

Ingenta.com Ingenta.com offers access to article summaries from over 25,000 publications linked to the full text of over 5,200 titles. Full text access is set by each of our 170 publisher partners, but typically individual subscribers, or individuals within institutions that subscribe, can access the full text of their publications for free. Non-subscribers can, for the majority of articles, pay-per-view choosing from electronic, fax or Ariel delivery.

Ingram A wholesaler of trade books, books-on-tape, and periodicals to libraries, booksellers, and specialty retailers, Ingram passes on economies of scale to its customers in the form of a substantial discount off the list price.

Inhabited initial An initial letter in an illuminated

manuscript containing within its contours decorative figures of human, animal, or imaginary beings, not necessarily related to the content of the text, often depicted fancifully. Compare with figure initial and historiated initial..

Inherent vice A weakness in the chemical or physical composition of a document or other object that causes it to deteriorate from within over time, for example, acid in the lignin contained in papers made from untreated wood pulp, or the chemical instability of cellulose nitrate film. If conservation measures fail, preservation of the item may require reformatting.

In-house archives The unit within a company, agency, or institution responsible for retaining the noncurrent records of the parent organization, and sometimes those of other corporate bodies and individuals with which it is closely associated, as opposed to an outside repository.

In-house building Bound by the preservation lab as opposed to being bound by a commercial binder.

In-house use The number of times an item is used within the walls of a library during a given period of time (usually a month or year), as opposed to the number of times it is checked out. In-house use is tracked by counting the number of times an item is left lying on a table, carrel, or reshelving cart in a public area of the library, to be reshelved by a member of the library staff. Although this method is never completely accurate (some patrons return materials to the shelf after using them), statistics on in-house use can be helpful in developing periodical and reference collections. Compare with circulation statistics

Initial article An article appearing in first-word position in a title or corporate name (usually a, an, or the, or the equivalent in another language), ignored in indexing. In the MARC record, the second indicator position following a tag indicates how many characters are to be ignored when the title or name in the field is sorted or filed.

Initial letter A large capital letter at the beginning of the first word of a chapter or paragraph. In medieval manuscripts, initial letters are often ornamented and illuminated. In incunabula, a rubricator inserted them in spaces left blank when the sheets were printed.

Initialism A shortened form of a phrase or compound term, composed of the initial letters of its words or parts spoken letter-by-letter, rather than pronounced as a word (example: IPO for initial public offering or ADA for Americans with Disabilities Act). Compare with abbreviation and acronym.

Initialize To start a computer system, program, or disk anew, an operation that usually requires erasing all or part of the data stored in memory. In Apple Macintosh computers, initializing a disk formats it. In computer programming, a variable is initialized when it is given its first value.

Initializing (formatting) Setting up a disk (any kind) to receive information. When a disk is initialized (formatted), its magnetic media is divided into tracks and sectors, and structure files that your computer uses to keep track of data are created.

Ink A colored liquid used for writing and in printing to create an impression on a flat surface, usually a sheet or roll of paper. Up to the late 19th century, printing ink was traditionally made from lampblack (pure carbon) mixed with a linseed oil base. To create colors, lampblack was replaced with other substances, such as vermillion to produce red. The quality of printing ink depended on the quality of the oil base, which varied because prior to the mid-19th century most printers made their own ink according to recipes handed down from master to apprentice. Although lampblack remains the basic ingredient of black printing ink, the complex formulas used today are the product of chemical technology. The typographer must carefully match choice of ink to grade of paper in planning a print job.

Ink ball A large round pad made of buckskin or sheepskin firmly stuffed with a wad of cotton or wool and fastened to a short wooden handle, used by the pressman in hand printing to apply ink to type set in wooden formes. Most pressmen worked two-handed with an ink ball in each hand.

Inlay A picture or decorative element of contrasting color, set into the cover of a book, usually in leather with or without tooling. Also, an illustration set into a border or frame of paper, the overlapping edges shaved thin to make the resulting sheet uniform in thickness. Compare with onlay.

Inline An elegant display typeface in which each broad stroke has a white line down its center. Compare with outline letter.

Inline images Graphics that are contained within a document's textual information. In a Web document, these graphics can either be loaded automatically when the page is accessed or loaded manually by clicking on the image's icon.

INNOPAC Also known as "Triple I" or "III". The Library's integrated library system which was implemented in 1996. The public catalog is called SAGE. Innovative Interfaces, Inc., located in Emeryville, California, is the company that developed and maintains INNOPAC.

INNOPAC prism OCLC software used to search for and download bibliographic records at the point of ordering. A PRISM record will have a complete bibliographic MARC record.

Innovative Interfaces Inc. (III) Founded in 1978 by Jerry Kline and Steve Silberstein, Innovative Interfaces has become one of the leading vendors of online catalog software and automation support for libraries worldwide. A significant number of library consortia in the United States prefer III software (example: ohiolink). Also known as Triple I.

In-process material: newly acquired items in a library which are undergoing technical processing such as cataloging, marking, etc. Patrons who need an in-process item can place a rush request for it with Circulation; it will usually be available within a day.

Input Data transferred to or entered into a computer system for processing, as opposed to the results of processing, known as output. The most commonly used input devices in personal computing are the keyboard and mouse. Scanners are also becoming more widespread and significant advancements have recently been made in voice recognition technology.

Input standards OCLC has established the following set of standards for entering bibliographic data into its online union catalog:

Inscribed copy A copy of a book that bears, as a presentation inscription, the name of the recipient and sometimes an appropriate comment or remark, followed by the signature of the donor, who may be the author. The inscription is usually written on the flyleaf. Abbreviated insc. Compare with presentation copy.

Inscription A brief, informal dedication written inside a book, usually on the flyleaf. Also, words engraved in stone or on some other hard surface, usually as a greeting or to commemorate an important event or person (example: the Rosetta Stone).

In-service training Formal instruction provided by a company, agency, organization, or institution at its own expense to enable its employees to become more proficient or qualified, especially in a new skill or set of skills. The sessions may be designed in-house and conducted on the premises by employees with the necessary expertise, presented by a vendor's traveling representative, or conducted by an outside training firm hired specifically for the purpose

Inset In bookbinding, a section of two or more leaves placed within another section in such a way that the back folds of both are sewn in the same pass of the thread. The inset section can wrap around the outside of the main section ("outsert"), or be placed in its center or at some intermediate location within it. Insetting is used to include plates without having to go through the time-consuming process of tipping them in. Also refers to a small diagram, map, or illustration printed within the area of a larger illustration, usually enclosed in a border of ruled lines.

Inset map A small map drawn or printed within the border of a larger map, usually showing in greater detail a specific feature or portion of the larger one, for example, a major metropolitan area within the borders of a map of a state or province. The same purpose may be served by an ancillary map printed on the same sheet or page outside the borders of the main map.

Installer A utility that copies system software or an application from floppy disks or a CD-ROM to your hard disk. An Installer may also decompress the new files, remove obsolete files, place extensions and control panels in their proper folders, and/or create new folders.

Installment One portion of a literary work divided into parts for publication in consecutive issues of a periodical, or one part or fascicle of such a work published separately, usually at regular intervals. During the 19th century, novels were often published in this fashion.

Installment sale A sale in which the purchaser pays for an item in two or more payments, usually at regular intervals of a month or more. Under this arrangement, the item is shipped when the order is received, without waiting for final payment. In the book trade, this practice is usually limited to very expensive multi-volume reference works.

Instant book A book published within weeks of an important event to capitalize on popular interest in the subject. Because careful research usually requires considerable time and effort, works prepared in haste may contain errors of fact and lack depth of treatment. An experienced reviewer will note such deficiencies.

Instant messaging (IM) A real time computer conferencing system that enables two or more persons to "chat" online via the Internet, IM allows the user to add the name of another person to a messaging list and be instantly notified whenever the person logs on. A chat session is initiated by typing a message in a designated window or "chat room" generated by the IM software. The message is displayed almost instantaneously on the screen of each person on the list, and the recipient(s) may respond quickly by typing a message. Most IM systems are designed to emit an auditory signal whenever a message is transmitted or received. Some systems allow the user to exchange data files, synchronize Web browsing, send images and video, and play computer games. Instant messaging is used in libraries to deliver electronic reference services to remote users and to persons who prefer to communicate online.

Institute for Scientific Information Established by Eugene Garfield in 1958, ISI is a commercial company providing citation indexing, current contents services, and information management tools in the sciences, social sciences, and arts and humanities

Institute of Museum and Library Services An independent federal grant-making agency created under the Museum and Library Services Act of 1996 to foster leadership, innovation, and lifelong learning by supporting museums, archives, and libraries of all types, and encouraging partnerships among them. IMLS administers four grant-in-aid programs for libraries, including LSTA grants to state library agencies. IMLS publishes the monthly e-mail newsletter Primary Source.

Institute of Physics Journals search Search for articles appeared in all the journals published by Institute of Physics can be made. The coverage of database is from 1874 till date. Full text access to current articles is available for registered members at free of cost. Full text articles are available in the first 30 days of publication.

Institution record Record in a union catalog that pertains to one of the cooperating institutions only.

Instruction group The reference service unit

responsible for organizing and developing library instruction services and programs for all CSU constituents

Instruction lab A library instruction classroom equipped with computer workstations (pcs or laptops) for the hands-on use of students, usually with an instructor station connected to an LCD projector for the demonstration of online search techniques.

Instruction: library department responsible for coordinating and conducting the library's orientation and instruction efforts, including: building tours; credit classes in research; short courses on databases, programs, and specific subject areas; and course-specific sessions requested by faculty.

Instructional Video Acces Centre (IVAC) Instructional video viewing center. While in the IVAC, students can directly phone Instructional Services on campus and view instructional videos and classroom instruction recordings.

Intaglio A printing technique used mainly for graphic purposes in which the areas to be printed are engraved or etched below the surface level of a plate. The plate is inked and then the surface is wiped clean, leaving a residue only in the engraved portions, which is transferred to a sheet of paper or other printing surface under pressure, usually on a rolling press. The only intaglio printing process still in commercial use is photogravure.

Integral Said of a leaf or page sewn or bound into a book or pamphlet when the publication was first printed. Compare with insert.

Integrated access An information retrieval system that allows users to search for books, periodical articles, and electronic resources such as computer files and Web sites, in one operation using a single interface, instead of searching online catalogs, bibliographic databases, and Web search engines separately. Seamless access is a goal yet to be realized in most libraries.

Intel 80x86 A type of microprocessors used in IBM PC or compatibles. The 80286 was introduced in the mid-1980s, followed by the 80386 and 80486. The Pentium processor is the next step up.

Intellectual Freedom Round Table (IFRT) Founded in 1973 as a permanent round table of the American Library Association, IFRT advocates freedom of access and expression in libraries, and provides support to librarians and other library employees who become embroiled in controversies involving censorship. IFRT also serves as a forum for the discussion of intellectual freedom issues at the state and local levels, and monitors developments in intellectual freedom that affect libraries, including legislation and court decisions. IFRT is affiliated with the Office for Intellectual Freedom of the ALA which publishes the Library Bill of Rights, the Freedom to Read Statement, and other ALA policies concerning the freedom to read.

Intellectual freedom The right under the First Amendment to the U.S. Constitution of any person to read or express views that may be unpopular or offensive to some people, within certain limitations (libel, slander, etc.). Legal cases concerning free speech issues are heard by the U.S. Supreme Court.

Intellectual Property Digital Library The Intellectual Property Digital Library Web site provides access to various intellectual property data collections currently hosted by the World Intellectual Property Organization. These collections include Madrid, PCT and JOPAL (non-patent reference) data and support fully searchable information retrieval and display by users on demand. The access is free of cost by user name and password as guest.

Intellectual property The expression of ideas defined by federal and international law as property. Though ideas themselves cannot be owned, the manner in which a particular author, film director, or other creator expresses ideas belongs to him or her and is protected by copyright law from unauthorized reproduction. Materials in the public domain are freely available. Those that are not in the public domain have stringent restrictions (called fair use) on how much of a work and under what circumstances copies can be made without payment to the owner. **Interactive** A computer interface designed to respond to input from a human being, usually in the form of commands and/or data. A back-and-forth dialogue between a computer program and its human user is an interactive session. Highly interactive systems, such as computer games, are designed to anticipate the user's needs, instead of responding in a prescribed way. Once started, a program that is not interactive proceeds without further human input.

Interactive map A map in digital format, designed to allow the user to view a portion of its surface on another scale or gain access to additional information, usually by selecting a hot spot on its surface with a pointing device such as a mouse (example: Mapquest).

Intercom Public Announcement System (PA) at the Loan Desk. (Technically not an intercom, but often called that by staff).

Interdisciplinary number A class number in Dewey Decimal Classification, used for works that cover a subject from the point of view of two or more disciplines, for example, 305.231 in sociology, reserved for interdisciplinary works on child development. In the schedules, such works are identified by an interdisciplinary works note. They are to be used only when the author devotes a significant amount of content to the discipline in which the number is found.

Interdisciplinary Research or course work requiring the resources of more than one academic discipline, for example, a topic in American studies, a field that overlaps American history, politics, literature, art, music, popular culture, etc. Although most indexing and abstracting services limit their scope to a specific discipline (example: Psychological Abstracts) or field (Child Development

Abstracts & Bibliography), pertinent literature from allied disciplines may also be included. Also refers to a reference work on a subject that overlaps two or more disciplines (example: Encyclopedia of Violence, Peace, and Conflict).

Interest profile A list of keywords or descriptors selected from a subject thesaurus, representing topics of interest to the user of a current awareness service. As part of the service, regular searches are performed on the terms. Based on the results, the user is notified of the existence of new publications as soon as they are indexed, and current information is forwarded on the desired topic(s). Synonymous with user profile.

Interface The point or process that joins two components of a data processing system, for example, the screen display that functions as an intermediary between a software program and its human users. Some interfaces are more user-friendly than others.

Interleaving In fine editions, a protective sheet of tissue or blank paper pasted or inserted loose between a plate and a page of text to prevent rubbing. Interleaving is sometimes done with buffered paper between acid materials to prevent acid migration. Also refers to blank leaves that are sometimes bound between the printed pages of a book for use in note-taking.

Interlibrary Loan (ILL) The process through which a library borrows material from another library or organization. If the item that you are looking for is not owned by the University Library in print or electronically, and you are a current faculty, staff or student at UW-Whitewater, you may request the item via Interlibrary Loan. Use of the online Interlibrary Loan request form is recommended, since it speeds up retrieval time.

Interlibrary Loan Services (ILL) - A lending and borrowing service which provides access to materials in other libraries. You can request books, journals, theses, etc., through ILL at local public libraries or through NSU. The service specifically designed for distance students at NSU is called Distance Library Services. The Electronic Library (http://www.nova.edu/library) has electronic request forms that you can use.

Interlinear Explanatory notes or translation handwritten or printed between the lines of a text, usually in small lettering or type. Compare with gloss.

Intermediary A person or software program that functions between the end-user and an online bibliographic retrieval system to assist in database selection, establish telecommunication connections, formulate useful queries in correct syntax, and evaluate the relevance of information retrieved. Mediated searching is provided on request in most academic libraries by a public services librarian specially trained in online searching.

Intermediate records Records used so infrequently by an agency or individual in the conduct of business or affairs that normal operations are not hampered by their transfer to a storage area less accessible than the location where active records are housed. Synonymous with semicurrent records.

Intermediate storage In archives, a separate area where inactive or intermediate records are stored temporarily prior to final disposition, often less accessible than the location where active records are housed. Synonymous with secondary storage.

Internal document A document, such as a memorandum or report, intended for distribution within an organization, rather than for wider publication. Sensitive internal documents may be classified to restrict access to authorized personnel.

International Association of Technological University Libraries (IATUL) Founded in Germany in 1955, IATUL provides an international forum for the exchange of ideas pertinent to librarianship in technological universities, and the discussion of opportunities for collaboration in the solution of common problems. Its member libraries are represented by their directors and senior managers. IATUL publishes the quarterly newsletter IATUL News.

International copyright Copyright protection extended to works published outside a country's borders, currently governed by international copyright law and international agreements, most notably the Berne Convention and the Universal Copyright Convention.

International Copyright Information Centre A clearinghouse with headquarters in Paris, established by UNESCO in 1971 to offer assistance to publishers from developing countries in securing rights to books and other publications protected by copyright in other countries.

International Database (IDB) It is a computerized data bank containing statistical tables of demographic and socioeconomic data for 227 countries and areas of the world.

International Federation of Classification Societies (IFCS) Founded in 1985, IFCS is a federation of national, regional, and linguistically-based classification societies devoted to promoting research in classification. The IFCS publishes the IFCS Newsletter and supports the Journal of Classification published by the Classification Society of North America.

International Federation of Film Archives (FIAF) Founded in Paris in 1938, FIAF has an international membership of the world's leading museums and film archives. Its goals are to preserve the moving image in all its forms, facilitate research on the history of motion pictures, encourage the collection of documents on cinema history and film preservation, foster the accessibility and exchange of films and cinema-related material, and help create new film archives around the world. FIAF publishes the biannual Journal of Film Preservation.

International Federation of Library Associations and Institutions (IFLA) An independent international nongovernmental association of library associations, libraries and related institutions, sponsors, and individuals,

IFLA was founded in 1927 by fifteen countries as the International Library and Bibliographical Committee to promote global cooperation, communication, and research in library science and librarianship. With association and institutional members in over 130 countries, IFLA has a democratic structure in which a general assembly of members (the Council), is the highest governing organ. The organization maintains a Secretariat headed by a Secretary-General in The Hague and sponsors an annual conference in a different member country each year.

International Labour Office ILO database (LABORSTA) on labour statistics covering economically active population (data since 1945) employment, unemployment, hours of work, wages, labour cost, consumer prices, occupational injuries, occupational accidents, and strikes and lockouts (data since 1969) of different countries of the world. Also gives access to one more database, which contain data on 'Economically Active Population, 1950-2010' of different countries of the world.

International League of Antiquarian Booksellers (ILAB) An organization encompassing twenty national associations representing antiquarian booksellers in 30 countries, ILAB was founded in Amsterdam in 1947 to uphold and improve professional standards in the antiquarian book trade, promote honorable conduct in business, and contribute to a broader appreciation of the art and history of the book.

International Literary Market Place (ILMP) A directory of the international book publishing industry issued annually by R. R. Bowker, ILMP provides information on publishers, literary agents, book manufacturing, book clubs and dealers, major libraries and library associations, and literary associations, periodicals, and awards for over 180 countries. The directory also includes an industry yellow pages. The most recent edition of ILMP is usually shelved in the reference section of most large academic and public libraries.

International Organization for Standardization (ISO) A name derived from the Greek word isos meaning "equal." Founded in London in 1947 with headquarters in Geneva, ISO is a nongovernmental federation of national standardization organizations in 130 countries, dedicated to establishing international standards to facilitate commerce and cooperation in scientific, technical, and economic endeavors. The United States is represented in ISO by the American National Standards Institute (ANSI). ISO operates through approximately 160 technical committees and 2,300 subcommittees which recommend standards and standardization policy to its national members

International Poster Collection Special collection of posters, slides, ephemera and digital images housed in the Poster Room within Archives and Special Collections, Morgan Library. The collection is created from posters received from the Colorado International Invitational Poster Exhibition held biennially on campus. The majority of the posters are available on the International Poster Collection Web site.

International Relations Round Table (IRRT) A round table of the American Library Association created in 1949, IRRT develops the interests of librarians in activities and problems related to international library relations by providing hospitality to visitors to the United States from the library community abroad and by facilitating communication between the International Relations Committee of the ALA and individual ALA members

International Satandard Serial Number (ISSN) Eight digit number separated into two groups of four assigned by the National Serials Data Program to provide a unique identification number to each serial title. SAGE can be searched by ISSN.

International Serials Data System (ISDS) An intergovernmental network established under the auspices of UNESCO to develop and maintain an international registry of serial publications containing the information necessary for identification and bibliographic control, including the International Standard Serial Number (ISSN) and key title. The ISSN center for the United States is the National Serials Data Program (NSDP) administered by the Library of Congress.

International Standard Bibliographic Description (ISBD) A set of standards adopted in 1971 by the International Federation of Library Associations (IFLA), governing the bibliographic description of items collected by libraries. The general standard ISBD(G) serves as a guide for describing all types of library materials. Standards have also been developed for specific formats: ISBD(CM) for cartographic materials, ISBD(PM) for printed music, ISBD(S) for serials, etc. Isbds have been integrated into several catalog codes around the world, including AACR2.

International Standard Book Number (ISBN) ISBN is assigned by designated agencies in countries publishing books to provide each book with a unique identification number by which the item can be ordered. The number consists of 10 digits separated into 4 functional parts as follows; 1) One or more digits to represent the country or group of countries in which the item was published; 2) 2-7 digits of the publisher's prefix; 3) one or more digits to identify a particular title and to expand the number to nine digits; 4) and a check digit for a computer validity check. SAGE can be searched by ISBN.

International Standard Serial Number (ISSN) International Standard Serial Number, a unique eight-digit standard number assigned by the International Serials Data System (ISDS) to identify a specific serial publication (example: 0363-0277 for Library Journal). The ISSN is usually given in the masthead of each issue. When a serial undergoes a title change, a new ISSN is assigned. In AACR2, the ISSN is given in the standard number and terms of availability area of the bibliographic record. Compare with ISBN.

Internet A worldwide network of computers that can be accessed via the campus computer network. The Internet allows local computer users to find and use information resources on computers of other academic institutions, research institutes, private companies, and government agencies.

Internet address The unique code assigned to a specific computer connected to the Internet to identify it as a sender and/or receiver in the transmission of data or program files. Two categories of addresses are used: e-mail addresses of specific individuals (example: presleyelvis@aol.com) and the urls of FTP sites, Telnet sites, and Web sites (example: www.aol.com). The form of Internet addresses is governed by the Domain Name System (DNS).

Internet cafe A retail business that sells coffee, snacks, and light meals, and provides computer equipment and Internet access to customers while they dine, at no charge or for a reasonable fee. Some large academic and public libraries have installed such facilities on their premises to allow patrons to read their e-mail without monopolizing equipment needed in other locations for library research.

Internet Explorer A client program from Microsoft that comes preinstalled on most new IBM PC or compatible computers; enables you to browse the World Wide Web.

Internet note Field within SAGE order record used to determine processing when received. This may include information relating to another edition which has already been cataloged and VENDOR notification.

Internet resource A digital document (Web page, FTP file, e-mail message, etc.) That can be downloaded from a remote server over the Internet. Rules for cataloging Internet resources are available online from OCLC in Cataloging Internet Resources: A Manual and Practical Guide edited by Nancy Olson. Most writing style manuals have been updated to include a section on citing electronic sources (electronic style).

Internet service provider (ISP) A company in the business of providing Internet access to computer users who do not have a direct connection, usually via a telecommunication channel in exchange for payment of a modest monthly fee. The **ISP** with the largest number of subscribers is America Online (AOL). Most isps also provide proprietary software to facilitate use of the Internet..

Internet Society an international nonprofit organization that governs such issues as the assignment of IP addresses.

Internet Telephony Internet telephony (IPT) is the transport of telephone calls over the Internet. IPT could use traditional telephony devices, multimedia pcs or dedicated terminals to take part in the calls. The calls could entirely or partially be transmitted over the Internet.

Internship A limited period of supervised training in a library or other information agency, intended to facilitate the application of theory to practice following completion of formal course work toward a master's degree in library and information science. An intern may be paid and/or receive graduate credits based on the number of hours worked

Interoperability The capability of a computer hardware or software system to communicate and work effectively with another system in the exchange of data, usually a system of a different type, designed and produced by a different vendor.

Interpolation Information added to the bibliographic description of an item by the cataloger, not explicitly stated in or on the item, for example, the number of pages in a book without page numbers, or a publication date not given in the item but believed on the basis of investigation to be correct. In the bibliographic record, interpolations are made inside square brackets (examples: [32] p. And [1974?]). Compare with extrapolation.

Interrupt A brief interruption of the computer's activity so that an urgent task can be performed.

Intralibrary loan The loan of an item by a library to another library within the same library system, or directly to a patron of another library in the same system, on request, usually faster than interlibrary loan if the system has its own delivery service. In some online catalogs, the user may initiate this type of transaction without staff assistance.

Intramural card (IMO CARD) An account card owned by the Libraries for use at the CSU Bookstore only for pre-approved purchases of supplies. Available through the accounts office.

Intramural order (IMO) A form to use when purchasing items or services on-campus that are to be paid for by the Libraries. Issued through the accounts office.

Intranet A private network inside a company or organization that uses the same kinds of software that you would find on the public Internet, but that is only for internal use. Compare with extranet.

Introduction The part of a book in which the subject and purpose of the work are briefly stated, and the reader prepared for the treatment of the subject that follows in the text, usually written by the author or by a recognized authority in the field. The introduction normally appears in the front matter, following the preface or foreword, but may sometimes take the form of the first chapter. In either case, it is considered an integral part of the work and is not necessarily changed in subsequent editions, as is the preface. Abbreviated introd. Compare with prologue.

Introductory offer A promotional tool used by book clubs to attract new subscribers by allowing the customer to select a certain number of books at a very low price (sometimes at no charge), usually from a list of popular titles, in exchange for a commitment to purchase a minimum number of additional titles within a designated period of time, usually one year.

Introductory price A lower price offered by the publisher of a new book or other publication prior to the announced publication date, or for a limited period before and after publication, to encourage advance sales, after which the item is sold at list price. The period during which an introductory price is offered may be extended if advance orders warrant, in contrast to a prepublication price that expires on a specific date designated by the publisher.

Inventory The process of checking all the items on a library's shelves against a list of holdings to identify for replacement or deselection those missing and not checked out. A similar procedure is used to check other library property such as furniture and equipment against an authority list to identify missing items. Also refers to the list itself, which may include descriptions, quantities, prices paid, etc.

Inverted heading In indexing, a multiword heading in which conventional word order is transposed to bring the most significant word into first-word position, for example, the Library of Congress subject heading Combustion, Spontaneous human.

Inverted title A title divided by a bibliographer or indexer into two parts and transposed to bring a significant word into first-word position, for use as an entry in a bibliography or as a heading in an index (example: Language and Linguistics, Dictionary of).

Invoice A document or form sent to a purchaser by a vendor indicating the order number, description, quantity, price, terms of sale, method of delivery, cost of shipping, and total amount owed for items shipped and/or services rendered. Most libraries require an invoice before payment can be authorized. Compare with purchase order.

IP Address Network addresses are usually of two types: (1) the physical or hardware address of a network interface card; for Ethernet this 48-bit address might be 0260.8C00.7666. The hardware address is used to forward packets within a physical network. (2) The logical or IP Address is used to facilitate moving data between physical networks and is made up of a network number, a subnetwork number, and a host number. All Internet addresses at SDSU have a network number of 130.191, a subnet number in the range of 1-254, and a host number in the range of 1-254.

IP Datagram The basic unit of information passed across the Internet. An IP Datagram is to the Internet as a hardware packet is to a physical network. It contains a source and destination address along with data. Large messages are broken down into a sequence of IP Datagrams.

IP Number (Internet Protocol Number) Sometimes called a dotted quad. A unique number consisting of 4 parts separated by dots, e.g. 165.113.245.2, Every machine that is on the Internet has a unique IP number - if a machine does not have an IP number, it is not really on the Internet. Many machines (especially servers) also have one or more Domain Names that are easier for people to remember.

IP recognition The method by which a subscription service (such as a database) recognizes its subscribers (such as a college library or an individual licensed and authorized to use the database). Many subscription databases, such as firstsearch, identify legitimate users by matching their IP address to a list of subscribing institutions. To access services using IP recognition, users generally must be connected to the Internet through the subscribing institution.

IP Validation -The database vendor verifies that the user is coming from a Internet address that has permission to use the database.

IPAC The Library's online catalog. IPAC is available on our web site at www.mesalibrary.org.

IRC (Internet Relay Chat) Basically a huge multi-user live chat facility. There are a number of major IRC servers around the world which are linked to each other. Anyone can create a channel and anything that anyone types in a given channel is seen by all others in the channel. Private channels can (and are) created for multi-person conference calls.

IRIS A consortium of three libraries, the University of Kentucky, the University of Tennessee, Knoxville, and Vanderbilt University.

IRQ Interrupt request; refers to a number associated with a serial port on an IBM PC or compatible computer. It usually can be changed by flipping a dip switch. Occasionally, when you're using a modem connect to the Internet, you may need to adjust the IRQ number assigned to the serial port which connects the modem to avoid conflicts with another device like your mouse.

Irregular serial a serial publication which is not issued on a regular, predictable schedule; there may be several issues in one year, or only one every several years.

Irregular The frequency of a serial publication issued at intervals of uneven length which do not follow an established rule. The opposite of regular.

Irreversible A change in the chemical or physical state of an item, which cannot be undone, for example, an embossed or perforated ownership mark or worming in a book. In conservation, reversibility is a priority in the treatment of materials for which the original condition is of evidential or historical value.

ISAAC Information System for Advanced Academic Computing. Serves as a clearinghouse for information about the use of IBM-compatible hardware and software as aids to instruction and research in higher education. Membership is free to all students, faculty, and staff at these institutions.

ISBN International Standard Book Number: A unique number assigned to every book published in this country, and many in other countries. The ISBN system is recognized internationally. An ISBN has nine or ten digits; the first digit denotes country of publication, the next several the publisher, the remainder identify the item.

ISDN (Integrated Services Digital Network) Basically a way to move more dataover existing regular phone lines. ISDN is available to much of the USA and in most markets it is priced very comparably to standard analog phone circuits. It can provide speeds of roughly 128,000 bits-per-second over regular phone lines. In practice, most people will be limited to 56,000or 64,000 bits-per-second. Unlike DSL, ISDN can be used to connect to many different locations, one at a time, just like a regular telephone call, as long the other location also has ISDN.

ISID Index to Indian Social Science Journals Indexes 85 Indian Social Science journals enabling users to search for references on the basis of string (series of characters) either for author's name, or words in titles for selected journals. Most of the journals are indexed from the first volume. Also indexes press clippings taken out from 14 India's English dailies. Access is free with simple registration.

ISO International Organization for Standardization, the group that developed the OSI protocols.

Isogram A line on a graph or map connecting points of equal or corresponding average value for a specific variable. Isorithms show amount, for example, temperature (isotherms), barometric pressure (isobars), sunshine (isohels), etc. Isopleths show frequency (hurricanes, marriages, power plants, etc.). Synonymous with isoline.

ISP Internet Service Provider. A company that provides access to the Internet. A service provider can offer simple dial-up access, SLIP/PPP access, or a dedicated line.

ISSN International Standard Serial Number; sequence of eight numbers which are assigned to a serial title as its unique identifier.

Issue date The specific date or period (spring, summer, fall, winter) by which a particular issue of a serial publication is identified, usually printed on the front cover and on each page as a running foot.

Issue number The number assigned by the publisher to a separately issued part of a serial publication to distinguish it from other parts published at different times. Issue numbers are assigned consecutively, starting with the first issue of each publication period. When a serial is published in volumes, issue numbers recommence with each volume.

ISSUE Single piece of a SERIAL.

Issue To produce books or other printed materials for public sale or distribution.

IT See: information technology.

IT8 Industry standard color reference target used to calibrate input and output devices.

Italic A cursive form of type, first used in an Italian edition of Virgil, which slants heavily to the right, used in combination with roman type for emphasis and to indicate foreign words or phrases in a text. In the preceding sentence, the word "emphasis" is in italic, and in the following sentence, the book title appears in boldface italic. Warren Chappell states in A Short History of the Printed Word (1970) that italic is rooted in a variety of humanistic script known as cancellaresca or "chancery" that reached its highest state of development in 16th century Italy when rounded letterforms were elongated to become elliptical. Abbreviated Ital. Or It. See also: bibliographic item and record item.

Item Record A record in the library catalog which describes a book, document, periodical or other material of which the library owns a copy or to which its users may have access. It consists of fields specifying for each item the author's name(s), title(s), place of publication, publisher name, edition statements, date of publication, physical description. Also included in the item record is the location of the item in the library, its call number, and its status, or if it is accessible via the Internet, a link to it.

Item specific request A request on a particular copy (using a specific barcode number) of a title. Item specific requests can only be placed by library staff. Please call 480-644-2207 or stop at the Ask Here Desk for assistance.

Item type A code in the item record for a bibliographic item in a library collection which, in conjunction with patron type, determines the loan rule applied when the item is checked out by a specific borrower. Each library or library system develops and maintains its own set of item types based on the nature of its collection(s).

ITV Interactive Television.

IUCAT Indiana University Libraries' online catalog, containing more than 5 million entries for books, edited volumes, periodical titles, videos, sound recordings, and other library materials.

IUG Innovative User's Group — Users of Innovative software and systems.

Jacket cover A removable covering made of thin, transparent, flexible plastic, designed to fit over the dust jacket of a book published in hardcover, to extend the life of the binding and enhance the visual appeal of the jacket design, available from library suppliers in a range of sizes. Used more extensively in public and school libraries than in academic and special libraries, it allows the outside surface of a book to be easily cleaned with a damp rag or paper towel and disinfectant cleaning solution. The ends should be securely fastened to the cover with adhesive tape of a type that can be removed without damage.

Jargon The specialized vocabulary and idioms of a group of people engaged in the same activity or line of work, for example, the marcese used by library catalogers in reference to the bibliographic record and its component fields. In a more general sense, speech that is unintelligible or incoherent. Compare with slang.

Java A simple platform-independent object-oriented programming language used for writing applets that are downloaded from the World Wide Web by a client and run on the client's machine. Developed by Sun Microsystems, Java is a programming language that is specifically designed for writing programs that can be safely downloaded to your computer through the Internet and immediately run without fear of viruses or other harm to your computer or files. Using small Java programs (called "Applets"), Web pages can include functions such as animations, calculators, and other fancy tricks. Java is a simple, robust, object-oriented, platform-independent multi-threaded, dynamic general-purpose programming environment. It is best for creating applets and applications for the Internet, intranets and any other complex, distributed network. A network-oriented programming language invented by Sun Microsystems that is specifically designed for writing programs that can be safely downloaded to your computer through the Internet and immediately run without fear of viruses or other harm to our computer or files. Using small Java programs (called "Applets"), Web pages can include functions such as animations, calculators, and other fancy tricks. We can expect to see a huge variety of features added to the Web using Java, since you can write a Java program to do almost anything a regular computer program can do, and then include that Java program in a Web page.

Java Script This is a language very close to Java that allows for more interaction with the viewer. It is much more forgiving than Java as doesn't require it's own window in which to work. A scripting language developed by Netscape and Sun Microsystems that is loosely related to Java. Javascript code can be embedded in a Web page along with HTML code and is easier to write than Java, especially for novice programmers. Javascript, however, is not a true programming language and has limited functionality in comparison with Java. A javascript-compliant Web browser, such as Netscape, is necessary to run javascript code. Javascript is an interpreted programming or script language from Netscape. It is somewhat similar in capability to Microsoft's Visual Basic, Sun's Tcl, the UNIX-derived Perl, and IBM's REXX. In general, script languages are easier and faster to code in than the more structured and compiled languages such as C and C++ and are ideal for programs of limited capability or that can reuse and tie together existing compiled programs. Example: The date on the bottom of the page (Page Last Updated) & all pages here change each time I save the file. I do not manually type in the date each time I edit a page. Handy because just saving the file changes the date displayed!

Jaz drive A removable disk drive from Iomega Corporation; the cartridges it uses are capable of holding 1GB of data.

JDK (Java Development Kit) A software development package from Sun Microsystems that implements the basic set of tools needed to write, test and debugjava applications and applets

Jeremiad A fierce denunciation of a particular evil, or the evils of society in general, in which current misfortunes are considered a just penalty for past misdeeds, and repentance extolled as the only road to a happier, more secure future. The term is derived from the Lamentations of Jeremiah in the Old Testament. The sermons of Puritan preachers in colonial New England provide abundant examples of this literary form.

Jestbook A collection of jokes, witty anecdotes, epigrams, exempla, and ribald tales, usually with didactic endings. Introduced into Europe from the Muslim world during the 8th century, jestbooks enjoyed greatest popularity during the 16th and 17th centuries. Because of their ephemeral nature, few early examples survive. Also spelled jest book. Synonymous with facetiae.

Jewelled binding A binding in which the boards are covered in designs done in gold or silver inset with ivory and precious or semi-precious stones, usually with a similarly decorated clasp to keep the vellum leaves of the body pressed firmly together (example: Heures Francoises et Latines pour Madame L. Gallois). During the medieval period, this style was used for devotional s commissioned by the Catholic Church and members of the nobility from the 6th century onwards. The lavish use of costly materials was considered an act of religious piety, rather than ostentation, and the colors of the gems often had symbolic meaning. Extremely valuable, the rare survivals are sold by the world's most prestigious auction houses.

Job description A detailed description of the duties and responsibilities associated with a specific position in an organization, used in training, performance evaluation, and the allocation of workload. Compare with position description.

Job lot Copies of a book or other publication offered by the publisher at lower than list price to a wholesale bookseller known as a jobber, usually to reduce or close out stock of a particular title. Compare with remainders.

Jobber In the United States, a wholesaler that stocks large quantities of new books and nonprint materials (audiobooks, videotapes, music cds, etc.) Issued by various publishers, and supplies them to bookstores and libraries on order, usually at a substantial discount (10-40%). Titles out of print from the publisher may still be available in limited quantity from a book jobber. Large jobbers also offer customized services such as continuation orders, approval plans, cataloging, technical processing, etc. Using a jobber allows a library to operate more efficiently by consolidating book ordering. Directory information on book wholesalers is available in the reference serial Literary Market Place. Synonymous in the UK with library supplier. Compare with dealer.

Joint author In AACR2, a person who collaborates with one or more others to produce a work in which all who contribute perform the same function. The contributions of the individual collaborators may not be indicated and are usually not separable. In cataloging, the main entry is made under the name of the author listed first on the chief source of information (the primary author), with added entries for the other authors, unless the primary responsibility clearly rests with one author. Bibliographic style manuals differ in the maximum number of joint authors named in a citation.

Synonymous with coauthor. Compare with composite work.

Joint imprint The imprint of two or more publishers, appearing on the title page of the same edition of a work. In most instances, the co-publishers market and distribute the work in different countries or regions of the world. For a recent example, see The Great Libraries: From Antiquity to the Renaissance, published in 2000 by Oak Knoll Press and The British Library, assigned separate isbns for the US and UK.

Joint In bookbinding, the narrow portion of covering material affixed directly to the endpaper along the groove separating the board from the inlay over the spine, forming the hinge that allows the cover to open and close like a door. A book has a front joint connecting the front board to the spine, and a back joint connecting the back board to the spine. On the inside, the hinge is formed by the fold in the endpaper, reinforced in some editions with a cloth strip.

Joint publication Publication (by prior agreement) of the same work by two different publishers in separate editions, often in hardcover by a university press and in paperback by a trade publisher. Compare with co-edition.

Joint use A cooperative arrangement between a library and another institution, such as a school, community college, or university, in which both institutions share the same facility and/or collections for example, the Dr. Martin Luther King, Jr. Library in San Jose, California, a partnership between the City of San Jose and San Jose State University in which the San Jose Public Library and the University library share the same building and collections.

Journal A periodical published by an academic press, learned society, government agency or professional organization, intended for scholars, students, professionals or experts, and featuring articles which disseminate results, critical interpretations or reviews of scholarly or scientific research in a particular subject discipline or profession.

Journal of commentary A periodical that specializes

in the publication of news analysis and discussion of political, social, and cultural issues, usually from an editorial position somewhere on the political spectrum, for example, the National Review on the right or The Progressive on the left. Journals of commentary are usually issued monthly and sold at news stands, in bookstores, and by subscription. Compare with magazine and journal.

Journal pagination In journal publishing, page numbers often begin with the first page of the first issue in a volume, and continue in a single numeric sequence through the last page of the last issue in the volume. This means that the pagination in each issue (except the first) begins where the previous issue ended. Since most journals are published quarterly and bound into annual volumes, continuous pagination makes it easier for the user to find a specific article by page number in the appropriate volume. Compare with magazine pagination.

Journalese The rather trite style of writing used by some newspaper and broadcast journalists, who rely on cliches and hackneyed expressions to pitch a story to the widest possible audience ("rattlesnake roundup rattles rights groups"), avoided in serious journalism.

Journalism The art of gathering news, writing and editing copy, or directing the publication of a newspaper, magazine, or journal. A person who turns news into copy is a journalist (also refers to the person who keeps a journal or diary). A photographer who specializes in capturing news on camera is a photojournalist. In the United States, Pulitzer Prizes are awarded annually for distinguished public service in journalism, and for reporting in a variety of categories (feature writing, commentary, criticism, editorial writing, cartooning, and photography).

Journals consortium An organization that handles the production and distribution of a number of journals, but does not necessarily exercise editorial control over them if they are owned by other organizations. In the United States, perhaps the best-known example is the journals publishing division of the Johns Hopkins University Press which provides online access through Project MUSE to the full-text of its own journals, plus sixty titles from other scholarly publishers.

Journals Specialized, scholarly publications written by professors, scholars and experts for researchers and professionals; examples include American Economic Review, Journal of the American Medical Association, Journal of Psychology, etc. Journal articles are based upon research and usually have extensive footnotes and bibliography. Journals are often refereed or peer reviewed.

JPEG An acronym which stands for Joint Photographic Experts Group, a standard for compressing still images in digital format at ratios of 100:1 and higher. Data compression is accomplished by dividing the image into small blocks of pixels, halved again and again until the desired ratio is reached. Data is lost each time the compression ratio increases. Pronounced "jay-peg." Compare with MPEG.

JSTOR A nonprofit organization that began as a digital text initiative of the Andrew W. Mellon Foundation, JSTOR provides searchable bibliographic databases containing the complete full-text back files of core scholarly journals in a wide range of disciplines, current to within 2-5 years.

JUL Joint University Libraries; the name of the library system from 1941 until the merger of Peabody College and Vanderbilt University on July 1, 1979.

Jumbo file A collection of prints, pictures, and/or documents of unusually large size, organized for ease of access in a folder, portfolio, or other container of a size sufficient to accommodate them.

Jump page The page of a newspaper, magazine, or other periodical on which a story or article that begins on the first page (or near the front of the issue) is continued, usually indicated by the references "Continued on page..." and "Continued from page..." at the break in the text.

Junior Collection Collection of children's books. Divided into two areas : non-fiction and fiction.

Junk mail Unwanted e-mail messages, usually advertising not solicited by the recipient.

Just received Item status which indicates that we have physically just received an item and are starting to process it for inclusion in our collection. Holds may be placed on items with this status.

Justification In typesetting, the equal and exact spacing of words and letters in a line of type to make the text block appear even vertically at the right- and/or left-hand margins. Type aligned with the left margin is said to be left-justified. Aligned with the right-hand margin, it is said to be right-justified. Type can also be centered on a page, as in headings. Compare with alignment.

Justified A word processing format in which text is formatted flush with both the left and right margins. Other options include left justified (text is lined up against the left margin) and right justified (text is lined up against the right margin).

Juvenile collection A library collection of books and other materials intended specifically for children under 12-13 years of age, shelved separately from the adult and young adult collections, sometimes in a children's room with separate sections for juvenile fiction and nonfiction, beginning readers and easy books, picture books, and books for very young children (alphabet books, counting books, board books, cloth books, etc.). Juvenile collections are usually managed by a librarian with specialized training in children's services.

Juvenilia Works produced during the childhood or youth of an artist or writer, which may reveal literary or artistic immaturity, but often compensate with an abundance of youthful enthusiasm and a style or approach that is highly innovative.

K An abbreviation for kilobyte; it contains 1,024 bytes; in turn 1,024 kilobytes is equal to one megabyte.

Kanji A subset of approximately 5,000 Chinese ideograms borrowed or adapted by the Japanese for use in their own written language. In 1946, the Japanese government selected a smaller subset of 1,850 for use in official publications and in newspaper/magazine publishing. Also refers to any one of these loan characters.

Kardex Historically, a manual file for checking in serial issues, no longer used. Now all CHECK-IN is done online in SAGE.

Kb **kilobit.** 10^3 bits of information (usually used to express a data transfer rate; as in, 1 Kilobit/second = 1Kbps = 1Kb).

Kbps Kilobits per second; a measure of data transfer speed; one Kbps is 1,000 bits per second. Example: a 28.8 Kbps modem. Standard telephone lines are capable of transmitting data at a maximum speed of about 33.6 Kbps, although with newer technologies this limit is increasing.

Keep down In typesetting, an instruction to the typesetter to use capital letters sparingly in the titles of works mentioned in the text. The opposite of keep up.

Keep up In typesetting, an instruction to the typesetter to use capital letters at the beginning of each word of the title of any work mentioned in the text. Prepositions, conjunctions, and initial articles are usually kept down, making "The Adventures of the Huckleberry Finn" an all up setting. In modern British practice, only the first word and proper names are capitalized ("The adventures of Huckleberry Finn"). In French, only the first word following the initial article and proper names are capitalized. In Italian, only the initial article is capitalized. In German, all nouns are capitalized. The opposite of **keep down**.

Kelmscott Press A private press founded in 1891 by the architect, designer, writer, calligrapher, and typographer William Morris (1834-1896) who sought to revive, in modern book production, the aesthetic of the medieval period and early printing. Although the press survived only until 1894, the 53 books it issued set a very high standard of beauty and craftsmanship. For more information about the Kelmscott Press, please see the entry in A Dictionary of Book History (1986) by John Feather. For images of works produced by the Press, see the exhibit catalog William Morris and the Art of the Book (1976) published by the Pierpont Morgan Library.

Kerberos: An authentication system developed at the Massachusetts Institute of Technology (MIT); it enables the exchange of private information across an open network by assigning a unique key called a "ticket" to a user requesting access to secure information.

Kerf A shallow groove cut into the binding edge of the sections of a book, perpendicular to the spine near the head and tail of the text block, to allow the kettle stitching to be recessed.

Kermit An asynchronous communication protocol developed and maintained by the Kermit Project at Columbia University, which enables files to be transferred from one computer system to another. Accurate, flexible, and customizable, Kermit includes terminal emulation and can be installed on almost any operating system. Although it is not in the public domain, Columbia University allows Kermit to be used as shareware, but encourages users to purchase the product in support of the Project.

Kermit An error-checking file-transfer protocol used to copy files from one computer to another. Also the name given to the public domain software distributed by Columbia University, which supports this protocol.

Kern The portion of the face of a unit of type that extends beyond the edge of its body to overlap an adjacent character (example: the lowercase italic f in many typefaces). Kerning is also refers to the practice in typesetting of backspacing to tuck one character into another to avoid the appearance of irregular spacing in a line. Pairs of letters close-fitted in this way include AT, AV, Ta, Wa, etc. The term is also used in typesetting for the practice of reducing the space between characters to make copy fit a given line length.

Kernel Size The number of pixels sampled as a unit during image manipulation and sharpening processes.

Kerning: The amount of space between characters in a word; in desktop publishing, it is typically performed on pairs of letters or on a short range of text to fine-tune the character spacing.

Kettle stitch In hand-binding, a special end stitch taken near the head and foot of each section to lock the sewing thread after it passes down the fold, linking adjacent sections through their folds and producing two rows of kettle stitches perpendicular to the binding edge, one near the top and the other at the bottom of the spine. In some editions, a shallow groove called a kerf is cut into the binding edge at each end of the spine to recess the kettle stitching. Synonymous with catch stitch.

Key control The process of establishing and maintaining the list of persons authorized to access keys to the door locks and lockable equipment in a library, as a means of securing the facility's locking system. A full survey of all locks and lock locations must first be conducted and an inventory made of all existing keys. Then key distribution is carefully recorded, including keys retrieved from employees who leave library employment. Access to master keys is limited to essential personnel, using a two-key system in areas where security is especially important (rare books, special collections, computer equipment rooms, etc.). When not in use, keys are stored in a secure cabinet, with a log for recording name of borrower, date of issue, and date of return.

Key title The unique name assigned to a serial publication, linked to the International Standard Serial Number (ISSN) under the International Serials Data System (ISDS), usually (but not always) the same as the title proper. In library cataloging, the key title is given immediately following the ISSN in the bibliographic record. If there is no ISSN, the key title is not added. Also spelled key-title.

Keyboard A thin flat peripheral device that allows a computer user to enter input by manually depressing keys marked with letters, numerals, and special characters. The keys can be arranged in a single set of parallel rows, or split into two sets of rows (fixed or adjustable) to make them more ergonomic. A computer keyboard can be built-in, as in a laptop, or a separate piece of equipment, as in most desktop personal computers.

Keypad A small hand-held infrared device used in large-screen demonstrations of online systems to enable the instructor to control electronic equipment installed on the demonstration console. Also, the part of a full-size computer keyboard consisting of a set of programmable numeric keys, usually arranged in four rows on the far right-hand side.

Keyword - A word or term, chosen by the user, that best summarizes the information being sought. A user can search the library catalog or other database for either a single keyword or a combination of keywords in order to retrieve records containing the keyword(s).

Keyword Searching - Refers to the instructions given to the computer to search for words in multiple fields of a record, i.e. Author, subject or title fields.

Keywords The most significant words in a topic, book or article title, etc. Keywords are used as terms when searching databases.

Kilobyte (Kb) 1,024 bytes of digital data

Kinescope A motion picture made by filming the images displayed on a television monitor.

Kiosk A small circular pavilion, usually located near the entrance to a library, used for displaying announcements, dust jackets removed from new books, reading lists, comments and suggestions from library users (sometimes with responses from library administration), and other information concerning library operations and programs.

Knowledge base A database where information common to a particular topic is stored online for easy reference; for example, a frequently-asked questions (FAQ) list may provide links to a knowledge base.

Knowledge Information that has been comprehended and evaluated in the light of experience, and incorporated into the knower's intellectual understanding of its subject.

Known-item search A search in a library for a specific work, as opposed to a search for any work by a known author or for works on a particular subject. If the title of the work is known, the easiest way to locate a copy is to search a library catalog or bibliographic database by title. When the user is uncertain of the precise wording of the title, the best strategy may be to search by author's name. If at least 2-3 significant words in the title are known with certainty, a keywords search may retrieve an entry for the work.

Kraft paper A heavy, unbleached grade of coarse paper, usually mocha brown in color, used for paper bags and wrapping paper. In publishing, kraft paper is used for the outer wrapper on magazines to protect the glossy cover from damage in mailing. In binding, a narrow strip of kraft paper may be used as a second lining to reinforce the layer of thin fabric called crash (or super) affixed to the binding edge of the sewn sections as the first lining to hold them firmly together.

Kunstlerroman From the German word Kunstler ("artist") and the French word roman ("novel"), a novel that traces the growth of a writer's creative genius from childhood to maturity, with particular attention to major trials and obstacles, and their influence on the development of the artist's character and work (example: A Portrait of the Artist as a Young Man by James Joyce). Compare with Bildungsroman.

KWAC An acronym for Keyword and Context (also known as Keyword alongside Context), an algorithmically generated index in which keywords from the title (and sometimes the text) of a document are printed as headings along the left-hand margin of the page, with the portion of the title or text following each keyword indented under the heading, followed by the portion of the title or text preceding the word. Unlike KWOC indexing, this method preserves multiword terms and phrases in the alphanumeric sequence of headings. Compare with KWIC.

KWIC An acronym for **Keyword in Context**, a type of permuted index in which the title of a document (and sometimes the text) is used to illustrate the meaning of a keyword used as an entry. Tagged by hand or extracted from the document algorithmically, keywords are printed in alphabetical order at a fixed position in a line of fixed length (usually at the center), so that they appear in a column, with as much of the context as can be accommodated preceding and following each word. The keywords in the column may be distinguished typographically to make them easier to read. Keyword and context are usually coded to identify the document indexed. Compare with KWAC and KWOC.

KWIC Index Short for keyword In Context. An index produced by rotating each significant word in the title of a document so that is appears alphabetically in the index. The general reference area has a KWIC Index of the holdings in the area for general, science and technology, and documents reference materials. (No longer being maintained — June 1999)

KWOC An acronym for **Keyword out of Context**, a variation on the KWIC (Keyword in Context) index, in which keywords extracted algorithmically from the title of a document (and sometimes the text) are printed as headings along the left-hand margin of the page, with the titles or portions of text containing each keyword indented under the corresponding heading. A symbol may be substituted for the keyword in the string of text. Unlike KWAC indexing, this method does not preserve multiword terms and phrases in the alphanumeric sequence of headings.

Lab manual A book of exercises that includes instructions for laboratory experiments to be carried out, usually under the supervision of an instructor, by a student enrolled in a course in the sciences, often published in softcover in conjunction with a textbook.

Label A small paper form on which information can be written, typed, or printed, designed to be affixed to the surface of an item such as a book, usually for purposes of identification or classification. Libraries use labels extensively in technical processing. They are available precut from library suppliers in various colors, shapes, and sizes, either blank or preprinted, with or without adhesive backing. Labeling tape is also available for making customized labels mechanically. When labels are used in preservation, they should be acid-free. In a broader sense, any identifying mark attached to a thing to set it apart or provide information to those using or viewing it (see labeling).

Label type Indicates label format for printed label for each periodical title.

Labeling The controversial practice of affixing a warning mark or label to library materials considered unsuitable for young children or that contain language or images which some readers or viewers might find offensive or distressing. The practice is followed by some public television stations in the United States when programs containing adult language or graphic images of sex and/or violence are broadcast at times when children are likely to be watching.

Lacuna A gap in a library collection, usually in the holdings on a specific subject or by a particular author, which the library seeks to fill in order to meet the needs of its users. Also refers to a missing portion of a page, or missing pages, in a manuscript or text, especially when caused by damage or normal wear and tear. Plural: lacunae.

Lai In medieval French literature of the late 12th to 13th century, a short poem composed in octasyllabic couplets.

Provencal lais were love poems composed to be sung to music. Marie de France, who wrote in old French at the court of Henry II (Plantagenet), is famous for her short romantic narratives on themes drawn from Arthurian and other Celtic legends.

Laid in A single sheet inserted but not glued into a book or other printed publication. Compare with integral.

Laid paper Handmade paper which, when held up to a light source, reveals a pattern of fine, faintly translucent parallel lines intersecting at right angles in a grid made by the wires of the papermaking frame. The same effect is achieved in machine-made paper by the dandy roll, a cylinder that smooths the surface and impresses designs such as the watermark and countermark. Compare with wove paper.

LAMAR Faculty, staff, and graduate student computer accounts reside on this machine at CSU. Libraries employees may obtain a Lamar account by completing an application form available in the front office.

Lambda Book Report A monthly review publication published by the Lambda Literary Foundation, a nonprofit organization supporting gay and lesbian literature. The Foundation also sponsors the annual Lamda Literary Awards and Behind Our Masks, an annual writers conference.

Lamination A method of preserving old and fragile documents in which a layer of thin transparent plastic film is adhered to one or both sides of a sheet of paper or board by means of heat and/or pressure, sealing it against dust and atmospheric conditions. Processes of deterioration inherent in the object are not arrested by lamination. Encapsulation is preferred in preservation work because it is reversible. Lamination is also used in libraries to protect and enhance the appearance of dust jackets on hardcover books and the covers of paperback editions. Available in rolls from library suppliers, laminate is applied by hand or on a machine called a laminator.

Lampoon A biting satire written in prose or verse, usually directed against an individual in public life or an institution that has become the object of public scrutiny. Lampoons written in verse were popular in England during the 18th century. The form was given new life in 20th century by publications such as the Harvard Lampoon and its close relative, the National Lampoon. Because this form of humor exposes its subject(s) to public ridicule, libel laws impose restraint.

LAN Local Area Network. A network of directly-connected machines (located in close proximity), providing high speed communication over physical media such as fiber optics, coaxial cable, or twisted pair wiring.

Landmark building A library facility preserved because it has architectural and historical significance, for example, the New York Public Library building at 5th Avenue and 42nd Street in Manhattan which houses the humanities and social sciences research collections. Designed in the beaux-arts style by John Merven Carrere and Thomas Hastings, and constructed on the site of the old Croton Reservoir, the building opened in the spring of 1911.

Landsat map high-altitude satellite photograph-like

Language dictionary A dictionary that lists the words of one language, in alphabetical order, with definitions in another. Some language dictionaries are divided into two parts, first listing the words of a language with definitions in another, and then vice versa.

Language The system of conventional sounds and symbols developed over time by a specific human population as a means of expressing and exchanging thoughts, feelings, information, and knowledge. A language consists of a vocabulary and rules of grammar, syntax, and orthography. A national language is the official language of a specific country, used in its government publications and educational institutions. Some countries have more than one national language, for example, Canada where both English and French are officially recognized.

LAPSE Issues of a serial are no longer being received; requires claiming with VENDOR/publisher to reestablish receipt.

Lapsit services Library services and programs designed for very young children (12-24 months old) in conjunction with their adult caregivers, including nursery rhymes, songs, finger plays, and storytelling, often with the aid of a flannel board or puppets.

Laptop A small portable battery-operated personal computer, usually equipped with a built-in keyboard and mouse, and a flat panel monitor that folds over the keyboard to form a cover. Modern research libraries are retrofitting study areas to provide network connectivity for patrons who use laptops, and some academic libraries are installing them in classrooms used for bibliographic instruction. Synonymous with notebook. Compare with personal digital assistant (PDA).

Laptop Computer Check-out Morgan Library's laptops are available for use in the Library by current Colorado State University faculty, staff, and students.

Large paper edition An edition in which the leaves are larger in size than the trade edition (and usually printed on better quality paper) making the margins wider than normal. Limited and deluxe editions are often printed in this way.

Large print (LP) Any type size larger than 16-. Also refers to books printed in type larger than the 9-, 10-, or 11-point size normally used for text, mostly publications for visually impaired, elderly, and young readers (picture books, beginning readers, etc.). The National Association for Visually Handicapped has established standards for LP materials. English-language LP materials currently in print (and forthcoming) are listed in The Complete Directory of Large Print Books and Serials, a reference serial published by R. R. Bowker, arranged by subject, with author and title indexes, and printed in 14-point type to facilitate use by sight-impaired readers.

LARS Automated Binding Preparation System. Used to produce bind slips.

Laser printer An output device introduced by IBM in 1975 that uses a laser beam and electrostatic imaging to print text and/or image(s) by transferring and fusing toner to the surface of paper, one sheet at a time. Resolution is determined by the spot size of the laser. Print quality is superior to that of dot-matrix and ink-jet printers. Hewlett-Packard is currently the major manufacturer of personal laser printers, from low-end desktop models capable of printing 4-8 pages per minute, to large office units capable of printing up to 32 pages per minute.

Laubach Literacy (LL) A nonprofit educational corporation dedicated to helping adults of all ages improve their lives and communities by learning essential literacy skills (reading, writing, math, and problem-solving). Its publishing division, New Readers Press, distributes over 500 titles to literacy programs, libraries, schools, prisons, and religious organizations in the United States. LL is an affiliate of the American Library Association.

Law binding A style of binding used for law books in which the boards are covered in leather or imitation leather of a medium to light color, with two contrasting bands of a darker color on the spine (usually dark red, green, or blue).

Law library A type of special library with a collection consisting primarily of materials for legal research and study, including case law, federal and state statutes, international legal agreements, treatises, reference works, legal periodicals, and electronic search tools. A law library maintained by a court, law school, or legal firm is normally managed by a law librarian who may hold a J.D. degree in addition to the M.L.S. or M.L.I.S.

Law/Tax Collection Noncirculating collection of legal and tax materials located in Morgan Library, 1st floor, west wing. Included in the Law/Tax Collection are sources for judicial opinion, statutory law, and reporting services dealing with Federal and Colorado taxation.

Layout In typography, the overall plan of a printed publication showing the placement of text blocks, illustrations, captions, running heads, etc., and indicating fonts and font sizes, intended to be followed by the printer. Also refers to the process of preparing copy for typesetting, and to the preliminary rough sketch and eventually to the more precise drawing called a "comprehensive" showing the general appearance of a printed page, usually done on special paper ruled in 12-point squares. Compare with make-up.

LBC Libraries Budget Committee. Recommends one-time expenditures to the DEAN. Members are the assistant dean, chair of LFC, and the Director of Fiscal Service.

LC copy Cataloging information issued by the Library of Congress showing how they cataloged a book or serial. Available on-line from RLIN and OCLC, and in book form in the National Union Catalog.

LCD Liquid crystal display, a technology used in display panels and projectors that enables the output from a computer or other digital device to be projected onto a large screen. LCD technology is used in laptops because it requires less power than a conventional light-emitting monitor and occupies less space, allowing a flat panel to be used as the display unit; however, an external light source is required (ambient light is usually sufficient).

LCSH (Library of Congress Subject Headings) - A controlled vocabulary used to describe the contents of works. Materials classified with Library of Congress call numbers use these subject headings.

Lead story The most important item of news reported in an issue of a newspaper or news magazine, or in a television news broadcast, usually printed on the front page, featured on the front cover, or introduced in the opening minutes of the program. The lead story is usually longer and more detailed than the other stories published in the same issue or broadcast on the same program.

Lead term In indexing, the first word in a heading or content descriptor, which determines the position of the heading when it is listed or filed in alphanumeric sequence. In headings of two or more words, conventional word order is sometimes inverted to bring the most significant word into first-word position (example: Law, Spartan as opposed to Spartan Law).

Leader The first field of a MARC record, consisting of 24 character positions, each of which encodes data of a specific type, mostly information of use to catalogers, such as record status (new, corrected or revised, deleted, etc.) And descriptive cataloging form (AACR2, ISBD, etc.), or codes to facilitate record retrieval (character coding scheme, base address of data, etc.). Cataloging software usually provides prompts or windows to assist catalogers as they enter information in the leader.

Leaders In typesetting, a line of dots or dashes intended to direct the reader's eye across the page, as from a chapter title listed in a table of contents to the appropriate locator (usually a page number) in the right-hand column. Also, a publishing term for the most important titles on a publisher's frontlist.

Lead-in title Backlisted titles offered in a book club mail advertising campaign at very low prices or no charge, as an inducement to potential subscribers, or as bonuses or dividends to existing members. Synonymous with introductory title.

Lead-in vocabulary In a thesaurus of the controlled vocabulary used in indexing the literature of an academic discipline (or group of disciplines), cross-references are included to direct or "lead" the user from synonyms and quasi-synonyms to the authorized subject heading or descriptor, usually by means of an instruction to see or USE the preferred term. A thesaurus containing such cross-references is said to have syndetic structure.

Leading In printing, the amount of vertical space allowed by the typesetter between lines of type in a column or on a page. Pronounced "ledding."

Leaf In book production, a sheet or half-sheet of paper or parchment when folded in half forms two leaves, each of single thickness with two pages, one on each side, either blank or printed. In early books, the leaves were consecutively numbered only on the recto or right-hand page of an opening (foliation), but in modern book production, the recto usually bears an odd page number and the verso or left-hand page an even number (pagination), sometimes reversed in reprints.

Leaflet a publication of two to four pages, unstitched and unbound, usually folded or stapled together, as in the program notes distributed to attendees at a performance. Also refers to a thin pamphlet of comparatively small size.

Leak In information systems, the loss of confidentiality that results when security precautions are breached. When sensitive information falls into unauthorized hands, the consequences can be devastating for those who have a stake in maintaining secrecy, but leaks can also be intentional (to divert attention, pre-empt criticism, etc.).

Lean matter A printer's term for copy that takes longer than usual to set because it does not contain much white space, for example, a scholarly essay or treatise, as opposed to dialogue or poetry. The opposite of fat matter.

Learning curve A graphical representation of the rate at which learning occurs, particularly in a new environment or subject area. A learning curve may be steep, moderate, or gentle depending on the amount of new knowledge to be acquired, its complexity, and the time available to complete the task.

Learning management system (LMS): Software used for developing, using, and storing course content of all types.

Information within a learning management system often takes the form of learning objects (see "learning object" below).

Learning object A chunk of course content that can be reused and independently maintained. Although each chunk is unique in its content and function, it must be able to communicate with learning systems using a standardized method not dependent on the system. Each chunk requires a description to facilitate search and retrieval.

Leased Line Refers to line such as a telephone line or fiber-optic cable that is rented for exclusive 24-hour, 7-days-a-week use from your location to another location. The highest speed data connections require a leased line.

Leather The skin of an animal (calf, sheep, goat, pig, seal, etc.), processed for use in bookbinding. Often dyed an attractive color, the leather used on book covers may also be embellished with inlay and/or tooling, blind or highlighted in gold or silver. Leather-bound books were common up to the mid-19th century. Today, cloth, paper, or synthetic material is used to cover the boards of trade books published in hardcover. Real leather is used only in hand-binding. Compare with imitation leather and leatherette.

Leather-bound A book bound, fully or partially, in the processed skin of an animal, with the back of the spine always in leather. Medieval manuscripts and early printed books were bound in wooden boards covered in leather or parchment. In modern book production, leather is used mainly in hand-bound books of fine quality. Leather bindings can be plain or tooled, with any tooling left blind or gilt. Compare with imitation leather and leatherette.

Leatherette A durable bookbinding material available in various colors, made from strong machine-glazed paper, embossed to give the appearance of a leather surface.

Leave request form Teal leave request form for professional leave, obtained from the front office and submitted in duplicate to one's immediate supervisor.

Leave without pay To take Leave Without Pay means taking time off from one's (state classified) job without pay. No type of leave shall be earned during periods of leave without pay (i.e. Leave Without Pay affects sick and annual leave accruals). All accrued leave does not have to be exhausted in order to take Leave Without Pay.

Lectern A reading desk in a Christian church, especially one from which portions of the Scriptures are read aloud during services. In a more general sense, any sloping desk or stand, usually with a narrow ledge called a book stop along the bottom edge to support an open book or sheaf of papers, and to allow the reader free use of the hands.

Lectionary A liturgical book containing selections from the Christian Scriptures, indicating the sequence in which they are to be read by a congregation during services throughout the year.

Legal value utility in the conduct of future legal proceedings, or as evidence of past legal decisions

Legend A visual aid that explains to the reader the symbols used on a map or in a diagram. Also refers to the title or caption printed below an illustration, or on a coin or medal.

Legibility The cumulative visual effect of the physical appearance of written or printed text, which depends on the size, shape, and darkness of the characters, their distance from each other, length of line, and the amount of spacing between words and between lines. Other factors that determine legibility are the color and finish of paper, available illumination, and the experience and skill of the reader. In printing, the legibility of text is enhanced by no more than thirteen words per line, adequate type size (9- to 12-point), margins of sufficient width and balance, clarity of type, density of ink, and a paper finish that reduces glare (matte rather than smooth).

Legible Writing or printing that can be easily read or deciphered by the human eye, the opposite of illegible.

Legibility is an important consideration in the design of printed material. Compare with readable.

Legislative history A chronological account of the steps involved in the passage of a bill into law, including events leading up to the first draft, committee hearings, lobbying efforts, floor debates, compromises, final vote, enactment, and any subsequent history, such as a presidential veto or court test.

Legislative reference service An agency or unit of government that provides research assistance to legislatures and other government agencies on issues related to proposed legislation. This function may include assistance in drafting and indexing bills. At the federal level, legislative reference service is provided by Congressional Research Services, a division of the Library of Congress.

Lender string In interlibrary loan, a list of the OCLC symbols of up to five libraries, selected by the borrowing library from the holdings display in the OCLC worldcat database as potential lenders for an item requested by a library patron. OCLC queries the first prospective lender on the list and if the request is not filled, the second is automatically queried, and so on. Should the request remain unfilled after the first five libraries have been contacted, the borrowing library has the option of selecting a second string of five new OCLC symbols from the holdings list and repeating the process.

Lending library A library or other institution that sends materials on request to another library, usually via interlibrary loan. Compare with borrowing library.

Lending service Access services, including reserve, are provided with a minimal staff; other library services are not provided when the Libraries are open on this basis.

Letter In writing and printing, a character or symbol used to represent a speech sound. All the letters of a written language constitute its alphabet. The Latin alphabet used to write the English language contains 26 letters, each with an uppercase and lowercase form.

Letter to the editor A letter, usually printed at the discretion of the publisher on the editorial page of a newspaper or magazine, in which a reader expresses his or her views on the subject of a previously published article or editorial, or on the editorial policy of the publication in general, sometimes followed by a brief response from the editor(s).

Letter-by-letter A method of alphabetization in which any punctuation marks and divisions are ignored in a heading consisting of two or more words, and the heading treated as a single word ("newt" appearing before "New Testament"). The Chicago Manual of Style recommends a modification in which the method is followed only to the first comma or parenthesis, to keep identically spelled surnames together. Most dictionaries are alphabetized in this fashion. Synonymous with all through and follow through. Compare with word-by-word.

Lettered Inscribed with letters of the alphabet, especially the title on the spine of a book, usually done in letters of contrasting color or gilt. Also refers to a person who is educated or literate.

Letterform The shape of the uppercase and lowercase letters of the Latin alphabet, especially with reference to their evolution in calligraphy and their design in typography. Also spelled letter form. For a brief but informative treatment of the history of letterforms, please see the entry on "Letters" in Geoffrey Glaister's Encyclopedia of the Book (Oak Knoll/ British Library, 1996).

Lettering The act of making letters or of inscribing with letters, numerals, and special characters, especially by hand-printing, painting, or calligraphy. In binding, the process of marking the cover of a volume with the title, name of author, volume number, etc. To remain sharp and legible, lettering on the outside of a book should be applied with sufficient pressure, temperature, and dwell to ensure permanent adhesion of the stamping foil to the covering material.

Letterpress The original printing process invented by Johann Gutenberg in which the raised surface of metal type, or an image on a block or plate, is coated with ink transferred directly to paper (or some other printing surface) by the application of pressure. After a press run, type may be left standing for subsequent reuse, or broken up and used for another job. In modern printing, letterpress had been largely replaced by offset. Also spelled letter-press.

Letters patent A written document of record, issued by a government or monarch to confer a right, privilege, title, office, or property on a person or corporate entity, in a manner that is open for inspection.

Letters The handwritten, typewritten, or printed personal or business messages of one or more persons. A letter is usually enclosed in an envelope and sent to the addressee by post or courier. In AACR2, the collected letters of a single person are cataloged under the name of the writer, with an added entry for the editor or compiler. If the letters are addressed to the same person, an added entry is also made under the name of the addressee. The collected letters of several writers are cataloged under the name of the editor or compiler. Compare with correspondence.

Levant A high-quality open-grained morocco leather made from the skin of the Angora goat, used in bookbinding to achieve an elegant, highly polished look.

Level of description In library cataloging, the amount of detail given in a bibliographic record, indicated by the number of data elements included in the bibliographic description of the item. Anglo-American Cataloging Rules specify three distinct levels of description: full level, core level, and minimal level.

Lexicography The process of writing and compiling a dictionary or glossary, including the selection of terms and the preparation of an entry for each word, giving the correct spelling, pronunciation, derivation, one or more definitions, and sometimes antonyms and examples of usage. The person who writes or compiles such a work is a lexicographer. Compare with lexicology.

Lexicology The field of study devoted to the origins, form, and meaning of words in any language. Compare with lexicography.

Lexicon Originally, a dictionary of Greek, Hebrew, Arabic, or some other literary language. In modern usage, a specialized dictionary or glossary of the words of a specific subject or field of study. In linguistics, a list of all the lexical items (lexemes) in a given language.

Liaison In academic libraries, librarians are often assigned one or more academic departments for which they serve as intermediary between the teaching faculty and the library. Liaison responsibilities may include bibliographic instruction, collection development (including reference and electronic resources), current awareness, and faculty training in the use of library resources. Most liaison librarians have academic preparation or at least some level of expertise in the disciplines they serve.

Libdex The Library Index A searchable worldwide online directory of library homepages, Web-based opacs, Friends of the Library homepages, and library e-commerce affiliates, maintained by Peter Scott of the University of Saskatchewan Library

Libel A written or printed statement or representation intended to expose a person, group of persons, or corporate entity to public ridicule or contempt, or to damage in some other way the reputation of its subject. Also refers to the act of publishing such a statement. Burden of proof is on the plaintiff to show that actual damage occurred. In the United States, the constitutional guarantee of freedom of speech and press provides no protection to libelous statements. Slander is defamatory words spoken but not published in writing or in print.

Librarian A professionally trained person responsible for the care of a library and its contents, including the selection, processing, and organization of materials and the delivery of information, instruction, and loan services to meet the needs of its users. In an online environment, the role of the librarian is to manage and mediate access to information which may exist only in electronic form.

Librarian of Congress An office created in 1802, two years after the Library of Congress was established, for which no qualifications were specified. The position is filled by presidential appointment for no fixed term. In 1897, the Senate acquired the power to approve the President's nomination, and the Librarian of Congress was given the authority to appoint the staff of the Library of Congress and to establish its rules and regulations. In the 20th century, a precedent was established for appointing the Librarian of Congress for life.

Librariana A catch-all term for the body of information, works, and memorabilia that has accumulated on the subject of libraries, librarians, and related topics, particularly items of historical interest.

Librarianship The profession devoted to applying theory and technology to the creation, selection, organization, management, preservation, dissemination, and utilization of collections of information in all formats. In the United States, often used synonymously with library science. A person formally trained or certified to perform such services is a librarian.

Libraries Faculty Council (LFC) A deliberative and advisory group consisting of all Library faculty members which meets regularly to consider problems and innovations in the Libraries. The group has no power to act, only to recommend to the dean.

Libraries personnel Responsible for administering the full range of personnel services and functions for faculty, classified and student staff categories; for implementing and monitoring personnel policies and practices for students and staff; for ensuring that the Libraries is in compliance with all relevant university, state, and federal regulations and requirements as they pertain to students and classified staff; and for developing, implementing and monitoring staff development/training activities for faculty and classified staff.

Libraries Unlimited (LU) Founded in 1964 by Bohdan S. Wynar, Libraries Unlimited serves the needs of the library profession through the publication of bibliographies and reference books, library science textbooks, information science materials, and practical handbooks, manuals, and monographs for library educators, practicing librarians, media specialists, and teachers. In July 2001, LU joined the Greenwood Publishing Group Inc., a division of Elsevier.

Libraro of Congress Classification The system made up of letters and numbers which divides knowledge into subject areas. The system was devised by the Library of Congress and is used at Colorado State University to arrange books on the shelves. Finding a book on the shelf (Library of Congress call number)

Library Administration and Management Association (LAMA) A division of the American Library Association founded in 1957, LAMA has a membership consisting of library directors and persons with an interest in improving the quality of administration and management in libraries of all types. LAMA publishes the quarterly journal Library Administration & Management (LA&M).

Library administration The control and supervision of a library or library system, including planning, budgeting, policy-making, personnel management, public relations, and program assessment, with responsibility for results. Also refers collectively to the persons responsible for managing a library, usually a board of trustees or dean, library director, and his or her immediate staff..

Library advocate A person who appreciates libraries and their role in society, to the extent of speaking and acting publicly in their support, especially when funding and the freedom to read are at stake.

Library and Information Science Abstracts (LISA) An indexing and abstracting service devoted to the literature of library science and information science, published quarterly from 1950-1968 under the title Library Science Abstracts, and bimonthly since 1969 under the current title by the Library Association of Great Britain (ISSN 0024-2179). Available online from R. R. Bowker, LISA provides abstracts of articles from over 550 periodicals published in over 68 countries worldwide and papers from major English-language conference proceedings, updated biweekly.

Library and Information Science Technology Association (LITA) A division of the American Library Association since in 1966, LITA has a membership consisting of librarians and other information professionals concerned with all aspects of the acquisition, organization, storage, retrieval, and dissemination of information in electronic formats, including digital libraries, metadata, authorization and authentication, electronic journals and electronic publishing, telecommunications, networks, computer security and intellectual property rights, technical standards, online catalogs and bibliographic databases, optical information systems, desktop applications, software engineering, etc. LITA publishes the quarterly journal Information Technology and Libraries (ITAL) and also the LITA Newsletter.

Library association A membership organization consisting of a group of librarians, library directors, and other persons involved with libraries, who meet periodically to discuss matters of professional interest. Library associations elect officers, sponsor conferences, select committees to address specific issues, publish newsletters and professional journals, and charge dues to support the organization's activities. The largest library association in the United States is the American Library Association (ALA). Its counterparts in Canada and Great Britain are the Canadian Library Association (CLA) and the Chartered Institute of Library and Information Professionals (CILIP).

Library award Special honor and recognition given to an individual for outstanding librarianship and/or service to the library profession. If an award includes a monetary prize, it is usually funded by an individual or corporate donor, or by a library association. Recipients of library awards and scholarships are listed annually in the Bowker Annual Library and Book Trade Almanac. A less extensive list is provided in the reference serial American Library Directory.

Library Awareness Program An attempt by the FBI to recruit librarians in the United States as "cold warriors" during the 1970s and 1980s, by suggesting that they restrict public access to unclassified scientific research, particularly information available from the National Technical Information Service (NTIS). Librarians were asked to report on individuals requesting certain categories of scientific information, especially foreign nationals from countries in the Soviet Union. The FBI had the support of the National Commission on Libraries and Information Science (NCLIS) in this effort, which undermined the confidentiality of library lending records and open access to library resources.

Library Bill of Rights A formal statement adopted by the American Library Association in 1948 and amended in 1961, 1990, and 1996, affirming the right of libraries in the United States to provide, to all members of the communities they serve, materials expressing diverse points of view, and to remain free of censorship. Implementation of the Library Bill of Rights is the work of the Office for Intellectual Freedom of the ALA

Library binder A commercial binder that specializes in serving the needs of libraries. Most libraries regularly send their periodical back files to a library binder to be bound into annual volumes. Special binding may also be needed for heavily used items and trade paperbacks. Library binders are organized in the Library Binding Institute.

Library binding An especially strong, durable binding used for periodical back files and for rebinding worn volumes and new paperbound publications for which circulation is expected to remain high over a comparatively long period of time. Includes pre-library binding.

Library Binding Institute (LBI) A trade association of commercial library binders doing business in the United States, Canada, and the U.K., LBI was established in 1935 to create and maintain standards for library rebinding and prebinding, improve binding methods, and facilitate cooperation between library binders and between binders and their customers. Membership is also open to suppliers of library binders and organizations with an interest in the preservation of books and periodicals. LBI developed the ANSI standard for library binding in cooperation with the American Library Association. The Institute publishes the magazine The New Library Scene and technical papers on binding and related topics..

Library bond An interest-bearing or discounted security issued by a library district, or by the government entity of which a library or library system is a part, usually to finance the construction and/or renovation of facilities, or some other major capital project. A bond places the library district under a general obligation to pay the bondholder (investor) a specified amount of interest, usually at regular intervals, and to repay the principal amount of the loan within a designated period of time. The bond is backed by a majority of voters in the district, who consent to be taxed at a slightly higher rate to raise sufficient revenue to pay the interest and principal on the loan. Bond measures pass more easily in times of prosperity than in economic recession.

Library card A small paper or plastic card issued by a library to a registered borrower, which must be presented at the circulation desk in order to check out materials from its collections. Identification is usually required of new applicants. In most libraries in the United States, library cards are barcoded for electronic circulation. Periodic renewal may be required to verify current street address and telephone number. Synonymous with borrower card.

Library card number The 8-digit numerical code found on the back of your library card. Mesa library card numbers all begin with the numeral 9.

Library classes a variety of courses and one-shot classes and workshops offered by the

Library closure The closing of a library or branch in a library system, temporarily or permanently, usually due to budgetary constraints or demographic changes in the area served. Library closings are announced in the news section of American Libraries, the monthly magazine of the American Library Association.

Library collection The total accumulation of books and other materials owned by a library, cataloged and arranged for ease of access, which often consists of several smaller collections (reference, circulating books, serials, government documents, rare books, special collections, etc.). The process of building a library collection over time is called collection development. Synonymous with holdings. Compare with collection.

Library conference A formal gathering of librarians, library directors, and others associated with libraries, for the purpose of meeting colleagues, discussing issues and events, and learning about new products, services, technologies, and recent developments in the library science and information science profession. Most library associations sponsor regular conferences at which officers are elected, committees and task forces formed, policies formulated, awards announced, etc. Conferees are generally charged a registration fee based on the sections of the conference they plan to attend..

Library connection The Libraries' newsletter to communicate new developments and events to faculty and graduate students; it is published during the fall and spring semesters. It is cataloged at Z732 C63 C62.

Library cooperation Methods by which libraries and library systems work together for the mutual benefit of their users, including centralized processing, cooperative cataloging, international exchange of bibliographic information, union catalogs, resource sharing, etc.

Library director The person who has overall responsibility for supervising the operations of a library or library system, including planning, budgeting, policy-making, personnel management, and program assessment. In public libraries, the library director is usually subject to the oversight of a board of trustees; in academic libraries, by a dean of academic affairs or provost.

Library discount A discount off the list price of a book or other publication, given by most publishers and jobbers on purchases made by an institutional library. Most publishers offer a flat rate, usually 5-10%. Jobbers may link the discount rate to size of order or volume of purchasing. As a general rule, specialized titles are given a shorter discount than trade books, or not discounted at all because of their limited sales potential.

Library district An officially delineated geographic area in which the residents decide by popular vote whether to provide tax support for a public library or library system, or one of the geographical areas into which a state is divided for the purpose of administering libraries in accordance with a comprehensive state-wide tax plan.

Library edition An edition of a book published in a binding stronger and more durable than the usual publisher's binding, for marketing specifically to libraries, usually more expensive than the trade edition of the same title.

Library education Educational programs designed to prepare students for the post-baccalaureate degree of M.L.S. or M.L.I.S., taught by the faculty of a university department known as a library school (or school of librarianship). Modern library education began in 1887 when Melvil Dewey founded the first school for training professional librarians at Columbia University.

Library equipment Mechanical and electronic devices purchased by a library for staff use, or to facilitate patron use of its services and collections, including photocopy machines, microform reader-printers, video and CD players, projection equipment, computers and computer peripherals, security devices, etc.

Library extension Programs and activities that enable a library or library system to deliver traditional services outside the physical walls of its facilities, including bookmobiles, books-by-mail, and direct delivery of library materials to patrons. Compare with library outreach.

Library faculty The professionally trained librarians employed at an academic institution that grants faculty status to librarians. One of the advantages of faculty status is the right to participate in governance. At some institutions, library faculty are members of the same collective bargaining unit as the teaching faculty. Whether they are eligible for tenure and promotion to the same ranks as the teaching faculty depends on the contract governing employment

Library fines The date your library materials are due is stamped in each item as you check them out. For most library items, CSUL has a no-fines policy for short-term overdues.

Library From the Latin liber meaning "book" (in Greek and the Romance languages the corresponding term is bibliotheca). A collection or group of collections of books and/or other materials organized and maintained for use (reading, consultation, study, research, etc.). Institutional libraries, organized to facilitate access by a specific clientele, are staffed by librarians and other personnel trained to provide services to meet user needs. By extension, the room, building, or facility that houses such a collection, usually but not necessarily built for that purpose. Directory information on libraries is available alphabetically by country in World Guide to Libraries, a serial published by K. G. Saur. Two comprehensive worldwide online directories of library homepages are libdex and Libweb. Abbreviated lib.

Library Gateway The Library Gateway is a web site that

allows electronic access to Cornell University Library 24 hours a day. It performs three major functions:

Library hand A highly legible, uniform style of handwriting traditionally used by librarians for making entries in manuscript catalogs before the typewriter came into widespread use. With the conversion of card catalogs into files of machine-readable records, catalog cards have fallen into disuse and handwritten catalog entries are rarely seen.

Library historian A researcher who writes about the history of libraries and librarianship, from ancient to modern times. Librarians with an interest in library history are organized in the Library History Round Table (LHRT) of the American Library Association.

Library History Round Table (LHRT) A round table of the American Library Association dedicated to facilitating communication among scholars and students of library history, supporting research in library history, and addressing current issues of concern to library historians, such as conservation and preservation. LHRT publishes the semiannual LHRT Newsletter..

Library Home - **A button in the library catalog that, when clicked, returns the user to the library home page.**

Library hours The hours during which a library is open to its users, and any days when it is not open, usually posted near the entrance or at the circulation desk. Libraries also make their hours available by telephone and via their Web pages. Because staffing is required to keep a library facility open, hours often reflect budgetary constraints. Most libraries are equipped with a book drop for returning items when the facility is closed.

Library humor Jokes, cartoons, anecdotes, unusual reference questions, witticisms, satire, occupational folklore, etc., having to do with libraries and librarianship.

Library Instruction Round Table (LIRT) A round table of the American Library Association dedicated to promoting formal and informal library instruction in all types of libraries, as a means of helping library users acquire the information literacy skills essential for lifelong learning..

Library Journal (LJ) Founded in 1876, Library Journal is a combination trade journal/review publication published in 20 issues per year by Cahner Business Information, a division of Elsevier. LJ publishes news and announcements of interest to library professionals, feature articles, commentary, analysis of trends, regular columns, and approximately 7,500 reviews per year of new books, magazines, databases and CD-roms, videocassettes, and books-on-tape suitable for general library collections aimed at adult readers. The reviews are short but evaluative, written by and for librarians. Materials published for children and young adults are reviewed in School Library Journal.

Library legislation Laws passed by a federal or state legislative body, pertaining to or affecting the interests of libraries and related institutions (example: Digital Millennium Copyright Act of 1998). Through their professional associations, librarians and library advocates seek to influence legislative decision-making in ways that will benefit libraries and their users.

Library Literature & Information Science (LLIS) Published since 1934 by H. W. Wilson, Library Literature & Information Science is an author and subject index to the English-language literature of library science and information science, covering books, periodical articles, pamphlets, and library school theses, with book reviews listed in a separate section at the end of each volume. Published from 1934-1998 under the title Library Literature, LLIS is available in print in bimonthly paperback supplements cumulated annually. It is also available as an online database directly from the Wilson Company or via OCLC firstsearch (1980 to the present

Library market The portion of the market for books and other publications generated by sales to libraries, library systems, and related organizations such as museums, archives, and research institutions. The library market is segmented by type of library (public, academic, school, special, etc.). Publishers and jobbers market their products to libraries by exhibiting at library conferences, advertising in library trade journals and review publications, offering special library discounts and prepublication prices, and direct mail advertising (trade catalogs and brochures).

Library materials All the items purchased by a library or library system to satisfy the information needs of its users, including books, periodicals, reference materials, music scores, maps, microforms, and nonprint media, as distinct from equipment and supplies. Some libraries include subscriptions to electronic resources in the materials budget, others fund them separately. Except for gifts and special endowments, the acquisition of library materials is normally funded through the operating budget. The rapid escalation of journal subscription prices over the past decade has forced many academic libraries to cancel periodical subscriptions to maintain balance between expenditures for books and serials.

Library of Congress (LC) Classification System - A system using a combination of letters and numbers to indicate the subject content of library materials. Materials are shelved by the call numbers of the LC classification system. NOTE:·Most academic libraries use LC classification system (including the LRITC) while most public libraries use the Dewey Decimal classification

Library of Congress (LC) Classification: The call number system that uses a combination of letters and numbers to identify the broad subject and shelf location of items in the library collection.

Library of Congress (LC) Established by Congress in 1800 to function as a research library for the legislative branch of the federal government, the Library of Congress eventually became the unofficial national library of the

United States. Located in Washington D.C., LC houses a collection of over 120 million items and administers the U.S. copyright system, serving as the nation's copyright depository. LC is also the primary source of original cataloging in the United States. The machine-readable cataloging (MARC) and cataloging-in-publication (CIP) programs originated at the Library of Congress.

Library of Congress Control Number (LCCN) When the Library of Congress began printing catalog cards in 1898 and distributing them in 1901, a unique Library of Congress Card Number was assigned to each item for identification and control. With the development of machine-readable cataloging in the late 1960s, LCCN became the Library of Congress Control Number. It is used in bibliographic records and also in authority and classification records. The **LCCN** is assigned to a publication after the deposit copy is received by the U.S. Copyright Office, or in advance of the publication date if a publisher requests cataloging-in-publication..

Library of Congress Rule Interpretations (LCRI) A loose-leaf service that provides current information on recent decisions of the Library of Congress concerning the interpretation of the most recent revision of Anglo-American Cataloging Rules (AACR2). **LCRI** is published in print and as part of Cataloger's Desktop available on CD-ROM.

Library of Congress subject heading (LCSH) A descriptive word or phrase selected by a subject specialist at the Library of Congress from the list of Library of Congress Subject Headings and assigned to a book or other item when first published to indicate its subject. Multiple subject headings are assigned when necessary or desirable. The complete list of LC subject headings is published annually in a multi-volume set known to librarians as "the big red books," usually available in the reference section of most large public and academic libraries, and in the cataloging department of smaller libraries. Compare with Sears subject heading.

Library portal Software that allows a computer user to customize online access to collections of information resources by creating a list of Internet connections, much like a personalized directory of street addresses and telephone/FAX numbers (example: mylibrary). The purpose is to reduce information overload by allowing patrons to select only the resouroes they wish to display on their personal interface.

Library publication A work produced and distributed by a library, for example, a brochure intended for users, describing the library facility, its resources, and the services provided by its staff. Most library publications are ephemeral, but large academic and research libraries publish more permanent works. A recent example: Alixe Bovey's Monsters and Grotesques in Medieval Manuscripts published by the British Library in 2002.

Library rate A significantly lower postal rate charged to libraries and related nonprofit institutions by the U.S. Postal Service for books and other educational materials sent by mail. The law was amended in 1976 to allow publishers and distributors to use the rate when shipping books and other materials to libraries. The lower rate has allowed public libraries to offer books-by-mail programs to homebound patrons, and has helped keep down the cost of interlibrary loan service. Compare with media mail.

Library Rechnology Service (LTS) The services unit in the Libraries reporting to the ASSISTANT DEAN for Administrative Services that is responsible for technology support of all computers and computer applications in the Libraries.

Library representative A publisher's sales representative responsible for calling on libraries, usually within an established territory, to solicit orders for titles on the publisher's list. Contacts are made, usually by telephone or in person, with librarians responsible for collection development and acquisitions. Also refers to a vendor's representative, responsible for soliciting subscriptions to online bibliographic databases and full-text resources, usually trained to give demonstrations to library selection committees. Abbreviated library rep.

Library Research Round Table (LRRT) Founded in 1968 as a permanent round table of the American Library Association, LRRT is dedicated to fostering library research by providing program opportunities for researchers to describe and disseminate their work, and by informing and educating ALA members about research techniques and the importance of research as a foundation for effective administrative decision-making and problem-solving. LRRT also gives annual awards for distinguished published research and excellence in doctoral research.

Library research Systematic study and investigation of some aspect of library and information science, in which conclusions are based on the statistical analysis of data collected in accordance with a pre-established research design and methodology. Results are usually published in a professional library journal, or presented at a library conference and subsequently published in its proceedings. Library research helps expand the theoretical base of library and information science, and also provides data necessary for effective administrative decision-making and problem-solving. Research on libraries and librarianship published in the previous year is reported in an essay in the Bowker Annual Library and Book Trade Almanac.

Library school A professional school or department qualified to grant the post-baccalaureate degree of M.L.S. or M.L.I.S., supported and administered by an institution of higher learning to prepare graduate students for employment in professional positions in libraries and as information service providers. The first modern library school was established by Melvil Dewey at Columbia University in 1887. Library schools may be accredited or approved (or both). Length of program varies. Synonymous with school of librarianship. Library schools in the United States and

Canada are listed by state and province in a section of the American Library Directory, published annually by R. R. Bowker.

Library science The professional knowledge and skill with which recorded information is selected, acquired, organized, stored, maintained, retrieved, and disseminated to meet the needs of a specific clientele, usually taught at a professional library school qualified to grant the post-baccalaureate degree of M.L.S. or M.L.I.S. The term is used synonymously in the United States with librarianship. Compare with information science.

Library Services and Construction Act (LSCA) Passed by Congress in 1956, the Library Services Act (LSA) provided federal funding for the extension of public library services to the unserved, mainly in rural areas. In 1964, Congress expanded its scope to permit federal grants-in-aid for construction and expansion of library services in all areas with inadequate services, including urban communities. Over a period of thirty years, the effect of LSCA on public library construction was comparable to the earlier era of Carnegie philanthropy. In its final phase, LSCA funding was extended to adult literacy programs and outreach services to the children and youth of poor families, homeless persons, and the physically disabled.

Library Services and Technology Act (LSTA) A section of the Museum and Library Services Act of 1996, LSTA promotes access to learning and to the information resources provided by all types of libraries, by distributing federal funds to state library agencies under a formula based on population. State libraries may use the appropriations to support state-wide initiatives and services, or distribute funds to public, academic, research, school, and special libraries within their state, through sub-grant competitions and cooperative agreements. In the year 2000, more than $138 million in LSTA funds was distributed to state library agencies.

Library staff The entire group of paid employees responsible for the operation and management of a library or library system, including its director, librarians, paraprofessionals, technical assistants, clerical personnel, and pages or student assistants. In academic libraries at institutions that grant librarians faculty status, a distinction is usually made between faculty members and nonfaculty staff. In other types of libraries, a distinction may be made between professionally trained librarians and support staff. Volunteers are not considered part of the staff because they are unpaid.

Library statistics Numerical data assembled, classified, and tabulated to present useful facts and information about the operation of a library or library system, or about the activities of libraries at the local, state, provincial, or national level, usually in the form of a periodic report

Library supplies Expendable materials such as labels, book cards and pockets, date due slips, rubber stamps, mending tape, magnetic strips, plastic sleeves, laminate, paper for printing and photocopying, etc., which a library must order from a library supplier in order to prepare new items for circulation, maintain collections, and provide services.

Library survey A written or oral question-and-answer instrument designed to elicit feedback from library users. Library surveys are administered by staff, or by an outside agency, to determine how well the library's services, programs, and collections meet user needs and any objectives established by the library administration and/or governing institution. They are also used to generate data in library research. Also refers to the report produced as the result of such a study.

Library system A group of libraries administered in common, for example, a central library and its branches or auxiliary outlets. Also, a group of independently administered libraries joined by formal or informal agreement to achieve a common purpose. Under such an arrangement, each library is considered an affiliate. Compare with consortium.

Library technician III Position in the state classified personnel system representing the highest level non-professional class in library activities. Library Technician III's usually serve as assistants to professional librarians and are responsible for planning, developing, and implementing procedures, methods, and systems to effect improvements in efficient operation.

Library tour A guided walk through a library facility, usually conducted by a librarian or library assistant, to orient new users to the location of services and resources. Some libraries have installed online library tours on their Web sites, which include clickable floor plans linked to photographs and descriptive text. Not to be confused with bibliographic instruction.

Library trustee A member of an appointed or elected board responsible for overseeing the growth and development of a library or library system, including long-range planning and policy-making, public relations, and fund-raising. Trustees are usually library advocates but may sometimes be political appointees.

Library use only A circulation status code written on or affixed to a physical item in a library collection and entered in the item record in the catalog, indicating that it is available for use within the walls of the library, but may not be checked out and removed from the premises except by special arrangement. The use of reference books, periodical indexes, and in some cases bound and/or unbound periodicals is generally restricted to the library. Use of items in special collections, such as rare books and manuscripts, may even be restricted to a designated room or area of the library. Compare with noncirculating.

Library website A collection of links and resources

compiled by a library and designed to be viewed via a browser for the World Wide Web (such as Netscape or Internet Explorer). The UNLV Libraries website links to information about the library and tools that will help with research and learning and it has this address: http://www.library.unlv.edu

Library Workstations Computers in the library that provide access to the IUCAT online catalog, Helmke Library's homepage, and other Web resources.

Libretto The words or text to which a cantata, oratorio, opera, operetta, or other work for the musical stage is set, often published in the form of a small booklet for enthusiasts who wish to follow along while attending a performance or listening to a sound recording. The person who writes a libretto is the librettist (example: Edna St. Vincent Millay for The King's Henchman, an opera composed by Deems Taylor). To find librettos online, try a keywords search on the term "librettos" in Yahoo!

LibSys libsys is a software package for library automation. It has been developed by a New Delhi based software company - Info-Tek Consultants Pvt. Ltd., engaged in providing software solutions for General Insurance and ERP/CRM since 1984. Its continuous growth for the last 12 years, has made libsys a defacto standard for libraries in India. Its acceptance in global market further strengthens its popularity across the country as the most field proven library system in a wide spectrum of libraries with unmatchable depth in functionality and features. With an open system architecture (3-tier) since its inception and its continuous transition from a host multi-user system to Client-Server implementation and finally a total web-based solution, makes libsys an advanced multidimensional library system. A powerful and user friendly Web-OPAC along with Windows based OPAC, makes it an outstanding choice for a Library system. Libsys handles Indian languages/scripts using ISM Publisher and GIST of C-DAC. There is an additional 'Unicode' support in libsys that facilitates handling of both International and Indian languages/scripts.

Libweb A very comprehensive worldwide directory of library homepages, updated daily on the Berkeley Digital Library Web site.

Licensed book A book in which the author makes use of a character or product subject to copyright restrictions, for example, a children's book based on a motion picture character (Mickey Mouse) or a commercially successful toy (Barbie). Use is by permission of the copyright holder under the terms of a licensing agreement handled by the copyright owner's licensing agent. Although the sales potential of licensed books makes them popular with retail booksellers, they are as a general rule not purchased for library collections.

Licensing agreement A formal written contract between a library and a vendor for the lease of one or more proprietary (copyrighted) bibliographic databases or online resources, usually for a fixed period of time in exchange for payment of an annual subscription fee or per-search charge. Vendors typically charge libraries on a sliding scale based on number of registered borrowers or FTE enrollment, number of institutions or facilities served, and number of simultaneous users. Most licensing agreements limit remote access to registered users. For more information about licensing, see the final draft of Principles for Licensing Electronic Resources developed by the AALL, ALA, AAHSL, ARL, MLA, and SLA. Compare with site license.

Lifelong learning One of the goals of bibliographic instruction and information literacy programs is to help library users obtain the skills they need to pursue knowledge at any age, independent of a formal educational institution. Public libraries play an important role in meeting this need because they provide access to materials in a wide range of subjects at various reading levels, not only for students enrolled in a formal curriculum, but for anyone interested in reading and learning.

Ligature Two or more letters joined together in

printing, such as the double ff joined at the cross-stroke in some fonts. Also refers to the stroke that joins the two letters. In letterpress, a ligature is cast as a single unit of type.

Light pen Pencil-like wand attached to a computer terminal used to read barcode labels.

Lightface A typeface in which the characters are the same size as medium-weight and boldface type of the same font, but composed of thinner strokes that do not appear as dark on the printed page.

Light-pen A metal stylus equipped with a light sensor on one end for scanning barcodes at the circulation desk. Some models require an external decoder. Synonymous with bar code wand.

Lignin An organic substance contained in wood pulp, considered undesirable in all but the lowest grades of paper because it contains acid which weakens the cellulose in vegetable fiber, causing paper, board, and cloth to yellow and become brittle over time. Lignin is removed in the manufacture of chemical pulp, but not in the production of groundwood pulp from which inexpensive papers such as newsprint are made.

Ligue des Bibliotheques Europeenes de Recherche (LIBER) The European version of the Association of Research Libraries, LIBER is a nongovernmental association of the national, university, and research libraries of Europe, founded in 1971 by an IFLA steering group under the auspices of the Council of Europe. Its goal is to assist in establishing a functional network of research libraries throughout Europe, improve access to research collections and services, facilitate research librarianship, and help preserve the European cultural heritage. LIBER publishes LIBER Quarterly and sponsors a conference in a different country each year.

Limerick A five-line poem written in light verse in which the rhymes (in a/a/b/b/a scheme) are highly original and often irreverent to the point of being unprintable. The earliest examples are from the 18th century nursery rhyme collection Mother Goose Melodies for Children ("Hickory dickory dock..."). A brief discussion of the limerick form is available online compliments of the English Department at Emory University.

Limitation The statement that certifies the total number of copies printed in a limited edition, usually appearing on the verso of the leaf preceding the title page. The statement usually notes any special qualities of the edition (large paper, special binding, etc.) And provides a blank space for the number of each copy to be entered by hand. Synonymous with certificate of issue.

Limited edition An edition consisting of a predetermined number of copies (usually 200 to 500, seldom more than 1500) which the publisher intends not to reprint in exactly the same form. If the individual copies are consecutively numbered, each copy usually bears a certificate of issue on the verso of the leaf preceding the title page, indicating the size of the edition and copy number. Individual copies may also be autographed by the author. If a trade edition of the same work is also issued, the limited edition is usually printed on finer paper, given a better quality binding, and sold at a higher price. In the antiquarian book trade, a copy of a limited edition usually commands a higher price because of its rarity. Compare with deluxe edition.

Limited retention Serial issues kept for a designated amount of time and then discarded; are not bound.

Limited service efrence serviceand circulation services are provided with minimal staffing, from 8:00 a.m-5:00 p.m., Monday-Friday, during Intersession schedule.

Limiting A feature of a well-designed online catalog or bibliographic database that allows the user to employ various parameters to restrict the retrieval of entries containing the terms included in the search statement. Limits may be set before a search is executed, after results are displayed, or both, depending on the design of the system.

Limiters are not standardized but typically include: publication date, material type, language, full-text, peer-reviewed (journal articles), and locally held.

Limits In the library catalog and some other databases, a means to restrict a search to include only items that contain a certain characteristic. Common characteristics for limiting a search include: date of publication, periodical title, type of resource (book, video, periodical, etc.), language, and availability in full-text. In the library catalog, the limits feature is not available for Author, Subject or Call Number searching.

Limp binding A book bound without boards in flexible leather, vellum, or cloth covers, lined or unlined, a style used mainly for diaries, devotional works, and light verse. The squares in limp binding often extend further beyond the edges of the sections than in a normal binding. Compare with flexible binding.

Line art In printing, an illustration of reproduction quality done in black-and-white, as opposed to a half-tone in which the range of tonal values in the original is rendered by converting the image into a field of minutely graded dots.

Line drawing A drawing executed entirely in lines without the use of shading, hatching, or some other graphic technique to add depth or volume to the image. Cartoons, caricatures, and diagrams are often done in this style.

Linear feet Measurement of the size of library holdings. General Library holdings usually average 8 to 10 volumes per linear foot.

Line-item budget A method of budgeting used in some libraries and library systems in which anticipated expenditures are divided into discrete functional categories called "lines" (salaries and wages, materials, equipment, etc.) For the purpose of systematically allocating resources and tracking operating expenditures.

Lining Materials applied to the binding edge of a book with adhesive, following rounding and backing, to hold the sewn sections together securely, usually a piece of thin, loosely woven fabric called crash (gauze, mull, super), followed by a strip of kraft paper as a second layer in better quality bindings. Synonymous in this sense with back-lining. The term is also used synonymously with endpapers.

Link A direct connection in a hypertext document to the Internet address (URL) of another document, embedded as a word or phrase in the text, or appearing as a symbol, icon, or other graphic element which can be activated by the click of a mouse or some other pointing device. Text links usually appear underlined and in blue on the computer screen. A link is broken if it does not take the user to the desired destination when clicked. Link rot is a colloquial expression for the tendency of links to become broken due to address changes and the removal of HTML files from public access. The remedy is regular link checking. Synonymous with hyperlink.

Link checking The process of testing the links in an HTML document to determine if they are functioning properly. Software has been developed to check links automatically. Without regular checking and updating, URL changes and dead links may accumulate in a Web page.

Link system A video networking teaching enhancement that enables instructors to broadcast their computer screen contents to each student workstation. The Link System is installed in the Electronic Information Labs #1 and #2.

Linux A widely used Open Source Unix-like operating system. Linux was first released by its inventor Linus Torvalds in 1991. There are versions of Linux for almost every available type of computer hardware from desktop machines to IBM mainframes. The inner workings of Linux are open and available for anyone to examine and change as long as they make their changes available to the public. This has resulted in thousands of people working on various aspects of Linux and adaptation of Linux for a huge variety of purposes, from servers to TV-recording boxes.

LION Library Internet Online Network. A menued front-end system at SDSU that allows access to a number of databases such as library on-line catalogs, periodical indexes, and Internet gophers.

LIS An abbreviation of "library and information science.

LISA Library and Information Science Abstracts.

List All the publications currently available for purchase from a given publisher, including the frontlist and backlist, but not forthcoming titles.

List price The undiscounted price at which a new publication is offered for sale to the public, established by the publisher at the time the edition is issued. The list price is quoted in the publisher's catalog and printed on the front flap of the dust jacket in hardcover editions, and usually on the back cover in softcover editions. Discounts offered to libraries, booksellers, and jobbers are computed as a percentage off the list price. In library cataloging, the list price of an item is indicated (when available) in the standard number and terms of availability area of the bibliographic description (field 020 or 022 of the MARC record). Synonymous with published price and retail price.

List server a program that sends and receives messages for subscribers of an e-mail discussion list.

Listening room A special soundproof room or area in a library, equipped with playback equipment (players, speakers, headphones, etc.) For listening to audiorecordings (compact discs, audiocassettes, lps, etc.). Registered borrowers and sometimes members of the general public are permitted to use the equipment, individually or in groups, usually for a limited period of time.

Listprocessor A program that manages electronic mailing lists; OIT is responsible for the listprocessor software and also handles requests from the OSU community or new mailing lists.

Listserv A distribution list management package whose primary function is to operate mailing lists. It allows groups of computer users with a common interest to communicate among themselves.

LITA Library and Information Technology Association.

Literacy The ability to read and write with a minimal level of proficiency. Illiteracy is the inability to read and write. The literacy rate of a nation or other geographic area is usually expressed as the percentage of its adult citizens who know how to read and write. In the United States, adult literacy programs have been available for many years and public libraries have been heavily involved in promoting literacy. In recent years, such efforts have focused on adults for whom English is not the first language. Compare with information literacy and computer literacy Volunteers of America (LVA) A national network of over 350 locally based programs that provide professionally trained volunteer tutors to teach basic literacy and English to speakers of other languages. LVA is an affiliate of the American Library Association.

Literal Following the exact words and ordinary meaning of a text or speech, without taking into account possible figurative or symbolic use of language, as in a literal interpretation of a passage from the Bible. The interpretation of words or statements according to their denotation rather than their connotation. Also refers to an approach that is prosaic or matter-of-fact, rather than intuitive.

Literary agent An organization or person in the business of offering professional advice to writers on the suitability of manuscripts for publication. An agent may also provide guidance and/or assistance in locating and selecting a publisher, negotiating a book contract, arranging the sale of subsidiary rights, and handling the business of authorship in general, usually in exchange for a commission paid by the author, or a portion of the proceeds derived from the work. A literary agent may also act on behalf of a publisher to find works to fill a specific need. Not all authors use an agent—some prefer to deal directly with the publisher. Directory information for literary agents is available in the reference serials Literary Market Place and Writer's Market.

Literary award A special honor and/or reward given to an author or illustrator for creating a specific work, or in recognition of a distinguished career, usually based on the decision of a qualified panel of judges. Most literary awards and prizes given annually are funded by private individuals or foundations. Rewards may include a medal, grant, and/or cash prize. Recognition usually boosts the sale of the recipient's works and can mean larger advances on royalties from publishers..

Literary Market Place (LMP) Published annually by R. R. Bowker, LMP is a directory of the book publishing industry in the United States and Canada, containing an alphabetic list of U.S. publishers, indexed by subject, type of publication, and geographically by state. It also lists Canadian publishers, small presses, editorial services, literary agents, book trade associations, writer's conferences and workshops, literary awards and prizes, fellowships and grants, and provides a calendar of book trade and promotional events. The section on advertising, marketing, and publicity lists book review publications, news services, book clubs, book exhibits, etc. LMP also includes an industry yellow pages, with separate sections for companies and key personnel. Bowker also publishes the companion International Literary Market Place. The most recent edition of LMP is shelved in the reference section of most large and medium-sized academic and public libraries.

Literary warrant The quantity of works that have been written on a specific subject or topic. In library cataloging, the development of portions of a classification system in response to the content of materials requiring classification. In indexing, the addition of a subject heading or content descriptor to an indexing language, based on the frequency of occurrence of the concept it represents in the title or text of documents indexed. Compare with user warrant.

Literary work A nonsacred work written in literary form (poem, play, essay, novel, story), recognized and appreciated by educated readers and lovers of literature for the superior quality of its style and treatment of an enduring theme. Compare with popular fiction and pulp fiction.

Literati Men of letters. Scholarly, learned, and/or well-educated people.

Literature Collections, reviews, popularizations, textbooks, encyclopedias, handbooks, etc., and tools which point the user to primary sources (abstracts, indexes, bibliographies). Secondary literature provides broader dissemination of information that has already appeared in another form.

Literature Enduring works of poetry or prose that express ideas and emotions of universal human interest in a form and style embodying excellence. Also refers to the body of works written and/or produced on a subject, in a given field of inquiry, or in a specific language, country, period, etc.

Literature guide A reference work that describes special features of the scholarly literature in a given discipline, including important standard reference materials and serials.

Literature review A comprehensive survey of the works published in a field of study, or related to a particular line of research, usually in the form of a bibliographic essay or annotated list of references in which attention is drawn to the most significant works. An annual review is a form of serial devoted entirely to the publication of literature reviews. Synonymous with review of the literature.

Literature search An exhaustive search for published information on a subject, conducted systematically using all available bibliographic finding tools, aimed at locating as much existing material on the topic as possible, an important initial step in any serious research project. Compare with ready reference.

Lithography The process of creating illustrations or prints by drawing on a zinc plate or the surface of fine-grained limestone with a water-repellent substance to which ink adheres, a technique developed in Germany in the early part of the 19th century. When the stone is wetted, ink is repelled by the moist areas and attracted only by the design. An impression is made by applying dampened paper to the stone under pressure. In chromolithography, separate stones are used to produce multiple colors.

Litterateur A man of letters, especially one who devotes himself to the study and writing of literature in the capacity of an amateur or dilettante.

Little magazine A periodical of limited circulation, devoted to experimental or avant-garde poetry, fiction, essays, humor, photography, and art. Little magazines flourished in the United States, Britain, and France during the 1920s, but most disappeared before the beginning of World War II. Desktop publishing has given new life to this form of publication. According to Magazines for Libraries, over 5,000 little magazines are currently published in the United States, with some available online (example: Ploughshares). For libraries, indexing is a problem because they fall outside the mainstream press. Synonymous with literary magazine. Compare with zine.

Liturgical work A book used in the worship services of an organized religion. In AACR2, liturgical works are entered under the name of the body with which they are associated (example: Catholic Church). If a well-established title exists in English, it is used as the uniform title (example: Breviary). If there is no well-known title in English, or the name of the body is given in another language, a brief title is entered in the language of the liturgy, followed by a word or phrase in parentheses indicating the variant or special text (if applicable), for example, Book of hours (Ms. Rohan). Compare with sacred text.

LMC Library Management Council; composed of the University Librarian, auls, division directors, personnel officer, budget officer, development officer, and assistant to the University Librarian.

Loan and reserve Access service desk where library materials are checked out and returned.

Loan character A character from one writing system, used in writing another language, for example, the Chinese characters used by the Japanese to write their own language (kanji).

Loan Period The amount of time a patron may borrow a book or other item from the library. The time varies depending on the type of material borrowed and the status of the borrower.

Loan rule In library circulation systems, the decision governing the prescribed period of time for which an item of a specific item type may be checked out by a borrower, depending on the patron type. The loan rule also determines the form of the notice sent when an item is kept past its due date, and the amount of any overdue fine charged to the patron. The cost of replacing a lost or damaged item may also be determined in part by the loan rule. Each library or library system establishes and maintains its own set of loan rules for the various categories of materials in its collections.

Loan status The type of loan in effect at a particular time for a specific item in a library collection. Most items are available for general circulation, but some may be on reserve or on loan to other libraries via interlibrary loan. Noncirculating items such as reference books are for library use only.

Loc.cit. Latin, abbreviation for loco citato: "in the place cited." In a footnote, used with the author's last name; stands for the title of a work, and the page, cited in an earlier footnote. EXAMPLE: 41 Gross, loc.cit.

Local area network (LAN) A communications network restricted to a relatively small geographic area, often within a single building or group of adjacent buildings such as a college, university, or corporate campus, consisting of at least one high-speed server, client workstations, a network operating system, and a communications link. Lans handling communication over the Internet use optical fiber as a transmission medium. Compare with wide area network (WAN).

Local bibliography A bibliography of books and other materials about a specific geographic area smaller than a country, usually including material about the history, geography, architecture, and environment of the area, as well as works about the people born or residing in it. Useful in genealogical research.

Local collection A library collection of books, prints, maps, photographs, and other materials related to a specific geographic area and its inhabitants, usually the community in which the library is located, useful in historical and genealogical research.

Local system The system you are using. Interactions between your computer and another computer on the Internet are sometimes described using the terms "local" and "remote" systems. The local system is your computer and the remote system is the other computer.

Location Where the physical item is housed. In homer UCAT, Location is given in the left-hand column of the item record.

Location code Word or abbreviation beneath or beside the call number which is used on spines of books that are shelved in special places; examples are archive, REF, VET, ATMOS. All location symbols are listed on the library locator.

Location symbol A code consisting of a few letters or a word displayed in a catalog record or added to an entry in a bibliography, indicating the specific location or collection in which the item is shelved (example: Ref for items in the reference stacks). In a union catalog, location symbols are used to indicate the libraries in the system or consortium owning at least one copy of the item. Synonymous with location code.

Locator The portion of an entry in a catalog or index that gives the location of the unit indexed. In the library catalog, it is the call number. In a single index, the locator is usually a page or paragraph number, or a figure or table number. In an abstracting service, the locator is the abstract number under which the full bibliographic description of a document can be found. In an open-end index, the locators may be the bibliographic descriptions themselves.

LOCIS Library of Congress catalog system. The Library of Congress has an extensive and useful congressional legislation system that you can use to look up the bills that are in Congress, as well as having nearly any book ever published in the United States.

Locked case books books shelved in a locked room due to high vulnerability to theft or vandalism; some are entirely non-circulating, others may circulate on an exit permit. There are locked case materials in the Science, Fine Arts, and Middle East collections; ask for them at the respective desks.

Locked up Said of assembled type and display matter made up into pages and imposed in a chase once it has been tightly secured by adjusting small expandable wooden or metal boxes called quoins positioned between the imposed type and the sides of the chase. The resulting forme is ready to be placed on the bed of the press for printing.

LOEX An acronym for Library Orientation exchange (pronounced "low-ex"), a "library outreach" office established in 1971 at Eastern Michigan State University with the aid of a grant from the Council on Library Resources (CLR) and the National Endowment for the Humanities (NEH). Since its inception, LOEX has sponsored the annual LOEX Conference, attended by bibliographic instruction librarians and other individuals with an interest in library instruction, and has served as a clearinghouse for bibliographic instruction materials and resources.

Log off The procedure by which a user closes or terminates communication with a remote computer system. The opposite of log on. Also spelled log-off or logoff. Compare with exit.

Log on The procedure by which a user gains access to and initiates communication with a remote computer system, usually by typing or entering an authorized username and/or password. The opposite of log off. Also spelled log-on and logon.

Logical difference In Boolean logic, the result obtained when the NOT command is used to separate members of a set of entities from those of another. It is the search strategy used to determine which records in a library catalog or bibliographic database contain term A but not term B. Synonymous with logical subtraction and negation. Compare with logical product and logical sum.

Logical sum In Boolean logic, the result obtained when the OR command is used to find all the members of two or more sets of entities. It is the search strategy used to determine which records in a library catalog or bibliographic database contain term A or term B, or both A and B. Synonymous with logical addition and union. Compare with logical difference and logical product.

Login Noun or a verb. Noun: The account name used to gain access to a computer system. Not a secret (contrast with Password). Verb: the act of connecting to a computer system by giving your credentials (usually your "username" and "password")

Logo An emblem or graphic design used in publications and on promotional materials by a company, organization, agency, or institution as a trademark or symbol of its identity. Web sites often include a logo to indicate affiliation with a host organization, or to suggest the nature of the site's content.

Logogram A symbol or character that stands for an entire word, for example, $ for dollar and # for number.

Logon script a small program that executes a set of commands when a user logs on to the system; at Marriott, Systems sometimes uses logon scripts to automatically provide user ID and password information when users access

Logon, logoff to begin or to end operation of a computer or program.

LOL: Commonly used in electronic communications to express humor; an acronym meaning "laughing out loud". Can be written in either upper- or lower case.

Long discount The standard discount given by a publisher to a bookseller on trade books, usually 40%. Compare with short discount.

Long page In printing, a page containing more lines of type matter than specified. In books, a typesetter may add an extra line (or lines) to avoid setting an orphan or widow. Compare with short page.

Longitudinal study A research methodology in which the same phenomenon is observed continuously or at intervals over an extended period of time, usually to discern temporal patterns or identify changes that occur in response to altered conditions.

Long-playing record (LP) A sound recording medium in which music or spoken words are recorded in a continuous spiral groove on the surface of a thin, flat vinyl disk that can be played back at 33 rpm using a device called a record player equipped with a stylus, cartridge, and speakers to amplify the sound. Long-playing records have been superseded, first by audiocassettes and then by audio compact discs. They are retained by libraries for archival purposes.

Long-Term Disability (LTD) Available to stste classified employees on a voluntary basis and available to general faculty as part of their cafeteria benefit package. Benefits are payable for disabilities occurring due to accident or sickness either on or off the job. The amount of LTD is 60% of earnings.

Loose leaf services Volumes containing news, court opinions, or reference material on special subjects, updated by regular supplements.

Loose Sheets of paper, parchment, etc., that are unbound, usually filed in a folder or container. The opposite of bound..

Loose-leaf A rigid or flexible mechanical binding that can be manually opened and closed by the user to remove or insert, at any location in the sequence of pages, one or more leaves or sections with holes or slots punched along the back margin. The most common varieties are ring binding and post binding. Loose-leaf binding is used in libraries for reference serials, government documents, legal publications, instruction manuals, etc., which must be updated on a regular basis. Compare with comb binding and spiral binding.

Lossy Image compression that functions by removing minor tonal and/or color variations, causing visible loss of detail at high compression ratios.

Lost A code used in a library catalog record to indicate the circulation status of an item no longer available because it was checked out to a previous borrower and never returned. Most libraries bill the patron an amount based on the cost of replacement after a number of overdue notices have been sent without result. In some libraries, the charge may be refundable if the item is found and returned within a reasonable time. Compare with missing.

Lot A regular shipment of books, periodicals, or other printed material sent by a library to a bindery for binding or rebinding. The phrase "closing the lot" refers to the point in time after which no further items are added to a shipment. Only when the lot is closed can the necessary paperwork be prepared to accompany the shipment.

Low Key A dark image that is intentionally lacking in highlight detail.

Lowercase The small letters as opposed to the capital letters of a type font. The opposite of uppercase. Type matter set in lowercase can be read more rapidly than the same text set in uppercase. The words "lowercase" and "uppercase" are derived from the relative positions of the compartments within the wood or metal case designed to hold elements of type bearing small letters and capital letters at a typesetter's bench in the days when typesetting was done by hand (letterpress). Also spelled lower case. Compare with minuscule.

LPI/LPCM Lines per inch or per centimeter. Units of measurement for screen ruling.

LUC Library Use Card; card used for access to libraries and for borrowing privileges.

Lurk To receive and read messages posted to an online discussion forum, or observe the exchanges in a chat room, without actively participating in the discussion. In some mailing lists, there may be more lurkers than active correspondents.

Lurker Slang term for someone who regularly reads newsgroup, BBS, or mailing list discussions, but rarely participates in them.

Lurking To read a network newsgroup or electronic mailing list and not post any messages; usually considered to be good netiquette for those unfamiliar with the newsgroup. Most regular participants appreciate new contributors getting the feel of the discussion before jumping in.

Lynx A type of browser designed to work with text-only Internet connections like dial-up UNIX shell accounts. LZW The Lempel-Ziv-Welch image compression technique.

Lyric In classical Greece, a song or poem performed to the accompaniment of a harp-like stringed instrument called a lyre. In contemporary usage, a relatively short poem in which a single speaker expresses a personal emotion or state of mind, as opposed to narrating a sequence of events. The form includes sonnets, elegies, odes, and hymns.

GLOSSARY OF LIBRARY AND INFORMATION SCIENCE (Vol. II)

Dr. Amjad Ali
Deputy Librarian
Aligarh Muslim University, Aligarh

Ess Ess Publications
4837/24, Ansari Road, Darya Ganj,
New Delhi-110002
✆ : 23260807
Fax : 23274173
E-mail: info@essessreference.com
url:http://www.essessreference.com

First Published 2004

ISBN: 81-7000-410-1 (Set of 2 Volumes)

Rs.1700/- (Set of 2 Volumes)

Published by:
Ess Ess Publications
4837/24, Ansari Road, Darya Ganj,
New Delhi-110 002.
Phone: 23260807
Fax: 23274173
E-mail: info@essessreference.com
url: http://www.essessreference.com

Printed in India at:
Printline, New Delhi

Dedicated to

My Parents

Preface

Libraries are affected by changes taking place in the society. The change is reflected in their services, practices and techniques of information management. The last two decades witnessed adoption of a record number of new terms for library and information related activities as influenced by the application of computers and advent of Internet.

This Glossary of about 4,500 terms includes traditional as well as the latest items which will be useful for the students of library and information science, working librarians and information professionals at every stage of their career from students life to management positions.

My thanks are due to the individuals and organizations which have put the relevant resources on the Net as I referred some of them to compile this Glossary. My thanks are also due to M/s Ess Ess Publications, New Delhi for bringing out this multi-volume book in a very short time.

Dr. Amjad Ali

E-Mail: amjad_alig@yahoo.co.in

GLOSSARY

M.L.I.S. The post-graduate degree of Master of Library and Information Science, granted by a library school upon completion of a required course of study. To be considered for a professional position in most public and academic libraries in the United States, a candidate must have earned either an M.L.I.S. or M.L.S. degree.

M.L.S. The post-graduate degree of Master of Library Science, granted by a library school upon completion of a required course of study. To be considered for a professional position in most public and academic libraries in the United States, a candidate must have earned either an M.L.S. or M.L.I.S. degree

M2's Access Service Monitors who have been promoted to a second level Monitor position. M2's are members of the department's managerial team and perform duties of greater scope. Oversight/supervision is one major assignment and another is special projects. One may find M2's diagramming floorplans, revising emergency procedure manuals, coordinating other MONITORS and students, etc.

Mac Short for "Macintosh" - a range of personal computers from the Apple company which use a graphical user interface. In Marriott, teaching lab 1745 is equipped with Macs, and there are Macs available for student use in the Multimedia Center.

Machine Readable Cataloging (MARC) Conversion of printed material into a format that can be stored in a computer for access and display upon a computer terminal. See also MARC format.

Machine-aided indexing A method of indexing in which a computer is programmed to select possible descriptors from a thesaurus of preferred terms, based on an analysis of words and phrases appearing in the title and/ or text of a work. Each suggestion is evaluated by a human indexer and either accepted or rejected. The indexer is also free to select additional authorized terms for indexing. Compare with automatic indexing.

Machine-Readable Cataloging (MARC) An international standard digital format for the description of bibliographic items, developed by the Library of Congress during the 1960s to facilitate the creation and dissemination of computerized cataloging from library to library within the same country, and between countries. By 1971 the MARC format had become the national standard for dissemination of bibliographic data, and by 1973 the international standard. Widespread use of the MARC standard has helped libraries acquire predictable and reliable cataloging data, make use of commercially available library automation systems, share bibliographic resources, avoid duplication of effort, and ensure that bibliographic data will be compatible when one automation system is replaced by another.

Machine-readable data file (MRDF) Information stored in a form that can be used directly as computer input, without conversion from a format that is not machine-readable, for example, bibliographic records in MARC format as opposed to printed catalog cards. Storage medium varies (magnetic tape, magnetic disk, etc.).

Machine-readable Data in a form that can be recognized, accepted, and interpreted by a machine, such as a computer or other data processing device, whether created in such a form or converted from a format that a machine cannot read. Usually refers to digital information stored on hard disk, floppy disk, or magnetic tape.

Macintosh The family of computers introduced by Apple in 1984 which popularized the graphical user interface (GUI), setting a precedent for the design of user-friendly graphical applications and operating systems that other software companies like Microsoft were quick to follow.

Although Apple commands only 5% of the market for desktop computers, the company produces the largest series of nonibm-compatible personal computers. "Macs" remain popular in desktop publishing and graphic design because of the usability of the interface. In libraries, Macs are used mainly in the children's room and curriculum room.

Macro computing, a method of customizing user input in which a series of recorded keystrokes, commands, or menu options are assigned a brief name or key combination (usually **Ctrl** or **Alt** plus a specific character) to enable the user to execute a pre-determined sequence of steps quickly by simply typing the name or key combination.

Macroform A general term for any storage medium bearing text and/or images large enough to be easily read without magnification. Macroforms can be opaque (example: photocopies) or transparent (overhead transparencies). Compare with microform.

Made-up copy A copy of a book assembled from parts taken from one or more defective copies of the same edition, or a copy in which imperfections are corrected by adding or substituting parts taken from other copies of the same edition.

Mag stripe Magnetized stripe; a magnetized strip for use in automated machines, on which data can be recorded. Used on VU library cards to record patron ID information for access control.

Magazine A popular interest periodical usually containing articles on a variety of topics, written by various authors in a nonscholarly style. Most magazines are heavily illustrated, contain advertising, and are printed on glossy paper. Articles are usually short (less than five pages long), frequently unsigned, and do not include a bibliography or list of references for further reading. Most magazines are issued monthly or weekly for sale at newsstands, in bookstores, and by subscription. English-language magazines are listed by subject in Magazines for Libraries published by R. R. Bowker. Abbreviated mag. Compare with journal and journal of commentary.

Magazine pagination Numbering the pages of a periodical, starting with one at the beginning of each issue. Magazines and trade journals are usually paginated in this way, making it more difficult to locate a specific article in a bound volume by page numbers, compared with a publication that uses journal pagination.

Magazines for Libraries Published irregularly since 1969 by R. R. Bowker, Magazines for Libraries is a subject list (with title index) of over 8,000 English-language periodicals, selected by the editors from over 170,000 possibilities as the most useful for the average public, academic, government, school, or special library. Coverage includes general interest magazines, research journals, trade journals, zines, and children's periodicals. Each entry includes a basic bibliographic description; an annotation explaining the purpose, scope, and audience of the publication; and a brief evaluation. Libraries usually place this collection development tool on continuation order and shelve it in the reference section.

Magnetic strip A thin magnetized strip of plastic firmly affixed to a book or other bibliographic item at the time it is processed, which can be set to trigger a security alarm whenever someone attempts to remove the item from the library without checking it out. Synonymous with security strip and tattle-tape.

Magnetic tape An electronic storage medium consisting of a thin strip of flexible plastic to which a metallic coating is applied which can be selectively magnetized to record information sequentially in linear or helical tracks. Magnetic tape is mounted on open reels or in cartridges. To retrieve a specific record or file on tape, all the records (or partitions) preceding it must be sequentially searched. Magnetic disk storage is faster because it allows data to be accessed randomly. For this reason, data in current use is usually stored on disk, but tape is often used for archival storage because it is more economical and has greater capacity.

Magnum opus Latin for "great work." A literary or artistic work considered by discerning critics to be of major importance, usually the crowning achievement of its author, composer, or creator (example: **Ulysses** by James Joyce). Not all authors and artists produce a work that is considered superior to their others (William Shakespeare). The opposite of opuscule. Compare with masterpiece.

Mail Merge The merging of database information (such as names and addresses) with a letter template in a word processor, in order to create personalized letters.

Mail server A networked computer dedicated to supporting electronic mail. At OSU,there are two major servers used for processing e-mail: 1) smtp.service.ohio-state.edu which handles outgoing messages; and 2) pop.service.ohio-state.edu which handles incoming messages. You use a client program like Eudora for retrieving new mail from the server and for composing and sending messages.

Mailing list A collection of e-mail addresses identified by a single name; mailing lists provide a simple way of corresponding with a group of people with a common interest or bond. There are two main types of lists: 1) one you create within an e-mail program like Eudora that contains addresses for two or more individuals you frequently send the same message; and 2) a Listserve type that requires participants to be subscribed (e.g., a group of collaborators, a class of students, or often just individuals interested in discussing a particular topic). For information about obtaining a Listserve mailing list, contact OIT at 688-HELP.

Maillist A (usually automated) system that allows people to send e-mail to one address, whereupon their message is copied and sent to all of the other subscribers to the maillist. In this way, people who have many different kinds of e-mail access can participate in discussions together.

Main class One of the highest-level divisions of a classification system. In Library of Congress Classification, the 20 major classes are indicated by letters of the English alphabet:

Main entry in a card catalog, the card with the most complete bibliographic information on an item, listing subject headings and tracings such as other authors; usually the main entry is filed by first author.

Main heading In pre-coordinate indexing, the first part of a composite heading that includes at least one subheading. In the Library of Congress subject heading Information science—Research—Methodology, the phrase Information science is the main heading, Research is the subheading, and Methodology is the sub-subheading..

Main memory The amount of memory physically installed in your computer. Also referred to as "RAM".

Main schedule The list of classes used by a cataloger or indexer, individually or in combination, to classify documents by subject under the rules of a given classification system, arranged in the order of their symbolic notation. In a hierarchical classification system, the logical divisions, subdivisions, etc., of the main classes are displayed. Compare with auxiliary schedule.

Mainframe A large computer system capable of supporting many terminals that do not have independent processing capability, used to run complex applications that require a considerable amount of computing power. Mainframes are classified by size (small, medium, and large). Compare with microcomputer, minicomputer, and supercomputer.

Maintenance contract A formal agreement in which an outside company agrees to check designated equipment on a regular basis after any warranty has expired, and to maintain it in good working order, including major repairs as needed, in exchange for payment of a monthly or annual fee, an arrangement common in libraries that own their own photocopiers, reader-printer machines, computer equipment, etc.

Major A descriptor or identifier in an index entry or bibliographic record, representing a main focus or subject of the document indexed, usually indicated by an asterisk or other symbol, or distinguished typographically. Minor descriptors and identifiers representing less significant aspects of the content are left unmarked.

Major Orchestra Librarians' Association (MOLA) Founded in 1983 by representatives of the Philadelphia Orchestra, Boston Symphony, and Minnesota Orchestra, MOLA is an international organization devoted to improving communication among performance librarians and helping them provide better service to their orchestras. The association also presents a unified voice in relations with music publishers. Its membership includes over 170 libraries associated with orchestras, opera and ballet companies, military bands, and music conservatories. MOLA publishes the quarterly newsletter Marcato and hosts the molalist electronic mailing list

Majordomo An Internet mailing list program designed to run on the UNIX operating system. Compare with Listserv.

Majuscule A large capital or uncial letter used in Greek and Latin manuscripts of the 4th and 5th centuries A.D., as distinct from a small letter or minuscule

Makeready The process of preparing the printing press for a press run, including adjustment of the forme or plates to produce a uniform impression.

Make-up In letterpress printing, the process of removing type from the galleys and arranging it in page format, including the positioning of text, illustrations, notes, and running heads in accordance with the typographer's layout, done by a worker known as a compositor. Also spelled makeup.

Malapropism The accidental or intentional misuse of words, especially two words of similar pronunciation but very different meaning. The term is derived from Mrs. Malaprop, the name of a character in Sheridan's play The Rivals (1775) who had a habit of using polysyllabic words incorrectly ("...don't attempt to extirpate yourself from the matter"). Earlier examples can be found in the utterances of the constable Dogberry in Shakespeare's

Managed book A book on a topic chosen by the publisher, who controls and directs every aspect of its creation. If a paid staff writer or freelancer is used for the text, the structure of the work is usually based on an outline provided by the publisher. In books with a preponderance of pictorial content, the name of the author or editor may not be given on the title page. Compare with packaged book.

Management information system (MIS) A computer-based information system developed and maintained by a commercial enterprise to integrate data from all its departments (product development, production and inventory, marketing and sales, personnel administration, etc.) To support managerial and supervisory decision-making with real time analysis. MIS systems are designed to track progress towards achievement of the company's goals and objectives, including the identification of problems or obstacles that must be resolved by upper-level management. In the plural, the term refers to the study and teaching of such systems. Courses on MIS are offered as a major at some business schools in the United States.

Mandatory (M) A field or subfield of the MARC record in which data must be entered to meet OCLC input standards for a given encoding level. Compare with optional and required if applicable or readily available.

Mania Library staff accounts and Libraries network is housed on this computer server.

Manifestation As defined in FRBR (Functional Requirements for Bibliographic Records), the result of a single act of physical embodiment/production of a specific expression of a creative work, for example, an edition of one of the variant texts of a literary work (1993 Yale University Press edition of Hamlet), or a recording of a specific performance of a musical work (1998 recording of West Side Story released by Sony/Columbia on compact disc). A manifestation consists of all the physical objects (items) possessing the same characteristics with respect to intellcctual/artistic content and physical form, in most instances a set of multiple copies produced for commercial distribution. However, for some expressions there may be only a single exemplar, as in the case of an archival oral history recording, an author's manuscript, or a one-of-a-kind art book.

Manifesto A public declaration, in writing or in speech, of beliefs, motives, plans, and/or intentions, made by an individual, group, or government

Manila A thick, durable buff-colored paper, originally manufactured from Manila hemp fiber, used mainly for file folders and mailing envelopes. Also spelled manilla.

Manual A book of compact size, especially one describing in considerable detail the government of a state or the structure and functions of a government agency (example: The United States Government Manual published annually by the U.S. GPO).

Manual Authority File (MAF) Largely replaced by online authority records, in the past these files were established to record the proper form of entry for a name. The file is divided into three sections: 1. Personal names; 2. Corporate and geographic names; and 3. Uniform titles. The file originated with the Title IIC project, and later expanded to include authority records established by the bibliographic control and electronic service department. Manual authority file includes information on cross references and the history of a name, and the cataloging code under which the name was established. The corporate and geographic file remains in card form, replaced in part and updated by the online authority file.

Manufacturer In library cataloging, the agency responsible for actually making a bibliographic item. In the case of books and other printed publications, the printer is the manufacturer. Compare with producer.

Manuscript An abbreviation of the Latin phrase codex manu scriptus. Strictly speaking, a work of any kind (text, inscription, music score, map, etc.) Written entirely by hand. Also refers to the handwritten or typescript copy of an author's work as submitted for publication, before printing. In the United States, bibliographic control of manuscript collections is provided by the National Union Catalog of Manuscript Collections (NUCMC), a cooperative cataloging program of the Library of Congress. In AACR2, manuscripts are cataloged under the rules for printed books. Abbreviated ms. And mss. In the plural.

Manuscript book A book written entirely by hand, particularly one produced prior to the invention of printing from movable type, usually copied by medieval monks or scribes on leaves of parchment or vellum, bound in leather-covered wooden boards. Medieval manuscript books were often rubricated, illuminated, and/or embellished with miniatures.

Manuscript collection university archives has a number of manuscript collections on a variety of subjects. For a list, see the most recent edition of "A Guide to Manuscripts at Colorado State University," Libraries Publication no. 24.

Manuscript Society, The Founded in 1948 as the National Society of Autograph Collectors, The Manuscript Society has since grown to a membership of over 1,800 scholars, authors, dealers, private collectors, librarians, archivists, and curators. Its membership also includes historical societies, museums, special libraries, and academic libraries with manuscript collections. The Society publishes the quarterly journal Manuscripts and the newsletter Manuscript Society News.

Manuscripts The division responsible for the collection, cataloging, and maintenance of the Library's unpublished historical collections, including diaries, autobiographies, correspondence, business and personal records. Subject areas covered in Marriott's Manuscripts collections include Politics; Communications; Architecture; Ethnic groups; Science, Engineering and Medicine; History, Philosophy, and Religion; Outdoor Recreation; Mining; Visual and

Map and Geography Round Table (MAGERT) A round table of the American Library Association established in 1980, MAGERT is the world's largest organization devoted to map and geography librarianship. Membership is open to ALA members who work with or have an interest in map and geography collections and information related to maps and mapping. MAGERT publishes the semiannual journal Meridian and the bimonthly newsletter Base Line.

Map Any two-dimensional representation of all or a portion of the earth's surface, the heavens, or another celestial body, normally done to scale on a flat sheet. Early maps were drawn on parchment stored in rolls. In modern libraries, maps are usually stored flat or folded in a specially designed map case with wide, shallow drawers. Maps are also included as inserts or pocket parts in books and periodicals. As illustrations, they may be printed as plates with the text, or on the endpapers. An atlas is a book consisting almost entirely of maps, with the content usually indexed in a gazetteer at the end. The largest mapping agency in the United States is the U.S. Geological Survey.

Map case A library furnishing, usually made of wood or metal, containing a number of wide, shallow drawers in which large sheet maps can be stored flat, with a large smooth top on which they can be spread for examination.

Map collection The map collection at CSUL includes

maps and atlases published by the U.S. government and private publishers, U.S. Geological Survey quadrangle maps and maps for all areas of the world, including thematic maps such as soils or vegetation.

Map index An alphabetical list of the place names written or printed on a map or series of maps, giving the location of each feature, usually as grid coordinates. Compare with index map.

Map library A library or unit within a library which has collections consisting primarily of cartographic materials that are of current or historic interest, including maps, atlases, gazetteers, charts, globes, relief models, digital data, remotely sensed images, etc., for example, the Perry-Castaneda Library Map Collection at the University of Texas. Map librarians are organized in the Map and Geography Round Table (MAGERT) of the American Library Association.

Map projection an arrangement of the longitude and latitude grid to enable part or all of the globe's curved surface to be represented on a flat surface. (For example, Mercator's Projection.)

Map room Collection of maps located in the Science and Engineering Library including topographic, nautical, and geological series, as well as a variety of special subject maps.

Map series A series of sheet maps, all drawn to the same scale and specifications, encompassing a clearly defined geographic area when complete, identified collectively by the mapping agency that produced them.

MAPI Application Programming Interface; a system built into Microsoft Windows that enables different e-mail programs to interface to distribute e-mail. When both programs are MAPI-enabled, they can share messages.

Mapping agency An organization that produces and publishes maps and other cartographic information, usually under the sponsorship of a national government or its armed forces. The largest mapping agency in the United States is the U.S. Geological Survey. In AACR2, name of mapping agency is given in the statement of responsibility area of the bibliographic description of a cartographic item.

MARBI Machine-Readable Bibliographic Information Committee, the body within the American Library Association responsible for developing official ALA standards for the representation of bibliographic information in machine-readable format. Its membership includes nine voting members from ALCTS, LITA, and RUSA, and three interns. Members of the MARC Advisory Committee to the Library of Congress also participate in its deliberations, including ex-officio representatives of the national libraries and bibliographic utilities, and several dozen nonvoting liaisons from other units within the ALA and from non-ALA organizations with an interest in issues related to library automation standards.

Marbling A style of decorative endpaper used in hand bookbinding, bearing a design produced by water colors floated on the gummed surface of a sheet of paper. The liquid pigments are swirled with a special comb in a pattern resembling the surface of cut marble. The technique is also used on book covers, and to decorate the edges of the sections of a book. Developed in the 17th century, probably in France, marbing was particularly popular during the Victorian period. As a less expensive alternative, endpapers are sometimes printed with a pattern resembling hand-marbled paper.

MARC machine Readable Cataloging MARC records contain data in standardized format and allow conversion to automated cataloging and circulation systems.

Margin Any one of the four blank borders around the matter written or printed on a page or sheet, known as the top or head margin; the bottom, foot, or tail margin; the outer, outside, or fore-edge margin; and the inner, inside, back, or binding margin. The combined inner margins of facing pages form the gutter. The relationship of the widths of the four margins is an important factor in the design of a legible, aesthetically pleasing page. Standard proportions are: bottom margin double the top and inside margin 1/2 or 2/3 of the outside. Rebinding may require trimming the inner margin of a book.

Marginalia Headings or notes written or printed on the margins of a page, usually in writing or type of a size or style distinct from that of the text. Marginalia include footnotes, side notes, and shoulder notes.

Mark up In publishing, to prepare copy for printing by specifying details of typeface, fonts, layout, etc., in a code comprehensible to the compositor or typesetter.

Marking Process of attaching a call number to the PIECE, security taping, and property stamping; also called preparations. Section of reservation service responsible for preparing materials for shelving.

Marvel Machine-Assisted Realization of the Virtual Electronic Library. The Library of Congress' gopher. It presents information about the Library of Congress such as facilities and services, reading rooms, copyright, services to libraries and publishers, etc., as well as other Internet resources.

Marvive Company that provides shipping list services and bibliographical records for depository items.

Masque A lavish form of court entertainment that originated in Renaissance Italy and was particularly popular during the reigns of Elizabeth I, James I, and Charles I of England. Masques combined music, song, dance, and poetic drama in a spectacular display of costume and elaborate staging held together by a loose allegorical plot, usually based on a mythological theme (example: Masque of Blacknesse by Ben Jonson). The name is derived from the face masques worn by the members of court who played the main characters. This costly form of royal amusement ended with the Puritan revolution of 1642.

Mass-market paperback A new work or a reprint of a title previously published in hardcover, produced and distributed in paperback for sale at newsstands and in supermarkets, drugstores, chain stores, etc., rather than trade bookstores. Copies are usually of standard rack-size (4 × 7 inches), printed on poor quality paper, bound with hot melt adhesive, and priced to sell to the widest possible audience. The format is used extensively for popular fiction and genre fiction. Libraries prefer them for books-by-mail programs to keep mailing costs down. In some public libraries, mass-market paperbacks received as gifts are circulated on the honor system. Compare with trade paperback.

Master In reprography, the plate, stencil, negative, or document from which copies are made, usually more than once. The quality of a master copy usually deteriorates with extended use.

Master negative In microfilm, the first generation negative, developed from the film used to shoot the image, from which at least one print master is made, usually stored in a separate location under controlled conditions and used as little as possible

Masterpiece A work of art, craftsmanship, or writing universally recognized as embodying the highest skill of a great master or group of masters. An artist, composer, or writer may produce a single masterpiece (examples: Charlotte and Emily Bronte) or more than one masterpiece in a lifetime (Jane Austen). Synonymous with chef-d'oeuvre. Compare with magnum opus.

Master's Theses Directories and in Disseration Abstracts International. They can also be located in the worldcat database via OCLC firstsearch. Compare with dissertation.

Masthead A box or column printed in each issue of a periodical, stating the title of the publication, its publisher, ownership, editors, frequency, ISSN, subscription rates, and giving notice of copyright, usually with contact information.

In a newspaper, the mastehead is found on the editorial page or on page one. In magazines and journals, it is usually printed on or near the page bearing the table of contents. Compare with flag.

Mat Two pieces of board, hinged along one edge for mounting a print, photograph, etc., the bottom piece providing support (backing) and the top piece cut in the shape of a window through which the image is viewed. In quality framing, prints are often double- or triple-matted in boards of contrasting color.

Matalibb A cross-database searching tool. It allows you to search up to eight database and catalogs at once; create a personalized resource list; and save, email and download search results. Metalib software was created by the Ex Libris group.

Matching grant A grant made by a foundation, government agency, or individual, contingent on the recipient raising sufficient funds to match the donor's contribution. Although the ratio of grant funds to contributions may vary, most are dollar-for-dollar up to a fixed amount, with a time limit imposed on fund-raising activities. Some federal LSTA grants-in-aid are structured in this way.

Material budget Funds allocated for the purchase and maintenance of print serials and monographs as well as electronic resources.

Material selector (subject selector) Librarian designated to do collection development for an academic department or program..

Material specific details (MSD) A generic term for the area of a bibliographic record reserved for elements of bibliographic description specific to certain types of material (musical presentation, mathematical data, and numeric and/or alphabetic, chronological, or other designation) recorded in field 254 of the MARC record for music, field 255 for cartographic materials, and field 362 for serials.

Material type An option available to users of some online catalogs and bibliographic databases that allows search results to be limited to materials of a specific physical format (book, periodical, videocassette, sound recording, map, music score, etc.). In cataloging, material type is assigned to the item from a list established by the local library (or library system) and is not necessarily the same as the item type used for circulation purposes.

Materials budget The portion of a library's operating budget allocated for the purchase of books, media, serials, and other information resources for the use of its clientele and staff, as opposed to expenditures for salaries and wages, equipment, supplies, and services. Some libraries include electronic resources in the materials budget, others make a separate allocation.

Math Coprocessor Another name for a floating-point processor.

Mathematical data The field within the materials specific details area of a bibliographic record in which mathematical elements in the bibliographic description of cartographic materials are entered (scale, projection, coordinates, etc.).

Matrix This often refers to a 2-dimensional array of CCD elements.

Matte Paper that has a dull unreflective finish, easier on the eye of the reader than glossy finish, but not as visually appealing for printed graphics. Also spelled matt.

Matter In printing, copy in the process of being set in type, or already set (standing). Live matter has yet to be used in printing; dead matter has been used and is ready to be broken up. The terms fat matter and lean matter refer to the proportion of white space or broken lines on a page. Printers also differentiate between body matter and display matter. Also refers to copy that is to be printed, in manuscript or typescript form.

Matweb matweb, the FREE materials information database with data on 24,704 materials including metals, plastics, ceramics, and composites.

Maximize A feature of a graphical user interface that allows the user to enlarge a window to its fullest size by clicking on a small button in the upper right-hand corner of the window. The opposite of minimize.

MCA Microcomputer Consultation Area; located in 512 Baker Systems. Walk-in consultation for Windows and Macintosh hardware; word processing; e-mail; web browsing; spreadsheet; database software; and Internet connections.

Mcbee CARD Manual key sort charge card used to check out materials not entered on the online circulation system i.e., unbound periodicals.

Mcluhan, Marshall (1911-1980) The University of Toronto professor of literature and culture who became famous for his innovative theories about how methods of communication influence society. In 1963, his analysis of the effect of movable type on the culture of 15th century Europe (The Gutenberg Galaxy: The Making of Typographic Man) won the Governor-General's award for critical writing. In 1964, mcluhan gained considerable attention in the popular press for Understanding Media: The Extensions of Man in which he argued that the communication media used by humans are extensions of the physical senses which, by their very nature, introduce changes in the way societies function and in human consciousness, apart from the content they convey. His assertion that "the medium is the message" eventually became "the medium is the massage." For more about his life and work,

Mean line In typography, the imaginary horizontal line running along the tops of the x-height lowercase letters of a type font that lack ascenders. Synonymous with x-line. Compare with cap line.

Mechanical binding A form of binding in which the

leaves of a publication are held together by some type of mechanism, usually metal or plastic wire or rings threaded or inserted through holes or slots punched along the back margin parallel to the binding edge, to allow the volume to open flat. The category includes loose-leaf binding, comb binding, and spiral binding.

Media A generic term for nonprint library materials (films, filmstrips, slides, videorecordings, audiorecordings, CD-roms, machine-readable data files, computer software, etc.). Microforms are not considered media because they are reproductions of print documents. The person responsible for managing a media collection and associated equipment is a media specialist. Reviews of newly published media titles are indexed annually by type of medium in Media Review Digest. Synonymous with audiovisuals. In a more general sense, material in any format that carries and communicates information content.

Media center A facility within an educational institution, responsible for providing a full-range of media resources, equipment, and services, staffed to assist students and instructors in utilizing its collections, usually supervised by a media specialist. A media center can be a separate facility, a separately administered unit located in the same building as a library, or an integral part of the library. Synonymous with learning resources center.

Media mail A special rate available from the U.S. Postal Service to businesses and the public for mailing books of at least eight pages, film (16 mm or narrower), printed music, printed test materials, sound recordings, play scripts, printed educational charts, loose-leaf pages and binders containing medical information, and computer-readable media, lower than the rate charged for parcels of comparable weight which do not contain such items. Advertising restrictions apply. Synonymous with book post and book rate. Compare with library rate.

Media resources Material that is not in paper or in

print format. Videos, audio cassettes, and microforms are referred to as media items.

Media specialist A librarian or other individual with specialized training in the creation, selection, organization, maintenance, and provision of access to media of all kinds, who may also be responsible for supervising a media center or the media department of a library, including collections, equipment, and facilities for listening and/or viewing.

Media Viewing & Music Listening Equipment Check out headphones and cartridges, along with music cds and videos at the Service Desk. The third floor offers a viewing and listening area, or use headphones for some applications in the student-access computer lab.

Mediated search A systematic search in which a trained intermediary, such as an online services librarian or information broker, assists the end-user in locating desired information, by helping to formulate and execute appropriate strategies for searching online catalogs and databases, and by using more traditional bibliographic finding tools. Compare with end-user search.

Medical book A book published in print or on CD-ROM for the use of medical practitioners, researchers, and/or students (example: Physician's Desk Reference), or for laypersons with an interest in health care (Harvard Medical School Family Health Guide). The category includes textbooks, reference works, and consumer guides, often published in successive editions. Currency is essential in maintaining medical collections.

Medical library A type of special library maintained by a university medical school, hospital, medical research institute, public health agency, or medical association to serve the information needs of students, researchers, and practitioners in the health sciences (medicine, nursing, dentistry, pharmacy, etc.), with collections that include print and online resources related to medicine and allied health. The largest medical library in the United States is the

National Library of Medicine, located in Washington, D.C. Medical librarians are organized in the Medical Library Association. Synonymous with health science library.

Medical Library Association (MLA) Founded in 1898, MLA has a membership of librarians and other individuals engaged in professional library or bibliographic work in medical libraries and allied scientific libraries. An affiliate of the American Library Association, MLA publishes the quarterly Bulletin of the Medical Library Association (BMLA).

Medium In information storage and retrieval, the physical substance or material on which data is recorded (parchment, paper, film, magnetic tape or disk, optical disk, etc.) Or through which data is transmitted (optical fiber, coaxial cable, twisted pair, etc.). In a more general sense, the material or technical means by which any creative work is expressed or communicated, in print or nonprint format. Plural: media.

Medium of performance The voice(s) and/or instrument(s) for which a musical work is composed, recorded in the note area of the bibliographic description in the order given on the actual item (example: soprano and piano).

Mediumistic writing A written work transmitted through a psychic medium who claims to have received it as a communication from the spirit of a dead person or entity. In libraries, such works are cataloged under the name of the medium with an added entry under the name of the purported author(s).

MEDLARS An acronym for medical Literature Analysis and Retrieval Service, a collection of databases maintained and leased to libraries and research institutions by the National Library of Medicine (NLM), including MEDLINE, AIDSLINE, TOXLINE, etc.

Medley A musical composition consisting of a string of well-known melodies or passages from various pieces which share a common characteristic (composed by the same person, during the same period, in the same genre, etc.), arranged so that the end of one coincides with the beginning of the next, with no break in continuity.

MEDLINE Created and maintained by the National Library of Medicine, MEDLINE is the largest bibliographic database in the world, indexing the literature of the biomedical sciences. It includes Index Medicus, Index to Dental Literature, and International Nursing. It also covers allied health, biological and physical sciences, humanities, and information science as they relate to medicine and health care, communication disorders, population biology, and reproductive biology. MEDLINE contains over 11 million bibliographic records representing articles indexed since 1966 from over 3,900 journals, as well as monographs published as the result of biomedical congresses and symposia. Approximately 67% of the records in MEDLINE include abstracts.

Meeting room Rooms in the library available for meetings. Library staff employee meetings are scheduled internally.

Megabyte (MB) megabyte. A unit of data storage size which represents 10^6 (one million) characters of information.

Megahertz (mhz) A measurement of the transmission speed of electronic devices, named after the German physicist Heinrich R. Hertz. One mhz equals one million cycles per second. In computing, a megahertz is usually equal to one million bps (bits per second). When used in reference to a computer's clock, the number of mhz indicates the speed of the central processing unit (CPU).

Melodrama From the Greek word melos meaning "music." The term originally referred to all dramatic works that included music, but in 19th-century England it was applied to a play in which the characters are stereotyped (good or bad), the action exaggerated and emotional, and the plot improbable and/or sensational, interspersed with catchy songs and orchestral accompaniment, with an invariably happy ending (example: Sweeney Todd, the Demon Barber of Fleet Street). Melodrama bears the same relationship to tragedy as farce to comedy. In contemporary usage, the adjective melodramatic is applied to any performance or literary work in which the characters are overdrawn and the action taxes the credulity of audience or reader.

Melvyl An on-line catalog system containing books, music scores and recordings, audiovisual materials, maps, and computer files from UC libraries and the California State Library. Also featured are periodicals from several sources.

Member copy A bibliographic record cataloged and/ or input by a library other than the Library of Congress where the cataloging library is a member of OCLC.

Member library cataloging Cataloging information provided by a library that is a member of a network or cooperative program. In our case, it is from OCLC.

Memoirs A narrative of events or reminiscences based on the author's own observations or personal knowledge of the world in which he (or she) lived, including events witnessed, people known or observed, places visited, etc. The life need not have been historically significant, but one which placed the writer in a position to observe first-hand significant events as they unfolded. Unlike a private diary or journal, memoirs are usually written for publication long after the occurrence of the events described, and do not necessarily provide a day-to-day account. Compare with autobiography.

Memorabilia Materials of sentimental or historical value to the person who created or collected them, including personal books and papers, clippings, photographs, sketches, correspondence, diaries, journals, notes, invitations, etc. Memorabilia are usually added to special collections, in accordance with a library's collection development policy.

Memorandum A formal note distributed internally to one or more persons in a company, agency, organization, or institution, with a header indicating the date it was sent and stating to whom it is addressed (To:), from whom it is sent (From:), and the subject of the text (Re:). Unlike a letter, a memo does not require a full salutation or signature at the end of the text—the sender may simply initial his or her name in the header. Plural: memoranda.

Memory The space available for holding or storing data on a computer. External memory consists of permanent storage space on hard disks and floppy disks. Main memory (RAM) stores data only during a single work session, which is why files must be saved before ending a session. Because main memory also allocates space to the operating system, the amount of usable memory is usually less than total RAM, which may limit the size of application programs that can be run on a given computer, and the maximum speed at which it can process data.

Mending Minor restoration of a book's condition, not requiring replacement of material or removal of the bound sections from the cover. When mending of library materials is done in-house, the job should be given to a person who is properly trained, to avoid permanent damage to items in need of attention. Compare with repairing and rebinding.

Mending tape A generic term for various kinds of adhesive tape designed specifically for making minor repairs on books and other printed materials, available by the roll from library suppliers, either single- or double-sided, with pressure-sensitive or water-based adhesive. For mending tears in paper, acid-free tape is preferred. In conservation, reversibility may require the use of a tape that can be easily removed without damaging the item.

Mending-CQ Item status which indicates that the item is damaged and being evaluated for repair. Sometimes item with this status are not repairable and are not returned to the regular collection, therefore no holds are allowed on items with this status.

Mental map A map depicting a geographic area of any extent according to the subjective perceptions of a particular person or group of people, rather than in relation to physical reality, for example, a New Yorker's view of the United States west of New York City. This category also includes maps in which an area is sized according to the quantity of the subject involved, for example, human population per square mile, which would, in a map of the United States, make Texas considerably smaller and New York much larger than is actually the case.

Mentor An experienced, trustworthy person who willingly provides useful advice to a new member of a community, profession, or organization, to assist the person in achieving success in his or her new position and environment. Mentoring relationships can either be established informally by the participants, or under the formal sponsorship of the organization. Mentoring of recent library school graduates can be arranged through the New Members Round Table (NMRT) of the American Library Association.

Menu bar A list of menu names, usually displayed horizontally below the title bar in a graphical user interface, with corresponding menu options hidden from view. When the user selects one of the menu names, the appropriate list of options is displayed in a drop-down, pop-up, or sidebar menu.

Menu Bar The horizontal bar that contains the names of available menus. The menu bar is located below the title bar.

Menu is a list of options from which a computer user can choose. This saves the user from having to memorize a set of commands. It also reduces the decision down to the basic information required (note the etymology from the French word minuet meaning small).

Menu-driven A computer interface that provides a hierarchical sequence of lists of possible choices (options) from which the user must make the appropriate selections to accomplish the desired result. Menu-driven interfaces are easier for novices to negotiate, but slower and less sophisticated than command-driven systems and consequently less attractive to experienced users.

Merge To combine in logical sequence two or more separate files of information into one, either manually or by an automated process. When such a combination includes the recognition and removal of duplicate files, the process is known as merge/purg.

Merger The combination of two or more serials into one. A note is included in the bibliographic record for the new serial (Merger of:) indicating the titles of the publications that merged, and a companion note is added to the record for each of the serials that merged (Merged with: to become:) indicating the title(s) with which it merged and the title of the publication created as the result of the merger. The opposite of split. Compare with absorption.

Mesh An acronym for Medical Subject Headings, the controlled vocabulary used by the National Library of Medicine in its MEDLINE database (available on the Web as pubmed). The mesh headings are published in print by NLM in an alphabetically arranged annotated list and in tree structures.

Message A collection of data that is ordered according to the rules of a given protocol suite, such that it is intelligible to the sending and receiving software.

Messenger service A unit of the Office of the University Librarian responsible for the pickup and delivery of mail and library materials among libraries. This includes handling U.S. mail, Federal Express and UPS shipments, as well as bindery shipments.

Meta Search Engines Search several other search engines all at once. This may not allow you to access some features of the individual search engines, however.

Meta Tag A specific kind of HTML tag that contains information not normally displayed to the user. Meta tags contan information about the page itself, hence the name ("meta" means "about this subject") Typical uses of Meta tags are to include information for search engines to help them better categorize a page. You can see the Meta tags in a page if you view the pages' source code.

Metacrawler Search engine at http://www.webcrawler.com.

Metadata Strictly speaking, data about other data. In a functional sense, structured data about data. More specifically, a description of a set of data (how and when it was collected, who collected and organized it, the format in which it is presented, etc.). In libraries, any database or machine-readable data file used to identify, describe, and locate networked electronic resources (example: askjake). At the present time, no standardized format exists, but the Dublin Core Metadata Initiative (DCMI) is working to establish an international cross-disciplinary consensus on methods of bibliographic control for electronic resources. For more information.

Metadatabase A database of databases, usually formed by aggregating two or more smaller databases to allow the user to search their contents as a whole, instead of repeating the same search in each separately (example: onefile from Gale Group which consolidates the infotrac bibliographic databases into a single very large finding tool). The pace of aggregation has accelerated as very large vendors have dominated the market for access to periodical databases, but however helpful "one-stop searching" may be in interdisciplinary research (and to users who lack the skill to select the optimum databases for a specialized topic), segmentation still offers significant advantages for the experienced researcher.

Meta-index An index of indexes. For a meta-index of indexes to Web sites, see the WWW Virtual Library.

Metallic ink Printing ink to which finely ground particles of metal (aluminum, bronze, copper, etc.) Have been added to produce a decorative metallic effect.

Metaphor From the Greek word metapherein meaning to "to carry across." A figure of speech in which a word or phrase denoting a specific object, person, idea, etc., is applied to something with which it is not normally associated, to attribute one or more of its qualities to the other without using "like" or "as" to make an explicit comparison. The identification or substitution can be direct ("Oaths are straws, men's faiths are wafer-cakes" Henry V 2.3.51) or merely suggested ("Upon the heat and flame of thy distemper sprinkle cool patience" Hamlet 3.4.123). Metaphor has been used as a literary device since the earliest works of recorded literature ("rosy-fingered dawn"), to enable imaginative writers to expand the literal meaning(s) of a word or phrase. When the elements compared are so dissimilar as to be incongruous, the resulting mixed metaphor ("mixaphor") can be amusing ("rusty lips"). A dead metaphor has become so commonplace as to have lost its impact ("time marches on"). The history and grammar of metaphor is studied in the discipline of linguistics. Metaphors are sometimes collected and indexed, usually thematically (Metaphors Dictionary edited by Elyse Sommer and Dorrie Weiss).

Meta-Search Engines Parallel Internet query engines which are used to submit questions to several search engines at one time. In a recent (May, 2001) study, Danny Sullivan of Search Engine Watch found that many metasearch engines are now including paid placement sites in their results lists.

Metonymy A figure of speech in which the name of one thing is used for another to which it is related, of which it is an attribute, with which it is associated, or which it suggests (example: "White House" for Presidency or "Crown" for King). Reverse metonymy is the use of the name of a thing to refer to one or more of its attributes.

Mhz Megahertz. A million cycles (occurrences, alterations, pulses) per second. Used to describe the speed at which a computer's processor (or CPU) operates. A 25-mhz processor can handle 25 million operations per second.

Mhz or mhz Megahertz; a measurement of a microprocessor's speed; one mhz represents one million cycles per second. The speed determines how many instructions per second a microprocessor can execute. The higher the megahertz, the faster the computer.

Microcard Opaque card on which microcopies have been reproduced photographically, arranged in rows.

Microclimate The isolated environment (light, temperature, relative humidity, dust, etc.) Within a small confined space such as a display case, enclosed bookcase, drawer, box, or other storage container, easier to control than a large storage area when conservation is a high priority.

Microcomputer A generic term for a programmable computer designed to handle relatively small operations, usually a desk-top machine containing a single-chip microprocessor on a printed circuit board, which may be part of a larger computer system or connected to a network. The term may have been coined to distinguish personal computers from more powerful minicomputers.

Microfiche A small card-shaped sheet of photographic film, designed to store miniaturized text and/or microimages arranged sequentially in a two-dimensional grid. Microfiche is available in color or black-and-white (negative or positive). Various formats exist, but ISO recommends 75 x 125 mm (48 frames in four rows of twelve) or 105 x 148 mm (60 frames in five rows of twelve). Although each sheet usually includes a title and/or index number in a heading across the top that can be read without magnification, the text itself can be read and copied only with the aid of a microform reader-printer machine. User resistance can be mitigated by keeping equipment in good repair and providing point-of-use assistance.

Microfiche envelope A small paper envelope, open at the top and right end, or at the top only, with a high throat for storing one or more sheets of microfiche so that only the title strip on the first sheet is visible. Archival quality microfiche envelopes are made of acid- and lignin-free paper.

Microfilm A continuous roll of 16 mm photographic film used for storing miniaturized text and/or microimages in a single row (cine format) or double row (comic format) of frames that can be magnified and copied only with the aid of a specially designed reader-printer machine. Microfilm is available in color or black-and-white (negative or positive). In some libraries, periodical back files are routinely converted to microfilm to save space. Microform reader/printers are available in libraries with microfilm holdings for viewing and making hard copies. User resistance can be mitigated by keeping equipment in good repair and by providing point-of-use assistance. Compare with microfiche.

Microform A generic term for a highly reduced photographic copy of text and/or images stored on a translucent medium (microfiche or microfilm), or on an opaque medium such as card stock (microopaque or aperture card). Microforms can be original editions or reproductions. Reader-printer machines are required to view and make hard copies. Digital storage media such as magnetic tape and disk, CD-ROM, etc., are superseding microforms in information storage and retrieval but the transformation is far from complete. Microforms currently available for purchase are listed by author/title and subject in the serial publication Guide to Microforms in Print. Compare with macroform.

Micrographics A general term for the techniques used to photographically reduce text and/or graphic images to a size too small to be read by the human eye without magnification, usually for the purpose of preservation or compact storage, as in the conversion of periodical back files from print to microfilm or microfiche. Micrographic formats also include microopaque and aperture card. Compare with micrography.

Micrography The art and practice of writing in microscopically small characters. Compare with micrographics.

Microopaque A sheet of opaque material, such as paper or card stock, bearing miniaturized text and/or microimages arranged in a two-dimensional grid which can be magnified and copied only with the aid of special equipment. Reader-printer machines for viewing and making hard copies are usually provided in libraries with microopaque holdings. Compare with microfiche.

Microprint An obsolete form of microphotograph which can hold many pages of text on a 9"x6" card, viewed with the aid of a microprint reader. It is similar to a microfiche, but has positive images of the pages printed on an opaque card. Marriott's materials in microprint are not actually accessible at present, as there are no functional readers and the machines are no longer being manufactured.

Microprocessor A central processing unit (CPU) etched or printed on a single silicon microchip. To function as a computer, a microprocessor requires a power supply, a clock, and memory. Microprocessors are used in most digital devices (pcs, personal digital assistants, clock radios, etc.).

Microscope slide A small piece of transparent material (usually glass) designed to hold a very small object for viewing through the lens of a microscope or microprojector. In AACR2, microscope slides are cataloged according to the rules for three-dimensional artifacts and realia. Compare with microslide.

Microscopic printing Printing done in a very small type size. Although the first works printed in Europe were in large type, early printers soon realized that with smaller typefaces, more matter fitted on a page. By 1825, the French type-founder Henri Didot had cast type that produced 25 lines to the inch. Because the casting of extremely small type has physical limitations, most microscopic reduction is now done photographically

Microslide A slide consisting of a single mounted frame of microfilm. Compare with microscope slide.

Microsoft word Word processing application software that includes spelling and grammar checks. Available for public use in the Electronic Information Centre.

MIDI: Musical Instrument Digital Interface; enables a computer to control devices, such as synthesizers and sound cards, that emit music. Computers with a MIDI interface can record sounds created by a synthesizer and then manipulate the data to create new sounds. A variety of programs are available for composing and editing music conforming to the MIDI standard.

Midlist The portion of a publisher's list consisting of literary fiction and serious nonfiction titles which are not expected to become bestsellers, often written by new and emerging authors. Studies suggest that although publishers are issuing as many new midlist titles as ever, the failure of bookstore chains to market them competitively has resulted in a decline in percentage of total book sales.

Mildew The growth of micro-organisms whose spores remain dormant under cool, dry conditions inside libraries and other facilities, but are stimulated by warm, moist air to feed on the leaves and bindings of books and other printed materials. The growth of mildew produces an acid harmful to paper and materials used in binding. It also produces a characteristic musty odor that can be prevented in libraries by maintaining good air circulation, low relative humidity, and adequate lighting. Once started, an infestation of mildew can be difficult to eradicate.

Military library A library maintained by a unit of government responsible for national defense, maintaining collections for the use of military staff, but which may have a broader mandate, including accessibility to the general public (example: Nimitz Library at the U.S. Naval Academy).

Military librarians are organized in the Federal and Armed Forces Libraries Round Table of the American Library Association.

Milling Cutting away a small portion of the binding edge of a book (usually less than 1/8 inch) to prepare the sections for adhesive binding or oversewing, an operation done in a bindery by moving the inner edge of the clamped text block over the rotating blades of a milling machine. In first-time binding, the back folds of the sections are cut away, producing loose leaves. In rebinding, the old adhesive, thread, staples, etc., are cut away along with the folds to prepare the leaves for reattachment.

MILNET Military Network. A network used for unclassified military production applications. It is part of the DDN and the Internet.

MIME (Multipurpose Internet Mail Extensions) Originally a standard for defining the types of files attached to standard Internet mail messages. The MIME standard has come to be used in many situations where one cmputer programs needs to communicate with another program about what kind of file is being sent. For example, HTML files have a MIME-type of text/html, JPEG files are image/jpeg, etc.

MIME mappings A list of file extensions and the types of files they belong to. When the server sends an HTTP reply, it sends a type/subtype header according to the requested file's extension.

MIME type/subtype An HTTP header sent with a reply that determines how a client will view or use the message. The MIME type tells the general type of document, such as image or application, and the subtype tells the specific type such as GIF or ZIP.

Mini bib A brief bibliographic record for staff use.

Miniature book A book conceived on a very small scale, measuring no more than three inches along its greatest dimension (height or width), usually printed in 6-point type or smaller and illustrated on the same scale. Not uncommon, miniature books include Bibles, almanacs, poetry, classics, juvenile literature, tokens, etc. Very tiny books, such as those used in doll houses, are usually produced photographically. Of interest to collectors, miniature books have an enthusiastic following in the United States. For more information, see the Web site maintained by the Miniature Book Society.

Miniature edition An edition of very small size (three inches or less in height and width), usually printed in 6-point type or smaller, and illustrated on the same scale. Synonymous with lilliput edition and microscopic edition.

Miniature score A music score printed in small type to allow the pages to be reduced to pocket size. Miniature scores are designed to be used by music lovers for study and enjoyment, rather than by performers in their work.

Minicomputer A medium-sized computer introduced in the 1960's, capable of serving up to several hundred users. A dedicated minicomputer is used to run the online catalog in many libraries. Synonymous with midrange computer. Compare with microcomputer, mainframe, and supercomputer.

Minimal level cataloging (MLC) An encoding level that allows more severe limitations on the description and classification of an item (and on the amount of authority control) than in core level cataloging, resulting in a less than complete bibliographic record. MLC was designed to provide access to materials unavailable due to cataloging arrears, as well as items worthy of retention but not considered worth the expense of full level cataloging.

Minimize A feature of a graphical user interface that allows the user to reduce a window to a tab in the taskbar, or to an icon on the desktop, by clicking on a small button in the upper right-hand corner of the window. The opposite of maximize.

Minor A descriptor or identifier assigned in a bibliographic record to represent one of the less significant aspects of the content of the document (form, methodology, etc.). A minor descriptor or identifier is not marked with an asterisk or distinguished typographically in the list of preferred indexing terms, as is a major descriptor or identifier representing a primary focus or subject of the document. Some indexing systems do not provide minor descriptors and identifiers.

Minors card Borrowing card issued to library users junior high school age through the age of 17.

Mint In the antiquarian book trade, a copy in the same immaculate, unaltered condition as when it was first published, new and virtually unused—the highest possible grade in any assessment of condition. Used books in mint condition command a higher price than copies showing signs of wear. Synonymous with as new and pristine. Compare with fine copy

Minuscule In medieval cursive handwriting, one of the small letters from which the modern lowercase letters of the roman alphabet evolved by way of the Carolingian script introduced by Alcuin of York in Europe in the late 8th century.

Minutes Under parliamentary procedure, a written chronological account of the business conducted at a formal assembly, such as a library faculty or staff meeting, usually written from notes taken by an elected or appointed secretary, or other designated member, for distribution to all the other participants in advance of the next meeting for their correction and approval. The minutes of important meetings may be archived as a matter of record.

MIPS Millions of Instructions Per Second.

Miracle play A form of medieval religious drama performed on a movable wagon from a script giving an account of a divine miracle, usually one believed to have occurred in the life of a Christian saint or character from the Bible. Compare with morality play.

Mirror Generally speaking, "to mirror" is to maintain an exact copy of something. Probably the most common use of the term on the Internet refers to "mirror sites" which are web sites, or FTP sites that maintain copies of material originated at another location, usually in order to provide more widespread access to the resource. For example, one site might create a library of software, and 5 other sites might maintain mirrors of that library.

Mirror sites Web sites that keep exact copies of material from another site, to provide improved access.

MIS See: management information system.

Misbound A book in which a map or illustration, a number of leaves, or a complete section has been folded incorrectly, gathered in incorrect sequence, bound in upside down, or omitted. The publisher will normally send a replacement if such a copy is returned by a bookseller or retail customer.

Miscellany A collection consisting of an assortment of writings on diverse subjects. The term also appears in the titles of books containing literary works of various forms, usually related to a specific subject (A Miscellany of Women's Wisdom), person (A James Joyce Miscellany), place (A Handful of Spice: A Miscellany of Maine Literature and History), etc. Compare with anthology.

Misquote To repeat incorrectly words that another person has spoken or written, inadvertently or by intention. A quotation made out of context may be misleading, but it is not necessarily a misquote. Quotations included in written works should be properly cited and double-checked for accuracy before publication.

Missal A liturgical work containing all the prayers used in celebrating the Catholic Mass during the period of a year. The earliest medieval examples were copied by hand on parchment or vellum and beautifully illuminated. In a more general sense, any book of prayers or daily devotions.

Missing A code used in a library catalog to indicate the circulation status of an item not checked out, which cannot be found anywhere in the library. If a thorough search by library staff fails to locate the item within a reasonable time, a replacement copy may be ordered, provided demand persists and an edition of the work is still in print. Compare with lost.

Missing copy Parts of a book, such as the index or appendices, which may not be ready when a publisher sends the typescript and specifications to the printer. If additional copy is to follow, allowance must be made in estimating the cost of printing.

Mission The basic purpose or role of an organization, expressed succinctly in abstract terms. A clearly written mission statement is the basis for formulating achievable goals and objectives in strategic planning, and serves as a constant reminder of the organization's primary reason for existing.

Missionary book Publisher's slang for the first book published on a subject. To catalog such a work, a new class number and subject heading may be required.

Missive A formal or official message, especially a detailed and lengthy one, such as a letter sent by a superior authority conveying a mandate, recommendation, permission, or invitation to a specific individual or group of persons concerning an action (or actions) to be undertaken. Also refers to a legal document in the form of a letter, exchanged by parties to a contractual agreement.

Miter In hand bookbinding, to bring materials together at an angle (usually 45 degrees) along a straight line without overlap, as in folding the leather or cloth covering material over the edges of the boards at the corners toward the inside, and pasting it down before the endpapers are applied. Also refers to the joint formed by fitting together two pieces beveled at an angle along a straight line. Also spelled mitre.

Mixed notation A classification notation in which two

or more kinds of symbols are used, for example, the letters of the English alphabet used to indicate the main classes and first-level subdivisions in Library of Congress classification and the arabic numerals used for further subdivisions (example: ND2893.A78 2000). Compare with pure notation.

Mixed responsibility In AACR2, a collaboration in which two or more persons or corporate bodies contribute to the content of a work, each performing a different function, for example, the author responsible for writing the text of a children's picture book and the artist who creates the illustrations. Compare with shared responsibility.

MLA (1)Medical Library Association ; (2)Music Library Association

MLA Handbook for Writers of Research Papers

MLA style A format for typing research papers and citing sources in the humanities, developed by the Modern Language Association of America and published in the MLA Handbook for Writers of Research Papers, available in the reference section of most academic libraries.

MLS Master's Degree in Library Science; also represented as MSLS and MLIS.

MLS/MLIS Master of Library Science degree. The terminal degree for the profession of library science.

Mnemonic From the Greek mnemon meaning "mindful." A code in which the abbreviation(s), symbol(s), or formula(s) are easy to remember (example: DEL for "delete" and REF for "reference"). Also, a word or rhyme composed by a person to be used as a mental aid in recalling something.

Mnemonic notation A classification notation in which the characters representing the classes are directly linked to the name of the class, making it easier for the user to learn and recall the way the classification system is organized. Most notations used in library cataloging and indexing are not mnemonic.

MNP Microcom Networking Protocol; a standard that provides error correction and data compression in modems. Different levels of MNP provide a range of capabilities. Level 4 provides error correction and automatically varies the transmission speed based on the quality of the line. Level 5 incorporates the first four levels and adds a data-compression algorithm. Levels 6 and above provide enhanced error correction and data compression.

Mock-up A rough but accurate physical representation in wood, cardboard, papier-mache, plastic, canvas, etc., of a device, apparatus, structure, or process, usually on the same scale, with movable parts that can be manipulated or modified for the purpose of analysis, testing, demonstration, or instruction. Compare with model and reproduction.

Model An accurate three-dimensional representation, usually on a smaller scale, of the physical appearance of a real object of any size, particularly useful in depicting very large objects (e.g., the solar system). Compare with mock-up and realia.

Modem A contraction of modulator-demodulator, originally a peripheral device capable of converting digital pulses into analog frequencies for transmission over telecommunication lines, and data received in analog frequencies into digital pulses for display on, or processing by, a digital computer. A modem also dials the telephone line, answers calls, and controls transmission speed. Modem speed is measured in baud. Although external modems are still available, most new microcomputers come equipped with a built-in modem.

Modem connection A modem is a device or program that enables a computer to transmit data over, for example, telephone or cable lines. The Libraries' has two active telephone lines available for patron's, located in the area just west of the EIC.

Moderator A person who reviews and has the authority to block messages posted to a supervised or "moderated" network newsgroup.

Module One of several parts of an online tutorial designed in separate units, to be completed in a certain sequence. Each unit is sufficiently self-contained that advanced students may skip it if they are already familiar with its content, or complete it out of sequence, although continuity may be lost in doing so. Some tutorials include a self-quiz at the end of each module.

Moire A repetitive interference pattern caused by overlapping symmetrical grids of dots or lines having differing pitch or angle.

Mold A group of microscopic lower plants whose reproductive spores are abundant in most environments, but require certain conditions of temperature and humidity to germinate and grow. In libraries and archives, the best way to keep molds from infecting materials is to provide good air circulation and keep the relative humidity below 70-80%. Once established, molds can be eliminated by using a fungicide or by fumigation. Also spelled mould.

Monaural Sound reproduced from a single channel by an audio playback device with one amplifier or speaker. The result is less realistic than stereophonic or quadraphonic sound recording. Synonymous with monophonic.

Monetary value worth in the market place, based on appraisal by a person experienced in making such judgments

Monitor An output device consisting of an electronic display screen which, when attached to a computer, enables the user to view text and/or images. Computer monitors vary in size, shape, and resolution. A recessed monitor is mounted below the surface of a desk or table, usually beneath a glass panel at an angle to allow the user's line of sight to remain unobstructed in a classroom equipped with a wall screen and LCD projector. Laptop computers have a flat panel monitor that folds down to cover the keyboard. A television monitor is an analog device designed to display signals from a television receiver, or signals prerecorded on videocassette for playback using a VCR.

Monochrome plate An illustration printed separately from the text in a single color, usually listed by number with any other plates in the front matter of the book. Compare with duotone and color plate.

Monochrome Single-colored. An image or medium displaying only black-and-white or greyscale information. Greyscale information displayed in one color is also monochrome.

Monograph A relatively short book or treatise on a single subject, complete in one physical piece, usually written by a specialist in the field. Monographic treatment is detailed and scholarly, but not extensive in scope. The importance of monographs in scholarly communication depends on the discipline. In the humanities, monographs remain the format of choice for serious scholars, but in the sciences and social sciences where currency is essential, journals are usually the preferred means of publication.

Monographic series A series of monographs, usually issued under a collective title by a university press or scholarly society. Each volume in the series may contain more than one monograph, each with its own title in addition to the series title.

Monographs and identification Section of acquisition services responsible for searching, acquiring and receiving monographs.

Monoline A typeface in which the strokes of which the characters are composed, whether straight or curvilinear, are all of the same thickness, including any serifs. Compare with block letter.

Monologue From the Greek monologos meaning "speaking alone." A play, skit, or recitation in which all the lines are spoken by a single actor, or a long sequence of lines within a play, spoken by one of the characters alone on the stage. In drama and narrative fiction, an interior monologue reveals a character's private thoughts and feelings. Compare with soliloquy.

Montage A composite image made by juxtaposing two or more images, or parts of images (drawings, photographs, pictures, etc.), without separation lines, in a composition that gives new meaning to the whole but preserves the distinctiveness of the individual elements, a technique originally developed as an art form but now used extensively in advertising and graphic design.

Monthly catalog (MOCAT) Monthly Catalog of U.S. Government Publications. A periodical indexing by author, title and subject federal documents published by the superintendent of documents in Washington, D.C. Also accessible on CD-ROM.

Monthly Issued once a month (twelve times per year) with the possible exception of one or two months, usually during the summer. Many magazines and some journals are published monthly (example: Monthly Labor Review). Also refers to a serial issued once a month.

MOO (Mud, Object Oriented) One of several kinds of multi-user role-playing environments.

Morality play A form of drama popular during the Middle Ages and Renaissance in which the characters are engaged in an allegorical struggle over the condition of the human soul. Unlike mystery plays and miracle plays, which were presented on mobile wagons, morality plays were usually performed on a stationary platform.

Morgue A library maintained by the publisher of a newspaper, usually consisting of back issues, reference materials, indexes and databases, clippings, notes, photographs, illustrations, and other resources needed by reporters and staff to research, write, and edit articles for publication. The term originally referred to the repository of biographical materials collected on persons of interest, for the purpose of writing obituaries. The first newspaper library in the United States was established at the office of the Boston Pilot in 1831.

Morocco A fine pebble-grained leather made from goatskin tanned with sumac, believed to have been introduced to Europe by the Moors. One of the most durable leathers used in bookbinding, it is strong yet flexible. Older books bound in morocco are often rare and valuable. Compare with calf and pigskin.

Mosaic The first WWW browser that was available for the Macintosh, Windows,and UNIX all with the same interfacc. Mosaic really started the popularity of the Web. The source-code to Mosaic was licensed by several companies and used to create many other web browsers. Mosaic was developed at the National Center for Supercomputing Applications (NCSA), at the Univeristy of Urbana-Champange in Illinois, USA. The first version was released in late 1993.

Motherboard The heart, soul, and brains of a computer. This plastic board resembles a miniature city, but its buildings are actually chips for things like the processing, RAM, and ROM, and the tiny roads connecting them are circuit traces. Also called the logic board. There are no fatherboards or sonboards, but see daughterboard.

Motif A term borrowed from art and music (leitmotif) to refer to a textual element that symbolically represents a specific theme in a literary work by virtue of repetition, usually presented in the opening verse, chapter, or paragraphs and subsequently elaborated.

Motion picture A length of film from which an unbroken sequence of still photographs can be projected at speeds of 16 to 24 frames per second, producing the illusion of continuous motion. Motion pictures made in color or black-and-white, with or without recorded sound, on film 8, 16, 35, or 70 mm wide. They include documentaries, feature films, and short films. Synonymous with cinefilm. Compare with cinema.

Motorola 680 × 0 A line of microprocessors that powered all Apple Macintosh computers from the first 68000 to the 68040 in the mid-1990s. New Macintosh computers now contain the Power PC chip.

Mottled calf Calfskin used in bookbinding, which has been dabbed or sprinkled with colored dye or tanning acid to give it a decorative spotty appearance.

Mottling A texture similar to orange peel sometimes caused by sharpening. It is particularly visible in flat areas such as sky or skin.

Mounted An illustration or photograph tipped onto a blank page in a book or album. Also, a fragile or damaged leaf, illustration, map, etc., strengthened with backing made of paper, card, or thin cloth.

Mouse A small handheld input device which, when rolled across a hard, flat surface, allows the user to direct the motion of a cursor or pointer on a computer screen, and initiate an operation or select an option displayed in a graphical user interface by pressing down on one of its buttons. Because the button makes a clicking sound when pressed, such programs are called point-and-click applications. In graphics programs, the mouse can be used like a pen, pencil, or paintbrush. Most mouse operations can be executed more slowly using the keyboard. Basic models are designed to be used by a right- or left-handed person. Contoured models are available for either the right or left hand. In laptops, the mouse is usually built-in.

Mouse type Very tiny, barely readable type used for the fine print in sales contracts, coupons, contest entry forms, etc., to notify the reader of legal restrictions, expiration dates, and other information that the seller is required to display but wishes to downplay.

MOV A file extension found on the World Wide Web that denotes that the file is a movie or video in quicktime format.

Movable shelves Electronically operated compact storage shelving.

Movable type Metal type cast as individual units, each bearing a single character, assembled by a typesetter into words, lines, and pages of text, then disassembled for reuse once a print job is completed. Although there is evidence that printing from wood blocks originated in China, probably during the 11th century, Johann Gutenberg is credited with the invention of modern movable type in Germany in the mid-15th century.

Moving company A professional mover hired to transfer the contents of a library from one location to another, usually selected in a competitive process in which the company is given the opportunity to inspect the sites before submitting a bid. Unless stated otherwise in the bid specifications, the contractor determines the methods used and provides both personnel and equipment. Professional movers with experience moving libraries work very methodically and quickly because, as the move slows or stops, their costs increase.

Moving The transfer of all or a portion of the contents of a library (collections, equipment, furnishings, and personnel) from one facility to another, temporarily or permanently. Most libraries hire a professional moving company with library experience to do the actual work, but advance planning is required for a move to be executed smoothly. Library literature is available on the moving process to assist planners in avoiding common pitfalls.

MPEG Moving Picture Experts Group, a standard for compressing full-motion video in digital format. More efficient than JPEG (the standard for compressing still images), MPEG is used to transmit a wide range of audio-video formats including DVD motion pictures. MPEG-2 requires bandwidth of 4-15 MB per second and an MPEG board for playback in most computers. Pronounced "em-peg."

MPLA Mountain Plains Library Association. Its mission is to further the development of librarians, library employees and trustees and to promote quality library service in the states of the Mountain Plains Region (Arizona,

Colorado, Kansas, Montana, Nebraska, Nevada, New Mexico, North Dakota, Oklahoma, South Dakota, Utah and Wyoming.)

MRF Machine readable format, e.g. MRF cataloging records.

MUD Multi-User Dimension; a virtual reality site on the Internet where multiple users can interact.

MUD (Multi-User Dungeon or Dimension) (usually text-based) multi-user simulation environment. Some are purely for fun and flirting, others are used for serious software development, or education purposes and all thatlies in between. A significant feature of most muds is that users can create things that stay after they leave and which other users can interact within their absence, thus allowing a world to be built gradually and collectively.

MUD, Object-Oriented a multi-user role-playing environment (MUD) with an object-based environment (e.g. Biomoo).

Multicast In telecommunication, to transmit data simultaneously to more than one individual or site connected to the same network, for example, to all who subscribe to an e-mail mailing list, as opposed to broadcasting messages to all who own the appropriate receiving equipment (radio and television).

Multimedia A combination of two or more digital media (text, graphics, audio, animation, video, etc.) Used in a computer application, such as an online encyclopedia, computer game, or Web site (example: A 2 Z 4 Birders Online Guide). Multimedia applications are often interactive. Synonymous in this sense with digital media.

Multimedia Center (MMC) the facility which houses and provides access to

Multimedia map A map available electronically that includes audio, video, and/or animation, in addition to graphic images and text (example: the wildworld Web site maintained by the National Geographic Society).

Multipart volume A work published in two or more physically separate parts that together constitute a single bibliographic volume. Reference works too large to be bound as a single volume are published in this manner (example: some volumes of Dictionary of Literary Biography). Compare with multivolume work.

Multiple access More than one point of access to a file of data (example: a library catalog or bibliographic database searchable by author, title, subject, keywords, etc.), as opposed to a resource that has only one point of access (example: the headwords in a printed dictionary of the words of a language). Compare with multiple user access.

Multiple user access A file of data that can be used independently by more than one person at the same time, for example, a multi-volume print encyclopedia as opposed to a single-volume dictionary. Access to online catalogs, bibliographic databases, and full-text electronic resources by more than one simultaneous user may be governed by licensing agreement. Compare with multiple access.

Multiplex The division of a single transmission medium into multiple logical channels supporting many apparently simultaneous sessions.

Multitasking The ability of a CPU to perform more than one operation at the same time; Windows and Macintosh computers are multitasking in that each program that is running uses the CPU only for as long as needed and then control switches to the next task.

Multivolume work A work published in two or more numbered or unnumbered volumes under a single title (example: Oxford English Dictionary), sometimes over an extended period (Dictionary of American Regional English). A multivolume work is cataloged as a single entity, with the volumes owned by the library listed in a holdings note. Compare with multipart volume and series.

MUSE (Multi-User Simulated Environment) One kind of MUD - usually with little or no violence.

Museum library A type of special library maintained by a museum or gallery, usually within its walls, but sometimes in a separate location, containing a collection books, periodicals, reproductions, and other materials related to its exhibits and fields of specialization. Access may be by appointment only. Borrowing privileges may be restricted to museum staff and members.

Museum publisher A museum or historical society that issues books, exhibit catalogs, and other publications under its own imprint or in cooperation with other publishers, for example, the Metropolitan Museum of Art in New York City. Museum publications are usually of fine quality, often issued in both hardcover and softcover editions to appeal to collectors and casual buyers.

Music library A library containing a collection of materials on music and musicians, including printed and manuscript music scores, music periodicals, recorded music (cds, audiocassettes, phonograph records, etc.), books about music and musicians, program notes, discographies, and music reference materials.

Music Library Association (MLA) Founded in 1931, MLA promotes the establishment, growth, and use of music libraries and collections of music, musical instruments, music literature, music recordings, and related materials in both print and nonprint format. An affiliate of the American Library Association, the organization also seeks to advance music librarianship, scholarship, and publishing. MLA publishes the monthly Music Cataloging Bulletin.

Musical presentation statement An optional area of the bibliographic record representing a musical work, in which the physical form of the music is described (full score, miniature score, piano score, etc.) As it appears on the chief source of information. If such a statement is an integral part of another area of bibliographic description, and recorded as such, it is not repeated.

Musical work Three definitions are recognized in

AACR2: 1) a musical composition created as a single unit intended by its composer to be performed as a whole; 2) a set of musical compositions with a collective title, not necessarily intended for performance as a whole; and 3) a group of musical compositions assigned a single opus number. In cataloging musical works, main entry is under the name of the composer, with added entries for arranger, librettist, major performer(s), etc.

Mutilation Damage, defacement, or destruction of library materials inflicted intentionally, rather than accidentally, including tearing covers and pages; cutting out illustrations or passages of text; marking or writing on margins or text; and removing labels, bookplates, protective covers, date due slips, etc., all actions that drain library resources. The motives for such acts range from an attitude of entitlement, to monetary concerns (libraries generally charge for photocopying), disapproval of the library's collection development decisions, to outright malice.

My account Section of the library catalog where a patron can look up their due dates, renew items, change their PIN or email address, and view their patron profile.

My list Area of the library catalog which is used to temporarily store a book list for future reference. MY lists are created in the library catalog, either in IPAC or webpac, and if attached to your library card record, remain for one month before they are automatically deleted.

Mystery A popular novel, story, or drama about an unusual event or occurrence, such as a murder or disappearance, that remains so secret or unexplained as to excite popular curiosity and interest. The plot in mystery fiction often hinges on an attempt by a sleuth to uncover the truth. The Sherlock Holmes stories of Sir Arthur Conan Doyle are classic examples. Subgenres include detective fiction and suspense.

Mystery play A form of medieval religious drama, popular from the 14th to the 16th century, usually performed on a mobile wagon from a script based on a story from the Scriptures or a sequence of episodes from biblical history. In England, the performance of. mystery plays was often financed by the local trade guilds in connection with important feast days, such as Corpus Christi. Compare with morality play.

Myth From the classical Greek word mythos meaning "story." A narrative rooted in the traditions of a specific culture, capable of being understood and appreciated in its own right, but at the same time part of a system of stories (mythology) transmitted orally from one generation to the next to illustrate man's relationship to the cosmos. In traditional societies, myths often serve as the basis for social customs and observances.

Mywebct A portal or entry page that gives you access to all your webct courses on a particular server using a single username and password. From here you can see whether there are any new assignments, quizzes, mail, or discussion items for each course (updated on a daily basis).This page also contains current announcements of interest to webct users, as well as links to related information.

NAL Window Network Application Launcher. The window on the computer desktop that provides access to a staff member's software applications.

NALA Nashville Area Library Alliance; a consortium of academic, school, the Public Library of Nashville, and the Tennessee State Library and Archives established to share collections.

Name authority file An authorized list giving the preferred form of entry for names (personal, corporate, and geographic) used as headings in a library catalog, and any cross-references from variant forms.

Name index A list of the personal names appearing of a work, arranged alphabetically by surname, with reference to the page number(s) on which each name can be found in the text. Not all books have a separate name index—personal names may be included in a general index or in the subject index. When present in a single-volume work, the name index is part of the back matter. In a a multi-volume work, it is usually found at the end of the last volume. Compare with author index.

Nameserver A computer that runs a program for converting Internet domain names into the corresponding IP addresses and vice versa.

Name-title added entry In AACR2, an added entry in a library catalog that gives the name of a person (or corporate body) and the title of a work, to identify: 1) a work that is included in or the subject of the work being cataloged; 2) a larger work of which the work being cataloged is part; or 3) another work to which the work being cataloged is in some way relatcd.

Naps Network Access Points; these interconnect the commercial isps.

Narration The telling of a story or account of events, in speech or writing, usually in the first or third person. Most documentary films and television programs include a scripted narration, with the name of the narrator given in the credits. Celebrity narrators may be employed to enhance the appeal of a work.

Narrative A written or spoken work in the form of a story or account (real or imagined) told by one or more narrators as a continuous, episodic, or broken series of related events, usually in the first or third person. Narratives can be short, as in a brief anecdote, or as long as a full-length novel. A narrative poem is one that relates a story (ballad, epic, etc.). The narrative structure of a work is the sequence and voice in which the author unfolds events, for example, in a series of flashbacks.

Narrow The shape of a book in which the width of the cover is less than two-thirds its height, a format commonly used in the design of field guides and travel guides. Compare with square.

Narrowcast Selective use of communication media to target a highly specialized audience, in contrast to a mass media broadcast intended to reach as many listeners or viewers as possible.

Narrower term (NT or N) In a hierarchical classification system, a subject heading or descriptor representing a subclass of a class indicated by another term (example: "Music librarianship" under "Librarianship"). A subject heading or descriptor may have more than one narrower term (also "Comparative librarianship" under "Librarianship"). Compare with broader term (BT) and related term (RT).

National Agricultural Library (NAL) Established as a federal library in 1862 under legislation signed by President Lincoln, NAL is part of the Agricultural Research Service (ARS) of the U.S. Department of Agriculture (USDA). With a collection of over 3.3 million items, NAL is the primary source of agricultural information in the United States and the largest agricultural library in the world. Located in Beltsville, Maryland, NAL works closely with libraries at land-grant universities to improve access to, and utilization of, agricultural information by researchers, policy-makers, educators, farmers, consumers of agricultural products, and the general public.

National Archives and Records Administration (NARA) The national archives of the United States, a federal agency established by Congress in 1934 to oversee the management of all federal records, including the public's right of access to documents and information not specifically exempted under the Freedom of Information Act. NARA's 33 facilities house approximately 21.5 million cubic feet of original textual materials collected from the executive, legislative, and judicial branches. It also includes nonprint materials, such as motion pictures, sound and videorecordings, maps and charts, aerial photographs, architectural drawings, computer data sets, posters, etc. NARA is administered by an Archivist of the United States appointed by the President with the approval of Congress, and advised by a National Archives Council.

National archives The central archives of a nation, charged with collecting and preserving documents and records of historical significance to its citizens and government. The first national archives was established in France in 1790. In the United States, the National Archives and Records Administration (NARA) has statutory responsibility for the preservation of archival information of national importance. Compare with national library.

National Association of Government Archives and Records Administrators (NAGARA) Founded in 1984, NAGARA is a nationwide association of local, state, and federal archivists and records administrators, and individuals with an interest in improving the management of government records. Its members are local, state, and federal archival and records management agencies. NAGARA publishes the quarterly newsletter NAGARA Clearinghouse..

National Association of Media & Technology Centers (NAMTC) A nonprofit association devoted to assisting specialists responsible for managing media and technology centers, through networking, advocacy, and support activities intended to enhance equitable access to nonprint media, technology, and information services to educational communities. Membership in NAMTC is open to regional, K-12, and higher education media and technology centers, as well as commercial media vendors.

National bibliography An ongoing list of the books and other printed materials published or distributed in a specific country, especially works written about the country and its inhabitants, or in its national language, for example, the British National Bibliography which has provided, since 1950, a weekly list of new works published in Great Britain.

National biography A publication containing biographical information about people of noteworthy accomplishments living in or associated with a particular country. Most national biographies are multi-volume reference works.

National Book Award An honor awarded since 1950 by the National Book Foundation, a consortium of book publishing groups, to enhance public awareness of exceptional books written by Americans. Awards are given in four categories: fiction, nonfiction, poetry, and children's literature. Decisions are made by an independent panel of five judges. The prize in each category is $10,000 and a crystal sculpture.

National Commission on Libraries and Information Science (NCLIS) An independent agency within the executive branch of the U.S. federal government, established in 1970 to advise the President and Congress on national library and information policy, conduct studies of library and information needs, assess the adequacy of current resources and services, promote research, develop plans for meeting the nation's information needs, and help coordinate library-related activities at the federal, state, and local levels.

National Endowment for the Humanities (NEH) An independent grant-making agency established in 1965 by the National Foundation on the Arts and the Humanities Act, NEH supports research, education, and public programs in the humanities, with attention to the diverse heritage, traditions, and history of the United States, and the relevance of the humanities to current conditions and events affecting American society. Each state has an Humanities Council that establishes its own guidelines and application deadlines. The state councils support a variety of projects, including library reading programs, lectures, conferences, seminars and institutes, media presentations, and museum and library traveling exhibitions. The national office is located in Washington D.C.

National Federation of Abstracting and Information Services (NFAIS) Founded in 1958 at the instigation of the Director of BIOSIS, NFAIS has a membership of 55 leading nonprofit, commercial, government, and academic producers and distributors of online bibliographic databases and other digital information services for research and professional use, as well as organizations that provide access to electronic databases in a wide range of disciplines. NFAIS publishes the monthly NFAIS Newsletter..

National Film Preservation Board (NFPB) A nonprofit organization created by Congress to support nationwide efforts to preserve the film heritage of the United States and improve access to film for study, research, education, and exhibition, NFPF began in 1997 with the support of grants from the Academy of Motion Picture Arts and Sciences and the Film Foundation. In 2000, the organization began distributing federal matching grants to film archives to preserve endangered films and collections.

National Film Registry (NFR) A list of up to 25 films selected each year by the Librarian of Congress, with the assistance of the National Film Preservation Board, for preservation in the archives of the Library of Congress. The films must be at least ten years old, but need not be feature-length or have been released to a theater audience to be eligible for selection. The National Film Preservation Act of 1988 authorizes the Board to consider the broadest possible range of films in its deliberations.

National Genealogical Society (NGS) Founded in 1903 with headquarters in Arlington, Virginia, NGS is a service organization devoted to collecting, preserving, and disseminating genealogical information, encouraging interest in genealogical research, fostering careful documentation of genealogical data, and promoting education and training in the field of genealogy. NGS publishes the NGS Newsmagazine and the journal NGS Quarterly.

National Information Standards Organization (NISO) A nonprofit association accredited by the American National Standards Institute (ANSI) to develop voluntary standards in library science, information science, publishing, and other information services, NISO is designated by ANSI to represent U.S. interests to the Technical Committee on Information and Documentation of the International Organization for Standardization (ISO).

National Law School Library Article Index Indexes articles from the journals subscribed by National Law School Library, Bangalore. At present it is having around 11,000 records in its database.

National library A library designated and funded by a national government to serve the nation by maintaining a comprehensive collection of the published and unpublished literary output of the nation as a whole, including publications of the government itself. Most national libraries are also responsible for compiling a national bibliography, and some serve as the legal depository for works protected by copyright in their country. The national library of the United States is the Library of Congress, located in Washington D.C. Three other libraries—the National Agricultural Library, the National Library of Education, and the National Library of Medicine—contain national collections in specific subject areas.

National Library of Canada/Bibliotheque nationale du Canada (NLC/BNC) The national library of Canada, established by act of Parliament in 1953. Located in Ottawa, NLC/BNC is charged with acquiring, preserving, and promoting the published heritage of Canada for all Canadians. Its collections are focused primarily on Canadiana (works written by, about, or of interest to Canadians, published in Canada or abroad).

National Library of Education (NLE) The largest library in the world devoted solely to the collection, preservation, and effective use of research and other information in the field of education. Located in Washington D.C., NLE is funded by the U.S. federal government. It serves the U.S. Department of Education, Congress, and the Office of the President, as well as the general public, and is the center of a national network of libraries, archives, and other information providers in education.

National Library of Medicine (NLM) The largest medical library in the United States, administered by the National Institutes of Health (NIH). Located in Bethesda, Maryland, NLM provides public access to an online version of its MEDLINE bibliographic database at no charge under the title pubmed.

National Library Service for the Blind and Physically Handicapped (NLS) A national library program administered by the Library of Congress that produces and distributes Braille and recorded library materials at no charge to eligible borrowers through a national network of cooperating regional and local libraries. Established by Congress in 1931 to serve blind adults, NLS was expanded in 1952 to serve visually impaired children, in 1962 to provide music materials, and in 1966 to serve individuals with other physical impairments that prevent them from reading print of standard size.

National Library Week Sponsored for the first time in 1958 by the National Book Committee and the American Library Association, National Library Week is an officially recognized seven-day period in the spring of each year during which special attention is given to promoting libraries of all types in the United States. Most public libraries celebrate the event by displaying posters and exhibits, issuing press releases, and sponsoring book talks and other promotional activities. In the UK, a similar event known as National Libraries Week is celebrated in the fall of each year.

National Storytelling Network (NSN) Formed in 1998 when the National Storytelling Association split into the National Storytelling Network and Storytelling Foundation International, NSN is an organization dedicated to improving the quality of storytelling wherever it can contribute to the quality of life. An affiliate of the American Library

Association, NSN sponsors the annual National Storytelling Conference in cooperation with its local and regional members. NSN also publishes Storytelling Magazine and hosts the storynet Web site.

National survey A government agency that specializes in mapping, surveying, and providing scientific information about the topography natural resources of a country. In the United States, the national surveys are the U.S. Geological Survey (USGS) and the National Geodetic Survey (NGS).

National Technical Information Service (NTIS) Located on the outskirts of Washington D.C., NTIS is an agency within the Technology Administration of the U.S. Department of Commerce that is the largest centralized source of scientific, technical, engineering, and business information produced or sponsored by U.S. and international government agencies. Its collection of over 3 million items includes technical reports, statistics, business information, publications of the U.S. military, multimedia training programs, computer software, and electronic databases.

National Union Catalog (NUC) A series of printed catalogs issued by the Library of Congress, that began in 1948 as an author list of printed cards and titles reported as held by other libraries in North America—a heroic pre-digital attempt to create a union catalog of national scope to facilitate resource sharing. With the development of machine-readable records, the nucs have been largely superseded by the availability of holdings information in the large bibliographic databases maintained by utilities such as OCLC

National Union Catalog of Manuscript Collections (NUCMC) A cooperative cataloging program sponsored by the Library of Congress since 1959, NUCMC provides cataloging of archival and manuscript materials at no charge to repositories in the United States which meet its eligibility guidelines. MARC records are created by NUCMC catalogers in the RLIN national-level database, based on cataloging data supplied by eligible repositories.

Native Software that's written specifically to run on a particular processor. For example, a program optimized for a 68K processor runs in native mode on a Quadra, but it runs in emulation mode (which is slower on a Power PC-based Power Mac). Also, the file format in which an application normally saves it documents. The native format is generally readable only by that application (other programs can sometimes translate it using filters).

Natural language A human language in which the structure and rules have evolved from usage, usually over an extended period time, as opposed to an artificial language based on rules prescribed prior to its development and use, as in a computer language. In search software designed to handle input expressed in natural language, the user may enter the query in the same form in which it would be spoken or written. Compare with controlled vocabulary.

Nautical chart A map for use in navigation of waterways, which includes such features as depth contours, loran lines, and beacon locations. To find these in

Navigation bar A series of options, usually in the form of clickable buttons, icons, or text links arranged in a row across the top or bottom of the screen or window, or along the right- or left-hand side, indicating the main categories under which the information contained in the subpages of a Web site is organized. In a well-designed site, the navigation bar is repeated on each subpage to enable the user to select from the list of main options without having to return to the initial page. Compare with toolbar.

Navigation Tools Allows users to find their way around a website or multimedia presentation. They can be hypertext links, clickable buttons, icons, or image maps.

Navigation Using the hypertext links, icons, and menu options displayed on a Web page to move to other resources available on the Internet. When the user proceeds in a casual way, the activity is called surfing; when approached purposefully, it is a search.

Neatline The line that marks the edges of a map, separating it from the margin (if there is a margin), usually a thin rule in black or dark-colored ink.

Need to know In information security systems, the underlying principle restricting access to sensitive or classified materials to persons who have an essential and justifiable need to be informed. Under conditions of extreme secrecy, such a need may be substantiated by various levels of security clearance and the issuance of identification (badges, passwords, etc.).

Neer-Reviewed Journals Journals where the quality of the articles is maintained by a review process by experts prior to publication. The article submitted to refereed or peer reviewed journals are examined by one or more people with expertise in the field with which the article deals. The purpose of this is to give some assurance that the information in the article is valid.

Negative The image that results when negative photographic film is developed, producing tonal values (black and white) that are the reverse of the original subject and of any positive print of the same image. Negative color film not only reverses tonal values, but also the colors of the subject, making them appear as complementary colors (red as green, blue as yellow, etc.).

Neologism A new word coined from an existing term or terms (example: netiquette from "network" and "etiquette"), or a new meaning given to an existing word (example: "quark" from Finnegan's Wake used in physics as the name of a subatomic particle). Acronyms are neologisms. Also refers to the use of this form of new word or meaning.

NEON Nevada Education Online Network is the former name of the library website.

Nesting In Boolean searching, the use of parentheses to embed a logical operation within another logical operation, as a means of indicating the sequence (syntax) in which the logical commands are to be executed by the computer. In the following example, the Boolean "or" command will be executed first, followed by "not" and then "and."

Net borrower A library that borrows more items via interlibrary loan than it lends to other libraries over a designated period of time. The opposite of net lender.

Net lender A library that lends more items via interlibrary loan than it borrows from other libraries during a designated period of time. Net lenders are more likely than net borrowers to charge a fee for interlibrary loan service. In the OCLC ILL system, each time the status of an item requested is updated to "shipped," a small credit is given per transaction to the lender, providing some compensation to libraries that are net lenders.

Net price A bookseller's cost for a book or other publication, usually the publisher's list price or suggested price, less any discount. The cost of shipping is usually added to the net price.

Net Terms of sale in which a publisher specifies that a book must be offered at no retail discount or reduction in price. Synonymous with net published price. Compare with non-net. Also used as a shortened form of "Internet," usually capitalized (Net).

NETFIX System for reporting technology problems to the Library Technology Team.

Netiquette A neologism formed by shortening the phrase network etiquette. The rules of civility and good manners that apply to communication via the Internet, an environment in which the visual cues available in face-to-face communication and the auditory cues perceptible in voice communication are lacking

Netizen Derived from the term citizen, referring to a citizen of the Internet,or someone who uses networked resources. The term connotes civic responsibility and participation.

Netlibrary A collection of electronic books (EBOOKS). The Libraries purchases electronic books from netlibrary and creates a record in SAGE linking to the ebook. CSUL currently has approximately 10,500 ebooks. Search SAGE by the word "netlibrary" to display the set. You can preview ebooks for 15 minutes for quick reference, or check them out for a 24 hours time period.

Netscape A company that produces a free Web browser. Netscape is often used generically to refer to the browsers themselves: Netscape Navigator and Netscape Communicator.

Netscape Navigator A popular software program designed to facilitate browsing for information available at sites on the World Wide Web. Netscape Navigator allows the user to bookmark Web sites for future reference, print and download search results, and includes many other user-friendly features. Its primary competitor in the Web browser market is Internet Explorer from Microsoft.

Network A group of physically discrete computers interconnected to allow resources to be shared and data exchanged, usually by means of telecommunication links and client/server architecture. Most networks are administered by an operations center that provides assistance to users. The largest "network of networks" in the world is the Internet, allowing users of computers of all types and sizes to communicate in real time.

New adult reader A person of mature years who has recently learned to read, usually by enrolling in an adult literacy program. Public libraries try to meet the needs of new adult readers by selecting materials appropriate to their reading level, and by developing services to acquaint them with available information resources.

New age book A generic term used in publishing to refer to contemporary titles written on subjects outside mainstream American culture, such as holistic health and alternative medicine, nontraditional exercise and fitness techniques, natural foods and alternative diets, self-help psychology, astrology and numerology, and non-Western spiritual practices (yoga, meditation, tai chi, etc). New age books are selected mainly by public libraries.

New book A new title issued for the first time, usually in hardcover, announced by the publisher in book trade journals and review publications and promoted through book signings, author interviews, etc. Recently published titles make up a publisher's frontlist. Some new books make the bestseller list. Compare with backlist.

New construction A completely new library facility, designed from scratch and constructed from the ground up, as opposed to the renovation or expansion of an existing structure. New construction allows the architect to use state-of-the-art design concepts and the latest materials, furnishings, and equipment, within the constraints imposed by the project budget. The old facility is usually converted to some other purpose once the library has moved to its new location. New library construction is reported annually in Library Journal and the Bowker Annual Library and Book Trade Almanac.

New edition pending (NE or NEP) A code used on a publisher's invoice to indicate that a new edition of the title ordered is in preparation, but has not yet been issued.

New Members Round Table (NMRT) Established in 1931 as a round table of the American Library Association NMRT assists persons who have been ALA members for under ten years to become active in the Association and in the library profession at the national, state, and local levels In addition to providing a resume review service and mentoring program, NMRT sponsors the electronic mailin list NMRT-L.

New Search - A button in the library catalog that, wher clicked on, takes the user to a blank search screen for the same search mode that was previously used. For example, if the most recent search was a Basic Search by Keyword, clicking on the New Search button would take the user to a blank Basic Search screen with Keyword already selected.

New serial title (NST) Union catalog listing periodicals and a record of the Holdings in United States and Canadian libraries.

New Technologies in Libraries Citations Provides citations/bibliography of articles on recent developments in Library and Information Science field. The articles are selected from a sizable number of LIS journals. The coverage is from 1998.

New York Public Library (NYPL) The largest public library system in the United States, NYPL is composed of Research Libraries supported largely by private funds, and Branch Libraries serving the boroughs of Manhattan, the Bronx, and Staten Island operated mainly from public funds allocated by the city and state of New York.

New York Review of Books (NYRB) Published since 1963 in 20 issues per year by NYREV, Inc., NYRB provides in-depth commentary on literature, culture, politics, and science in the form of lengthy book reviews written for the educated reader by well-known authors and scholars. NYRB also includes announcements of new books published by trade and university presses.

New York Times Book Review (NYTBR) One of the most influential review publications in the United States, NYTBR is published weekly as part of the Sunday edition of the New York Times. It is also available by subscription as a separate section. Reviews are long and scholarly, written for the educated reader by well-known writers and scholars. Some publishers consider it the most important medium in the country for advertising new trade books..

Newberry Library Located in Chicago, the Newberry Library is a privately funded independent research library devoted primarily to the humanities. Free and open to the public, it contains an extensive noncirculating collection of rare books, maps, manuscripts, and other materials related to the civilizations of Western Europe and the Americas. The Library was established in the late 19th century at the bequest of the wealthy Chicago businessman and philanthropist Walter Loomis Newberry.

Newbery Medal A literary award given annually since 1922 under the auspices of the American Library Association to the author of the most distinguished children's book published in the United States during the preceding year. Sponsored by the family of Frederic G. Melcher, the medal is named after John Newbery (1713-1767), the British publisher who first published books written specifically for children.

Newbery Newbery Award Winner. Juvenile Book Award for story or content. Newbery winners are indicated in the library catalog.

Newbery, John (1713-1767) The English writer, publisher, printer, and bookseller who first recognized the potential commercial market for books written specifically for children. Newbery began publishing works for children in 1744 with A Little Pretty Pocket-Book, containing rhyming fables and rules of conduct, followed by the didactic favorites The History of Little Goody Two-Shoes (1765) which may have been written by his friend Oliver Goldsmith. Illustrated in color, the titles in his inexpensive Juvenile Library series were very popular in England. He also published the first children's encyclopedia, The Circle of the Sciences in seven volumes (1745-48), and the first children's periodical, The Lilliputian Magazine (1751). Newbery's contribution to children's literature is commemorated in the Newbery Medal, awarded annually since 1922 to the most distinguished children's book by an American author published in the United States during the preceding year.

Newbie A slang term for a person who is a newcomer to e-mail, electronic mailing lists, newsgroups, the World Wide Web, or the Internet in general, or to any computer application or system.

News A term often used to denote USENET news, a popular forum for discussion on the Internet.

News library A type of special library maintained in the offices of a newspaper publisher, or other news agency, which includes in its collection newspaper and magazine clippings, photo files (sometimes with negatives), maps, pamphlet files, microforms, reference materialss, and online databases related to news and current events. Most are open to subscribers and librarians at the discretion of the news librarian, usually by appointment. News libraries are listed in The International Directory of News Libraries, a serial published in cooperation with the News Division of the Special Libraries Association.

News magazine A general interest magazine devoted to the publication of news and editorial comment, usually on a wide range of subjects, from politics to entertainment (example: U.S. News & World Report and Maclean's in Canada). Most news magazines are published weekly and sold at newsstands, in bookstores, and by subscription. Some are available in an online version (example: Newsweek or Time)..

News service A method of pooling news-gathering resources, first developed in the mid-19th century when six highly competitive New York City newspaper publishers decided to cooperate to lower the expense of collecting and transmitting international news via telegraph to the United States. Most wire services operate through overseas bureaus to which news reporters submit their copy and photographs

Newsgroup An Internet message board, usually devoted to a specific topic, to which a participant may post comments or queries, then view the replies of other participants, responses to the replies, and so on. A sequence of related postings is called a discussion thread. The most common types are Usenet and netnews which use the Network News Transfer Protocol (NNTP). Unlike e-mail mailing lists, most newsgroups are unmoderated, so postings are not filtered on the basis of content, nor are they limited to a list of registered subscribers. The cyberfiber Newsgroups Directory or the Google Groups search engine can be used to locate newsgroups on a specific topic.

Newsletter A serial publication consisting of no more than a few pages, devoted to news, announcements, and current information of interest primarily to a specialized group of subscribers or members of an association or organization who receive it as part of their membership, for example, The National Teaching & Learning Forum, available in print and in an online edition. Newsletters are listed in the Oxbridge Directory of Newsletters, a reference serial published by Oxbridge Communications. Most periodical indexes and bibliographic databases do not cover newsletter content.

Newspaper A serial publication, usually printed on newsprint and issued daily, on certain days of the week, or weekly, containing news, editorial comment, regular columns, letters to the editor, cartoons, advertising, and other items of current, often local, interest to a general readership. Some national newspapers are issued twice daily in early and late editions, or in different editions for different regions of the country.

Newspaper index A list of the editorial content (news stories, articles, editorials, and columns) published in one or more newspapers, usually arranged alphabetically by subject (including names). Indexes to major U.S. dailies are available in print (example: New York Times Index). Newspaper indexes are also available online (examples: datatimes and Newspaper Abstracts in OCLC firstsearch).

Newspeak A neologism coined by the journalist and writer George Orwell in his anti-utopian novel 1984 (published in 1949) to refer to the artificial language of government slogans, especially authoritarian propaganda. The term is also applied to euphemisms used by politicians, bureaucrats, and military personnel in public pronouncements to evade public scrutiny and deflect criticism of their actions (incursion instead of "invasion"), and by broadcasters to lull audiences into complacency.

Newsprint A grade of coarse, absorbent, unsized paper made primarily from groundwood pulp, used in printing newspapers and newsletters to keep costs down. Because it is bulky, yellows quickly, and becomes brittle with the passage of time, libraries convert newspaper back files to microfilm or microfiche, and provide reader-printer machines for enlarging and making hard copies.

Newsreader A software program that lets you subscribe to newsgroups as well as read and post messages to them.

Newsreel A short film, 10-20 minutes in length, providing brief documentary-style coverage of a series of news events or topics of general interest. Newsreels preceded the feature film in commercial movie theaters until the 1950s when television broadcast news replaced them. In the United States and Europe, the newsreel was an important propaganda tool during the first and second world wars. They are preserved in archival film collections.

Newswatcher A client program for Macintosh distributed with via the OIT Software To Go web site; enables you to read network newsgroups and to submit postings.

Nexlib Library Management System nexlib is a full-featured library management system. It is Windows-based with simple point-and-click navigation; the system is easy and fun for library users and staff. Nexlib is designed with a consistent, intuitive interface familiar to anyone who has used Microsoft Office. You can explore the entire system with just a few mouse clicks, yet behind the simple interface lies a powerful database engine capable of maintaining millions of records. Nexlib is designed to meet the needs of all information seekers. Academic researchers can search the entire library collections like, books, magazines, research reports, Company annual reports, CD materials etc. For the librarian, nexlib provides simple interfaces to catalog new books, manage users, create reports, and control budgets & acquisitions.

NFS Network File System. A protocol developed by Sun Microsystems which allows a computer system to access files over a network as if they were on its local disks. This protocol has been incorporated in products by more than two hundred companies, and is now a de facto Internet standard.

NIC Network Information Center. A organization that provides information, assistance and services to network users.

Niche publishing The activities of small presses and divisions within large publishing companies that limit their scope to a relatively narrow subject area (example: auto repair manuals or travel guides) or type of literature (example: genre fiction), producing publications intended to meet the needs of a specific market segment. Some niches are broader than others.

Nickname A short, easy to remember name you can create within an e-mail program like Eudora; it can contain any combination of letters and numbers. Nicknames can be used in place of an individual's full e-mail address in the To:, CC:, or Bcc: lines of a message.

Nickname A familiar name of a person, usually a diminutive form of the full given name (example: "Bill" for William). Also, a popular name sometimes given in derision or to highlight a special attribute of the person ("Wild Bill"). Corporate entities can have nicknames ("Big Apple" for New York City). Information on nicknames can be found in the latest edition of the Pseudonyms and Nicknames Dictionary published by the Gale Group. Compare with conventional name.

Nihil obstat A Latin phrase meaning "nothing hinders" appearing on the verso of the title page of works that have been examined by officials of the Roman Catholic Church and found to contain no offense that merits censorship, still used in books that present official Catholic doctrine (example: New Catholic Encyclopedia).

Nipping In bookbinding, the step in which the text block and case (or covers) are pressed firmly together to expel air from between the leaves, giving the volume its desired shape. When done after sewing to reduce swell before the covers are applied, the process is called smashing.

NISO NISO is the abbreviation for the National Information Standards Organization. It is a non-profit association that identifies, develops, maintains, and publishes technical standards to manage information. An example of a NISO standard is Z39.50, an information retrieval standard that defines the way two computers communicate and share information.

Nitrate film A flexible base made of cellulose nitrate, produced by Eastman Kodak from about 1890 until 1950 for use in film negatives and motion picture film. Because it is chemically unstable and highly flammable, organizations such as the National Film Preservation Foundation provide grant assistance to film archives to facilitate the copying of moving image collections from nitrate film to a more permanent base, such as acetate or polyester.

NLM (1) National Library of Medicine(Bethesda, Maryland); (2) The classification system devised by the NLM and used in the Biomedical Library for books published after 1970.

NNTP (Network News Transport Protocol) The protocol used by clientand server software to carry USENET postings back and forth over a TCP/IP network. If you are using any of the more common software such as Netscape, Nuntius, Internet Explorer, etc. To participate in newsgroups then you are benefiting from an NNTP connection.

No date A phrase abbreviated n.d., used in a bibliographic record to indicate that the publication date is unknown. If no publication date appears on a book or other item, but the correct date is ascertainable from other sources, it is indicated in the edition area of the record, is a bracketed interpolation (example: [1956]).

Nobel Prize in Literature A literary award established and funded in 1900 by Alfred B. Nobel, who made his fortune from the invention of dynamite. The Nobel Prize in Literature is given annually by the Swedish Academy in Stockholm to "the person who shall have produced in the field of literature the most distinguished work of an idealistic tendency

NOC Network Operations Center. A location from which the operation of a network or internet is monitored. Additionally, this center usually serves as a clearinghouse for connectivity problems and efforts to resolve those problems.

Node From the Latin nodus meaning "knot" or "knob." In botany, the point on the stem of a plant from which a leaf or twig grows. In communications, a junction point in a network, such as a personal computer connected to a LAN or a terminal connected to a mainframe. Each node has its own unique network address and the capacity to send, receive, and store messages. In an indexing language, the point in a tree structure at which two or more lines meet.

Noise In the scanning context, this refers to random, incorrectly read pixel values, normally due to electrical interference or device instability.

Non exempt A status of employment as defined by the Wage and Hour Division of the Department of Labor. Employees in this category are paid overtime (time and a half for any hours worked over 40 in a week) and by the hour.

Nonbook A collective term for library materials not bound in codex form like a book, including but not limited to maps and other cartographic materials (except atlases), prints, photographs, slides, filmstrips, motion pictures, videorecordings, sound recordings, kits, models, realia, etc. Compare with nonprint.

Non-Book Materials Those Library materials which do not come within the definition of a book, serial or pamphlet and which require special handling, e.g. Audio-visual materials, charts, maps, etc.

Non-circulating items Include archival material, rare books, reference material, current periodicals and other items which must remain accessible within the library at all times.

Noncirculating Materials which may not be charged to a borrower account except by special arrangement, but are usually available for library use only, including reference books, periodical indexes, and sometimes the periodicals themselves. Whether materials in special collections are designated circulating or noncirculating depends on the policy of the individual library or library system, but their use is nearly always restricted to library premises.

Noncurrent Recurring information, materials, or records that are no longer up-to-date, for example, corporate annual reports from previous years or earlier editions of a reference serial, often retained in libraries and archives for their archival value. Noncurrent holdings of print periodicals, called back files, are often converted to microfilm or microfiche to conserve space. The opposite of current. Compare with outdated.

Nonfiction Prose literary works describing events that actually occurred and characters or phenomena that actually exist or existed in the past. In a more general sense, any piece of prose writing in which the content is not imagined by the author. In libraries that use Library of Congress Classification or Dewey Decimal Classification, nonfiction is shelved by call number. Compare with fiction.

Nongap break An indication in a library catalog or union catalog record that a hiatus exists in the publication or in the numbering of a serial, despite the fact that no items issued are missing. This circumstance can arise when publication ceases and then starts up again under the same or a different title, sometimes with a change in numeration. Compare with gap.

NON-GPO Government document not published in the U.S. Government Printing Office, i.e. Printed at field agency locations; Non-depository items.

Nonlinear Dynamics Bibliography The bibliography contains about 12617 references.

Non-lossy Image compression without loss of quality.

Non-net Copies of a work (usually a textbook) which a bookseller is permitted by the publisher to sell in bulk quantities to schools for educational use at a discretionary discount. Compare with net.

Nonprint Materials published in a format other than writing or print on paper, including microfiche and microfilm, slides, filmstrips, films, videorecordings, audiorecordings, and information in digital format such as machine-readable data files. Most nonprint library materials require special equipment for listening and/or viewing. Compare with nonbook.

Nonrepeatable (NR) A MARC field which may appear only once in the same bibliographic record, for example, the 250 field reserved for the edition statement and other information pertaining to edition. A nonrepeatable subfield may occur only once in a field. The opposite of repeatable (R).

Nonresident's card A borrower's card issued to a person who does not reside within the legal boundaries of the district or area served by the library or library system, usually in exchange for payment of a modest fee, renewable at regular intervals.

Nonsorting character A character, such as the apostrophe, ignored in arrangement when it appears in a word, phrase, heading, or descriptor.

Non-study hourly Employees hired by the hour. They must punch a computerized time clock at the Loan Desk, cannot work over 40 hours per week, or more than six months during a 1-year period, and do not receive fringe benefits such as sick leave or vacation time.

Nonsupplier A library or other participant in the OCLC Interlibrary Loan network that does not respond to requests from other libraries to borrow returnable materials. In the OCLC worldcat database, the three-letter OCLC symbols of nonsuppliers appear in lowercase in the holdings display attached to the bibliographic record for an item, in contrast to the symbols suppliers which appear in uppercase.

Nontraditional student A student who enrolls at an institution of higher education after several years of little or no contact with the system of formal education. Nontrads are usually older than traditional students who enter college out of high school and complete their undergraduate degree without a break. Because nontrads often lack the library skills of their younger classmates, they may require instruction and reference assistance at a more basic level, but once they gain self-confidence, they can be highly motivated. Compare with adult learner.

North American Serials Interest Group (NASIG) Established in 1985, NASIG is an independent organization that facilitates the sharing of information and ideas among individuals involved with serial publications, including serials publishers, librarians, subscription agencies, producers and vendors of catalog software and periodical indexes/databases, representatives of bibliographic utilities, educators, and binders, mainly in the United States, Canada, and Mexico. NASIG sponsors an annual conference, hosts the electronic mailing list NASIG-L, and publishes the NASIG Newsletter.

North American Sport Library Network (NASLIN) Founded in 1989, NASLIN is dedicated to facilitating communication and resource sharing among sports libraries, archives, and information services through conferences, educational programs, and other cooperative projects. Its members are librarians, archivists, and information specialists involved in the publication, acquisition, organization, retrieval, and dissemination of information related to all aspects of sports, physical education, and recreation. NASLIN publishes the semiannual newsletter NASLINE.

North pointer A standard graphic device in the form of a small cross or wheel with an arrow pointing north, printed on maps, charts, blueprints, plans, etc., usually in or near the legend to indicate compass orientation.

Nos An abbreviation of the phrase "not on shelf," used by library staff to refer to an item listed as available in the catalog, which cannot be located in correct call number sequence in the stacks. When this occurs, the patron may request that the staff conduct a search for the item. If it is not found, the circulation status is changed to "missing" in the item record and a replacement copy may be ordered or the bibliographic record removed from the catalog.

Not Charged If a library item is not checked-out, the online catalog will indicate that the status of the item is Not Charged. This means that the item is available in its call number location in the library.

Not our publication (NOP) A term used on a publisher's invoice to indicate that the title ordered cannot be supplied because the library or bookseller apparently ordered it from the wrong publisher.

Not received Used in CHECK-IN CARD to indicate non-receipt of a serial issue; issue has been claimed but is now unavailable.

Not returnable (NR) A term used on a publisher's invoice to indicate that a book or other item cannot be returned once it has been received by the library or bookseller placing the order.

Not yet published (NYP) A term used on a publisher's invoice to indicate that the title ordered cannot be immediately supplied because it is in the process of being published and will be issued at some time in the future.

Notation The set of characters (usually numerals and/ or letters of the alphabet) used to represent the classes and subdivisions of a classification system. In library cataloging, the class notation assigned to a bibliographic item represents its subject and is the first element of the call number, determining its position on the shelf relative to other items of similar classificiation.

Notched binding In some adhesive bindings, shallow parallel grooves are cut into the binding edge perpendicular to the spine to enlarge the surface area exposed to the adhesive. Although notching strengthens the binding of a book, the additional adhesive has the disadvantage of restricting openability.

Note area The area following the physical description in a bibliographic record giving the contents of the work, its relationship to other works, and any physical characteristics not included in preceding areas of bibliographic description. Each note is given a separate paragraph in fields 5XX of the MARC record.

Note In writing and printing, a statement explaining a point in the text of a work, or giving the source of a quotation or idea that does not originate with the author. Notes are usually numbered consecutively and may be listed as footnotes at the bottom of the same page as the text to which they refer, or as endnotes at the conclusion of an article, chapter, or book.

Notebook A loose-leaf or spiral binder with flexible or inflexible board or plastic covers, usually filled with blank leaves, ruled or unruled, for taking notes. Some notebooks also include a pocket across the bottom inside the front and/or back cover for holding loose papers. Also used as a synonym for laptop.

Nothing but net Nothing But Net is a newsletter to inform library staff about the Libraries' WEB activities. Content includes training opportunities, technical tips for WEB design, announcements of new or substantially revised library WEB pages, and reports on DIGITAL projects. Nothing But Net is sent electronically to all library staff every other month (6 times a year).

Notices Forms produced by sage to be sent to patron (e.g., recall notices, available notices, overdue notices).

Notification slip A printed form sent to the acquisitions department of a library by an approval plan vendor to announce a new book that meets the needs profile established by the library. Under most plans, rejection of the title by the library within a designated period of time will prevent shipment.

Novel From the Italian novella, meaning "a new little thing." In most European languages, the word for novel is roman, derived from the literary tradition of medieval romance. The origins of the modern novel can also be traced to the picaresque narratives of 16th-century Spain, of which Cervantes' Don Quixote is a well-known example.

Novelette A novel of 30,000-50,000 words (example: Billy Budd by Herman Melville). Synonymous with short novel. Compare with novella.

Novelization A literary work converted into a novel from the form in which it was originally written (example: The Wave by Morton Rhue based on a teleplay by Johnny Dawkins based on a short story by Ron Jones). In AACR2, a novelization is cataloged under the name of the novelist with added entries for the author and title of the work on which it is based.

Novella An Italian word meaning "short story" or "tale." A short prose narrative comparable in length to a novelette or long short story, which often relates a surprising fictional event (example: Old Man and the Sea by Ernest Hemingway). Novellas often have a moral and may be written in a satirical style (Goodbye, Columbus by Philip Roth). Compare with novel.

Novice A person who uses an unfamiliar computer system for the first time, as opposed to an experienced user. In the design of Web sites and graphical user interfaces, libraries and computer software companies may conduct usability tests to judge the user-friendliness of the new system. In a more general sense, any patron for whom the procedures of a library are new and often confusing. Special consideration must be shown at the reference desk.

NSDP National Serials Data Program - A program of the Library of Congress, established in 1972, responsible for the assignment of ISSN and key titles to U.S. serials and control over the accuracy and uniqueness of these data elements.

NSFNET National Science Foundation Network. The NSFNET is a high speed network of networks which is hierarchical in nature. At the highest level is a backbone network which spans the continental United States. Attached to that are mid-level networks and attached to the mid-levels are campus and local networks. NSFNET also has connections out of the U.S. to Canada, Mexico, Europe, and the Pacific Rim. The NSFNET is part of the Internet

NT Windows N(ew) T(echnology). The operating system for desktop computers currently in use at the libraries.

NUC National Union Catalog; a catalog issued by the Library of Congress containing a record of titles cataloged at the Library of Congress plus location of these titles in other libraries throughout the U.S. and Canada.

NUCMC National Union Catalog of Manuscript Collections.

Number A quantity that can be counted, represented by a word, numeral, or combination of numerals—cardinal numbers indicate how many (1, 2, 3, 14, 154), ordinal numbers indicate relative position in sequence (1st, 2nd, 3rd, 14th, 154th). In text, the numbers zero to nine are usually spelled out, but numbers greater than nine are given in numerals. Also, to assign a number to each item in a series, for reference and to indicate sequence. Abbreviated no.

Number book A form of book, common in the 18th and 19th centuries, published in numbered parts or installments, usually at regular intervals..

Number building In Dewey Decimal Classification, the cataloger must construct a class number when no existing class in the schedules precisely represents the subject of the work. This is done by adding to a base number, notation found in the table of standard subdivisions (or in one of the other tables), or from another part of the main schedules, according to established rules, for example, the addition of the decimal fraction .5 to the base number 020 to create the class 020.5 for periodicals in the library and information sciences.

Numbered copy A copy of a book published in a consecutively numbered limited edition, bearing a copy number assigned by hand by the publisher and an indication of the total number of copies printed, usually in the colophon or in a certificate of issue on the verso of the leaf preceding title page.

Numeral In writing and printing, a character or set of characters used to represent a number (example: the arabic numeral 9 or roman numeral IX). General rules for the use of numerals in library cataloging are given in Appendix C of AACR2.

Numeric and/or alphabetic, chronological, or other designation In library cataloging, the material specific details area of the bibliographic description in which the publication history of a serial is given, usually in the form of an open or closed entry, as distinct from the holdings note indicating the issues owned by a specific library or library system.

Nursery rhyme A short metrical verse or ditty originating in the oral tradition of a specific culture, taught to very young children to help them learn to speak or count. Some nursery rhymes are derived from adult sayings that had a double meaning in the cultural context in which they originated. Nursery rhymes are usually published in collections shelved in the juvenile section of a public library, or in the curriculum room of an academic library.

Oacket: the basic unit of data transmitted over the

Internet; packets are transmitted independently and then reassembled at their destination.

Oak Knoll A company located in New Castle, Delaware that publishes, distributes, and sells books on bibliography, book collecting, book history, bookplates, the book trade, libraries, publishing, bookbinding, book design, book illustration, papermaking, typography, fine printing, forgery, and censorship. Its inventory includes over 12,500 antiquarian titles. Click here to learn more about Oak Knoll Books & Oak Knoll Press. Obiit Latin for "died," usually abbreviated ob. Before a date to indicate the year of a person's decease (ob. 1922).

Obituary A notice of a person's death, usually published in a newspaper or magazine, which may include a brief biographical sketch of the main events in the life of the deceased. The obituaries of well-known public figures may be researched and written long before the person's death, to be ready for printing on short notice. Obituaries are indexed under the last name of the deceased in Biography Index, a reference serial available in most large libraries in the United States and via OCLC firstsearch. Abbreviated obit.

Object In AACR2, an object is defined as a three-dimensional artifact, replica, or naturally occurring entity. In the British list of general material designations, the term also includes dioramas, games, microscope slides, models, and realia.

Objective A specific achievable outcome of actions taken to achieve a stated goal, usually expressed in measurable terms and subject to a time limit. Although an objective does not address the specific means by which the outcome is to be achieved, it should be based upon a realistic assessment of available resources. A good set of achievable objectives can serve as an inspiration and guide for an organization in planning for the future, allocating resources, evaluating progress, adjusting strategy, and persevering until the desired result is achieved.

Object-oriented Generally used to describe an illustration or font file as being created by mathematical equations. Also

Oblong A book wider than it is high. Children's picture books are often oblong in shape to allow the illustrator a wider canvas. In a more general sense, any publication bound on its shorter dimension. Synonymous in the printing trade with landscape. Compare with portrait.

Obscenity Speech, writing, or artistic expression considered indecent by conventional standards of behavior because it offends the modesty and delicacy of feeling of ordinary people. Synonymous with smut. Compare with pornography.

Observatory Library A unit of the Science and Engineering Library division; located on Oman Drive at Dyer Observatory; contains a majority of the astronomy collection. Closed collection materials may be requested at the Science and Engineering Library.

Occasional A document or publication issued on an irregular basis, sometimes numbered sequentially by the publisher (example: Occasional Publications in Archaeology and History of the Massachusetts Historical Commission).

OCLC control number Whenever the bibliographic utility OCLC enters a new record into its online union catalog (worldcat), a unique number is assigned to the record for the purpose of bibliographic control. The number appears in the leader of the MARC record and is system-supplied. Compare with LCCN.

OCLC Interlibrary Loan (ILL) The interlibrary loan service of OCLC, a network that facilitates the borrowing and lending of materials between libraries and other institutions that are OCLC members and participants in worldcat, the largest online union catalog in the world.

OCLC Online Computer Library Center. A nonprofit library computer service and research organization with the stated goals of helping libraries further access to information and reduce information costs. Thousands of libraries around the world participate in the OCLC system. OCLC offers a large number of databases through their firstsearch online system, including worldcat, a combined catalog of participating libraries with links to facilitate interlibrary loans, and many special subject periodical indexes. OCLC is also used extensively by libraries for obtaining cataloging information for processing materials.

OCLC Online Union Catalog (OLUC) The former name of worldcat, an online union catalog containing over 46 million bibliographic records representing items held by over 6,700 libraries and other institutions that are members and participants in OCLC, the largest bibliographic utility in the world.

OCLC symbol A unique three-letter code assigned by OCLC to identify a library or other institution that is a member or participant in its cataloging and interlibrary loan network (example: DLC for Library of Congress). Institutions with more than one library may have a different symbol for each library. OCLC symbols are used in bibliographic records to indicate cataloging source (MARC field 040) and in holdings displays in the OCLC worldcat database to identify libraries that have used a record for cataloging purposes. Symbols of interlibrary loan suppliers are displayed in uppercase, those of nonsuppliers in lowercase. OCLC publishes two alphabetically arranged print directories under the title OCLC Participating Institutions, one arranged by OCLC symbol and the other by name of institution. The list is also available on the World Wide Web in searchable format, updated weekly (purl.org/oclc/pi).

OCLC worldcat This database is an online catalog of the holdings of books, journals, and other materials held by thousands of OCLC member libraries. (OCLC is Online Computer Library Center.) Cornell researchers can identify and locate materials in other libraries and collections using worldcat, and request these materials through interlibrary loan.

OCLC/Firstsearch Comprehensive online remote databse offering over 70 different databases including worldcat, which has some 49 million records in over 400 languages from over 15,000 libraries worldwide.

OCR Label Optical Character Recognition. A numeral read by light pen to uniquely identify items. Used by the acess service staff to identify units of library materials.

OCR Optical character recognition; the act of using a visual scanning device to read text from hard copy and translate it into a format a computer can access (e.g., an ASCII file). OCR systems include an optical scanner for reading text and sophisticated software for analyzing images.

Octavo (8vo) A book approximately 6 x 9 inches in size, made by folding a full sheet of book paper in three right-angle folds, producing signatures of eight leaves (sixteen pages). If a 32-page section is desired, as in most children's picture books, double size sheets are folded four times. The precise size of each leaf in an octavo edition depends on the size of the original sheet. In modern printing, octavo is the most commonly used size for books published in hardcover. Compare with folio, quarto, duodecimo, and sextodecimo.

Ode A relatively long lyric poem of elaborate structure derived from songs performed by the chorus in ancient Greek dramatic performances, written to eulogize a hero (or heroes). In English literature, the object of praise may be a person or category of person (example: Ode to the Confederate Dead by Allen Tate), an abstraction (example: Ode to Beauty by Ralph Waldo Emerson), or an inner state expressed symbolically (example: Ode on a Grecian Urn by John Keats).

Off-duty Time when an employee is 1) scheduled but not working (usually on a break or lunch hour), 2) not scheduled on a shift, or 3) not working if employed part-time. Off-duty public services librarians are sometimes recognized as staff when passing through a public area of the library and approached by patrons in need of assistance. The opposite of on-duty.

Office of record The unit within an organization, responsible for systematically documenting an activity and preserving the resulting records for the normal period for which they are needed to conduct business or affairs, for example, a personnel office in the case current employment records. Synonymous with agency of record.

Official name The legal name of a company, agency, organization, institution, etc., which may differ from the form of name used in its publications, or in cataloging them for a library collection. Compare with corporate name.

Official publication A document issued in multiple copies by an official body, such as a government agency or intergovernmental organization, under its legal name, often retained by libraries for reference purposes (example: Budget of the United States Government issued annually by the Office of Management and Budget). U.S. federal government documents fall into this category.

Official records The formal written documents in which the ongoing activities of a company, government, organization, or institution are recorded, usually retained in archives for their evidential, legal, informational, or historical value, in accordance with instructions contained in a disposition schedule (example: Congressional Record).

Official title The full title appearing on the title page of a book or other printed publication, used by librarians in cataloging the item.

Official University ID card Get your picture ID card at the Walb Student Union Information Desk to use as your official IPFW identification, library card, and photocopy debit card.

Offline An automated service not connected to a network, for example, a stand-alone PC running bibliographic databases on CD-ROM or an intranet not connected to the Internet. Also refers to computer accessories or devices not connected to or installed on the central processing unit (CPU), or physically connected but not turned on or standing ready for use, for example, a printer or scanner that is turned off.

Offprint A copy of an article, chapter, or portion of a publication reprinted from the same plates, usually at the same time as the original, but issued separately, with or without a cover, usually for the author's personal use. Contributors to scholarly journals often receive a limited number of copies of their articles from the publisher, sometimes as a form of compensation. An offprint may or may not include a title page, but retains the original pagination. The sale of offprints provides an important source of revenue for some journal publishers. Also spelled off-print. Synonymous with overprint, run-on, and separate. Compare with reprint.

Offset A rotary printing process in which ink is applied to a thin plate wrapped around a rotating cylinder, which transfers the image to a second rubber-coated cylinder from which an impression is made on a sheet or roll of printing paper. Offset is faster, less expensive, and capable of printing much finer detail than letterpress.

Offset lithography A high-volume, ink-based printing process, in which ink adhering to image areas of a lithographic plate is transferred (offset) to a blanket cylinder before being applied to paper or other substrate.

Off-site storage Temporary or permanent storage of archival or library materials at a location outside the walls of the main facility, usually necessitated by a shortage of space. Stored materials may be temporarily unavailable or retrievable by courier upon request during certain hours. The most common criterion used in selecting items for off-site storage is low usage. Items may be shelved by a method that maximizes

OIS Office of Instructional Services at CSU. The University-wide organization responsible for providing media support for instruction, outreach, and other purposes for faculty, staff, and graduate teaching assistants.

Olla A type of writing material made in southern India and Sri Lanka from young leaves, especially of the palmyra palm, soaked in water and pressed flat, then cut into strips approximately three inches wide and one to three feet in length. Holes are made in one end of each strip through which they can be attached by a cord to wooden boards to form a book. The mixture of charcoal and oil rubbed into writing incised on the surface with a metal stylus may have helped preserve the earliest pre-Christian examples. According to Harrod's Librarians' Glossary (Gower: 1990), this type of book is still made by Buddhist monks in Sri Lanka. The term also applies to documents of this form and material. Also spelled ola.

Omnibus book A large single-volume reprint of two or more separately published novels or other literary works, usually by the same author.

Omnibus reference A cross-reference directing the user from a single heading to multiple headings in an index, as in the following example from the Library of Congress Subject Heading list:

Omnibus review An evaluative article in which a reviewer discusses and in some cases compares two or more books or other publications of a certain type, on a specific subject, in a particular field of study, or which have some other characteristic in common.

On approval An arrangement with a publisher or jobber that allows a prospective buyer, such as a library, to examine newly published items before deciding to purchase. Materials sent for inspection must be returned within a designated period of time if the recipient does not intend to purchase.

On order A term used in acquisitions to describe an item ordered from a publisher, jobber, or dealer, but not yet received by the library. After the item has been received and completely processed, the order record created by the library at the time the order was placed is eventually purged. In some online catalogs, the status of an item on order is indicated in a temporary catalog record.

On sale or return Terms given by a publisher to a bookseller allowing the return for credit of copies that remain unsold. The bookseller's account is normally charged for the sale, but payment is not expected until the items have sold or a designated time limit has expired

On-demand publishing The production of single copies or small quantities of printed publications in response to orders from customers, as opposed to supply from inventory. An example of such a service is Dissertation Express which provides single copies of Ph.D. Dissertations on demand for a fixed fee.

On-duty Time when an employee is expected to be at work, particularly the hours of a scheduled shift at a public service point, such as the circulation desk or reference desk. The opposite of off-duty.

One-act play A form of modern drama in which all the action occurs in a single act (example: Aria da Capo by Edna St. Vincent Millay). Established as a literary form by the experimental theater movement that began in the late 19th century, the one-act play is usually short (20-50 minites performed), with a limited number of characters, no breaks in the action, and little if any change of scene, analogous to the short story in narrative fiction.

One-of-a-kind book A book created in a single copy, as opposed to a production book issued in multiple copies. Art books created for display are usually of this type. Compare with limited edition.

One-on-one Services provided by a librarian or other library staff member working alone with a single patron, usually involving a high degree of interaction, as in most transactions at the reference desk. Synonymous with one-to-one.

One-person library (OPL) A library or information service operated and managed by a single individual, usually with minimal assistance, more common in special libraries than in other types of libraries. In public library systems, small branch libraries are sometimes run by a solo librarian or paraprofessional, often with the help of volunteers from the community. Bookmobiles are nearly always operated by a single person.

One-shot A periodical for which only a single issue was published. Also refers to a reprint of the entire text of a book or of an abridgment, published in a single issue of a periodical, as distinct from a serialized reprint.

Onionskin A very thin, tough, light-weight, translucent paper with a smooth glazed or cockle finish, used for airmail stationery, tracing paper, etc. Also spelled onion skin.

Onlay One or more decorative panels or thin pieces of leather or paper, often of more than one color, mounted on the cover of a book in relief, usually tooled around the edges to secure them to the surface and for decorative effect. Compare with inlay.

Online A computer connected to the Internet, an intranet, or some other network, via telecommunication links, as opposed to a stand-alone system. Also refers to computer accessories or devices physically separate from, but directly connected to and under the control of, a central processing unit (CPU) and ready for interactive use in real time. Sometimes used synonymously in libraries with automated, computerized, and electronic. Compare with offline.

Online bookstore A commercial enterprise that electronically markets and sells books and nonprint media (videos, cds, dvds, CD-roms, etc.) Mail order over the Internet. Some online booksellers have retail outlets (example: barnesandnoble.com), others do not (amazon.com).

Online catalog A library catalog consisting of a collection of bibliographic records in machine-readable format, maintained on a dedicated computer that provides uninterrupted interactive access via terminals or workstations in direct, continuous communication with the central computer. Most online catalogs are searchable by author, title, subject heading, and keywords. The software used in online catalogs is proprietary and not standardized. Synonymous with OPAC.

Online circulation system System which inputs checkout and discharges of library materials directly into a computer without manual intervention.

Online Computer Library Centre (OCLC) Computerized library service and research organization based in Ohio. The Center operates an international network that libraries use to acquire and catalog books, order custom-printed catalog cards, arrange interlibrary loans, and maintain location information on library materials. Formerly called Ohio College Library Center. CSUL is a member and uses their database for cataloging.

Online Database: an electronic database of either full-text documents or citations and abstracts which can be searched by telephone or internet connection.

Online learning: Also referred to as distance education; courses offered online that do not require the student to be on campus for most or all class participation. Students can work with course materials at their own convenience or they can work collaboratively on class projects using tools like chat and discussion groups (bulletin boards).

Online renewal Books can be renewed by email at libcirc@canes.gsw.edu. You must include your name and user id / bar code. In addition, you should include author, title, call number and bar code information for each item that you are renewing. Please be aware that bringing the books to the library to renew them is the safest way to insure that they are properly renewed.

Online searching In general, searching a computerized database. In libraries, may refer to a paid, librarian- mediated search of databases from a vendor such as STN (for Chemical Abstracts) or Dialog, in contrast to databases available for end-users to search on CD-ROM or Web-based subscriptions. At Marriott, there is very little demand any more for such paid searches because of the extensive availability of subscription databases.

On-line Service A commercial service that (for a price) provides goodies such as e-mail, discussion forums, tech support, software libraries, news, weather reports, stock prices, plane reservations, even electronic shopping malls. To access one, you need a modem. Popular on-line services include America Online, compuserve, and Prodigy.

Online services In libraries, the branch of public services concerned with selecting and providing access to electronic resources, such as online catalogs and bibliographic databases, including mediated searching, usually done by an online services librarian. Compare with systems librarian.

Online tutorial An instructional tool in electronic format, usually available via the Internet, designed to teach library users, in a step-by-step and sometimes interactive process, how to use a specific resource (usually an online catalog or bibliographic database), or all the services and resources needed to research topics in a specific discipline or subject area. Particularly helpful to students enrolled in distance education courses who may be unable to come to the library for bibliographic instruction, online tutorials are often modular in design, with a self-quiz at the end of each unit to give users the opportunity to assess their mastery of the content (example: TILT, provided by the University of Texas System Digital Library). Compare with pathfinder.

Online Used in conjunction with computer databases; generally means that the user is in direct contact with the database and can interact with it, usually through a computer terminal. Often used to distinguish remote databases such as those on SAGE, as opposed to CD-ROM locally loaded databases.

On-the-job Occurring in the course of one's

employment, for example, on-the-job training as opposed to instruction that takes place outside the normal work routine.

Ool kit A toolkit or a collection of buttons that typically make the more common tools for an application easily accessible.

Oonline Public Access Catalog Computer terminals used by patrons to access the Libraries' online catalog (SAGE) and the online catabase the Libraries subscribes to. Also: OPAC, PAC.

Oot-of Print Searching Attempting to purchase used copies of materials that are out-of-print through special used book dealers.

Ooze leather Calf or split sheepskin given a soft velvet or suede finish on the flesh side, used mainly in binding volumes of poetry, belles lettres, etc.

OP Out of print. The book or other material is no longer available from the publisher or a regular distributor.

Op. Cit. Latin for opere citato meaning "in the work previously cited." An abbreviation used in notes and bibliographic citations that allows a quotation or idea from the work previously cited to be referenced simply by giving the new page number(s).

OPAC An acronym for Online Public Access Catalog, a computer catalog of the books and other materials owned by a library. In most libraries, the largest concentration of OPAC terminals or workstations is located near the reference desk to make it easier for reference librarians to provide assistance. Synonymous with online catalog. Compare with webpac.

Open Archives Initiative (OAI) Supported by the Digital Library Federation, the Coalition for Networked Information, and a grant from the National Science Foundation (NSF), OAI develops and promotes interoperability standards to facilitate the exchange of information content in digital formats. The program had its origins in the desire to facilitate scholarly communication by improving access to digital archives.

Open catalog A library catalog in which there are no restrictions on the addition of new bibliographic records, and existing records are revised and corrected as the need arises. Compare with closed catalog and frozen catalog.

Open Content Copyrighted information (such as this Glossary) that is made available by the copyright owner to the general public under license terms that allow reuse of the material, often with the requirement (as with this Glossary) that the re-user grant the public the same rights to the modified version that the re-user received from the copyright owner. Information that is in the Public Domain might also be considered a form of Open Content.

Open entry A bibliographic record, holdings note, or entry in an index or bibliography that allows further information concerning the item to be added, used in the library catalog to describe serials for which the library does not own all the issues or parts. Open entries are indicated by a hyphen and a space following the first volume number and/or year owned (example: v.1- , 1936-). Compare with closed entry.

Open order In acquisitions, an order for library materials that remains active because it could not be completely filled by the seller at the time it was received.

Open reserve A reserve collection shelved in an open stack to afford library users unrestricted access. Compare with closed reserve.

Open source A computer program for which the source code is made available without charge by the owner or licenser, usually via the Internet, to encourage the rapid development of a more useful and bug-free product through open peer review. The practice also allows the product to be customized by its users to suit local needs (example: Linux operating system). To be certified "open source" under the Open Source Initiative (OSI), software must meet certain established criteria which include no restrictions on access.

Open Source Software Open Source Software is software for which the underlying programming code is available to the users so that they may read it, make changes to it, and build new versions of the software incorporating their changes. There are many types of Open Source Software, mainly differing in the licensing term under which (altered) copies of the source code may (or must be) redistributed.

Open stacks Shelving in a library to which users have unrestricted access. Synonymous with open access. The opposite of closed stacks.

Open System Interconnection (OSI) An ISO standard for network telecommunication developed during the 1980's to allow direct communication between computers of all types and sizes by defining a general framework for implementing communication protocols in seven layers. Although most network systems follow the OSI model, some have compressed two or three of the OSI layers into one.

Openability A binder's term for the ease with which the binding on a book can be opened at any page. In hardcover bindings, a volume with a hollow back can be opened more easily than one with a tight back. In adhesive bindings, an Otabind binding opens flat more easily than a perfect binding. In perfect bindings, an unnotched binding is easier to open than a notched binding. Most mechanical bindings are designed to open flat.

Opened Said of a book left uncut in binding, whose pages have to be slit by hand with a paper-knife, usually by the person who purchases the volume or receives it as a gift. Compare with unopened.

Open-end index An ongoing index covering a single publication (example: New York Times Index), works of a particular form (Biography Index), or the published literature of a specific discipline (Art Index) or group of related disciplines (MEDLINE), updated continuously or at fixed intervals. Compare with closed-end index.

Opening Any two facing pages in an open book or other printed publication. The right-hand page is called the recto; the left-hand page the verso. Compare with conjoint leaves.

Operating budget Funds allocated, usually on an annual or biennial basis, to cover the ongoing expenses incurred in running a library or library system, including the payment of wages and salaries, and the purchase of materials, equipment, supplies, and services. Compare with capital expenditure.

Operating system (OS) Software designed to control the basic operation of a computer and the exchange of data between the central processing unit and any peripheral equipment, mainly input and output devices. Loaded whenever the computer is started, the OS controls the running of all other programs, including any security systems designed to prevent unauthorized use. Commonly used PC operating systems include DOS, Windows, Macintosh, and UNIX.

Operations A management term encompassing all the activities and details involved in running a library or library system on a day-to-day basis, as opposed to functions requiring a long-range view of the institution's direction and priorities, such as planning and budgeting, policy-making, fund-raising, and public relations.

Operators symbols that represent operations. In computer science there are binary and unary operators depending on the number of elements or records an operator acts on. In database searching there are Boolean and Proximity operators. Boolean operators are a subclass of logical operators (Logical operators are binary operators that manipulate data at the bit level.). A Boolean operator manipulates the binary value "true/false".

Optical center In printing, the point slightly above the mathematical center of a page which the human eye perceives as the center. In page layout, the typographer fools the eye by designing around the optical center, rather than the mathematical center. The same rule applies in Web page design for computer screens.

Optical character recognition (OCR) A process by which characters typed or printed on a page are electronically scanned, analyzed, and if found recognizable on the basis of appearance, converted into a digital character code capable of being processed by a computer. OCR eliminates the time-consuming process of re-keying information available in print, but results can be unpredictable if the scanned copy is imperfect or contains diacritical marks or unrecognizable characters.

Optical disk A high-density storage medium consisting of a specially coated disk on which data can be encoded in a pattern of tiny pits burned into the surface with a laser, read by a device that reflects a laser beam off the pitted surface, and decoded by a microprocessor into digital or analog signals. Includes compact discs, CD-roms, and dvds. Synonymous with laser disk.

Optical fiber A thin, flexible cable containing a bundle of very fine, highly transparent, tubular glass fibers made of pure silicon dioxide, designed to transmit information encoded in pulses of laser light at very high speed (billions of bits per second) by means of internal reflection. Telephone companies are rapidly upgrading their transmission infrastructure from copper wire to fiber-optic cable. The advantages of optical fiber over coaxial and twisted-pair cable are high bandwiths, less attenuation of signal, and lighter weight, making it possible to transmit data in digital format at very high-speed from one computer to another over a network such as the Internet.

Optical Resolution In the scanning context, this refers to the number of truly separate readings taken from an original within a given distance, as opposed to the subsequent increase in resolution (but not detail) created by software interpolation.

Optical spacing In typesetting, the technique of

adjusting the distance between the individual letters in a line of capitals to create the optical illusion of even spacing, which requires placing some letter combinations closer together than others.

Optical Video Disc Compact discs which use lights to read information.

Option The privilege of purchasing the rights in a book or manuscript from the copyright holder for a specific purpose (example: the right to adapt a novel or short story for performance on stage or screen), usually granted for a fixed period of time designated in a legally binding agreement, in exchange for some form of compensation. Optional (O) A field or subfield of the MARC record in which data may be entered at the discretion of the cataloger, but is not required to meet OCLC input standards for a given cataloging level. Compare with mandatory and required if applicable or readily available.

Opus Latin for "a work" In the most general sense, any creative work or composition. In music, the term is usually followed by an opus number assigned by the composer or publisher to one of several works, or a collection of works related in form or medium, to indicate its place in the sequence in which they were composed or issued. Abbreviated op. Plural: opera or opuses.

Opus number A number assigned by the composer or publisher to one of several musical works, or a set of works related in form or medium, to indicate its place in the sequence in which they were composed or issued, usually included in the title following the abbreviation op. (example: Beethoven's Concerto for Violin, op. 61, D major). Special numbering exists for certain composers whose works were unnumbered when first published, for example, the universally accepted Kochel numbers devised by the 19th century Austrian botanist Ludwig von Kochel in his chronological thematic catalog of the works of Wolfgang Amadeus Mozart.

Opuscule A book or treatise of small size. Also refers to a musical work or literary composition of little significance. Compare in this sense with magnum opus.

Oracle time clock Colorado State University centralized timeclock system used to record hourly employees' time; system requires employees' supervisor approval before time is paid by the University.

Oral history A sound recording or transcription of an interview with a person whose memories and perceptions of historical events are considered worth preserving as an aural record for future research. Also refers to an historical work based on data collected orally, often preserved in archives and special collections (example: Hard Times: An Oral History of the Great Depression by Studs Terkel).

Orchestral score The full score of a musical work composed for orchestra, giving the parts for all the instruments.

Order Request to a publisher or vendor to purchase a publication, supplies, or services. Or the act of preparing an order.

Order canceled (OC) A term used on an invoice to indicate that the order for a book or other item has been canceled by the seller, usually because copies are no longer available. Compare with back order.

Order card Card used to request that publications be ordered; used by the librarians and/or faculty and students. Additional information on requested title is added by the mono/ID section of the acquisition.

Order packet Set of processing slips prepared by acquisition service, mono/ID section, or the SERIALS section with appropriate bibliographic information which is used for ordering and/or cataloging.

Order record In acquisitions, a record created and attached to the bibliographic record for an item at the time it is ordered, containing information needed to process the order (name of selector, budgetary fund, vendor, order date, estimated price, purchase order number, date received, special handling notes, date cataloged, and pertinent characteristics of the item). After the item is received and processed, the order record is eventually purged. Compare with item record.

Original binding A term used in the antiquarian book trade to indicate that a book retains the binding in which it was first issued, which may show definite signs of wear if the volume is an old one.

Original cataloging preparing catalog information directly from the item in hand, rather than obtaining the data from another source (see online cataloging). Original cataloging is labor-intensive and generally used only when the information is not otherwise available.

Original In literature, a work as written by the author or in the author's own words. In art, a finished work as completed by the artist and ready for reproduction. In science, a study that produces results never before reported, in some cases through the use of a new methodology or research design. In reprography, the source document from which the first copy is made or in some cases the first copy itself. In a more general sense, something new and fresh, not copied or based on a pre-existing model. Abbreviated orig.

OSI Open Systems Interconnection, a set of standard protocol grouped into seven layers: the physical, data link, network, transport, session, presentation, and application layers.

OSU Internet username All OSU faculty, staff, and students automatically are assigned a username in the format lastname.nn (e.g., doe.999). This username is part of what is referred to as your "osu.edu address" which is a generic e-mail address that can be set up to direct your incoming messages to whatever machine you actually use for reading mail. In most cases, it also is your OSU Internet username, and it must be activated before you can take advantage of services like access to various secure servers.

Other entries Catalog access points other than the main entry. There may be entries for the subject, authors, title, series, editor, illustrator, etc.

Other Terms USB Flash Drives are a generic term for the media. They are also known as: Jump Drives, Key Drives, Keychain Drives, USB Drives, Flash Drives, Thumb Drives, Micro-Vaults, Pen Drives, Micro Drives, Stick Drives, etc. Dependent upon vendor. This list is not definitive.

Outlook Microsoft's messaging and collaboration client; with Outlook, you can organize and manage information from a single location.

Overdue an item still charged to a patron after the due date (end of the loan period). Fines may be assessed on overdue items, and books that remain overdue for four weeks are declared lost and the responsible patron will be charged for the replacement cost of the item plus a $25.00 processing fee.

Oversized books: books too large to fit in the regular shelving. At Marriott, these are housed in a special Oversize stacks area on Level 2.

Oversized Items which are too large to be shelved in the regular shelves are cataloged as Oversized. Please ask a librarian to show you where the Oversized items are shelved. Oversized items may be checked out like regular items.

OVID Database vendor specializing in science, technology and medical information.

PAC Public Access Catalog. The SDSU University Library's on-line catalog which lists the books held here and the journals subscribed to (but not their contents. It also provides information on circulation status, books and journals ordered but not yet received, receipt of journal issues, and more.

Packet Switching The method used to move data around on the Internet. In packet switching,all the data coming out of a machine is broken up into chunks, each chunk has the address of where it came from and where it is going. This enables chunks of data from many different sources to co-mingle on the same lines, and be sorted and directed along different routes by special machines along the way. This way many people can use the same lines at the same time. You might think of several caravans of trucks all using the same road system to carry materials.

Packet The unit of data sent across a packet switching network. While some Internet literature use the term to refer specifically to data sent across a physical network, other literature views the Internet as a packet switching network and describes IP Datagrams as packets.

Page A request for a book to be delivered from a branch library or a community college library.

Pagination System of numbers or letters used to indicate the order of the pages in a book. Or that part of the physical description that states the number of pages contained in a book.

Paint The oldest and most limited Macintosh graphic file format, holding only black-and-white bit maps at 72 dpi. Paint files (file type PNTG) are limited to 8 by 10 inches.

PAL videotapes PAL is the term used to describe European VCR readable videos. Many PAL versions are stored in the Annex, and one can use equipment in the Media Center to view them. The Learning Resources Center converts PAL versions to VHS.

Palette The range of colors a computer or an application is able to display. Most newer computers can display as many as 16 million colors, but a given program may use only 256 of them. Also refers to a display box containing a set of related tools within a desktop publishing or graphics design program.

PAM box Pamphlet Box. Box used to support pamphlets or loose periodical issues on shelves. Usually made out of cardboard, but also available in metal, which are called Princeton Files.

Pamphlet File - File cabinets in the Reference Microform Room containing pamphlets and brochures on a variety of subjects, as well as annual and corporate reports. Arranged alphabetically by subject.

Parallel Cable/Parallel Port A cable used to connect peripheral devices through a computer's parallel port. A type of port that transmits data in parallel (several bits side by side).

Parallel port: An interface on a computer that supports transmission of multiple bits at the same time; almost exclusively used for connecting a printer. On IBM or compatible computers, the parallel port uses a 25-pin connector.

Parallel title The title proper in another language recorded in the title and statement of responsibility area.

Parameter A word, number, or symbol that is typed after a command to further specify how the command should function.

PARAPAR A conversion software package, PARAPAR has been developed in CALIBNET to support interchange of bibliographic data between USMARC, UNIMARC and CCF Files and also from non-standard formats to standard ones. Its primary objective is to convert data files, received from the participating libraries in variant formats, into a ISO-2709 compliant implementation through which the files are merged into the centralized Database of CALIBNET.

Parity A check bit used to make the sum of the bits in a unit of data either even or odd (including the parity bit). A unit of data that is 8 bits long would have no parity, and a unit of data 7 bits long would have an even parity bit to make an 8 bit word. Parity is used to check a unit of data for errors during transmission through phone lines or null modem cables.

Part Porton of a work in one or more volumes issued by a publisher as the work is completed for publication. It is distinguished from a fascicle by being a unit rather than a temporary portion of a unit.

Partner A feature of INNOPAC whereby a library user can execute a search in one library catalog and re-execute the same search in a different library catalog, if that library is a pre-defined "partner." CSUL's partners include U.Colorado, Boulder, University of Northern Colorado, Auraria, and other Colorado libraries that use INNOPAC.

Password A code used to gain access (login) to a locked system. Good passwords contain letters and non-letters and are not simple combinations such as virtue7. A good password might be: 5%df(29) But don't use that one!

Paste To insert information from the Clipboard. Information can be pasted multiple times.

Patent depository A collection of U.S. patents located in the Science and Engineering Library.

Path A route used in finding, retrieving, and storing files on a disk. The course leading from the root directory of a drive to a particular file.

PATH Database The California PATH Database provides access to the largest and most comprehensive collection of bibliographic information on Intelligent Transportation Systems (ITS).

Patron Record A record that contains information about the students, staff, faculty, and community borrowers who have borrowing priviledges with the University Libraries

Pay file A term used by INNOPAC to describe the file where invoice and other financial data is collected after it is entered by acquisition service staff through ordering and receiving functions. INNOPAC supports 4 pay files so that 4 different staff can work at any one time. When accounting staff "post" payfiles, INNOPAC updates the fund files, the order records, Payment History file, and the vendor file.

Pay for performance The performance management program mandated by the State of Colorado, and instituted by Colorado State University in 2001, which addresses the policies and procedures for classified personnel job performance planning and evaluation as well as associated merit salary increases.

PC Usually refers to an IBM PC or compatible, or when used generically, to a "personal computer". In a different context, PC also is an abbreviation for "politically correct."

PCMCIA A standard format for credit-card-size expansion cards, used to add features to laptop computers, hand-held computers, and desktop computers. The acronym stands for Personal Computer Memory Card International Association.

PDA Personal Digital Assistant; a small hand-held computer that in the most basic form, allows you to store names and addresses, prepare to-do lists, schedule appointments, keep track of projects, track expenditures, take notes, and do calculations. Depending on the model, you also may be able to send or receive e-mail; do word processing; play MP3 music files; get news, entertainment and stock quotes from the Internet; play video games; and have an integrated digital camera or GPS receiver.

PDF Portable Document Format is a file format developed by Adobe Systems. PDF captures formatting information from a variety of desktop publishing applications, making it possible to send formatted documents and have them appear on the recipient's monitor or printer as they were intended. To view a file in PDF format, you need Adob Acrobat Reader, a free application distributed by Adobe Systems.

Peer Review A process that articles in many scholarly journals go through before they are published. Once an article is submitted for publication, it is sent to an editorial board comprised of experts in the field to be evaluated. The submitted article must receive the approval of the editorial board before it is published. The editorial board is usually identified at the beginning of each issue of a journal. Peer-reviewed journals may also be called juried or refereed journals.

Peer Reviewed Journlas A publication, usually scholarly, in which articles are reviewed by a panel before being accepted for publication. Also sometimes called scholarly or refereed.

Peer-to-peer A network setup that allows every computer to both offer and access network resources, such as shared files, without requiring a centralized file server. Macintosh computers utilize this type of network setup.

PEGASUS The software application the library uses to manage e-mail.

Penalty Points When items are returned after the due date or due time, or are renewed after the due date, then penalty points are incurred. If the number of penalty points incurred by a borrower reaches a predetermined level, then the penalty becomes a fine. Penalty points are deleted at the end of each year.

Penn World Data Provides online access statistics covering 28 key variables on all the major world economies, from 1950 to 1998.

Pentium A type of microprocessor available in new IBM PC and compatible computers; it is the next step up from the Intel 80486 processor.

Performing Arts Skiing; Women's organizations; and Ranching.

Periodical - A serial published indefinitely at regular or stated intervals, generally more frequently than once a year. Each issue is numbered and/or dated consecutively and contains articles, stories, or other writings. Journals, magazines and newspapers are periodicals.

Periodical A regularly published magazine, journal, newspaper, or newsletter.

Periodicals Microform Room The room on the first

floor of the University Library where microfilm, microfiche and ERIC documents are filed.

Peripheral A piece of hardware that's outside the main computer. It usually refers to external hardware such as disk drives, printers, and scanners sold by a third party.

PERL The Practical Extraction and Report Language. An interpreted language for CGI scripts.

Permuterm a type of subject index generated by computer and showing paired combinations of the significant words in titles. Used in some major print indexes, notably Science Citation Index and Biological Abstracts.

Personality A method of setting up a computer or a program for multiple users. Example: In Windows, each user is given a separate "personality" and set of relevant files. Although Eudora Pro also has a feature called personalities, its use is geared toward a single user with multiple e-mail accounts.

PGP Pretty good privacy; a technique for encrypting e-mail messages. PGP uses a public key to give to anyone who sends you messages and a private key you keep to decrypt messages you receive.

Ph A type of directory service often referred to as a "phone book". When accessing this type of directory service, follow the directions from the particular site for looking up information. Phone, fax and video calls (IP telephony) can now be placed over the Internet (or any IP network) using market available client software or hardware. In most instances, users will only need to make a one-time purchase of client software or hardware to begin placing unlimited long distance calls for the cost of an Internet connection. The quality of the calls will not match that of calls placed over the traditional phone network. However with additional hardware and software purchases, higher quality communications can be achieved.

Photocopiers Photocopy machines located on the first, second, and fourth floors accept coins or bills to make copies at $0.10 per page, or $0.08 using a debit card. A color copier is available on campus at Printing Services.

Photographic archive Archival collection of Vanderbilt photographs; housed in Special Collections.

Phrase - More than keyword, searched exactly as typed (all terms required to be in documents, in the order typed). NOTE: Some search engines such as altavista and infoseek enclose keywords in quotes ("") to form a phrase. Firstsearch uses a w (i.e.,

PICS The standard macintosh graphic file format for animations. Essentially a collection of bit-mapped PICT images in sequential order, much like movie frames.

PICT/PICT 2 PICT is the standard macintosh graphic file format for graphics that are cut or copied to the Clipboard and for drawings that won't be output on postscript printers. This format is ideal for on-screen presentations, but page layout programs sometimes have problems with PICT files. Files are sometimes called metafiles because they can contain both bit maps and quickdraw-based objects.

PIECE Single unit of library material. Generic term is used loosely to describe items, both bound and unbound (the latter generally of a cumulative nature) that are undergoing processing in the technical services division.

PIN A password created by users of the Sage system. (PIN=Personal Identification Number)

PING Packet Internet Groper a utility used to determine whether a particular computer is currently connected to the Internet. It works by sending a packet to the specified IP address and waiting for a reply.

Ping To check if a server is running. From the sound that a sonar systems makes in movies, you know, when they are searching for a submarine.

Pixe Short for "picture element"; one of the dots that make up a digitized image. A pixel may be binary (black and white) or multivalued for colored displays. The number of pixels in a display determines resolution, more pixels providing higher resolution.

Pixel Stands for one picture element (one dot on a computer monitor); commonly used as a unit of measurement.

Pixel Skipping A means of reducing image resolution by simply deleting pixels throughout the image.

PKUNZIP A utility used to decompress a file a zipped file (e.g., a file with a ".zip" extension).

PKZIP A common file compression utility for IBM PC and compatibles. Compressed files are referred to as "zipped" and usually end with a ".zip" file extension. A special kind of zipped file is self-extracting and ends with a ".exe" extension.

PKZIP/PKUNZIP A software compression utility for the PC. It allows you to compress or "zip" a file or a number of files into one archive file in the ZIP file format.

Plagiarism is the passing off as your own, the work of others'. Original sources are not given credit.

Plagiarism The unattributed use of a source of information that is not considered common knowledge. Three acts are considered plagiarism: (1) failing to cite quotations and borrowed ideas, (2) failing to enclose borrowed language in quotation marks, and (3) failing to put summaries and paraphrases in your own words.

Plug-in a software module that adds a specific feature to a larger system, for example plug-ins for the Netscape Navigator that enable it to display audio and video files. Plug-ins display the files within the browser window, without having to open a separate window as helper applications do. (see Enliven,

Plug-in A small program that can be downloaded to give a browser additional capabilities, such as the ability to play audio files or display special graphics formats.

PMT Photomultiplier tube. The light sensing device generally used in drum scanners.

PNG (Portable Network Graphics) PNG is a graphics format specifically designed for use on the World Wide Web. PNG enable compression of images without any loss of quality, including high-resolution images. Another important feature of PNG is that anyone may create software that works with PNG images without paying any fees - the PNG standard is free of any licensing costs.

Pocket label Label on the back of each periodical issue indicating title, date, date of receipt, and CSU Libraries ownership.

Pocket part Updates to a title that is inserted in a pocket inside the back cover which are usually superseded.

Poor text complete, but so worn that it can be sold only as a reading copy; missing parts must be noted.

POP (Point of Presence, also Post Office Protocol) Two commonly used meanings: Point of Presence and Post Office Protocol. A Point of Presence usually means a city or location where a network can be connected to, often with dial up phone lines. So if an Internet company says they will soon have a POP in Belgrade, it means that they will soon have a local phone number in Belgrade and/or a place where leased lines can connect to their network. A second meaning, Post Office Protocol refers to a way that e-mail client software such as Eudora gets mail from a mail server. When you obtain an account from an Internet Service Provider (ISP) you almost always get a POP account with it, and it is this POP account that you tell your e-mail software to use to get your mail. Another protocol called IMAP is replacing POP for email.

Popular Source Information, especially articles, written to entertain or inform the general public. Some examples of popular magazines include Time, Newsweek, and People Weekly.

Population Index It presents an annotated bibliography of recently published books, journal articles, working papers, and other materials on population topics.

The coverage is from 1986-2000, containing total of 46,035 citations.

Port A place where information goes into or out of a computer, or both. E.g. The serial port on a personal computer is where a modem would be connected. On the Internet port often refers to a number that is part of a URL, appearing after a colon (:) right after the domain name. Every service on an Internet server listens on a particular port number on that server. Most services have standard port numbers, e.g. Web servers normally listen on port 80. Services can also listen on non-standard ports, in which case the port number must be specified in a URL when accessing the server, so you might see a URL of the form: gopher://peg.cwis.uci.edu:7000/ This shows a gopher server running on a non-standard port (the standard gopher port is 70). Finally, port also refers to translating a piece of software to bring it from one type of computer system to another, e.g. To translate a Windows program so that is will run on a Macintosh.

Portal Usually used as a marketing term to described a Web site that is or is intended to be the first place people see when using the Web. Typically a "Portal site" has a catalog of web sites, a search engine, or both. A Portal site may also offer email and other service to entice people to use that site as their main "point of entry" (hence "portal") to the Web.

Posting A single message entered into a network communications system.

Post The act of sending a message to a particular network newsgroup.

Posterization The conversion of continuous tone data into a series of visible tonal steps or bands.

Postscript A page description language primarily used for printing documents on laser printers; it is the standard for desktop publishing because it takes advantage of high resolution output devices. Example: A graphic design saved in postscript format looks much better when printed on a 600 dpi printer than on a 300 dpi printer.

Postscript fonts Called outline or scalable fonts; with a single typeface definition, a postscript printer can produce many other fonts. Contrast to non-postscript printers that represent fonts with bitmaps and require a complete set for each font size.

Power PC A line of microprocessors developed by Motorola, Apple, and IBM; this chip is used in Power Macintoshes.

Ppi/ppc Pixels per inch or pixels per centimeter. Units of measurement for scanned images.

PPP (Point-to-Point Protocol) - Protocol that handles the sending of data packets over dial-up and leased-line connections to your ISP. PPP gets you online. NOTE: People in Broward country can use PPP access to dial directly to NSU and access NSU's Web system. People outside the Broward area would have to pay long distance charges to use this access.

PRAM Parameter RAM (pronounced pee-ram). A small portion of the Mac's RAM set aside to hold basic information such as the date and time, speaker volume, desktop pattern, and key-board and mouse settings. PRAM is powered by a battery, so it doesn't lose the settings when you shut down. Sometimes, however, the PRAM data gets corrupted, causing crashes or other problems.

Prepay Payment in advance of receipt of ordered item.

Prepayment discount Fr payment with the order (usually 5% or free shipping)

Preprint A portion of a work printed and issued before the publication of the complete work; for example, a copy of an article issued before the journal is published or a conference paper issued prior to the holding of the conference.

Prepublication discount On orders placed prior to the publication date to encourage advance sales

Preservation A multi-pronged approach to long-term

care of the library's collections. It involves preventive care as well as repair and restoration treatments.

Preservation lab Section of preservation services responsible for conservation treatment, replacement of pages and selecting materials for commercial rebinding.

Preservation services Unit of the Libraries responsible for the preservation of the collection, making certain it is housed under the best possible conditions, and for determining what materials need special facilities or restoration to prevent their deterioration. The Unit consists of stacks, the preservation lab, the bindry, and marking.

Primary color A base color that is used to compose the other colors.

Primary literature The original research or writings on a subject. Includes technical reports, conference literature, patents, theses, and journals (the main medium for the dissemination of new knowledge). See secondary literature.

Primary record a resource created by the same people that initially experienced or used it. They create the records for their own purposes, records that often remain unpublished. Sometimes they witness an event, sometimes they are involved in an event, and sometimes the record is directly created by the event.

Primary source An original source, such as a speech, diary, novel, legislative bill, laboratory study, field research report, or eyewitness account. While not necessarily more reliable than a secondary source, a primary source has the advantage of being closely related to the information it conveys and as such is often considered essential for research, particularly in history.

Printkey Software program that allows the user to capture screens and save them as graphic files by pressing the "Print Screen" key on the computer keyboard.

PRISM Cataloging database of OCLC. See INNOPAC PRISM.

Process Ink Colors CMYK pigments used in printing processes, chosen to produce the widest range of color mixtures.

Professional journal A journal addressed to a particular professional audience such as doctors, lawyers, teachers, engineers, or accountants.

Profile The color characteristics of an input or output device, used by a CMS to ensure color fidelity.

Proforma invoice Invoice received for checking and approval prior to receiving the forma invoice. It is used as a checklist for serials renewals and then returned to the vendor for authorization to renew.

Program: A set of instructions that tells a computer how to perform a specific task.

Promptcat An automated service provided by OCLC whereby MARC records are delivered and holdings set for purchased titles identified by a library's participating material vendors. Libraries may request that titles arrive shelf-ready with a call number and physical processing.

Proper names personal and geographical names.

Properties Information about an object, including settings or options for that object. For example, you look at properties of a file for information such as the file size, file type, and file attributes.

Prospector A global catalog based at the Colorado Allieance for Research in Denver, CO. The actual system is a Triple I product similar to SAGE . Prospector pulls together the library catalogs of 16 different Colorado libraries and the University of Wyoming for ease in searching. Users are also able to request materials from other library sites much the same way that CSU patrons can request items from S.O.S.

Protocols When data is being transmitted between two or more devices something needs to govern the controls that keep this data intact. A formal description of message formats and the rules two computers must follow to exchange those messages. Protocols can describe low-level details of machine-to-machine interfaces (e.g., the order in which bits and bytes are sent across wire) or high-level exchanges between application programs (e.g., the way in which two programs transfer a file across the Internet).

Proxy Refers to a special kind of server that functions as an intermediate link between a client application (like a web browser) and a real server. The proxy server intercepts requests for information from the real server and whenever possible, fills the request. When it is unable to do so, the request is forwarded to the real server. Example: OIT supports an HTTP proxy server called wwwcache.service.osu.edu; its function is to speed up requests for the same web pages. If someone else has recently requested the same page, it's much faster to download the page from the proxy server instead of forwarding the request over the Internet to the place where the page really is located.

Proxy Server A Proxy Server sits in between a Client and the "real" Server that a Client is trying to use. Client's are sometimes configured to use a Proxy Server, usually an HTTP server. The clients makes all of it's requests from the Proxy Server, which then makes requests from the "real" server and passes the result back to the Client. Sometimes the Proxy server will store the results and give a stored result instead of making a new one (to reduce use of a Network). Proxy servers are commonly established on Local Area Networks

Pseudunym Name assumed by authors to conceal or obscure their identity.

PSF Public Service Flyer Compiled by material selector in various subject areas.

PSN Packet Switch Node; a store-and-forward packet switch (formerly called an IMP).

PSTN Public Switched Telephone Network: The regular old-fashioned telephone system.

Psycarticles Psycarticles is an online database containing more than 26,000 entries from 49 peer reviewed journals published by APA and allied organizations from 1988 to the present. Full text articles covered in it are available for price.

Public domain software Uncopyrighted software, freely accessible to all users.

Public domain The status of works that are freely available and not governed by copyright restrictions. Most government documents are in the public domain, as are works for which copyright has expired. Many classic works of literature and primary sources available in full text on the Internet are in the public domain and thus can be copied without restriction. However, many (if not most) of the texts and other works in print and on the Internet are protected by copyright law; users must request permission of the copyright holder to reproduce such works. See also fair use and intellectual property.

Public Information Reference Service (PIRS) An integrated set of Web pages that guides users to selected local, state, U.S., and international government documents, statistical compendia, and other resources.

Public service division Division of the libraries composed of the following departments: access service, interlibrary loan and document delivery, reference service (collection management, information and reference, instruction, outreach and staff training), and government documents specialist.

Public service The aspect of library work including assisting patrons in the use of a library and the physical care of collections to make possible this service; may include reference, circulation, stack maintenance, and related services.

Public temp A directory on Guppy, one of the Libraries' servers, available from any public station for users to temporarily store their documents.

Publication - Any work issued to the public, including books, serials, newspapers, pamphlets, etc.

Publication date In a book — the date appears at the bottom of the title page (as opposed to the copyright date which is on the verso of the title page). Or in a periodical — the day or month, etc., it was issued.

Publication Manual of the American Psychological Association

Public-domain Software that has no copyright or fee, which means you can copy, use, and even alter and sell it.

Publisher Person, corporate body, or firm responsible for issuing a work.

Publisher's series Series of books whose only link may be the collective title assigned by the publisher.

Pubscience Provides access to a collection of scientific and technical publishers and journal literature.

Purchase order An official University order issued to a vendor by the purchase department for the supply of products and/or services. All purchase orders must go through the purchasing department except for library materials (monographs and serials), which are issued by acquisition services.

Purchase plan Agreement with a vendor where they send us materials according to predefined profiles in which the library keeps all materials received

Purchasing department The department within the University which is authorized by the State to conduct purchasing operations and to ensure compliance with State policies and regulations.

Push Frequently used to describe data sent over the Internet; the act of sending data to a client computer without the client requesting it. Example: a subscriptions service that delivers customized news to your desktop. Contrast to browsing the World Wide Web which is based on "pull" technology; you must request a web page before it is sent to your computer A software program that retrieves information from web sites and deposits a copy on the user's computer to view offline. This is in contrast to traditional pull technology, where the user must manually seek and find information on the World Wide Web. See also channel. The technology that puts pre-selected content directly on your computer screen from the Internet without your need to browse for it. With this technology, introduced by pointcast and Individual, Inc.and added to 4th generation browsers, you can program your desktop, for example, to automatically receive such things as local weather, news headlines, selected stock reports, and sports scores for selected teams or events.

Q - RRECALL A notice sent out to borrowers which changes the due date of a borrowed book or other material, usually because it is desired by another patron.

Quads nickname for USGS topographical maps, or "quadrangle" maps, so named because of the grid pattern they are based on.

Quality Factor A multiplication factor (between 1 and 2) applied to output screen ruling to calculate scanning resolution for optimum output quality. This is also known as the halftoning factor.

Quantity discount - on purchases of a required number of copies or titles

Quarter Tones Tones between shadow and midtones are known as 3/4 tones and those between highlight and midtones are known as 1/4 tones.

Quarterly periodical published at regular intervals four times a year.

Query The process by which a web client requests specific information from a web server, based on a character string that is passed along.

Questia Online library of Books and Journals It holds an over 45,000 books and 360,000 journal, magazine, and newspaper articles. Search for this database is free, however access to full text of the documents is priced.

Quicktime A video format developed by Apple

Computer commonly used for files found on the Internet; an alternative to MPEG. A special viewer program available for both IBM PC and compatibles and Macintosh computers is required for playback.

Qvtnet A program for Windows distributed via the OIT Software To Go web site; enables you to open a telnet connection to a remote computer.

QWS3270 A program for Windows distributed via the OIT Software To Go web site; provides IBM3270 terminal emulation when you connect to an IBM mainframe. Example: fullscreen TSO and WYLBUR sessions.

R Required if applicable or readily available - must be entered if appropriate under AACR2 and available on the item or from other records.

R. R. Bowker Founded in New York City in 1872, the publisher R. R. Bowker specializes in reference works on publishing, libraries, and the book trade. The company is known for its long-standing reference serials (Books in Print, American Library Directory, The Bowker Annual Library and Book Trade Almanac, Literary Market Place, Magazines for Libraries, Ulrich's International Periodicals Directory, etc.). Bowker has also served as the official ISBN agency for the United States since 1968.

RAM Random Access Memory. RAM is the most common type of computer memory, and it's where the computer stores system software, programs, and data you are currently using. It's formally called dynamic RAM (DRAM) because it's volatile, that is, the contents are lost when you turn off the computer (or crash). It's pronounced ram and measured in megabytes.

Ranganathan Shiyali Ramamrita Ranganathan (1872-1972) is one of the most influential figures in the field of library and information sciences. This paper argues that Ranganathan is a thinker ahead of his time. The fact that his ideas and his Colon Classification scheme are not well received and practised can probably be attributed to his vision being too advanced for his contemporary world of technology. Considering the progress that has been made since his times, Ranganathan's ideas deserve another investigation. Upon comparing the nature of his classification scheme with the various technologies like relational databases, online retrieval systems, or the World Wide Web, it is quite evident that Ranganathan's ideas of classification are more applicable now than before.

Rare book room is a room on the 1st floor of the library which has a collection of old gift books as well as many books on Georgia History. The vertical file for GSW and University System of Georgia material is also located in the Rare Book Room.

Rare Books Books that are valued for the significance of their contents, their scarcity, their imprint or date of publication, their physical characteristics or condition, or their associations (signed or annotated by a famous author, for instance). Cornell's primary collections of rare books are are located in the Rare Books & Manuscripts Collections in Kroch Library.

Raster A synonym for grid. Sometimes used to refer to the grid of addressable positions in an output device.

RDF (Resource Definition Framework; A set of rules (a sort of language) for creating descriptions of information, especially information available on the World Wide Web. RDF could be used to describe a collection of books, or artists, or a collection of web pages as in the RSS data format which uses RDF to create machine-readable summaries of web sites. RDF is also used in XPFE applications to define the relationships between different collections of elements, for example RDF could be used to define the relationship between the data in a database and the way that data is displayed to a user.

Read Only Memory (ROM) A memory chip containing instructions and/or data that cannot be changed or erased because the manufacturer created it in unalterable form.

Usually contains the programs required to start the computer. Compare with CD-ROM.

Reader-copiers Machines in the microform reading room that project and enlarge images for reading, and produce photocopies. The cost is $0.10 per page, payable at the Service Desk.

Reader-printer A machine designed for enlarging, viewing, and making printed copies of microforms (microfiche, microfilm, microopaque), usually coin-operated (fee varies). Libraries with microform holdings usually provide at least one reader-printer for patron use. Compare with photocopier.

Readers' advisory Services provided by an experienced public services librarian who specializes in the reading needs of the adult patrons of a public library. A reader's advisor recommends specific titles and/or authors, based on knowledge of a patron's past reading preferences, and may also compile lists of recommended titles and serve as liaison to other adult education agencies in the community. The same type of information is provided by reference works such as Reader's Adviser: A Layman's Guide to Reading published by R. R. Bowker. Compare with bibliographic instruction.

Readership The total number of people who read, or are estimated to read, a given publication, not necessarily equal to the number who purchase or subscribe to it. In periodical publishing, total readership equals base circulation plus pass-along. The term is also used to refer to a particular class of reader, for example, educated readership as opposed to general readership.

Reading copy A complimentary copy of a forthcoming book sent at no charge by the publisher to selected booksellers in advance of the publication date to promote sales. Reading copies may be printed as part of the regular edition and distributed in the same binding as the trade edition. Compare with advance copy.

Reading group An organized group, usually sponsored

by a library, school, church, or bookstore, whose members meet to talk about books they have read. Most groups coordinate their reading so that everyone has read the same book, or a work by the same author, in advance of meeting. In some groups, a facilitator is selected, sometimes on a rotating basis, who begins the session with a brief talk about the author or new book, then opens the floor for discussion.

Reading lamp A man-made light source specifically designed to provide the optimum amount of illumination for a person sitting and reading in a chair or at a desk, shaded to direct the light downward onto the page without glare. Very small models designed to clip onto the cover of a book can be purchased for reading in bed.

Reading level One of several degrees of proficiency in reading, usually defined in reference to a specific academic grade level (e.g., third-grade level) or stage of reading development, applicable to both reader and reading material. Factors determining reading level include vocabulary, sentence structure, length of text, and difficulty of content.

Reading list A list of recommended resources (books, articles, Web sites, etc.) On a topic, usually compiled by a teacher or librarian with an interest in or expertise on the subject, for distribution to students enrolled in a course of study, or available to readers on a library display rack, kiosk, or bulletin board, not as comprehensive or scholarly as a research bibliography. Compare with pathfinder and research guide.

Reading matter Anything that can be read, from the back of a cereal box to a philosophical treatise. Reading material need not be written or printed on paper, merely text-based (example: a news report published on a Web Site). Choice of reading material reflects a person's interests, tastes, education, and experience.

Reading preference A reader's taste in reading matter, as to format (books, magazines, comic books, etc.), genre (fiction or nonfiction), and subject (biography, crime, travel, etc.). Although reading preferences often change as a person grows older, studies have shown that in some individuals, they remain remarkably constant. Publishers use survey research to study the choices consumers make in purchasing reading material. Niche publishers may depend on consumers who have developed specific preferences. In public libraries, experienced public services librarians, having learned the reading habits of regular patrons, may order new materials with the preferences of specific individuals in mind.

Reading Rainbow A television series designed to interest children 4-8 years of age in the pleasures of reading outstanding books for children, Reading Rainbow is broadcast daily (M-F) for one-half hour by 95% of the public television (PBS) stations in the United States. Its fast-paced magazine-style format has garnered over 150 awards since its inception, including 13 Emmy Awards.

Reading room A specially designated room in a library, usually furnished with comfortable chairs, study tables, and reading lamps, where a person can study or read quietly without being disturbed. Reading rooms may also contain library materials such as reference books. Some libraries have wired their reading rooms to accommodate patrons using laptops, who require Internet access. Reading rooms in very large libraries, such as the New York Public Library at 5th Avenue and 42nd Street, are often beautifully designed and furnished.

Readme A small text file containing important instructions on how to use a computer program, or information about new developments affecting the user of a software system, which may not be included in the printed documentation. To avoid computer viruses, caution should be exercised when opening a readme file sent as an e-mail attachment.

Read-only A digital storage medium capable of being

read but not modified or erased, used for data that is to be retained permanently, for example, ROM (read only memory) and CD-ROM. The opposite of rewritable.

Ready reference A reference question that can be answered by a reference librarian in one or two minutes by providing a fact or piece of information found in a single source, a type of question which sometimes turns out to be an opening gambit that develops into a more comprehensive search.

Real Time Communication Communication occurring at the moment messages are generated. Real Time is a characteristic of synchronous communication.

Real time Happening immediately, in the present moment. An electronic process, operation, or routine that occurs quickly enough to affect or respond to a related process taking place simultaneously in actual time. The opposite of asynchronous.

Realaudio: client-server software from Progressive Networks, for selecting and playing back audio files; realaudio has a very short download time, allowing use in "real time" as opposed to previous technology which took many minutes to download one minute of audio material.

Realia Three-dimensional objects from real life such as artifacts, specimens, samples, and naturally occurring objects, sometimes borrowed or purchased by libraries for use in classroom instruction. In AACR2, the term is added inside square brackets [realia] as a general material designation following the title proper in the the bibliographic description. Compare with replica.

Realplayer A program or plug-in that gives you access to multimedia files, both on the Internet and those stored locally on your computer. With the program you can find and play clips (e.g., video, audio, video with audio, etc.) Without having to launch your web browser first. The plug-in works in conjunction with your web browser to allow you to access streaming media files.

Ream As originally used in papermaking, the term referred to a unit of measurement consisting of twenty quires or 480 sheets of handmade paper, but the number of sheets in a ream eventually became standardized at 500 sheets of machine-made paper. More recently, European papermakers have adopted 1,000 sheets as the standard number.

Rebacked A book given a new spine and mended hinges, usually because the spine was cracked or the hinges weakened. Rebacking is not as extensive as rebinding since some of the original binding materials (usually the boards) are retained.

Rebel card A debit card for making copies. Rebel Cards can be purchased for a dollar from dispensers or at the circulation service desks in Lied or branch libraries.

Rebinding The complete rehabilitation of a book too worn to be mended or repaired, a process that usually entails removing the case or cover, resewing the sections, and applying a new cover. The steps involved in preparing a book for rebinding are collectively known as pulling. Very large libraries are often equipped to perform rebinding in-house, but smaller libraries must rely on the services of a commercial bindery. Compare with recased and recover.

Reboot To cause the files in the operating system of a computer to be re-executed, usually by selecting the option to "Restart" or "Reset," or by pressing Ctrl+Alt+Del on the keyboard. This procedure is sometimes helpful in getting a computer "unstuck" after it locks up unexpectedly during processing. If it fails, the user can cold boot the system, but powering down will result in the loss of unsaved data. Synonymous with warm boot.

Rebus A type of puzzle in which certain words in a sentence are replaced by pictures of objects whose names suggest the meaning or sound of the words they are intended to represent, for example, a picture of a bed to suggest "sleep" or of an eye to represent the pronoun "I." According to James Bettley, editor of The Art of the Book (London: V&A

Publications, 2001), the earliest known example appears in a treatise on penmanship by Giovambattista Palatino printed in 1540.

Recall A request made by the library to one of its patrons to return a borrowed item before its due date. Any item may be recalled at any time for Course Reserve or after two weeks if requested by another Cornell patron. This service is available through the Requests link at the top of any online catalog record.

Recased A book that has come loose in or fallen out of its case or cover and been reglued into it, a process that usually requires new endpapers, but not resewing. Compare with recover and rebinding.

Recataloging The process of making substantial revisions in bibliographic records for items that have already been cataloged, usually in response to changes in the needs or policies of a library, for example, the addition of contents notes in records representing anthologies and other collected works. Compare with reclassification.

Received from the shipper in damaged condition are returned by the library to the seller for credit or replacement.

Receiving In acquisitions, the initial processing of an item shipped to the library by a publisher, jobber, or vendor, including verification that the correct item was shipped with all parts included, routing the invoice to the appropriate accounting office for payment, and updating the order record, usually with date received, number of parts received, and an indication of where the item was sent for the next step in processing.

Recension A revision of the text of a work, often a literary classic, based on a critical examination of earlier texts and authoritative sources, usually undertaken only after a consensus has developed among scholars concerning the weight of evidence. Compare with redaction.

Recent Advances in Manufacturing [RAM] Database Recent Advances in Manufacturing (RAM) is a database of bibliographic information for manufacturing and related areas. It covers items in well over 500 niche and mainstream journals and magazines, and also details of books, videos and conference proceedings.

Recently returned A code used in online catalogs and circulation systems to indicate the circulation status of an item returned by a borrower and checked in by library staff so recently that it may still be on a holding shelf or in the process of being reshelved. The temporary designation assists staff in tracing the item if it cannot be located by call number in the stacks.

Reciprocal agreement A mutual understanding between libraries, usually concerning fees for lending via interlibrary loan, typically "we will not charge you, if you do not charge us."

Reciprocal borrowing privileges Loan privileges granted by independent cooperating libraries to members of each other's user groups, sometimes for a modest fee.

Reclassification Revision of the call numbers assigned to selected items to make their relationship to other items in the collection more consistent, for example, to reflect the merger of two classes very similar in subject. Also refers to the conversion of a collection (or part of a collection) originally cataloged under one classification system to another, for example, from Dewey Decimal classification to Library of Congress classification, or vice versa.

Reclassify Revision of a call nuber due to a change in the classification schedule or an error in the cataloging when the call number was first assigned.

RECON Retrospective conversion of manual cataloging records to machine-readable format.

Reconfigure To change the way data is structured in a computer system.

Record A collection of related data fields organized and accessible as a single entity. Examples of data fields are author, title, publisher, abstract, call number, etc. In a periodical index, which is a collection of article citations, each citation is a record. In the CU Library Catalog, each reference retrieved per title is also a record.

Record group In archives, an aggregation of all the records of a particular agency or person, or a body of records known to be related on the basis of provenance, usually stored together in their original order (see respect des fonds). A record subgroup consists of records within a record group, related in some way (functionally, chronologically, geographically, etc.) Or produced by a subordinate unit of the agency responsible for creating, receiving, or accumulating the group. Subgroups may be further subdivided.

Record item In archives, the smallest separate and distinct unit of recorded material which, when accumulated, constitutes a record series, for example, a file in a group of related files. Compare with bibliographic item.

Record series In archives, records of the same provenance, determined upon inspection to belong together because they 1) are part of a recognizable filing system, 2) have been stored together because they were produced by the same activity, 3) are related to the same function or activity and are similar in format, or 4) comprise a set logically grouped in some other way. A record series is usually identified by a unique series number and may in some cases consist of a single record item.

Record structure The pre-established sequence of fields and subfields used to describe a single item in a library catalog or bibliographic database, each field containing one or more related elements of description. For example, the journal title, volume number, date of issue, and page numbers in the source field of a record representing a journal article in a periodical database. Most catalogs and databases include textual field labels in the record display to help users distinguish the various categories of description.

Record suppression The ability to remove a record

from public view, while keeping that record in SAGE, e.g., records for withdrawn books remain in the online catalog for a period of time, but cannot be viewed by the public.

Recordkeeping system The methods and procedures used in creating, arranging, and maintaining records of the activities of an agency or individual, usually in some kind of systematic order (alphabetical, chronological, topical, functional, etc.) Which may appear idiosyncratic to outsiders unfamiliar with the system..

Records Documents in any form, created or received by an agency or person, accumulated in the normal conduct of business or affairs, and retained as evidence of such activity, usually arranged according to a discernible system of recordkeeping.

Records management The field of management devoted to achieving accuracy, efficiency, and economy in the systematic creation, retention, conservation, dissemination, use, and disposition of the official records of a company, government agency, organization, or institution, whether in physical or electronic form, usually undertaken by a professionally trained records manager on the basis of a thorough records survey. Security and disaster preparedness are essential elements of a good records management program.

Records survey The systematic process of examining archival records in their administrative context to determine their content, format, provenance, original order, physical quantities and condition, rates of accumulation, and other characteristics, before beginning the work of describing and arranging them. The information gained in such a survey is also of use in developing disposition schedules, planning conservation, determining access policy, and estimating the amount of space required to store them.

Recover To apply a new cover to a volume, without resewing the sections. The process of making the new cover and attaching it to the sections is called recovering. Compare with recased and rebinding.

Recruitment The process of attracting qualified personnel to work in a library or library system, by posting a notice and position description in library journals and to library-related electronic mailing lists, and by publicizing the vacancy at job fairs and word-of-mouth. Also refers to the efforts of library schools and professional library associations to attract promising students to the career of librarianship.

Recto The upper side of a leaf of parchment, vellum, or paper, or the right-hand page in a bound volume when opened, usually assigned an uneven page number. The opposite of verso. The title page and dedication, and the first page of the preface, introduction, table of contents, chapters, appendices, indexes, and other major parts of a book are printed on the recto. Also, the side of a single printed sheet intended to be read first, unless both sides are identically printed. Also known as the obverse.

Recycled paper Paper manufactured from reclaimed wastepaper that has been reduced to pulp and processed to remove ink and other impurities. Recycled paper is used in printing and as writing paper, to conserve natural resources and reduce the volume of refuse in sanitary landfills. Book publishers consider the highest grades suitable for printing fiction.

Red book The popular name given to a manual containing official lists of state employees or other eminent people, for example, members of the British peerage, known by the color of its cover. Compare with blue book.

Redaction The process of editing, revising, and/or arranging to publish a work left incomplete or in a condition not suitable for publication, usually at the death of the author, done by a redactor. Also refers to the result of such an endeavor. Compare with continuation and recension.

Reduction A reproduction or copy produced on a smaller scale than the original, usually indicated as a percentage of the initial size (a 50% reduction of an 8 x 10-inch original produces a copy measuring 4 x 5 inches). Most photocopiers available in libraries have reduction capability for the convenience of users. The opposite of enlargement.

Reduction ratio In microphotography, an indication of the number of times the size of a document or other object is reduced to form a microimage. For example, 25X means that the image is 25 times smaller than the linear dimensions of the original. Reduction ratios are classified as follows:

Redundancy In communication, the use of repetition to reinforce a message and prevent misunderstanding, as in a sign that reads, "This Way to the Library" instead of simply "Library" or "To the Library." In a more general sense, any words or symbols not essential to the meaning of a message. In computer systems, devices that stand ready to handle transmission or processing, if and when the units normally used for the purpose fail or have to be taken offline.

Reel A flanged circular holder with a hole running from end-to-end onto which a roll of processed film is wound, usually designed to be inserted in a projector, reader, reader-printer, or other display device. Open reels were once used for magnetic tape, but have been largely replaced by cartridges. Compare with spool.

REF This abbreviation is used after a call number to indicate that a work shelved in the reference area and is non-circulating.

Referee In scholarly publishing, an expert whose areas of specialization include the subject of a journal article or book, usually a professional peer of the author, to whom the editor or publisher sends the manuscript for critical evaluation before accepting it for publication.

Refereed Journal - A publication, usually scholarly, in which articles are reviewed by a panel before being accepted for publication. Also sometimes called scholarly or peer reviewed.

Refereed publication A publication for which every submission is screened through a peer review process. Refereed publications are considered authoritative because disinterested experts have reviewed the material in advance of publication to determine its quality.

Reference A conventional word or phrase used in a work to refer the reader to another part of the text (see above or see below), or a similar word or phrase used in an index, catalog, or reference work to direct the user from one heading or entry to another (see or see also). Also refers to any Latin phrase used in footnotes, endnotes, and bibliographies to refer the reader to works previously quoted or cited, for example, ibid. And op. Cit. Sometimes used synonymously with citation.

Reference and User Services Association (RUSA) Established as a division of the American Library Association in 1972, RUSA has a membership consisting of librarians and other individuals committed to promoting the delivery of reference and information services to all persons, regardless of age, in libraries of all kinds. RUSA publishes the journal Reference and User Services Quarterly (RUSQ) and maintains the online newscenter RUSA Update. Click here to connect to the RUSA homepage.

Reference area This area contains atlases, guidebooks, bibliographies, directories, dictionaries and other information sources. The location symbol for these materials is REF.

Reference Assistance Services designed to teach skills and concepts that help you use and evaluate a variety of information resources best suited to your needs.

Reference book A book designed to be consulted when authoritative information is needed, rather than read cover-to-cover. Reference books often consist of a series of signed or unsigned "entries" listed alphabetically under headwords or headings, or in some other arrangement (classified, numeric, etc.). The category includes almanacs, atlases, bibliographies, biographical sources, catalogs, concordances, dictionaries, directories, discographies and filmographies, encyclopedias, glossaries, handbooks, indexes, manuals, research guides, union lists, and yearbooks, whether published commercially or as government documents. Long reference works may be issued in multivolume sets, with any indexes in the last volume. Reference works that require continuous updating may be published serially, sometimes as loose-leaf services.

Reference Books Bulletin (RBB) A separate section at the end of the review publication Booklist, providing reviews of approximately 500 reference books and electronic reference materials annually. General encyclopedias and certain types of dictionaries are often reviewed together to facilitate comparison. RBB has its own editorial board and, unlike Booklist, publishes reviews of items not recommended for purchase.

Reference collection Books not meant to be read cover-to-cover, such as dictionaries, handbooks, and encyclopedias, shelved together by call number in a special section of the library called the reference stacks. Reference books may not be checked out because they are needed by librarians to answer questions at the reference desk. Their location and circulation status is usually indicated by the symbol "R" or "Ref" preceding the call number in the catalog record and on the spine label.

Reference Consulting Area A place equipped with library workstations and printers for librarians to work with you one-on-one, located on the first floor near the Service Desk and the reference collection.

Reference desk collection Formerly known as "Ready Reference Collection" or "Ready Ref". Reference books used frequently by staff and/or patrons, shelved at the reference desk. Wooden dummies on the regular reference shelves indicate where the books are shelved.

Reference desk When a person has a question about

how to find specific information or how to use library services and resources, assistance can be obtained by contacting the public service point located near the reference collection of the library (in person, by telephone, or in some libraries via e-mail). A professionally trained reference librarian scheduled to work at the reference desk will try to provide an answer or refer the inquirer to a knowledgeable source. In large public and academic libraries, the reference desk may be staffed by two librarians, especially during periods of peak use. Compare with information desk.

Reference Desk/Reference Collection The reference desk is the place where librarians answer questions, give directions and guide patrons through their research. Often, there is a reference collection of books, computers, and other resources located near the reference desk. Librarians and patrons use these print and electronic materials to help find answers to questions and to help in the research process. A few examples of items found in a reference collection are dictionaries, encyclopedias, directories and almanacs.

Reference interview The interpersonal communication that occurs between a reference librarian and a library user to determine the person's specific information need(s), which may turn out to be different than the reference question as initially posed. Because patrons are often reticent, especially in face-to-face interaction, patience and tact may be required on the part of the librarian. A reference interview may occur in person, by telephone, or electronically (usually via e-mail) at the request of the user, but a well-trained reference librarian will sometimes initiate communication if a hesitant user appears to need assistance.

Reference librarian A librarian who works in public services, answering questions posed by library patrons at a reference desk, by telephone, or via e-mail. A reference librarian may also be called upon to provide point-of-use instruction on the use of library resources and information technology. Most reference librarians also assist in the selection of a balanced collection of reference materials to meet the information needs of the library's clientele.

Reference mark A printer's symbol used in text to refer to material printed in a different place, for example, in a footnote or in another passage on the same page. When more than one reference is given on a page, the order of symbols is: asterisk, dagger, double dagger, section mark, parallel mark, and paragraph mark. Numerals in superscript are preferred by most publishers to indicate the sequence of multiple references.

Reference Material Material designed to be consulted for brief items of information such as facts, statistics, background information, etc. Reference material can either be general in nature, such as the Encyclopedia Britannica or more specific, such as the Encyclopedia of Women and Sport in America.

Reference Microforms Room The area of the library that contains the pamphlet file and government documents that were published on microfiche.

Reference question A request from a library user for assistance in locating specific information or in using library resources in general, made in person, by telephone, or via e-mail. In most libraries, reference questions are answered by a professionally trained reference librarian during a regularly scheduled shift at the reference desk, but in small libraries this function may be performed by a paraprofessional. A reference interview may be required to determine the precise nature of the information need. Questions are usually recorded for statistical purposes by category (directional, informational, instructional, referral) in a transaction log.

Referencc Section A separate location for encyclopedias, handbooks, guides, directories, etc. These items do not circulate so that they will always be available for use in the library.

Reference serial A publication used by reference librarians to find authoritative information, which is issued successively at regular or irregular intervals with no indication of an ending date. The category includes dictionaries and encyclopedias (example: Contemporary Authors), directories (AV Market Place), annuals (Europa World Year Book), loose-leaf services (Facts on File), etc. Reference serials are normally placed on continuation order and shelved with other reference materials in the reference stacks.

Reference services All the functions performed by a trained librarian employed in the reference section of a library to meet the information needs of patrons (in person, by telephone, or via e-mail), including but not limited to answering substantive questions, instructing users in the selection and use of appropriate tools and techniques for finding information, conducting searches on behalf of the patron, directing users to the location of library resources, assisting in the evaluation of information, referring patrons to resources outside the library when appropriate, keeping reference statistics, and participating in the development of the reference collection.

Reference stacks The area of a library in which the reference collection is shelved in call number order, usually located near the reference desk, open to the public in most public and academic libraries in the United States. Printed periodical indexes may be shelved separately from the reference book collection, usually alphabetically by title or in a classified arrangement.

Reference statistics In most libraries, the librarians who work at the reference desk keep a daily transaction log in which they record reference questions, usually by hour and type of question (informational, directional, instructional, referral, etc.). Compiled by week, month, and year, the results are analyzed to reveal patterns and trends helpful in anticipating staffing needs, scheduling the reference desk, developing the reference collection, and planning new services. The librarian responsible for supervising reference services may also cite them in reports submitted to the library administration.

Reference transaction A reference transaction is an information contact that involves the knowledge, use, recommendations, interpretation, or instruction in the use of one or more information sources by a member of the library staff. The term includes information and referral service. Information sources include (a) printed and nonprinted material; (b) machine-readable databases (including computer-assisted instruction); (c) the library's own catalogs and other holdings records; (d) other libraries and institutions through communication or referral; and (e) persons both inside and outside the library.

Referral A type of reference transaction in which a patron with an information need is directed to a reputable person or agency outside the library, better qualified to provide assistance. In some public libraries, a list or index of referral agencies and resources, with contact information, is maintained at the reference desk for this purpose.

Referred Journals - Journals where the quality of the articles is maintained by a review process by experts prior to publication. The article submitted to refereed or peer reviewed journals are examined by one or more people with expertise in the field with which the article deals. The purpose of this is to give some assurance that the information in the article is valid.

Reforma Established in 1971 as an affiliate of the American Library Association, Reforma actively promotes the development of Spanish-language and Latino-oriented library collections, recruitment of bilingual and multicultural librarians and support staff, development of library programs and services for the Latino community, public awareness of library services among Latinos, lobbying on behalf of the information needs of Latinos, and liaison with other professional organizations.

Reformat To convert a document from one format to

another without changing its content, for example, a journal article published in print to microform for compact storage, or from print to ASCII text for inclusion in a full-text periodical database. In preservation, reformatting is usually undertaken when the long-term survival of a document in its current format is unlikely, for example, a work published electronically in a medium rapidly becoming obsolete, or a document printed on acid paper which is in an advanced state of deterioration.

Regional book A term used in the publishing industry for a book written to appeal to readers who live in, or have an interest in, a specific geographic area. Regional books are often published by small presses for sale in local bookstores or by mail-order. They include local histories, biographies, genealogies, directories, cookbooks, travel guides, field guides, etc. Some public libraries shelve them in a separate section to make them more accessible.

Regional library A public library serving the information needs of a group of communities or counties in the United States, supported by public funds provided by the units of government within its service area (example: the King County Library System in the Seattle metropolitan area).

Register The alignment of pages back-to-back during the printing of the second side of a sheet, to make the text blocks coincide exactly. In multicolor printing, the precise alignment of the impression for each color with the one(s) preceding it to produce an image that is in register (sharp), rather than out of register (blurred). Also refers to the list of symbols by which the signatures of a book are marked to indicate their sequence in binding.

Regular The frequency of a serial publication issued at intervals governed by an established rule, usually of uniform length, expressed in days, weeks, months, quarters, years, etc. (example: monthly with the exception of August and December). The opposite of irregular.

Reimburse To pay back money spent by another

person or compensate someone for damages or expenses incurred, usually upon presentation of a receipt verifying the amount. In libraries, employees may be reimbursed for travel expenses, office supplies purchased out of pocket, etc.

Reinforced binding A publisher's binding that has been strengthened, usually by adding a strip of cloth to each hinge and using stronger thread to sew the sections, but which does not meet the standards for prelibrary binding.

Reinstate To return something to a former condition, or a person to a position from which he or she has been removed, sometimes in compliance with the outcome of a grievance procedure or lawsuit.

Reinstatement A serial title which was dead is reactivated.

Reissue A second or subsequent impression of a previously published edition in which the text remains substantially the same, but the title page may be redesigned and the front matter and back matter altered.

Rejection slip A printed slip sent by a publisher with a returned manuscript to inform the author that the work has not been accepted for publication.

Rel Recorder element. The minimum distance between two recorded points (spots) in an imagesetter.

Related body A corporate body associated with another corporate body, but not functioning under its direct authority, for example, a Friends group that supports a library through volunteer work, fund raising, advocacy, and other activities, but is not a unit within its organizational structure. Compare with subordinate body.

Related term (RT or R) A descriptor or subject heading in a hierarchical classification system, closely related to another term conceptually, but not hierarchically (example: "Media Specialists" under "School Libraries"). A descriptor or subject heading may have more than one related term (example: "Children's libraries" under "School Libraries"). Compare with broader term (BT) and narrower term (NT).

Relationship As defined in FRBR (Functional Requirements for Bibliographic Records), the nature of the link between entities, for example, between one work and another (a "prequel to" Shakespeare's play Hamlet), between a work and one of its expressions (the film version of Hamlet "adapted and directed by" Kenneth Branagh), between an expression and one of its manifestations (Branagh's adaptation of Hamlet "embodied in" the videorecording released in 1997 by Columbia tristar Home Video), or between a manifestation and one of its items (a set of videocassettes "exemplifying" the 1997 videorecording of Branagh's interpretation of Hamlet).

Relative index A subject index to a classification system, indicating the classes under which subjects are listed, with their notations. In the Dewey Decimal Classification schedules, subjects are arranged by discipline. At the end of the schedules, an alphabetical index of subjects is provided (the Relative Index), indicating the disciplines in which each subject is found, listed in alphabetical order and indented under the heading for each subject, with the corresponding class numbers listed in a column on the right-hand side of the page. For example, the entry for the subject "Books" directs the cataloger to the discipline "Bibliographies" which has the notation 011, and also to "Publishing" (070.5), "Sociology" (302.232), and "Technology" (686).

Release date The date on which a motion picture or videorecording is officially made available for distribution to theaters for public viewing, or to wholesale and retail outlets for sale. In library cataloging, year of release is entered in the publication distribution, etc. Area of the bibliographic record representing the item. Compare with publication date.

Release print The final version of a motion picture, intended for distribution to public audiences, in some cases shorter than the director intended. In some cases, an initial print found to be too long is rereleased after having been cut (example: Disney's Fantasia). On very rare occasions, a motion picture from which important scenes were cut is rereleased after having been restored to its original length (Frank Capra's Lost Horizon). When such an item is cataloged by a library, the phrase "original restored version" is added as a note in the bibliographic description. Synonymous with showprint.

Release To allow copies of a recorded work to be issued, shown, or sold to the general public for the first time. In the case of motion pictures and videorecordings, to permit copies to be distributed for public viewing. In exceptional cases, a motion picture may be rereleased in significantly altered form. In library cataloging, the release date is used as the publication date in the bibliographic description..

Relevance ranking A feature of some search software which weights the documents or records retrieved in a search according to the degree to which they meet the requirements of the query. Ranked results are normally presented in decreasing order of relevance, computed on the basis of the number of occurrences of each search term in the document or record, and the weight assigned to the field(s) in which each term appears (title, subject headings, abstract, or full-text).

Relevance Search One of the search options available in the library catalog. When searching by Relevance, the retrieved records are automatically ranked according to how relevant they are to the keywords that were entered. The scheme give more importance to records that have the words in the title and subject headings, and records that have frequent occurrences of the words.

Relevance The extent to which information retrieved in a search of a collection or a resource, such as an online catalog or bibliographic database, is judged by the user to be "about" the subject of the query. Relevance depends on the searcher's subjective perception of the degree to which the document fulfills the information need, which may or may not have been expressed fully or with precision in the search statement. Measures of the effectiveness of information retrieval, such as precision and recall, depend on the relevance of search results. Compare with pertinence.

Relief map A topographic map showing the elevation of an area of the surface of the earth by means of standard graphic techniques, such as linear contour lines, hachures, shading, or tint. The U.S. Geological Survey (USGS) issues relief maps of the fifty states, available in the government documents collections of larger depository libraries. Compare with planimetric map.

Relievo binding A binding made from leather that is softened, then molded and deeply embossed, a technique used in 19th century England to introduce designs reflecting the Victorian revival of Gothic style. In Italian, relievo means "relief

Religious book A work of fiction or nonfiction in which the main theme is based on a particular religious faith. Included in the category are sacred texts, devotional works, materials for religious professionals, textbooks for religious education, and inspirational titles intended for laypersons. Some publishers specialize in religious works (examples: Zondervan, Judaica Press, and Kazi Publications). Large publishers may have a division devoted to religious publishing (example: Schocken Books within Random House). New Christian fiction is reviewed regularly in a separate section of Booklist. Religious books are sold in religious bookstores, through religious book clubs, and increasingly in trade bookstores. Public libraries select judiciously with an eye toward maintaining a balanced collection.

Relocation In Dewey Decimal Classification, the editorial decision to shift a subject from one class number to another in a new edition of the schedules, resulting in more than just a change in length of notation (example: "sociolinguistics" relocated in the 20th edition from 401.9 to 306.44).

Remainder mark A mark made by the publisher on the

bottom edge of a book, usually with a stamp, permanent marking pen, or spray paint to indicate that it has been remaindered, as a means of distinguishing it from copies sold at list price or regular discount.

Remainders A publisher's overstock (unsold copies of a book or other item) purchased by lot by a remainder dealer on the understanding that they may be offered for sale at a substantially reduced price. Bound remainders may be marked to distinguish them from copies sold at list price. Unbound remainders may be bound in an inexpensive remainder binding or reduced to pulp if there is no market for them.

Remake In printing, to rearrange the typographic elements on a printed page or in an entire publication, or to repaginate a publication (or a portion of it) from beginning to end..

Remboite From the French word remboiter meaning "to fit back into." A descriptive term for a book that has been rebound in covers removed from another volume, usually a binding that is in better condition, or more valuable or attractive.

Remote access Communication with a distant computer system or network as if one were a local user. To log on, the user may be required to enter an authorized username and/or password. Special communications software and/or hardware, such as a modem, may also be necessary. In most online library catalogs, a certain number of ports are reserved for remote access.

Remote assistance phones Phones available at remote locations ring directly to the Libraries' loan/reserve desk on the first floor. Each phone location has been given a Colorado Ghost Town name. Patrons may use phones to request assistance.

Remote login An interactive connection from your desktop computer over a network or telephone lines to a computer in another location (remote site).

Remote sensing image Image made by sensors, usually form an aircraft or spacecraft, which records features on the earth's surface.

Remote system Another computer on the Internet to which you connect. Interactions between computers are often described using the terms "local" and "remote" systems. The local system is your computer and the remote system is the other computer.

Remote users Distance Users are those members of the CSU community (faculty, staff and students) who are accessing library resources from a distance whether enrolled in a distance learning program or not.

Removes A printing term for notes or quotations set in smaller type at the foot of a page of text, for example, a book set in 12-point might have footnotes or endnotes set in 10-point or smaller type.

Renaissance librarian A librarian who cultivates a broad and deep understanding and appreciation of, and lively interest in, all aspects of librarianship, despite having developed at least one specialization.

Renew To extend the amount of time materials can be borrowed. Renewals can be done electronically on SAGE or by telephoning the loan desk. However, this applies only to materials owned by Colorado State University. Requests to renew interlibrary Loan items must be made through interlibrary Loan.

Renew To extend the period of time for which a book or other item is loaned by a library, usually by the length of the normal loan period. Renewal policies vary, but most libraries allow at least one renewal for most types of materials. To avoid fines, items checked out must be renewed by the borrower on or before the due date.

Renewal An extension of the loan period for a book or other item, usually for the length of the normal borrowing period. Also, the reregistration of a borrower at the end of an established period of library membership. Also refers to an extension of the period during which a periodical subscription is to be delivered following payment of a renewal fee by the subscriber.

Renewal notice A notice sent by the publisher of a periodical to inform a subscriber or subscription agent that unless a renewal fee is paid before a designated expiration date, the subscription will end.

Renovation A major refurbishing of existing facilities to make them appear new or like new. In a library, this can mean anything from repainting, recarpeting, and installing new ADA-compliant furnishings and equipment, to the complete gutting of an old building and reconstruction to meet current needs and contemporary design standards. Extensive renovation may require moving the library to a temporary location until alterations are completed. Major renovations are reported annually in Library Journal and in the Bowker Annual Library and Book Trade Almanac. Compare with expansion and new construction.

Rental collection Books in such high demand that they are circulated by a public library for a small fee, usually in multiple copies. Not all public libraries provide rental collections. Some use a waiting list or allow holds to be placed on high-demand items.

Reorder In library acquisitions and bookselling, any order for a stock item placed after the initial order has been received. Reordering is necessary when the original order is lost or canceled (usually because the item was unavailable when the order was first placed).

Repackaging Reissuing a previously published book in a different format to enhance its appeal to readers outside its primary market, sometimes by making it more affordable, as in a paperback edition, or easier to read, as in a large print edition.

Repaginated A book or other publication in which the numbers originally assigned to successive pages have been changed. Synonymous with repaged.

Repair flag A flag placed in a book or serial issue indicating the item or piece needs repair; to be sent to preservation.

Repairing The partial rehabilitation of a worn book or other item, including restoration of the cover and reinforcement of the hinges or joints, more extensive than mending, but less extensive than recasing or rebinding. In most libraries, repairs are done in-house.

Repairs Section within preservation service that has charge of mending materials for which rebinding is not necessary. Also known as the preservation lab.

Repeatable (R) A MARC field that may occur more than once in the same bibliographic record, for example, the 600 field, reserved for personal names used as subject added entries. A repeatable subfield may occur more than once in the same field. The opposite of nonrepeatable (NR).

Replacement A book or other item purchased by a library to take the place of a lost, damaged, or worn-out copy of the same title, not necessarily of the same edition if the original edition is out of print. Also, a copy sent by a publisher or jobber as a substitute for one found by a library or other purchaser to contain imperfections.

Replacement fund Officially called the Lost and Damaged Library Books Fund. This is an account used primarily to replace books, photocopy missing pages in books and journals, and aid in preservation of materials.

Replevin The recovery of archived property (records, manuscripts, documents, etc.) By an organization or institution claiming ownership. Also refers to the writ or legal action by which such property is recovered.

Replica A reproduction or copy of a work of art, especially one made by the artist who created the original, or produced under the artist's supervision. In a more general sense, any very close reproduction or copy of an object, especially one made on a smaller scale than the original.

Synonymous with doublette. Compare with facsimile and realia.

Report A separately published record of research findings, research still in progress, or other technical findings, usually bearing a report number and sometimes a grant number assigned by the funding agency.

Reporters Volumes containing opinions of particular courts or of courts in particular states (Law Library).

Repository The physical space (building, room, area) reserved for the permanent or intermediate storage of archival materials (manuscripts, rare books, government documents, papers, photographs, etc.). To preserve and protect archival collections, modern repositories are equipped to meet current standards of environmental control and security. Whether a repository is open or closed to the public depends on the policy of the parent institution. Sometimes used synonymously with depository.

Repository: synonymous with depository.

Representative fraction (RF) In cartography, the relationship of scale between distance on a map or chart and the actual distance on the surface of land or sea represented on the map, given in the legend as a ratio understood to be in standard units of measurement (example: 1:1,00,000).

Reprint A new impression of an existing edition, often made by photographic means, or a new edition made from a new setting of type which is a copy of a previous impression, with no alterations in the text except perhaps the correction of typographical errors. The work may also be given a redesigned title page and cover. The date of reprinting is usually included in the details of publication on the verso of the title page. The review publication Library Journal includes a "Classic Returns" section in each issue, highlighting recent reprints. Compare with reissue.

Reprint book A collection consisting of articles previously published in one or more magazines or journals. The articles are used in their original format as camera-ready copy, rather than reset by the printer in uniform typographic style.

Reprint publisher A publishing company that specializes in new impressions of previously published titles which the original publisher has allowed to go out of print, despite continuing demand. Reprint rights must be negotiated with the copyright holder. The number of copies in a reprint edition is usually less than in the original edition.

Reproduction A close copy of a work of art made mechanically or by hand for the commercial market, for example, a printed poster of a painting or drawing. Reproductions of large works are usually done on a smaller scale than the original. Price usually depends on quality and fidelity to the original. Also refers to an exact copy of a written or printed document made by mechanical or electronic means, for example, a photocopy.

Reprography A general term encompassing the processes of document reproduction or copying, by any method except large-scale professional printing, including photography, microphotography, photocopying, and photoduplication. For a more detailed overview of the various methods, please see the entry by J. E. Davies in the International Encyclopedia of Information and Library Science (New York: Routledge, 1997).

Republication The process by which a previously published work is reissued by a different publisher, without alteration of the text. Sometimes refers to the reprinting of such a work in another country. Also refers to any publication reissued in this manner.

Request An online service on SAGE which allows patrons to request items that are checked out or in storage. You must establish a PIN number to use this service. See also RECALL.

Request codes/names Specific areas or persons designated to be notified when a piece has been cataloged and is available.

Request form Form used by faculty, student, or staff requesting purchase of a book or other library materials.

Request item Command used when a borrower wants the library to hold an item for him or her. Patrons are able to place their own requests in IPAC and webpac using their library card number and PIN.

Required if applicable and readily available (R) Under OCLC input standards, a field or subfield of the MARC record in which data must be entered if 1) appropriate in AACR2 or essential for efficient access or effective processing, and 2) it is available in or on the item at hand, from other bibliographic records in the OCLC online union catalog, or from OCLC authority file records. Compare with mandatory and optional.

Requisition A written request, usually submitted to the acquisitions department of a library on a standardized form, for the order of materials, equipment, supplies, or services. Compare with purchase order.

Rerun In printing, a job redone because the quality of the first press run was not acceptable. Also refers to the rebroadcast of previously released television programming, more common during the summer months than at other times of the year.

Res A term used to define image resolution instead of ppi. Res 12 indicates 12 pixels per millimeter.

Resampling An increase or reduction in the number of pixels in an imge, required to change its resolution without altering its size. See also down-sampling and interpolation.

Research collection A library collection sufficiently comprehensive to support specialized research in an academic discipline or field. A good research collection includes primary sources, secondary sources, and the bibliographic tools needed to conduct an exhaustive search of the literature. Development of such a collection requires considerable time, and the knowledge and experience of one or more subject specialists.

Research guide A printed or online resource that provides detailed information, instructions, and advice concerning the best strategies, techniques, and resources for research in a subject or field of study. Book-length research guides are usually shelved in the reference section of a library (example: Shakespeare: A Study and Research Guide by David M. Bergeron and Geraldo U. De Sousa). Most academic libraries provide one- or two-page handouts on a display rack near the reference desk, explaining research techniques and listing finding tools appropriate to each discipline.

Research Index researchindex is a scientific literature digital library that aims to improve the dissemination and feedback of scientific literature. Includes over 400000 documents and over 5 million citations.

Research Libraries Group (RLG) Founded in 1974, RLG is a consortium of over 160 universities, national libraries, archives, historical societies, museums, and related institutions with substantial collections for research and learning. Devoted to improving access to information through collaboration, RLG maintains the RLIN online bibliographic database of nearly 88 million items and publishes Research Libraries Group News in three issues per year.

Research Libraries Information Network (RLIN) An information management and retrieval system consisting of an online union catalog of the holdings of members of the Research Libraries Group (RLG) combined with the English Short Title Catalog (ESTC) and authority files. RLIN contains over 88 million records and is used by hundreds of libraries, archives, and museums for cataloging, interlibrary loan, and control of manuscript and archival collections.

Research library A library containing a comprehensive collection of materials in a specific field, academic discipline, or group of disciplines, including primary and secondary sources, selected to meet the information needs of serious researchers (example: Folger Shakespeare Library in Washington D.C.). The primary emphasis in research libraries is on the accumulation of materials and the provision of access services to scholars qualified to make use of them. In most large research libraries, access to collections containing rare books and manuscripts is restricted

Research Library Information Network (RLIN) Machine-readable database including information from the CSUL card catalog as well as from the catalogs of other RLG member and user institutions, and the Library of Congress. CSUL previously used this database; currently uses OCLC.

Research paper A written composition, usually five or more pages in length, assigned as an exercise in a formal course of study. The writer is expected to state a thesis and advance a logical argument based on supporting information found in a systematic investigation of the topic. The source of quotations, facts, and ideas not those of the author must be documented in footnotes or endnotes, and a bibliography.

Research Systematic, painstaking investigation of a topic, or in a field of study, often employing techniques of hypothesis and experimentation, undertaken by a person intent on revealing new facts, theories, or principles, or determining the current state of knowledge of the subject. The results of original research are usually reported in a primary journal, in conference proceedings, or in a monograph by the researcher(s) who conducted the study. In the sciences, methodology is also reported to allow the results to be verified.

Researcher A person who conducts a careful, systematic investigation of a subject, or inquiry in a field of study, to establish facts, reveal underlying principles, and determine the current state of knowledge.

Reserve Bank of India Provides free of cost online access and download to vast amount of data related to banks and banking in India.

Reserve desk Section of access services where books selected by faculty for required class reading are segregated and loaned for limited periods.

Reserve Materials Specific books, periodical articles, and other materials which faculty require students to read for a particular course. These materials are set aside for short term use in the library for specific courses and are available at the Circulation Desk.

Reserve recall Recall used when a book is needed for Reserve.

Reserves - Material that has been set aside in the library by an instructor for the use of her students. Reserves may either be available in print/hard copy (ask at the circulation desk) or online (accessible via the "Service Forms" page, which is linked from the Andersen Library home page). NOTE: MS Word, or a program than can read MS Word files, is required to view this document.

Reshelve area: stacks in which materials that have just been gathered up after use are rough-sorted and held until shelvers return them to their homes. Marriott's reshelve area is located on Level 2 in the former auditorium.

Reshelving cart A double-sided wheeled cart equipped with 2-3 shelves to hold recently returned items until they are aready to be transported to the stacks and placed back on the shelf. If a book or periodical volume is listed as available in the catalog but is "not on the shelf" (nos), it may be on a cart waiting to be reshelved. Some online catalogs indicate in the catalog record the circulation status of items recently returned. Synonymous with book truck.

Reshelving The job of returning books and other items to the shelves of a library in correct call number sequence after they have been used, usually performed by a student assistant in an academic library or by a staff member called a page in a public library.

Residuum The portion of an author's total body of work, considered by scholars and critics to be of lasting value.

Resignation Formal notice of an employee's intention to terminate employment, usually given to the employer in writing, effective on a specific date. Most employment contracts require 30-60 days notice to allow the employer sufficient time to reallocate workload while a search for a replacement is conducted. Compare with retirement.

Resized A printed sheet or leaf in a book that has been washed, usually to remove writing, stains, or acid from the paper, and then recoated with a sizing compound to add stiffness and provide a protective finish.

Resnet A direct network connection available in OSU residence halls. Resnet is supported by OSU Housing, Food Services and Event Centers.

Resolution In general, this refers to how sharp and clear an image looks on screen or on paper, and how much detail you can see. It's usually determined by the number of dots (or pixels) per square inch (the more there are, the higher the resolution) and is used to describe printers, monitors, and scanners.

Resource sharing The activities that result from an agreement, formal or informal, among a group of libraries (usually a consortium or network) to share collections, data, facilities, personnel, etc., for the benefit of their users and to reduce the expense of collection development.

Resources services An operation of the library that provides services which are related to materials and their use by library patrons and staff. Comprised of the Annex, the former General Technical Services, and the Library Technology Team.

Respect des fonds A French term for the principle of provenance under which the archival records of an agency or individual are maintained separately according to source, rather than combined or intermingled with those of different origin.

Respondent A candidate for an academic degree who must defend, against one or more opponents, a thesis proposed by a faculty moderator acting as the praeses in a formal disputation.

Response time In computing, the amount of time that

elapses between the submission of input (a query, command, data, etc.) And the return of results (output) by the system. On the Internet, response time depends on speed of connection and amount of traffic on the network, which varies with time of day, day of week, etc. When a server goes offline, response time may be delayed indefinitely. Compare with turnaround time.

Restoration In conservation, the physical process of returning a damaged, worn, or otherwise altered document to its original condition, or as close an approximation of the original condition as possible. Before restoration can begin, deterioration must be stabilized by whatever method is most appropriate. To preserve the evidential value of an item in its altered condition, care should be taken to make repairs both visible and reversible (if possible).

Restricted access The privilege of using a library collection under specific conditions established as a matter of library policy. In archives and special collections, the use of rare books, manuscripts, and other unique and valuable materials may be limited to a particular room or a certain method, or by appointment only. In the United States, large private university libraries may limit access to the stacks to registered students, faculty, and staff, and to outside researchers granted special permission to use specific collections. The opposite of unrestricted. Compare with controlled access.

Results Ranking The order in which search results appear. Each search tool uses its own unique algorithm. Most use "fuzzy and" combined with factors such as how often your terms occur in documents and whether they occur in title or how near the top of the text. Ranking of the same sort of items is automatic in almost all systems.

Resume A summing up. In hiring, a statement of the experience and qualifications an applicant brings to the position. Handbooks on resume preparation are available in the reference section of most public and academic libraries. The New Members Round Table (NMRT) of the American

Library Association provides a resume review service for recent library school graduates.

Retention Holding or keeping materials in possession, usually in a desired state or condition, as opposed to disposing of them. In archives, the retention period for documents is usually indicated in the disposition schedule. Academic and research libraries generally purchase materials with the intention of retaining them indefinitely; public libraries weed on the basis of circulation. Long-term retention of library materials may require preservation measures, such as reformatting.

Retention period In archives, the length of time that records of a specific category or origin must be retained before they are transferred to intermediate storage or given some other disposition. In the absence of statutory or regulatory stipulations, the period is usually determined by current usage and projected need.

Retirement Resignation from a position of employment with the intention of ending a career, a step usually taken at an age when the retiree is in a position to live on other income (pension, retirement savings, social security, etc.). Early retirement is resignation before the age at which most employees cease working, sometimes in response to a special offer of eligibility or compensation made by management ("golden handshake"). Under a policy of mandatory retirement, employees are not allowed to continue working beyond a certain age.

Retitled edition All the copies of a book reissued under a title that is not the same as the title of the original edition. In AACR2, the original title is entered as a note in the bibliographic description when the item is cataloged.

Retro order Retrospective order. The one-time ordering of back issues of a journal or serial to complete the set.

Retrofit To adapt an older library facility to accommodate improvements in information technology, a process that often involves not only the installation of new equipment and furnishings, but may also require structural alterations, reallocation of space, changes in lighting and HVAC, additional electrical and telecom wiring, and attention to noise control, traffic patterns, etc.

Retrospective bibliography A bibliography restricted to materials published in the past, usually limited to a specific period of time (example: Agriculture and the GATT: A Retrospective Bibliography, 1948-1980 by Wayne K. Olson). The opposite of current bibliography.

Retrospective conversion The process of converting existing bibliographic records from manual, human-readable form, such as a cards in a card catalog, into machine-readable format, usually by matching the old records one-at-a-time to those contained in an authoritative database of machine-readable records. Once a match is made, the cataloger downloads as much of the machine-readable record as the library needs, usually for a modest fee. In the United States, OCLC provides most of the MARC records used in retrospective conversion. Abbreviated recon. Compare with recataloging.

Retrospective Including works created or published in the past, rather than current or recently issued materials, as in a retrospective bibliography. In a more general sense, anything pertaining to events or activities that occurred in the past, rather than the present, as in the retrospective conversion of existing bibliographic records to another format.

Retrospective search A search for information that is no longer current. Bibliographic databases that support this type of searching usually index information in repositories and archival collections in which documents may be added but are rarely modified or removed. Some search software allows the user to specify a publication date range, to exclude current materials.

Return policy The conditions established by a publisher under which items ordered, shipped, and delivered may be returned for credit by a library or bookseller. Items received in damaged condition, not the fault of the receiver, are understood to be returnable. The return policy for undamaged items is normally stated on the publisher's invoice, usually in code, NR or XR indicating no returns or nonreturnable. Items that have been processed or specially bound at the request of the purchaser are not returnable unless a major defect is found within a reasonable time. When an item is returned for a valid reason, a replacement copy is usually sent by the publisher.

Return to Andersen Library Catalog A button that appears in the Andersen Library Catalog when using Universal Borrowing. When clicked, the portal to other UW-system library catalogs is closed, and the user is returned to the Basic Search screen prepared to search only local holdings.

Returnable In interlibrary loan, materials that the lending library expects the borrowing library to return, usually within a designated period of time unless renewed, as opposed to materials, such as photocopied articles, provided without expectation of return.

Returns Books or other items sent back to the publisher by a bookseller who purchased them under terms allowing unsold stock to be returned for credit. Also, items returned to a publisher or jobber by a library under an approval plan or book lease plan, or because they were found upon delivery to be damaged or defective. The conditions under which items may be returned for credit are stated in the publisher's return policy. On the invoice, the symbol **NR** or **XR** indicates that returns are not allowed.

Reverse chronological The arrangement of data, records, items, headings, entries, etc., according to their relation in time, from the most recent to the earliest. In online catalogs and bibliographic databases, the default display of records retrieved in a keywords search is often reverse chronological order. The opposite of chronological.

Reversibility In document conservation, the degree to which a procedure can be undone without adversely affecting the condition of the item. As a general rule, reversible procedures are preferred because future research or legal developments may require that the item be restored to its original condition. However, since complete reversibility may be difficult to achieve, it must be balanced against other priorities.

Review An evaluative account of a recent artistic performance or exhibit, or of a newly published literary or scholarly work, usually written and signed by a qualified person, for publication in a current newspaper, magazine, or journal. The account can be descriptive, reportorial, comparative, critical, or serve as a vehicle for a lengthy essay in which the reviewer discusses several recently published works (omnibus review) or a broader topic for which the works reviewed serve as a springboard. In libraries, selection decisions are based primarily on reviews. Synonymous with critique. Compare with puff.

Review article an article that evaluates the published research on a topic. The purpose of a review article is to select the most important publications on the topic, sort them into categories, and comment on them so that a researcher can gain a quick overview of the state of the art in that area.

Review copy A complimentary copy of a new book or other work in its final form, sent by the publisher at no charge to a person who writes reviews, to the editor(s) of a periodical that publishes reviews, to an opinion leader in the field covered, or to a bookseller in the hope of attracting favorable comment, often with a review slip laid in. Synonymous with press copy. Compare with advance copy.

Review lag The interbal of time between the publication of a new book, or the release or first performance of a creative work, and the appearance of reviews. For popular fiction and nonfiction written by well-known authors, the delay may be a matter of days or weeks, especially if galleys or review copies are distributed by the publisher to prospective reviewers in advance of the publication date, but for scholarly titles, the lag may exceed a year.

Review publication A newspaper, magazine, or journal devoted primarily to publishing reviews of new books and other publications (serials, nonprint media, etc.). Some also provide feature articles, regular columns, author interviews, literature reviews, etc., and most include book announcements and other advertising. Directory information for review publications is available in Literary Market Place.

Review slip A brief notice or form letter sent by the publisher of a new book to a book reviewer or bookseller with a free copy of the work, informing the recipient that the item is a review copy and requesting its consideration.

Reviewer A person who writes a brief or extended evaluation of a new book or other creative work, usually at the request of the editor of a publication that includes reviews. Scholarly works are usually reviewed by the author's peers. Reviews published in library review publications, such as CHOICE, Library Journal, and Booklist, are written by librarians and academic professionals actively engaged in collection development. In the performing arts, reviews are written by critics whose response can determine the success or failure of a production.

Revised edition An edition in which the text of a previously published work is substantially altered by correction, deletion, and/or addition, either by the original author or editor, or by another writer, usually to expand the content or bring it up-to-date. Some revised editions are not as "revised" as they claim to be (caveat emptor). The extent of revision may be indicated in a new foreword or preface. Frequency of revision usually depends on the amount of new material available, but may also be linkd to a decline in sales of the preceding edition. In library cataloging, the abbreviation Rev. Ed. Is given in the of the bibliographic record to indicate that an edition is revised. Usually synonymous with second edition. Compare with expanded edition.

Revision Text that has been altered by the original author, or by another writer, usually to correct, amend, update, or otherwise improve it. In books, the result may be published as a revised edition. Compare with rewrite.

Rewritable A digital storage medium capable of being written, erased, and rewritten repeatedly, for example, magnetic tape or disk, as opposed to a medium that is read only or write once, read many (WORM).

Rewrite To put text already written into different words or form, making more extensive changes than in a revision. In journalism, to convert news copy submitted in rough form by one or more reporters into a version suitable for publication.

RFC In the Internet community, Request For Comments are the working notes of the Internet research and development community. These documents contain protocol and model descriptions, experimental results, and reviews. All Internet standard protocols are written up as rfcs. The document series, begun in 1969, which describes the Internet suite of protocols and related experiments. Not all (in fact very few) rfcs describe Internet standards, but all Internet standards are written up as rfcs. The RFC series of documents is unusual in that the proposed protocols are forwarded by the Internet research and development community, acting on their own behalf, as opposed to the formally reviewed and standardized protocols that are promoted by organizations such as CCITT and ANSI. A complete list of rfcs can be found at http://www.internic.net/rfc/. FYI An abbreviation for the phrase "for your information." There is also a series of rfcs put out by the Network Information Center called fyis; they address common questions of new users and many other useful things. See section Requests for Comments for instructions on retrieving fyis. Internet Relay Chat (IRC) . A protocol that allows users to converse with others in real time. IRC is structured as a network of servers, each of which accepts connections from client programs. It is a program for synchronous (real-time) communication. Users can log on to an IRC server and choose a channel to participate in or create a new channel.

RGB Red, green, and blue; the primary colors that are mixed to display the color of pixels on a computer monitor. Every color of emitted light can be created by combining these three colors in varying levels.

Rhyming dictionary A dictionary in which the words of a language are listed alphabetically by phonetic ending to assist writers of verse. In libraries, rhyming dictionaries are usually shelved in the language section of the reference collection. They are also available online (see rhymezone from Lycos).

Riddle A puzzle or problem in the form of a misleading statement or question containing clues expressed in a manner requiring ingenuity and a sense of humor to arrive at the correct answer or solution (in the parlor game "Charades" the clues are visual). Exceedingly popular with young readers, collections of riddles are available in the juvenile section of most public libraries.

Rights The exclusive privilege of receiving the benefits associated with ownership of a literary property, the most important of which is the right of first publication, protected under copyright law in most countries. In the case of books, volume rights give the publisher the exclusive right to publish a work in volume form within a specific geographic territory, including the right to reprint in paperback, book club, or textbook edition, and to reprint the work in its entirety in a single issue of a periodical or in an anthology. Subsidiary rights include serialization, abridgment, translation, foreign publication, excerpt, quotation, reproduction, commercial exploitation, and adaptation for performance on stage, as a motion picture, or on radio or television. Rights may be transferred or sold by the owner to another person or entity.

Ring binding A form of loose-leaf binder consisting of a number of metal rings (usually three) fixed in a metal or hard plastic spine. The rings are designed to open, usually at the center, by means of pressure tabs at the top and bottom of the spine, allowing prepunched leaves to be individually added or removed, used in libraries for materials such as loose-leaf services that require frequent updating. Unlike post bindings, ring bindings open flat.

RIP Routing Information Protocol used by Berkeley UNIX systems to exchange routing information among a set of computers attached to a network. RIP packets are sent and received by a program called routed.

RLIN (Eureka) The Research Libraries Information Network (RLIN), is an information management and retrieval system used by hundreds of comprehensive research libraries, archival repositories, museums, academic, public, law, technical, and corporate libraries to build an international database of bibliographic information. The RLIN database indexes books, journals, and other materials held by full-member Research Library Group (RLG) libraries. Cornell researchers can identify and locate materials in other research libraries and collections using RLIN, and order these materials through interlibrary loan. As a member of RLG, records for many of the Cornell University Library's holdings will show up in this database. RLIN is available through the catalog and Find Databases.

RLIN ILL Subsystem This subsystem allows electronic mail delivery delivery of an interlibrary loan request to member institutions, automatically transferring it to up to six libraries.

RLO Responsible Library Officer. By policy, this is the most senior supervisor in access services at the time of an emergency, safety or security issue. A master list of RLO names and phone numbers is updated regularly. An RLO is typically the on-site senior person, but guidance/instruction can also come remotely. The Coordinator of access services is the chief RLO

Road atlas A book of maps showing the roads, highways, towns, and cities in a specific state, province, region, or country, often with mileage between major destinations (example: Rand mcnally Road Atlas and Vacation Guide). Updated annually for retail sale to motorists and travelers, most include an index of place names (gazetteer) at the end, giving the location of cities, towns, and other geographic features by means of grid coordinates on the road maps. For an interactive online road atlas, see mapquest.

Road map A map showing the location of the roads and highways passable to motorized vehicles within a given area (county, state, province, country), for the use of motorists and travelers. Smaller in scale than a city map, a road map usually includes a table of distances between major towns and cities, a gazetteer, one or more larger-scale inset maps of major metropolitan areas, and symbols indicating service and rest areas, scenic routes, toll roads, major parks and museums, campgrounds, airports, etc. A road atlas is a collection of road maps covering a large area, usually bound in the form of a book or pamphlet.

Roan A thin, soft, flexible sheepskin, usually dyed a dark color, used in bookbinding from the late 18th century as a substitute for morocco which was more elegant, but also more expensive.

ROGER On-line catalog at UCSD for books and other material in the libraries at the University of California at San Diego.

Roll A manuscript written on a sheet of vellum or parchment, not folded but rolled up for storage on a shelf or in a box or cylindrical receptacle called a scrinium. Compare with scroll. Also refers to a list of names, especially the members of an organization, assembly, or official body, used to "call the roll" in a roll-call vote.

ROM Read Only Memory; a special type of memory used to store programs that start a computer and do diagnostics. Data stored in ROM can only be read and cannot be removed even when your computer is turned off. Most personal computers have only a few thousand bytes of ROM. Contrast to RAM (random access or main memory) which is the amount of memory available for use by programs on your computer.

Roman a clef French for "novel with a key." A form of novel in which real people or institutions are given fictitious names, but depicted in such a way that well-informed readers can penetrate the disguise. Such works are often satirical, for example, Robert Penn Warren's thinly veiled characterization of the Louisiana demagogue Huey Long in All the King's Men. Compare with historical fiction.

Roman a these French for "novel with a thesis." A form of novel in which the author presents a moral dilemma or social problem in order to advance a specific point of view or programmatic solution, instead of leaving the resolution to the reader (example: The Grapes of Wrath by John Steinbeck). Synonymous with problem novel and protest novel.

Roman numeral A system of numerals developed by the ancient Romans, used throughout Europe prior to the introduction of arabic numerals in the 11th century. Capital letters of the Latin alphabet are used to indicate number, either alone (I=1, V=5, X=10, L=50, C=100, D=500, and M=1,000) or in combination, according to established conventions (IV = 4, VI = 6, IX=9, XI=11, etc.). In printing, roman numerals are used for chapter headings, lists, dates, and in lowercase to paginate the front matter of a book.

Roman The formal Latin alphabet consisting of minuscule (lowercase) and majuscule (uppercase) letters, as distinct from gothic or black letter. Minuscules were adapted from the noncursive book hand used in medieval Europe; majuscules evolved from the capitals used in the inscriptions carved on tombs and other stone monuments by the ancient Romans.

Romance A type of narrative in which the primary themes are passionate love and adventure, usually depicted in an exotic rather than realistic setting, involving characters that are larger than life stereotypes. Most contemporary romance is written to appeal to female readers. The origins of romance as a literary form can be traced to the gothic novel of the 18th century and the earlier tradition of medieval chivalry. Nineteenth century romanticism revived the romance in verse form, and also in the visual arts.

Roman-fleuve A French term for a form of novel in which the narrative covers the fortunes of an entire family, sometimes over several generations (example: One Hundred Years of Solitude by Gabriel Garcia Marquez).

Romanization The transliteration of words, names, titles, or text from non-roman script into the letters of the roman alphabet.

Root The first directory in a hierachy of directories and subdirectories.

Rosetta Stone A smooth slab of black basalt, approximately 2.5 feet wide and 3.75 feet high, bearing the same inscription, a decree honoring Ptolemy V Epiphanes written in 196 BC in two languages: Greek and Egyptian. The Egyptian version of the text is carved in hieroglyphs and in the demotic cursive script. Discovered in Egypt in 1799 by a party of French soldiers under the command of Napoleon Bonaparte, the stone was subsequently used by the British physicist Thomas Young and the French Egyptologist Jean-Francois Champollion to decipher the meaning of Egyptian hieroglyphic writing.

Rotated display An alphabetically arranged display of all the significant words contained in the descriptors listed in a thesaurus of indexing terms, in which each word is treated as a filing unit. Descriptors are repeated in the alphabetic sequence under each of their significant words, single-word descriptors appearing only once. Word order within terms is not altered. The following example is from the Rotated Descriptor Display in the Thesaurus of ERIC Descriptors.

Rotating display A highly compact bookcase with shelves on four faces, mounted on a cylindrical spindle that allows it to be turned by the person browsing its contents, used in libraries for displaying paperbacks and media items (videocassettes, cds, etc.). Synonymous with rotor display and revolving case.

Rotation A method of scheduling shifts at a library service point in which a group of librarians or other staff members take turns, usually in predetermined sequence. Evening and weekend reference desk hours are often scheduled in this manner to distribute workload equitably.

ROTF Commonly used in electronic communications to express humor; an acronym meaning "rolling on the floor". A similar acronym is "ROTFLML" which means "rolling on the floor madly laughing". Can be written in either upper- or lower case.

Rotulus A manuscript in the form of length of papyrus, parchment, or vellum written on one side only and stored in a hollow roll. The oldest examples are from ancient Egypt. Compare with scroll.

Rotunda A type of gothic script developed in Italy and Spain during the Middle Ages. The broad, round letterforms of rotunda retained some of the features of the earlier Carolingian script. Widely used by scribes for copying theological, legal, and scholastic texts, its use eventually spread north of the Alps. After the invention of printing from movable type in the mid-15th century, it was adapted for use in typefaces.

Rough Calfskin given a suede-like nap, instead of the usual polished surface, used in binding from the 17th century onwards. Synonymous with reversed calf.

Rough edges A generic term used in bookbinding to refer to the irregular deckle edges of paper left uncut by the binder in some editions, more difficult to clean than trimmed edges when books are exposed to dust.

Round table In modern usage, a group established to discuss on an ongoing basis a range of topics and/or issues of concern to its members, usually within the context of a larger organization. The original "Round Table" preserved at Winchester, England is believed to have been the center around which the King Arthur of medieval legend met with his knights, its shape intended to prevent quarrels over pre-eminence.

Rounding In bookbinding, a procedure performed after first gluing, before the lining is applied to the back. In rounding, the binding edge of the sewn sections is hammered or otherwise physically manipulated to give the spine a convex shape in preparation for backing. The procedure gives the book a concave fore-edge, diminishes swell, and prevents the binding edge from falling forward with extended use, or from the force of gravity as a result of standing upright for years on the shelf. Compare with flat back.

Router A special purpose computer that attaches to two or more networks and routes packets from one network to the other. A router uses network layer addresses (such as IP Addresses) to determine if packets should be sent from one network to another. Routers send packets to other routers until they arrive at their final destination.

Routine A component of a computer program, written to execute a given operation or function under specific conditions, for example, an error routine. Also refers to an operation or procedure which, if performed regularly in the same manner, increases efficiency.

Routine revision - Updates terminology, clarifies notes, provides modest expansions of existing notation

Routing slip A list attached to the front cover of a new document or periodical issue, giving the names of the people within a department or organization who would like to receive it. Each person crosses his or her name off the list when finished, then sends the item to another on the list. After the last person has seen the item, it is returned to the person responsible for processing, filing, or disposing of it.

Routing The routine circulation of new publications, such as the current issues of library journals, to a list of library staff in accordance with their preferences, to allow them to keep abreast of recent developments in their field(s) of interest and specialization.

Roving In the delivery of reference services, the practice of discreetly walking about the reference area of a library in search of users who need assistance, as opposed to remaining seated at the reference desk, waiting for patrons to approach with their questions. Experienced reference librarians learn to tell by body language and other nonverbal cues when a user is experiencing difficulty. They may initiate a reference interview by politely asking if the person is finding the information needed. In large libraries, when two librarians are scheduled on reference duty at the same time, one may rove while the other remains at the desk.

Royalties A term used in the book trade for the regular payments made by a publisher to the author or creator of a work for copies sold, based on a percentage of the published price (usually 10-15 percent). Negotiated in advance by the parties or their agents, royalties and advance on royalty are stipulated in the book contract. Most publishers have an established policy concerning royalty percentage, but in the case of books with high sales potential, a higher percentage may be offered as an inducement to sign.

Rpi Rels (recorder elements) per inch. A measurement of the number of discrete steps that exposure units in imagesetting devices can make per inch.

Rpm Revolutions per minute, a unit of measurement indicating the playing speed of a phonograph record. The most common speed is 33 rpm (long-playing).

RS-232 Interface between Data Terminal Equipment (DTE) and Data Communications Equipment (DCE) employing Serial Binary Data Interchange, a standard set by the international standards organization - Consultative Committee on International Telegraphy and Telephony. The interface between a terminal to a modem for the transfer of serial data.

RSIG Resource Services Implementation Group; body made up of representatives from different units of Resource Services charged with resolving issues of workflow, policy, etc. For Resource Services.

RSS (Rich Site Summary or RDF Site Summary or Real Simple Syndication) XML-based summary of a web site, used for syndication, etc.

RTF Rich Text Format; a type of document formatting that enables special characteristics like fonts and margins to be included within an ASCII file. May be used when a document must be shared among users with different kinds of computers (e.g., IBM PC or compatibles and Macintoshes).

Rubbed The condition of a book that has a visibly chafed binding, but is otherwise undamaged. Compare with scuffed.

Rubber stamp A small block of wood or metal covered on one side with a thin layer of rubber into which letters, numbers, and/or a design have been cut in relief. When inked and pressed against a smooth, clean surface, the block leaves a mark, used in libraries to stamp ownership marks on books and other materials, and to stamp the due date on items at the time they are checked out. Some models are self-inking.

Rubric An initial letter, word, chapter heading, title, or other part of a work, written in red or blue ink, in contrast to the text which is written or printed in black, a technique used to embellish hand-copied medieval manuscripts and early printed books. A book decorated in this way is said to be rubricated. A person who pens such letters is a rubricator or rubrisher. Compare with illuminated initial.

Rule A thin metal strip of type-height, used to print continuous lines, or lines of dots or pattern, as in a plain or decorative border around a title page. Rule-borders on bindings can be in blind or gilt. Thickness of rule (measured in points) determines thickness of line. A rule may be thicker at the center with tapered ends.

Rule interpretation (RI) A formal explanation, clarification, or expansion of existing cataloging rules, usually resulting from a case that raises questions concerning the applicability of established policy and/or procedure. Ris are issued by the cataloging agency responsible for administering the catalog code; in the case of AACR2, by the Cataloging Distribution Service of the Library of Congress.

Rule of application The instruction in Dewey Decimal Classification to classify works about the application of one subject to another under the second of the two, for example, the classification of a monograph on the literary influence of Ovid on Chaucer with works about Chaucer.

Rule of three The instruction in Dewey Decimal Classification to classify works in which equal treatment is given to three or more subjects (all subdivisions of a more general subject) under the first higher class number encompassing them all..

Rule of zero In Dewey Decimal Classification, when two or more class numbers are found to be equally suitable for a work, the cataloger is instructed to avoid subdivisions beginning with zero if there is a choice between 0 and 1-9 at the same point in the notation, and to avoid subdivisions beginning with 00 when there is a choice between 00 and 0.

Rums A slang expression used by London booksellers of the 18th century for a miscellaneous assortment of unsaleable books, probably derived from the tell-tale odor imparted by the previous contents of the wooden barrels used to store them.

Run In printing, the number of impressions taken from

a plate or setting of type at one time. A completed job is said to have been run-off.

Run on chapter A chapter that does not begin on a new page, but is set immediately following the end of the text of the preceding chapter, usually to minimize the amount of paper required to print the work. In quality printing, it is standard practice to begin a new chapter on the recto of the leaf following the last page of the preceding chapter.

Run-around In printing, a reduction in the line width of a column of type, on either the left- or right-hand side, to accommodate an illustration or note set into the text. Synonymous with set-around.

Rune A letter or character of the earliest Scandinavian and Anglo-Saxon alphabet. Also refers to the characters carved on metal, wood, or stone by the ancient Teutonic peoples of northern Europe. In a more general sense, an aphorism, riddle, or saying believed to have mystical meaning or magical powers.

Runners A sequence of numbers or letters printed at regular intervals down one or both side margins in a book to indicate the position of any line on a page. Used in long poems, dramatic scripts, and text in a foreign language, to enable the reader to reference a specific line (or lines) by page number.

Running foot The line of type printed below the text at the bottom of a page in a book or periodical, uniform in style and content, usually giving the same information as a running head. Synonymous with footline.

Running head The line of type printed above the text at the top of a page. In a book, it usually gives the title of the work on the verso and the chapter title on the recto. In periodicals, the running head gives the name of the publication, issue date, and page number, and may also include the volume number and issue number. Synonymous with headline and page head.

Running time The duration of a motion picture, including the credits but not any trailer(s) or supplemental material. In library cataloging, running time is given under extent of item in the physical description area of the bibliographic record. Compare with playing time.

Running title The title or abbreviated title of a book, or section of a book, repeated in uniform style at the head or foot of each page or verso, usually the same as the drop-down title. Also known as a running head.

Rural library A library or library system that serves a population living primarily on farms and ranches, and in remote communities, rather than in a town or city. Rural libraries typically provide outreach services such as bookmobiles and books-by-mail to bring library resources and services to users.

Rush to expedite the availability of a new item; patrons may place a rush request for an item that is presently on order or in process, and it will be obtained, processed and held for them as quickly as possible, often within a day or two. Selector librarians may place a rush order for urgently-needed items.

Rush order A request made by a library to a publisher, jobber, or dealer that a specific title be supplied as quickly as possible, usually because it is needed by a professor for course reserves, to meet heavy demand, or to satisfy a patron who has requested it. Compare with special order.

Rush processing In acquisitions, an item sent to cataloging to be processed as soon as it is received, usually a rush order or an item for which a patron is waiting.

Rustic capital One of the lighter and less formal capital letters used as a book hand by scribes from the 1st to the 6th century A.D., in contrast to the heavy square capitals used in formal documents, derived from Roman inscriptions. Vertical strokes were thinned by holding the pen at an acute angle, condensing previously rounded letterforms to allow more text to be copied on a page, a distinct advantage when writing material (parchment or vellum) was costly and in limited supply. Latin: capitalis rustica.

S. L. (sine loco) Without place. (Used in the MARC 260 tag when the name of the place of publication is unknown).

Sabbatical A paid leave of absence granted to an academic professional for the purpose of research or scholarly endeavor, usually for one semester or a full academic year, following six or seven years of full-time service, sometimes involving travel. At many colleges and universities, applications are evaluated on a competitive basis by a faculty committee, or in some other manner determined by institutional governance. Librarians employed in academic libraries may be eligible for sabbatic leave depending on the provisions of the contract governing terms of employment.

Sacred text A written work revered by people who believe in one of the world's organized religions. In library cataloging, such works are entered under a uniform title (Bible, Talmud, Koran, Vedas, etc.). Most libraries in the United States keep at least one English translation of the Bible in the reference collection, usually with commentaries, concordances, etc. The sacred books of the other major world religions may be available in the circulating collection of academic libraries, especially at universities offering a major or graduate degree in comparative religion. Compare with liturgical work.

Saddle-stitching A technique used to bind INK "http://www.wcsu.edu/library/" \l "openability" open flat, but its strength is not sufficient to bind publications of more than 100 pages. Synonymous with stapling and saddle-wire stitching. Compare with sewing.

Saga From the Old Norse word for "thing said," a lengthy narrative in prose or verse, telling of adventure and heroic events, usually involving the history of a legendary Norse lineage. In modern usage, any long, complicated tale in which the plot has many unexpected twists and turns, particularly one recounting the fortunes of an extended family (example: The Forsyte Saga by John Galsworthy).

SAGE The name for the online catalog that identifies materials owned by Colorado State University. It includes books, periodicals, government documents microforms and Sage

Sage Coordination Group (SCG) Group in the libraries whose primary function is coordinating the functions of Sage.

Salary A sum of money paid to an employee on a regular basis (weekly, biweekly, monthly) for performing a specific job. In the United States, most full-time librarians and technical support staff are salaried. Statistical information on salaries for librarians employed in the U.S. and Canada is reported annually in Library Journal (usually in the October 15th issue) and in the Bowker Annual Library and Book Trade Almanac. Compare with wages.

Salvage Measures taken to recover materials, equipment, and furnishings damaged outside of normal use, for example, by water as a result of a major leak or flood. Salvaged materials may require special conservation procedures such as vacuum freeze drying or fumigation. Items not salvageable are usually discarded. Also refers collectively to the materials recovered.

Same size Instructions from the publisher to the printer to reproduce an illustration submitted as copy without enlargement or reduction in size.

Sample issue An issue of a periodical, usually the first of an entirely new publication, sent at no charge by the publisher to a potential subscriber for inspection. In libraries, such copies are usually received and evaluated for selection by the serials department. In academic libraries, they may be routed to the appropriate department of the teaching faculty for evaluation.

Sampling The process of converting analog data into

digital data by taking a series of samples or readings at equal time intervals.

Sanjay Sanjay is a software package developed by NISSAT in collaboration with DESIDOC to help the libraries and centres in India to improve their house-keeping and service functions through automation. The package is totally menu driven and can be used even by non-professionals. The package was released for marketing in September 1995, and it has an installation base of many sites.

SANJUKTA A multi-user storage and retrieval software developed to support CALIBNET's Centralised Database and to provide online access from remote locations. SANJUKTA has been designed and implemented by A Mukhopadhyay, Technical Consultant, CALIBNET and his associates based on MOD+, a software he developed earlier to support management of small/medium-size libraries. The software has been developed, using 4 GL Code and designed to provide the user with options and flexibility in generating records, organizing and searching information viewing the search outputs, and interchanging data files with external databases with least manual interference.

Sans-serif See: block letter. Also spelled sanserif.

Satellite transmission A method of data transmission; the sender beams data up to an orbiting satellite and the satellite beams the data back down to the receiver.

Satire The use of sarcasm, irony, and wit to expose to ridicule the weaknesses or foibles of a person, group, or institution, often used to call public attention to a moral lapse or abuse of public trust, to damage the reputation of the victim for political or personal reasons, or as entertainment (example: The Ideal Husband, a comic drama by Oscar Wilde).

Saturation The extent to which one or two of the three RGB primaries predominate in a color. As quantities of RGB equalize, color becomes desaturated towards grey or white.

Save To preserve a data file by copying it from main memory (RAM) to a permanent storage medium, such as a hard disk or floppy disk, at the end of a session on a computer. Unsaved data may be lost when the application is closed or the computer powered down.

Scale In cartography, the ratio of distance shown on a map, photograph, or other graphic representation of a given geographic phenomenon, to its corresponding dimension on the ground, or to another graphic representation. On maps, the scale is usually printed beneath the title in the legend, in the form of a bar scale or as a representative fraction (example: 1:24,000). When a map is cataloged by a library, the statement of scale is given in the mathematical data area of the bibliographic description.

Scanner In data processing, a peripheral device that reads and converts handwritten or printed text, graphics, or barcodes into digital format (a bitmap) for processing or display on a computer screen, without actually recognizing the content. In libraries, optical scanners are used to create digital images of materials for interlibrary loan, document delivery, and electronic reserves, and in circulation to read the barcode on the patron's library card and on items in the collection. Some barcode scanners require an external decoder.

Scatter note A note in a classification schedule instructing the cataloger to classify works in multiple locations. For example, in Dewey Decimal Classification, reviews of works on a specific subject are classed with the subject or discipline, rather than under a general class for "Reviews."

Scatter The separation of entries on the same subject in a catalog or index, a condition that occurs when entries are made under 1) both the singular and plural forms of a heading, 2) variant forms of a name or title, or 3) a broad heading in one instance and a more specific heading in another. Scatter may also occur when there is inadequate control of synonyms or lack of precision in the assignment of subject headings or descriptors. Scatter is reduced by authority control and vocabulary control.

Scenario An outline or sketch of the plot of a dramatic work (play, opera, ballet, etc.), indicating the order of scenes and the characters involved in the action. Compare with treatment.

Schedule a classification schedule; a printed list (in a hierarchial order) of all the main classes and divisions of the system, such as the Library of Congress Classification Schedule.

Schedule reduction The elimination of some of the provisions made in a previous edition of a classification schedule, resulting in the discontinuation of certain classes, usually because the literature on the subject has dwindled significantly or because the class represents a distinction no longer recognized in the discipline or field.

Schematic A clear, simple line drawing or diagram used in textbooks and technical books to illustrate an operating principle or mechanism (or one of its parts).

Scholarly article An article, usually in a scholarly journal, that deals with academic subject matter at an advanced level.

Scholarly book A publishing term for a book that is: 1) written in a scholarly style, 2) about a specialized subject, 3) aimed at relatively narrow clearly-defined market segment, 4) sold primarily within that market, 5) often purchased on the basis of imprint, 6) not price-sensitive, 7) not highly profitable for the publisher, 8) usually published by a university press or the publishing arm of a scholarly society, 9) reviewed mainly in scholarly journals, and 10) indexed, with a bibliography or list of references for further reading at the end. Scholarly books normally generate little income from the sale of subsidiary rights, but attract a more sustained readership than most trade titles (adapted from Bodian's Publishing Desk Reference, NY: Oryx Press, 1988).

Scholarly communication The means by which individuals engaged in academic research and creative endeavor inform their peers, formally or informally, of the work they have accomplished. Scholars communicate by writing monographs and journal articles for publication, presenting conference papers which are subsequently published in proceedings and transactions, submitting reports in fulfillment of grant requirements, creating and maintaining Web sites aimed at the academic community, and corresponding with peers via e-mail and electronic mailing lists. One of the missions of academic libraries (and librarians) is to facilitate scholarly communication in all its forms.

Scholarly journal A journal that is primarily addressed to scholars, often focusing on a particular discipline. Scholarly journals tend to be refereed publications and for some purposes may be considered more authoritative than magazines. Scholarly journals tend to have articles that are substantial in length, use specialized language, contain footnotes or endnotes, and are written by researchers (whose academic credentials are often provided) rather than by journalists. See also refereed publications.

Scholarly Publishing and Academic Resources Coalition (SPARC) An international alliance of approximately 200 universities, research libraries, and library associations, SPARC was created in 1998 by several Association of Research Libraries (ARL) directors to address the pricing practices and policies of scientific, technical, and medical (STM) journal publishers. The coalition seeks to educate faculty on academic serials issues, fosters competition in the scholarly communication market, and advocates fundamental changes in the system and culture of scholarly communication.

Scholarly source Scholarly sources are publications written by subject experts for other researchers in the discipline. Scholarly sources include most journals but not the other types of periodicals (magazines and newspapers).

Scholary sources are often peer-reviewed or refereed, and generally include a bibliography. Compared to popular sources, scholarly sources are generally considered more appropriate for college-level research.

Scholium A marginal note explaining, interpreting, or commenting on a text, especially an annotation added by a classical grammarian on a passage from a work by Greek or Latin author of antiquity. Plural: scholia.

School library A library in a public or private elementary or secondary school that serves the information needs of its students and the curriculum needs of its teachers and staff, usually managed by a school librarian or media specialist. A school library collection usually contains books, periodicals, and educational media suitable for the grade levels served.

School Library Journal (SLJ) Published by R. R. Bowker, SLJ is a monthly trade journal and review publication for school, children's, and young adult librarians. In addition to regular columns, feature articles, and news of interest to the profession, SLJ reviews approximately 4,000 general trade books for children and young adult readers each year, and over 1,000 educational media titles, including CD-roms. The reviews are short but evaluative, written by and for librarians.

Scibase Scibase gives free access to a unique collection of the world's premier databases of scientific, technical and medical research literature. Scibase currently covers more than 30 million articles published since 1965 in more than 30,000 journals. Scibase is updated daily with approximately 10,000 new article records. Also gives access to full text of articles from selecte jouranls of few publishers.

Science and Engineering Library Sarah Shannon Stevenson Library for Science and Engineering; a division of the library whose collections support the natural and physical sciences, mathematics, and engineering; includes the Map Room and the Patent Depository; located in the Stevenson Science Center.

Science fiction A highly imaginative form of fiction and motion picture based on scientific speculation, usually depicting life and adventure in the future or on other worlds, not outside the realm of possibility, sometimes prophetically (example: 1984 by George Orwell) or as a commentary on contemporary conditions (Brave New World by Aldous Huxley). Science fiction is so popular that most large cities in the United States have at least one bookstore specializing in the genre. Abbreviated sci fi. Compare with fantasy.

Science Information Center This library-within-a-library reference service and collection on the fourth floor delivers specialized science, technology, and health science information.

Sciences: astronomy, biology, chemistry, computer science, earth sciences, mathematics, medicine and health, physics

SCODE 3 Frequency code – if holdings are closed on the serials check-in record.

Scope note (SN) One or two sentences of text added to an entry in a thesaurus of indexing terms or list of subject headings to indicate the intended use of a descriptor or subject heading, including any special rules for assigning it in indexing. Scope notes are usually added to clarify ambiguity or restrict the use of a term to one of several possible meanings. Not all terms require a scope note, but if one is given, it normally precedes any synonyms (UF), broader terms (bts), narrower terms (nts), or related terms (rts). Compare with parenthetical qualifier.

Scope The area or field within which a specific activity occurs. Also, the range or extent of action, observation, meaning, inquiry, etc. In libraries, the range of subjects or fields covered in a catalog, index, abstracting service, bibliographic database, reference work, etc. Compare with coverage.

Score A record of a musical work in which the parts to be played or sung are written or printed in musical notation on separate staves, vertically aligned to enable them to be read at the same time.

Scoring To make a linear indentation on a piece of paper or card to allow it to turn or fold more easily without damaging the fibers. When done with a dull rule or disk, the process is called creasing. When a sharp rule is used, the fibers are partially broken, producing an effect similar to perforation, which allows the paper to tear more cleanly along the fold. In binding, to compress the fibers of a leaf in a line along the inner edge to allow the volume to open more easily.

SCORM Sharable Courseware Object Reference Model A set of technical standards that enable Web-based learning systems to find, import, share, reuse, and export learning content in a standardized way. Elements which are compliant can easily be merged with other compliant elements to generate a modular collection of training materials.

Scout A person with experience in the book trade, employed by a publisher to seek out new writers and illustrators whose early works show promise, and to explore with them possibilities for new books. Compare with book scout.

SCR Serial Control Record.

Scrapbook A blankbook, usually of large-size, containing unprinted leaves for mounting or inserting photographs, pictures, clippings, letters, invitations, and other memorabilia, usually to preserve them for sentimental reasons. Compare with album.

Screen dump The process of saving as a file, or sending to a printer, a copy of the image displayed on the monitor of a computer, usually to create a record that can be used to document and/or diagnose a malfunction. Synonymous with screen capture.

Screen Frequency The number of rows or lines of dots in a halftone image within a given distance, normally stated in lines per inch (lpi) or lines per centimeter (lpm). A frequency of 200 lpi would only be used in high-quality printing.

Screen reader A software program that translates text on a Web page into audio output; typically used by individuals with vision impairment.

Screen Ruling Another term used for screen frequency.

Screen saver A utility program that blanks out the image displayed on the monitor of a computer, or replaces it with a continuously changing pattern, to prevent ghosting, the permanent etching of a still image on the monitor. Most screen savers can be set to commence after a designated period of inactivity and remain on the screen until the mouse is moved or a key is depressed, restoring the original image.

Screenplay A story written in a form suitable for motion picture or television production, or adapted for that purpose from an existing novel, short story, or stage play by a screenwriter whose name is given in the credits.

Screenwriter The person responsible for writing the screenplay for a motion picture, videorecording, or television program, or the scripted narration for a documentary, whose name is usually given in the credits. In library cataloging, the name of the screenwriter is entered in the note area of the bibliographic record representing the item.

Scribal copy A written manuscript produced by a scribe or copyist, as opposed to the original manuscript written by the author, or at the author's dictation.

Scribe A professional penman who copied manuscripts by hand before the invention of printing from movable type. During the Middle Ages, most copyists were monks who worked in the scriptoria of Roman Catholic religious establishments.

Scrinium A container in the shape of a cylinder with a removable top, used by the Romans of antiquity for storing manuscripts in the form of scrolls.

Script The text of a play, motion picture,

videorecording, or television or radio program, indicating the lines to be spoken by each character, with directions for staging the work. Compare with acting edition and promptbook.

Scriptorium The room in a medieval monastery reserved for the preparation of manuscripts by scribes. In some religious houses it was a single large room; in others, the space was partitioned into individual cells. To minimize distraction, absolute silence was maintained while work was in progress.

Scripture Originally, any written composition, but the term is now used mainly for the Old and New Testaments of the Christian Bible, sometimes in the plural (Holy Scriptures). In a more general sense, any religious or sacred text or record.

Scroll A manuscript in the form of a length of papyrus, usually rolled around a sturdy wooden rod with knobbed ends called the umbilicus, with a tag attached to one end for identification. In antiquity, texts were written in columns on papyrus sheets glued together to form a continuous roll which the Romans called a volumen. The codex (book with pages) replaced the scroll after animal skin (parchment and vellum) came into widespread use as a writing surface. Compare with rotulus.

Scroll Bar The bar that appears at the right side or the bottom of a window that contains more information that can be displayed. The scroll bar is used to scroll an object or parts of a document into view when the entire object or document does not fit in the window.

Scuffed The condition of a book with a binding so badly scraped that it has become frayed or roughened in places. Compare with rubbed.

SDI An abbreviation of "selective dissemination of information..

SDSL (Symmetric Digital Subscriber Line) A version of DSL where the upload speeds and download speeds are the same.

Sdsunet San Diego State University Network. The backbone network that connects multiple buildings on the SDSU campus.

Search A systematic effort on the part of a library user or librarian to locate desired information by manual or electronic means, whether successful or not, as opposed to browsing a library collection with no clear intention in mind.

Search committee A group of people, usually three or more library staff members, elected or appointed to assist in the process of selecting a candidate (or list of candidates) to fill a vacant position in the library. Their responsibilities may include drafting the position description, posting the vacancy, evaluating applications, selecting candidates for interviewing, drafting interview questions, conducting interviews, and selecting and recommending finalist(s) to library administration.

Search engine A hardware device designed to search a text-based database for specific character strings typed as input by the user. More recently, computer software designed to help the user locate information available at sites on the World Wide Web, by selecting categories from a hierarchical directory of subjects (example: Yahoo!) Or by entering appropriate keywords (Google, Hotbot, etc.). Most Web search engines allow the searcher to use Boolean logic and truncation in search statements.

Search history A feature of some search software systems and Web browsers that allows the user to view a consecutive list of all the searches executed during the current search session, or all the sites visited in a browsing session. Some systems allow the user to select a previous search from the list and re-execute it, or print or save the search history, if desired.

Search service A business that specializes in locating out of print books at the request of libraries and private collectors. Acquisitions librarians must rely on such services when a replacement copy is needed for an item that is still in demand but no longer in print. Some rare books dealers also offer this service.

Search software A computer program designed to execute a search for information when queried by a user. User-friendly search software provides both a menu-driven interface for novices and a command-driven interface for experienced searchers. Sophisticated search software permits the use of Boolean logic, nesting, truncation, wildcard, and proximity operators in search statements, and allows the user to limit search results by various parameters. Compare with search engine.

Search Statement A phrase or combination of words that are entered into the library catalog or other database in order to find information.

Search statement In information retrieval, an information need or query entered as input in a form acceptable to the search software used by the retrieval system. Most online catalogs, bibliographic databases, and search engines allow Boolean logic, nesting, truncation, wildcard, and proximity operators to be used in search statements, and permit the user to limit search results.

Search strategy In information retrieval, a systematic plan for conducting a search. In most cases, the first step is to formulate a clear and concise topic statement. The next step is to identify the main concepts in the topic. Then the most appropriate finding tools for the subject must be identified and located. Lists of authorized subject heading(s) and descriptors in the appropriate indexing systems can then be consulted to find preferred terms to represent the main concepts.

Search term A word or phrase representing one of the main concepts in a research topic which, when combined with other terms in a search statement, can be used to query an online catalog or bibliographic database and retrieve relevant information. Search terms can be authorized subject headings or descriptors selected from a prescribed list (thesaurus), or keywords supplied by the user.

Searchable An electronic resource running on software designed to allow the user to type a word, phrase, or string of words or phrases, as input to find all the records, entries, or text containing the search term(s). Most online catalogs and bibliographic databases can be searched by author, title, subject heading (descriptor), and keywords. Boolean logic and truncation are permitted in a keywords search in most library catalogs and databases.

Sears subject heading A subject heading from a list created by Minnie E. Sears, first published in 1923 for use in school libraries and small public libraries. Although it is based on Library of Congress subject headings, the Sears List of Subject Headings published by H. W. Wilson is narrower in scope and its headings are more general. Small libraries supplement it with LC headings as needed.

Season One of the annual cycles in the publishing industry. When publishers introduce their frontlist in the spring and fall of each year, the previous year's frontlist titles move to the backlist. New and backlisted titles are described in the seasonal publisher's catalog distributed by mail to libraries and booksellers.

Secondary binding When potential sales of a new book are difficult to predict, the publisher may decide to bind an edition in batches over a period of years. The color or quality of the binding material and the lettering on the spine may differ slightly from one batch to another. To distinguish the primary binding from subsequent bindings, the order in which the batches were bound must be determined, if possible. Compare with remainder binding.

Secondary Color Color obtained by mixing two primary colors. Although known as primary colorants, C,M, and Y are the secondary colors of light. Red plus green produce yellow, for example.

Secondary literature Material published about the primary

Secondary source source that comments on or relies

on primary sources. An article in a newspaper that reports on a scientific discovery or a book that analyzes a writer's work is a secondary source.

Secondary Source Works that are not original manuscripts or contemporary records or documents associated with an event, but which critique, comment on, or build upon these primary sources.

Secondary values In archives, the values of records for the activities of users other than the office of record or its successors. Compare with primary values.

Section In library cataloging, a separately published part of a serial, usually representing a subject category within the whole, designated by a topical heading or an alphabetical or numerical code (or both). Also, a similar division within a law book. Also refers to one of the separately folded parts of a newspaper, for example, the Entertainment Section.

Section title See Divisional title. Security In computing, the technology developed to prevent unauthorized persons, particularly hackers and crackers, from gaining entry to protected systems and files, including data encryption, virus detection, firewalls, and the authentication of authorization codes (usernames, passwords, pins, etc.). In a more general sense, all the measures taken to prevent unauthorized persons from accessing confidential information.

Secure server A special type of file server that requires authentication (e.g., entry a valid username and password) before access is granted. Example: At OSU, most Software To Go files are stored on a secure server.

Security audit A thorough on-site inspection in which a person (or persons) trained and experienced in library security critically examine and analyze all the existing security systems and procedures used in a library, to ascertain current status, identify deficiencies or excesses, and make recommendations based on findings. A professional security audit may include the analysis of crime statistics.

an assessment of insurance needs, and discussion of sensitive topics, such as internal theft and personal security issues.

Security Certificate A chunk of information (often stored as a text file) that is used by the SSL protocol to establish a secure connection.

Security gate A device installed near the entrance and/or exit of a library, usually in the form of a swing-arm or pair of uprights positioned in such a way that persons entering or leaving the premises must pass through a magnetic detection system designed to trigger an alarm if an attempt is made to remove library materials without checking them out. Less obtrusive laser systems are also available. Some security gates include a counter that provides traffic statistics.

Security guard An employee responsible for patrolling the premises of a library to discourage disruptive behavior and illegal activities, such as vandalism and the unauthorized removal of materials (theft), and to deal with individuals who do not comply with library policies and rules. Most security guards wear uniforms and are trained to handle problem patrons and various types of emergency situations. Synonymous with security officer.

Security socket layer (SSL) A protocol developed by Netscape for securely transmitting documents via the Internet. Urls that require an SSL connection start with https: instead of http:.

Security system An electronic alarm system installed at the entrance and exit of a library facility to detect the unauthorized removal of library materials (theft). Most security systems use a swing-arm or pair of uprights called a security gate, activated by a magnetic strip affixed to each item, which must be desensitized by circulation staff at the time an item is checked out to avoid triggering the alarm. Some security systems include a counting device for gathering statistics on traffic patterns.

See A cross-reference in a library catalog, index, or reference work directing the user from a synonym (or other equivalent term) to the preferred heading or descriptor for a given name, place, or subject (example: Beyle, Marie Henri see Stendahl, 1783-1842). Synonymous with search under. Compare with USE.

See also A cross-reference in a library catalog, index, or reference work directing the user to a heading under which related information can be found on a given subject (example: Treaty of Versailles, 1919 see also Paris Peace Conference, 1919). Synonymous with search also under.

Selection criteria The set of standards used by librarians to decide whether an item should be added to the collection, which normally include a list of subjects or fields to be covered, levels of specialization, editions, currency, languages, and formats (large print, nonprint, abridgments, etc.). Selection criteria usually reflect the library's mission and the information needs of its clientele, but selection decisions are also influenced by budgetary constraints and qualitative evaluation in the form of reviews, recommended core lists, and other selection guides.

Selection Service of Articles on Metallurgy and Moulding The SESAMM bibliographical database gives access to the entire CTIF information holdings made up of more than 33,000 documents.

Selection The process of deciding which materials should be added to a library collection. Selection decisions are usually made on the basis of reviews and standard collection development tools, by librarians designated as selectors in specific subject areas, based on their interests and fields of specialization. In academic libraries, selection may also be done by members of the teaching faculty in their disciplines. Very large academic and public libraries may use an approval plan or blanket order plan to assist selectors. Library patrons also recommend titles for purchase, especially in libraries that provide a suggestion box. The opposite of deselection.

Selective bibliography A bibliography that includes

only a portion of the relevant literature, usually based on predetermined selection criteria, such as the needs of a particular group of users, desire for current versus retrospective material, or an evaluation of quality.

Selective Chosen in preference to another or others on the basis of a special characteristic or quality. In library research, a finding tool such as an index or bibliography that includes only a portion of the available literature, usually limited to sources that meet certain pre-established criteria (quality, currency, reading level, degree of specialization, etc.). Compare with comprehensive

Selector codes/names Librarians identified by abbreviations and assigned to various subject areas and funds. These codes are used in order record in Sage to compile and produce reports.

Self end In bookbinding, an endpaper that is not separate from the text, but rather part of the first or last section and therefore of the same paper stock as the text.

Self-Check stationbar-code reading machines for patrons to check out materials themselves, rather than checking materials out at the circulation desk. Self-check stations are available at Olin and Hotel School libraries. A Cornell ID card is required to use self-check. A receipt is printed indicating when the materials are due back at the library.

Self-checkout An automated circulation system that allows registered library patrons to check out circulating materials without the assistance of staff, usually by scanning the barcode on the individual's library card and on each of the item(s) to be borrowed.

Self-citation A reference made in a written work to one of the author's previous publications, an accepted practice in scholarly communication, provided important works written on the subject by other authors are not neglected or ignored.

Self-cover A pamphlet or periodical covered in the

same paper stock used to print the text, rather than a heavier grade of paper.

Self-extracting file A type of compressed file that you can execute (e.g., double-click on the filename) to begin the decompression process; no other decompression utility is required. Example: on IBM PC or compatibles, certain files with an ".exe" extension and on Macintoshes, all files with a ".sea" extension.

Self-help publication A book, audiotape, or videotape intended to assist the reader, listener, or viewer in solving a personal problem, for example, finding the best treatment for a physical illness or condition, or the answer to a legal question without having to pay for professional services. Some publishers specialize in self-help publications (example: Nolo Press, providing legal books for laypersons). Compare with how-to publication.

Self-publishing The design, printing, and marketing of a work at the author's own expense, without the assistance of a commercial publisher, often undertaken out of devotion to the subject. Sophisticated desktop publishing software and high-quality photocopiers have made this option easier and less expensive than it once was. Also refers to the electronic publication of a work by its author, usually installed on a server publicly accessible over the Internet.

Self-service Library functions that can be initiated, controlled, and/or executed by the patron without the assistance of library staff, including automated checkout, patron-initiated interlibrary loan service, and online catalogs that allow users to view their own patron records, place holds, renew items on loan, etc. Synonymous with disintermediated service.

Se-Lin labels White labels bearing the call number, usually on the spine of a book. Se-Lin refers to the brand name of the labeling system.

Semantic factoring An indexing technique in which a compound heading or descriptor is divided into its constituent parts (example: Annotated bibliography —> Annotation + Bibliography). In some cases, semantic factoring yields false drops (Library + Research —> "Library research" and "Research library").

Semantic relation The connection in meaning between two or more concepts, and between the terms (subject headings or descriptors) used to represent them in an indexing language.

Semantics The branch of linguistics concerned with the meaning of the words, signs, and symbols that constitute the elements of change and evolution in a spoken or written language. Also, the branch of semiotics that deals with relationships of meaning between signs and between signs and their referents within a system of communication.

Semiannual Issued at intervals of six months. Also refers to a serial issued every six months. Synonymous with half yearly.

Semicurrent Archival materials too old to be considered current, but still useful and therefore retained for a certain period, usually in a location reserved for intermediate storage, pending final disposition.

Semimonthly Issued twice each month, or every two weeks. Also refers to a serial issued twice a month, with the possible exception of certain issues (example: Library Journal). Synonymous with biweekly.

Seminal From the Latin word for "seed." An idea or work so original when first expressed, composed, created, released, or published that it has considerable influence on the thought and work of contemporaries, and on succeeding generations of writers, scholars, or artists who may give it further development in their own works.

Semiotics The systematic study of the linguistic and nonlinguistic signs and symbols used in both natural and artificially-constructed languages. The three branches of semiotics are: 1) pragmatics (how signs are used by those who make use of them), 2) semantics (relationships of meaning between signs and their referents), and 3) syntactics (how signs are combined). Each of the branches has pure (theoretical), descriptive, and applied aspects.

Semipublished Works such as reports, internal documents, theses, etc., which are difficult if not impossible to obtain through regular market channels because they were never intended for publication, but which may be available via interlibrary loan, document delivery service, or some other method of retrieval. Compare with unpublished.
Semiweekly Issued twice each week. Also refers to a serial publication issued twice a week. Synonymous with twice weekly.

Send To transmit data from one node to another on a computer network, as in the exchange of e-mail messages or the export of bibliographic data from an online catalog or bibliographic database to an e-mail account. Also refers to the command in a computer program that initiates such a transmission. The opposite of receive.

Sensitize To prepare an item for the electronic detection system. Sensitized material will trigger the alarm at the exit.

Sentencing The application of the appropriate disposition schedule to a group or collection of archival records.

Sentimental novel A work of serious fiction, popular in 18th century England and 19th century America, in which the author portrays the afflictions of one or more heroes and/ or heroines of unblemished character, to demonstrate the rewards virtuous conduct (example: Uncle Tom's Cabin by Harriet Beecher Stowe). Synonymous with domestic novel.

SEO — (Search Engine Optimization) The practice of designing web pages so that they rank as high as possible in search results from search engines. There is "good" SEO and "bad" SEO. Good SEO involves making the web page clearly describe its subject, making sure it contains truly useful information, including accurate information in Meta tags, and arranging for other web sites to make links to the page. Bad SEO involves attempting to deceive people into believing the page is more relevant than it truly is by doing things like adding inaccurate Meta tags to the page.

Separately paginated Numbering the pages of each volume or part of a set, or of each issue of a single volume of a periodical, in a separate sequence, starting with number one. Compare with continuous pagination.

Separately published An item issued by a publisher or distributor as an independent entity, usually under its own title and copyright, as opposed to a work published in a collection or as a serial. For example, the individual works in a monographic series, each published under a separate title.

Septennial Issued every seven years. Also refers to a serial publication issued every seven years.

Sequel A work of narrative fiction, in most instances a novel, which although complete in itself, continues a previous work in plot, setting, and characters, usually (but not always) beginning where the action in the previous work left off (example: Let the Circle Be Unbroken by Mildred D. Taylor, sequel to Roll of Thunder Hear My Cry). In a more general sense, anything that follows; a subsequent series of events or course of affairs. The opposite of prequel. Compare with continuation.

Sequential The arrangement of a series of entries or items in prescribed order based on a predetermined system of priority, for example, reverse chronological order. In computing, sequential access refers to data stored in a manner that allows pieces of it to be accessed only in a certain order, as in the medium of magnetic tape. Compare with random access memory (RAM).

Serendipity A word first coined by the English writer Horace Walpole in The Three Princes of Serendip to refer to the knack of making fortunate discoveries unexpectedly, by accident or coincidence. In information retrieval, this usually depends on the ability of the browser to recognize the relevance or utility of data not actively sought at the time it is encountered. Flexibility is one of the qualities of a good researcher.

Serial Catch-all term for anything that is published on a regular basis. It can be a publication issued in successive parts, at more or less regular intervals, and to be continued indefinitely. This may be weekly, monthly, quarterly, semi-annually, or annually. Magazines, journals, conference proceedings, trade publications, yearbooks, newsletters, and indexes are all serials.

Serial bibliography A bibliography published in successive parts, at fairly regular intervals, usually limited to a specialized field of study (example: Bibliography of Asian Studies published every one or two years).

Serial Cable/Serial Port A cable used to connect peripheral devices through a computer's serial port. Normally a 25-pin connector on each end, yet can be a 9-pin on one. A Serial Port can either be plugged into an expansion slot on the motherboard of your computer or built into the motherboard itself. Serial ports are used for such devices as printers, mice, and modems.

Serial cancellation Notice given to a publisher or subscription agency that a library no longer wishes to subscribe to a specific serial publication. In recent years, the relentless increase in subscription prices and the inability of acquisitions budgets to keep pace with inflation have forced academic and research libraries to cancel periodical subscriptions to maintain balance in the purchase of serials and monographs. The scientific disciplines most affected by such cuts because they are more serial-dependent than the arts and humanities, and because average subscription price is highest for scientific journals.

Serial In AACR2, a publication in any format issued under the same title in successively numbered and/or dated parts or issues, appearing at regular or irregular intervals and intended to be continued indefinitely. Serials include print periodicals (newspapers, newsletters, magazines, and journals) and their electronic counterparts, as well as annuals, yearbooks, transactions, proceedings, and monographic series cataloged separately. When serials split, merge, or are absorbed, a change of title may result.

Serial index An index to the content of a publication issued in successively numbered parts, usually a cumulative author and/or title index compiled by the publisher, appearing at the end of the last issue of the publication year. Most magazines (and some journals) do not provide such an index.

Serial number A number identifying the place in sequence of a publication issued as part of a series. Also refers to a unique identification number assigned to a serial title for identification purposes, such as the International Standard Serial Number (ISSN).

Serial rights Under copyright law, the subsidiary rights of an author or publisher to control the publication of a work in installments, usually in a magazine or newspaper. Serial rights can be sold or transferred by the owner.

Serial set Special edition of United States Senate and House journals, reports and documents, grouped in series and numbered consecutively, which Congress orders printed after each congressional session.

Serial title The name of a publication issued in successive parts, usually printed on the front cover and in the masthead of a periodical issue or on the title page of a monographic serial. In electronic periodicals, the title appears on the welcome screen. Title changes are more frequent in serials than in other types of publications. In most libraries in the United States, periodicals are shelved alphabetically by title.

Serialized A work published in installments, usually at regular intervals. During the 18th and early 19th centuries, books were often published in numbered parts or fascicles, but by the late 19th century most serialized works appeared in consecutive issues of newspapers and magazines

Serials collection Section of acquisition service which handles most aspects of acquiring periodicals and serials other than Colorado state and U.S. Government titles. This department encumbers orders, approves invoices, maintains SAGE files of receipt of issues or volumes, claims items not received, and prepares periodical issues for shelving.

Serials desk A service point, usually located near the periodicals section in a library, staffed by a person trained to assist patrons in locating serials and in using equipment for making copies of articles (photocopiers, microform reader-printers, etc.).

Serials Directory, The A directory issued annually by EBSCO in print, online, and on CD-ROM, providing bibliographic information and pricing for a classified list of over 140,000 serials currently published in the U.S. and internationally. Indexed alphabetically by serial title, ceased title, ISSN, and peer-reviewed title, The Serials Directory is usually shelved in the reference section of large libraries

Serials list A list of all the serials held by a library, including any titles that have ceased publication or been canceled for which the library retains back files, usually arranged in alphabetical order by title, with holdings indicated in open and closed entries, and cross-references to and from changed titles.

Serials review A systematic examination of a library's serials list to identify titles to be retained and subscriptions to be canceled, usually conducted by a serials librarian or serials department, ideally with input solicited from persons likely to be affected by the decisions. Titles suggested for addition or substitution may also be considered, depending on the amount budgeted for serials expenditures. In some libraries, serials reviews are scheduled on a regular basis (usually every 1-3 years), but in others, the process occurs irregularly. Decisions are based on usage, subscription price, importance to the discipline, and availability of full-text in online databases.

Series A group of separately published works related in subject and/or form, issued in succession by a single publisher or distributor, usually in uniform style, each bearing, in addition to its own title, a collective or series title applied by the publisher to the group as a whole. The individual volumes or parts may not share the same author or editor, nor is it necessary for them to be published at regular intervals, or numbered. The series title is given on a separate series title page, usually the verso of the leaf bearing the half-title. It also appears at the top of the title page or on a page following the title page. Some reference books are published in open-ended series (example: Contemporary World Issues from ABC-CLIO). In library cataloging, information describing series (title proper, statements of responsibility, ISSN, number, etc.) Is given in the series area of the bibliographic record. Abbreviated ser. Compare with serial.

Series area The area of bibliographic description reserved in library cataloging for information about a work separately published as one of a group of items, including the title proper of the series, statements of responsibility concerning the series, ISSN, and the number within the series (if the individual items are numbered). In the MARC record, series statements are entered in the fields tagged 4XX.

Series author A writer of works published in series (example: J. K. Rowling, author of the Harry Potter books for children).

Series authority file Largely replaced by the online authority file, this continues to be used for older series. Record of proper forms for series to keep the entries uniform. Also gives information as to whether or not to trace a series, i.e. Make added entry in the catalog. File is located in the bibliographic contro and electronic service department.

Series authority record worksheet Form used for

various stages of establishing and/or upgrading a series according to AACR2 cataloging code.

Series statement The portion of a bibliographic record reserved for description of the group of which the publication is a member (if applicable), including the title proper of the series, statements of responsibility concerning the series, ISSN, and number within the series (if the items are numbered). In the MARC record. series statements are entered in fields tagged 4XX.

Series title A collective title applied to a group of separately published materials issued in succession in uniform style by a single publisher or distributor. In books, the series title is usually printed on the verso of the leaf bearing the half-title, often with a list of previously published works in the same series. In the bibliographic record, the title proper is given in the series statements (MARC fields 4XX).

Series title page An added title page appearing before the main title page in a work issued as part of a group of publications, giving the title of the series and, in some cases, additional information, such as a list of previously published titles in the series, names of authors, dates of publication, numeric designations, etc. The series title page is usually the verso of the page bearing the half-title.

Serif From the Dutch Schreef meaning "stroke" or "line" in writing—a fine, short line crossing or projecting as a finishing touch from the end of one of the main strokes of a letter of the Latin alphabet in a typeface that includes such extensions. Warren Chappell describes the serif as "a terminal device, functionally employed to strengthen lines which otherwise would tend to fall away optically" (A Short History of the Printed Word, Boston: Nonpareil Books, 1970). Serifs enhance the legibility of printed text matter. The opposite of sans-serif and block letter.

SERMLP Southeastern Regional Medical Library Program.

Server A computer, or a software package, that provides

a specific kind of service to client software running on other computers. The term can refer to a particular piece of software, such as a WWW server, or to the machine on which the software is running, e.g. "Our mail server is down today, that's why e-mail isn't getting out." A single server machine can (and often does) have several different server software packages running on it, thus providing many different servers to clients on the network. Sometimes server software is designed so that additional capabilities can be added to the main program by adding small programs known as servlets.

Service (NT service) A process that performs a specific function in Windows NT and can be called by various other programs. Windows NT provides tools to monitor and administer services.

Service area The geographic area served by a public library or library system, from which it derives a major portion if not all of its funding, usually through taxation.

Service charge A fee added by some jobbers to orders placed by libraries for materials sold by the publisher at little or no discount, or for special services provided by the jobber in filling the order. Also refers to a fee charged by a subscription agency for filling orders for periodical subscriptions, usually 5-10% of the total annual amount paid by the library for subscriptions.

Service contract An arrangement in which the supplier (or some other service provider) agrees to regularly maintain and repair one or more pieces of equipment after any warranties have expired, usually in exchange for payment of an annual or monthly fee. Libraries enter into such agreements to keep photocopiers, microform reader-printer machines, security devices, automation equipment, etc., in working order. Synonymous with service agreement.

Service copy A third generation microfilm copy, produced from a print master to be cataloged, stored, and used as an information source in a library.

Service Desk The service point on the first floor where

staff will help you check out library materials and course reserves, use equipment, and get started on library research.

Service point A fixed location within a library or information center, staffed to provide a specific service or services to users (examples: circulation desk, reference desk, serials desk, interlibrary loan office, etc.).

Servlet A small computer program designed to be add capabilities to a larger piece of server software. Common examples are "Java servlets", which are small programs written in the Java language and which are added to a web server. Typically a web server that uses Java servlets will have many of them, each one designed to handle a very specific situation, for example one servlet will handle adding items to a "shopping cart", while a different servlet will handle deleting items from the "shopping cart."

Session laws Laws arranged in order of passage (Law Library).

Set discount The price charged by the publisher when all the volumes in a multivolume set are ordered at the same time, as opposed to the higher price charged per volume when one or more volumes are purchased separately. The price difference is usually 5-20%.

Set Two or more related bibliographic items in any format, published or issued as a single entity in uniform style and cataloged as a unit, for example, a multivolume dictionary or encyclopedia. Normally, all the volumes in a set are published at the same time, but there are notable exceptions (Dictionary of American Regional English). Compare with series.

Setting The overall locale and historical period in which the action in a narrative work occurs. In a specific scene or episode, the setting consists of the actual physical surroundings (indoors or out), an element of the atmosphere. For example, the general setting of the play Hamlet by Shakespeare is medieval Denmark, with the duel scene at the end of the play set inside the castle at Elsinore. In a theater production, the setting is the scenery and properties, synonymous with the French term mise-en-scene.

Sewing A method of binding in which the sections of a publication are held together with thread, usually machine-stitched through the back fold before the lining is glued to the back. In quality binding, the sewn sections are stitched to two or more narrow cotton tapes spaced at intervals across the binding edge of the text block. Sewing allows the leaves to open without pulling loose, as they often do in adhesive bindings. For a well-illustrated description of the sewing process, please see the entry on "Machine sewing" in Geoffrey Glaister's Encyclopedia of the Book (Oak Knoll/ British Library: 1996). Compare with saddle-stitching and side-stitching.

Sexennial Issued every six years. Also refers to a serial publication issued every six years.

Sextern In bookbinding, a gathering consisting of six sheets of paper, parchment, or vellum folded once to create twelve leaves, used in some manuscript books and early printed books.

Sextodecimo (16mo) A small book, approximately 6 inches in height, made by folding each sheet of book paper to form signatures of sixteen leaves (thirty-two pages).

Sexual harassment Any unwelcome sexual advance, request for sexual favors (explicit or implicit), or other verbal or physical conduct of a sexual nature, when submission to such conduct is made a condition of employment or used as the basis for employment decisions affecting the recipient, or when such conduct interferes with an employee's work performance or creates an intimidating, hostile, or offensive work environment. Libraries deal with sexual harassment by formulating and disseminating clear policies, screening applicants carefully, providing in-service training, keeping complete and accurate personnel records, and taking appropriate disciplinary action.

SFX SFX allows you to click on a citation in a database

and view a list of services for that item. SFX stands for "special effects." SFX is an electronic service which service which allows you to view the full text of an article online; request delivery of the book; article or document through interlibrary loan; check the SAGE Library Catalog to see if CSUL owns the item; SFX also provides citation index, which allows you to enter information for an article citation and see if CSUL has electronic access to it.

Shaded letter In printing, an outline letter made to appear three-dimensional by the presence of a dark shadow along the same side of each stroke, used mainly in display work.

Shadow The darkest area of an image.

Shaken A book in which the leaves are beginning to come loose but are still attached to the binding, usually caused by loosening of the sewing threads or wear on the hinges, a condition more advanced than started, but not yet sprung.

Shared cataloging Program by a group of libraries to share the intellectual effort of cataloging by contributing records to a central database, from which each library can draw.

Shared responsibility In AACR2, a work in which two or more persons or corporate bodies collaborate in creating the content, each performing the same type of activity, with the contribution of each participant either distinct or indistinguishable from that of the others. Synonymous with shared authorship. Compare with mixed responsibility

Shareware Software available over the Internet which the user may download and try on the "honor system" before deciding to purchase. Payment of a nominal registration fee is expected following a reasonable trial period, entitling the user to receive documentation, technical support, and updated versions as they become available.

Sharing violation An attempt by a computer user to open a data or program file currently in use in another application, an action that generates a message on the screen saying the file must be "closed" before it can be used in the other application.

Sheehy Common reference to the following work: Sheehy, Eugene P., Guide to Reference Books. The guide is an annotated bibliography of reference works, classified by subjects.

Sheet As used to describe an item cataloged under AACR2, a single whole piece of thin, flat opaque or transparent material other than a broadside, bearing printed and/or handwritten matter on one or both sides. In printing, a unit of paper as manufactured, whether printed or blank. In hand papermaking, a unit of paper the same size as the physical mold used to make it. In microforms, a single piece of fiche (microfiche, superfiche, ultrafiche), usually 4 x 6 inches in size.

Sheet map A map printed on one side of a single sheet of paper, with or without explanatory matter printed on the reverse side. In libraries, sheet maps are usually stored flat or folded in a map case with wide shallow drawers.

Sheet music A musical work written or printed on one or more unbound sheets of paper. Libraries usually place sheet music inside a protective folder or binder in physical processing.

Shelf capacity The average number of volumes that will fit on a book shelf, depending on the width of the shelf from upright to upright, the average depth (thickness) per volume, and the portion of each shelf left empty to facilitate reshelving. Total stack capacity can be computed by multiplying shelf capacity by the number of available shelves in the library stacks.

Shelf dummy A piece of wood, cardboard, or plastic in the shape of a book, placed on a shelf in a library, with a spine label directing the user to the location of a title shelved out of normal sequence. Shelf dummies are often used in reference stacks to indicate the location of items shelved in ready reference, and in periodical stacks to indicate that back files are located elsewhere, for example, in microfilm or microfiche cabinets. Compare with dummy.

Shelf guide A sign or label attached to the end or edge of a shelf in a library indicating its contents, usually by call number, or alphabetically by title (periodicals) or last name of author (fiction). Synonymous with shelf label.

Shelf height The vertical distance between two shelves. Adjustable shelving allows the distance to be altered to accommodate items of varying height. Average shelf height is one of the factors determining stack capacity.

Shelf list Record, usually a card file, of titles in a library with the entries arranged in the order of the items in the shelves—in other words, in call number order. This record can be produced from SAGE. Formerly, this record was on catalog cards; now is being eliminated through the Shelf List Reduction Project.

Shelf reading Periodic examination of the arrangement of books and other materials in the stacks of a library to ensure that items are in correct call number sequence on the shelf, usually performed by a student assistant or staff member called a page, during slack periods. An item shelved out of order may be lost to users until the shelves are read. Synonymous with shelf checking. Compare with inventory.

Shelf reserve Reserve materials that cannot be scanned onto electronic reserve. E.g. Entire personal and library books, video tapes, and CD-roms.

Shelf-cocked A permanent deformation in the binding of a book that develops when it is allowed to lean at an angle against a shelf upright or nearby volume over a prolonged period of time. The condition is caused by the force of gravity and can be prevented by using a sturdy bookend at the end of each row on shelves that are not full. Also known as spine lean Compare with cocked.

Shelflist A nonpublic catalog of a library collection, containing a single bibliographic record for each item, filed in the order in which the items are arranged on the shelf (usually by call number), used for inventory because it contains the most current information on copy and volume holdings. Card shelflists are being phased out by libraries that have converted their public catalogs to machine-readable records.

Shelf-sitter A slang term used by librarians for an item in the circulating collection that is seldom if ever checked out, or a reference book that is rarely used. In public libraries with limited shelf space, items with low circulation are eventually weeded, but in the collections of academic and research libraries, they may be retained indefinitely.

Shelf-worn The condition of a book that shows visible signs of having been repeatedly removed and replaced on the shelf, usually along the edges of the binding. In libraries, the most shelf-worn volumes are often well-loved children's books, standard dictionaries, general encyclopedias, and other heavily used reference works. Library binding increases the shelf life of a book.

Shelving by size Storing books by height rather than by subject classification, usually in four or more groups ranging from the smallest to the largest. This method increases shelf capacity by up to 25%, but when subject access is sacrificed, browsing capability is diminished. For this reason, shelving by size is used mainly in storage locations inaccessible to the public.

Shepards Publications used to determine which court opinions mention an earlier opinion (Law Library).

Shift The length of time spent working at one job in any 24-hour period, no more than eight hours for full-time employment in most workplaces. Also refers to the length of time a person performs a particular task before being relieved by the next person scheduled to do the same work. Librarians scheduled at a service point such as the reference desk may rotate shifts, especially in the evening and on weekends.

Shifting The laborious process of moving an entire

collection, or sections of a collection, from one location to another in the stacks of a library, usually to create shelf space in classifications that have become overcrowded.

Shipping and receiving Section of the fiscal service responsible for mail collection and distribution, including receipts and shipments of all mail and freight and the mailing of all interlibrary loan materials.

Shipping The delivery of materials, equipment, or supplies ordered from a publisher, jobber, dealer, or supplier to a library by post or some other method. Also refers to the charge for delivery, usually included as a separate amount on the invoice. Directory information for shipping services is available in annual reference serial Literary Market Place.

Shockwave a group of interactive multimedia players from Macromedia that provide streaming audio and animation (see Enliven, quicktime).

Shoe One of a set of four metal sheaths custom-fitted to the corners of a large hand-bound book to protect the leather binding, usually made of brass or silver, plain or decorated.

Short discount In the book trade, a discount less than the one normally allowed by the publisher, jobber, or bookseller, usually 5-35%. Professional books, textbooks, and reference books are normally sold at short discount, as are items on special order. Compare with long discount.

Short film Any motion picture with a running time of less than 30 minutes (three reels or less). The category includes cartoons, newsreels, documentaries, and experimental films. The once common practice of showing one or more shorts before a feature film has ceased in commercial movie theaters. Short films are now shown mainly at film festivals. Synonymous with short subject.

Short list A small group of candidates chosen from a larger group, from which the final selection is made when filling a vacant position, awarding a prize, or determining the winner of a competition.

Short page In printing, a page with fewer lines of type matter than the specified number, as at the end of a chapter. In contemporary books, the unfilled space is usually left blank, but in older editions.it was sometimes adorned with a printer's ornament. Compare with long page.

Short score A sketch of an ensemble work in which the composer sets forth on a few staves its main elements, with the intention of elaborating on the themes at some time in the future. Compare with close score and condensed score.

Short shipment An order shipped with one or more items lacking, usually because they were out of stock at the time the order was filled. The absent titles, known as shorts, are usually placed on back order to be shipped as soon as they become available.

Short short story A fictional prose narrative of 500 to 1,500 words, containing all the elements of a short story in very concise form (example: "The Mad Woman" by Guy de Maupassant).

Short story A work of short fiction, usually 2,000-10,000 words in length, in which the author limits the narrative to a single character (or group of characters) acting in a limited setting, usually at a single point in time, to achieve a unified effect. Short fiction is published in literary magazines and collections. Stories considered outstanding by editors and critics may be anthologized following initial publication. Short stories published in collections are indexed in Short Story Index published annually by H. W. Wilson. Compare with novelette and short short story.

Short term disability (STD) Short-term disability insurance is an added benefit for all state classified employees. The program is 100% employer paid and benefits are payable for disabilities occurring due to accident or sickness occurring either on or off the job. The amount of STD benefit is 60% of an employee's pre-disability earnings.

Short title An abbreviated title of a book or other publication, usually enough of the full title to enable the item to be identified in a catalog or bibliography, or on a price list or order form.

Shortcut Some operating systems allow the user to create an icon or pointer on the desktop which can be double-clicked to directly access a program or document, without having to click the Start button and select the application or filename from a menu or directory system.

Shoulder In bookbinding, the ridge along the binding edge of the text block, made to accommodate the boards of the cover by bending the backs of the sewn sections from the center toward the front and back, a process called backing, done in with a hammer in hand-binding, and by machine in commercial binding, after the back has been rounded, and before the lining is applied. Also called an abutment, flange, groove, or ledge.

Shoulder note A note written or printed on the outer corner of the head margin of a page, usually in handwriting or a type size (or style) that distinguishes it from the text.

Shouting When specific words within an e-mail message (or its entire text) are typed in uppercase, the tone may be inerrupted by its recipient(s)..

Show through A printing defect in which text or illustration printed on one side of a leaf is visible through the paper from the other side, usually the result of a mismatch between paper stock and ink, on the part of the typographer.

Sibling In indexing, a descriptor or subject heading that shares a broader term (one level up in hierarchy) with one or more other descriptors in the same indexing language. The meanings of sibling terms may overlap (example: "Children's librarians" and "School librarians" under the broader term "Librarians"). Compare with orphan.

Sic The Latin word for "thus" written inside brackets [sic] or parentheses (sic) after a quotation to indicate that a misspelled word or grammatical error has been reproduced verbatim. In continental Europe, the exclamation mark (!) Is used for the same purpose.

Side note A note written or printed on one of the side margins of a page, opposite the passage of text to which it refers, usually in writing or type that distinguishes it from the text. A cut-in side note is set in from the left- or right-hand margin, with text surrounding it on three sides. Synonymous with marginal note. Compare with gloss

Side sewing In binding, to fasten sections or loose leaves together by sewing the entire text block through the side along the binding margin in a single pass, a method that considerably restricts openability. The ANSI standard for library binding specifies that a lock-stitch be used in side sewing, and does not recommend the method for text blocks over 1/2-inch thick or when the binding margin is less than 3/4-inches wide. Compare with fold sewn.

Side title The title impressed on the outside of the front cover of a book, sometimes a shortened version of the title printed on the .

Sidebar Information printed alongside a text and set apart visually, usually inside a box or by shading. Sidebars are used in magazines, textbooks, popular reference books, how-to books, etc., to present related or supplementary material which the author does not wish to include in the text. Compare with side note.

Side-stitching A method of binding in which flat wire staples are driven by machine through the entire thickness of the sections of a publication, parallel with the back fold, close to the binding edge. Used primarily for textbooks and periodical issues of more than one section, the method is stronger than saddle-stitching, but does not allow the leaves to open easily. For this reason, side-stitched publications must have a wide gutter margin. Synonymous with side-wire stitching.

Signage A collective term for all the static visual symbols and devices posted in a library to direct patrons to specific resources, services, and facilities, and to inform them of library hours, policies, programs, and events, including their size, design, and placement. Signs which are clear, concise, consistent, courteous, and appropriately placed can significantly reduce the number of directional questions received at the reference desk and make using the library less stressful, especially for inexperienced patrons.

Signatory A government or agency that has the legal right to sign an official document, such as a treaty or trade agreement. Also refers to a person whose signature appears on such a document.

Signature In printing, a single sheet of paper folded one or more times to become, with the addition of any plates or other inserts, one section in a bound publication. In modern book production, signatures are usually in multiples of 8 pages, with 32 the norm. A signature mark called a register is applied by the printer to alert the binder to the order in which the folded sheets are to be gathered.

Signed An entry in a reference work, or article in a periodical, in which the name of the author (or authors) is given, usually at the beginning or end of the text. In a more general sense, any written document that indicates the identity of the person who wrote it, such as a letter or legal instrument bearing the author's signature. The opposite of unsigned.

Silent film Any motion picture produced without sound, usually from the period before "talkies" were introduced (1895 until about 1927). Also refers to the entire body of motion pictures produced during this early period. Classic American examples include the early films of comedians Charlie Chaplin and Buster Keaton, and the works of D. W. Griffith. When early silent films were shown to live audiences, the movie theater usually hired an orchestra or pianist to provide musical accompaniment. Projection speed for silent films is usually 16 fps (frames per second). In library cataloging, lack of sound track is indicated by the abbreviation si. In the physical description area of the bibliographic record for a film.

Silk screen A method of stencil printing in which the areas of a design to be left unprinted are masked on the underside of a screen made of fabric, plastic, or woven metal stretched on a frame. Ink or paint is forced through the unmasked areas onto the printing surface by hand or by machine. Each color must be applied separately using a different stencil. Screen printing is used for signs and posters, and for printing on surfaces such as glass, metal, plastic, wood, etc. Synonymous with serigraphy.

Silking The process of affixing chiffon silk, or some other gossamer material, to one or both sides of a sheet of paper, or to a leaf in a book, to repair or preserve it. The result is said to have been silked.

Silverplatter A commercial vendor that provides access to a wide range of bibliographic and full-text electronic databases to libraries of all kinds via a proprietary interface.

SIMM: Single In-line Memory Module; a small circuit board that can hold a group of memory chips; used to increase your computer's RAM in increments of 1,2, 4, or 16 MB.

Simple Search Engines - They allow you to type in a single word or phrase and shows you the Web pages that contain that word or phrase.

Simplex In communications, a channel that has the capacity to transmit signals in one direction but not in the other. Compare with duplex.

Simplified edition An adaptation that makes the text of a previously published work easier to read, usually for a specific age group or category of reader, by substituting less difficult words, shortening the narrative, and adding a glossary, commonly used in ESL (English as a second language) instruction. Compare with abridgment.

Simultaneous publication Publication of the hardcover and paperback editions of a new book at the same time. Normally, the softcover edition is published months or even years after the cloth edition. Compare with parallel publishing.

Simultaneous submission Submission of a completed manuscript by the author or the author's agent to more than one publisher at the same time. A journal publisher's policy concerning simultaneous submission is usually stated in its guidelines for contributors.

Simultaneous user A person who accesses a bibliographic database or other online resource at the same time as other users. Licensing agreements usually specify the maximum number of users who may log on simultaneously at a given subscription rate. Most vendors have designed their proprietary search software to deny access when the limit is exceeded.

Sine loco A Latin phrase meaning "without place." In library cataloging, the abbreviation s.l. Is used inside square brackets [s.l.] In the publication, distribution, etc. Area of the bibliographic description to indicate that there is no known place of publication. Compare with sine nomine.

Sine nomine A Latin phrase meaning "without name." In library cataloging, the abbreviation s.n. Is used inside square brackets [s.n.] In the publication, distribution, etc. Area of the bibliographic description to indicate that the name of the publisher or distributor is unknown. Compare with sine loco.

Single index An index compiled all at one time, to facilitate access to the content of a single publication, for example, an index at the back of a book or at the end of the last volume of a multivolume reference work. Compare with cumulative index and open-end index.

Single title continuation Set that comes out in part over a period of time with a definite end in view. Acquisition service places a standing order for the set; term is used for processing purposes.

Sinkage In printing, the amount of space left blank above the first line of type at the top of a page of text, for example, at the beginning of a chapter or other major division of a book.

Site A collective term covering all the Internet facilities offered by one organization.

Site license Official permission granted to a company, agency, organization, or institution by a software producer or vendor to use a software product under specified conditions on all the computers at a designated IP address, or range of IP addresses, usually in exchange for payment by the licensee of an annual fee. Compare with software license.

Site licensed software A collection of inexpensive software packages available to the OSU community from OIT; programs included are a result of site license agreements, bulk purchases, and educational discounts by vendors as well as public domain software. For more information, call 688-HELP.

Site-license Through negotiations with a vendor, a renewable fee has been paid to allow a fixed number of copies of copyrighted software at one site.

Sitesearch Collection of tools from OCLC that the library uses for creating electronic resources. Examples of library projects using sitesearch software are IRIS and Athena.

Sized Paper treated in manufacture with a substance that makes its surface less porous, reducing its capacity to absorb moisture. Blotting paper is left unsized. Also refers to book cloth treated with a stiffener.

Sizing Substances such as resin or gelatin added to paper stock in manufacture to promote the bonding of cellulose fibers, or as a coating to fill pores in the surface after sheets have been formed. Sizing makes paper less permeable to water, preventing the ink used in printing from bleeding. Sizing also gives definition to the printed image. Some sizings are acidic and contribute to the deterioration of paper.

Skeleton staff The minimum number of employees required to operate a library, usually those necessary to staff essential service points and maintain security. Libraries chronically under-staffed may be forced to operate with minimal staff in the evening and on weekends, or remain closed.

Sketch A brief essay, story, or play, developed in less detail than a more complete work of the same literary form. A character sketch captures the essence of one or more individuals, with little or no plot. Also refers to a drawing that provides a rough outline of its subject without adding much detail, usually done rapidly, in a single sitting, sometimes as a study for a more elaborate treatment of the same subject.

Skyline In newspaper publishing, any headline printed across the top of the first page above the flag. Compare with banner.

Slang An informal or colloquial expression peculiar to a specific group, often unintelligible to outsiders but sometimes decipherable from its context. Slang expressions are subject to linguistic fashion. Most serious authors use slang terms only in dialogue or when writing informally. In libraries, dictionaries of slang are available in the reference section.

Slash In writing, printing, and computing, a character in the form of a line slanting diagonally from upper right to lower left, used to indicate division, fractions, and ratios (miles/hour); to combine dates (1905/06); to indicate alternatives (and/or); and to separate the parts of an Internet address (http://www.myuniversity.edu/library). Synonymous with forward slash, solidus, and virgule. Compare with backslash.

Sleeper In the retail book trade, a trade book that sells slowly when first published, but develops a strong, steady market over a period of months or even years. In libraries, a new book that circulates slowly when first added to the collection, but in time attracts a strong, steady readership. In the antiquarian book trade, a valuable item priced well below its market value in a dealer's catalog or on the shelf because the seller is unaware of its actual worth.

Sleeve A transparent plastic covering designed to fit snugly over the paper dust jacket of a hardcover book. Applied by a library staff member during physical processing, plastic sleeves are used in public libraries to a greater extent than in other types of libraries, to protect book covers and enhance their visual appeal.

Slick A term used in publishing to describe a heavily illustrated consumer magazine of high circulation, printed in color on glossy paper, for sale at newsstands, in bookstores and supermarkets, and by subscription.

Slide A small transparent, positive image in color or black-and-white, produced on film or glass, usually mounted in a rigid cardboard or plastic frame of standard size (2 x 2 inches), designed to be projected one-at-a-time on a large screen using a slide projector, with or without recorded sound. Modern slide projectors are designed to hold carousels for queuing dozens of slides. Most models have an automatic advance that can be activated remotely by the presenter. Models designed for professional use include a microprocessor that enables slides to be accessed randomly. Slides may also be viewed in a slide viewer, a smaller device with built-in rear-screen projection. Some models have audio and automatic advance capability similar to slide projectors. Compare with filmstrip.

Slide mount A rigid cardboard or plastic frame, usually of standard size (2 x 2"), designed to hold a single slide to protect it from damage and make it easier to label, store, and handle.

SLIM++ SLIM++ is an integrated, multi-user, multi-tasking library information software for the Windows environment. SLIM++ helps catalogue books, films, sound recordings, drawings, clippings, articles, reports, letters, pamphlets, serials publications... All those things that contain information so vital to your organization. SLIM++ cataloguing adheres to popular international standards. This means you can exchange data with the world. Retrieval of the data is simple, fast and efficient. Even a catchy phrase in the description of the catalogued item can be used for searching.

SLIP Serial Line Internet Protocol A standard for using a regular telephone line (a serial line) and a modem to connect a computer as a realinternet site. SLIP has largely been replaced by PPP.

Slip law Law in its first printed form after passage in Congress prior to its publication in the U.S. Statutes. Available in documents stacks.

SLIP Serial Line Internet Protocol. A protocol used to run IP over serial lines, such as telephone circuits or RS-232 cables, interconnecting two systems.

Slipcase A sturdy cardboard box, covered in paper, cloth, or leather, designed to snugly contain a single book or set of books, with an open front to expose the spines, allowing the title(s) remain visible. Intended to keep volumes together and protect them from damage, slipcases are more common in deluxe editions and videocassette sets than in trade book editions. Also spelled slip-case. Compare with pull-case and solander.

SLJ See: School Library Journal.

Small capital A capital letter of x-height, about 2/3 as large as the full-size capital of the same type size, used for emphasis in printed text. Abbreviated small cap. Abbreviated s.c.

Small press, the trade publication of small publishers, provides approximately 100 reviews of small press books in each bimonthly issue. Directory information on small presses is available in Literary Market Place and Writer's Market.

Smartboard A general term for several types of

electronic whiteboard, the most sophisticated of which can be synchronized with a computer to function like an oversize touch screen, allowing users to interact directly with the display, instead of using a keyboard, mouse, or other input device. Smartboards are used for bibliographic instruction in very well-equipped academic libraries. Also spelled smart board.

Smashing See: nipping.

SMDS Switched Multimegabit Data Service; A standard for very high-speed data transfer.

Smiley A whimsical sequence of punctuation marks and special characters, arranged to suggest the expression on a human face, used in e-mail messages to symbolically communicate emotion or humor. Frequently used examples include:

SMTP Simple Mail Transfer Protocol. Internet standard protocol for transferring electronic mail messages from one computer to another. SMTP specifies how two mail systems interact and the format of control messages they exchange to transfer mail.

Snail mail A colloquial term for paper mail handled by the U.S. Post Office.

SNMP Simple Network Management Protocol);A set of standards for communication with devices connected to a TCP/IP network. Examples of these devices include routers, hubs, and switches. SNMP is defined in RFC 1089

SO Standing order; all successive volumes of a work have been ordered to be supplied automatically when published.

Sobriquet A nickname, assumed name, or other imaginative appellation applied to a person (example: Sachmo), group (Copperheads), place (Dixie), thing (Old Ironsides), or institution (Uncle Sam). An author is occasionally known by such a name (The Bard). Compare with pseudonym.

Social Responsibilities Round Table (SRRT) Established over 25 years ago as a permanent round table of the American Library Association to make the organization more democratic and to establish progressive priorities for the library profession, SRRT has been particularly active on issues involving civil and economic rights. SRRT publishes the quarterly SRRT Newsletter and is affiliated with the Alternative Press Center (APC) which publishes of the Alternative Press Index.

Social Science Research Network e-library Contains over 34,400 abstracts for papers submitted to SSRN. Also gives access to few full text articles.

Social sciences Anthropology, criminology and criminal justice, economics, international relations, law, political science, psychiatry, psychology, public administration, social work, sociology, urban studies, women's studies

Society A corporate entity consisting of a group of people who meet periodically to share a common interest, especially one that is academic or professional. The most comprehensive directory of such organizations is the Encyclopedia of Associations, available in the reference section of most libraries in the United States.

Society for Scholarly Publishing (SSP) An organization that grew out of the Association of Scientific Journals (ASJ) and the Innovation Guide project of the National Science Foundation during the 1970s, SSP is devoted to advancing scholarly communication and publishing, and the professional development of its members through education, collaboration, and networking. Its members include scholarly book and journal publishers, librarians, manufacturers, booksellers, and Web editors.

Society for the History of Authorship, Reading and Publishing (SHARP) Created in 1991, SHARP provides a global network for book historians. Its membership includes literature professors, historians, librarians, publishing professionals, sociologists, bibliophiles, classicists, booksellers, art historians, reading instructors, and independent scholars from over 20 countries. SHARP sponsors an annual conference, maintains an online discussion forum, and publishes the quarterly newsletter SHARP News.

Society of American Archivists (SAA) Founded in 1934, SAA is the oldest professional organization of archivists in North America, dedicated to promoting the identification, preservation, and use of records of historical value. SAA publishes the newsletter Archival Outlook and the semiannual journal American Archivist.

Socket Logical address of a communications access point to a specific device or program on a host.

Softcover A publication bound in covers that are not rigid, usually a paperback, but the term also includes limp and flexible bindings. Most periodicals are issued in softcover. In trade books, the softcover edition is published separately from the hardcover edition, usually at a later date, and is sold at a lower price. Synonymous with paperbound.

Software A generic term for computer programs and their associated documentation, as opposed to data used as input and generated as output. In computing, data is "processed"—software "runs." A software product consists of a set of instructions written by a programmer, distinct from the manufactured hardware used to run it. The term includes systems programs such as operating systems (OS), database management systems (DBMS), utilities that control the operation of the computer itself, and application programs designed to process data and accomplish specific tasks for the user.

Software license A formal agreement between the producer and purchaser of a software product concerning permissible use, especially with regard to sharing and making copies. Software piracy is the unauthorized copying of licensed software, usually for sale in a country other than the one in which it is copyrighted. Compare with site license.

Solander A box in the shape of a book, wide enough to stand upright, used for storing books, pamphlets, maps, plates, papers, etc., designed in two parts with a slide-on top, or hinged to open at the front or side, with a clasp or spring catch. Named after Daniel C. Solander, the 18th century Swedish botanist who designed it for storing specimens at the British Museum. Compare with pull-case and slipcase.

Soliloquy A long sequence of lines addressed by an actor or actress, not to the other players on stage, but directly to the audience, revealing private thoughts, feelings, or intentions. Perhaps the best known example is the "To Be or Not to Be" speech in Hamlet in which the protagonist expresses the personal dilemma posed by the unexpected allegation of murder made by his father's ghost. A shorter speech intended to be inaudible to the other characters in a scene is an aside. Compare with monologue.

SOLINET Southeastern Library Network; regional library consortium.

Solo librarian A librarian solely responsible for managing a small library, without the assistance of other paid staff. Solo public librarians often rely on the assistance of volunteers from the community served. Running even a small library single-handedly requires energy, initiative, versatility, and self-sufficiency. Solo librarians are organized in the Solo Librarians Division of the Special Libraries Association.

Songster A type of broadside or chapbook popular during the 18th and 19th centuries, containing poems and ballads sung to popular tunes.

Sonnet A lyric poem of fourteen lines, written in iambic pentameter. A sonnet sequence is a group of sonnets written by a single poet, usually on a common theme. The form originated in Italy in the 13th century. The most common rhyme schemes were developed by Petrarch and Shakespeare.

Sorting In a search of a online catalog or bibliographic database, the default display is normally alphabetical order by author or title, or reverse chronological order by publication date. However, in some online catalogs and databases, the user may select the sequence in which results will be displayed, usually from a list of options, either before or after the search is executed. Compare with ranking.

Sound archives A permanent collection of sound recordings, preserved for research purposes (example: Stanford Archive of Recorded Sound). Materials collected include wax cylinders, shellac and vinyl phonograph records, audiotape, digital compact discs, etc. One of the earliest comprehensive archives of sound recordings was established in the early 20th century by the British Broadcasting Corporation (BBC).

Sound recording A generic term for sounds that have been mechanically, electromagnetically, or digitally recorded onto a medium designed for playback with the aid of audio equipment. The category includes phonograph records, audiotapes, compact discs, and the sound track on motion pictures, videorecordings, dvds, etc. Libraries collect sound recordings of music and human speech (poetry, drama, speeches, interviews, broadcasts, books-on-tape, etc.). The proceedings of meetings and conferences are sometimes recorded for archival purposes.

Sound track The sound component of a motion picture or video, usually recorded along one or both edges of the film or tape, on a magnetically coated stripe, synchronizing sound with image. Also refers to the music score of a motion picture, released separately on audiocassette or compact disc, sometimes under a slightly different title. Silent films have no sound track.

Source Any document that provides information sought by a writer, researcher, library user, or person searching an online catalog or bibliographic database. Also refers to a document that provides information copied or reproduced in another document, for example, a quotation or excerpt. In literature, the story, legend, or work that inspires or provides elements of plot or characterization for another literary work, for example, the chronicles of English history on which Shakespeare based some of his history plays.

Source document In reprography, the original document from which copies are made, usually containing text and/or graphic material that can be read by the human eye without magnification. Compare with master.

Source field In the record structure of most bibliographic databases, the data field containing the journal title, volume number, date of issue, and page numbers of a periodical article; the book title, publisher, publication date, and page numbers for an essay in a collection; or the title, publisher, and publication date for a book or book chapter. In the record display, the field label may be abbreviated SO:

Source language The original language of a text that has been translated into one or more other languages. In library cataloging, the language of the original work is indicated in a parallel title or Translation of: note in the bibliographic description.

Spacing The use of one or more blank characters to separate words in printing and typing. Also refers to one or more lines left blank at the beginning of type matter, or between lines of type, for example, the three lines left blank at the top of a typed or printed catalog card, or the double space before the first note and before the tracings. In AACR2, the use of spacing in catalog records is governed by the general rules for punctuation, and by the specific rules for punctuation in each area of bibliographic description.

Spam Unsolicited e-mail messages mass-mailed to large numbers of newsgroups and/or mailing lists with little concern for the burden such activity places on subscribers. Spamming is considered one of the worst violations of netiquette because it forces Internet users to waste valuable time scanning and deleting unwanted messages. The person who sends such messages is a spammer. For more information on this nuisance, please see: spam.abuse.net.

SPARC Scholarly Publishing and Academic Resources Coalition.

Spatial Data Spatial data is data pertaining to the location and spatial dimensions of geographical entities. Examples of spatial data files can be found within the Cornell University Geospatial Information Repository (CUGIR), accessible through the Library Gateway.

Special collections Some libraries segregate from the general collection rare books, manuscripts, papers, and other items which are 1) of a certain form, 2) on a certain subject, 3) of a certain time period or geographic area, 4) in fragile or poor condition, or 5) especially valuable. Such materials are not allowed to circulate and access to them may be restricted.

Special edition An edition or issue of a work (or works) produced in a format that differs from previous editions, usually for a special purpose and sometimes under a distinctive title, with a new introduction and sometimes additional notes, appendices, or illustrations. The term is also used synonymously with library edition.

Special interest magazine A magazine devoted to a specific topic of interest to a fairly narrow, well-defined audience, for example, golfing enthusiasts (Golf Digest) or yoga teachers and practitioners (Yoga Journal). Public libraries usually subscribe to special interest titles on the basis of demand, as indicated by patron requests and usage statistics for related items. Compare with general interest magazine.

Special issue An issue of a periodical devoted wholly or substantially to a specific subject or occasion. When published more than once on the same topic, a special issue usually appears at the same time in consecutive years, for example, the annual swimsuit issue of Sports Illustrated, a high-demand item in public libraries.

Special Libraries Association (SLA) Founded in 1909,.SLA has an international membership of information professionals employed in special libraries serving business, research, governments, universities, newspapers, museums, and institutions that use or produce specialized information. SLA publishes the monthly magazine Information Outlook

Special library A library established and funded by a commercial firm, private association, government agency, nonprofit organization, or special interest group to meet the information needs of its employees, members, or staff in accordance with the organization's mission and goals. The scope of the collection is usually limited to the interests of its host organization. Special librarians are organized in the Special Libraries Association. Information on special libraries in the United States and Canada is available in the Directory of Special Libraries and Information Centers published by the Gale Group.

Special offer An offer by a supplier or vendor to sell goods and/or services at a lower price, usually for a limited period of time, or to provide a trial period, premium, or other inducement to purchase or subscribe. Other restrictions, such as minimum purchase amount, may apply.

Specialization Concentration on a limited aspect of a subject or discipline, often to the exclusion of related areas of study or inquiry. The breadth of librarianship is so great that most librarians decide to focus on one or two aspects of the profession. In library school, students usually select a functional specialization (public services, technical services, automated systems, etc.). Each of these tracks is divided into narrower branches, for example, subject analysis within technical services, or bibliographic instruction within public services. In public libraries, librarians specialize in services for adults, young adults, or children. Librarians employed in special libraries focus on a particular subject or field (art, business, engineering, law, medicine), type of material (government documents, film and video), type of institution (correctional, military, museum), or type of collection (archives, special collections). The professional organizations and journal literature of librarianship reflect these divisions.

Specific entry In subject analysis, the principle that a work is listed in a library catalog, index, or bibliographic database under the most specific subject heading(s) or descriptor(s) that fully describe its content. For example, a book about poets would be entered under "Poets" not "Writers" and a work about French poets under "French poets" or "Poets, French" rather than "Poets." Compare with coextensive entry.

Specific material designation The most specific designation of the type of material to which an item belongs, given under extent of item in the physical description area of the bibliographic description, for example, "videodisc" under the general material designation "videorecording."

Specifications The instructions sent by a publisher to a printer with the typescript of a work regarding its characteristics as a prospective publication, including its dimensions, paper stock, typeface, quantity of illustration, extent of front and back matter, etc., from which the printer creates a specimen page to indicate the proposed style of typesetting. Cost of production is determined by specs and size of edition. In a more general sense, detailed instructions concerning work to be done, products or services to be supplied, etc., especially when a contract is to be signed.

Specificity In indexing, the degree to which the meaning of a descriptor or subject heading matches the content of the document to which it is assigned. For example, although the Library of Congress subject heading "Gardening" applies to a book about gardening inside the house, the heading "Indoor gardening" describes the content more precisely. Specificity in this sense is relative to the work described. An indexing term may be specific, whether broad or narrow, as long as it matches closely an important subject of the work.

Specimen A single individual or member of a group or class, selected as an example or sample of the whole, for example, an item of a specific type selected to represent a group of items, or an entire collection, in a library display or exhibit. Compare with artifact.

Specimen case A wide flat storage container, usually with a transparent top, divided into compartments usually backed with soft material, used for for mounting and storing specimens in rows to facilitate comparison. Some models are lockable. In museums, specimen cases may be built to specific dimensions to allow them to be stored, one atop another inside a specially designed cabinet.

Specimen page One of several sample pages submitted by the printer to the publisher to show the proposed typographic style for a prospective publication, usually four in number, including the first page of a chapter and at least one subhead to show display type. Also refers to a copy of a page from a book or other publication, reproduced on any scale for use by the publisher in marketing.

Speckling Isolated light pixels in predominantly dark image areas, sometimes caused by incorrect readings or noise in the scanning device.

Spectral Highlight A bright reflection from a light source containing little or no detail.

Spectrophotometer An extremely accurate color measurement device using a diffraction grating to split light into its components wavelengths, which are then measured by numerous light sensors.

Speech recognition See: voice recognition.

Spell checker A feature of most word processing software that automatically checks the spelling of words typed in a document against a built-in dictionary, alerting the user to any misspelled words and even correcting typos on the fly. Spell-checkers are not infallible. A misspelling will not be flagged if it is itself a word ("their" for "there"). The option can usually be turned "off" by the user if not desired.

Spin little A title appearing on the spine of an item.

Spine label A small typed or printed label affixed to the lower spine of a book or other bibliographic item at the time it is processed, displaying its location symbol and call number, for use in reshelving and to assist the user in retrieving the item from the shelf once its call number has been found in the library catalog.

Spine rounded or flat part of the binding on a book, connecting the front and back covers and protecting the binding edge, the only part of the cover visible when the volume is placed alongside others on the shelf. It usually bears the spine title or an abbreviated title, and the last name or full name of the author. In libraries, a label bearing the location symbol and call number is affixed to the lower spine of each volume to facilitate retrieval and reshelving. In some bindings, the spine is covered in a different material than the boards (see: half-binding, quarter binding, and three-quarter binding). Synonymous with backbone and shelf back. Compare with back.

Spine title The title appearing on the spine of a book, sometimes shorter than the title impressed on the cover or printed on the title page. Synonymous with back title.

Spine-out Books displayed on a shelf with their spines facing the front, usually one alongside the other with a bookend at the end of the row to keep them upright—the shelving method used in the stacks of most libraries because it allows the spine title and call number on each volume to be seen at a glance. Compare with face out.

Spin-off An independently published book or set of books containing material selected from a longer work published by the same company, for example, the three-volume New Grove Dictionary of Musical Instruments containing entries that are nearly identical to those in the much longer New Grove Dictionary of Music and Musicians. Compare with abridgment.

Spiral binding A form of mechanical binding in which

a continuous coil of wire or hard plastic is drawn through small holes or slots punched in the binding edge of the covers and leaves of a publication to hold them together, used mainly for reports, manuals, workbooks, and notebooks containing blank or ruled pages. Spiral bindings open flat. Synonymous with coil binding. Compare with comb binding.

Split The permanent division of a serial into two or more parts. The note Continues in part: is included in the bibliographic record for each of the parts to indicate the title of the publication that split, and the corresponding note Split into: is added in the record for the serial that split to indicate the titles of the publications created by the division. The opposite of merger

Spoilage In book production, printed sheets or entire copies discarded because they contain imperfections or were damaged in printing or binding. Allowance for spoilage is included in the size of printing and binding orders.

Sponsor A person or corporate entity that subsidizes or provides encouragement, funding, or some other form of practical assistance in the production of a radio or television program, Web site, or other creative work, usually in exchange for some form of publicity. Compare with patron.

Sponsored book A book issued by an established commercial publisher for which the cost of publication is subsidized by an organization or company with an interest in seeing it published. The subsidy may be a direct payment to the publisher to cover losses in the event of disappointing sales, or an agreement to purchase enough copies at an established price to make the publication profitable. Compare with vanity publisher.

Spool A cylindrical flanged wheel with a hole running from end-to-end onto which a roll of unprocessed film is wound, designed to be inserted in a camera or processing machine. Compare with reel.

Spread The full expanse of facing pages in an opening

in a book or other bound publication. The page on the right-hand side is the recto; the one on the left is the verso.

Spreadsheet A number-related document whereby calculations and formulas are applied to the data organized in rows and columns of cells.

Spreadsheet Application software that allows textual information and numeric data to be displayed and computed in two-dimensional tabular format (rows and columns), widely used in budgeting and statistical analysis. Also refers to the result of using such a program, in print or electronic format.

Sprinkled In binding, a book on which the cut edges of the sections have been irregularly sprayed or spattered with flecks of color as a decoration, a technique used mainly on large dictionaries and expensive reference sets. The visual effect makes dust and any natural discoloration less noticeable.

Sprung The condition of a book in which the text block has separated from its cover, either in the process of rebinding or through wear on the hinges. Mending may require new endpapers. Compare with shaken.

Spurious work A written work known to be counterfeit (not genuine), usually one uncritically ascribed to a known author and subsequently discovered to be of unknown or uncertain authorship.

SQL (Structured Query Language) A specialized language for sending queries to databases. Most industrial-strength and many smaller database applications can be addressed using SQL. Each specific application will have its own slightly different version of SQL implementing features unique to that application, but all SQL-capable databases support a common subset of SQL.

Square A book in which the width of the cover is more than three-quarters (but not greater than) its height, a shape often used in art books and children's picture books. Compare with narrow and oblong.

Square bracket One of a pair of angled lines [ ] enclosing a word, phrase, or numeric figure in text, usually to indicate insertion. In library cataloging, square brackets are used to indicate an interpolation made by the cataloger (example: [48] p.) And around the general material designation following the title in a bibliographic record representing a nonbook item (example: [sound recording]). Compare with parenthesis.

Square capital A letter f the Latin alphabet used in Europe as a book hand from the 3rd to the 5th century, adapted from the lapidary capitals used in antiquity to carve inscriptions on monuments. The pointed serifs incised in stone were replaced with wider square serifs, easier to execute with a reed or quill pen, and the contrast between thick and thin strokes was greater in square capitals. Even so, the difficulty of writing square capitals led to the use of rustic capitals during the same period. Latin: capitales quadrata.

Squares In bookbinding, the edges of the boards of a cover, extending beyond the text block at the head, fore-edge, and tail to protect the bound sections from damage. Cased books have equal margins of cover around the edges, usually 1/8 to 3/16 of an inch. The term is also used for the part of the cover that is turned in on the inside, but not covered by the endpapers after they have been pasted down. Compare with cut flush.

SS System-supplied - data generated by the cataloging system which cannot be altered by the cataloger.

Ssearch A systematic examination of data make in order to locate specific information; can be done "manually" or on a computer.

SSL Secure Socket Layer; A protocol designed by Netscape Communications to enable encrypted, authenticated communications across the Internet.

Stabilization Chemical or physical methods applied in conservation to maintain the integrity of a document by arresting deterioration already in progress, for example, the neutralization of acid in the paper used for printing books and other publications. The stability of a document is its ability to resist changes of physical state when exposed to normal use and storage conditions. Compare with restoration.

Stack A unit of connected book cases or shelves, usually arranged in rows, for storing the library's collection.

Stack capacity The amount of material that can be contained in the stack area of a library, expressed as the total linear or square feet of available shelving, or the maximum number of volumes or other physical units that can be accommodated, sometimes computed by means of a formula.

Stack maintenance All the duties involved in keeping the books and other materials stored in the stacks of a library in good order, including reshelving, shelf reading, shifting the collection when certain classifications become overcrowded, and relabeling shelf ranges to indicate their contents.

Stack Space saving storage area where items in little demand are housed. Ask at the **Loans Desk** for all items you require from stack.

Stacked advertising Advertising that appears only in the front or back, or in the front and back, of a periodical and nowhere else in the issue (example: National Geographic). In custom binding of periodicals, unpaginated advertisements appearing in the front and/or back of each issue may be removed to reduce bulk.

Stacks Rows of bookshelves in a library.

Stacks The shelving areas in a library where books, periodicals, and other materials are stored when not in use. In some libraries, the stacks are closed to the public, but most libraries in the United States allow patrons to browse all or part of their primary collections in open stacks.

Staff retreat An opportunity provided by the administration of a library for the professional, technical, and administrative staff to meet in a comfortable location away from the workplace, usually once or twice a year for at least a full or half day, to discuss issues affecting the library and the clientele it serves. To avoid distraction, strategic planning is often conducted in such a setting.

Staff room A room in a library, usually equipped with comfortable furniture and a kitchenette, where staff members can go when they are not on-duty to eat, relax on a break, or meet informally. Synonymous with staff lounge.

Staircasing See Aliasing.

Stand-alone A computer not connected to a network, which functions independently of other computers and systems. In libraries, bibliographic databases on CD-ROM may be installed on a stand-alone PC workstation, especially when licensing agreements restrict usage to one simultaneous user.

Standard An acceptable level or criterion according to which something is compared, measured, or judged. Also refers to an amount, extent, quality, pattern, criterion, etc., fixed by usage or convention, or established as the norm by prevailing authority, as in the standard size of a catalog card used by libraries prior to the development of machine-readable cataloging. A de facto standard is one that becomes generally accepted without the formal endorsement of a standard-setting organization. Compare with benchmark.

Standard author An author whose literary works have earned such a respected place in the national literature of a country that they are frequently taught in literature courses and included in anthologies (examples: William Faulkner, Jane Austen, Gustave Flaubert, Henrik Ibsen, Anton Chekhov, etc.).

Standard deviation In statistical analysis, a quantitative measure of how far a variable differs from the norm, calculated as the square root of the variance.

Standard format The most common form of a specific type of document, for example, the sequence in which the parts of a journal article reporting the results of original scientific research are presented (review of existing literature, research methodology, results or findings, discussion or analysis of results, conclusions, suggestions for further research, and list of works cited).

Standard Generalized Markup Language (SGML) Established in 1986, SGML is an ISO standard governing the rules for defining tag sets that determine how machine-readable text documents are formatted. Not dependent on a specific computer system or type of software, SGML is widely used in preparing machine-readable text archives. The HTML code used to create Web pages is an SGML language that uses a fixed set of predefined tags. XML is a subset of **SGML** in which the tags are unlimited and not predefined.

Standard Industrial Classification (SIC) A system of four-digit product codes developed in the 1930s by the Statistical Policy Division of the U.S. Office of Management and Budget to represent categories of products and services sold by commercial companies, for the purpose of compiling economic statistics. In 1997, the OMB adopted the North American Industry Classification System (NAICS) to replace the SIC, a change that has affected some business reference books.

Standard list A list of titles recommended for any library collection of a particular type and size, usually published under the auspices of a library association (example: Books for College Libraries). Standard lists are difficult to keep current. Synonymous with selection guide

Standard number and terms of availability In AACR2, the area of bibliographic description in which the standard number (ISBN, ISSN, etc.), list price, and any other terms under which the item is available are entered (field 020 or 022 of the MARC record).

Standard number The unique identification number

assigned to an edition at the time of first publication, in accordance with an internationally standardized identification system, usually appearing somewhere on the item. In hardcover books, the International Standard Books Number (ISBN) is printed on the verso of the title page and usually on the front flap of the dust jacket. In softcover editions, it appears on the verso of the title page and on the back cover (usually in the lower right-hand corner). In periodicals, the International Standard Serial Number (ISSN) is included in the masthead or with the table of contents. In AACR2, the standard number is given in the standard number and terms of availability area of the bibliographic description.

Standard subdivision In the Library of Congress Subject Headings list, a subheading applied uniformly to one or more categories of main heading, for example, the subheading "Influence" under headings for personal names, corporate bodies, uniform titles of sacred texts, religions, wars, types of organizations, and forms and movements in the arts (example: Hardy, Thomas, 1840-1928—Influence).

Standard work A work widely recognized as a model of excellence in its field, which libraries may order in multiple copies or editions (example: The Elements of Style by William Strunk, Jr.). A standard reference work is usually published in revised editions (example: The Columbia Granger's Index to Poetry in Anthologies). Compare with classic.

Standardization The process of establishing uniform procedures and standards in a specific field of endeavor, usually to facilitate exchange and cooperation, and to assure quality and enhance productivity. In librarianship, standards are established by professional associations, accrediting bodies, and government agencies.

Standards Criteria established by professional associations, accrediting bodies, or agencies of government for measuring and evaluating library services, collections, and programs (example: Information Literacy Competency Standards for Higher Education published in 2000 by the

Association of College and Research Libraries). Also refers to any code of rules or procedures established by national and international library organizations to govern bibliographic control, such as the MARC record format, CIP, and the ISBN/ISSN adopted by the publishing industry.

Standing committee A permanent committee appointed by management or selected according to established procedures to handle specific ongoing responsibilities, usually in support of an organization's mission and goals, as opposed to an ad hoc committee established to address a particular issue or accomplish a specific task, then dissolved once its goals and objectives have been met.

Standing order a book order placed with a dealer who will automatically supply the parts of a continuing item as they are published until instructed not to.

Standing room In the Dewey Decimal Classification schedules, topics considerably less extensive in scope than the subject(s) represented by the class, usually given immediately following the notation and heading, in a note that begins with "Including," "Contains," "Example(s)," or "Common names." Standing room provides a location for topics for which the number of published works is limited, but expected to grow, possibly to the point of warranting a separate class number. Catalogers are not permitted to add standard subdivisions to such topics, nor are other number building techniques allowed (adapted from DDC). Compare with approximate the whole.

Star map See: astronomical map.

Start A binding defect in which one of the sections of a book projects beyond the others at the fore-edge because it has not been properly secured at the binding edge. Also refers to a crack between sections at the binding edge, usually the result of forcing the leaves open while they are held down, instead of pressing gently along the inner margin to form a fold at the binding edge.

Start/Stop Bits A start bit signals the start of a unit of data in asynchronous communications. A stop bit signals the stop of a unit of data. The unit can vary in length depending on the protocol.

Started A book in which a portion of the body is so loose in the binding that it protrudes beyond the fore-edge but remains attached, a condition not as advanced as shaken.

Statbase Statbase provides access to a comprehensive set of key statistics drawn from the whole range of official United Kingdom government data sets. Topics covered include population, income, balance of payments, birth and death rates, consumer expenditure, marriage and divorce rates, economic activity, employment and unemployment, education and training, etc.

State accounts Books, periodicals and other materials originating in, or bearing the imprint of, an office or agency of a state government.

State Board of Agriculture (SBA) Board (Board of Governors of the Colorado State University System) appointed by the governor as the governing body of Colorado State University as well as the University of Southern Colorado. State Board of Agriculture records from 1879 on are located in the university archives.

State classified All permanent University employees not included in the academic faculty or administrative personnel staff are in the state classified personnel system.

State library In the United States, a library supported by state funds for the use of state employees and citizens, usually located in the state capital, containing a comprehensive collection of the state's official documents, books written by authors living in the state, and newspapers published in the state. The first state library was established in Pennsylvania in 1816.

State manual A publication issued annually or semiannually by a state government, usually containing the text of the state charter and/or constitution, election statistics, and information about government structure, elected and appointed officials, voting districts, and the towns or boroughs, cities, and counties within the state. Also known as a blue book.

State Part of an edition that differs from other copies of the same edition by virtue of minor changes in the make-up or typesetting made during printing or binding, usually additions, deletions, corrections, and transpositions. In the 16th and 17th centuries, variations in state were often the result of allowing the author to visit the press room while printing was in progress. They are used in historical bibliography and the antiquarian book trade to determine priority of issue. In this sense, state has no relation to condition. Compare with variant.

Statement of responsibility In library cataloging, the portion of the bibliographic record indicating the person(s) or corporate body responsible for creating the intellectual or artistic of the item, for example, the author, editor, or compiler of a written work, or the composer or arranger of a musical work. In most cases, the statement of responsibility is transcribed from the chief source of information in or on the item. In AACR2, when more than one kind of responsibility is indicated (multiple statements of responsibility), the names are transcribed in the order in which they appear on the chief source of information.

State-of-the-art A product, system, or design that represents the most advanced degree of technical achievement in its field at the present time. In the construction of new facilities, libraries typically strive for state-of-the-art design and technology, but must often settle for what is financially feasible.

Stationer In Europe, the earliest nonmonastic producer and lender of manuscript books for profit. Stationarii (Latin) were licensed by medieval universities to oversee the copying, binding, distribution, and repair of officially approved texts. In England, the earliest commercial booksellers, who sold their wares from market stalls, were known as stationers

Stationery: A template you can create within Eudora Pro for outgoing messages; if you repeatedly send the same message, using a stationery file saves time. Instead of retyping the message or cutting and pasting, you just open a pre-written stationery file and edit it as necessary.

Statistical abstracts a compilation summarizing social, political, economic or other statistics for a given geographic, political, or other entity. For example, the indispensable Statistical Abstract of the United States.

Status code Codes used in the online catalog defined by the Library to have particular meanings; e.g., status codes may indicate if a book is checked out, lost, being bound, etc.

Status See: borrower status, circulation status, and loan status.

Statutory copy See: deposit copy.

Stave The set of five parallel horizontal lines on which musical notation is written or printed. In the full score of an ensemble work, each part is written on a separate stave.

Steady state A library collection in which the number of items weeded equals the number acquired over time. Libraries with a limited amount of shelf space and no prospect of expansion must maintain a constant collection size. Synonymous with no growth or zero growth.

Steering committee A group of people appointed or elected to take charge of a complex project, for example, the task of planning the renovation of an existing library or organizing a move into a new library facility. Their responsibilities include setting priorities and establishing the sequence in which various stages of the work are to proceed.

Stem The root of a word used as a search term in a query entered as input in information retrieval, to which one or more truncation symbols are added to retrieve variant forms (example: *witch* to retrieve bewitch, bewitched, bewitching, witch, witches, witchery, witchcraft, etc.).

Step index A series of shallow indentations resembling a staircase, cut into the fore-edge of a book, bearing a sequence of characters or headings, sometimes printed against a dark ground to facilitate reference. Synonymous with cut-in index. Compare with tab index and thumb index.

Stereograph A visual medium in which a transparent or opaque image, or two slightly different images of the same scene arranged side-by-side, appear three-dimensional when seen through the lenses of a binocular instrument called a stereoscope. In AACR2, stereographs are cataloged as graphic materials. Synonymous with stereogram.

Stereophonic Sound reproduced by an audio device simultaneously from two separate channels with two amplifiers or speakers. Stereophonic sound separation produces a more realistic effect than earlier monaural recording, but not as realistic as quadraphonic sound.

Stereotype A fixed impression which may have little basis in fact, but is nevertheless perpetuated by persons unwilling to look more deeply into the matter. Librarians are often cast in a mold by the mass media because few people outside the library profession understand what librarians do when they are not shushing people. Library humor often makes light of the absurdities inherent in the notion of the "typical librarian."

Stick A sturdy hardwood rod about three feet long, divided lengthwise down the center, usually into four thin shafts, with a handle on one end and a rubber ring at the other to hold the most recent issue of a newspaper securely along the fold. When not in use, the rods are designed to rest horizontally in a rack high enough to allow the leaves to hang freely without touching the floor. Synonymous with newspaper rod.

Stick wicket File kept at the reference desk and the journal room assistance desk giving answers to difficult and/ or recurring questions; is maintained by members of reference service.

Sticker A small preprinted adhesive label placed inside a book imported from another country, usually on the title page to indicate the name of the domestic distributor. Stickers are also used by publishers and booksellers to indicate price changes.

Still A single frame from a motion picture or videotape, often used for promotional purposes. Also refers to a single photograph taken with a conventional camera, especially one in which the subject is a performer, for use in publicity.

Stipple A pattern of small dots of varying color and/or density, used in drawing, painting, or printing to create the impression of gradations of light and shadow in an image.

Stipple engraving A graphic technique that combines etching and engraving to produce designs in which outlines are etched by hand and shading is produced by a pattern of small dots of varying size and density, cut into the same plate with a graver. Also refers to a print made by this technique.

STM An abbreviation used in the publishing trade for the scientific, technical, and medical segment of the market for journals, books, and other forms of scholarly communication. Leading STM publishers include Elsevier Science and Springer-Verlag.

Stock photograph A photograph taken in the past, kept on file for use when no current picture is available, in contrast to one taken specifically for the purpose at hand. Newspapers usually maintain a file of stock photographs, especially portraits of well-known individuals, pictures of landmarks, etc., for use as the occasion arises. Directory information for stock photo agencies is available in Literary Market Place. Copyright law applies.

Stop word/stop list Also "noise word". Words not indexed in the computer system due to too many entries or lack of meaning. (e. G., and, or, the).

Stopword A a, an, as, at, by, for, from, of, on, the, to). Some systems frequently used word—usually an article, conjunction, or preposition with little semantic content—

ignored when a keywords search is executed because it adds little value to the search statement and is not helpful for retrieval (common examples: have a predetermined list of stopwords, which may be given in the help screen(s). In some systems, a stopword may be context-dependent, for example, the word "education" in a bibliographic database providing access to materials on education, but not in a database indexing articles published in newspapers or general interest periodicals. Also spelled stop word.

Storage A facility on Guardsman Way where infrequently used materials are kept in order to free up shelf space in the library stacks. Items in storage are listed in UNIS. Patrons may request retrieval of materials in storage at the Circulation desk; items are retrieved once a day.

Storage Building for the storage of lesser-used library materials.

Storage area A location within a library building or outside its walls where infrequently used materials and equipment are housed until needed. In some libraries, items in storage may be retrieved by courier at the user's request. The status of items in a storage collection may be indicated in the catalog record.

Story hour A period of time set aside for reading and telling stories to the youngest members of a library's clientele, a regularly scheduled event in some public libraries. The storyteller is usually a trained children's librarian, but storytelling may also be done by a particularly talented or experienced assistant or volunteer. In some public libraries, the children's room includes a special room or corner with soft furniture, designed to put young listeners at ease. Also spelled storyhour. Synonymous with storytime.

Storyboard A series of pictures or rough sketches with accompanying text, used in the production of an audiovisual or multimedia work to help the creators visualize the sequence of its parts. Also spelled story board.

Storybook A book of stories for children. often an

illustrated collection of well-known fables, fairy tales, nursery rhymes, and poems, sometimes devoted to a specific topic or theme (example: The Japanese Children's Storybook on the Bombing of Hiroshima by Toshi and Iri Maruki). The term is also seen in the titles of collections of Bible stories written for children. Compare with picture storybook.

Storytelling of telling and reading stories to young children, for pleasure and to interest them in books and reading. The practice was first introduced in libraries by Caroline Hewins at the Hartford Public Library in Connecticut in 1882. Storytelling is sometimes done with the aid of a flannel board or puppets. In audiobooks for children, the story is sometimes told by a celebrity narrator whose voice is easily recognized.

Strategic alliance A collaborative partnership between a library and one or more external departments, agencies, organizations, etc., for the mutual benefit of all the participants. Examples include mentoring relationships between undergraduate libraries and athletics programs; digitization projects involving libraries, archives, museums, and historical societies; and library events involving authors, sponsored in conjunction with local booksellers.

Strategic planning The systematic process by which a company, organization, or institution (or one of its units) formulates achievable policy objectives for future growth and development over a period of years, based on its mission and goals, and on a realistic assessment of the resources, human and material, available to implement the plan. The process may require the collection and analysis of data on current operations and user preferences in order to evaluate competing options. A well-developed strategic plan is the basis for effective performance evaluation.

Strawboard A coarse board used in case binding, made from unbleached straw and repulped waste fiber. Binder's board is preferred in trade editions.

Streaming Audio/video that plays as it arrives, rather

than waiting until the whole file has downloaded (see realaudio and Shockwave).

Streaming (streaming media): A technique for transferring data over the Internet so that a client browser or plug-in can start displaying it before the entire file has been received; used in conjunction with sound and pictures. Example: The Shockwave plug-in from Macromedia gives your computer the capability for streaming audio; realplayer is used for viewing sound and video.

Streaming video A method of sending a sequence of compressed moving images one-way over a data network, at the user's request or broadcast at a fixed time, which allows viewing to begin before the entire file has been transmitted. To counteract any delays caused by packet switching and maintain the impression of continuous motion, a buffer on the client computer is used to store a few seconds of video before it is displayed on the screen. Unlike video that is downloaded for subsequent playback, streaming video is stored as a temporary file and deleted when the application used to view it is closed. Videoconferencing differs from streaming video in providing two-way transmission in real time.

Stripe A narrow band of magnetic material applied as a coating along one or both edges of a length of motion picture film, on which the sound track is recorded.

Stub The narrow strip of paper remaining along the inner edge when a leaf is sliced cleanly out of a book, used to tip in another leaf when a replacement is required. Also refers to a narrow strip of cloth or paper sewn between the sections of a book to attach a folded map or illustration, or bound into the front or back to secure a pocket. In binding, the process of adding such strips to a text block is called stubbing.

Student assistant part-time employee in an academic library, school library, or media center, enrolled as a student at the institution served by the library. Student assistants are usually paid an hourly wage for performing routine tasks such as stack maintenance and checking items in and out at the circulation desk.

Study prevelege State classifiedemployees and general faculty employees have the privilege of registering for up to 6 credits per academic year at no charge.

Stuffit A common file compression utility for Macintoshes. Compressed files are referred to as "stuffed" and usually end with a ".sit" file extension. A special kind of stuffed file is self-extracting and ends with a ".sea" extension. Stuffed binary files can be converted to ASCII format for transfer over the Internet; such files have a ".sit.hqx" or ".sea.hqx" extension.

Style guide a publication which specifies details of writing style required by a particular publishing house or professional organization, including such matters as punctuation, capitalization, and rules for citing references. For example, the ACS Style Guide : a Manual for Authors and Editors.

Style manual A guide to a prescribed set of rules for typing research papers and theses, usually written for a specific academic discipline or group of related disciplines, covering the mechanics of writing (punctuation, capitalization, quotations, plagiarism, etc.), format (spacing, headings, tables and illustrations, etc.), and correct form of documentation (footnotes, endnotes, and bibliographies), usually including pertinent examples. In academic libraries, the latest editions of leading style manuals are available on reserve or in the reference section. For electronic style, see the Style Guides section of Yahoo! Compare with style sheet.

Style sheet A list of the rules of spelling, punctuation, usage, and citation employed by the publisher of a periodical, to which an author who submits a manuscript for publication is expected to conform. In book publishing, adherence to house style is usually checked by the copy editor in the process of marking up a manuscript for the printer. Compare with style manual.

Stylus The earliest known writing implement, consisting of a sharp, pointed stick made of wood, bone, metal, or reed, usually with a small flat spatula on the nonwriting end for making erasures, used in ancient Mesopotamia to cut or impress straight, wedge-shaped pictographic characters into the surface of clay tablets, and later by the ancient Greeks and Romans to write on wax tablets. As clay gave way to papyrus, parchment, and paper as a writing surface, the stylus was replaced by brush, quill, and pen.

Subclass In classification, a class of which each and every member is a member of another, usually more encompassing, class (example: Periodical / Publication). In close classification, subclasses are subdivided into sub-subclasses (Magazine / Periodical) and so on (News magazine / Magazine).

Subcommittee Two or more members of a larger committee, elected or appointed to address one or more specific issues or needs on behalf of the larger group and report back in a timely manner. A subcommittee that begins ad hoc may eventually become permanent or develop into an independent committee.

Subdirectory An area on a hard disk that contains a related set of files; on IBM PC or compatibles, a level below another directory. On Macintoshes, subdirectories are referred to as folders.

Subdivision A more specific aspect of a class or subject heading, indicated by additional notation or by a subheading following a dash or some other mark of punctuation (example: History in the heading Libraries—History). The most common varieties are form subdivisions (Libraries—Directories), geographic subdivisions (Libraries—United States), and period subdivisions (Libraries—United States—History—19th century) .

Subfield Because most variable fields in the MARC record contain two or more related pieces of information, they are subdivided to allow each element of bibliographic description to be recorded separately. A subfield contains the smallest logical unit of descriptive data pertaining to a bibliographic item. Each subfield is preceded by a delimiter ($ for Library of Congress or double dagger for OCLC) followed by a subfield code, usually a lowercase alphabetic character although arabic numerals are permitted. For example, subfield **$c** of the physical description (field 300) is reserved for the dimensions of an item. Since the first subfield is implicit at the beginning of each field, the subfield code **$a** is not displayed.

Subfield code A one-character code used in the MARC record to indicate the portion of a variable field reserved for a single data element, usually a lowercase alphabetic character (although arabic numerals are permitted), preceded by a delimiter sign, for example, **$c** to indicate date of publication in the publication, distribution, etc. Area (field 260) of a Library of Congress record. Because the first subfield is implicit at the beginning of each field, the subfield code **$a** is not displayed.

Subgenre A subcategory of an existing class of literature or art, which has its own distinguishing characteristics, for example, detective fiction within the mystery genre.

Subhead Any secondary heading in a written work, intended to subdivide the text of a chapter or other major division, usually printed in a smaller size of the typeface used for the main heading. In textbooks and long entries in reference books, subheads may be further subdivided into sub-subheads indicated by an even smaller type size. Also spelled sub-head. Compare with subheading.

Subheading A secondary heading added to a main subject heading or descriptor in a pre-coordinate indexing system, usually following a dash or some other mark of punctuation, to allow documents to be indexed more specifically. Subheadings may be further subdivided. For example, in the Library of Congress subject heading United States—History—Civil War 1861-1864, United States is the main heading, History is the subheading, and Civil War 1861 1864 the sub-subheading. In a printed list of indexing terms, subheadings and sub-subheadings are indented to visually represent the hierarchic relations between terms. Compare with subhead.

Subject analysis Examination of a bibliographic item by a trained subject specialist to determine the most specific subject heading(s) or descriptor(s) that fully describe its content, to serve in the bibliographic record as access points in a subject search of a library catalog, index, abstracting service, or bibliographic database. When no applicable subject heading can be found in the existing headings list or thesaurus of indexing terms, a new one must be created.

Subject Any one of the topics or themes of a work, stated explicitly in the text or title, or implicit in its message. In library cataloging, a book or other item is assigned one or more subject headings as access points, to assist users in locating its content by subject. In indexing and abstracting services, and in bibliographic databases, the headings assigned to represent the content of a document are called descriptors. In a more general sense, any topic of study or discussion, or theme expressed in writing, painting, etc. Abbreviated subj.

Subject bibliography A list of resources (books, articles, reports, etc.) On a specific topic, usually compiled by a librarian or researcher with specialized knowledge of the subject, to acquaint other researchers with the existing literature. A retrospective subject bibliography may be selective or comprehensive within a designated publication period. A current subject bibliography quickly becomes outdated unless updated, usually in supplements. Book-length subject bibliographies may be shelved in the reference section of the library. Compare with reading list.

Subject collection An extensive collection of library

materials related to a particular subject or group of closely related subjects, for example, the South Asia collection at the UC Berkeley Library or the collection on printing history at the Newberry Library in Chicago. Special security precautions may be taken to protect subject collections if they contain rare and/or valuable items. For a list of subject emphases, as reported by university, college, public, and special libraries and museums in the United States and Canada, please see Subject Collections, a directory published by R. R. Bowker. Compare with special collections.

Subject directory An hierarchical grouping of related subject headings. The tree structure shows relationships between subject headings. They can be found either inside a database or separate from a data base. Generally a thesaurus is a book of synonyms, often also containing antonyms. An example is Roget's Thesaurus. In database searching, a thesaurus strategy is to use multiple iterations to search for related words and generate results. The database will often suggest synonyms and related words to try.

Subject encyclopedia An encyclopedia in one or more volumes devoted to a specific subject, field of study, or academic discipline, as opposed to a general encyclopedia containing information on a broad range of subjects. Entries in a subject encyclopedia are usually written and signed by an expert on the topic and may include a brief bibliography.

Subject heading A descriptive word or phrase assigned to an item in a database using controlled vocabulary. Most academic library catalogs use The Library of Congress Subject Headings to describe the subjects of books in the catalog. Other databases create their own list, or thesaurus, of accepted descriptive terms. In some databases subject headings are called descriptors. Researchers can benefit by examining subject headings as they search a catalog or database. Subject headings provide content information that can help the researcher evaluate whether a book or article is worth further examination. Subject headings also suggest alternative terms or phrases to use in a search.

Subject librarian Librarian designated to do collection development for an academic department or program.

Subject or Professional Magazines Fall in between the categories of magazines and journals, with articles written by experts but intended less to advance the field than to report on developments of interest.

Subject search: to seek information by topic (as opposed to author or title). In many indexes and catalogs, a "subject" search implies searching by the use of standardized subject headings assigned by the indexers, as opposed to keyword searching, where the user essentially guesses at words included in titles or abstracts of relevant items.

Subject subdivision Restrictive word or phrase added to a subject headings to limit it to a more specific meaning.

Subnet Address An extension of the Internet addressing system that allows a site to subdivide a single Internet address to cover multiple physical networks. This is done by dividing up the host address part of an IP Address into a local network number and host address number.

Subscribe Commonly refers to the act of selecting a network newsgroup as one you want to read on a regular basis or of sending a request to join a mailing list (discussion group) that interest you. The opposite action is called "unsubscribing".

Subscription database A database that can be accessed or licensed only through a subscription. Libraries provide a wealth of information freely to their patrons, but most of the electronic materials they provide are paid for by the library through a subscription. Often the material provided in a subscription database is more selective and quality controlled than sources that are freely available on the Web. Because databases are often provided through a license agreement, these databases are sometimes referred to as licensed databases.

Substantial revision Major redefinitions and relocations in a class

Substrate The base material used to carry out or support an image, for example, paper or film.

Subtitle: an explanatory phrase following a main.

Subtractive Primaries Another term for primary colorants.

Successive title Type of serials cataloging in which the previous title entry is closed, and complete new descriptive cataloging is done for the new title. Successive title cataloging occurs when a serial changes its title.

SUDOCS Abbreviation referring to the U.S. Government superintendent of documents, the federal government printer. Classification designation for government documents is called the sudoc number.

Sudocs Classification Superintendent of Documents Classification. A string of letters and numbers used to identify and label publications issued by the United States federal government. The letters beginning each sudocs classification number refer to the government agency responsible for the publication.

Suggestion box Receptacle for deposit of suggestions from patrons are located throughout the Libraries at service points and on the Comment Box of Sage. Responses to electronic suggestions made on sagege are posted online. Suggestions are answered and posted online and at service points by the coordinatorof information/reference.

Superintendent of Documents (SUDOC) Classification: The call number system that uses a combination of letters and numbers to identify the issuing agency and shelf location of items in the library's U.S. Government Publications collection.

Supersampling The capture of more grey levels per color than is required for image manipulation or output. This additional data allows shadow details to be heightened, for example.

Superuser SAGE system user empowered with all

available functions; usually reserved for the two co-administrators

Supplement (SUPPL) Complementary part of a book or article, which adds information to, or continues the text of the original. Supplement often refers to additional issues of a journal, which may or may not be distributed as part of the journal subscription. Some supplements require a separate subscription.

Suspended publication SERIAL publication not currently being published, but which has not formally ceased publication or merged with another title. Publisher intends to resume publication at a later date.

SVGA Super VGA (Video Graphics Array); a set of graphics standards for a computer monitor that offers greater resolution than VGA. There are several different levels including 800 x 600 pixels, 1024 by 768 pixels, 1280 by 1024 pixels; and 1600 by 1200 pixels. Although each supports a palette of 16 million colors, the number of simultaneous colors is dependent on the amount of video memory installed in the computer.

Synchronous communication Communication in which messages are sent, received, and responded to simultaneously. Online chat is a form of synchronous communication.

Syndetic structure in a catalog or index, the system of "see" and "see also" cross references to other headings. TCP/IP: Transmission Control Protocol/Internet Protocol; the communication program common to most connected

Syntax Error Occurs when a user (or programmer) has put words in an order that a program does not understand.

Synthesizer An electronic musical instrument capable of generating sound using real-time control over the key parameters of sound: frequency, timbre, amplitude, and duration. Today most synthesizers include a MIDI interface. Also may refer to an internal sound card or external box for use with multimedia sequencing software.

Sysop (System Operator) Anyone responsible for the physical operations of a computer system or network resource. For example, a System Administrator decides how often backups and maintenance should be performed and the System Operator performs those tasks.

T-1 A leased-line connection capable of carrying data at 1,544,000 bits-per-second. At maximum theoretical capacity, a T-1 line could move a megabyte in less than 10 seconds. That is still not fast enough for full-screen, full-motion video, for which you need at least 10,000,000 bits-per-second. T-1 lines are commonly used to connect large lans to theinternet.

T1 An AT&T term for a digital carrier facility used to transmit a DS-1 formatted digital signal at 1.544 megabits per second.

T-3 A leased-line connection capable of carrying data at 44,736,000 bits-per-second. This is more than enough to do full-screen, full-motionvideo.

T3 A term for a digital carrier facility used to transmit

Table book A luxurious edition, usually covered in silk or velvet, intended for display in the private drawing rooms of wealthy people of the 19th century. Its modern counterpart is the coffee table book.

Table of contents (TOC) A list of the contents of a printed publication in the order of their appearance, usually with page numbers as locators. In a book, the TOC lists the front matter, chapters or other major divisions of the work, and the back matter. In an anthology or collection, the TOC lists the titles of the works included by the editor(s) (stories, poems, plays, essays, etc.), in order of appearance. In books, the TOC is printed in the front matter on the first recto following the dedication or title page. In periodicals, the TOC appears near the front of each issue or on the back cover, listing the editorial content (articles, columns, reviews, etc.), but not any advertising.

Table With reference to web design, a method for formatting information on a page. Use of tables and the cells within also provide a way to create columns of text. Use of tables vs frames is recommended for helping to make your web site ADA-compliant.

Tabloid A newspaper printed in a format half the size of an ordinary broadsheet newspaper, containing short news stories of a highly sensational and improbable nature, abundantly illustrated (usually with photographs), sold mainly at newsstands and in supermarkets. Also refers to an advertising preprint of 4 or more pages, normally one-half the size of the newspaper into which it is inserted.

Tactile materials Reading materials in which the text is provided as a series of raised symbols, as in braille, or in surfaces of different texture, for the use of visually impaired persons

Tag A three-character numeric code in the range of 0XX-9XX with XX=01-99, used in the MARC record to identify the kind of data contained in a field. The numbering system allows fields to be grouped by function in hundreds. In fields requiring authority control, the second and third character positions in the tag indicate parallel content. According to Betty Furrie, approximately ten percent of all MARC tags are used in most bibliographic records; the other ninety percent are used infrequently (Understanding MARC Bibliographic Machine-Readable Cataloging). For books, the most frequently used tags are:

Tag group The three-digit content designators (called tags), used to identify fields in the MARC record, are grouped by function in hundreds as follows, with XX in the range of 00-99:

Tags Formatting codes used in HTML documents. These tags indicate how the parts of a document will appear when displayed by a Web client program.

Tail The bottom edge of a book, on which it rests when

shelved in an upright position. Also refers to the margin at the foot of a page, as opposed to the margin at the head.

Take down The process of preparing a book for rebinding by removing its cover, boards, endpapers, sewing threads, and lining, including any cleaning or repair. When a volume has been reduced to its original sections, it is said to have been taken down. Synonymous with pulling.

Take-over The acquisition of exclusive rights in a book or other work by a new publisher, following initial publication by another company.

Tale A narrative account of a real, imaginary, or legendary incident, usually told in the first person in a rambling style, with more attention to plot and setting than to character development. Most tales are works of short fiction (example: "The Legend of Sleepy Hollow" by Washington Irving), but the term has also been applied to novels (Tale of Two Cities by Charles Dickens). In a tall tale, the plot is deliberately far-fetched, usually for comic effect ("Cannibalism in the Cars" by Mark Twain).

Tapes Narrow strips of tightly woven cotton material to which the sections of a book are sewn in quality binding. Two half-inch wide strips spaced at intervals across the binding edge are the norm, but in larger volumes, as many as five may be used. Tapes are no longer used in most trade bindings. Compare with bands.

Target audience The group or category of person for which a literary or artistic work is written or produced, or for which a library collection is developed (students, professionals, recreational readers, a particular age or interest group, etc.).

Task force A group of individuals drawn from various units within an organization, charged with accomplishing a specific objective or set of objectives. Once the task is completed, the group is disbanded and its members return to their former units. Compare with ad hoc committee.

Taskbar A row of tabs in a graphical user interface,

usually located across the bottom of the screen, with text labels indicating the applications and files currently open. In multitasking, a tab can be clicked by the user to bring the corresponding window to the foreground or to restore it to its original size after it has been minimized. In the Windows operating system, the Start button is also located in the taskbar, which may contain other information such as date and time.

Taxonomy The science of classification, including the general principles by which objects and phenomena are divided into classes which are subdivided into subclasses, then into sub-subclasses, and so on.

TCC Technology Coordinating Committee.

TCP Transmission Control Protocol. This is a transport layer protocol that establishes a reliable, full duplex, data delivery service used by many TCP/IP application programs. The TCP software uses the IP protocol to transmit information across the Internet.

TCP/IP An initialism for Transmission Control Protocol/Internet Protocol, a set of communications protocols developed by the U.S. Department of Defense and implemented in 1982 to allow the users of host computers of different types and sizes to communicate with each other and exchange data via the Internet and other networks (intranets and extranets). Supported on most platforms, TCP/IP has become the protocol of the Internet. TCP ensures that the total amount of data (bytes) sent is received correctly, and IP provides the mechanism for routing the packets

TCP/IP Transmission Control Protocol/Internet Protocol; This is the suiteof protocols that defines the Internet. Originally designed for the UNIX operating system, TCP/IP software is now included with every major kind of computer operating system. To be truly on the Internet, your computer must have TCP/IP software.

Teach team Composed of staff who regularly work in the EIC and Journal Room, the Tech Team meets twice each month to remain current in technical skills, enhance communication, and optimize service to the public.

Teacher's manual A booklet or softcover book issued in conjunction with a textbook, to assist instructors in using the text to teach their classes. In library cataloging, the presence of a teacher's manual is recorded as accompanying material in the physical description area of the bibliographic record representing the textbook.

Technical library A library that supports one or more of the applied sciences, such as engineering or computer science. A technical library can be a branch library in a large university, a major collection within a large academic or public library, or a special library maintained by a private corporation or government agency.

Technical processing All the activities and processes concerned with acquiring, organizing, preparing, and maintaining library collections, including cataloging and physical processing, usually accomplished "behind-the-scenes" by the technical services department of a library. When the department is understaffed, arrears may accumulate.

Technical report A scientific paper or article describing research or other significant developments in a field of the applied sciences. When submitted to a military agency, such a report may be "classified" or subject to other access restrictions. .

Technical reports Publications which report results of research or development, often conducted or sponsored by the U.S. Government. Considered to be "unpublished" in part because of their limited distribution, rapid obsolescence, and method of reproduction (multilith, mimeograph, xerox, MICROFICHE, etc.)

Technical services (TS) Library operations concerned with the acquisition, organization (bibliographic control), physical processing, and maintenance of library collections, as opposed to the delivery of public services. Technical processing is performed "behind-the-scenes," usually in a technical services department.

Technical services The aspect of library work concerned with ordering, receiving, cataloging, and processing of materials. In the Heard Library this work is performed in Resource Services.

Technical Services The departments which handle acquisition, cataloging, processing, and maintenance of the materials in the library.

Technician A person who has special expertise in the maintenance of high-tech machines, particularly computer and scientific equipment. Libraries with automated systems require the services of a "techie" to keep hardware and software running smoothly. Compare with systems librarian

Telecommunication The process of sending and receiving signals or messages at a distance via telegraph, telephone, radio, television, cable, microwave, or any other electromagnetic method on which modern information technology depends. Also, any transmission, emission, or reception of signals by such means. Compare with telecommunications.

Telecommunications The individual messages transmitted and/or received via telegraph, telephone, radio, television, cable, microwave, or other electromagnetic means. Sometimes used synonymously with telecommunication.

Telecommute To work from home using a computer and telecommunication links, instead of traveling to an office to conduct business. Some library functions, such as the design and maintenance of Web sites can be accomplished at a distance, but most library personnel work on-site.

Teleconference A live, two-way conference of two or more people using audio and video transmission technology that enables the participants to see and hear each other in real time without having to meet in the same physical location.

Telephone directory A large format paperback publication distributed annually by a telephone company at no charge to its customers, containing an alphabetic list of the names, telephone numbers, and street addresses of people served in a given city, town, or geographic area in a section called the white pages, and an alphabetic list of businesses with phone numbers and addresses in the yellow pages at the back. For very large cities, the white pages and yellow pages may be published in separate volumes.

Teleplay A drama written to be recorded in a studio and broadcast on television, rather than for live performance on stage or to be filmed as a motion picture. Synonymous with television drama.

Teleric The library's automated telephone renewal system.

Teletext A type of one-way broadcasting service that allows digital information provided by a television station, such as closed captions or continuously updated news, to be displayed on a television receiver specifically adapted to allow text and graphics to be superimposed over regular programming, usually in frames. Compare with videotex.

Television new archive Videotape collection of the national network, evening news broadcasts and other news specials beginning in 1968. Formerly a department of the Heard Library.

Tellus: Marriott's suggestion box - patrons may give us their questions and suggestions either physically by dropping them off in the Tellus box on level 3, or by e-mail; comments and responses are posted on the Tellus board by the level 3 entrance.

Telnet Terminal emulation software governed by the TCP/IP protocol, which allows the user to to a remote computer or terminal and use its systems as if on-site. Designed to transmit ASCII text, Telnet was once widely used in libraries to provide remote access to online catalogs, but has been largely superseded by graphical Web-based access to electronic resources.

Temporarily out of print (TOP) A term used on a publisher's invoice to indicate that the title ordered cannot be supplied because the last printing is sold out, and to inform prospective purchasers that additional copies are expected from the printer in the near future. Compare with out of print at present.

Temporarily out of stock (TOS) A term used on a publisher's invoice to indicate that the title ordered cannot be supplied because current inventory is exhausted, but additional copies are expected, usually from the binder or manufacturer. Compare with out of stock.

Temporary control number A number that appears in the "status" line in UNIS for items that are on order or in-process, but not yet available on the shelves. Patrons may request rush ordering or processing of such items by giving the temporary control number to the circulation desk.

Temporary records Documents intended by their creator to remain useful for a short time only, which have no archival value and can be discarded or destroyed when no longer needed without loss to the individual or organization (example: draft versions not required to document a process).

Temporary storage A space within an archive or library facility, or located off-site, where materials, equipment, or supplies are kept for a short time until they can be processed, installed, distributed, transferred to a permanent location, or disposed of in some other way (example: a large gift collection awaiting examination by selectors).

Tennshare an organization of all types of libraries and information agencies in Tennessee to promote resource sharing programs to provide citizens with a wider range of information sources.

Tenure Facility Committee (TFC) Elected by tenured members of the Libraries Faculty to advise the DEAN of

Libraries on reappointment, award of tenure, and promotion of CSU librarians.

Tenure The guarantee of permanent employment, granted by an academic institution to a faculty member for satisfactory performance upon completion of a specified number of years of service. A position for which tenure is granted is classifed as tenure-track. Academic librarians who have faculty status are eligible for tenure; those with academic status usually are not. In a more general sense, the length of time a person has been employed, or may be expected to be employed, by a company, agency, organization, or institution. Compare with **promotion.**

Terabyte 1000 gigabytes.

Term A word, phrase, or symbol, especially one used to represent, in a dictionary, catalog, index, or database, a subject or other feature of a work.

Term frequency (TF) The number of times a search term occurs in a record or document included in a database, one of the variables used in assigning a weight to the record or document in relation to others retrieved in the same search.

Terminal An electronic device consisting of a computer keyboard and screen or optical scanner, which can be used to enter data (input) and display output from a central computer (usually a minicomputer or mainframe), but is not capable of independent processing. Synonymous with **dumb terminal** and **visual display terminal (VDT).** Compare with **personal computer** and **thin client.**

Terminal emulation The act of using your desktop computer to communicate with another computer like a UNIX or IBM mainframe exactly as if you were sitting in front of a terminal directly connected to the system. Also refers to the software used for terminal emulation. Examples: the Telnet program for VT100 emulation and QWS3270 (Windows) and TN3270 (Macintosh) for IBM3270 fullscreen emulation.

Terminal Mode Many communications programs allow you to mimic a computer terminal, which is basically a keyboard and CRT display and/or a printer. A common terminal mode emulator is VT-100.

Terminal Ready (TR) This light is illuminated when your computer has turned on the RS-232 (serial) interface. Sometimes this light will not come on until you have loaded your communications software into memory.

Terminal Server A special purpose computer that has places to plug in many modemson one side, and a connection to a LAN or host machine onthe other side. Thus the terminal server does the work of answering thecalls and passes the connections on to the appropriate node. Mostterminal servers can provide PPP or SLIP services if connectedto the Internet.

Terminal A device that allows you to send commands to a computer somewhere else. At a minimum, this usually means a keyboard and a display screen and some simple circuitry. Usually you will use terminal software in a personal computer - the software pretends to be (emulates) a physical terminal and allows you to type commands to a computer somewhere else.

Terminal Server A small, specialized, networked computer that connects many terminals to a LAN through one network connection. A terminal server can also connect network users to asynchronous ports or a host.

Terminology Words, phrases, and symbols representing the concepts and subjects used in a specific field of research, study, or activity, for which the meaning (established by convention or explicit agreement among its practitioners) is clearly defined, sometimes in a published glossary or lexicon. Synonymous with nomenclature.

Terms of availability The conditions under which a bibliographic item is available for sale in the market place, usually the list price, entered in field 020 or 022 of the MARC record.

Ternion In bookbinding, a gathering consisting of three sheets of paper, parchment, or vellum folded once to create six leaves, used in some manuscript books and early printed books.

Tertiary source A written work, such as a chapter in a textbook or entry in a reference book, based entirely on secondary sources, rather than on original research involving primary documents. Whether a source is secondary or tertiary can be determined by examining the bibliography (if one is provided). Another clue is that secondary sources are almost always written by experts, but tertiary sources may be written by staff writers who have an interest in the topic, but are not scholars on the subject.

Test collection A library collection consisting of assessment instruments used by researchers and practitioners in education, psychology, counseling, and allied fields. Information on test collections is available in the Directory of Test Collections in Academic, Professional, and Research Libraries (2002) published by the Association of College & Research Libraries. Tests are reviewed in the Mental Measurements Yearbook published by the Buros Institute of Mental Measurements.

Tete-beche A form of binding in which the text of one work begins at the "front" of the book and the text of a second work at the "back," inverted (upside-down) with respect to the other so that their last pages meet somewhere in the middle of the sections. Also, a volume bound in the same manner, which contains different versions of the same text. Compare with dos-a-dos.

Text block The gathered signatures of a book, sewn or adhered in a single unit and trimmed before attachment to the case or cover, not including any paper added by the binder, such as endpapers or doublures. Compare in this sense with book block.

Text Encoding Initiative (TEI) Introduced in 1987, TEI is an international interdisciplinary standard intended to assist libraries, museums, publishers, and scholars in representing literary and linguistic texts in digital form, to facilitate research and teaching. The encoding scheme is designed to maximize expressivity and minimize obsolescence. TEI began as a research project organized cooperatively by the Association for Computers and the Humanities, the Association for Computational Linguistics, and the Association for Literary and Linguistic Computing, funded by research grants from the National Endowment for the Humanities, the European Union, the Canadian Social Science Research Council, the Mellon Foundation, and others.

Text encoding initiative Initially launched in 1987, the TEI is an international and interdisciplinary standard that helps libraries, museums, publishers, and individual scholars represent all kinds of literary and linguistic texts for online research and teaching, using an encoding scheme that is maximally expressive and minimally obsolescent. See also XML.

Text In a written, printed, or digital work, the words or (in the absence of words) signs or symbols used to express the author's thoughts, feelings, and ideas. Compare with wordless.

Text type Type used to print reading material, for example, the body of a book or other publication, as opposed to the display type used to print headings, running titles, etc., or the extract type used to print notes and long quotations. Synonymous with body type.

Textbook A limited edition, or a book club item. The "hyper" in Hypertext comes from the fact that in HTML you can specify that a block of text, or an image, is linked to another file on the Internet. HTML files are meant to be viewed using a "Web Browser". The coding language used to create Hypertext documents for use on the World Wide Web. HTML looks a lot like old-fashioned typesetting code, where you surround a block of text with codes that indicate how it should appear. The protocol for moving hypertextfiles across the Internet. Requires a HTTP client program on one end, and an HTTP server program on the other end. HTTP is the most important protocol used in the World Wide Web (WWW). These indexes are very commonly used by faculty in their tenure process to indicate the impact of their publications on others' research. Citation indexes can also be used for standard author/subject searching. Textbooks are usually ordered by college bookstores in quantity, based on projected course enrollment. The standard publisher's discount on textbook orders is 20%. Used copies in good condition may be sold back to the bookstore for resale at a lower price than new copies.

Textbook edition A trade book issued in a separate edition specifically for the use of students enrolled in a course of study. The format may be altered to make it more useful, for example, by the addition of study questions and bibliographies at the end of each section or chapter. Textbook editions are sold at short discount, usually 20% when ordered in quantity. Synonymous with text edition.

Textile binding A style of bookbinding popular in Europe from the 12th-15th century in which the boards were covered in velvet and/or silk brocade, usually adorned with gold or silver clasps. In the 16th and 17th centuries, embroidered velvet and silk bindings were popular. Because luxury fabrics are fragile and deteriorate with age, few examples survive in good condition.

Textual bibliography - the relationship between the text as conceived by the author and the text as published

Textual criticism Close study and comparison of the various texts of a literary work to determine the version that reflects most faithfully the writer's intentions, particularly important in the case of older works for which the original manuscript is missing or incomplete, or for which multiple versions exist.

Textura In printing, the most formal of the gothic or

black letter type fonts, used in early editions of the Bible and liturgical works.

Textus receptus Latin for "received text." The version of a work which, in the absence of indisputable proof to the contrary, is considered by scholars to represent the author's intentions to a greater degree than other versions known to exist.

Theatre Library Association (TLA) Established in 1937, TLA has an international membership consisting of curators, librarians, archivists, writers, historians, stage designers, actors, booksellers, collectors, and other individuals with an interest research in the performing arts, and in the collection, preservation, and use of performing arts materials. Based in New York City, TLA is an affiliate of the American Library Association. Its publications include the annual journal Performing Arts Resources and the quarterly newsletter Broadside.

Theft The unauthorized removal of materials from library premises, a persistent problem controlled by restricting access to the technical services department and installing a security gate at the public exit with an alarm automatically activated by a magnetic strip affixed to the item, which must be desensitized by library staff at checkout. Unfortunately, determined thieves learn to locate and remove the strips to avoid detection. In most states in the U.S., theft and vandalism of library materials is punishable as a misdemeanor..

Thematic atlas A book of maps devoted to a specific topic, subject, or theme, usually including text, illustrations, and other graphic material explaining their meaning and significance (examples: The Atlas of Endangered Species).

Thematic catalog A list of the works of a composer, arranged chronologically or by category, in which the major theme is given for each composition, or section of a long composition, usually in a few bars. Some thematic catalogs are devoted to musical works of a particular form and period, usually arranged alphabetically by name of composer. Compare with thematic index.

Thematic index A list of the major themes in a musical composition, or group of compositions, usually printed in the front or back of the score, with references to the work(s) in which they appear. For short s, the theme is usually given as the first few bars. Compare with thematic catalog.

Thematic map A map showing one or more features or aspccts of a given area of the surface of the earth or of another celestial body. Thematic maps can be quantitative, illustrating statistical data, such as average annual precipitation, or qualitative, indicating the distribution of characteristics such as predominant language, ethnic group, religious affiliation, etc.

Thermal Wax Transfer A printing process using small heating elements to melt dots of wax pigment on a carrier film, which are then transferred to paper or transparent film by contact. This differs from the dye sublimation process in that individual dots do not fuse together, so thermal wax transfer appears to be of a lower resolution.

Thesaurus A list of subject headings or descriptors that are used in a particular catalog or database to describe the subject matter of each item. A thesaurus is useful to researchers because it identifies which term among a variety of available synonyms has been used by the database compilers to describe a subject. Some databases provide a searchable thesaurus that helps researchers choose the most effective search terms before they start searching.

Thread A list of postings in electronic communications that deal with a common topic. A thread is usually used in the context of newsgroups and discussion lists and often contains a common or slowly evolving subject line.

Theses often refers to the treatises written by candidates for the Master's Degree, as distinct from doctoral dissertations. Marriott has 2 copies of theses completed at the University of Utah, a circulating copy and an archival copy kept in Special Collections. We do not generally own copies of theses completed at other institutions; these must be obtained by interlibrary loan or purchase.

Thesis A proposition advanced and defended in a formal disputation, especially by a candidate in partial fulfillment of university requirements for a master's degree. Master's theses are indexed annually by discipline, subject, and author.

Thesis play A dramatic work in which the playwright consciously attempts to illustrate a social problem and suggest to the reader or audience a possible solution (example: Mrs. Warren's Profession by George Bernard Shaw).

Thesis statement: a one or two sentence description of the main point you intent to make in the paper or dissertation. It is usually found very near the beginning of the work. An example is "In this paper I will provide evidence that...".

Thin client A computer connected to a client-server network, which does very little independent processing, all or most of the application processing being done on the server. Also refers to a client computer capable of downloading a program from a server and processing data like a PC, but which does not store data locally. Compare with terminal.

Thomas Named in honor of Thomas Jefferson, Thomas is a database designed and maintained since 1995 by the Library of Congress to make legislative information, such as the Congressional Record, more accessible to the public. Available on the Internet 24 hours a day free-of-charge, Thomas also provides answers to faqs, links to the full-text of historical documents such as the Declaration of Independence and the Constitution of the United States, and a section on bills recently in the news.

Thread A theme or topic that generates an ongoing e-mail discussion among the participants in an Internet newsgroup or mailing list, usually repeated in the header of each message posted on the subject. In literature, an idea or theme that connects the various parts of a narrative.

Three-decker A novel published in three octavo volumes. First issued in paper-covered boards without illustration, and later in cloth-covered boards, three-deckers became the standard format for fiction published in England between about 1850 and 1870. According to Geoffrey Glaister, circulating libraries kept this type of publication going until inexpensive reprint editions became widely available (Encyclopedia of the Book, Oak Knoll/British Library: 1996).

Three-quarter binding A style of bookbinding in which the spine and corners are bound in a different material than the sides, usually a more durable covering such as leather. Similar to half binding except that the corners are larger and the material covering the spine extends up to half the width of the boards. Compare with full binding and quarter binding.

Threshold The point at which an action begins or changes. The threshold setting used in scanning line art determines which pixels are converted to black and which will become white. The threshold defined in the USM process determines how large a tonal contrast must be before sharpening will be applied to it.

Thriller A novel, play, or motion picture that produces feelings of intense excitement in the reader or audience by depicting dangerous action (crime, espionage, etc.), usually culminating in a narrow escape in which a high level of suspense is maintained up to the final denouement (example: Alfred Hitchcock's film North by Northwest).

Throw-out A leaf wider than normal, usually bearing a map, table, diagram, wide-angle photograph, or other illustration mounted and folded so that it can be opened out for reference while the corresponding text is read. Also spelled throwout. Synonymous with fold-out and pull-out.

Thumb index A series of semicircular thumb-sized notches cut into the fore-edge of a book, bearing a sequence of letters, words, numbers, or symbols, usually printed against a dark background to show the alphabetic, subject, numeric, or other arrangement of the text and facilitate reference, seen most often in hardcover editions of language dictionaries and handbooks. Compare with step index and tab index.

Thumbnail A very small image of a page of text or graphic element, used in a Web page as a link to the same image in larger format. Since thumbnail graphics take less time to load, they are often used in Web pages to provide the option of enlarging an image without significantly increasing the time required to transmit the document.

Tie-bound periodicals volumes loosely bound in cardboard covers because one or more issues of the "run" are missing.

Tier One of two or more distinct levels, as of shelves in a section of library shelving, priorities for resource allocation or acquisition, payment or benefit options in a health care plan, etc.

TIFF An acronym for Tagged Image File Format, a widely supported data format developed by Aldus and Microsoft for storing black-and-white, gray-scale, or color bitmapped images on a personal computer. Files in TIFF format are compressed and usually have the extension .tif or .tiff added to the filename.

Tight back A method of binding in which the back of a volume is glued to the cover, leaving no hollow to allow the binding to flex as it is opened. Books bound by this method do not open flat. Another disadvantage is that the lettering printed on the spine tends to crack with extended use. For these reasons, hardcover editions are nearly always bound with a hollow back.

Tight The condition of a book so tightly bound that the spine is inflexible, preventing the leaves from opening and staying open at a particular page. As new books are used, their bindings gradually loosen allowing them to open flat at any page. Library bindings are usually tighter than trade bindings. Compare with tight back.

Tilde A mark in the form of a horizontal inverted "s" used as a diacritical mark over certain letters in the Spanish and Portuguese languages to indicate pronunciation, as a symbol in logic and mathematics to indicate negation, and in urls, usually followed by the name of the person responsible for creating and/or maintaining the Web page.

Tilte entry Record of a work in the catalog under the title.

Time-expired records In archives, temporary records assigned a specific date for destruction that has passed without the occurrence of appropriate action, usually due to a backlog in processing.

Timeout In computing, a routine that automatically terminates a period of waiting when a screen requiring user input receives no response within a designated time, for example, an interface that logs off whenever a predetermined period of inactivity occurs during an online session. The term is also used in communications to refer to the automatic termination of a waiting period when no response is received. Also spelled time out.

Times Literary Supplement (TLS) First published in 1902, TLS is one of the most influential book review publications in the UK. Published weekly in newspaper format, it provides in-depth reviews of current fiction and nonfiction on a wide range of subjects, as well as reviews of contemporary theater, opera, and film. Like its American counterparts, the New York Review of Books and the New York Times Book Review, TLS is noted for its coverage of literary works. It also carries announcements of new books published by scholarly and university presses.

Times Series Data Library It is a collection of about 800 time series, drawn from many different fields viz. Agriculture, Crime, Finance, Health, Labor market, Macroeconomics, Production, etc.

Tintype A positive photographic image made with a wet collodion emulsion on a thin iron plate darkened with black lacquer. As in a daguerrotype, the image is reversed laterally. Inexpensive and fast, the process was widely used for portraiture from the 1850s to the end of the 19th century, bringing photographic images within reach of the masses. In the 1880s, the wet emulsion was replaced by a dry gelatin. Synonymous with ferrotype.

Tipped in A single leaf, errata slip, or separately printed map or illustration trimmed to page size and glued into a book against the following page without using a guard, after the text has been printed and bound, usually by applying a thin line of adhesive along the inner margin, near the binding edge. A tipped in leaf (called a "paste in") may be somewhat restricted in its openability.

Tissue A sheet of very thin paper inserted loose between the leaves of a book or affixed to the inner margin, usually to protect the surface of a plate or prevent the offset of fresh ink onto the facing page.

Title A word, phrase, sentence, character, or characters appearing on an item, naming the work (or works) for identification and reference. Choice of title usually reflects the content of the work, distinguishing it from others of similar subject. A subtitle may be included following a colon or semicolon. Translations may have a parallel title in the original language. The full title is usually printed on the title page of a book or at the beginning of an article or essay published in a book or periodical. The title given on the title page may differ from the one printed or impressed on the spine or cover. In a film or videorecording, the title is usually given in the first few frames.

Title and statement of responsibility In library cataloging, the area of bibliographic description in which the title proper of a work and information concerning authorship (statement of responsibility) are recorded (field 245 of the MARC record).

Title bar The horizontal bar at the top of a window. The title bar shows the name of the window.

Title change Usually a SERIAL publication, which has undergone a change in its title proper.

Title Distinguishing name of a work.

Title frame One or more frames usually found at the beginning of a work produced on film (motion picture, filmstrip, etc.), containing textual information distinct from the subject content, used as the chief source of information in library cataloging when the bibliographic record is created to describe the item. Compare with title screen.

Title index An alphabetically arranged list of the titles of the works covered in a serial or nonserial work (example: the Book and Film Title Index in America: History and Life). Title and author indexes are sometimes combined.

Title leaf The leaf of a book bearing the title page on the recto and the publisher's imprint, notice of copyright, cataloging-in-publication (CIP), ISBN, and printing history on the verso. In the front matter of a book, the title leaf follows the half-title and precedes the dedication.

Title List - A button in the library catalog that, when clicked, returns the user to the list of titles that were retrieved by a search.

Title merge Two or more SERIAL titles merge to form 1 (one) single title.

Title page The page at the beginning of a manuscript, book, or other printed publication (usually the recto of the leaf following the half-title) bearing the title proper of the work and usually (but not necessarily) the names of the author(s), editor(s), translator(s), and publisher. The title page may also indicate the volume number (if applicable) and the date and place publication. The verso of the title leaf usually gives the notice of copyright, publication date, publisher's imprint, CIP, ISBN, and in some cases the printer's imprint. According to Geoffrey Glaister, the first complete title pages appeared in early printed books around 1500. By the late 16th century the decorative possibilities of the title page had been fully realized (Encyclopedia of the Book, Oak Knoll/British Library: 1996). Abbreviated tp. Also spelled title-page..

Title proper The primary name of a bibliographic item, usually found on the chief source of information, including any alternative title, but not parallel titles or any additional title information. In AACR2, the title proper is entered in the title and statement of responsibility area of the bibliographic description (field 245 of the MARC record

Title screen In a machine-readable data file such as a bibliographic database or Web page, a screen display of text giving the title proper of the work and in most cases the name of the author(s) or editor(s), and details of its publication, used in library cataloging as the chief source of information in creating the bibliographic description of the item. Compare with title frame.

Title search to search for an item by its title, generally in an alphabetical listing.

Title spilit One SERIAL title which splits into two or more different titles.'

Title statement of a work, plus the optional general material designation and remainder of the title (if applicable), given in the title and statement of responsibility area of the bibliographic description (field 245 of the MARC record). In AACR2, the wording, order, and spelling of the title proper is followed exactly as it appears in or on the item, but punctuation and capitalization may be changed by the cataloger.

Titulus Introductory words added in capital letters by a rubrisher in red or blue ink in a space left blank at the beginning of a chapter when the text of a medieval manuscript was hand-copied, often filling several lines. Gold leaf was used in more important works.

TLD- (Top Level Domain) The last (right-hand) part of a complete Domain Name. For example in the domain name www.matisse.net ".net" is the Top Level Domain.There are a large number of TLD's, for example .biz, .com, .edu, .gov, .info, .int, .mil, .net, .org, and a collection of two-letter TLD's corresponding to the standard two-letter country codes, for example, .us, .ca, .jp, etc.

TN3270 A program for Macintosh distributed via the OIT Software To Go web site; provides IBM3270 terminal emulation when you connect to an IBM mainframe. Example: fullscreen TSO and WYLBUR sessions.

To bind (A periodical): To join several issues of a magazine or journal in one volume with a hard cover.

Tome Originally, any volume of a work published in more than one volume. In modern usage, a book of very large size, also weighty in subject or treatment.

Tone Curves Also known as gamma curves. These are used to smoothly adjust the overall tonal range of an image, or the individual tonal ranges of each color channel.

Toolbar A narrow band along one side or across the top or bottom of a window or frame in the graphical user interface of a microcomputer application, displaying a row of buttons or icons that can be clicked with a pointing device such as a mouse to access menus and open other windows, allowing the user to select options, set parameters, and perform functions. Compare with navigation bar.

Tooling In finishing, decorative designs hand-stamped with a heated brass tool on the surface of the material covering the boards of a book (usually cloth or leather). Tooling can be blind or highlighted in ink, or in gold leaf or foil.

Toolkit A printed or online guide that brings together in one place practical information for accomplishing a goal or beginning a project, including but not limited to case studies, action plans, policies, learning modules, resource lists, useful terminology, important contacts, etc. (example: The Ethnographer's Toolkit, edited by Jean Schensul and Margaret lecompte). Also spelled tool kit.

Top term (TT) The most general term in a hierarchical classification system, indicated by the abbreviation TT in the thesaurus of indexing terms (example: INSPEC Thesaurus) or by the narrowest indention under the heading to which it applies.

Topic A subject for research or discussion. The first step in a library research project is the formulation of a workable topic statement. As a literature search progresses, the topic may require refinement (change of specificity or focus), depending on the amount of published information available and the time constraints of the researcher.

Topical guide A printed or online list or description of the best bibliographic tools and resources available to a researcher for conducting a literature search on a specific topic, presented in the sequence in which they would optimally be used. Also known as a pathfinder.

Topographic map A map on any scale showing in relief the geographic features of a given area of the surface of the earth (or another celestial body), usually by means of contour lines. When unbound, such a map is called a topographic sheet. Abbreviated topo.

Topographic series A group of topographic sheet maps showing the geographic features of the surface of a country at scales of 1:10,000 to 1:250,000, usually issued by an agency of civilian or military government, such as a national survey or mapping division of a defense department. Topographic series are also issued internationally at scales of 1:1,000,000 to 1:5,000,000.

Total circulation In publishing, the entire distribution of any issue of a periodical publication, including copies sent to paid subscribers, single-copy retail sales, in-house use, and complimentary copies distributed for promotional purposes.

Total publication An agreement between an author and publisher in which a work is issued in hardcover and also in a mass market paperback edition under the publisher's separate paperback imprint, as opposed to leasing the paperback rights to an independent publisher for which the author is usually paid a higher royalty. The term does not apply to simultaneous publication under a single imprint of hardcover and softcover trade editions, or to the subsequent issuance of a trade paperback edition in which the text and illustrations remain the same as in the hardcover edition.

Touch screen A computer screen covered with a clear touch-sensitive panel that enables the user to make selections from a menu of options or initiate specific operations by touching the part of the screen that displays the appropriate word, phrase, symbol, icon, or button. Pressure-sensitive cells in the panel transmit data to the screen software, activating the selection. Also spelled touchscreen. Compare with touchpad.

Touchpad An electronic pointing device consisting of a small flat surface connected to a computer, which the user can activate with the touch of a finger, instead of depressing the keys on a keyboard or moving a mouse. Synonymous with touch panel. Compare with touch screen.

Toy book A small, illustrated book for young children, published in 19th century England and America, usually consisting of eight leaves of vivid, hand-colored pictures with very little text (alphabets and simple tales were popular). Originally issued in paper covers, later variations included cloth books printed on sturdy fabric, pop-up books, and flicker books. Toy books were often published in series to encourage gift buying and collecting.

Toy collection A collection of toys, puppets, games, etc., sometimes available for loan in the children's room of a public library, especially helpful in serving families in low-income communities.

Trace Item status which means that the item was not found on the shelf and we are conducting a further search for the item. Holds may be placed on items with this status. You will be notified if the item cannot be located.

Tracings A record of the additional headings under which a bibliographic item is listed in a library catalog, usually associated with the main entry. Also, a list in an authority file of all the cross-references made to and from a heading used in a file of bibliographic records, to enable the cataloger to "trace" all the entries referring to the item whenever a change or correction is necessary, or when the item is withdrawn from the collection.

Track In information storage and retrieval, one of the concentric rings or spirals on the surface of a magnetic disk, on which data is recorded. A standard floppy disk has either 80 tracks (double-density) or 160 tracks (high-density). In sound recording, one or more optical or magnetic bands running parallel with the long dimension of an audiotape, videotape, or film on which signals are recorded for playback as synchronized sound.

Tract A book or pamphlet containing a treatise or discourse on a political, social, or religious topic, usually issued as propaganda or for doctrinal purposes. Also refers to a pamphlet made from a single sheet of printing paper folded one or more times to create leaves.

Trade association An organization dedicated to promoting a specific line of business, such as the book trade, for example, the Association of American Publishers or the American Booksellers Association. Most trade associations publish a trade journal to keep members informed of new products and developments affecting their interests. Directory information on book trade associations is available in the annual reference serial Literary Market Place.

Trade book A general term encompassing quality fiction and nonfiction for adults, trade paperbacks, and children's books published for the general public, as distinct from mass market paperbacks sold at newsstands and reference books, scholarly books, and textbooks intended for a narrow segment of the market. The standard publisher's discount on trade books is 40%.

Trade bookstore A bookstore that sells books of good quality, published for the general public rather than for a narrow segment of the market. Large chains may also sell newspapers, general interest magazines, videorecordings, dvds, music cds, road maps, calendars, greeting cards, etc. (examples: Barnes and Noble and Borders Books & Music). Trade bookstores normally do not stock expensive reference books, scholarly and technical books, and textbooks. Mass market paperbacks are stocked selectively, based on reputation of author.

Trade catalog A list of all the books (currently in print), published in a specific country or in other countries for which domestic publishers act as agents (example: Books in Print). Also, any publication that lists and describes the products manufactured and sold by a commercial company, with prices, illustrations, and information on how to order, for use in sales. The publisher's catalogs sent by post to booksellers and libraries are a prime example. Some booksellers also publish their own trade catalogs for distribution to potential retail customers, or make catalog information available on the Web (example: Amazon.com).

Trade directory A serial publication, usually issued annually, listing the companies and organizations engaged in buying, selling, or exchanging a specific category of goods and services. Entries include the official name, mailing address, phone/FAX numbers, key personnel, and other important information (example: American Book Trade Directory published by R. R. Bowker).

Trade discount Given by publishers to jobbers and retail outlets

Trade edition An edition produced by a trade publisher in hardcover and/or paperback publisher's binding for sale to quality booksellers and libraries. Trade editions are published for the general reader, rather than a specific segment of the market. Compare with mass-market paperback, scholarly book, and textbook.

Trade Journals Serials that fall in between the categories of magazines and journals, but their focus includes more product and business information. Articles are written by staff or experts in the field for members of a specific business or organization; examples include Internet World, Flying, Buttons, Popular Mechanics, PC Magazine, etc.

Trade magazine A periodical dedicated to the interests of a specific trade or industry, often providing such information as news of the field, descriptions of products and services, lists of new publications, legislative activities, etc.

Trade name The name used to designate a specific business enterprise and the reputation it has acquired in the market place (example: Microsoft), as distinct from any trademark associated with the firm's products (Windows).

Trade paperback A softcover edition published by a university press or trade publisher, in larger format and better quality binding than a mass-market paperback, for retail sale in college and trade bookstores. Most trade editions are published first in hardcover, then reprinted in paperback from the same plates after sales potential in hardcover has been realized. In some instances, paperback rights are sold by the original publisher to a trade paperback publisher. Synonymous with quality paperback. Compare with mass-market paperback.

Trade publisher A publishing house that issues books of interest to the educated reader, for sale in college and quality retail bookstores (example: Farrar, Straus and Giroux or St. Martin's Press). Few large trade publishers remain independent. A case in point is Alfred A. Knopf, now owned by Random House, which is in turn owned by the international publishing and entertainment conglomerate Bertelsmann AG. Compare with popular press and university press.

Trademark A letter, numeral, word, phrase, logo,

device, design, sound, or symbol (or combination of these) used in connection with a product or service to signify, directly or by association, the identity of the owner, usually a commercial enterprise that has reserved to itself the use of the distinctive mark by registering it with the U.S. Patent and Trademark Office. Trademarks of successful products and services are jealously guarded by their owners to prevent competitors from imitating them. Registration, indicated by an "R" enclosed in a small circle following the name ("TM" if registration is pending), gives the owner the right to legal redress in case of infringement. Also spelled trade mark.

Tragedy A literary work in prose or verse in which a catastrophe or sudden reversal of fortune befalls the protagonist, usually due to uncontrollable circumstances (example: Arthur Miller's Death of a Salesman) or as a result of an error of judgment or serious flaw in character (Macbeth). In classical Greek drama, the weakness that brings about the downfall of the tragic hero (or heroine) is typically hubris (pride). Compare with comedy and tragicomedy.

Tragicomedy A form of drama that originated in Elizabethan and Jacobean England, combining the forms and conventions of tragedy and comedy, usually by including characters of both high and low social position, and by unfolding unfortunate events that unexpectedly result in a happy ending (example: Shakespeare's Merchant of Venice).

Trailer A very short film used primarily for advertising purposes, consisting of carefully selected extracts from a longer motion picture to be shown at a later date. In library cataloging, the term is added inside square brackets [trailer] following the title proper in the bibliographic description to indicate material type. Compare with film clip.

Training Instruction designed to teach a person or group of people (trainees) a specific skill or set of skills, for example, how to check books and other materials in and out at the circulation desk of a library, or how to reshelve items in correct call number sequence. In-service training occurs in the workplace during normal working hours, sometimes in the context in which the skill(s) will be used.

Transaction log A continuous record of the operations initiated by users of an automated system during a designated period of time (week, month, year). In online catalogs and bibliographic databases, the "transactions" are usually searches recorded by type (author, title, subject, keywords, etc.) Which can be analyzed to reveal usage patterns and longitudinal changes in search behavior.

Transactions The published papers or abstracts of papers presented at a conference or meeting of a society or association, usually including a record of what transpired. Compare with proceedings.

Transcribe To make a written or typewritten copy, usually of a speech, broadcast, sound recording, or other oral presentation, or a copy of notes taken on the content of such a presentation.

Transcript A copy of an original, usually made by hand or typewritten, particularly a legal document or official record. Also refers to the written record of words spoken in court proceedings or in a speech, interview, broadcast, or sound recording.

Transfer A change in the physical custody of archival materials from one location or agency to another, usually without a corresponding change of legal ownership and responsibility, for example, the relocation of records no longer current to temporary storage to await final disposition.

Translation A passage from a speech or written work, or an entire speech or work, put into the words of another language (English into Spanish), or into a more modern form of the same language (Old English or Middle English into contemporary English), usually to make the text more accessible to individuals who are unable to read it in the original language. Translations differ in the degree to which they follow the original. The name of the translator usually appears on the title page of a book, following the name of the author. A translation may have a parallel title in the source language. In library cataloging, the note Translation of: is added in the bibliographic description, giving the title in the original language. Abbreviated trans.

Transliteration Rendering the characters of one alphabet in characters representing the same sound (or sounds) in another alphabet (example: Greek or Cyrillic into Roman). Each character is treated independently of the others. Compare with romanization.

Transparency A sheet of transparent film, usually 8½ × 11" in size, bearing text and/or images in color or black-and-white, designed to be projected on a large screen using an overhead projector or document camera. Presentation software has superseded overhead transparencies, but a well-prepared presenter brings them to use as backup in case of equipment or network failure. Synonymous with overhead transparency. Compare with overlay.

Transportation Research Information Services Online Provides access to over 420,000 bibliographic records covering transportation research published in books, journal articles, technical reports and other media. Literature covered from 1960 to present. Also selected links to full text or sources of full text have been given.

Travel guide A handbook designed for persons interested in touring a foreign country, or an unfamiliar city, state, province, or region of their own country. In addition to describing major attractions, most travel guides include maps and directions, information about dining and overnight accommodations, and advice about currency exchange, immunizations, personal safety, and communication with the local inhabitants. Some guides specialize in a particular type of travel, such as bicycle touring or ecotourism.

Treasure hunt An exercise in which students are

required by their instructor to use the resources of the library to find answers to a list of very specific and often unrelated questions, sometimes as a contest. This type of assignment usually puts a temporary strain on the reference desk, especially when a large number of students converge on the library, all needing the same information at the same time. For this reason, it is one of the "pet peeves" of reference librarians who believe library skills are best learned in the context of a more meaningful research assignment.

Treatise A book or long formal essay, usually on an abstruse or complex subject, especially a systematic well-documented presentation of facts or evidence, and the principles or conclusions drawn from them. The term is sometimes used in a pejorative sense to refer to a written work in which the treatment is dry and scholarly or unnecessarily thorough or detailed.

Treatment A narrative account of the screenplay for a motion picture or television broadcast, including a detailed description of characters, scenes, sets, camerawork, etc., but without the dialogue. Compare with scenario.

Treatment history A record of the conservation procedures applied to an item (deacidification, fumigation, rebinding, restoration, etc.), usually including date of application and any details concerning the treatment process which might be of future use to conservators, particularly in cases requiring reversal.

Treaty A formal written agreement between two or more governments concerning peace, military alliance, trade relations, economic assistance, etc., often the result of protracted negotiations. Also refers to the signed document serving as the official record of such an agreement. The texts of important treaties are available in the government documents or reference section of large libraries. The originals are usually housed in national archives or in the special collections of national libraries.

Tree structure A classified display in a thesaurus of

indexing terms showing the complete hierarchy of descriptors, from the broadest to the most specific, usually by indention, sometimes with a tree number indicating the location of the heading in the tree, as in the Medical Subject Headings. Tree Structures developed and maintained by the National Library of Medicine

Trial A test conducted for a limited period of time to determine the suitability of a new person in a position, or the quality or feasibility of a new system, product, or service. Database vendors usually offer a free 30-day trial to libraries as an inducement to subscribe.

Trial user A person or organization asked to use a new service or computer system, usually for a limited period of time, to test its usefulness and effectiveness, and to help identify problems that need to be corrected before the final version is released for general use.

Trianon collection Large private collection of rare books purchased from the Trianon Foundation in Colorado Springs. It is now housed in university arvive.

Triennial Issued every three years. Also refers to a serial publication issued every three years.

Trilogy A set of three narrative works related in theme or plot, which together form a larger work (example: the **Oresteia** of Aeschylus). Four similarly related works are called a tetrology (The Alexandria Quartet by Lawrence Durrell).

Trim size The finished dimensions of a printed sheet or publication after waste has been trimmed away to prepare it for binding, usually indicated in the specifications for the print job.

Trimmed A term used in the book trade to indicate that the leaves of a book have been cut down to a size smaller than the publication as originally issued.

Trimming In bookbinding, the process of slicing approximately 1/8 of an inch from the head, tail, and fore-edge of the body of a book to remove the folds of its signatures, done on a machine called a guillotine. In paperback books, the cover is usually cut flush or even with the sections. Compare with uncut.

Trojan Horse A computer program is either hidden inside another program or that masquerades as something it is not in order to trick potential users into running it. For example a program that appears to be a game or image file but in reality performs some other function. The term "Trojan Horse" comes from a possibly mythical ruse of war used by the Greeks sometime between 1500 and 1200 B.C. A Trojan Horse computer program may spread itself by sending copies of itself from the host computer to other computers, but unlike a virus it will (usually) not infect other programs.

Trolling: The act of deliberately posting false or inflammatory information in a network newsgroup to elicit responses from other serious readers.

True crime story A nonfiction genre in which the subject is an actual crime or event (disappearance, kidnapping, murder, etc.) So bizarre or inexplicable that it excites popular interest and curiosity (example: Small Sacrifices: A True Story of Passion and Murder by Ann Rule). Compare with mystery.

Truetype A technology for outline fonts that is built into all Windows and Macintosh operating systems. Outline fonts are scalable enabling a display device to generate a character at any size based on a geometrical description.

Truncate In shortening a word, to cut off at a given point as opposed to abbreviation. Used in computer searching to retrieve variants of a word or a list of items beginning with a phrase or string of characters.

Truncation is the shortening of a search word, field, or record. In the case of truncating a search word, this is a strategy used to search among multiple variants or spellings of a word. The asterisk (*) is generally used as a wildcard to replace a letter or letters. An example is invest* which will pick up instances of invest, investor, investments, investigations, etc. In some databases the asterisk must be accompanied with a number that define the number of characters that can be truncated.

TSO An interface on the MVS system maintained by OIT for numerical and statistical processing and programming. For information about accounts, call 688-HELP or send e-mail to 8help@osu.edu.

Ttechnical services division One of the divisions of the Libraries, composed of the following services: acquisition, cataloguing and preservation.

Turabian style A set of rules and guidelines for citing references as well as preparing and submitting manuscripts for publication developed by Kate L. Turabian. These rules are detailed in A Manual for Writers of Term Papers, These, and Dissertations (the most recent version is available at the reference desk).

Turnaround time In data processing, the amount of time that elapses between the initiation of a process or operation and its completion. Compare with response time.

Turn-in In bookbinding, the portion of the covering of a book folded over the outer edges of the boards, from outside to inside, mitered at the corners, and covered to within 1/8-3/16" of the edge by the paste-down. On library corners, the turn-in is folded; on Dutch corners, it is cut.

Turnover The rate at which employees leave a company, organization, or institution and are replaced. A high turnover rate may be a sign of difficult working conditions, inadequate compensation, poor management, burnout, etc.

Tutorial A printed or online instructional tool designed to teach novices how to use a computer system or electronic resource, usually in a self-paced step-by-step manner, often with questions at the end for testing proficiency. Online tutorials have been developed by instruction librarians to accommodate distance learners and students who prefer online library instruction. Compare with help screen.

Twisted pair A cable of relatively low bandwidth used in older telephone networks and less costly lans, consisting of two separately insulated thin-diameter wires twisted around each other, one to carry the signal and the other grounded to absorb interference. Most computer networks use coaxial cable and/or optical fiber which provide the higher bandwidth required for high-speed data transmission. Telephone companies in the United States are upgrading their infrastructure to coax and fiber-optic cable.

Twisted pair cable A type of cable that is typically found in telephone jacks; two wires are independently insulated and are twisted around each other. The cable is thinner and more flexible than the coaxial cable used in conjunction with 10Base-2 or 10Base-5 standards. Most Ohio State UNITS telephone jacks have three pairs of wires; one is used for the telephone and the other two can be used for 10Base-T Ethernet connections.

Two on A sewing method used in hand-binding in which two sections are sewn along the fold with a single length of thread, alternating between the sections from kettle stitch to kettle stitch. Today, the technique is used mainly in fine binding to minimize swell (most trade bindings are sewn all along). Hand sewing three sections together in similar fashion is known as three on.

Two-double fold test A simple trial used by conservators to detect brittle paper. One corner of a leaf is gently folded diagonally forward and back twice about 1/2-inch in from the point where the edges meet. Paper is found to be brittle if the corner breaks off or detaches with a slight pull after the fourth fold.

Type facsimile A reprint of a work made from a new setting of type in which every detail of the appearance of printed matter in the original edition is copied as precisely as possible. Synonymous with facsimile reprint. Compare with facsimile edition.

Type family In printing, all the variants of the same

basic type design, including uppercase, lowercase, and small capitals in both roman and italic in all sizes and weights (lightface, medium, semi-bold, boldface, condensed, expanded). Compare with font.

Type of recording In AACR2, the method used to encode sound on a disc or tape (analog, digital, magnetic, or optical) is given in the physical description area of the bibliographic record created to represent the item in the library catalog, as in the following examples:

Type page The area or part of a printed page that is printed upon, excluding the margins, headlines, footlines, and page numbers.

Type size The dimensions (height and width) of the body size of a type font, usually given in points. Most books are printed in type sizes ranging from 5-point to 22-point. Larger types sizes are used mainly for display matter. On the old-fashioned typewriter, pica was the most common type size.

Type Small, separately cast rectangular metal units, each bearing on its face a single character cut in relief. In letterpress printing, the units are assembled by a typesetter into pages of text, locked in a chase and transferred to the bed of a printing press, where they are inked and an impression of the type matter made under pressure on a printing surface such as paper. After the print job is completed, the units are disassembled for reuse. Johann Gutenberg is credited with inventing movable type in Germany in or around the year 1456.

Typeface The upper surface of a unit of type, bearing in relief the character to be printed. Also refers to the general design or style of the characters of a font of type, including all the sizes and weights in which the font is made. Designing a new typeface is a major undertaking, even for an experienced typographer. It is therefore not unusual for a typeface to be named after the person who designed it (example: Garamond). There does not appear to be universal agreement on the classification of typefaces. Also spelled type face. Sometimes abbreviated face.

Typescript An author's original typewritten copy of a work, in the form in which it is submitted for publication, or a typewritten copy of the original commissioned by the author or publisher, as opposed to a manuscript written by hand. Abbreviated ts. And tss. (plural).

Typesetting In printing, the setting of type from copy, either by hand or by machine, done by a person called a

Typographical error A mistake in a printed work made by the typesetter. Also refers to a similar error made by a person using a keyboard to type a text. Most word processing software includes an automatic spell checker to alert writers to such errors. Abbreviated typo. Synonymous with misprint.

Typography The art and craft of setting and arranging type, and making impressions from the result, which began with the invention of movable type by Johann Gutenberg in Germany in the mid-15th century. Also refers to the general style, arrangement, and appearance of a work printed from type, and to the skill involved in selecting a suitable ink and grade of paper, choosing an appropriate typeface and type size, determining page layout, etc. The person responsible for the final appearance of a printed publication is the typographer.

U.S. Copyright Office The agency of the U.S. federal government responsible for administering copyright law, a unit of the Library of Congress. Although the first federal copyright law was passed in 1790, copyright functions were not centralized under the Library of Congress until 1870 and the Copyright Office did not become a separate department of the Library of Congress until 1897. In addition to administering federal law protecting the intellectual property rights of American citizens, the Copyright Office also provides expertise to Congress on matters related to intellectual property, advises and assists Congress in drafting proposed changes in U.S. copyright law, advises Congress on compliance with international copyright agreements, serves as a depository for works registered under U.S. copyright law, and furnishes information to the general public on copyright law and registration.

UALC Utah Academic Library Consortium; an organization made up of representatives from all academic libraries in Utah, formed to work on issues of concern to all the institutions (such as journal pricing) and improve access to materials for the state as a whole through initiatives such as consortial subscriptions to electronic products.

UDP User Datagram Protocol; One of the protocols for data transfer that is part of the TCP/IP suite of protocols. UDP is a "stateless" protocol in that UDP makes no provision for acknowledgement of packets received.

UKM The OCLC symbol for the national library of Great Britain.

Ulrich's International Periodicals Directory An annual reference serial published since 1932 by R. R. Bowker, Ulrich's International Periodicals Directory provides bibliographic information and pricing for a classified list of over 164,000 regularly and irregularly issued periodicals currently published in the U.S. and internationally, including titles available electronically. The directory is indexed by title and ISSN, with separate sections for cessations, title changes, refereed journals, and titles available in various digital formats. Ulrich's is also available on CD-ROM and online by licensing agreement.

Ultrafiche A card-shaped transparent microform with a reduction ratio considerably greater than that of standard microfiche or superfiche (up to 3,000 frames per 4 x 6-inch sheet). A special ultrafiche reader-printer machine is required to view and make hard copies of documents stored in this medium.

Ultraviolet (UV) Electromagnetic radiation beyond the spectrum visible to humans as light, shorter in wavelength than violet light but longer than X-rays. The sun is the chief source of natural ultraviolet radiation. Because UV radiation can damage photographs and accelerate the deterioration of certain grades of paper, prolonged exposure of library materials to direct sunlight should be avoided and incandescent lighting installed when possible in storage areas where preservation is a high priority. UV filters can be used to reduce exposure.

Umbilicus In antiquity, a knobbed wooden rod attached to one end of a papyrus scroll around which a manuscript was rolled when not in use. A vellum tag was usually attached to one end, bearing a note indicating the title or contents.

Unabridged A version of a written work that has not been shortened and is therefore considered to be complete. The fact that an edition is unabridged is sometimes indicated on the title page of long works issued in paperback, but unless otherwise stated, a published work is assumed to be unabridged. An unabridged dictionary is the version containing the most words (example: Webster's Third New International Dictionary). Compare with abridgment.

Unabridged dictionary A dictionary that attempts to include all the words of a language. For the English language, there are only three, Webster's Third New International Dictionary (1961), Random House Unabridged Dictionary (1993), and the Oxford English Dictionary (1989), the latter concerned more with etymology than with definition. First published in 1909, Webster's Third has about 450,000 entries (down from 600,000 in the second edition). The Random House Unabridged Dictionary has fewer words, but more illustrations. Compare with desk dictionary.

Unauthorized biography A biographical work written without the consent of its subject or the subject's family if the biographee is deceased, sometimes more objective in its analysis than an authorized biography because the biographer does not have to make concessions to gain access to confidential sources. However, an unauthorized biography may be less detailed or complete if the author was denied important information.

Unauthorized edition An edition printed without the consent of the author, the author's legal representative, or the original publisher, but not in violation of existing copyright law. Compare with authorized edition.

Unbacked Printed on only one side of a blank sheet of paper, as in a poster.

Unbound A printed publication issued without a binding or cover, or with its cover removed. Prior to the 19th century, books were sold in the form of printed sections, to be bound to the purchaser's specifications. Also refers to an issue of a periodical or part of a serial that will eventually be bound, usually with others, to form a volume. Compare with disbound and loose.

Uncataloged loan When titles on SAGE are "On Order" or "In Process," the process by which an uncataloged loan request is completed at the reference desk. "On Order" items are rush cataloged when they arrive and sent directly to the patron; "In Process" items are located by monograph staff, rush cataloged for patron, and delivered to the loan/reserve desk where patron are notified that they are ready for pick up. There occasionally are times when patron need the book immediately and the 2-3 day processing time for rush cataloging is not sufficient. In these instances, the monograph staff property the book and loan the uncataloged books to the patron for 2 weeks for undergraduates and 6 months for faculty and staff. Patron return uncataloged items directly to monograph where it is then processed and sent to cataloging and eventually to the stacks.

Uncial From Latin uncialis meaning "of an inch" or "inch-high." A large, full majuscule script used in the earliest Biblical codices and as a book hand in manuscripts written and copied from about 300-700 A.D., in which capital letters were rounded and modified in ways suggestive of later lowercase letters, probably to increase writing speed. Half uncial gradually replaced uncial as a book hand after the 6th century. Also refers to manuscripts written in this script.

Uncover A database of book reviews, magazines, and articles, including FAX article delivery. It provides table of contents information for over 14,000 journals in all disciplines held by the libraries in the Colorado Academic and Research Libraries consortium and provides on-line access to ERIC, at education database. Coverage for most journals begins with 1989.

Uncut A volume in which the bolts are not trimmed to uniform size in binding, leaving the leaves to be separated by hand by the owner of the book, with a paper knife or other thin-edged instrument. Synonymous with unopened and untrimmed.

Underfunded An organization, institution, or project allocated insufficient monies to accomplish its goals and objectives. Chronic underfunding can lead to a decline in quality of service and is demoralizing for staff and management.

Undergraduate library A separate library established, supported, and maintained by a university to serve the information and research needs of its undergraduate students and the instructional requirements of the undergraduate curriculum. Sometimes administered as a branch library. Compare with graduate library.

Underground press A publisher that issues printed publications unofficially or clandestinely, usually to members of a group or organization that opposes the policies of an established government or other authority, more common during periods of civil unrest than in times of peace and prosperity. Eventually, most underground presses either disband or become "above ground" publishing houses.

Underlining Words, phrases, or passages of text underscored in pencil or ink by a previous reader, usually for future reference. As a general rule, libraries do not add heavily underlined gift books to the collection. Also refers to a formatting option available in word processing software that can be used to place a line beneath a single character, word, phrase, line, or entire passage of text. Compare with highlighting.

Underrun A press run that produces fewer copies than the number ordered, sometimes causing a shortage of publisher's inventory. The opposite of overrun.

Underserved Persons within the geographic area or clientele served by a library or library system who use its services infrequently for a variety of reasons, including limited awareness of available resources and services, lack of familiarity with the national language, illiteracy, poor health, lack of transportation, etc. Outreach programs help bridge these gaps.

Understaffed Having an insufficient number of employees to do the work required. Signs of overwork (fatigue, absenteeism, arrears, etc.) Can be the result of understaffing. Synonymous with short-staffed and short-handed. The opposite of overstaffed.

Underutilized A library service, resource, or item used less often than it ought to be, usually because its usefulness is not widely appreciated, or because it is not as accessible as other alternatives, for example, collections of theses and dissertations in some academic libraries.

Undocumented Lacking official papers or other tangible evidence in support of existence, identity, validity, authenticity, provenance, etc.

UNESCO UNESCO gives access to its data sources on education, literacy, science and technology and culture and communication of different countries of the world.

Unexpurgated A text or edition that includes passages omitted from other versions or editions, usually because they were considered offensive to some readers. Compare with expurgated.

Unfinished A work left incomplete at the death of the author, composer, or creator. Unfinished literary works are sometimes published posthumously (example: The Last Tycoon by F. Scott Fitzgerald).

UNICORN The library automation software developed by SIRSI that underlies ACORN, the libraries' on-line catalog.

UNICOS A version of the UNIX operating system adapted for CRAY computers.

Uniform edition Two or more books printed, bound, and jacketed in the same style to show that they constitute a single entity, such as a multivolume encyclopedia, or that they are related to each other in some other way, for example, the individual titles in a monographic series or the collected works of an author.

Uniform Resource Locator (URL) A URL (Universal Resource Locator) is a general-purpose Internet addressing protocol, used in WWW (HTTP) service. It is of the form: protocol://hostname.domain.name/directory or file names/file name.file extension One could say a URL is what a telephone number is to a telephone or a street address is to a house. Although Web site urls are sometimes long and hard to read let alone remember, browsers like Netscape have a bookmark feature, which gives you the opportunity to save the location (URL) of Web sites you want to return to.

Uniform style The appearance of publications printed in the same typographical style on the same grade of paper, issued in a binding of the same size and design. Volumes published as a set or series are usually produced in this fashion.

Uniform title In authority control, the distinctive title selected for cataloging purposes to represent a work issued under more than one title, usually in more than one expression or manifestation. Uniform titles are commonly used to catalog sacred texts (example: Bible) and liturgical and musical works.

Union catalog A list of the holdings of all the libraries in a library system, or of all or a portion of the collections of a group of independent libraries, indicating by name and/

or location symbol which libraries own at least one copy of each item. When the main purpose of a union catalog is to indicate location, the bibliographic description provided in each entry may be reduced to a minimum, but when it also serves other purposes, description is more complete. The arrangement of a union catalog is normally alphabetical by author or title.

Union list A complete list of the holdings of a group of libraries of materials 1) of a specific type, 2) on a certain subject, or 3) in a particular field, usually compiled for the purpose of resource sharing (example: Union List of Serials in the Libraries of the United States and Canada and its continuation New Serial Titles issued by the Library of Congress). The entry for each bibliographic item includes a list of codes representing the libraries owning at least one copy. Union lists are usually printed, but some have been converted into online databases.

UNIS Marriott Library's online public-access catalog. It does not appear to be an acronym standing for anything.

Unitary term A heading or indexing term composed of two or more nouns joined by the conjunction "and," treated as a single subject because their meanings overlap to such an extent that the literature about them is not clearly separated. Each part is seen as approximating the whole, as in the Library of Congress subject heading Forests and forestry. Not all headings of this form are unitary (example: Forestry and community).

United Nations United Nations provides data on different countries. Its data sources include social indicators, population statistics, and monthly bulletin of statistics.

Universal Borrowing - (UB) This service is a type of Interlibrary Loan that allow students, faculty and staff of the UW-Whitewater to borrow materials from other UW-System libraries for free. Not all materials are available (reference, periodicals, periodical articles, special collections, etc.) Via this service. To use UB, begin in the Andersen Library Catalog and click on the UB & Other Catalogs button.

Universal Copyright Convention (UCC) An international copyright convention drafted in 1952 under the auspices of UNESCO, revised in 1971 and ratified by over sixty-five countries, including the United States. Under its terms, each signatory nation extends to foreign works the same copyright protection it gives to works published within its territory by one of its own citizens.

Universal Decimal Classification (UDC) An elaborate expansion of Dewey Decimal Classification in which symbols are used, in addition to arabic numerals, to create longer notations used in subject classification, making it more flexible than DDC and particularly suitable for specialized collections. Developed by Henri La Fontaine and Paul Otlet of the Institut Internationale de Bibliographie, UDC was first published in a French edition in 1905. Adopted by the International Organization for Standardization (ISO), it has been translated into many languages, is revised regularly by an international group, and has become the most widely used classification system in the world.

Universal Machine-Readable Cataloging (UNIMARC) The most comprehensive version of the MARC format for cataloging bibliographic items, UNIMARC was first published in 1977 and is currently developed under the sponsorship of the IFLA Universal Bibliographic Control and International MARC Core Activity (UBCIM) program to facilitate the international exchange of bibliographic records between national bibliographic agencies.

Universal Serials and book Exchange Formerly, along with the United States Book Exchange, a clearinghouse of publications, accepting, holding and distributing publications from various libraries.

University Archives University Archives, located in the Rare & Manuscripts Collections in Kroch Library, collects and preserves records of historical, legal, fiscal, or administrative value to Cornell University. Holdings include official records and reports of the university, its officers, and component parts; private papers of faculty, students, staff, and alumni; official and student publications; maps and architectural records; audiovisual materials including still photographs and negatives, motion picture film, oral history interviews, and audio and video tapes; and artifacts and ephemera documenting Cornell's history.

University library A library or library system established, administered, and funded by a university, to meet the information, research, and curriculum needs of its students, faculty, and staff. Some large universities maintain separate undergraduate and graduate libraries. Compare with college library.

University press A publishing house associated with a university or other scholarly institution, specializing in the publication of scholarly books and journals, particularly works written by its faculty (example: Johns Hopkins University Press). Most university presses operate on a nonprofit basis, relying on a committee of senior faculty members to select manuscripts for publication. The trade association of university presses in North America is the Association of American University Presses

Unix A computer operating system (the basic software running on a computer, underneath things like word processors and spreadsheets). Unix is designed to be used by many people at the same time (it is multi-user) and has TCP/IP built-in. It is the most common operating system for servers on the Internet.

Unknown authorship A work for which the author (or authors) are unknown or cannot be identified with certainty, including works emanating from a corporate body that is unknown or lacks a name. Libraries catalog such works under the title (example: Chanson de Roland). In AACR2, if the work is attributed to one or more persons or corporate bodies, added entries are made under their names. Synonymous with Compare with diffuse authorship.

Unlettered A binding that has neither the title nor the

author's name is displayed on the spine, making its content difficult to identify when placed upright alongside other volumes on the shelf.

Unopened A book in which the bolts are left uncut in binding. Once the leaves have been slit by hand with a paper knife or other thin-edged implement, the volume is said to have been opened.

Unpaged Pages of a book or other publication not assigned individual page numbers, usually found in the front matter. The cataloger records the number of such pages in the physical description area of the bibliographic record, as an interpolation inside square brackets (example: [15] p.). Compare with unpaginated.

Unpaginated A book or other publication in which the pages of the text are not numbered or sequentially marked. The total number of pages in an unpaginated work is noted by the cataloger as an interpolation inside square brackets in the physical description area of the bibliographic record (example: [118] p.). The opposite of paginated. Compare with unpaged.

Unprintable A word or phrase considered unfit to be printed, usually for reasons of obscenity, sometimes indicated in text by the first letter followed by an asterisk substituted for each of the remaining letters (h***).

Unprotected Data accessible to modification or deletion by unauthorized persons because it is stored in a file or on a disk that is not secured.

Unpublished A work in the process of publication that has yet to be issued. Also, a manuscript or typescript never published, either because it was not intended for publication or because the author was unable to find a publisher. Compare with semipublished.

Unsigned A written work, such as an entry in a reference book or article in a magazine, that does not include the name of the author, usually an indication that the piece was written by a paid staff writer. In a more general sense, any written document that does not indicate the identity of the author, especially a letter or legal instrument lacking a signature. The opposite of signed. Compare with anonymous.

Untouched A term describing early printed books (incunabula) that have been neither rubricated nor illuminated.

Unzipping Expanding files that have been compressed.

Up time The time when a computer is in operation.

Update To make a news story, data file, reference work, or other information source current, usually by revising existing content or substituting new material. Bibliographic databases are updated on a regular basis by adding records representing newly published items. Frequency of update is usually given in the database description. Printed indexes and abstracting services are updated in monthly or quarterly paperbound supplements, usually cumulated annually. Legal publications (statutes, case law, etc.) May also be updated in supplements, but most reference works are revised and republished in a new edition.

Updated A work from which outdated information has been removed and current information substituted, or to which more recent information has been added. Printed publications may be updated in supplements (example: legal statutes and case law) or revised and republished in a new edition. The currency of information provided on a Web site is indicated in the note "Last updated on [date]" usually found near the bottom of the welcome screen.

Upgrade To improve existing hardware or software by replacing it with a model or version that has new features and/or additional capabilities. Software upgrades are usually indicated sequentially by a decimal number added to the name of the application. Compare with migration.

Upload To transmit a copy of one or more files from a local computer to the hard disk of another (usually more remote) computer, such as a mainframe or network server, a process that may require terminal emulation software. The opposite of download.

Uppercase Capital letters, as opposed to the small or lowercase letters of a type font. The terms uppercase and lowercase are derived from the relative positions of the compartments in the wood or metal case containing elements of type bearing capital letters and small letters at a typesetter's bench in the days when type was set by hand (letterpress). Also spelled upper case.

UPS Uninterruptible Power Supply. A unit that switches to battery power whenever the power cuts out.

Urban Libraries Council (ULC) Founded in 1971, ULC is an association of approximately 150 public libraries located in metropolitan areas of the United States with 50,000 or more inhabitants, and the corporations that serve them, organized to solve common problems, take advantage of new opportunities, and foster applied research to improve professional practice. ULC is an affiliate of the American Library Association

URL Uniform Resource Locator; a means of identifying resources on the Internet. A full URL consists of three parts: the protocol (e.g., ftp, gopher, http, nntp, telnet); the server name and address; and the item's path. The protocol describes the type of item and is always followed by a colon (:). The server name and address identifies the computer where the information is stored and is preceded by two slashes (//). The path shows where an item is stored on the server and what the file is called; each segment of the location s preceded by a single slash (/). Examples: The URL for the OSU home page is http://www.osu.edu.

URN Uniform Resource Name; A URI that is supposed to be available for along time. For an address to be a URN some institution is supposed to make a commitment to keep the resource available at that address.

USA and Canada Trade Data Online Trade Data Online provides access and the ability to generate customized reports on Canada's and U.S. trade with over 200 countries. The data types include imports, exports, trade balances by product and industry.

Usability testing Quantifiable methods used to determine the ease with which the design of a computer interface, such as an online catalog or Web site, meets the needs of its users, including direct observation of actual search behavior, interviewing, surveys, and exploratory activities in which volunteers are asked to organize categories of information according to their own preferences. Without usability testing, librarians tend to design systems from a trained perspective, based on assumptions about information-seeking behavior that do not necessarily reflect the experiences of actual users.

Usability The ease with which a computer interface can be efficiently and effectively used, especially by a novice. The first priority in designing for usability is to provide clear, consistent navigation of content. Some libraries employ usability testing to evaluate the user-friendliness of their Web pages.

Usage The number of times a bibliographic item is used by library patrons during a given period of time, including the number of times it is checked out and any in-house use measured by the number of times it is picked up from a desk or table in a public area for reshelving. In academic libraries, high-use materials may be given a shorter loan period, or placed on reserve or in the reference section. In some libraries, low-use items may be candidates for weeding. Usage statistics are also helpful in collection development.

USAID Global Education Online Database 2000 GED Online provides education data in two ways. Users can select a single indicator for multiple years and multiple countries by clicking on one of the bulleted groups of indicators under the UNESCO or DHS headings.

USB flash drivesremovable media that uses an EEPROM chip to transfer and store data via a USB port using plug and play technology. Utilizing the USB port, these devices are powered by the computer's power supply and are capable of high speed data transfer. Flash devices have the capacity of holding more data than a floppy disk and can be used on Windows, Mac and Linux stations and on almost any version of operating system. For older operating systems, it is necessary to download the USB support drivers from Microsoft or Apple. Consult your USB device manual.

USB Short for Universal Serial Bus, an external bus standard that supports data transfer rates of 12 Mbps. A single USB port can be used to connect up to 127 peripheral devices, such as mice, modems, and keyboards. USB also supports Plug-and-Play installation and hot plugging.

Use An instruction used in an entry in a subject headings list or thesaurus of controlled vocabulary to direct the user from a synonym or quasi-synonym to the preferred term under which items on the topic are cataloged or indexed (example: Reading Therapy USE Bibliotherapy in the Thesaurus of ERIC Descriptors). Compare with see.

Use life The length of time or number of times an item can be used before it becomes so worn that it is no longer fit for use and has to be discarded. For books, use life depends on quality of paper, strength of binding, and actions taken to protect the cover, such as enclosing the dust jacket in a washable plastic sleeve.

Used book A book that has had at least one previous owner. The condition of the cover and leaves is an indication of the amount of use a volume has received. Sometimes used books are found upon appraisal to be rare and valuable, especially copies of a first edition. Synonymous with secondhand book.

Used bookstore A bookstore that specializes in books that have had at least one previous owner, sometimes limited to a particular genre, such as mystery or science fiction. Unless a used book is rare or out of print, it is usually priced on the basis of condition, lower than the list price of a new copy. Some bookstores sell both new and used books. Synonymous with secondhand bookstore.

Used for (UF) A phrase indicating terms synonymous with an authorized subject heading or descriptor, not used in cataloging or indexing to avoid scatter. In a subject headings list or thesaurus of controlled vocabulary, synonyms are given immediately following the official heading. In the alphabetical list of indexing terms, they are included as lead-in vocabulary followed by a see or USE cross-reference directing the user to the correct heading.

USENET A network of newsgroups. There are thousands of newsgroups available through USENET. Each one covers a specific topic or subject area.

Usenet news: A method of exchanging information on the Internet. Similar topics are arranged into a wide variety of newsgroups. Also referred to as "network news"or "electronic bulletin boards".

User area The amount of floor space in a library that can be assigned for use by patrons, as opposed to the area required for the use of staff, closed stacks, automation and HVAC equipment, maintenance, storage, etc.

User education All the activities involved in teaching users how to make the best possible use of library resources, services, and facilities, including formal and informal instruction delivered by a librarian or other staff member one-on-one or in a group. Also includes online tutorials, audiovisual materials, and printed guides and pathfinders. A broader term than bibliographic instruction.

User group The individuals within the population served by a library who actually make use of its services and collections on a fairly regular basis. Synonymous with clientele. Compare with constituency.

User Id The string of characters that identifies you. The name by which you are known to the network. Also known as username.

User survey A questionnaire administered to users of a library or library system to find out what brings them to the library, how they normally use the resources and services it provides, their subjective evaluation of the quality of their experiences, and any suggestions for improvement (feedback). In a longitudinal study, the same or a similar survey instrument is administered more than once, after a suitable interval of time has elapsed, to measure changes in usage patterns, attitudes, etc.

User warrant The addition of a term to an indexing language, or the assignment of an existing descriptor to documents by an indexer, based on the frequency with which it is requested or included in the search statements entered as input by the users of an information retrieval system. Compare with literary warrant.

User-friendly Computer software or hardware designed to be easy to use or operate, even by a complete novice. Most user-friendly systems include point-of-use instruction and readily accessible help screens, written in language that is clear and easy to comprehend. User-friendliness was a prime consideration in the design of the graphical user interface (GUI) that made the Windows and Macintosh operating systems a commercial success.

Username A name used in conjunction with a password to gain access to a computer system or a network service. Example: At OSU, your main username is referred to as your "OSU Internet username" and it usually consists of your last name, a period, and a unique number (e.g., doe.999). This username is required for accessing a variety of secure servers across campus.

USM Unsharp masking. A process used to sharpen images.

Utility A small program that expands the capability of a computer's operating system by enabling it to perform an additional task, usually something as routine as managing a disk drive, printer, scanner, or other peripheral device. Unlike the basic operating system, utilities can be added and removed as needed. A utility differs from an application program in being less complex, usually limited to a single function.

Utility Commonly refers to a program used for

managing system resources such as disk drives, printers, and other devices; utilities sometimes are installed as memory-resident programs. Example: the suite of programs called Norton Utilities for disk copying, backups, etc.

Utopia A term coined by Thomas More from the Greek ou ("no" or "not") and topos ("place"). A literary or artistic work in which the setting is an ideal society, usually one existing in a future time or imaginary place (example: Looking Backward by Edward Bellamy). Utopias are created by authors who feel nostalgia for an idealized past, or who wish to call attention to the need to reform existing social, political, or economic institutions. The opposite of dystopia.

UUCP UNIX-to-UNIX Copy Program. This was initially a program run under the UNIX operating system that allowed one UNIX system to send files to another UNIX system via dial-up phone lines. Today, the term is more commonly used to describe the large international network which uses the UUCP protocol to pass news and electronic mail.

UUENCODE (Unix to Unix Encoding) A method for converting files from Binaryto ASCII (text) so that they can be sent across the Internet via email.

Uuencode A method of converting files into an ASCII format that can be transmitted over the Internet; it is a universal protocol for transferring files between different platforms like UNIX, Windows, and Macintosh and is especially popular for sending e-mail attachments. The Eudora e-mail program automatically encodes and decodes (uudecodes) such files.

V.34 A standard for modem transmission speed up to 28,800 bps; V.34 modems automatically adjust their transmission speeds based on the quality of the line. .

Uuncompression Expanding files that have been compressed.

V.42 A standard that applies to error control in relation to high-speed modems.

V.42 BIS A standard that applies to data compression in relation to modems; it roughly corresponds to MNP Level 5.

Vacuum freeze dry An expensive conservation procedure in which wet library materials are frozen, then placed in a chamber from which the air is extracted, causing the water (in the form of ice) to vaporize.

Vade mecum Latin for "go with me." A small book, such as a guidebook, handbook, or manual, meant to be carried about and used for quick reference. In a more general sense, any item that is regularly carried by a person. Also spelled vade-mecum. Plural: vade mecums.

Vandalism Damage to library collections, furnishings, or facilities which is intentional rather than accidental, usually motivated by anger or malice on the part of the perpetrator. Vandalism detracts from the physical appearance of a library and its resources. The cost of repair or replacement puts an unwelcome burden on the budget. To avoid detection, most acts of vandalism are committed in unstaffed locations or after hours. Some libraries employ a security guard to keep an eye on areas not visible from at least one public service point when the library is open.

Vanilla text Text written on a computer, usually with the aid of a text editor or word processing software, in a standard font with no formatting (boldface, italics, etc.), usually with a filename ending in .txt. Synonymous with plaintext.

Vanity publisher A type of publisher, more common in the United States than in other countries, that specializes in producing books at the author's expense, used mainly by writers whose works have been rejected by commercial publishers, and by individuals of private means who are convinced they have an important message to impart to the world. In England, vanity publishing is used primarily for poetry. Books published by vanity publishers are avoided by reviewers and rarely purchased by retail booksellers and libraries. Synonymous with vanity press. Compare with private press and self-publishing..

Variable control field A variable field of the MARC record (tagged 00X with X in the range of 1-9) containing neither indicators nor subfields codes, reserved for a single data element or series of fixed-length data elements identified by the relative position of characters. For example, field 008 containing 40 characters of encoded information about the record as a whole, such as the date it was entered into the database, frequency of publication, etc. Compare with variable data field.

Variable data field A variable field of the MARC record (tagged 1XX-9XX with XX in the range of 00-99) that has two indicator positions following the tag and usually contains textual rather than coded information, consisting of one or more elements of bibliographic description, each recorded in a separate subfield preceded by a two-character subfield code. Compare with variable control field.

Variable field A field of the MARC record that varies in length, containing either coded data or text, subdivided into logical elements recorded in separate subfields. All the fields in the MARC record are variable except the 24-character leader and the 005, 007, and 008 fields which are of fixed length. Variable fields are of two types: variable control fields (tagged 00X) which include neither indicators nor subfield codes, and variable data fields (tagged 1XX-9XX with XX in the range of 00-99) which include two indicator positions following the tag and a subfield code at the beginning of each data element.

Variant A copy of a book that differs slightly in one or more points from others of the same impression, or from a previous printing of the same edition. The differences may occur in the sections, binding, or both. Once priority of publication has been conclusively established, such variations are referred to as issues and states. Also refers to one of two or more slightly different early texts of a literary work, for example, the plays of Shakespeare that survive in multiple versions. Abbreviated var.

Variant edition An edition that includes changes made in the work by the author, sometimes ranging from first composition all the way to publication in a definitive edition, allowing the reader to see the evolution of the text. Compare with variorum edition.

Variorum edition From the Latin phrase cum notis variorum meaning "with notes from various persons." An edition based on scholarly comparison and interpretation of several previously published versions of the text, which also includes commentary written by various editors. Compare with variant edition..

Various dates (v.d.) A phrase used to indicate that a set or series of volumes contains works that have different publication dates.

Varnish The glossy coating applied to the printed surface of the paper cover or dust jacket on a new book, for protection and to enhance its visual appeal. Varnish can be expensive when applied in a separate press run. A second pass is not required when varnish is added to gloss ink.

Vatican Library Although the Catholic popes always had private libraries, in the 15th century Pope Nicholas V created a library specifically for the clerics and scholars who lived and worked in and around the papal palace. A suite of rooms was set aside, and he began collecting the most beautiful manuscript books of the time. Pope Sixtus IV continued the work, and the library's holdings grew rapidly from about 1,200 books in 1455 to 3,500 in 1481 when the first handwritten catalog was made by the librarian Platina.

V-chip A microchip installed in a television set, designed to allow parents to block access to programs containing content considered unsuitable for children (violence, explicit sex, adult language, etc.). In 1996, Congress passed legislation requiring manufacturers of television receivers to install the V-chip in sets sold in the United States

(13-inch or larger). However, according to the Christian Science Monitor, a survey released in July, 2001 found that only 7% of parents with children 2-17 years old use the V-chip in their television set, either because they own an older set, do not know if their set has a V-chip, or find it difficult to use. 56% said they use the rating displayed on the screen before a program begins to make decisions about their children's viewing.

VCR An initialism for video cassette recorder, an electronic device designed to record onto videotape (in VHS format) signals received by a standard television receiver, for playback on a television monitor. Vcrs are also used to play prerecorded videocassettes (feature films, documentaries, etc.). Although vcrs are analog machines, adapters are available that enable digital data to be stored on videotape as computer backup.

VCR Video cassette recorder.

Vellum A thin, fine parchment made from the polished skin of a newly born lamb, kid, or calf, dressed and polished with alum for use as a writing surface before paper came into widespread use in Europe, and also in bookbinding. Also refers to a manuscript written on fine parchment, and to a fine-quality off-white paper made to resemble the animal membrane.

Vending machine A machine designed to automatically dispense goods when the correct amount of money, or a credit or debit card, is inserted and a selection made. In libraries, copy cards are often dispensed in this way.

Vendor A company in the business of providing access to a selection of bibliographic databases, online or on CD-ROM, by subscription (examples: EBSCO, proquest, Gale Group, silverplatter) or on a per search basis (OCLC firstsearch and DIALOG), usually under licensing agreement. Providers of nonprint media are also commonly referred to as vendors.

Venn diagram A graphical device in which closed circles (or ovals) are used to illustrate the logical relationship between sets of data: nonintersecting circles for sets with no elements in common; overlapping circles for sets with some but not all elements in common; and a circle within a circle for a set that is subset of another. Invented by Johann Sturm in 1661 and named after the English logician John Venn (1834-1923) who used them from 1880 onwards, Venn diagrams are used in bibliographic instruction to help students visualize the results of Boolean logic in keyword searching.

Verbatim et literatim A Latin phrase meaning "word for word and letter for letter," precisely as written or printed. More loosely, a quotation, transcription, or translation that is faithful to the original. Also refers to a literal translation.

Verbatim In exactly the same words as the original source or text, word for word, as in a direct quotation.

Verification The process of using bibliographic sources to ascertain that an author actually exists, or to determine the proper form of a name or the correct title of a work, usually prior to ordering or cataloging the item for a library collection. Compare with pre-order searching. In a more general sense, checking the truth or accuracy of any fact or statement, usually by consulting an authoritative source of information.

Vernacular From the Latin vernaculus meaning "native." In literature, works written in the daily language of a group of people, particularly the inhabitants of a specific geographic region, as distinct from the official language of the same population or area, for example, the language of the novels of Thomas Hardy, in which English country folk speak and act in a manner appropriate to their rural origins.

Vernacular name The form of a person's name used in reference sources published in his or her country of birth or permanent residence. In AACR2, the cataloger is instructed to use the form of the name that has become well-established in English-language reference sources, and to make appropriate references from other forms (example.

Veronica (Very Easy Rodent Oriented Net-wide Index to Computerized Archives) Developed at the University of Nevada, Veronica was a constantly updated database of the names of almost every menu item on thousands of gopherservers. The Veronica database could be searched from most major gophermenus. Now made obsolete by web-bases search engines.

Versal In medieval manuscripts, a large ornamental capital letter written on the inner margin or extending partly into the text, to indicate the beginning of a paragraph, verse, or important passage. The earliest examples were outlined in dots, ornamented with flourishes, or written in ink of contrasting color, but by the 15th century versals had developed into elaborately illuminated initial letters. The larger size meant that a versal occupied several lines, with its top usually aligned with the minuscules of the word to which it belonged.

Verse A sequence of words arranged in accordance with established rules of metrical composition, rhyme, etc. Also, a set of lines comprising one unit in the overall pattern of a metrical composition (song, ballad, etc.) Written in several sections of similar form, aside from any refrain. Synonymous in this sense with stanza. Also used as a general term for light poetry.

Versification The transformation of a prose work into poetic or metrical language. Also, the overall structure or style in which a poetic work is composed.

Version One of several variations of an intellectual work, possibly created for a purpose or use other than the one originally intended. Also, a variant form of a work of unknown or uncertain authorship, such as a fairy tale or legend. Also refers to a specific translation of the Bible, or any of its parts (example: King James Version). Abbreviated vers. Compare with adaptation and edition.

Verso From the Latin phrase verso folio meaning "with the page turned." The back side of a book or the left-hand page of an opening in a book or other publication, usually assigned an even page number. Publisher's imprint, publication date, notice of copyright, ISBN, and CIP are usually given on the verso of the title page of a book. Also refers to the reverse side of a single printed sheet, the side intended by the printer to be read second. The opposite of recto.

Vertical file A collection of loose clippings, pictures, illustrations, pamphlets, or other materials of an ephemeral nature which, because of size and format, are filed on edge in drawers or in a box, usually organized in folders by subject or some other classification system to facilitate retrieval. Also refers to the filing cabinet in which such materials are stored.

Very Good (VG) Shows some signs of wear, but has no tears in paper or binding; defects are noted.

VGA An initialism for Video Graphics Array, a standard video adapter in an IBM PC, capable of producing resolutions of 640 x 480 pixels in up to 256 colors. Superseded by SVGA.

VHS An initialism for Video Home System, a video recording and playback format consisting of hard plastic cassettes containing half-inch videotape. Introduced by JVC in 1976 to compete with Sony's Beta format, **VHS** has since become the industry standard for both home and commercial use. SVHS (Super VHS) was developed to improve resolution.

Vide The imperative form of the Latin verb videre, "to see." Used in the sense of "refer to" in footnotes to direct the reader's attention to a specific passage, page, chapter, or work. Abbreviated v. Or vid.

Video clip A short section of a longer work produced on videotape, used in a broadcast or incorporated into another work such as a Web page, usually for promotional purposes or to give the viewer a brief impression of the whole. Compare with film clip.

Video Round Table (VRT) A round table of the American Library Association, VRT provides leadership on issues related to video collections, programs, and services in all types of libraries, including copyright, pricing, censorship, and preservation. VRT also forms alliances with the film and video production and distribution industry to promote diverse, high-quality video production.

Videocassette A recorded videotape permanently enclosed in a hard plastic case containing two take-up reels to which the ends of the tape are permanently attached for playback and rewinding. In the United States, the standard format for videotapes is VHS. Most libraries shelve videocassettes in a separate section, but in some libraries they are integrated into the circulating collection by call number. To satisfy demand and encourage prompt return, the loan period for videocassettes may be shorter and the overdue fine higher than for books. Compare with videorecording.

Videoconference A meeting of two or more participants, conducted in real time at a distance using a video camera, microphone, and large television monitor or computer screen installed at each location, linked by satellite or digital network. Videoconferencing can save time and travel expense, especially in distance learning and in organizations with geographically separate units. Also spelled video conference.

Videodisc A large optical disk, usually made of plastic with a reflective metal coating, on which visual images and associated audio signals are recorded for subsequent playback on a videodisc player attached to a television receiver and monitor. Compare with videorecording. Synonymous with optical digital disk.

Videorecording A generic term for an electronic medium in which visual images, usually in motion and accompanied by synchronized sound, are recorded for playback by means of a television receiver and monitor. The category includes videotape and videodisc. Videorecordings are listed by title and indexed by subject, credits, awards, and special formats in Video Source Book, an annual reference serial published by the National Video Clearinghouse.

Videotape Magnetic tape on which visual images and accompanying sound are recorded for subsequent playback via a television receiver and monitor, usually sold in the form of a videocassette. The industry standard is one-half inch wide tape (VHS). Compare with videorecording.

Videotex An interactive (two-way) telecommunication system in which a television receiver is adapted to enable computer databases to be searched over a telephone line or cable, using a menu-system or keyboard for input. Search results are displayed on the television screen. Synonymous in Britain with viewdata. Compare with teletext.

View In cartography, a representation of a landscape from a perspective that makes details appear as if projected on an oblique plane, for example, a bird's-eye view, panorama, or worm's-eye view, sometimes used for comic effect.

Viewer another name for helper application.

Viewing room A special room in a library, equipped with projection equipment for viewing motion pictures, videorecordings, or dvds, individually or in a group. Viewing equipment may include a film projector and screen, and a VCR and/or DVD player attached to a large-screen television monitor or LCD projector. Use of the equipment is usually limited to registered borrowers and may be by appointment only.

Vignette A small illustration or decoration appearing on or before a title page, or at the beginning or end of a chapter in a book. In illuminated manuscripts, a small design, usually circular or oval in shape, consisting of vine leaves and tendrils, used to decorate an initial letter, border, or miniature.

VIRTUA Virtua is an ILS (Integrated Library System) with visionary technology such as FRBR (Functional Requirements for Bibliographic Records), Update Notifications through SDI, User Reviews & Ratings—a peer review feature, and a Smart Device (PDA) interface to the catalog.

Virtual An adjective referring to activities, objects, beings, and places that have no actual physical reality because they exist only in digital form (in cyberspace), for example, an e-mail "box" or an electronic "shopping cart."

Virtual classroom An online environment where students can have access to learning tools any time. Interaction between the instructor and the class participants can be via e-mail, chat, discussion group, etc.

Virtual library A "library without walls" in which the collections do not exist on paper, microform, or in any tangible form, but are electronically accessible in digital format. Such libraries exist only on a very limited scale, but in most traditional print-based libraries in the United States, catalogs and periodical indexes are available online, and the full-text of some periodicals and reference works may also be available electronically. Some libraries and library systems call themselves "virtual" because they offer online services (example: Colorado Virtual Library).

Virtual memory: A technique that enables a certain portion of hard disk space to be used as auxiliary memory so that your computer can access larger amounts of data than its main memory can hold at one time.

Virtual reality An electronic environment created especially for computer users, through the use of software that simulates the visual appearance of three-dimensional reality, but lacks physical substance, used mainly for training purposes and popular entertainment.

Virtual Reality Modeling Language (VRML) A language for coding three-dimensional HTML applications.

Virtual Server Also called a Web site. A virtual computer that resides on an HTTP server but appears to the user as a separate HTTP server. Several virtual servers can reside on one computer, each capable of running its own programs and each with individualized access to input and peripheral devices. Each virtual server has its own domain name and IP address and appears to the user as an individual Web site or FTP site. Some Internet service providers use virtual servers for those clients who want to use their own domain names.

Virtual tour An online tour of a library's facilities, usually available over the Internet. Formats vary, but some include clickable floor plans linked to photographs with accompanying text describing the collections and services available at each location.

Virus Software intended to harm the computers connected to a network, usually disseminated with malicious or hostile intent by persons who try to conceal their identity to avoid detection and prosecution. Most viruses are designed to attach to programs or parts of the operating system, where they replicate with destructive effect. To prevent this type of damage, LAN administrators install anti-virus software that automatically checks for viruses and eliminates them whenever possible. Anti-virus software can also be purchased by individual computer users who wish to protect their pcs.

Visual aid An item, such as a motion picture, videocassette, slide, photograph, map, chart, model, specimen, etc., used by an instructor or pressenter to allow the audience to view an example or representation of what is being taught. Instruction librarians sometimes bring to the classroom reference books containing information pertinent to course content, to enable students to recognize them by sight.

Visual dictionary A dictionary in which words and phrases (grouped by subject, theme, or activity) are illustrated, usually in a line drawing on the same or the opposite page, with each term keyed to the corresponding feature of the diagram by a thin line or small reference number printed on the illustration. Dorling Kindersley has made a specialty of publishing this type of book for children. The format is also used in language dictionaries in which the terms corresponding to the illustrations are given in two languages. Synonymous with pictorial dictionary and picture dictionary.

Visual Resources Association (VRA) An international organization established in 1982 to advance knowledge, research, and education in the field of visual information resources, VRA has a membership consisting of information media professionals, including digital image specialists; art, architecture, film, and video librarians and museum curators; slide, photograph, microfilm, and digital archivists; architectural firms; museums and galleries; publishers and image system vendors; rights and reproduction officials; photographers and artists; art historians; and scientists. VRA sponsors an annual conference and publishes the quarterly VRA Bulletin.

Visually impaired A person whose sight makes using library materials in conventional formats difficult, if not impossible. Library services designed to meet the needs of visually-impaired persons include Braille, large print, books-on-tape and other recorded media, and radio reading service. In the United States, these services are available through the federally-funded National Library Service for the Blind and Physically Handicapped (NLS).

Vital records Records essential to an agency in the ongoing conduct of its business or affairs, without which it would cease to function effectively (example: the file of patron records used by a library in circulation transactions). For archivists, identifying and protecting vital records under every conceivable circumstance is a primary concern in records management and disaster planning.

Viz. An abbreviation of the Latin videlicet meaning "namely," "that is to say," or "to wit," used in text and footnotes to introduce a word or phrase added to explain more completely or precisely a previous word, phrase, or statement.

VMS Digital Equipment Corporation proprietary operating system which runs on the VAX series of machines.

Vocabulary All the words used in a language. Also, all the words and phrases used by a particular person, group, or profession. Also refers to a list of words in a textbook for students learning a foreign language, usually printed at the end of the text containing them, or at the end of each chapter. Compare with glossary and lexicon.

Vocabulary control In indexing, the process of creating and maintaining a list of preferred terms to indicate 1) which of two or more equivalent terms will represent a concept as the authorized subject heading or descriptor in the classification system, and 2) the relations of hierarchy (broader and narrower terms) and association (related terms) among headings once they have been selected. Controlled vocabulary is recorded in a subject headings list or thesaurus updated as new concepts emerge and older terminology becomes obsolete. Compare with authority control.

Vocabulary mapping A function built into the search software of some bibliographic databases that allows the user to relate a specific search term to the appropriate subject heading(s) or descriptor(s), read a scope note explaining how each heading is used, view the hierarchical tree of headings to which it belongs, and select broader headings or narrower terms or subheadings to include in the search. Vocabulary mapping is available in large databases, such as MEDLINE and psycinfo, which have a well-developed controlled vocabulary.

Vocal score The score of a musical work composed for voice (opera, oratorio, cantata, etc.) In which all the parts are shown in normal size on separate staves, with any accompaniment (ordinarily written for orchestra) reduced to two staves for performance on a keyboard instrument. Compare with chorus score.

VOD Video On Demand.

Voice mail A messaging system that allows a person to send, receive, and store audio messages using a standard telephone receiver. Also spelled voicemail.

Voice Over Internet Protocol (VOIP) voip is a term used for a set of facilities designed to manage the delivery of voice information using Internet Protocol. In general, this means sending voice information in inconspicuous digital form rather than in the traditional circuit-committed protocols of the public switched telephone network (PSTN). A major advantage of voip and Internet telephony is that it eliminates ordinary toll charges. The delivery of voice information in the language of the Internet, i.e., as digital packets instead of the current circuit protocols of the copper-based phone networks. In VOIP systems analog voice messages are digitized and transmitted as a stream of data (not sound) packets that are reassembled and converted back into a voice signal at their destination. The killer idea is that VOIP allows telephony users to bypass long-distance carrier charges by transporting those data packets just like other Internet information. With VOIP, your PC becomes your phone and you can call anywhere in the world for the cost of a local call.

Voice recognition Technology capable of recognizing the sounds of human speech and converting them into digital signals for processing as input by a computer, used mainly in communications. In computing, command systems capable of recognizing a few hundred words eliminate the need for a mouse or keyboard in repetitive operations. Discrete systems, used in dictation, require the speaker to pause between words. Continuous recognition handles natural language at normal speed, but requires considerably more processing capability. Systems capable of understanding large vocabularies spoken at any speed are anticipated in the foreseeable future.

Voice-over In motion pictures, video, and television, a narration, commentary, or prepared text spoken by a person who is not seen on the screen, a technique widely used in advertising. In documentaries, the name of the narrator is usually given in the credits.

Volume In the bibliographic sense, a major division of a work, distinguished from other major divisions of the same work by having its own chief source of information and, in most cases, independent pagination, foliation, or signatures, even when not bound in a separate cover. In a set, the individual volumes are usually numbered, with any indexes at the end of the last volume. For a periodical, all the issues published during a given publishing period (usually a calendar year), bound or unbound. The volume number is usually printed on the front cover of each issue, and on the same page as the table of contents. In bound periodicals, it is impressed on the spine.

Volume number The number assigned to all the issues of a periodical published during a given publication period (usually a calendar year), beginning with number one for the period (year) in which the title was first issued. If the issues are bound in one or more physical volumes, the number is printed or impressed on the spine(s). In a multivolume reference work, such as an encyclopedia, the volume number appears on the spine and on the title page.

Volume rights The rights, usually negotiated with a publisher by the author or author's agent, to publish a work in volume form, including hardcover, paperback, book club, and textbook editions. Volume rights also include publication of the work in its entirety in a single issue of a periodical and reprinting, in full or in part, in an anthology. Compare with subsidiary rights.

Volunteer A person who works for a library or other organization without material recompense. Library volunteers are often retirees who wish to make a contribution by remaining actively engaged in their community. They perform a variety of tasks, depending on their skills and talents, including reshelving, physical processing, mending, storytelling, landscape maintenance, etc.

VPN (Virtual Private Network) Usually refers to a network in which some of the parts are connected using the public Internet, but the data sent across the Internet is encrypted, so the entire network is "virtually" private.

VRAM Video RAM. A type of memory dedicated to handling the image displayed on a monitor. VRAM is built into many Macs, and it also comes on display cards.

VT100 A type of mainframe terminal developed by Digital Equipment Corporation (DEC) which became the de facto industry standard, creating an environment in which other types of computers are required to use software that emulates VT100 in order to log on via Telnet to a mainframe.

VTLS stands for 'Virginia Tech Library System'. An automated library system used by many libraries, including USQ.

VUL Vanderbilt University Library. The name of the library system from 1979 to 1984.

Vulgate From the Latin vulgata meaning "popular." A Latin translation of the Bible prepared in the 4th century by St. Jerome, which remained for centuries the version authorized by the Roman Catholic Church. In 1546, the Council of Trent, after considering all extant Latin translations, reaffirmed the Vulgate as the official version. The first book printed in Europe, the Gutenberg Bible, was an edition of the Vulgate.

W.a.f. An abbreviation of "with all faults," used in the antiquarian book trade to refer to the condition of a book offered for sale as is, not returnable if found to be defective.

Wages Money paid to an employee for the total number of hours worked in a given period (weekly, biweekly, monthly), computed at an hourly rate. Library staff employed part-time are usually paid by the hour. Compare with salary.

WAIS Wide Area Information Servers, A commercial software package that allows the indexing of huge quantities of information, and then making those indices searchable across networks such as the Internet. A prominent feature of WAIS is that the search results are ranked (scored) accordingto how relevant the hits are, and that subsequent searches can find more stuff like that last batch and thus refine the search process.

Walford Common reference to the following work: Walford's Guide to Reference Material, V. 1-3. The guide, published in Great Britain, is an annotated bibliography of reference works.

Wall shelving Single-sided shelving placed against a wall and sometimes attached to it, as opposed to free-standing shelving (usually double-sided) designed to stand on its own away from a wall or other support. Shelving of both types is manufactured in sections to allow libraries to assemble ranges of varying length.

Wallpaper The decorative background pattern or image against which windows, menus, icons, and other visual elements are displayed and manipulated in a graphical user interface (GUI), usually created in JPEG or GIF file format. Some systems allow the user to select a wallpaper from a variety of different designs. Files of wallpaper designs are also available online from third-parties. Wallpapers can be custom-designed to display a distinctive element, such as a logo, trademark, or other symbol of institutional identity. Compare with screen saver.

WAN Wide Area Network; any computer network over an area larger than a single building or campus.

WAP Wireless Application Protocol; an application environment and set of communication protocols for enabling wireless access to the Internet.

Warping A twist or bend in a book cover that occurs after binding or casing, severe enough to prevent the volume from lying flat, usually caused by dampness. In newly bound books, the condition may be caused by differences in the expansion and/or contraction of the materials used in the case or cover. Warping can be minimized in binding by using well-dried boards, endpapers with the grain running from head to foot, and adhesives of low water content, and by proper pressing. In libraries, it is controlled by storing books in a dry, well-ventilated place.

Warranty A fixed period of time, specified in the sales agreement, during which the seller is required to repair or replace a piece of equipment that does not function properly. Once the warranty period has expired, the purchaser must pay for repairs unless a maintenance contract has been signed. As a general rule, length of warranty is an indication of the manufacturer's confidence in the product.

Washing A labor-intensive preservation technique in which an item printed on paper, such as a map or print, is treated with a mild chemical solution to remove stains, writing, foxing, or acid, then pressed and resized. For bound publications, the process usually necessitates rebinding.

Water resource archive A joint project of the Colorado State University Water Resources Archive and the University Libraries. The Colorado Water Resources Research Institute and the Colorado Agricultural Archives. Formally begun in 2001, the Archive consists of collections from individuals and organizations that have been instrumental in the development of water resources in Colorado and the West.

Water tear Paper separated along a moistened line to give the tear a soft, uneven, feathered edge as the fibers gently pull apart without breaking, a technique is used in making delicate paste repairs in books and other print materials.

Water-damaged Library materials that have been exposed to wet or damp conditions, usually as a result of leakage, flooding, or accident. Exposure of print materials to moisture can cause swelling, warping, staining, and contamination with mildew and mold. Water-damage can be very difficult to repair.

Watermark A faintly translucent papermaker's mark, consisting of lettering and/or a design that can be seen faintly in a sheet of quality paper when it is held up to a light source.

In hand papermaking, the design is made by sewing or soldering twisted wire to the mold, causing the layer of moist fiber to be thinner over the wire. In mechanized papermaking, the wire is impressed on the moist fiber by a cylinder called the dandy roll.

Waterstained The condition of a book or other printed publication which has leaves or binding discolored by contact with water.

Wavetable synthesis A method of translating digital data into analog sounds; it relies on recordings of real instruments to produce sounds.

Web browser Client software that interprets the hypertext (HTML) code in which Web pages are written and allows documents and other data files available over the Internet to be viewed in graphical, as opposed to text-only format. In the United States, the most widely used Web browsers are Netscape Navigator and Microsoft Internet Explorer. The appearance of a Web page may vary slightly depending on the type and version of browser used to view it.

Web Coordination group WCG - Group that advises add assists the Web Librarian regarding the development, design, policy, and function of the Libraries' Web pages.

Web Implementation Team The Web Implementation Team assists library staff in WEB PAGE creation, both in formal classes and with one-on-one point of need assistance. They check WEB PAGES for formatting guidelines and mount pages in a timely manner.

Web index A search engine that organizes Web sites by subject content in a hierarchy of subject categories, from the most general to the most specific. For example, links to Web sites for "library and information science organizations" are listed in Yahoo! Under:

Web page A document created with HTML that is part of a group of hypertext documents or resources available on the World Wide Web.

Web search To use one of the hierarchical subject guides or search engines available from a Web browser to identify and retrieve information housed on the

Web server A computer capable of providing Internet access to Web-based resources and services in response to requests from client computers on which Web browser software is installed. A Web server includes the necessary hardware, and also the operating system, TCP/IP protocols, server software, and information content of the Web sites installed on it. Web server software is designed to accept requests from users to download HTML text, image, and audio files.

WEB Short for World Wide Web.

Web site A group of related, interlinked Web pages installed on a Web server and accessible 24 hours a day to Internet users equipped with browser software. Most Web sites are created to represent the online presence of a company, organization, or institution, or are the work of a group or individual. The main page or welcome screen, called the homepage, usually displays the title of the site, the name of the person (or persons) responsible for creating and maintaining it, and date of last update. Also spelled Website.

Web walking Using a Web client program to move through the documents available on the World Wide Web. This casual browsing nature of navigating the WWW has also been referred to as strolling, crawling and jumping.

Webcast Simultaneous transmission of live or delayed audio or video programming over the World Wide Web to all who own the equipment needed to receive it, the Internet counterpart of broadcasting via radio or television. In a narrower sense, to send the same Web-based content (audio, video, graphics, text) to a group of Internet users, based on their individual needs or interests. Synonymous with netcast.

WEBCAT The representation of the library's catalog which is accessible on the Web. This is the public view of the catalog.

Webct An integrated set of tools that enables faculty to create web-based course content. The information can be used to supplement a class taught mostly face-to-face, or it can be the basis for an online course taught entirely on the web. Webct is the primary course management tool supported by TELR and OIT at Ohio State.

WEBCT An online course tool used by CSU instructors.

Webdewey An enhanced version of the full Dewey Decimal Classification database available to full members and partial users of OCLC in conjunction with the CORC online cataloging project, webdewey can be used to generate proposed Dewey class numbers for Web pages and other electronic resources.

Webliography An enumerative list of digital resources on a specific topic or subject, available in print or on the Web (example: Ralph Ellison Webliography by Claude H. Pott). Typically, the urls of any Web sites included in the resource list are embedded in the HTML document, enabling users to connect to the site by clicking on its hypertext link. The OCLC CORC project is creating a database of electronic pathfinders to assist librarians in integrating and organizing their print and digital topic-specific resource guides. Also known as a subject gateway.

Weblog A Web page providing a list of links and/or comments related to a topic or subject (broad or narrow in scope), arranged in reverse chronological order, the most recently added piece of information appearing first. An example in the field of library and information science is lisnews.com which accepts postings from its readers. A list of library Weblog sites is maintained by Peter Scott on libdex. Scott also manages the Weblog Library News Daily. Synonymous with blog. The process of maintaining a Weblog is known as blogging.

Webmaster The individual responsible for managing and maintaining a Web site, often the person who designed it, whose name usually appears near the bottom of the main page or welcome screen, usually with a contact link. In libraries, the Webmaster may be the systems librarian, a "techie," or a person who has acquired a knowledge of HTML and Web servers.

Webpac An online public access catalog (OPAC) that uses a graphical user interface (GUI) accessible via the World Wide Web, as opposed to a text-based interface accessible via Telnet.

Website The entire collection of web pages and other information (such as images, sound, and video files, etc.) That are made available through what appears to users as a single web server. Typically all the of pages in a web site share the same basic URL, for example the following urls are all for pages within the same web site: http://www.baytherapy.com/, http://www.baytherapy.com/whatis/, The term has a somewhat informal nature since a large organization might have separate "web sites" for each division, but someone might talk informally about the organizations' "web site" when speaking of all of them.

Webtv Microsoft trademark applied to technology that enables the user to search the Web via television, rather than a PC. A set-top box is installed containing an analog modem designed to make the connection to the Internet via a telephone line and convert data to a format that can be displayed on the television monitor, with navigation by hand-held remote control device or optional keyboard. To gain access, the user must establish an account with an Internet service provider. Synonymous with Internet TV.

Wedge-serif A typeface with serifs that are triangular in shape, also known as latin.

Weeding The process of examining items in a library collection title-by-title to identify for permanent withdrawal those that are outdated, in worn condition, or no longer circulating, especially when space in the stacks is limited. Public libraries usually weed routinely on the basis of circulation. In academic libraries, weeding is done less frequently, usually only when the shelves become overcrowded, in anticipation of a move, or when a significant change occurs in curriculum, such as the elimination of a major. Weeding should be undertaken judiciously because out of print titles can be difficult to replace. Compare with deselection.

Weekly Issued once a week. Also refers to a serial issued once a week (example: Publishers Weekly). Most news magazines and some newspapers are published weekly (Newsweek and Barron's).

Weight The relative thickness of a typeface, which determines how dark it will appear on a printed page, indicated in typography by gradation (extra-light, light, semi-light, medium, semi-bold, bold, extra-bold, and ultra-bold). In selecting an appropriate weight of type for a proposed publication, the typographer must consider grade of paper, type of ink, and method of printing. Most books are printed in medium type, with bold or semi-bold used for headings and emphasis.

Welcome screen The first screen a user encounters upon logging on to a database, Web site, or application program. A well-designed welcome screen gives the title, scope and coverage, name of author and/or producer, host, and a basic set of options, with instructions for using the system and a link to a more detailed help screen if needed. A well-designed interface includes a direct link back to the welcome screen on all the subordinate screens.

Western A short story, novel, motion picture, or television program (or series) in which the setting is the 19th century American West and the characters are cowboys, frontiersmen, "outlaws," settlers, and indigenous people. Also refers to the fiction genre comprising such works.

White letter A term used in early printing for roman type, as opposed to gothic or black letter.

White line In printing, a line of spacing equal in depth to a line of printed matter, used before and after headings, long quotations, etc., to set them apart from the text.

White pages The portion of a telephone directory in which the names, phone numbers, and street addresses of individuals residing in a specific city, town, or geographic area are listed alphabetically by surname, usually preceding the classified section (yellow pages) listing similar information for businesses and other organizations. White pages available on the Internet sometimes include e-mail addresses (see.whowhere? From Lycos).

White paper An official government report on any subject, especially one summarizing the results of an investigation or important policy decision of the British Parliament. Compare in this sense with green paper. The term is also used to refer to an authoritative report on a topic in technology, such as a new line of product development, sometimes available online, usually written by a person employed by a research company or vendor, or by an independent consultant.

White Point A movable reference point that defines the lightest area in an image, causing all other areas to be adjusted accordingly.

White space In printing, any area of a page (other than the margins) not occupied by type matter or illustration, for example, the unfilled space at the end of each line of a poem or at the end of a chapter. Compare with blank.

White stripe Bound volume marked with a white stripe on the spine indicates available for a 2-day loan. Bound journals housed in Morgan in the movable shelves are white-striped.

Whiteboard A modern version of the erasable chalkboard, with a surface that is white, rather than the traditional black or green, made of a smooth material that can be written upon with dry-erase marking pens in various colors, easy to erase and not as messy as chalk. However, the plastic pens cannot be refilled and become nonbiodegradable waste. Whiteboards are available from library suppliers in reversible freestanding and single-sided wall-mountable models. Porcelain steel models are available for use with magnets. Synonymous with markerboard.

WHOIS An Internet program which allows users to query databases of people and other Internet entities, such as domains, networks, and hosts. The information for people generally shows a person's company name, address, phone number and email address.

Who's Who A reference book or reference serial providing brief biographical information about well-known people who are still living. Who Was Who covers the lives of deceased persons of prominence. Titles beginning Who's Who in... Cover the lives of important persons in a given field or profession. Those beginning Who's Who of... Are usually devoted to individuals of a specific gender, nationality, or ethnic origin.

Wide area network (WAN) A communication network covering an extensive geographic area, such as a country, region, province, or state. Compare with LAN.

Widow In typography, a single word or phrase, or a line shorter than one-third the specified line length, at the end of a paragraph, when it appears at the head of a column or page of text matter. Skilled typographers consider fewer than three lines in this position awkward and avoid setting them if possible.

Width The dimension of a book or other bound item from spine to fore-edge, usually less than its height, the exception being volumes square or oblong in shape. In the library cataloging, the height of a book is given in the physical description area of the bibliographic record in centimeters, but not the width. Also refers to the horizontal dimension of a section of single- or double-sided shelving. Most library shelving is sold in sections 36 inches wide.

Wi-Fi Wireless Fidelity, A popular term for a form of wireless data communication, basically Wi-Fi is "Wireless Ethernet".

Wild card symbol used to substitute any letter or combination of letters in a search word or phrase. A wild card symbol may replace a single letter (as in wom*n, to search for women or woman in one search) or any number of letters (as in psycholog*, to search for psychology, psychologist, and psychological). Though an asterisk is frequently used as a wild card symbol, some databases use other symbols such as a question mark or an exclamation point. See also truncation. Abstract - A brief summary of the topics covered in an article or book.

WIMPS An acronym for "windows, icons, mouse, pull-down menus." Synonymous with graphical user interface (GUI).

Window On a graphical user interface system, a rectangular area on a display screen. Windows are particularly useful on multitasking systems which allow you to perform a number of different tasks simultaneously. Each task has its own window which you can click on to make it the current process. Contrast to a "dialog box" which is used to respond to prompts for input from an application.

Windows A user-friendly operating system developed in 1985 by Microsoft for pcs running on DOS, progressively upgraded to its current version. Windows got its start by emulating the graphical user interface (GUI) developed by Apple and has since become the industry standard for desktop microcomputers.

Windows Me In 2000 Microsoft released Windows Me, short for Millenium Edition, which is aimed at the home user. The Me operating system boasts some enhanced multimedia features, such as an automated video editor and improved Internet plumbing. But unlike Microsoft's Windows 2000 OS which offers advanced security, reliability, and networking features Windows Me is basically just an upgrade to the DOS-based code on which previous Windows versions have been built.

Windows NT Windows N(ew) T(echnology). The

operating system for desktop computers currently in use at the libraries.

Windows XP It is a new kind of Windows for consumers. Under the hood, it contains the 32-bit kernel and driver set from Windows NT and Windows 2000. Naturally it has tons of new features that no previous version of Windows has, but it also doesn't ignore the past—old DOS and Windows programs will still run, and may even run better. XP comes in two flavors: Home and Professional. XP Home is a $99 upgrade ($199 for the full version) and Professional is a $199 upgrade ($299 for the full version). Recognizing that many homes have more than one PC, Microsoft also plans to offer discounts of $8 to $12 off the price of additional upgrades for home users (the Open Licensing Program is still available for business or home users who need 5 or more copies). That's fortunate because you'll need the additional licenses since the Product Activation feature makes it all but impossible to install a single copy on more than one PC. Windows NT 4.0 is similar in appearance and style to Windows 95. Windows 3.11 and NT 4.0 share few of the same characteristics. So, if you have been using Windows 95 on your personal computer, the transition to NT 4.0 should be relatively easy. If you are only familiar with the Windows 3.11 environment, you may need to spend some extra time adapting to the new look of the NT 4.0 main screen. Windows NT Run Faster Than Windows 3.11?. Windows 3.11 is a 16-bit operating system and Windows NT is a 32-bit operating system. One big difference between the two systems is that Windows NT processes information twice as fast as the older Windows 3.11 system. This gives Windows NT the power to process higher-end applications, such as Word 7.0 and Access 7.0.

Winsock Short for Windows Socket; an Application Programming Interface (API) for developing Windows programs that can communicate with other machines via the TCP/IP protocol. New Windows computers have Winsock built in.

Winzip A Windows-based file compression utility for IBM PC and compatibles. Compressed files are referred to as "zipped" and usually end with a ".zip" file extension. A special kind of zipped file is self-extracting and ends with a ".exe" extension.

Wire coil A continuous length of metal wire threaded through holes punched along the binding edge of the leaves of a book or notebook in spiral binding. Flexible hard plastic is also used for this purpose.

Wireless (netwoking): The ability to access the Internet without a physical network connection. Devices such as cell phones and pdas that allow you to send and receive e-mail use a wireless Internet connection based on a protocol called WAP (Wireless Application Protocol). At this point, web sites that contain wireless Internet content are limited, but will multiply as the use of devices relying on WAP increases.

Wireless A method of connecting to the Internet via electromagnetic airwaves, rather than wire or cable. Telecommunication charges are eliminated, but an Internet service provider is still required to gain access to the Internet. Wireless technology enables the ISP to offer greater bandwidth without the expense of adding cable to its own connection. However, in most wireless systems "line of sight" is required, which means that the radio antenna installed at a library must have an unobstructed path to the antenna maintained by the ISP. Each client antenna can serve 50-100 workstations at T1 speed. Wireless technology is also be used internally by libraries with a direct connection to the Internet, for example, to network an instruction lab equipped with pcs or laptops.

Wireless network Also known as a WLAN (wireless local area network), wireless networks use high-frequency radio waves rather than wires and cables to connect computers and local computing resources together.

With all faults (w.a.f.) A term used by booksellers, book dealers, and auctioneers to inform prospective buyers that an item is offered for sale as is and may not be returned if found to be defective.

Withdrawal The process of deleting all references in a library catalog to an item that has been permanently removed from the collection without being replaced by another copy of the same edition. The item is usually stamped "withdrawn" to avoid confusion in the disposition process. Also refers to the item withdrawn.

Withdrawl file Card file near the shelf list, arranged alphabetically by title, that shows bibliographic works officially withdrawn from CSUL. Withdrawn items are now archived electronically and searchable via a Microsoft Access database.

Witness In bibliography, the version of a manuscript or incunabulum accepted as authoritative by most scholars qualified to speak on the subject. In binding, a book with the fore-edge so slightly trimmed that some pages are left rough.

Wizard A context-sensitive dialog box that automatically appears in some computer applications to ask the user if help is needed at a particular point in the program, as distinct from a help menu that can be selected by the user as needed. Wizards can usually be turned "off" if the user finds them intrusive.

Woodcut A method of printing from an inked block of medium-soft wood (usually pear or cherry) from which an artist has excised all but an illustration, working by hand with knife and gouge in the same direction as the grain of a plank cut lengthwise from the tree. The design may be drawn directly on the plank (usually in pencil), or transferred by rubbing a tracing made on paper. Also refers to the block itself and to the print made from it. By contrast, wood engraving is done with a tool called a burin or graver across the grain of a block of hardwood cut in cross-section.

Word processing A method of converting information into readable text in which personnel, procedures, and equipment are organized for maximum efficiency and effectiveness. Word processing systems usually include a microcomputer with a keyboard for typing input, a monitor for the display of text, and a laser printer for producing high-quality output. An interface with a photosetting machine allows offset plates to be produced for printing.

Word search SAGE allows you to search by words. Words may be from the title or they may be subjects, concepts, ideas and dates.

Word-by-word A method of alphabetization in which headings that begin with the same word are arranged in alphabetical order by the next word, and so on, with punctuation marks treated as spaces ("New Testament" filed before "New, William" before "newt"). Also known as nothing before something. Compare with letter-by-letter.

Wordless A book or other publication without words, in which the story is told in a sequence of illustrations, a format used mainly in children's picture books (example: Clown (1995) by Quentin Blake). Without text, the "reader" must interpret the meaning of the story from the visual images. Each reader may perceive a slightly different meaning in the pictures.

Work An expression of human thought or emotion in language, signs, symbols, numerals, images, or other medium for purposes of communication and record. When such an expression is issued to the public, it is a published work. If the original author or creator is unknown, the work is anonymous.

Work form In technical processing, a card or paper form that accompanies a newly acquired item from the beginning of cataloging to the point at which it is ready to be placed on the shelf, with space for library staff to note any special instructions and data necessary to prepare catalog records, add cross-references, and physically prepare the item for use. Synonymous with worksheet.

Work in progress A written or artistic work published

or exhibited in incomplete form, sometimes in parts, to be continued or completed by the author or creator at a later date. Large reference works requiring many years of painstaking research are sometimes published as the work progresses (example: Dictionary of American Regional English).

Work mark One or two letters added by the cataloger to the author mark at the end of a call number, consisting of the first letter or two of the first word of the title (initial articles excluded), to distinguish works by the same author which have the same classification (example: the d in the book number D548d to identify David Copperfield by Charles Dickens), or to subarrange editions of the same work. Synonymous with work number.

Work room Specific areas used by the stacks unit of preservation unit to sort books for reshelving.

Work week For payroll purposes, Saturday morning through Friday evening.

Workaholic A person who fails to balance work with activities that provide rest and relaxation. When chronic, this condition can eventually lead to burnout.

Workbook A separately published learning resource containing exercises, sample problems, worksheets, review questions, and other practice materials, usually with blank space for recording answers. When published in conjunction with a textbook, a workbook is usually bound in softcover, sometimes in a spiral or comb binding to allow it to open flat.

Worker's compensation Insurance Provided to all University employees to assist them with expenses resulting from any injury or occupational diseases incurred in connection with job performance.

Workflow The manner in which work is passed from one member of a department to another, or from one department to another within a company, organization, or institution, to allow the steps necessary for completion to be executed in proper sequence. Efficiencies can sometimes be achieved by systematic analysis of workflow.

Working balance Money allocated for funds such as a firm, replacement, retro serial, subscription or continuation.

Working conditions The surroundings in which work is accomplished, including factors affecting health and safety (lighting, sanitation, heating/cooling, noise, air quality, etc.) And comfort (parking, break time, child care, etc.). Companies, organizations, and institutions that employ large numbers of people often have a formal procedure or standing committee for handling complaints and suggestions concerning working conditions.

Working title The title provided by the author at the time a manuscript is submitted to the publisher, used during the editorial process, but sometimes altered slightly or changed completely before final publication to reflect the content more accurately or make the work more marketable.

Workload The amount of work to be completed in a given time by an employee or group of employees. How much is actually accomplished depends on speed, skill, motivation, working conditions, etc.

Workman Either the first letter of the first significant word of the title of a book, or an arbitrary letter. It is sometimes placed immediately after the Cutter number to distinguish different works by the same author.

Workroom A room closed to the public, where technical processes and routine tasks are carried out in the library, for example, the receiving area of the serials department, where current issues of periodicals are checked in and prepared for use, and back issues are boxed to be shipped to the bindery or discarded.

Workshop A meeting of people interested in learning more about a subject, or who wish to gain practical experience in the use of a technique, system, or resource, usually for the purpose of training or professional development. A workshop differs from a conference in being task-oriented and of shorter duration (usually one day or less), and may be open to attendees who do not necessarily share membership in a voluntary organization.

Workstation An area within a workplace, equipped with a personal computer and high-resolution monitor for accomplishing tasks that require the use of information in digital format (especially graphics), usually furnished with a desk, chair, and specially designed table to accommodate the PC and any peripheral equipment. If the microcomputer is networked, special wiring may be required. Also refers to a PC functioning as a client in a network. In this sense, compare with server.

Work-study student Students employed by the University on state or federal government awards, which covers 70 % of wages. The Libraries pay the remaining 30%.

World atlas A reference book, usually of large size, containing maps of all the countries and regions of the world, printed in color, sometimes accompanied by explanatory text and statistical information, with an index of place names (gazetteer) in the back (example: The Times Atlas of the World).

World Bank World Bank provides national statistics for countries and regions and country profiles of all its member countries pertaining to the aspects of agriculture, education, environment, finance, health, population, urban and social development etc.

World Biographical Index 7 This database contains 2,8 million records, each record covers brief biographical information of individuals.

World Crime Statistics United Nations World Crime Surveys of Crime Trends and Criminal Justice data sets are available here. Data is available in ASCII, Lotus 123, and SPSS formats.

World Health Organization WHO provides access statistics from its statistical system 'Whois'. The data types can be accessed from their databases are on mortality, basic health indicators, HIV/AIDS, statistical data from world health report, population etc.

World Intellectual Property Organization (WIPO) A specialized agency of the United Nations with headquarters in Geneva, WIPO is responsible for administering 21 international treaties concerning the protection of intellectual property through copyright, patent, and trademark law, for the benefit of its 177 member nations.

World Tourism Organization WTO Data Base covers statistics on international outbound tourism, international inbound tourism, and tourism indicators covering a wide variety of tourism trends.

World Trade Organization WTO provides online access to many of its data sources, which include international trade statis

World Wide Web (WWW) A global network of Internet servers providing access to documents written in a script called Hyper Text Markup Language (HTML) that allows content to be interlinked, locally and remotely. The "Web" was designed in 1989 by Tim Berners-Lee, working at the CERN high-energy physics lab in Geneva. Mark Andreeson, a student a the University of Illinois, later devised a simple point-and-click system called Mosaic that subsequently evolved into the Netscape Web browser.

Worldcat Formerly known as OLUC, worldcat is the online union catalog of materials cataloged by OCLC member libraries and institutions,. a rapidly growing bibliographic database containing over 48 million records representing materials published since 1000 BC in over 400 languages in a variety of formats (books, manuscripts, maps, music scores, newspapers, magazines, journals, theses and dissertations, sound recordings, films, videorecordings, computer programs, machine-readable data files, etc.). Updated daily, worldcat is used by OCLC members and participants for cataloging and interlibrary loan, and is available for general use by licensing agreement through OCLC firstsearch.

Worm A worm is a virus that does not infect other programs. It makes copies of itself, and infects additional computers (typically by making use of network connections) but does not attach itself to additional programs; however a worm might alter, install, or destroy files and programs.

Worming The condition of a book in which small insects called bookworms have bored holes through the text block or binding, or left other visible traces of their unwelcome presence.

Wove paper Handmade paper that reveals a faintly translucent, fine mesh pattern when held up to a light source, the result of wires woven evenly like cloth in the paper mold. The same effect is achieved in machine-made paper by the pressure of the dandy roll. Compare with laid paper.

Wrap-around A publishing term for a cover design extending all the way from the front edge of a book over the spine and across the back board, usually seen in volumes containing a large proportion of pictorial content.

Wrapper The printed or unprinted cover of a paperbound book or pamphlet, usually of a heavier grade of paper than the text and therefore not part of the printing that produced the publication. When made from the same paper as the text, it is known as a self-wrapper. Also refers to the outer covering on a magazine, usually made of kraft paper, added to protect the glossy cover from damage in the post. Compare with dust jacket.

Writ Historically, a command written in epistolary form, addressed to one or more officials under the seal of an English king, indicating that a specific action is to be performed or is prohibited. In a more general sense, any formal written document issued by a court or other judicial authority in the name of a sovereign or state, forbidding or ordering the person(s) to whom it is directed to perform a specific action (example: Writ of Habeas Corpus, known as the "Great Writ" in English common law).

Write-off A bibliographic item or other piece of library property so badly damaged that it cannot be repaired, for which the cost of replacement cannot be recovered. Also refers to a debt that cannot be recovered, for example, an overdue fine that remains unpaid for so long that the library must clear it from the circulation record.

Writer's Market An annual reference publication that provides directory listings for literary agents, book publisherss, small presses, book producers, consumer magazines, trade journals, scriptwriting, newspaper syndicates, writing contests and literary awards, and other resources for writers.

WS_FTP A program for Windows available via the OIT Software To Go web site; enables you to transfer files across the Internet to or from your desktop computer.

WYLBUR An interface on the MVS system maintained by OIT for numerical and statistical processing and programming. For information about accounts, call 688-HELP or send e-mail to 8help@osu.edu.

WYSIWYG What you see is what you get. The image you see on the screen matches what will print on paper. Pronounced wizzy-wig. X.25 A data communications interface specification developed to describe how data passes into and out of public data communications networks. The CCITT and ISO approved protocol suite defines protocol layers 1 through 3.

Xerography From the Greek xeros and graphos, meaning "dry writing." A method of reproducing text and/or images in which dry resinous toner transferred from an electrostatically charged plate is thermally adhered to a sheet of paper or some other copying surface inside a photocopier (originally called a xerox machine). The result is a photocopy or xerox copy. Xerography is a form of reprography.

X-height The mean height of the lowercase letters of a typeface that have neither ascenders nor descenders, sometimes used instead of point size as an indication of type size. The x-height letters of the roman alphabet are: a, c, e, m, n, o, r, s, u, v, w, x, and z. The tops and bottoms of some letters such as the "c" and "o" may extend slightly above the mean line and below the base line. Also spelled ex-height.

XML Extensible Markup Language A widely used system for defining data formats. XML provides a very rich system to define complex documents and data structures such as invoices, molecular data, news feeds, glossaries, inventory descriptions, real estate properties, etc. As long as a programmer has the XML definition for a collection of data (often called a "schema") then they can create a program to reliably process any data formatted according to those rules.

XPFE (Cross Platform Front End) A suite of technologies used to create applications that will work and look the same on different computer operating systems. A widely used XPFE application; is the Netscape web browser in version 7 and later. The primary technologies used in creating XPFE applications are Javascript, Cascading Style Sheets, and XUL.

X-rated A motion picture or videorecording containing material considered suitable for adults only, usually because it contains material considered pornographic. The term is also applied to print publications containing adult material (magazines, photographs, etc.).

XUL — (extensible User-interface Language) A markup language similar to HTML and based on XML. XUL used to define what the user interface will look like for a particular piece of software. XUL is used to define what buttons, scrollbars, text boxes, and other user-interface items will appear, but it is not used to define how those item will look (e.g. What color they are). The most widely used example of XUL use is probably in themozilla web browser, where the entire user interface is defined using the XUL language.

XVGA See: SVGA.

Xylography Printing done from blocks of wood, especially by the early process of wood engraving. The results are known as xylographica.

YA An abbreviation of young adult, an adolescent aged 12-18, usually in the ninth to twelfth grade.

Yahoo! Yet another hierarchically officious oracle, a worldwide directory of Web sites developed in 1994 by two Stanford University engineering students to organize Web content in a hierarchical system of subject categories. Yahoo! Also provides other Web-based services (news, weather, travel service, e-mail, shopping, games, etc.). It uses a smaller database than most other Web search engines, but searches in Yahoo! Usually have higher precision because the Web sites it lists are selected by human beings, rather than robot software.

Yapp binding A form of limp leather binding with rounded corners and squares that overlap the edges of the sections, sometimes by as much as half the thickness of the text block, named after William Yapp who used it on pocket Bibles sold in England in the mid-19th century. Geoffrey A. Glaister notes in Encyclopedia of the Book (Oak Knoll/British library, 1996) that a similar style of binding with tooled edges was used during the 16th century. Synonymous with circuit edges, divinity circuit edges, and divinity edges.

Yearbook An annual documentary, historical, or memorial compendium of facts, photographs, statistics, etc., about the events of the preceding year, often limited to a specific country, institution, discipline, or subject (example: Supreme Court Yearbook published by Congressional Quarterly). Optional yearbooks are offered by some publishers of general encyclopedias. Most libraries place yearbooks on continuation order and shelve them in the reference collection. Yearbooks of historical significance may be stored in archives or special collections. Also spelled year book. Compare with annual.

Yellow pages The portion of a telephone directory or trade directory following the white pages in which the names, phone numbers, and mailing addresses of commercial enterprises are listed, usually alphabetically by subject or in a classified arrangement, so named because the section is printed on yellow paper. Yellow pages are also available online (example: superpages.com from Verizon) and for specific professions (Librarian's Yellow Pages).

Yellow press A popular name for newspapers and periodicals of the early 20th century that published news stories of a vulgarly sensational nature, comparable to the modern tabloid. Synonymous with gutter press.

Yellowback An inexpensive popular novel bound in a shiny yellow paper or board cover with a picture printed on the front, usually a woodcut in three colors, a type of publication that originated in England in the 1850's and was used until the end of the century for inexpensive reprint editions. Also spelled yellow back. Compare with dime novel.

Yellowing A color change that occurs in the condition of certain grades of paper with age, particularly those made from unbleached or groundwood pulp, one of the reasons most libraries convert newspaper back files to microfilm or microfiche. The problem can be averted in libraries by purchasing materials printed on acid-free permanent paper.

Young adult book A book intended to be read and enjoyed by adolescents 12 to 18 years of age. Also refers to a book intended for adults, but considered suitable by reviewers and librarians for mature ninth to twelfth grade readers. Public libraries usually maintain a separate section of young adult literature managed by a librarian who specializes in YA services, including collection development. Compare with children's book.

Young Adult Library Services Association (YALSA) A division of the American Library Association founded in 1930, YALSA has a membership of librarians responsible for evaluating and selecting books and nonprint materials for young adults (age 12 to 18) and for promoting and strengthening library services for young adult readers. YALSA publishes the semiannual journal Young Adult Library Services.

Young adult services Library services intended specifically for adolescent patrons (ninth through twelfth graders), including collection development, programming, and readers' advisory. Public libraries usually have a room or section devoted specifically to young adult materials, managed by a librarian who specializes in providing services for this age group. Compare with adult services and children's services.

Youth collection A collection of materials written for children and young adults; located in the Education Library.

Z39.50 "Z39.50" refers to the International Standard, ISO 23950: "Information Retrieval (Z39.50): Application Service Definition and Protocol Specification", and to ANSI/NISO Z39.50. The standard specifies a client/server-based protocol for searching and retrieving information from remote databases.

Z39.50 The OSI client-server protocol established as a standard by the National Information Standards Organization (NISO), which allows computer users to query a remote information retrieval system using the software of their local system and receive results in the format of the local system. Click here to connect to the Web page on **Z39.50** maintained by the Network Development and MARC Standards Office of the Library of Congress.

ZAP Slang term meaning to sensitize or desensitize material in the electronic detection system. **Zebra number:** number from barcode label used by Circulation.

Zig-zag book A book made by folding a continuous strip of paper backward and forward accordion-style. When the pages are sewn at the back fold, the strip is printed on one side only. When both sides are printed, the folds are left unsewn to allow the volume to be opened to its full length. This form of book is called an orihon when made from a manuscript or printed document originally produced as a roll. Compare with concertina.

Zine Derived from "fanzine" (a contraction of "fan magazine"), pronounced "zeen." The term came into use during the 1980s to refer to a small, low-circulation magazine or newspaper, self-published out of passion for the subject rather than for personal gain, usually produced with the aid of desktop publishing software and high-quality photocopy machines.

Zip disk A 3.5-inch removable disk cartridge developed by Iomega, capable of storing 100MB or more of data (much more than

Zip drive A disk drive developed by Iomega that uses a 3.5-inch removable Zip disk capable of storing 100MB or more of data at relatively low cost, used for storing very large files and collections of files. The drive usually comes with software that catalogs the contents of the disk and provides file security.

Zip To compress a data file using PKZIP software or some other utility capable of compressing data into PKZIP format. When such a file is restored to an uncompressed format, it is said to have been unzipped.

Zoom In photography, to alter the size of an image from a stationary camera position without changing perspective by using a zoom lens to increase or decrease the focal length. In cinematography, this type of lens appears to make the camera advance toward the subject when zooming in, or retreat from it when zooming out.

Zoom text A screen enlarging program that enlarges the computer image up to 16X the original size. The user can choose to enlarge the entire screen or portions of the screen. Available in the assistive technology room and in the EIC.